Public Finance
in Theory and Practice

PUBLIC FINANCE

In Theory and Practice

A. R. PREST, M.A., Ph.D
Professor of Economics, London School of Economics and Political Science

N. A. BARR, M.Sc.Econ., Ph.D
Lecturer in Economics, London School of Economics and Political Science

WEIDENFELD AND NICOLSON
LONDON

First published 1960
Reprinted 1961
Second edition 1963
Reprinted 1965
Third edition 1967
Reprinted 1968
Fourth edition 1970
Fifth edition 1975
Reprinted 1976
Reprinted 1977
Sixth edition 1979

Weidenfeld and Nicolson
91 Clapham High Street, London SW4

ISBN 0 297 77648 7 cased
ISBN 0 297 77649 5 paperback

Set, printed and bound in Great Britain by
Fakenham Press Limited,
Fakenham, Norfolk

Contents

PART II – INSTITUTIONS

PART III – POLICY

Tables

Figures

Charts

Preface

As Chapter 1 of this book is called 'General Introduction' and Chapters 2 and 13 provide introductory material to Parts I and III, there is no need to take up space now to describe the contents.

All that need be said is that an attempt is made to discuss the basic theoretical issues of Public Finance fairly fully and then, after describing institutional arrangements, to apply them to specific topics of policy. No doubt some will find the applied part more to their taste than the theoretical, and vice versa, but it is absolutely vital that any book which attempts to range widely in this field should be concerned with both aspects.

Work on this volume started some five years ago, but for a variety of reasons made only slow progress until 1958. Leave of absence from University and College teaching duties and from College administrative duties for the Easter Term 1958 and a most generous grant from the Rockefeller Foundation to visit the US and Canada then enabled me to complete the manuscript. I have profited immensely from criticisms by Professor Sir D. H. Robertson, who read all the manuscript, and from Professor J. E. Meade and Mr M. J. Farrell, who each read substantial parts of it. No doubt many faults remain and for these I am responsible. There would have been many more if I had not been fortunate enough to receive such expert advice.

Christ's College, Cambridge *A. R. Prest*
January 1959

Preface to Second Edition

Almost all the changes in the second edition are of a factual and statistical character. In particular Part II has been extensively revised and some changes have been made in Part III, especially in Chapters 14 and 19. I have to thank Mr A. G. Armstrong, for most valuable help with the statistical revisions.

Christ's College, Cambridge *A. R. Prest*
April 1963

Preface to Third Edition

Extensive alterations have been made in this edition. In addition to a thoroughgoing revision of the factual material in Parts II and III, it has been necessary to re-write large sections of Part III. In particular, the former chapter on capital gains taxation has been cut down in size and amalgamated with that on personal income taxation. In its place, there is now a whole chapter on the various forms of capital taxation – the net wealth tax, estate duties, inheritance taxes and gift taxes. The chapter on company profits taxation has been completely re-written and substantial alterations have been made to those dealing with depreciation and overseas income. The opportunity has also been taken to make some small changes in Part I. I have to thank Mr J. Warford for invaluable assistance in making the statistical and factual revisions and Dr G. Jantscher for helpful comments on the chapter on capital taxation.

Manchester *A. R. Prest*
August 1966

Preface to Fourth Edition

The structure of the book is essentially unchanged in this edition. But the opportunity has been taken to review and amplify the theory chapters at some points as well as to bring Parts II and III up to date. I have to thank Mr J. M. Davis for carrying the burden of the statistical revisions so extremely well.

Manchester *A. R. Prest*
April 1970

Preface to Fifth Edition

A few changes have been made in the Analysis Part but the majority of changes occur in Parts II and III, especially in relation to the many taxation changes in the UK since 1970. The text of several chapters in Part III has been completely re-written; some discussion of EEC tax implications is also to be found there now. I have to thank a number of people for help with the statistical revisions.

London *A. R. Prest*
April 1974

Preface to Sixth Edition

The publication of an edition under joint authorship seemed an appropriate occasion for making very extensive changes, so that this edition differs radically from previous ones.

Part I (renamed *Principles*) has been reorganized, rewritten (particularly with respect to the discussion of income stabilization) and revised as necessary to take account of recent developments in the field.

Part II (renamed *Institutions*) has been changed in several respects. We now take the Government as a Whole first, before coming to the individual segments. The opportunity has also been taken to enlarge the old chapter on the National Insurance Fund considerably so that it is much more an account of the whole range of social security expenditures. To make room for these additions, we decided to drop the old chapter on the National Debt and also the short Appendix on the Public Finances of Canada.

Part III (*Policy*) has been very largely rewritten, both to take account of the many changes which have taken place since the last edition and to incorporate a new chapter on Income Redistribution and the Welfare State.

Although the general format of the book, and the total number of chapters, remain as before, the overall effect of the changes is to recognize such major developments of recent years as tax harmonization, negative income tax and tax-credit plans, and to incorporate much more material on and discussion of social security and related revenues and expenditures than before.

Finally, it remains to thank the many people who have given us help in reading our material and preparing it for publication. In particular, we are greatly indebted to officials of the Inland Revenue, Customs and Excise and the Department of Health and Social Security for advice on the factual material in Part II. But any errors which remain are our responsibility.

London
April 1979

A. R. Prest
N. A. Barr

1

GENERAL INTRODUCTION

1 HISTORY AND SUBJECT-MATTER OF PUBLIC FINANCE

Discussion of the various aspects and meanings of public finance has a long history in the works of economists. If we look at Adam Smith's *Wealth of Nations* we find a whole section (Book V) devoted to 'the revenue of the Sovereign or Commonwealth'. Similarly, the title of Ricardo's main work was, significantly enough, *The Principles of Political Economy and Taxation*. With such a long history, we are likely to learn a good deal about the subject-matter of public finance if we start by running quickly over the writings of some of the great economists of the past.

If we turn first to Adam Smith we find that he divides Book V into three chapters dealing respectively with 'the expenses of the sovereign or commonwealth', 'the sources of the general or public revenue of the society', and 'public debts'. The first chapter deals with the various types of public expenditure and the appropriate means of defraying them; in the second he classifies revenue into various categories and also enunciates his four famous canons or principles of taxation (that taxation should be 'equal' – and this should most probably be taken to mean 'proportional to income' – that tax levies should not be uncertain or arbitrary, that the State should not exact payment in a manner inconvenient to the taxpayer, and that taxes should be economical to collect). In the third chapter he discusses the origin and history of the 'public debt' and makes various proposals for reducing it.

In his *Principles*, Ricardo spends some ten chapters dealing with problems of taxation. Chapter VIII ('On Taxes') discusses the general effects of taxation, and the remaining chapters deal with the effects of particular taxes or types of taxes such as those on rent, houses, profits, wages etc. Although there is no connected discussion of public debt in the *Principles*, Ricardo does deal with this subject in a separate publication, his *Essay on the Funding System*.

With the publication of J. S. Mill's *Principles of Political Economy* in

1848, the period of the English classical economists may be said to have come to an end. Mill, like his predecessors, devoted a good deal of space to public finance. Book V of the *Principles* is in fact labelled 'The Influence of Government' and some seven chapters of this section are concerned with problems of government finance – the general principles of taxation, the classification of taxes into 'direct' and 'indirect', the comparative effects of different taxes, and various problems of the National Debt.

As far as the classical economists are concerned we can therefore say that there was recognition of the division of the subject-matter of public finance into its revenue, expenditure and debt aspects. But whereas Adam Smith put the discussion of expenditure at the forefront of his work, Ricardo and J. S. Mill concentrated much more on the other two aspects.

In contrast, we find relatively little systematic discussion of public finance as a *subject* by the major authors in the Marshall–Edgeworth era at the end of the nineteenth century. Marshall's *Principles* has no connected discussion of the problems of taxation, let alone any of the other aspects of public finance, even though he does spend a very considerable amount of time developing various aspects of the theory of taxation in different sections of the book. Again Edgeworth was very emphatic in declaring:[1]

> The science of taxation comprises two subjects to which the character of pure theory may be ascribed; the law of incidence, and the principle of equal sacrifice.

By the time that Economics had effectively replaced the older discipline of Political Economy the systematic exposition of the whole subject of public finance had disappeared from the major works of the great economists.

The corollary of this development was the appearance of books specifically devoted to public finance; the time had come for parturition, so to speak. One of the first of these in the United Kingdom was Bastable's *Public Finance*, published in 1892, but his general treatment of the subject is similar to that of a better known successor, Dalton's *Public Finance*, first published in 1922. Here the definition of the subject-matter of public finance is very explicit:

[1] *Papers Relating to Political Economy*, Volume II (Macmillan, 1925), p. 64.

Public Finance is concerned with the income and expenditure of public authorities and with the adjustment of one to the other.

The section on public income follows the general lines laid down by Ricardo and Mill in discussing general principles and the specific effects of particular taxes. In the remainder of the book, however, there is more of a return to the traditions of Adam Smith in that a good deal of space is devoted to public expenditure. Since the emergence of textbooks specifically devoted to public finance, it can therefore be said that there has been a clearer recognition of the right of the expenditure as well as the revenue side of public authorities to appear in any treatment of the subject.

More recent variations in the subject-matter of public finance can be seen from the contents of other well-known textbooks published in the next quarter of a century. The contrast between the first edition (1928) and the third (1947) of Pigou's *Public Finance* illustrates one fundamental change. In both editions, there is a treatment of the principles of taxation and the merits and demerits of particular taxes. But whereas most of the remainder of the first edition was taken up by discussion of the problems of war finance, on the grounds that in peacetime the only sort of permissible public borrowing was in respect of remunerative capital works, the contrast in the third edition is startling. Now instead of war finance we have a very full and thorough discussion (headed 'Public Finance and Employment') of the various ways in which the authorities may influence aggregate income by fiscal measures. This is just one instance of the form in which modern treatments of public finance are cast. Since the great depression of the 1930s and the inflationary period of wartime, and, above all, since the publication of Keynes' *General Theory*, it has been clearly recognized that the discussion of the effects of particular taxes and particular types of government expenditure is only part of the subject-matter of public finance, and that any complete treatment must include a full discussion of the influence of government fiscal operations on the level of overall activity and employment.

In the early post-war period it looked at one time as if fiscal aspects of short-term stabilization would dominate all other aspects of public finance. There was also a good deal of interest in the relationships between fiscal policy and long-term growth. However, the position changed again and the relative importance of macroeconomic policy declined for a number of reasons: the practical difficulties of applying it in the later 1960s and seventies, the monetarist counter-revolution in economic thought and the emergence or re-discovery of other topics in the public finance field. Of the latter, the ones which have commanded most attention have been mainly connected with public expenditure rather than taxation. A great deal of attention has been paid in recent years to the principles underlying the relative sizes of the public and the private sectors of the economy, the circumstances under which market failure occurs and so on. Another topic has been the division of any given size of public sector into different levels – central, state and local. The nature and consequence of subsidies from the public to the private sector have also come under intensive investigation. Nevertheless not all the limelight has been reserved for public expenditure matters. In recent years, there has been a recrudescence of interest in the design of income and commodity taxes which might meet optimality requirements, as dictated by the joint consideration of resource allocation and distribution.

There are many ways in which one can set out the constituent elements of public finance. One can say that it involves both micro and macro aspects and that the micro element in turn involves both matters of resource allocation and of the distribution of income, consumption and wealth. Or one can say that it embraces considerations of public expenditure as well as public revenue, both construed broadly to embrace the activities of spending agencies (e.g. social security funds) which may be outside a very narrow definition of government and of taxation; similarly, one can point to topics ranging from the highly theoretical to the most down-to-earth. And it follows without saying that there are many elements of normative as well as positive economic reasoning involved.

Given the immense range of the subject-matter, the difficulty comes in knowing where to draw the line and leave subjects out of account in this book. There are four particular points to mention. First, the establishment of areas where markets may not work effectively leads to consideration of the mechanics of decisions at governmental level – principles of voting, relationships between political masters and subordinate bureaucrats and so on. Although a great deal of high-grade mental effort has been devoted in recent years to these aspects of public choice – the spelling out of these processes and the applicability and incorporation of economic principles in such decision-taking – we shall not ourselves venture into this territory.

Secondly, National Debt considerations are of a borderline character. It can be argued that government borrowing is simply one form of raising revenue and therefore that it is rather illogical to include a discussion of taxes and fees, etc. but not borrowing. On the other hand, it can be argued that debt management involves many considerations of interest rates and similar matters which belong much more closely to the field of monetary theory and management than to fiscal policy. Regretfully, we shall have to omit the subject for reasons of space even though it raises many fascinating issues, not least the controversy about whether an increase in governmental indebtedness in any one year is effectively a burden on people living at that time or on a future generation.

A similar kind of problem arises with the treatment of public commercial enterprises of various kinds. We shall omit any connected discussion of such points as the pricing and investment policy of undertakings of this sort, but we shall have something to say about the points at which they make contact with the more clearly fiscal aspects of government activity. Finally, when we come to governmental machinery, we shall confine ourselves to those parts relating to revenue and expenditure decisions rather than extend our view to cover the whole range of economic decision-taking.

2 THE ORGANIZATION OF THIS BOOK

We have discussed the historical origins and growth of the main present-day constituents of the subject-matter of public finance. Now we turn to explain the particular way in which we shall divide it.

The first section of the book is concerned with problems of *Principles*. In the course of six chapters we try to assess the relative merits and demerits of the various types of government revenue and expenditure when judged by the standards of economic criteria such as the ideal allocation of productive resources, the distribution and stabilization of income and so on. In the second section we shall concentrate on *Institutions*, i.e. the main types of revenue and expenditure in the UK and the processes of controlling and organizing revenue and expenditure. We shall start by looking at the public sector as a whole and relating it to national activities. Then we shall deal with the central government and National Insurance together with related expenditures. Finally, we examine local authority finances in some detail. An Appendix will review, albeit very much more briefly, some of the features of the US revenue-expenditure system.

Part III will be concerned with important topics of current *Policy* in the UK, such as the taxation of personal income, income redistribution and the welfare state, the taxation of capital, the taxation of companies, the reform of indirect taxation and so on.

It will be seen therefore that we divide the subject-matter into the three heads of *Principles*, *Institutions* and *Policy*. It may very well be asked: why this division and why this order?

The distinction between *Principles* and *Institutions* is fairly clear-cut and there is no need to apologize for it. It might perhaps be wondered why the *Principles* section ranges more or less indiscriminately over the effects of individual taxes and expenditures and those of taxes as a whole, or why, to use the usual jargon, it does not separate off completely the micro- and macroeconomic aspects of the subject. The answer is simply that it seemed important to treat them together. There are various criteria for judging the relative effects of different taxes and unless it can be shown that one set of criteria is much more fundamental or much more important than another there seems little case for separating them. On the other hand, it clearly seems necessary to draw a distinction between *Principles* and *Policy*. Whilst *Principles* are concerned with the fundamental theory of public finance, *Policy* deals with the application of these principles (or sometimes their lack of application) to the topical problems of the day. It is possible to deal with the bare bones of *Principles* at an abstract level more or less applicable to any country. When we come to *Policy* we have to concentrate much more on a single country, looking at its major problems and taking full cognizance of the institutional background and intellectual climate of ideas on these matters. Inevitably, this also means that the level of discussion differs from that in the *Principles* section. In one sense it is lower, as there is less abstract and purely theoretical reasoning; in another sense it is higher, in that one has to blend one's knowledge of the real world with pure theory. These differences come to the front in the footnote arrangements; in *Principles* it is possible to dispense with them (more or less), in *Policy* we find it necessary to introduce footnote qualifications continuously.

The precise order of arrangement is based on the consideration that the general principles discussed under *Principles* are of wide and lasting interest, whereas matters of *Institutions* and *Policy* are bound to be narrower and more temporary. Therefore it would seem logical to take *Principles* first. Equally clearly, it would not be possible to discuss *Policy* issues at all sensibly without a grasp of the structure and mechanism of government finances in the UK and for this reason it is imperative to deal with *Institutions* before *Policy*.

Therefore our particular arrangement does cover the traditional field of public finance. Moreover, we believe it has some claims to be considered a reasonably logical system.

PART I
PRINCIPLES

2

PRELIMINARY MATTERS

1 THE PROBLEMS

The problems of *Principles* in public finance are those of knowing the effects, near and wide, short-term and long-term, of introducing and changing different kinds of government receipts and expenditures. If, for instance, an income tax is imposed for the first time in a country, will the level of output change, and if so, will some industries contract and expand more than others? What will happen to prices and wages? Similarly, if there is a large increase in government social security payments, how will the distribution of income between managers and workers, millionaires and tramps, Glaswegians and Londoners, be affected? And will people be encouraged to work harder, less hard or will they do just the same amount as before? Such are the kinds of question with which we have to deal in a *Principles* chapter.

In tracing out the ramifications of revenue and expenditure, it will obviously simplify our task considerably if we can agree on some principles of grouping, so that we can take whole blocks of revenue or expenditure at a time instead of trying to cope with each type separately. Therefore our first step must be to examine both the distinctions which can logically be made and the distinctions which are often in fact made. Subsequently, we shall outline and try to justify the organization of the *Principles* part.

1.1 *Logical distinctions*

If we glance at the annual accounts of any government organization, we can quickly see that a most general and far-reaching distinction can be made between those items which embrace both a movement of goods or services and a movement of funds, and those items which only cover one of these two categories, or, more briefly though less explicitly, between *bilateral* and *unilateral* flows. Thus all purchases or sales of goods and services will come under the first heading, as in these cases we have a movement of goods from the private sector of the economy to the public and a corresponding movement of funds from the public to the private sector. On the other hand, such items as government out-payments of interest and private payments of taxes to the government are unilateral flows taking place entirely on their own and therefore coming in the second category rather than the first. More generally, and rather more loosely, we can say that any *exchanges* of goods and services can and must be differentiated from *transfer payments*, a term which we can use as a generic description of those cases where no quid pro quo is involved. Thus, for instance we distinguish sharply between the absorption of goods and services by the National Health Service and transfer payments in the form of sickness benefit.

Some further aspects of this general distinction can now be examined. It can be seen very quickly that the differentiation which is frequently made between government current and capital transactions does not conflict with our more general distinction. Such items as the purchase of capital goods by the government or the sale of claims on itself in the form of War Bonds or other such titles are clearly a bilateral transaction and therefore come in our first category; on the other hand, capital grants, such as those paid to UK doctors after the introduction of the National Health Service to compensate them for the loss of the right to sell their practices, must be regarded as a transfer or unilateral payment. There is therefore no difficulty in reconciling the two classifications.

Nor does the distinction between transactions in money terms and in kind occasion any difficulty. The concept of a transfer payment is a perfectly general one embracing both types of transactions. Thus out-payments by the government, or *positive* transfers as we may call them, may be items such as widows' pensions or free milk for schoolchildren, whereas government receipts or *negative* transfers will embrace taxes and in-kind payments such as the surrender of works of art in lieu of payment of death duties, or wartime gifts of clothing for the Armed Forces. Normally, the distinction between money and in-kind items will not have much relevance for bilateral transactions as, except in cases of barter transactions, these consist by definition of a real flow matched by a money flow.

Another logical distinction is between payments and receipts which are optional and those which are obligatory. Most purchases and sales of goods and services are likely to be optional in the sense that there will generally be no compulsion to sell goods to or buy goods from the State. There are exceptions, such as the sale of services by conscripts, but by and large this is a fair generalization. Some transfer payments will always be obligatory. A poll tax (i.e. a fixed amount per head irrespective of circumstances) is one clear example; interest on the National Debt is another. On the other hand, there is no obligation to pay taxes on individual commodities, as these can always be avoided by not consuming them.

1.2 *Conventional distinctions*

If the basic logical distinction is between bilateral and unilateral flows, we now have to ask whether this does not imply that a number of time-honoured distinctions are more conventional than logical.

Suppose we take the distinction between receipts and payments first. A good deal of high-grade mental effort has been spent in the past in trying to show, for instance, the relative importance of government revenue in different countries or at different times. But once it is realized that there are many items which can be shifted in an arbitrary fashion from one side of the accounts to the other, many of these exercises which neglect this fact become quite valueless. It is just as reasonable to treat tax refunds as a negative item on the receipts side as it is to list it as a positive item on the expenditure side; similarly, tax receipts from government bondholders can be regarded as an item of positive receipts or negative expenditure. Examples like this can easily be multiplied. There is no need for us to do so, however, as the essential point is simply that only conventional distinctions, such as those given us by the government accounts, exist between some items of receipts and expenditure.

Familiar distinctions among the conventional revenue items may now be considered. The first is that between tax and non-tax receipts and the second is that between direct and indirect taxes.

Examples of the first distinction are the separation of court fines from liquor taxes, or the allocation of stamp duties on property transfers to the tax group and the operating surplus of a nationally owned enterprise to the non-tax group. When any justification for this sort of treatment is given it is usually argued that in the case of taxes there is no direct return of services to the taxpayer whereas in the case of non-tax items there is a much closer linkage.

The examples given above show the weakness of this argument. There is no sense in which a man who pays a fine for committing an assault can be said to receive any quid pro quo from the government; on the other hand, the transfer of the operating surplus of a nationalized industry to the government is exactly equivalent to a 100 per cent profits tax on that industry. The inherent logical difficulties of making this distinction are well demonstrated by the series of official estimates of UK national income since the war; the operating surplus of the Post Office has been treated in a series of different ways, without any change in the functions or position of the Post Office over the years. It may well be that in some cases there are good institutional reasons for making distinctions of this sort, e.g. fees and taxes may be collected by different agencies, but that is a rather different matter.

The classification of taxes into direct and indirect has a long history. In the *Principles of Political Economy*, J. S. Mill distinguished between direct and indirect taxes by asking whether a tax was actually paid over by the people on whom the burden fell or not. Direct taxes could, according to him, be levied on expenditure as well as income. A tax on house-services, for instance, would be rated as direct if paid by the tenant but as indirect if paid by the owner. Similarly, on this view, indirect taxes could be levied on incomes as well as on expenditure: a tax such as an employer's social insurance contribution, paid by the employer, but with effects on the conditions of employment, would presumably have to be treated as indirect.

The major difficulty about this approach is that it does presuppose some fairly extensive knowledge of the particular ways in which particular members of the community behave. Unless we are able to tell whether a tax is shifted from the immediate taxpayer to someone else, we cannot be certain whether to class it as direct or indirect. Further difficulties arise when a tax is partially, but not completely, shifted from the payer to others. It may be possible to shift a tax in some segments of an industry but not in others, if, say, the elasticity of demand for the goods produced is widely different in various regions of the country. In principle, Mill's distinction is logical enough, but without a much greater knowledge than we actually possess or are ever likely to possess about reactions to various taxes, it is extremely hard to apply.

Today, the distinction between direct and indirect taxes is more commonly drawn by reference to the *basis* of assessment rather than the *point* of assessment. Those taxes which are based on the receipt of income are termed direct, whereas those levied on expenditure are termed indirect. Income tax, profits tax and capital gains taxes are therefore direct; customs duties, excise taxes, value added taxes and stamp duties (based on capital expenditure) are indirect.

One obvious omission in this definition is the treatment of taxes based on the stock of capital, as distinct from those related to changes in the stock. Reference to income or outlay does not help us at all here. Nor does it get us much further in classifying an expenditure tax, i.e. a tax based on income *less* saving. Perhaps more fundamental is the criticism that no flow of funds in the economy can be indentified *solely* as an item of income or of outlay. Inevitably, it must be both simultaneously, and therefore any tax on someone's income must also be a tax on someone else's outlay. The distinction can be given meaning if we define income and outlay by reference to the household sector; in that case, taxes on wage incomes are unambiguously direct and taxes on beer consumption indirect. But there is no fundamental reason why the distinction between income and outlay should be orientated around households rather than business enterprises. One must clearly look at both types of entity. And in any case we are still left without a means of classifying taxes on income and expenditure flows between business firms.

Enough has now been said to show that the conventional distinctions drawn between taxes and other government receipts and between direct and indirect taxes do not have very good logical foundations. We must now turn to the items usually listed as government expenditures and ask whether the classifications commonly met are logically defensible or not.

We have already discussed the distinction between purchases of goods and services and transfer payments and we have seen that this is a perfectly valid classification. So too is the distinction between optional and obligatory transfers. But a further distinction is frequently made between those transfers in the form of grants and those in the form of subsidies, e.g. between old age pensions and disbursements of funds to British farmers. This distinction has very little basis in logic. This can be seen intuitively once it is realized that old age pensions can be thought of as a negative direct tax and farmers' subsidies as a negative indirect tax. If it is hard to draw a logical distinction between positive direct and indirect taxes, so must it be between negative direct and indirect taxes. More specifically, the usual distinction seems to rest on the assumption that one type of transfer only affects relative incomes of factors and the other only affects relative prices of goods. But to take a single instance, subsidies can easily have effects on the level of relative factor incomes, as we shall see later. Therefore this particular distinction seems to have no more validity than the corresponding one on the revenue side.

Wherever possible or relevant, we shall make use of the fundamental logical classification into bilateral and unilateral flows. As, however, it is convenient for some purposes to group various items together we shall use the terms 'direct' and 'indirect' taxes purely as shorthand expressions for conventionally defined groups of taxes ('direct' covering taxes assessed on wages, profits, rent and capital; 'indirect' covering taxes assessed on commodities) without any implication that these expressions correspond in any sense to a logical distinction.

2 THE METHOD OF ANALYSIS

We have completed our examination of the various forms of government receipts and expenditures, and we have seen the various ways in which they are interrelated and in which they can be classified. It is now time to turn to the means of judging the appropriate size of the public sector and the relative roles of central and subordinate units of government, together with the relative merits of different types of receipts and expenditures. Two questions seem to be involved: first the appropriate criteria and secondly, how to make use of the criteria. We shall explore each of these in turn.

2.1 *Appropriate criteria*

The first criterion is how far changes in different taxes and different types of expenditure influence the pattern of resource allocation inside an economy, assuming a given supply of resources. There are two dimensions to this subject. First, there is the allocation of resources between the public and the private sectors of the economy. This in turn is partly a matter of the diversion of real resources from private to public use and partly one of how far people are free to dispose of their incomes as they wish or, alternatively, how far purchasing power is siphoned away from them, whether for securing public absorption of real resources or for transfer of purchasing power from one set of individuals to another. Secondly, particular public revenue and expenditure decisions may themselves affect the allocation of resources between different uses within the private sector of the economy. We need to know which types of taxes cause the largest changes of this sort and which sort of changes should be considered beneficial and which not. Chapter 3 will deal with these subjects.

Secondly, we have to ask not only whether a change in government finance results in a reshuffling of existing productive resources but also whether it adds to or diminishes the supply of those resources. Will an increase in, say, unemployment benefit improve or impair the willingness of the population to work? Will larger profit taxes reduce the level of saving? All these questions centre round the supply of resources forthcoming for productive activity and Chapter 4 will be devoted to this topic.

Thirdly, changes in the level or form of government receipts and expenditures may affect the distribution of income and wealth among different sections of the community. Here again, we need to know the direction and extent of change, and we should also like to be able to judge the desirability of any such change. Many writers have dealt with this topic at great length and we shall examine it carefully in Chapter 5. Here again, there are close links with Chapter 3, for the effect of a tax is not simply to change the relative outputs of different goods and the allocation of different factors of production among the various end-products. In the process, it inevitably shifts the distribution of real incomes among the various factors of production and income groups by causing changes in relative prices of goods and factors. Nor is there just a one-way relationship here. Not only is it true that changes in resource patterns affect the distribution of incomes; but also tax-induced changes in the distribution of incomes have effects on consumption patterns and hence the allocation of resources. However, despite these linkages, it is much more conducive to clear thinking to separate the two criteria.

A fourth criterion is that of income stabilization. What are the relative merits and demerits of various expenditure increases as checks to depression or goads to inflation? And how far can tax policy be successful in smoothing out the fluctuations of income due to the trade cycle and how should tax policy be orientated to deal with long-term growth? Chapter 6 will deal with the complex issues of the subject.

The fifth criterion is that of administrative efficiency. It might well be, for instance, that some taxes are markedly superior to others in respect of all four of the above criteria but would be enormously costly to collect. Such issues as these will be dealt with in Chapter 7.

Obviously, these criteria are not the only ones, as there are many political and social criteria which could be brought forward. But we must restrict ourselves here to *economic* criteria, and it seems reasonable to claim that all the most important ones are subsumed under these five headings.

2.2 *Use of criteria*

The particular way in which we tackle the problem of analysis will already be apparent from the above discussion of criteria. Instead of taking individual taxes or expenditures one by one and considering their merits and demerits as a whole, we reverse the process and seek to ask how each type of tax or expenditure appears in the light of any one criterion. To put it another way, we divide the analysis horizontally instead of vertically, by economic criteria rather than by revenue or expenditure classification.

We believe there are some advantages in this approach. It is perfectly possible to set up some sort of hypothetically ideal tax arrangement and then compare the departures from it in respect of each tax. But there are some dangers in this course. One is that the ideal tax arrangement is by no means a straightforward concept, as we shall see from time to time. If sufficient can be gained from the comparison of the relative effects of different taxes, this is a much more clear-cut procedure. Another point is that when we are comparing pairs of taxes all the time, there is no danger of neglecting income effects, i.e. failing to recognize that some of the supposed effects of a change in the rate of any one tax are partly the result of the tax rate change and partly the result of the change in the budget surplus or deficit. Another point is that our approach enables us to treat revenue and expenditure problems symmetrically; although it is perfectly possible to examine the consequences of different types of expenditure by the alternative procedure, none the less it is rarely done. Another advantage is that policy issues are more concerned with marginal changes in the revenue or expenditure structure than with the supersession or introduction of a complete tax. Our method might therefore be deemed to have more advantages from this viewpoint.

3 THE CONCEPT OF INCIDENCE

One final topic remains. How do the criteria by which we have suggested that revenue and expenditure changes should be appraised fit into the traditional discussions about the shifting and incidence of taxation? We shall discuss the meaning of these concepts further in Chapter 5, but it may be useful for us to show now how the ideas developed above are related to these well-known general terms.

The main difficulty in answering this question lies in pinning down the precise meaning of 'incidence' which, like so many words in economic literature, has almost as many meanings as uses. Most writers have associated the word with the effects of taxes on prices. Thus Seligman devised a succession of finely wrought theories to show how various taxes were shifted forwards or backwards, thus influencing either prices of commodities or prices of factors of production. More generally, this approach is really concerned with the effects of taxes on the distribution of real income, for that is clearly what is involved when changes in prices of factors and of commodities are considered. There have at various times been attempts to define 'incidence' more broadly – to include, for instance, the effects on the allocation of factors between industries or even on the supply of factors coming forth for employment. As against these broader definitions, the Colwyn Committee of 1927 specifically attempted to narrow down the concept to the very immediate short run distributional consequences as distinct from the longer-term 'effects' on relative outputs and the supply of factors at work.

It can easily be seen, therefore, that whether the broader or narrower interpretation of 'incidence' is taken, we shall cover it in our succeeding chapters dealing with the allocation of resources, the supply of factors and the distribution of income and wealth. Because of the ambiguity surrounding the term we shall in general try to avoid using it, but where it is necessary to do so, we shall try to indicate how we interpret it.

3

THE ALLOCATION OF EXISTING RESOURCES

1 OUTLINE

It must be made quite clear from the beginning that we assume a given supply of all productive resources, i.e. a given labour force seeking work and a given level of saving, etc. In other words, we assume a zero elasticity of supply of resources to the economy as a whole, all questions of the labour force being able to choose at the margin between leisure and work and all questions of the influence of taxes, etc. on the level of saving being deferred to Chapter 4. We shall also postpone to Chapter 7 all the administrative difficulties of imposing different types of taxes and of organizing different types of government expenditure.

Resource allocation discussion falls into two parts. Section 2 will cover the principles governing the size and composition of public expenditure, the relative importance of public and private activities and so on. Then in section 3 we shall examine in detail how different types of taxes and expenditures affect the allocation of resources at the disposal of the private sector.

Although there has been a tendency in recent years to give a great deal of attention to the former topic, we shall follow historical tradition in spending more time on the latter. As a result of the growth of interest in the principles determining the optimum size of the public sector and the sort of situations where public intervention is needed in one form or another, many new and interesting questions have been raised, in particular the extent to which decision-taking by politicians and bureaucrats can be explained in terms of standard economic principles. But it is undoubtedly the case that economists have been better at raising new questions on this subject than settling them, or even for that matter settling old ones which have perplexed people for many years. This may well be inevitable given that one is dealing with a broad philosophical and political problem rather than a narrowly economic one. And even when economic issues are involved they tend to be of a very wide and general nature rather than a seriés of clear and close guides to practical action. Furthermore, one must keep opportunity costs in mind. The price of devoting more space to the determination of public expenditure would have to be a reduction in that devoted to other topics if the size of this book is to be kept within reasonable bounds. It is for reasons of these sorts that we shall devote less space to these recent developments than is fashionable in many quarters today.[1]

2 THE SIZE AND COMPOSITION OF PUBLIC EXPENDITURE

2.1 *Arguments for State intervention*

One very general way of approaching this question is to break it down into a series of smaller ones. First of all one has to ask: on what grounds of principle should the State interfere in economic matters at all beyond prescribing some very general rules of the game? Secondly, one needs to know the principles which determine whether any action which is agreed should be fiscal or otherwise. Thirdly, if fiscal action is considered desirable, should it involve absorption of goods and services by the State? To simplify, we leave on one side all questions of State interference to secure changes in the supply of resources, the stabilization of the income level, or the distribution of any given real income, although in fact these issues too can be discussed under the same headings as those we use. We also restrict ourselves to discussing the percentage of the flow of goods and services absorbed by the State and so leave on one side the desirability of State ownership of capital assets, i.e. our concern is with government *provision* rather than government *production* of goods and services.

To the first question, an infinite number of answers can be given depending on one's political and philosophical approach. But as a minimum, it seems possible to establish three different reasons why the State should be justified in stepping down from its dais into the economic arena. First of all, there are cases where economic activity is naturally carried on under conditions precluding competition and tending towards monopoly. Thus the scale and method of operations of a Post Office organization inside a country or a sewerage scheme inside

[1] Those wishing to explore these matters more fully should consult R. A. and P. B. Musgrave, *Public Finance in Theory and Practice*, second edition (McGraw-Hill, 1976) for incorporation of such matters in a standard work on public finance; and, for more specialized discussion, J. M. Buchanan, *The Demand and Supply of Public Goods* (Rand McNally, 1968) and J. G. Head, *Public Goods and Public Welfare* (Duke University Press, Durham, N. Carolina, 1974).

a town must be such as to make one, and only one, firm the effective unit of operation. Similarly, there are a limited number of channels in which sound broadcasting or television may take place; therefore *some* State control over their allocation is justified.

Secondly, there are many cases, as we shall see, where social costs or benefits exist which are not necessarily seen or taken into account by private individuals either in their role of consumers or as producers. In some cases, externalities are bound up with jointness of consumption; this brings us up against the problem of public or social goods, to which we shall return shortly. As for externalities *simpliciter*, elementary education is a good example. Living and working in a modern advanced society requires a certain minimum level of knowledge and training. But if any one individual fails to reach this standard the penalties for not doing so will be borne to some extent by the community in general as well as by the man himself. If, for instance, a man who cannot read is allowed to drive a car and because of his inability to observe traffic directions is involved in an accident, he suffers himself but so do the other parties to the accident. It is clearly better to devise means of anticipating and avoiding social losses rather than try to apportion responsibility for them afterwards.

Lastly, it is reasonable to argue that the State should always be prepared to help those who are incapable of economic reasoning or of having any perception of what is an advantageous and what a disadvantageous course of action economically. This principle of merit wants, as it is often called, justifies laws preventing employment of young children or legislation giving State support for the mentally handicapped.

Such, in the briefest outline, are the minimal grounds on which State interference may be justified. It should be emphasized that there is more than one way of setting out such principles; some authors, for instance, like to put great emphasis on the need to subsidize industries operating under decreasing costs. But whatever the precise formulation of these grounds for State action, we must now turn to the next question: what are the relative merits of fiscal as against non-fiscal action? Suppose, for instance, an important industry is dominated by a giant monopoly which is thought to be restricting output below the competitive level. Should attempts be made to 'trust-bust' by legislation, compulsorily dividing the organization into a number of sub-units or should subsidies be given to encourage potential rivals? There is little to say in terms of general economic principles. One can bring forward points such as the relative efficiency of the different government departments concerned, the speed with which action is desired and so on, but essentially these are much more in the nature of ad hoc arguments.

But supposing it is decided that State interference is necessary and that it should take fiscal form. How are we to decide between, say, a system of State subsidies and one of State purchases? Education is a good example here. One obvious reaction is that, to avoid the social burden of uneducated people, the State should itself hire the teachers, arrange school-building, school supplies and the like – and then make education available without payment. The alternative is a system of State subsidies (valid only for spending on education) to parents. Although it can be argued that the choice between the two methods can be made on the basis of taxpayers' preferences (i.e. that those who provide the finance may derive greater utility from government expenditure on education taking one form rather than the other) the practicality of such a proposition is not immediately obvious. It does not in fact seem that purely economic reasoning can take us very far in this discussion apart from genuflecting to the general principles of minimizing costs. This becomes even clearer if we remember that in practice the choice might lie between a larger number of alternatives (e.g. government loans or guarantees) than those already mentioned.[1]

This brief survey may be sufficient to give some idea of the general economic principles which should govern the size and composition of public sector expenditure. But the very bareness of the economic principles set forth will make it clear that we are now on the borderland where economic and political considerations meet and mingle inextricably with one another. Some economists have argued that the whole question could be settled by reference to ability-to-pay principles. Along with the propositions that tax burdens should be distributed so as to minimize sacrifices[2] and that public expenditure should be distributed on analogous principles to private consumption expenditures, it was maintained that the size of the budget could be settled by the simple test of comparing the marginal sacrifice due to extra taxation with the marginal gain from extra public spending. However, this approach seems to be sterile. Quite apart from all the difficulties of isolating and measuring sacrifices, no one ever demonstrated clearly

[1] The issues of market versus State provision, with some specific illustrations, are discussed in more detail in Chapter 14.

[2] See below, pp. 95–8

how the schedule of benefits from government spending was supposed to be constructed. Without such information, we are left with the emptiest of empty economic boxes.

2.2 *Pure public goods*

A great deal of effort has been devoted in recent years to attempts to elucidate the general considerations set out above by concentrating on the polar case of those pure public goods where the market mechanism is likely to break down altogether.

It is customary to distinguish three separate topics. First, we have to set out the conditions necessary to secure optimal provision of such goods. Second, we analyse why market failure takes place in these cases. Third, one comes to the nature of the political decisions needed to make the requisite quantity of such goods available through the political, rather than the market, process. We shall look at each of these topics but first of all we must set out exactly what is implied by a public good.

A pure public good is usually deemed to have three characteristics. First, there is an element of jointness or 'non-rivalness' in consumption, so that if a commodity is currently being supplied to individual A it can be made simultaneously available to individual B without extra cost, e.g. a nuclear deterrent weapon, or a television broadcast signal. Second, there has to be an element of non-excludability in the sense that B cannot be shut off from enjoyment of the commodity irrespective or not of whether he wishes to have it. In effect, this second property is exactly what we have in mind when singling out externalities – in the sense that these arise when one man imposes costs or benefits on another, for which financial compensation cannot be exacted. Third, it must be impossible to reject the supply of a particular good or service, so that if it is provided for A then B cannot fail to participate in it; he is a 'forced rider'. When all these conditions are satisfied, there can be no question of different people consuming different quantities of a good or service: each and every individual has to consume the same amount and this amount is also supplied to the totality of consumers. It should be noted that the third characteristic – impossibility of rejection – is a crucial element; without this stipulation, it would be *possible*, but not *necessary*, for consumption to be equal for everyone.

Taking up the first of the three topics listed above, the conditions for optimal output, we must begin by recapitulating the conditions necessary for optimal output in the market context, assuming for the time being that there is no discrepancy between private and social costs and benefits.

The notion of ideal output in the private sector is grounded in the concept of perfect competition, which implies an infinitely elastic demand for each of the products of any one firm and an infinitely elastic supply of each of the factors to that firm. If all those taking part in this perfectly competitive society act so as to maximize their satisfaction or returns, certain results follow when the system is in equilibrium.

As far as the consumer is concerned, relative consumption of different commodities should be such that the marginal values of different commodities will be proportional to their relative prices, i.e. no consumer can gain extra satisfaction by slightly altering the pattern of his expenditure. If producers act so as to maximize their profits, they will produce goods up to the point at which the marginal revenue from sales equals the marginal cost of production, and will so distribute their outlay on the factors of production that the marginal cost of any one factor is equal to the value of the marginal net product of that factor. Sellers of factors (or factor services) to firms will be in an optimum position if they allocate themselves so as to equate the marginal costs of their services to the prices offered for them.

Under the very special conditions of perfectly elastic supply of factors and demand for goods in the case of the individual firm, these actions will result in the marginal cost of a commodity being equated to its price and the value of the marginal net product of a factor being equated to its price. Alternatively, in indifference curve language, the optimum situation will be reached when the rate of substitution in consumption is equal to the rate of substitution in purchase on the market (i.e. the ratios of market prices of commodities) and this in turn is equal to the rate of substitution in production. Whichever formulation we use, it can easily be seen that it is impossible to increase the value of output of any one commodity without reducing the value of output of another commodity to a greater extent; and impossible to make one person better off, without making someone else worse off.

How do matters differ when we have to deal with a pure public good? The simplest approach to the problem is to contrast two figures, one showing the position with pure private goods and the other with pure public goods (Figure 3.1 (a) and (b)).

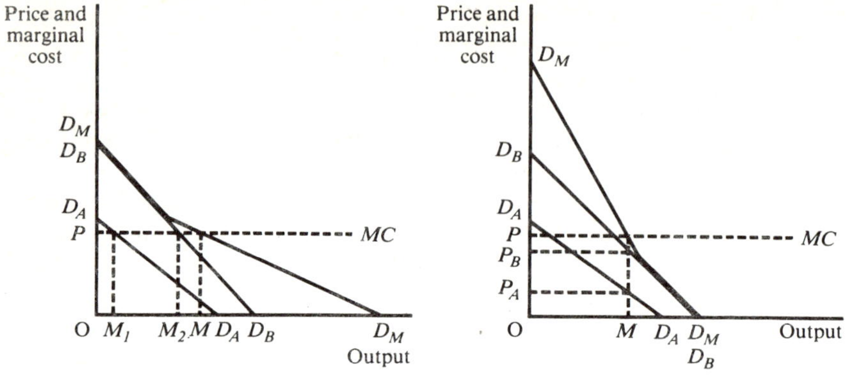

Figure 3.1 (a) Private goods

Figure 3.1 (b) Public goods

With pure private goods we add A's demand curve (D_A) horizontally to B's demand curve (D_B) to obtain the market demand curve (D_M). Total output is determined by the intersection of the marginal cost curve MC with D_M. All output is sold at price OP, with A taking OM_1 and B taking OM_2 to make up the total output of OM, i.e. prices are the same, but quantities differ.

With pure public goods, the critical feature is that everyone must consume the same amount – what is available for any one individual is available for everyone else – and so we have a situation where people can differ only in the marginal valuation they place on a given quantity of the commodity rather than in their consumption of it. Hence, demand curves now have to be added vertically rather than horizontally. Total output is given by the intersection of D_M and MC. Price OP represents the sum of the marginal valuations placed by A and B (P_A and P_B respectively) on an output of OM.

So we can summarize the contrast between the two cases by saying that with pure private goods we have the same price paid by A and B but different consumption levels; with pure public goods we have the same consumption level for A and B but they attach different marginal valuations to that level.

Although this method of explaining the difference between the two polar cases is useful as an introduction, it suffers, along with other analogous 'simple' explanations, from two major drawbacks. One is that it is a partial equilibrium approach which does not tie the output of private and public goods into the total production possibilities of the economy; the other is that there may be some fundamental difficulties in deriving the marginal valuations of public goods.

Leaving the latter problem on one side for the moment, the translation from partial to general equilibrium terms is fairly readily accomplished by a standard diagrammatic exposition originally due to Samuelson.[1]

The upshot is that we can reformulate the contrast between the pure private goods case and the public goods in a somewhat more sophisticated form.

If two consumers, A and B, allocate their budgets between two private goods X and Y, the standard equilibrium condition is that marginal rates of substitution in consumption should be equal to the marginal rate of transformation between the two commodities, i.e.

$$MRS_{xy}^{A} = MRS_{xy}^{B} = MT_{xy} \quad .$$

If, alternatively, A and B have to choose between one private good (Y) and one public good (X) the equilibrium condition then becomes

$$MRS_{xy}^{A} + MRS_{xy}^{B} = MT_{xy} \quad .$$

In other words, we now have a condition of additivity rather than equality between marginal rates of substitution in consumption, parallel to the partial equilibrium contrast between the horizontal and vertical summation of demand curves.

Further refinements can be made to this statement of optimality conditions, e.g. in showing that the sum of the differential prices to individual consumers of the public good should equal its marginal cost of provision. If prices are not uniform for all units purchased by any one individual, we then need to interpret price as meaning the price of the marginal unit purchased. One can also develop the analysis further if one is prepared to graft on the concept of a social welfare function.

We mentioned earlier that there are fundamental difficulties in deducing marginal valuations of pure public goods: demand curves may be of a pseudo-character only. The essential point, as Wicksell realized many years ago, is that people may be tempted to conceal their preferences. If a public good is supplied at all it is by definition available to everyone irrespective of whether any particular individual has expressed any interest in having it or any willingness to pay for it.

[1] P. A. Samuelson, 'The Pure Theory of Public Expenditures', *Review of Economics and Statistics*, November 1954; and 'A Diagrammatic Exposition of a Theory of Public Expenditure', *ibid*, November 1955. For expositions of the same technique, see R. A. and P. B. Musgrave, *op. cit.*, Ch. 3, and J. G. Head, *op. cit.*, Ch. 3.

So an individual will think that by keeping quiet about his needs he can enjoy the fruits of such output without paying a penny for it: this is the famous 'free-rider' problem, as it is often described in the literature. But the paradox is that if nobody at all shows any willingness to pay, then there will be no signal that any output at all should be provided. So we have a major contrast with the private goods position. Whereas in that case willingness to pay determines the maximum amount any one individual can consume, the same condition does not hold with pure public goods.

We now come to the second of the two main topics of this section: why is it that private provision of public goods is likely to be unsatisfactory?

If one thinks of such goods being produced privately for sale in the market, one must first of all ask whether the characteristic of non-rivalness in consumption is a fundamental drawback. Referring to Figure 3.1, one can see that the answer is 'no'. If it were possible to discriminate between A and B and charge B a much higher price than A, reflecting differences in marginal valuations, the total amount received from A and B together could suffice to cover the marginal cost of provision.

So although it would be correct to say that a perfectly competitive market solution, with all consumers paying identical prices, would be impossible in the face of non-rivalness, it would be incorrect to say that no market solution would be possible even though the result might be a smaller level of output than under a perfectly competitive regime. When, however, we consider non-excludability (whether allied with non-rejectability or not), it is easy to see that market solutions will be totally inapplicable if it is quite impossible to shut out consumers from whom payment cannot be exacted; or, alternatively, will be impracticable if the mechanism of charging is extremely expensive to operate. More generally, one might ask whether individuals might set up any market-type organization of any sort to arrange the supply of goods with public characteristics. But then we find ourselves in a Morton's fork situation. If there are a large number of people, any one individual has no motive to reveal his true preferences; he will feel that the quantity of public goods supplied will not be affected by any such concealment, or in other words that he may as well seize the opportunities of a free ride. But if everyone adopts this attitude, such goods as these will not be produced even though it is in everyone's interest (or, at least, everyone except those who positively abhor such things, e.g. pacifists and defence equipment) that they should be. On the other hand, if the number of people involved is small, strategic considerations will enter into preference revelation and so again no market-produced optimal solution is likely. So whether we are dealing with large or small numbers, there are formidable problems, probably insoluble, of disentangling by such processes the true nature of the demand for public goods.

Given this demonstration of possible market failure in whole or in part over a wide range of goods and services, a number of writers have tried to find whether the political mechanism would be likely to produce an optimal, or more nearly optimal solution. Although a great deal of effort has gone into this over many years (e.g. Wicksell's famous unanimity rule: that even if only one person was against a particular tax-and-expenditure proposal it should not be proceeded with), it would not seem that any agreed conclusions have been reached as yet. Problems of non-revelation of preferences arise in the political as well as the economic arena; and whereas some analysts have come to the conclusion that the political process would result in an over-supply of public goods, others have reached a diametrically opposite conclusion. It should also be noted that not much light is thrown on the question whether public intervention, if it is justified at all, should be pursued by transfers which affect the allocation of resources within the private sector or by public provision which also affects the allocation between the public and the private sector.

2.3 *Other public goods considerations*

It is frequently said that in reality the stringent conditions for pure public goods are unlikely to be met very often. Thus the importance of the non-revelation of preferences argument can easily be exaggerated. Some goods with marked public characteristics continue to be produced in the private sector; and in the normal situation where elected representatives express views on behalf of their constituents it is not altogether easy to visualize a process by which such spokesmen habitually misrepresent the views of those who have voted them into office.

It can be argued that goods exhibiting all of the relevant characteristics – non-rivalness in consumption, non-excludability and non-rejectability – are likely to be few in number, e.g. defence, the services of lighthouses, the anti-malaria spraying of a district or the provision of fluoride in an area water supply are standard examples. But this does not dispose of the problem; for even though there may be relatively few goods exhibiting all the basic attributes in full, there are many which do so in part. It may be that we have non-rivalness without non-excludability (e.g. a theatre performance[1] or a bridge, up to capacity); or that we have non-excludability without non-rivalness (e.g. separate oil wells tapping a common pool); or that we have non-rivalness and non-excludability but rejection is possible. It may also be that the degree of 'publicness' is a function of the size of geographical area; in a small area a particular service (e.g. fire protection) may be equally available to all whereas this is not necessarily so when an area is enlarged. In general, we can think of goods and services being distributed over the whole spectrum between the limiting cases of purely private and purely public goods.

Further complications arise when an individual's utility is not simply a function of his own consumption of private-type goods and of any pure public good which is available but is dependent on his own private and public goods consumption and on someone else's public goods consumption – in other words, when we have spillover or mixed-good relationships rather than pure public goods. Formally, in the pure public case, for the ith individual,

$$U^i = U^i\,(y_1^i, y_2^i, \ldots, x_n),$$

where $y_1, y_2 \ldots.$ are private goods and x_n is a public good equally available to all.

Whereas in the externality case,

$$U^i = U^i\,(y_1^i, y_2^i, \ldots, x_n^i;\, x_n^k),$$

i.e. the utility of the ith individual is dependent on consumption of x_n (equal for all), in the first case, but on the consumption of x_n by the kth individual as well as his own direct consumption of it, in the second case.

We now have a much more complex situation. Instead of the 'simple' optimality condition that the sum of the marginal rates of substitution of A and B between y (a private good) and x (a public good) should equal the marginal rate of transformation between x and y, we now have to stipulate that the sum of the two marginal rates of substitution between a private good and A's consumption of the public good should equal the sum of the two marginal rates of substitution between a private good and B's consumption of the public good; and both sum-

[1] For precision, we should specify a performance with an effective entrance barrier, e.g. we have non-excludability for anyone within hearing range, but outside any barrier, of an open-air performance.

mations should in turn equal the marginal rate of transformation.[1] In other words, it is no longer simply a matter of the allocation of productive resources between the public and the private good but also one of the amount of consumption of the public good by different individuals.

Nor are public goods considerations necessarily dissociated from merit goods principles. We can envisage public goods supply as being completely regulated by preferences of individuals; but we can also envisage situations which call for public overriding of such preferences. But in the latter case it is even harder than before to formulate a satisfactory political mechanism for determining optimum supply. But this is hardly surprising when we remember that the desideratum is a voting system which simultaneously caters for both the representation and the overriding of individuals' preferences.

2.4 *Other public expenditure issues*

Although much of the intellectual effort devoted to expenditure matters in recent years has been concentrated on the elucidation of the nature of public goods and the elaboration of appropriate political procedures in lieu of market ones ('the economics of politics'), other aspects of public expenditure have not been neglected. One major theme has been the examination of long-term trends in public expenditure and their explanation. Many explanatory hypotheses have been advanced such as the discrete jumps which take place at times of national emergency and are subsequently found to be irreversible, or the long-term tendency for public sector expenditure to increase as a proportion of GDP because productivity increases faster in the private sector (e.g. in manufacturing industry) than in the public sector (largely services) – the implication then being that public sector costs of provision are forced up disproportionately to the growth of GNP.

Another theme has been the investigation of the effects of changes in key variables, such as the size of the population or the size of the area served, on the costs of provision of any particular level of public goods and services. Thus one might expect an increase in population, area served constant, to reduce per capita costs of provision of a pure public

[1] Using the same terminology as on p. 27, we now write the condition for Pareto optimality as follows:

$$MRS^{A}_{x^{A}y} + MRS^{B}_{x^{A}y} = MRS^{B}_{x^{B}y} + MRS^{A}_{x^{B}y} = MT_{xy}$$

where x^{A} = A's consumption of the public good and x^{B} = B's consumption of the public good. See J. G. Head, 'Mixed Goods in Samuelson Geometry', *Public Finance*, no. 3, 1976, for a full discussion.

good available to all and sundry. Extension of a geographical area, population held constant, might reduce the dangers of a fire in one house affecting contiguous ones but, on the other hand, would increase the likelihood of any one fire in any one house doing more damage if fire appliances had farther to travel.

Yet another major theme has been the development of appropriate principles of public decision-taking in respect of major expenditure by the use of cost–benefit analysis.

But as we said earlier, we do not propose to dwell on these developments at length in this chapter. They are very adequately documented elsewhere.[1]

3 RESOURCE ALLOCATION IN THE PRIVATE SECTOR

3.1 *Preliminary matters*

3.1.1 *Ceteris paribus* A difficulty which constantly recurs in tax analysis is to know precisely what else is assumed to remain constant whilst the effects of a tax change are being traced. The essential point is that, in a sense, there is no such thing as ceteris paribus. For if we wish to trace the effects of an additional tax and simply postulate that government expenditure remains unchanged, the budget surplus must increase and there must be consequent effects on the level of money income and expenditure. In a very real sense other things have not remained unchanged. If the stock of money remains constant despite the increase in the budget surplus there may well be reductions in interest rates with further repercussions on the economy. On the other hand, if we assume that government expenditure increases pari passu with the tax, then even more directly other things are not being held constant, and it will usually be impossible to sort out the price and

[1] On long-term trends see A. J. Peacock and J. Wiseman, *The Growth of Public Expenditure in the UK*, second edition (Allen and Unwin, 1967); and H. C. Recktenwald (ed.), *Secular Trends of the Public Sector* (International Institute of Public Finance, Cujas, Paris, 1978). On detailed expenditure analysis see C. S. Shoup, *Public Finance* (Weidenfeld, 1969) Chs 4 and 5; and 'Collective Consumption and Relative Size of the Government Sector' in R. E. Grieson (ed.), *Public and Urban Economics* (D. C. Heath, Lexington, 1976). On cost–benefit analysis see A. R. Prest and R. Turvey, 'Cost Benefit Analysis: a Survey', *Economic Journal*, December 1965; R. A. Musgrave, 'Cost Benefit Analysis and the Theory of Public Finance', *Journal of Economic Literature*, September 1969; and P. R. G. Layard, *Cost Benefit Analysis* (Penguin, 1972).

quantity changes due to the tax from those resulting from the accompanying government expenditure.

There are several ways of dealing with this problem. One is to ignore it altogether, but this is hardly a suitable device for the furtherance of economic analysis. A second way is to assume that any tax increase is simultaneously compensated by a decrease in another tax in such a way as to leave the budget surplus or deficit unchanged. This immediately raises the questions 'which other tax is decreased', 'what will be the effects of this tax decrease' and 'how shall we separate these from those due to the tax increase'. To this the answer is sometimes given that we assume the compensating tax variation to be some kind of tax, which is known to have no effect on relative prices and quantities. But to this the reply is how does one know it has no economic effect unless one has at some time analysed its effects, *without any compensating variation*? This is a powerful line of argument and we should neglect it at our peril.

Another approach can be used when we are interested in *comparative* tax effects rather than the effects of a single tax considered in isolation. This is the very simple expedient of postulating either that the changes in government expenditure should be identical irrespective of the kind of tax change or alternatively that government expenditure remains unchanged and one tax is assumed to increase whilst the other is reduced. Therefore, if we are interested in comparing the effects of, say, a land tax and an equal-yield house-tax on the allocation of resources we simply assume that government expenditure changes in exactly the same way in each case. The *differential* change in relative quantities and prices of goods and factors will therefore be a reflection of the *comparative* effects of the two taxes. Similarly, the comparative effects of say, equal government expenditures on postmen and airfields can be traced by assuming an identical method of finance in each case.

Clearly this approach is only useful for *comparisons* between taxes or expenditures. But this is precisely what we often need and we shall therefore make use of this approach. Where this is insufficient we make use of a dummy tax which is conceived to be a tax of equal yield to that under consideration but without any effects on the allocation of resources. This is an artificial standard of reference, as it is in principle impossible to test any actual tax scheme to see whether it fulfils these criteria. The introduction or changing of a poll tax, for instance, necessarily implies some other change such as that due to an increased budget surplus, and any effects on output and prices will be the joint result of the poll tax and the associated change in the budget balance of government expenditure. We must therefore be extremely cautious about the reliance we put on this piece of scaffolding.

3.1.2 *Taxes versus charges* If it is decided that some particular expenditure should be the responsibility of the public rather than the private sector, the first question is whether those making use of this facility should be charged according to their consumption or whether the expenditure should be financed through taxation. In many cases the choice simply does not arise, as it is precisely the impossibility or undesirability of charging according to consumption which is the reason for government action. It is impossible to say how much benefit any one individual derives from defence expenditure. It is undesirable to charge people fully for the amount of education they receive. Where these sorts of considerations are not important and where the considerations of optimum allocation of resources according to private costs and benefits are deemed important, there is a prima facie argument for saying that charges according to use are likely to be more satisfactory than taxes not related to use. They can be thought of as the allocative mechanism which will most nearly simulate that of the private sector. Exactly how a system of charges should be organized would lead us into all the questions of public enterprise pricing, which is outside the scope of this book. But the general presumption must be that from the viewpoint of allocative efficiency, charging according to use is the right and proper system of paying for some forms of government-provided services.

3.2 *Direct versus indirect taxes*

We are now ready to turn to the first and best-known problem in tax analysis. This is the contention that the allocative effects of indirect or consumption taxes are inferior to those of direct or income taxes, both being interpreted in the conventional sense. Frequently, the argument is summarized by the epithet 'the excess burden of indirect taxation'.

To make our analysis logically precise we must state our basic assumptions. We start from a position where marginal costs are equal to prices throughout the economy and where factor rewards are equal to factor marginal net products, or in other words, where we have an optimum allocation of resources. We assume that there are no divergences between private and social costs and benefits. Finally, we assume zero elasticity of supply of the various factors of production to the economy as a whole. We now want to compare the relative effects of direct and indirect taxes. But there are many types of taxation subsumed under these general headings and it may be useful to fix our ideas more precisely by specifying particular forms of taxation. We shall compare an indirect tax based on one commodity (and levied at a specific rate per unit) with an income tax which is exactly proportional to income. Furthermore, in order to abstract from distributional considerations for the time being, it is assumed that each individual is an exactly similar microcosm of society as a whole in respect of his economic characteristics, i.e. everyone is alike in respect of ability, income and tastes. This will enable us to move easily from arguing at the individual level to arguing at the social level. Finally, we assume that the government collects exactly the same amount of revenue from either tax and spends it on exactly the same quantities of the same things in either case.

The difference between the effects of the two taxes is illustrated diagrammatically in Figure 3.2.

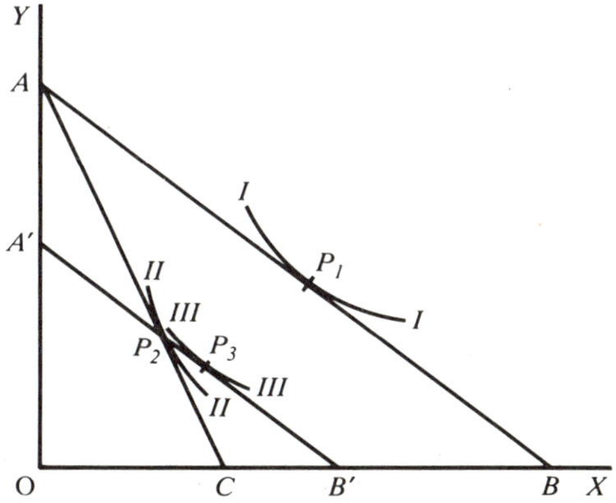

Figure 3.2. Excess burden of taxation (first approach)

Suppose we assume that a consumer spends the whole of his income on two goods X and Y, and that quantities of Y are measured on the vertical and quantities of X on the horizontal axis. The indifference curve I measures combinations of X and Y, between which the consumer has no preference and the price ratio line AB measures the relative prices of X and Y. The equilibrium position, from which any deviation must result in a less preferred position, will be P_1.

Now suppose a specific tax can be levied on X; imagine that the price of X increases so that now the price ratio line is AC. The equilibrium position will then be P_2 on the lower indifference curve *II*.

As an alternative, suppose an income tax be levied at a rate sufficient to produce an equal yield to the government. This will now give us a new price-ratio line $A'B'$ which will be parallel to AB if we assume that the imposition of such an income tax will not alter the relative prices of X and Y. This line will pass through P_2; for among the possibilities now open to the consumer is to buy the same amounts of X and Y as he did when X was taxed, since the income tax has been so fixed that his net income would just suffice to do so. But this is not in fact how he will behave; instead, equilibrium will be attained at P_3, where $A'B'$ is tangential to indifference curve *III*. As this curve represents a more preferred position than curve *II*, it must follow that a direct tax has less harmful effects on the allocation of resources than an indirect one.

Such is the argument which is often put forward to demonstrate the inferiority of indirect taxes. We now have to ask whether it is a general argument or whether it only holds under certain special conditions. This involves examination, first of all, of the conditions in which the taxes are levied and secondly, the particular form of the taxes.

It is useful to approach these further ramifications by means of Figure 3.3.

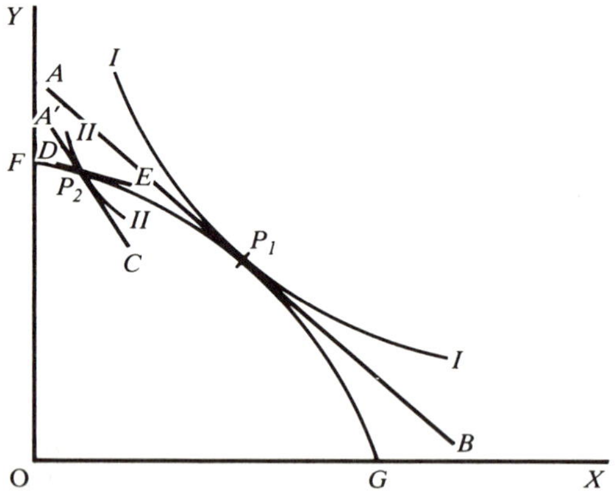

Figure 3.3. Excess burden of taxation (second approach)

In this diagram quantities of Y are again given on the vertical and those of X on the horizontal axis. *I* is an indifference curve for the representative consumer in a community; FP_1G is a production possibility curve showing the various combinations of X and Y which it is possible to produce with the resources available to the representative producer.[1] AB has the same meaning for consumers as before and for producers it represents a line of constant receipts, i.e. it shows the combination of X and Y which bring in the same total revenue to producers. P_1 is therefore the point of double equilibrium representing the most preferred position for the representative consumer and the most profitable position for the representative producer. Because of our assumption about the identical nature of each consumer and of each producer, this diagram can be thought of as applying to each individual in the community.

Now suppose a tax is imposed. The first proposition is that the production possibility curve will tend to remain unchanged, whatever the form of the tax and whatever the way in which it is spent. It is clear that, under the assumption made throughout this chapter about the fixed quantities of productive resources, there can be no change in the technical possibilities of production in the community. But it must also follow that the disposition of government expenditure will tend not to alter them either; for if the government simply transfers the receipts back to the private sector in equal lump sum grants the possibilities of producing X and Y clearly remain unchanged; if the government uses tax receipts to absorb real resources in producing another commodity, then strictly speaking we need a three-dimensional surface to show the possibilities of combining the new commodity (which we may call Z) with X and Y. But as an approximation we may use our original diagram to represent the new situation (in principle we can think of it as being drawn on a different scale after resources have been subtracted to meet the output of Z).

The effect of imposing an income tax in these circumstances is to leave the equilibrium point for both producer and consumer unchanged at P_1, for nothing has altered to change the relative prices of X and Y or the shape and position of the consumer and producer indifference curves. But if a tax is imposed on X then the equilibrium position is no longer P_1 but P_2. The new price line for consumers is $A'C$, and the fact that this is more steeply inclined than AB is directly due to the tax on X which must increase the price of X relatively to Y. $A'C$ is tangential to consumer indifference curve II at P_2 and therefore this is an equilibrium point for consumers. But the relevant price line for

[1] i.e. FP_1G can be thought of as the community production possibility curve drawn on a scale $1/N$th as large where N is the number of individuals in the community.

producers is not one which includes such taxes and so they will only be in equilibrium when the production possibility curve is tangential to a price ratio line net of taxes. The relevant line on Figure 3.3 is *DE*. This will normally be flatter than *AB* thereby indicating that part of the tax is borne by producers.

The point P_2 is therefore another position of double equilibrium giving tangency between FP_1G and *DE* for producers and tangency between *A'C* and *II* for consumers. But *II* is a lower indifference curve than *I*. Therefore, it follows that an indirect tax of a specific nature must produce a worse allocation of resources than a proportional income tax.

It may seem at first sight that we have spent a long time in travelling a circuitous way to end with a result which, apart from applying to the representative consumer and producer as distinct from the individual consumer, was derived much more simply a few pages ago. But this is not so. First of all we have brought production conditions directly into the picture; their absence from Figure 3.2 robs it of generality.[1] Secondly, supposing we were to assume that at the start of our whole investigation we were not in a position P_1 but rather one such as P_2, i.e. a position of equilibrium for both producers and consumers but not that which corresponds to an ideal allocation of resources. In these circumstances we consider the relative merits of an equal-yield proportional income tax and a specific tax on *Y*. By parity of reasoning with the previous case, the income tax will not cause any movement away from P_2, for nothing happens to change the producers' or consumers' indifference curves or the price ratio lines. But the specific tax on *Y* will clearly tend to flatten the consumers' price ratio line and to steepen the producers' price ratio line. And it is clearly conceivable that the new equilibrium situation might be something like P_1. But as we know, P_1 lies on consumer indifference curve *I* which represents a superior position to curve *II*. Therefore in these circumstances it must follow not that a specific tax and an income tax have the same effects but rather that a specific tax has better resource allocating effects than an income tax.

But it might well be asked whether in some sense or other P_1 is not a more reasonable initial assumption than P_2. If it were possible to maintain this view then it might be possible to dismiss the case where a

[1] The condition (p. 35) that the government buys the same quantities of the same things, whichever way it raises the revenue, could only be met if *X* and *Y* were both produced under conditions of constant costs.

specific tax has superior effects to an income tax as an academic curiosity without any relevance to the real world. Therefore, we must spend a little time outlining the circumstances under which there may be a difference in the slopes of *DE* and *A'C*, the producers' and consumers' price ratio lines respectively, even in the absence of a specific tax on *X* or *Y*.

First of all there will be a divergence between *A'C* and *DE* whenever marginal private costs diverge from price. In these circumstances the consumer will regulate his purchases by the market price but the producer will adjust output to the point where marginal cost equals marginal revenue. In other words, the consumer and producer face different price opportunities. Now this divergence of marginal cost (or revenue) from price is the fundamental characteristic of any form of restricted competition, ranging from pure monopoly through oligopoly to the case of relatively large numbers of sellers. The greater the divergence between marginal cost and price for any one firm, the greater is the extent to which resources are pushed elsewhere and hence the greater the divergence between the actual and the optimum allocation of the factors of production. In any situation where marginal costs are not proportional to commodity prices and marginal net products to factor prices, the allocation of resources is not ideal and therefore it is conceivable that a specific tax may improve rather than worsen the existing situation. The general principle is that a better allocation of resources can always be achieved by levying taxes on the products of the less monopolized industries (i.e. those where the ratio of marginal costs to prices is nearest to unity) thereby forcing more resources into the more restricted and monopolized industries. Therefore, if such circumstances prevail it is possible to show that indirect taxes levied in this way will have superior allocative effects to income taxes.

Another reason why the existing allocation of resources may not be optimum has already been mentioned, i.e. social costs and benefits may diverge from private costs and benefits. If the ratio of the social costs of production of two commodities is for any reason different from the ratio of the private costs, then the community production possibility curve will diverge from that of the representative producer, and tangency between the latter and the price ratio line will not be an indication of optimum factor utilization from the community point of view. Similarly if social benefits diverge from individual there will be a parallel divergence of the community indifference curve from that of private individuals. In either of these cases the situation existing before an indirect tax is imposed may not be optimum from a social viewpoint, and therefore the imposition of such a tax may improve rather than distort the allocation of resources, whereas an income tax would leave them unchanged.

It is clear that a non-optimum allocation of productive resources may well be an appropriate starting point for the analysis of the relative effects of income and specific taxes, and so no dogmatic statement can be made about the superior allocative effects of 'perfect' income taxes. It is time now to ask how the precise form of direct and indirect tax chosen for comparison affects the issue. To take the extreme case: would it be possible, even when the initial situation is one of optimum resource distribution, for direct taxes to cause as much or greater resource distortion than indirect taxes?

We shall find that once we relax the stringent initial assumptions of proportional income taxation applicable to all incomes and the identical nature of each producer and of each consumer, there are strong grounds for arguing that the imposition of an actual income tax in the real world will not conform to the pattern of the imaginary income tax in the imaginary world we have dwelt in so far. Furthermore, we shall find that in our comparisons we have to take account not only of the movements away from any given optimum pattern of resource distribution but also of tax-induced changes in the optimum pattern. These changes in the optimum pattern will result from the relative effects of different taxes on the distribution of income between income groups and hence on the preferred pattern of spending.

3.3 *Direct taxes*

Our next objective is to explore in some detail the various ways in which direct taxes may lead to a reallocation of resources. We shall assume throughout this discussion that the starting point is one of optimum resource distribution from a social, as well as a private, point of view. First of all, we shall discuss the various ways in which any actual income tax in the real world does not conform to the prototype which has no effects on the allocation of resources, and then subsequently we shall deal with the important ways in which resources do in fact tend to be shifted. Secondly, we shall make some comparisons between income taxes and expenditure taxes. Thirdly, we shall explore some of the contrasts between income and payroll and income and capital taxes.

3.3.1 *'Imperfections' of income taxes* There are two different sorts of reasons why any actual tax system may cause a diversion of resources by influencing the relative supplies of and demands for different products.

First of all, an income tax may not be applicable to all types of incomes. There have been examples in the past when taxes have been specifically aimed at individual industries – the South African diamond industry is an often-quoted example – and where, therefore, the failure to tax some incomes can be said to be a matter of deliberate policy. More often, however, failure to tax some types of income is a matter of chance rather than of policy. Sometimes conceptual difficulties stand in the way: e.g. which of the expense allowances granted to businessmen are really a concealed form of income or how should one treat casual receipts such as bequests and gambling winnings? Secondly, even if we agree in principle that a particular type of receipt is a form of income, it may be difficult to say how it should be measured, e.g. foodstuffs consumed by farmers. There are also plenty of cases where income is not taxed simply because of the administrative difficulty of doing so. We are all familiar with the landladies letting rooms to lodgers and the carpenter doing odd jobs for customers in the evenings. Sometimes, of course, income remains untaxed for a mixture of these reasons.

The opposite of the case where income escapes tax, i.e. that where income is taxed more than once, also frequently occurs. One example is income which is earned abroad and may be subject to income tax both in the foreign country and at home. Another apparent one is income earned by companies or corporations which is subject to tax both at the level of the company and at that of the shareholder, but, as we shall see later, there are in fact some complications in this example.

The second major reason why some types of income may suffer discrimination is that even though all types of income are taxed once and only once, some may be taxed at higher rates than others. The obvious contrast is that between a proportional income tax, where the tax taken is a constant proportion of income received and, on the other hand, a progressive income tax, where the proportion taken rises as income increases. The existence of progressive income taxes not only implies taking larger percentage slices away from the higher income groups in any one year, but may even mean taking more from people whose earnings fluctuate from year to year than from those whose earnings are constant over time. If, for instance, the tax system is such that incomes of £2,000 pay 10 per cent, those of £3,000 15 per cent and those of £4,000 25 per cent in tax, then Mr A who earns £2,000 in one year and £4,000 in the next will pay £1,200 in tax over the two years. Mr B, on the other hand, earns £3,000 each year and therefore over the whole period has the same total receipts, but only pays £900.

There are many other reasons why incomes may be taxed at different rates, either openly or effectively. Excess profits taxes which are usually based on the excess of actual profits earned over some more or less arbitrary standard are almost bound to imply differential rates of tax on growing and stagnant firms. Another example is the taxation of investment income at higher rates than earned income.

For all these sorts of reasons, and others too numerous to mention individually, we must expect to find 'imperfections' in real world income taxes. We now turn to explore the effects on the allocation of resources.

3.3.2 *Effects of income tax 'imperfections'* The first way in which any actual income tax may cause a diversion of resources is through effects on the structure of consumers' demand, a subject we have already discussed a little in our general comparison between direct and indirect taxes. Suppose, for instance, that the government has to meet additional expenditure of a given kind and can either impose an income tax which mainly hits rich people or one which mainly hits poor people. Then unless the changes in relative quantities of goods and services demanded are exactly the same in both cases – and this would be most unlikely as in general rich people do not have the same consumption patterns as poor people – there will be a differential effect on the quantities of resources employed in the various lines of production. However, this is a case of changing the optimum allocation, more than forcing a movement away from it, and therefore we are not concerned with it at this stage. We shall return to the whole issue of the effects of fiscal operations on the distribution of incomes in Chapter 5.

More important for our present purposes is the fact that different types of income taxes may have differential effects on the supply of resources to various industries. We can best examine this problem by looking at the relative effects produced by a poll tax and a proportional tax applicable to all incomes. In general, we should not on a priori grounds expect a poll tax, which has to be paid irrespective of the level of income and the nature of the industry, to have any effect on the distribution of resources. It must be re-emphasized that in the nature of things this is not a testable hypothesis, but it is none the less the best way of setting about the problem. For if our a priori reasoning about a poll tax holds, the effects of the proportional tax will be fully revealed and we shall not be confined to the *comparative* effects of the two. Further, as we shall briefly demonstrate, similar effects may be expected to hold, but a fortiori, in the case of progressive taxes. Finally, it is clear that if we can show that taxes levied on all incomes may have effects on the distribution of resources, then it will hold even more strongly that taxes levied on some incomes but not on others, or at varying rates on different kinds of income, must do so.

3.3.3 *The supply of labour to different industries* Let us first see how the supply of labour to the different industries in a country will be influenced by a tax proportional to income, as opposed to a poll tax. Suppose we assume that labour is distributed between two occupations, A and B, the wage-rates in the former being £80 a week and in the latter £40 a week. The conditions of working in A are so much more unpleasant than in B that this absolute wage differential is necessary to prevent labour flowing wholesale from A to B, and is, in fact, the differential which at the margin exactly offsets the non-monetary advantages of working in B. Now imagine a 20 per cent tax on earnings to be introduced in both occupations; the net rewards to labour will then fall to £64 and £32 respectively and the difference between the two will therefore now only be £32 and not £40. Therefore, we must expect to find that in the case of a proportional tax we shall have a tendency for labour to flow from A to B, a movement which would not be found in the case of a poll tax; for if the same sum of tax were collected by a poll tax the net rewards in A and B would be £68 and £28 respectively, thus preserving the £40 differential which is found in the no-tax position. Finally, a progressive tax can be seen to have even stronger effects in this respect than a proportional tax. Therefore, it clearly is the case that some types of income tax must cause some shifting of resources, and hence of outputs, away from the optimum position. Although our main illustration has been in respect of dirty, dangerous and disagreeable industries, the same reasoning can also be used to show that a proportional tax will have distorting effects, as compared to an equal-yield poll tax, in any case where there are differential non-monetary rewards which do not come within the tax net or expenses of earning a living which are not allowable for tax. In the case of progressive taxation, there will also be a further effect in that jobs with highly fluctuating monetary rewards from one year to another will be penalized compared to those offering stable incomes.

3.3.4 *The supply of capital to different industries* The next problem is the differential effects of proportional and poll taxes on the supply of capital to industry and in particular the distribution of capital between more risky and less risky industries. This is a complex subject and we can do no more than trace the outlines of the main issues here.

There seem to be two main points. First, will the imposition of a tax change the expectations of gain or loss from a risky investment? Second, how will investors react to such changes in expectations? It will be convenient to start with the assumption that in fact the mean expectation of gain or loss does change as a result of the tax and ask how investors will react. Later we shall question the validity of this initial assumption.

The traditional analysis of uncertainty-bearing rested on the principle of the diminishing marginal utility of money. If any man has a choice between a gilt-edged return of 4 per cent per annum and an equity return which may be 4 per cent but has equal chances of being 2 per cent greater or less per annum, he will choose the former, on the grounds that the increment in utility if he is lucky enough to reach the 6 per cent level will be insufficient to compensate for the loss of utility if he is unlucky enough to fall to the 2 per cent level. Therefore, in order to persuade people to undertake risky investments a premium has to be paid; to persuade people not to choose a gilt-edged investment yielding 4 per cent it may be necessary to tempt them with a mean expectation of 6 per cent, if the investment is a moderately risky one or, say, 8 per cent if it is extremely risky.

Now let us imagine a proportional tax of 50 per cent of incomes to be introduced. Instead of receiving a differential bonus of 2 per cent on moderately risky ventures and 4 per cent on mad-brained enterprises, the margins will be cut to 1 per cent and 2 per cent. Therefore, it was concluded that the effects of a proportional tax are to discriminate against risky enterprises; and, moreover, the greater the degree of risk the greater the amount of discrimination (in the example above, the margin is cut by only 1 per cent for the moderately risky but by 2 per cent for the most risky).

Arguments about risk-taking may also be cast in another form. If we take the widest definition of money income and include capital appreciation and depreciation of all kinds, then it seems reasonable to postulate that an asset which is completely free of risk of monetary loss or of inconvenience might be expected to yield a zero return. Although long-term gilt-edged stocks carry no risk of reductions of income in the narrow sense, they very definitely involve the purchaser in the risk of capital depreciation or at least the risk of losing the opportunity of buying stocks on more advantageous terms at some future date. In effect, therefore, with this approach, we take the return to holding wealth in the form of cash (i.e. a zero return) rather than in the form of government securities as our reference point. As against this, a moderately risky investment might offer equal chances of a return of, say, + £200 or − £200; a really risky one might lead to returns ranging from, say + £600 to − £600. In the absence of a tax, the mean expected return is zero in each case – the cash, the moderately risky and the really risky. But if a 50 per cent tax is imposed, the revenue authorities will share in the gains but not the losses from any venture. Therefore, in the moderately risky case the chances will now range from + £100 to − £200, giving a mean expectation of − £50; and, in the very risky case, the chances will now be from + £300 to − £600, with a mean expectation of − £150. Therefore, in the former case the result of the tax is to reduce the mean expectation from £0 to − £50; in the latter, from £0 to − £150. Hence, there is a greater discrimination against the more risky ventures.

There is, however, another issue to consider. The result of a 50 per cent tax is to reduce the net returns to all recipients of income; whether timid or adventurous, they will all be worse off than before. The result of this 'income-effect' may be to direct *more* investment into the riskier ventures in the hope of minimizing the reduction in the standard of living. It may also result in *less* investment of this type if people are now so much poorer that they feel they must play safe. Therefore the income effect may conceivably work in either direction and a priori we cannot say which will predominate. However, even if we did know it would not be relevant here, as we are interested in comparing a proportional income tax with a poll tax and by and large if there were a net income effect in one direction in the case of one tax it would also operate with the other. Therefore for *comparative* purposes we can neglect the income effects and confine ourselves to the substitution effects.

So far, therefore, we can say that if the imposition of a tax affects the mean expected return from ventures, there will be some tendency for capital to switch to the less risky industries. Now we have to question the initial assumption and ask whether it will always be true that proportional taxes will affect mean expected rates of return.

The major point is the possibility of offsetting losses against other income. Suppose we imagine, for instance, that our entrepreneur facing the possibility of a £200 gain or loss has a steady income of £2,000 per annum. In the absence of a tax, his expectations will range between £2,000 ± £200. In the presence of a 50 per cent tax, he will receive £1,100 [i.e. 50 per cent of (£2,000 + £200)] if he is successful and £900 [50 per cent of (£2,000 − £200)] if he is unsuccessful. In other words, he will have a chance of £1,000 ± £100, i.e. his mean expectation of income will be the same as if he did not expose himself to the risk of a loss. Then if we take the case of our more venturesome entrepreneur contemplating the venture with even chances of a £600 gain or loss we can see, if we imagine him to have a steady income of £2,000, that his pre-tax position will be £2,000 ± £600 and his post-tax position £1,000 ± £300. This immediately brings out the contrast between the case where loss offsets against other income are not possible and the case where they are. In the former the imposition of the tax reduced the mean expectation for the less risky venture from £0 to − £50 and for the more risky from £0 to − £150; in the latter, the mean expectation remains the same irrespective of whether any venture is undertaken and irrespective of whether any venture which is undertaken is of the more or less risky variety. Therefore, we must conclude that when losses can be completely offset in this way the imposition of a proportional tax on accruals of income will *not* reduce mean expectations below what they would be in the face of a lump sum levy and as a consequence the incentives to take risks will not be impaired.[1]

It may well be asked, however, whether it is realistic to assume that loss offsets are commonly possible. Obviously a distinction must be drawn here between the shareholder deciding which kind of shares to buy and the entrepreneur deciding which side of his activities to

[1] This conclusion is in fact over-simplified. Under some circumstances a proportional tax on accrued income with full loss offsets could lead to either more or less risk-taking than an equal-yield lump-sum tax.

There are also complications if we define freedom from risk of loss as being in real, as distinct from monetary, terms; in an age of inflation, cash-holding (except perhaps in Swiss francs) can then no longer be taken automatically as the appropriate reference point. Unpredictable rates of inflation are also likely to widen the spread of possible outcomes from any venture. See M. S. Feldstein, 'The Effects of Taxation on Risk-Taking', *Journal of Political Economy*, Sept–Oct., 1969.

expand. In the former case, we need to have a system which covers capital gains and losses as they accrue and not simply as they are realized.[1] It might, in the second case, be thought that there will be many cases of entrepreneurs who make such big losses that they cannot offset them against other profits in any one year. This rather takes us out of the field of principles but we can say here that even if losses are too big to be set against other forms of income in the same year, income tax laws frequently have 'carryforward' or 'carryback' provisions enabling losses to be offset in years other than those in which they are incurred. On the other hand, we must remember that we have been dealing entirely with a proportional tax system. Where progressive taxes rule, loss offsets cannot be complete except in the exceptional case where the whole range of possible outcomes lies within one tax rate. It must, therefore, in general be true that progressive taxes will tend to shift mean expectations of risky ventures downwards.

We may summarize our discussion of the effects of income taxes on resource allocation in this way. There are reasons to believe that in some circumstances even uniform proportional income taxes may cause a distribution of labour and capital among the various industries of a country different from that which would prevail if the same amount of revenue were raised by poll taxes. If this is true of a uniform proportional tax it will, in general, be true of a non-uniform or non-proportional tax, unless by design or chance it counteracts such effects as the tendency to drive labour from unpleasant industries or capital from risky ones.

This virtually concludes our discussion of the relative effects of different kinds of income taxes. Before we leave it, however, there is one further aspect to be mentioned. The Colwyn Committee Report of 1927 is perhaps the best known source of the argument that income taxes do not affect relative prices and quantities of goods and services.

[1] It is sometimes argued that a tax on realized capital gains (with allowances for realized losses) approximates more closely to a comprehensive income tax with full loss offsets than an income tax of the traditional British type, which made no systematic attempt to tax capital gains; and, as a consequence, the former tax is likely to have less adverse effects on risk-bearing than the latter. On the other side, it is argued that the most risky ventures are likely to yield part of their fruits in capital appreciation rather than income in the narrow sense and therefore a tax exempting realized capital gains is more conducive to risk-taking than one striking at them.

There seems to be no way of arriving at a definite conclusion on this point. The argument could go either way, depending on the extent to which risk is correlated with rewards taking the form of capital appreciation rather than ordinary income (the correlation is not always positive, e.g. National Savings Certificates), the opportunities for offsetting realized losses and the importance attached to such facilities.

Therefore it may be worth while considering the arguments put forward and examining their validity in the light of our treatment above. The essential schema of the Colwyn Committee argument was that a wholly general income tax could not alter the relative advantages of different industries and therefore would not shift resources between industries. In any given industry, the price level is determined by the marginal firm. As this makes no profit and pays no tax, its position will be unaffected and hence price is unchanged. Finally, each firm in an industry must be conceived to produce the same amount as before, for the marginal unit of output earns no profit, hence taxation cannot affect it and therefore output will be unchanged.

The objections to this form of reasoning may quickly be summarized. We have already argued at some length that even general income taxes may cause a movement of resources out of some industries and into others. The whole argument about the marginal firm appears to have been misconceived. It was never a part of accepted doctrine that the marginal firm was a no-profit firm and therefore it does not follow that a tax change has no effects on the position of such a firm. There appear therefore to be substantial gaps in the chain of reasoning which the Colwyn Committee tried to establish.

3.3.5 *Income taxes and expenditure taxes* By an expenditure tax we mean an income tax on personal incomes which specifically exempts current saving from taxation and specifically includes dissaving. The major effect of such a tax, as compared with a uniform income tax, is to alter the balance between spending and saving by giving greater encouragement to the latter. The most important repercussions are those on the supply of resources and these will be discussed in Chapter 4, but there is also something to be said on the allocation of existing resources. It has sometimes been argued that an expenditure tax will be more conducive to risk-bearing than a comprehensive income tax on accrued income on the grounds that, if equivalent rate[1] proportional income and expenditure taxes are compared, the fact that no tax is incurred when saving takes place in the latter case will mean that, provided the rewards to extra risk-taking are saved and not spent, the differentiation found against risk-taking in the case of an income tax is

[1] If 100 x per cent is the rate of income tax, then the equivalent rate of expenditure tax, 100 e per cent is given by $e = x/(1-x)$. Hence if $x = 0{\cdot}5$, $e = 1$. The income tax rate is on a 'gross' basis and the expenditure tax rate on a 'net' basis, in the sense that with the first a man with an *income* of £100 pays £50 in tax and in the second a man with *expenditure* of £50 pays £50 in tax.

not repeated with an expenditure tax. It is doubtful whether much weight should be attached to this point. First, as we have already argued, if a comprehensive income tax allows full loss offsets it does not discriminate against risk-bearing and so will not be inferior[1] to an expenditure tax in this regard. Secondly, as we shall argue in Chapter 4, the right comparison is not between a given rate of income tax and an equivalent rate expenditure tax but between a given income tax and an expenditure tax which raises the same amount of revenue. In a society where positive annual saving is the normal state of affairs, this will imply a higher rate of tax on the expenditure basis than on the income basis.[2] In the case where full loss offsets are not possible this will mean that at the margin additional risk-taking will yield a lower reward in terms of present consumption than in the income tax case; and the same may be true of the terms on which risk-taking may be exchanged for future consumption. Therefore, in this case, two conditions have to be satisfied for more risk-taking to be forthcoming with an expenditure tax: the terms of exchange between risk-taking and future consumption have to move in the 'right' direction and these terms of exchange have to count much more heavily in the mind of the investor or entrepreneur than those between risk-taking and current consumption.[3] There is no need to emphasize the stringency of these conditions.

Another resource allocation argument, and one which has received attention in the UK recently[4] is that the usual income tax system is riddled with a number of concessions to saving but that these are granted in a haphazard way and so one way of rationalizing this state of affairs would be to replace income taxation by expenditure taxation. However, this is a comparison of an imperfect system of one sort with a perfect system of another and so can hardly be thought of as an argument of fundamental principle. A further point[5] is that it is easier to index expenditure taxation, so that the real tax burden is invariant to inflation, than is the case with income taxation. There are some resource allocation implications here but we shall come to them in later chapters.

[1] Cf. C. S. Shoup, *Public Finance* (Weidenfeld and Nicolson, 1969), Ch. 12, for the argument that a comprehensive income tax with full loss offsets will actually lead to more risk-taking than a value-added tax or an expenditure tax.

[2] Now $e = x/[c(1 - x)]$, where c is the fraction of Personal Income (net of tax payable in the income tax case) consumed in the expenditure tax case.

[3] See p. 79 for a fuller explanation of this problem.

[4] See *The Structure and Reform of Direct Taxation*, Report of a Committee chaired by Professor J. E. Meade for the Institute for Fiscal Studies (G. Allen and Unwin, 1978).

[5] *Ibid.*

It may be worth spending a little time at this point on the relationship between an income tax, an expenditure tax and a value-added tax (i.e. a tax on the value added at each stage of the production process). A value-added tax can take a number of different forms; to simplify the discussion, let us assume initially that we are dealing with a closed economy. A uniform value-added tax which allows deductions for materials purchased and depreciation provisions in respect of plant, equipment, etc. corresponds closely to a uniform income tax. If value-added is reckoned after deducting not only material costs but also capital expenditure, whether for replacement or extension, this is equivalent to a tax on income which exempts private saving, if (to simplify) we assume there is no net lending between the public and private sectors. Although the correspondence to an expenditure tax is not exact – in the value-added case the exemption is in respect of private rather than personal saving – it is close enough to justify the conclusion that the allocative effects of value-added taxation will be essentially the same as those of expenditure taxation, e.g. in respect of effects on risk-bearing. In fact, as we go along, we shall see that the family of taxes between which there are close resemblances is a wider one. Value-added taxes of the consumption variety are very closely related to retail sales taxes; an income tax exempting investment income corresponds very closely to an expenditure tax;[1] and so does an income tax allowing immediate deductibility of capital expenditure. It is, in a fundamental sense, the general income tax which is the odd one out in this family.

3.3.6 *Payroll taxes* One proposition about payroll taxes (i.e. levies imposed on employer payrolls, sometimes, but by no means exclusively, for the purpose of financing social security benefits) due to Shoup[2] is that from an ex-ante viewpoint a uniform value-added tax exempting capital expenditure is very closely related to a uniform payroll tax. The argument runs as follows: at the margin the present value of the future cash flow from an investment will be equal to the current costs of investment. Therefore, exemption of the latter is equivalent to exempting the former. Therefore, a value-added tax of this type effectively has wages and salaries left as the tax base, provided that one can neglect items such as the rent of land.

Once the limitation of a closed economy is removed, the position is

[1] *Ibid.*

[2] *Public Finance, op. cit.*, Ch. 9.

more complex. A value-added tax may then be levied either on a *destination* basis (exports are not taxed, but imports are not deductible from the tax base) or on an *origin* basis (exports taxed, but imports deductible). If, as is more common, a value-added tax takes the destination form, the close relationship with the expenditure tax is preserved but not that with the payroll tax. If the origin base is taken, the reverse is the case.

Another important topic with payroll taxation is whether or not it leads to any substitution of capital for labour either inside any one industry or as a result of changes in product-mix. Whether one conceives of a payroll tax as working its way forward into prices, or backward into wages (or, temporarily, into profits) the general answer must be that it will not lead to any such substitution. A tax on labour costs affects the price of domestically produced capital goods (via the costs of labour employed in producing such goods) as well as the cost of labour simpliciter. So the first approximate answer must be that substitution effects of this sort are not likely. Complications arise in various ways, e.g. if capital goods are imported but even then there is no clear-cut conclusion that factor substitution is likely to take place.[1] So it follows that a tax on payrolls does not have to be compensated, as it is sometimes argued, by a tax on capital to avoid allocative inefficiency.

3.3.7 *Income taxes and capital taxes* Capital taxation is an ambiguous phrase used in a number of different senses. One sense, best avoided, in which the phrase is sometimes used is to indicate taxes which are assessed on income but actually paid at the expense of accumulated saving rather than by cutting down consumption. More correctly described as capital taxes are those which are assessed on capital but paid out of income, such as, say, a 2 per cent annual tax on all holdings of liquid assets. Then there are also those taxes which are both levied on capital and paid out of capital. These fall into two main categories; the once-for-all capital levy and the type of capital levy which, on the average, occurs once in a generation, i.e. death duties. To some extent, the distinction between taxes paid out of income and out of capital is a forced one, as it is conceivable that a small annual percentage tax on capital would be met by reductions in saving rather than consumption

[1] These arguments are set out more fully in C. S. Shoup, *Public Finance, op. cit.*, Ch. 16. See also P. A. Samuelson, 'A New Theorem on Non-Substitution' in his *Collected Scientific Papers*, Vol. 1 (MIT Press, Cambridge, Mass., 1965).

and that, on the other hand, death duties might, if the rates were not heavy, be met out of income rather than capital. For practical purposes, however, the distinction seems legitimate.

We shall now try to ask how the imposition of a capital tax is likely to influence the distribution of resources as compared to an equal-yield poll tax. First of all, we shall look at an annual tax on capital, and second, we shall take the case of death duties. As will soon be seen, there is not a great deal to be said at this stage about capital taxes. The more important problems fall into the province of Chapters 4 and 5.

The most important feature, as between a poll tax and an annual tax on capital, is that a tax on capital is bound to alter the relative returns from different types of investment. There is a wide range of types of capital assets which it is impossible to value in a sufficiently equitable manner to justify taxing them at all – perhaps the most obvious example is capital investment in human beings in the form of education and training. There are also many other assets where valuations, although more practicable, might be arbitrary: assets of family businesses, for which no stock market quotations exist, are an obvious example. Therefore, in all these cases we should expect to find a long-term tendency for a shift in the allocation of investible funds, as compared to a poll tax system.

There is one point that should be noted now, however. If the comparison were between a proportional income tax without loss offsets and an annual tax on capital, then it can be seen that the latter would have less serious effects on risk-taking than the former. If, for instance, the risky investor receives £10 from his £100 and the play-safe man only gets £10 from his £200, then a 50 per cent income tax will take £5 of income in each case (or, putting it differently, will reduce the differential yield from 5 per cent to 2.5 per cent). On the other hand, a capital tax of 3.3 per cent will take £3.3 away from the income of the first man but £6.7 from the second, which would clearly leave the differential income yield at 5 per cent, as now the first man will receive 6.7 per cent and the second 1.7 per cent. Therefore, a capital tax will tend to encourage the expansion of the riskier industries more than will an income tax. Once again it is important to specify that this will only hold when loss offsets are not fully possible. When they are fully possible, and when the basis of tax is comprehensive income, there is no reason in principle why an income tax should discriminate against risky investments more than a capital tax and in fact it might discriminate less.[1] Of course, it can be argued that loss offsets never are fully possible and that income taxes never do relate to comprehensive income, but these are empirical rather than theoretical matters.

Another thing should now be mentioned. A capital tax, by reducing the attractiveness of holding cash relative to income-yielding liquid assets, may help to increase the overall level of investment and not simply its distribution between different industries. However, this belongs mainly to the problem of income stabilization which we shall deal with in Chapter 6.

What of the relative merits of death duties and a poll tax? The major points here seem to be the effects on the level of saving and on the distribution of wealth and incomes, to which we shall return later. As far as death duties discriminate in favour of any one type of asset, either openly by differential rates of duty (as with agricultural land in the UK for many years) or covertly by under-valuation (as almost inevitably happens with house property and personal chattels) there will be some redistribution of investible funds into assets of this kind. Further effects on the distribution of resources may also follow from changes in Stock Exchange valuations due to sudden unloadings of large batches of securities. But, although substantial losses could obviously have effects on the relative attractiveness of different kinds of investment, such reactions are in general likely to be of a minor character.

3.4 *Indirect taxes*

3.4.1 *Introduction* We now turn to the field of indirect taxes to ask questions similar to those discussed in respect of direct taxes. Throughout most of the argument we shall make similar assumptions, i.e. that the existing distribution of resources is optimum in a social as well as a private sense, but we shall occasionally relax the assumption in order to explore particular points. We shall deal first with the relative merits of different taxes on consumer goods and then later compare consumer goods taxes with capital goods taxes. The order of the argument about consumer goods will be, first, to list the different types of tax, secondly to discuss the case of specific taxes on single commodities, then to deal with the problems of monopoly and

[1] Cf. pp. 46–7.

imperfect competition, to continue with lump sum and ad valorem taxes, and finally to examine general taxes on consumption.

3.4.2 *Types of consumer goods taxes* There are two distinctions to be made here. First, comes that between taxes closely geared to the level of output of a commodity and those which are not so arranged. At one end of the scale we have specific taxes levied at a certain rate per unit of output. At the other end, we have lump sum duties such as licence fees, payment of which may be a pre-condition of producing a particular commodity or rendering a particular service, e.g. shops selling tobacco or liquor are frequently subject to such conditions. Taxes based on the value rather than the quantity of sales, or ad valorem taxes, as they are usually called, correspond much more closely to the former than to the latter type, and where prices are constant over a wide range of output, they come to the same thing.

Secondly, and cutting across the previous distinction, we have the differentiation between the various types of goods which may be subjected to tax. The principal contrast is between *excise duties* levied on goods produced for home consumption and *customs duties* levied on goods entering (import duties) or leaving the country (export duties). A further distinction may also be drawn between those excise duties levied at the manufacturing stage of production and those levied at the wholesale and retail stage of selling, the latter frequently being known as sales taxes.

3.4.3 *Specific taxes* We shall now try to show the principles on which specific taxes on different commodities should be selected. To avoid unnecessary complications at this stage, we shall restrict ourselves to goods produced for home consumption.

Suppose that we assume that the elasticity of supply of each of a number of commodities is the same. If there is one commodity, and only one, for which demand is completely inelastic then it makes sense to tax only that commodity for it is precisely in these conditions that consumption will not be affected. And if we are postulating initially that the distribution of available resources among the different commodities is optimal, the objective should be to minimize any variations in consumption. There is, however, a hidden logical problem here in that there are far-reaching complications once one starts to ask how a given tax sum should be distributed between two or more commodities with differing elasticities of demand. Suppose, for instance, that there are three commodities with demand elasticities of 0.2, 0.3 and 0.4, respectively. Should the whole of the tax be placed on the first one – the most inelastic – and none on the other two? If not, how should it be shared between them?

This subject was the occasion of a famous article by F. P. Ramsey in the *Economic Journal* in 1927 and is also one which has received a lot of attention in the optimal taxation literature of the 1970s.[1] The essential distinction is between the situation where (as in this chapter) labour is taken to be inelastic in supply to the economy as a whole, and where it is not. In the first case, the answer is that the tax should be ad valorem and the rate should be the same on all goods and services, thereby resulting in differential percentage changes in consumption depending on demand elasticities. In the second case, the answer (on the basis of a number of restrictive assumptions such as low tax rates and compensated demand changes) is that the ad valorem tax rate should be inversely proportional to the elasticity of demand, so that the result is equi-proportional changes in consumption. An intuitive explanation is simply that if heavier taxes are levied on goods and services most nearly inelastic in demand, the substitution effects against work and the temptation to enjoy leisure instead of continuing to work are minimized. If the supply of labour, or demand for leisure, is not fixed, an equal-rate tax applying to all other items of consumption is inferior to a differential tax on the above lines.

Some of the limitations applying to the arguments in the preceding paragraph should be emphasized. First of all, it is an exercise concerned with relative rates of commodity taxes and says nothing about their merits compared to, say, a lump sum tax per head. Moreover, it is purely an argument about resource allocation and not an equity one. Secondly, the need for knowledge about demand and supply conditions necessary to implement 'the Ramsey rule' would be so enormous that one should not think that it has great practical significance.

Now let us reverse the process and assume that the elasticity of demand for each commodity is the same but that the supply elasticities differ. The argument now is that tax should be heaviest where elasticity of supply is least. The more inelastic the supply, the less will factors tend to move from that industry; the more elastic it is, the more will

[1] See, for instance, W. J. Baumol and D. Bradford 'Optimal Departures from Marginal Cost Pricing', *American Economic Review*, June 1970; A. Sandmo, 'Optimal Taxation: an Introduction to the Literature', *Journal of Public Economics*, No. 6, 1976; and A. B. Atkinson, 'Optimal Taxation and the Direct versus Indirect Taxation Controversy', *Canadian Journal of Economics*, November 1977.

factors be shifted. Therefore, in general, the movement from the optimum position will be smaller the greater is the proportion of the total tax sum collected from the commodities in inelastic supply.

This argument can easily be cast in Marshallian terms of loss of consumers' and producers' surplus. The essential diagrams are set out below.

Figure 3.4 shows the relative losses of consumers' surplus which occur under different demand conditions.

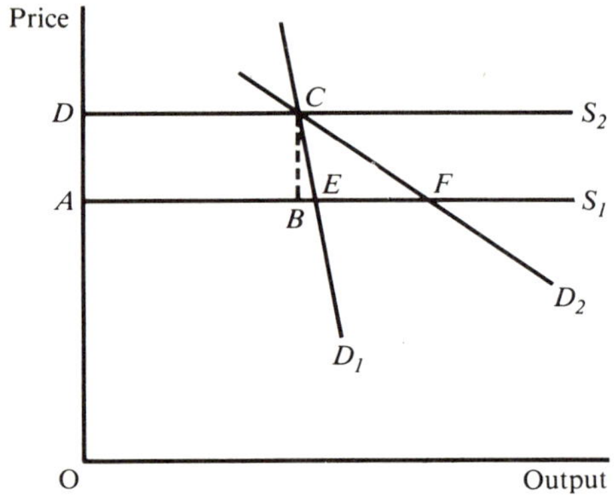

Figure 3.4 Indirect taxes and consumers' surplus (elastic and inelastic demand)

D_1 is a curve reflecting more inelastic demand; D_2 more elastic demand. S_1 is the supply curve before the imposition of tax; S_2 the supply curve including tax. In each case, the amount of tax collected is $ABCD$. But whereas in the case of more inelastic demand the loss of surplus is $ABCD + CBE$, in the other it is $ABCD + CBF$. Hence it can be ruled as a general proposition (ignoring the complication that the marginal utility of money may not remain constant for any one consumer or may not be equal as between consumers) that taxes on commodities with more inelastic demand occasion less loss of surplus than those on goods in elastic demand.

Figures 3.5 (a) and 3.5 (b) demonstrate a similar proposition about the relative loss of consumers' surplus under differing supply conditions. (It is clearer to demonstrate this comparison in two stages instead of one, both diagrams being drawn to the same scale.) In both cases, we have similar demand conditions and raise the same amount of taxation. Figure 3.5(a) shows CBE, the excess of loss of surplus over tax receipts, under perfectly elastic conditions of supply. In Figure 3.5(b), when supply is highly inelastic but *CB*, the vertical interval between S_1 and S_2, is the same as in Figure 3.5(a), the loss of consumers' surplus (less tax receipts) is negative, the area *GECD* being much smaller than the tax proceeds *ABCD*.

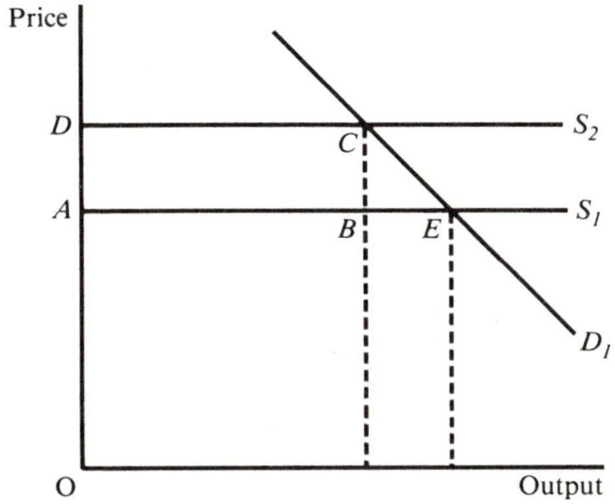

Figure 3.5(a) Indirect taxes and consumers' surplus (elastic supply)

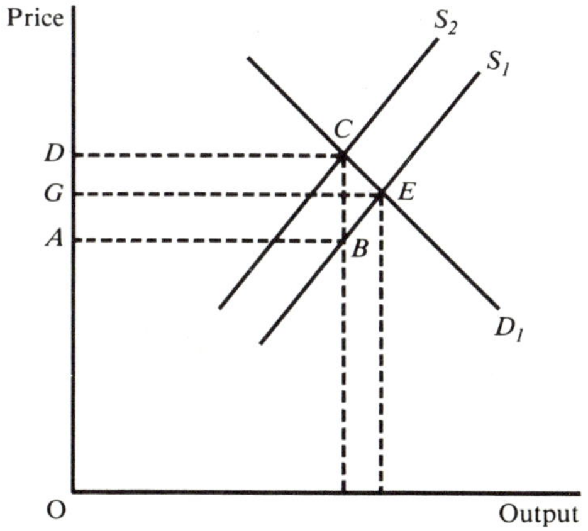

Figure 3.5(b) Indirect taxes and consumers' surplus (inelastic supply)

It must be realized, however, that exposition in this form does encounter all sorts of snags about measurement of surplus. If one is prepared to neglect these, there is no obstacle to this form of treatment. If, however, they are considered too formidable, the conclusions of our previous exposition, which are essentially similar to those deduced from considerations of surplus, must suffice.

3.4.4 *Monopoly and imperfect competition* We shall first of all try to show the relative effects of imposing a specific tax on a commodity sold under monopoly conditions as opposed to perfectly competitive conditions. Then we shall compare the oligopoly case with that of perfect competition. Finally, we shall try to appraise the precise significance of these results.

Economic theory tells us that, whereas in a perfectly competitive industry price and output are determined by the intersection of average cost and average revenue, output in a monopolized industry is determined by the intersection of marginal cost and marginal revenue and so is smaller. Comparisons between the effects of any given tax in the two cases can be made for certain types of revenue and cost functions. If we take first the case where average and marginal cost are constant, and where the demand function is linear, then price will rise by exactly the amount of the tax in the competitive case. In the monopoly case on the other hand, it can be shown[1] that the rise in price is equal to half the increase in marginal cost and that the increase in marginal cost is itself equal to the tax. Therefore, it must follow that the rise in price is only half what it is in the competitive case and consequently that the reduction in output is less than in the latter case.

If, on the other hand, we take the other extreme case where the supply curve is completely inelastic, then it will clearly be true that marginal costs and hence price and output will not change either under competitive or monopolistic conditions as a result of a tax. In all other conditions, no easy comparison is possible of the monopoly and competitive cases – it is, for instance, true that taxes tend to raise prices more when costs are falling than when they are rising in both cases, but it is not easy to say precisely how much difference there is between them for any given rate of change of costs. Nor, for that matter, is the conclusion clear that price rises are less under monopolistic than under competitive conditions when the elasticity of supply is infinite, except under the assumption of a linear demand function. If the demand curve is convex to the horizontal axis, there is a tendency for prices to rise to the full extent of the tax even under monopoly conditions. And, in fact, under still further hypotheses about the shape of the demand curve

[1] Cf. J. Robinson, *The Economics of Imperfect Competition* (Macmillan, 1933), especially Ch. 5.

(e.g. a constant elasticity curve) the price can be shown to rise more in the monopoly than in the competitive case. Therefore, any conclusion that prices will rise less under monopoly than under competitive conditions is subject to very stringent limitations.

Let us now see what happens in the case of oligopoly. A possible diagrammatic representation of the oligopolist's position is shown below (Figure 3.6).

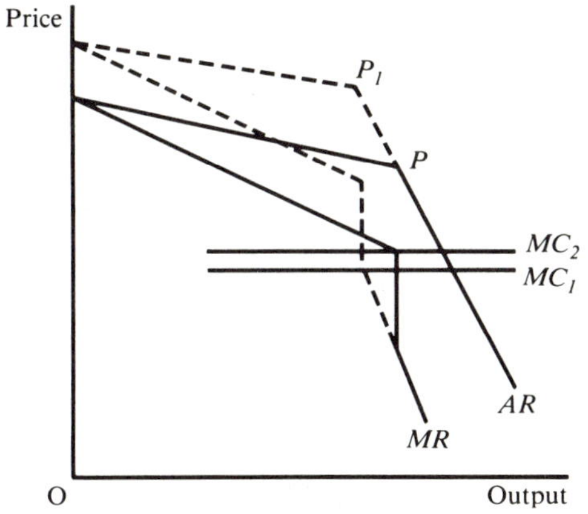

Figure 3.6 Indirect taxes under oligopoly

Such an oligopolist fears imitation if he reduces prices but also fears lack of imitation if he raises prices. Therefore, the elasticity of demand is greater for price increases than for price decreases. It will follow that the *MR* curve will be vertical over part of its length and if the tax is such that the new as well as the old *MC* curve cuts the vertical portion of the *MR* curve, price and output will be unaffected. It should be noted that this result will hold irrespective of whether marginal costs are constant, rising or falling with output. Therefore, when an industry consists of firms in this position, there will be less change of output than under competitive conditions, other than when either demand or supply is completely inelastic. If, however, each firm feels that on the occasion of a tax increase it can be quite confident that others will follow suit if it raises prices, we should have changes in price and output such as are represented by the dotted parts of the *AR* and *MR* curves and the new price P_1.

What is the significance of the conclusions reached above about the relative effects of a given rate of a specific tax under monopoly and competitive conditions? Supposing we actually have conditions under which taxes on monopolized industries have smaller effects on output than those on competitive industries. Would it follow that we should tax the products of the monopolized industries? The argument has only to be put in this way to be seen as a non-sequitur; for the very existence of monopoly implies (except in such cases as where there is an equal degree of monopoly all round, i.e. where marginal costs are proportional to price for all commodities) that the existing distribution of existing resources is not optimum and that too few factors will be employed in the monopolized industries and too many in the competitive ones. Therefore, it would obviously drive us further away from the optimum situation and not nearer to it, if one were to tax the product of a monopolized industry.[1] There would therefore seem to be little purpose in spending any more time on the comparison between monopoly and competition in order to deduce conclusions about the sort of commodities which may be taxed with the least diminution in economic efficiency.

3.4.5 *Specific and lump-sum taxes* We turn to consider the relative effects of equal-yield taxes imposed at a certain rate per unit of output, and lump-sum taxes, such as licence duties.

In general, we should expect to find, in the Marshallian type of short-period when equipment, etc. is fixed, that the latter type of tax will have no effects on output (assuming that changes in aggregate spending due to changes in taxes collected can be neglected). If manufacturers have adjusted output to the point of maximum profit, the imposition of a fixed licence duty can only reduce net profits – it cannot make it more profitable to increase or decrease output. The same conclusion will also hold in respect of a licence duty which is a fixed percentage of profits. In either case, therefore, a licence duty type of tax will be superior to a specific tax, unless conditions of zero elasticity of supply or demand prevail.

In the long period, however, we must expect to find that if profits are reduced below the normal level (as they will be if a licence duty is imposed under competitive conditions), then there will be a tendency for firms to leave the industry and therefore prices will tend to rise and output to fall. The superiority of a licence duty will therefore be a

[1] A lump-sum tax on monopolists to finance subsidies related to output of monopolists would be far more appropriate.

short-lived phenomenon, except in the case of monopolies earning surplus profits even in the long period.

3.4.6 *Specific taxes of various kinds* The principal contrast is between specific duties on home-produced goods (excise duties) and those on imports or exports (customs duties). Fundamentally, the same method of analysis applies. If the initial assumption is that the distribution of resources is not only optimum inside but also between countries, then any taxes falling on internationally traded goods with large demand or supply elasticities will cause a diversion of resources from the optimum in just the same way as excise taxes. There are many qualifications to this general principle but these belong to the field of international trade rather than public finance and we shall not attempt to deal with them here.

3.4.7 *Specific and ad valorem taxes* We have already made the point that equal-yield specific and ad valorem taxes will have identical effects when the elasticity of supply is infinite. In order to compare the effects of such taxes when these conditions of supply do not prevail, let us take first the supply curve of a commodity subject to diminishing returns. In this case, the absolute addition to supply price due to a given ad valorem tax increases as output increases, instead of being constant as in the specific tax case. When increasing returns prevail, the absolute addition to price decreases with increasing output. The implication of this is that ad valorem taxes will have more pronounced effects than specific taxes when supply price rises with output and less pronounced effects when supply price falls with output.

3.4.8 *Partial and general taxes* The practical distinction here is usually between sales taxes levied at ad valorem rates on a few commodities and those levied on a large range of goods and services.

The essential distinction between the case of a single commodity and that of the whole spectrum of production is that the elasticity of supply must be less in the latter than in the former case. Therefore, it must follow that, with given demand elasticities for the various products, the diversion of resources will be less in the case of a general than a partial tax yielding the same amount of revenue. Even in the case of taxes on single commodities, it should be noted that the likelihood of resource distortion is much less for those commodities which bulk large in total expenditure and for which, therefore, the elasticity of supply or demand is likely to be small, than in the case of commodities absorbing only a small fraction of the nation's productive resources or expenditures.

3.4.9 *General considerations* The specific assumption made at the beginning of our discussion of indirect taxes must now be recalled. It was expressly stated that we imagined the initial position to be socially optimum, i.e. that the same ratio of marginal costs to price was to be found throughout the economy and that no divergence was to be found between private and social costs and benefits or, alternatively, that the ratio of private to social costs and benefits was the same throughout the economy.

It must be explicitly stated that the whole of our discussion, except for the section on monopoly, rests on this base. Only under these circumstances do our conclusions about elasticities hold in the way which we have described. And only under these conditions will it be generally true that indirect taxes tend to produce an allocation of resources inferior to that obtained with a poll tax system. In the opposite case, when resources are not initially in their 'right' places it is perfectly possible that indirect taxes can improve rather than impair the allocation.

An example of the way in which a judicious system of indirect taxes may improve the allocation of resources is to be found in Marshall's famous proposition that taxes should be levied on those industries subject to diminishing returns, and subsidies given to those subject to increasing returns. The first point here is the principle of the elasticity of supply with which we are already familiar – clearly industries subject to diminishing returns more nearly approximate to conditions of inelastic supply than do the others and therefore are fitting subjects for the attentions of the tax gatherer. Secondly, there is the point that in addition to the gains of private individuals there may be further social gains to be taken into account. Subsidies to increasing returns industries will frequently render possible external economies and hence gains to the community over and above any to the entrepreneur. However Marshall's prescription is by no means universal. For instance, the principle of taxing diminishing returns industries must be severely qualified in so far as the usual reason for such a situation is the scarcity of factors rather than diseconomies of large-scale production. The really general conclusion is that a policy of selective taxes and subsidies may be justified on efficiency grounds, if it can be shown to offset distortions in the pattern of resource allocation due to monopoly elements or divergences between private and social costs and benefits.

3.4.10 *Taxes on capital goods* Fundamentally, the same principles apply to taxes on capital goods as to those on consumer goods, but there are some additional complications.

The most important difference is that not only are capital goods sold after manufacture in the same way as consumer goods, but the services derived from some of them are also sold on an annual basis, e.g. houses and other buildings are let at annual rentals. Therefore, when taxes are based on annual rental values (such as local rates in the UK) the relevant repercussions are those on the supply and demand for the services derived from the total stock of houses, and not simply those on the additions to that stock. Of course, upward changes in the stock of houses can only come about through an increase in the annual flow of new building (or, perhaps, a reduction in the rate at which old buildings fall into disuse) but the essence of the problem is that even large changes in the annual flow may only have small effects on the total stock when buildings are relatively long-lived. Therefore, the elasticity of supply of buildings for rental- and owner-occupation must inevitably be very small in any period shorter than that needed to make a substantial addition to or subtraction from that stock.

Moreover, this tendency for the elasticity of supply of services from capital goods to be small, due to the large ratio of the existing stock to the annual addition to the stock, will be reinforced when the period of construction of capital goods is lengthy or when changes in plans for building new capital equipment take a long time to come to fruition.

Therefore, in the short run the supply of services from capital goods may well be inelastic and so it can reasonably be argued that less distortion of resources will be caused by taxes on the services of capital goods than on consumer goods. But this is an argument with dangerous implications, for there must in the long run be reductions in the stock of capital goods in response to taxes on their services. Although reductions in the stock of houses do not directly affect productive potential, this is clearly not true of changes in the stock of commercial and industrial buildings, let alone changes in machinery and equipment. As we shall see, there are good reasons for believing that private investment in 'productive' capital may fall short of what is socially desirable and therefore one should argue for stimulating rather than restraining that output. It is really the housing component of investment to which the arguments of this section relate.

It might be convenient at this point to refer to the concept of tax capitalization. The argument here is that if a recurring tax is imposed on the annual income or capital value of an asset which is in very inelastic supply, then the whole burden of the tax falls on the man who happens to own the asset at the time the tax is imposed. An annual tax on land, for instance, will result in a reduction in the price of land to such an extent that the after-tax rate of return is as great as that prevailing before the tax was imposed. If this were not the case, existing owners would not be able to sell their land to new investors in land. Hence it can be said that the whole burden of the tax is capitalized on existing owners.[1] But it should be understood that this process only works exactly in the way described for an asset in fixed supply. Moreover, if the tax applied so widely that there was a consequential reduction in the discount rate employed to convert annual returns on assets into capital values, this would adulterate the pure milk of the argument still further.

3.5 *Relative expenditure effects*

Up to this point our analysis based on the criterion of resource allocation has all been conducted in terms of the comparative effects of different taxes with equal yields. In fact, some of the most important problems can be dealt with by this means, but it will nevertheless be instructive to reverse the process and ask about the relative effects of different kinds of government expenditure of equal total amount and financed in exactly the same way.

Suppose we look first at the relative effects of government transfers and subsidies, and to fix our ideas precisely let us contrast the outpayment of a lump sum transfer of equal amount to everyone with the payment of differential subsidies to various branches of industry. It can be seen at once that we have a parallel with the contrast between uniform poll taxes and indirect taxes. Instead of a loss of efficiency due to the diversion of resources from those commodities subject to, say, excise duties, we have a loss of efficiency due to the attraction of resources into those industries which are granted subsidies. Only in the case where subsidies were proportional to marginal costs would this not be the case – assuming, of course, once more that the initial

[1] Parallel arguments apply in the case of subsidies.

distribution of resources in the private sector of the economy is socially optimum.

It must be remembered that this is a contrast between differential subsidies and an equal lump sum transfer. If, on the other hand, transfers were proportional to income then we should expect to find the long-run consequence of more people moving into the objectionable and risky industries, in precise contrast to our findings about proportional taxes. Although some government transfers do take a form akin to this, e.g. the old income tax rebates for children in the UK were in effect greater for high income families than for low income families, the much more important cases in practice are those of equal-amount transfers or those where the sum transferred bears an inverse relation to the size of income, e.g. most educational grants or scholarships.

Although we do not have space here to develop the general subject of relative expenditure effects on resource allocation in the private sector, it is one which has received increasing attention in recent years with the growth of differential government outpayments and tax remissions geared to changes at macro levels (e.g. encouragement to substitute capital for labour) as well as micro levels (e.g. differential encouragement of individual firms as well as individual industries). In the USA, it has been mandatory for some years that the government should produce annual statements on tax-expenditures (i.e. expenditure by the government in the form of tax concessions rather than direct expenditure). The first official UK statement on such matters, though in much less detail, is to be found in a publication of January 1979.[1]

[1] *The Government's Expenditure Plans 1979–80 to 1982–83*, Cmnd. 7439 (HMSO, 1979).

4

THE SUPPLY OF RESOURCES

1 INTRODUCTION AND METHOD OF APPROACH

We have dealt at length with the way in which various types of revenues and expenditures affect the allocation of a given supply of resources inside a country. We must now turn to the next question: how do they affect the supply of resources forthcoming for productive use? We have stated in Chapter 2 that it is convenient to treat this question separately from the former. We must also clarify the distinction between the subject-matter of this chapter and that of Chapter 6. There we shall be concerned with all the issues of income stability and fiscal measures to secure full employment of labour. In this chapter we shall assume a given level of employment, or, more accurately, a given percentage of unemployment among the population seeking work, and we shall deal with the various other ways in which the supply of resources available for productive use may change.

1.1 *Internal and external resources*

We shall be principally concerned in this chapter with tax effects on the supply of labour and capital forthcoming inside any given country, but it must be realized at the outset that the real resources at a country's disposal may be augmented from without as well as from within. This may come about in two principal ways. First and more important, there may be a change in the terms of trade in favour of a country. Second, there may be an increase in the (real) value of the net dividends and interest received from abroad. Either of these two items can make a larger amount of goods and services available for disposal even though there has been no change in the supply or utilization of internal resources.

Although there is a good deal to be said on the relative effects of different types of revenues (e.g. export taxes as against import taxes) and expenditures (e.g. different kinds of subsidies to home producers) on the terms of trade, we shall not discuss this subject in any co-ordinated fashion in this book. To do so would inevitably take us into the field of international trade theory and widen our subject-matter enormously.

1.2 *Stocks and flows*

Now we come to a major distinction which demands careful analysis. 'A change in the supply of resources' is an ambiguous term which can be interpreted to mean *either* an addition to the existing stock of resources *or* an increased utilization of the services of the existing stock. It may be useful to trace out the various implications of this distinction in respect of labour and capital before proceeding further.

Taking labour to begin with, a change in the stock may come about first of all through a change in the size of the population, which in turn may be due to natural causes or to migration. Secondly, there may be changes in the population's capacity for work. The sort of factors involved here might be a change in the age-composition, influencing the proportions of working age (though this would usually be associated with a change in the size of the population) or a change in physical or mental abilities.

On the other hand, a differing degree of utilization of the existing stock of people may also come about through a variety of factors. The proportion of the population offering itself for work is one; the number of hours worked per week, the number of weeks per year and, for that matter, the number of years per lifetime are others. Finally, we have the intensity of effort per hour as another variable. As we are deferring all problems of involuntary unemployment until Chapter 6, under-utilization of this kind does not concern us for the time being.

Similarly, for capital, the distinction has several aspects. A change in the stock of capital potentially comes about when people decide to save a greater or smaller proportion of their income. The word 'potentially' is important here. A decision to save a larger fraction of income will not necessarily lead to an addition to the physical stock of capital, if the community's willingness to save outruns its willingness to invest. However, this also involves changes in involuntary unemployment and therefore can be left over to Chapter 6. Under our assumption of a fixed percentage of unemployment, we take it as axiomatic that an increased willingness to save will lead to a larger stock of capital equipment.

The utilization of any given stock of capital depends on factors very similar to those affecting labour. The proportion of a country's machinery in use, and the amount which is worked for three shifts per day, etc. are the typical problems.

It can now be seen that any discussion of tax effects on the supply of resources can be resolved into two components – one dealing with the stock of a factor and the other with the degree of utilization of that stock. There is, however, a little more to be said here. As far as public finance is concerned the relative importance of the two components is very different for labour and for capital. In the case of labour the influence of taxes, etc. on the size of the population is much less important than their influence on the utilization of a given population. Income tax rebates for children clearly have some effects on birth-rates, but common observation and experience suggest that this class of problems has nothing like the same importance as that involving marginal tax rates and their effects on hours and intensity of work. In the case of capital, it is exactly the other way round. Whereas different tax formulae may be immensely important in determining the flow of annual saving, it is unlikely that they will have any very direct influence on the extent to which the existing stock of capital is utilized. There are exceptions to these broad generalizations (e.g. it might be argued that additions to the stock of labour in the form of increased training and educational activities are a field where tax considerations are important) but nevertheless they do seem reasonably valid. It follows, therefore, that most of our tax and expenditure discussions will deal with the inducements to labour to work and with the problems of capital accumulation.

1.3 *Other types of resources*

It might be asked why we confine ourselves to the supply of labour and capital to the neglect of other types of resources.

It is traditional in economics to isolate land and enterprise as the two other boxes into which productive resources are sorted. Clearly, the characteristic features of the supply of enterprise are covered by our discussion of labour in this chapter and the preceding one. Similarly, our remarks about labour and capital can be applied mutatis mutandis to the supply of land.

Finally, although we shall not discuss one of the most important ways in which the available supplies of resources may be augmented, i.e. by changes in techniques due to innovations and of natural resources due to new discoveries, it would not seem that tax considerations which arise in this field are fundamentally different to those which we actually do discuss.

1.4 *The ideal conditions*

In Chapter 3 we spent some time specifying the conditions in which the distribution of the factors of production among their different possible uses would be optimum. Subsequently, we tried to show the relative effects of different kinds of taxes and expenditures in inducing shifts from this optimum position.

We shall not follow precisely the same route in this chapter, mainly because the concepts of an optimum population or stock of capital are much more difficult and much less agreed among economists than the relatively simple propositions we had to deal with in Chapter 3. It is perfectly true that there are many statements of these problems. For example, it is often stated that the optimum population to be combined with a given stock of capital, a given level of techniques, etc. is given by the point at which total welfare is at a maximum. But clearly any such brief statement bristles with difficulties. Quite apart from the extreme assumptions which have to be made to give any precision to this statement, it is certainly not crystal clear that this is a better criterion than the maximization of welfare per head. Similarly, it can be said that net saving should be undertaken so long as the marginal productivity of capital is greater than zero, and that the rate of net saving is less than the optimum if the present amount saved per year multiplied by the marginal utility of money is less than the excess of total welfare per year in the 'golden age' (when the marginal productivity of capital has been reduced to zero) over the total welfare per year which is currently enjoyed.[1] But it must immediately be said that this sort of notion is again extremely difficult to pin down. And in any attempt to spell out these matters more fully we run into the difficulty that we ought really to specify the conditions for optimum population and optimum saving jointly. Even though a great deal of high-grade intellectual effort has been applied to these problems in recent years, it is still not clear that one can specify such optima in purely economic, as distinct from political, terms. We shall, therefore, in the main have to content ourselves with discussing the relative effects of various taxes without any clear-cut guide about whether these effects constitute departures

[1] Cf. F. P. Ramsey, 'A Mathematical Theory of Saving', *Economic Journal*, December 1928, for the classic formulation of this problem; also E. S. Phelps 'The Golden Rule of Accumulation: a Fable for Growthmen', *American Economic Review*, Sept. 1961.

from an optimum or if they do, to what extent. This is a more restricted approach than was used in Chapter 3, but all things considered it seems to be the most satisfactory one to follow.

There is, however, one exception to the difficulty of specifying optimum conditions in these fields. The degree of utilization of labour is subject to fairly precise analysis and therefore we must set out the conditions necessary to secure the optimum division between work and leisure.

We assume for simplicity that a man can vary the amount of work he is willing to do per week into indefinitely small gradations. This is admittedly unrealistic but is a necessary simplification at the beginning. We can picture the situation in the way shown in Figure 4.1.

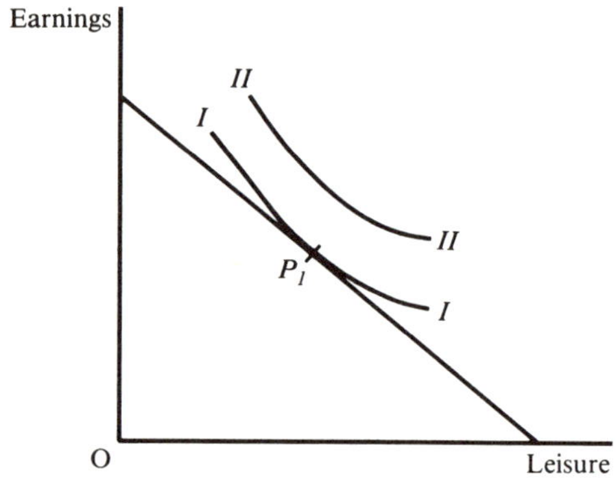

Figure 4.1 Earnings and leisure

If along the horizontal axis we measure leisure and on the vertical axis earnings, we can construct a price opportunity curve showing the amounts of income which can be obtained by sacrificing varying amounts of leisure. Thus if a man works a six-hour day he may receive £8, whereas a twelve-hour day may bring in £16. A series of indifference curves showing the relationship between leisure and earnings can be drawn, and we might expect them to be of the form *I*, *II*, etc. The most preferred point will be P_1, that of tangency between the price-opportunity line and the indifference curve *I*. At this point the marginal rate of substitution between income and leisure time is equal to the hourly wage-rate. Or, in older terminology, this represents the point at which the marginal utility of income has diminished and the marginal disutility of work has risen to such extents that they are exactly equal to one another. This shows us, therefore, how much work a man will decide to do, given his leisure preference and the market wage-rate. On the supposition that any man is in this equilibrium position – and this is, of course, a basic assumption – we now have a standard for judging whether and to what extent relative taxes cause deviations from this position.

1.5 *Method of approach*

As in the last chapter, we propose to examine *relative* effects of pairs of taxes and expenditures. We assume that a given amount of revenue has to be raised for a specific object of expenditure and we compare the relative consequences of collecting it by one means as against another. And conversely for the relative effects of different types of expenditure.

We shall first of all deal in detail with some of the major comparisons, and subsequently more briefly with some of the less important issues in this large field. Under *major comparisons* we include:

Proportional and progressive income taxes and the supply of labour.
Income taxes, excise taxes and the supply of labour.
Transfers, other expenditures and the supply of labour (all in section 2).
Income taxes, expenditure taxes and the supply of saving.
Income taxes, capital taxes and the supply of saving.
Income tax reliefs, subsidies and the level of company investment and saving (all in section 3).

2 TAXATION AND THE SUPPLY OF LABOUR

2.1. *Proportional and progressive income taxes and the supply of labour*

We shall concentrate on what we have called the degree of utilization of labour, or more specifically the effects of taxes on willingness to work. To begin with, we must make various simplifying assumptions. We shall deal first of all with the relative effects of a poll tax of £*x* per head and an income tax exactly proportional to income producing the same annual yield. Subsequently we shall turn to the comparison of proportional and progressive taxes. We shall deal initially with a single individual considered in isolation. We shall assume that he is paid on a system of straight time-rates, that the only choice is between working and not working and that he is free to vary his hours of work in infinitely small gradations. The complications of removing these restrictive assumptions will be examined later.

The essential distinction between an equal-yield poll tax and a flat rate income tax is that in the latter case the price of leisure can change relatively to other commodities, whereas it does not do so in the former. The 'income effects' are exactly the same in both cases but the 'substitution effects' differ. Figures 4.2(a) and 4.2(b) show this result.

As in Figure 4.1, P_1 represents the point at which the marginal rate of substitution between earnings and leisure is equal to the hourly rate of earnings before any tax is imposed. We may consider our individual to be spending QB hours of work per day in earning OR pounds. If an income tax of 50 per cent is now imposed on his earnings, the earnings-opportunity line will no longer be BA but BC, which has a slope half that of BA. The new point of equilibrium will be P_2, the point of tangency with indifference curve II.

In Figure 4.2(a) this is shown as lying to the left of P_1Q, thereby indicating that more work is being done than initially; in Figure 4.2(b) P_2 lies to the right of P_1Q, indicating less work than initially. In the former case, the income effects which are likely to make people work harder are assumed to outweigh the substitution effects working in the opposite direction; in the latter case, the reverse holds. Either of these results is possible and one cannot say a priori which is the more likely.

On the other hand, the imposition of an equal-yield poll tax will mean that our representative man will now face the earnings-opportunity line $A'B'$. As nothing has happened to alter the terms of exchange between work and leisure $A'B'$ must be parallel to AB; and as we are postulating an equal yield $A'B'$ must pass through P_2. Equilibrium will be obtained at P_3, the point of tangency with indifference curve III, which represents a position where more hours will be worked than at either P_1 or P_2, irrespective of whether we consider Figure 4.2(a) or 4.2(b). This brings out the essence of the contrast between the two taxes. With a lump sum tax, it is not open to the individual to vary his tax liability by modifying his hours of work; with an income tax the individual does have this choice. In the latter case, we have in fact a reduction in the marginal cost of leisure and hence greater consumption of it to an extent given by the strength of the substitution effects.

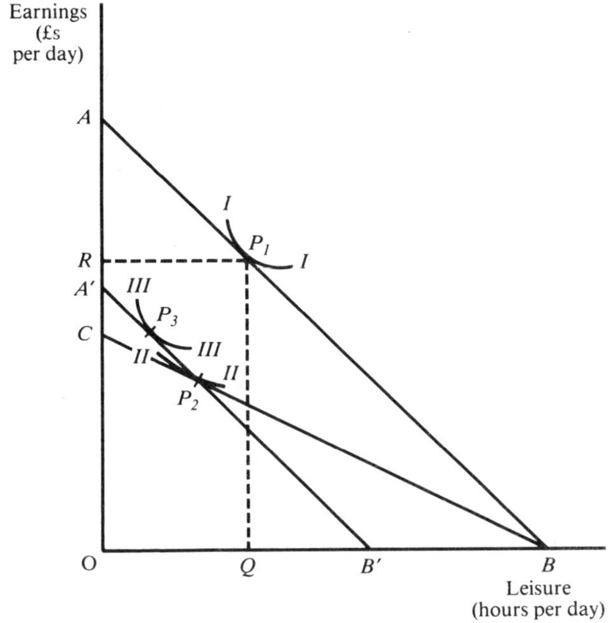

Figure 4.2(a) Earnings, leisure and taxation

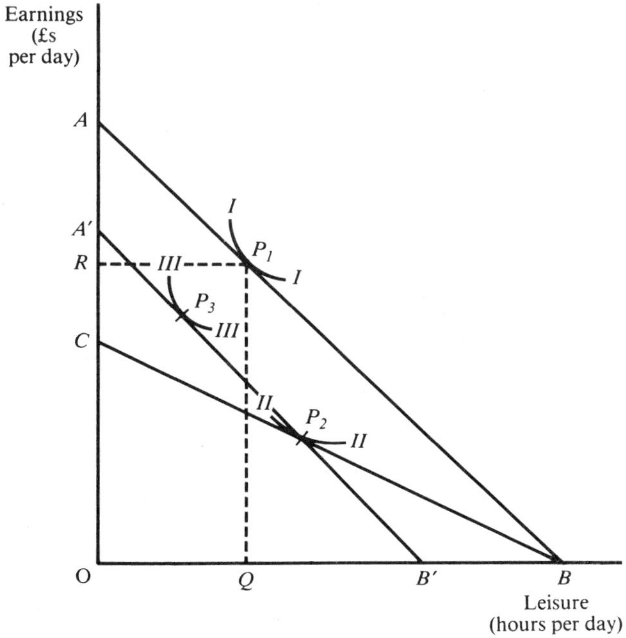

Figure 4.2(b) Earnings, leisure and taxation

The analogy with Figures 3.2 and 3.3 in Chapter 3 should be noted. In just the same way as a general proportional income tax can be shown to have better allocation effects than an excise tax on one commodity (at least when the relative outputs of commodities are initially optimum) so does a lump sum tax place workers on a higher indifference curve than an equal-yield income tax. In either case, the tax which alters the terms of exchange between the two alternatives pushes a man on to a lower indifference curve than one which does not so alter the terms of exchange.

In principle, we can also analyse the combined effects of a proportional income tax and a system of government transfers designed to return to each individual as a lump sum the exact amount of the proceeds collected in tax. It is clear that less hours of work will be done than initially, that is, once we abstract from income effects the substitution effect inevitably tends to make for a reduction in hours of work.[1] However, it must be realized that this sort of comparison is very artificial as it would be extremely difficult to organize a system whereby a man could be repaid the exact sum he has paid in income tax whilst retaining the lump-sum principle.

We must now relax some of the restrictive assumptions. First of all, we assumed that an individual could really make marginal adjustments to his hours of work. It is often argued that this is unrealistic and that in practice most people have the choice of working a fixed week or not at all, and that given such a choice the opportunities for substituting leisure for work or vice versa are relatively limited. This would seem to overstate the case, however. There are many ways in which marginal adjustments can be made to the amount of work done. Even those paid entirely on time-rates often have opportunities for overtime work, and they always have opportunities of absenteeism. Also, the opportunity for variations in output and earnings is obviously very much larger in the case of piece-workers. Then again we made the assumption that our individual guinea-pig has the straightforward choice between working and not working. When we take account of the fact that there is a whole range of activities which fall in an intermediate category (e.g. painting one's own house, executing small repair jobs for neighbours, etc.) the position becomes more complex. There is now a threefold margin to consider – income subject to tax, income not subject to tax

[1] Less work will also be done when income tax proceeds are returned to a man in the form of lump-sum transfers than when they are not so refunded. This reflects the view that if a man has a higher income he is likely to buy more leisure.

and no income. This means that the choice between work and leisure is no longer a clear-cut one, and that the concept of the substitution effect which looks so clear at first sight becomes blurred and ill-defined. It is not at all safe to deduce that if total numbers of hours spent on 'main' jobs diminishes, the amount of time devoted to leisure increases.

We can see, therefore, that modifications have to be made to the simple sort of diagrammatic picture even in the case of a single individual. And when we consider a whole community the problem becomes even more complicated. To start with, we now introduce another variable, the numbers seeking work. Not only may leisure be substituted for work through the medium of shorter hours per person but also through the number of persons seeking work. This, therefore, is a reinforcement of the argument that there are in practice considerable opportunities for the substitution effect to work itself out. The other sort of complication we have to consider for a community is whether the income effects do really cancel one another. Suppose we revert to the comparison between the poll tax and the proportional income tax with the same total yield. Clearly the amount taken from any one individual will not necessarily be the same under the two systems, even though the total from all the individuals taxed be the same. If there is exact symmetry between the reactions of those who gain relatively and those who lose relatively under the two systems, then it could still be assumed that the income effects would be the same in both cases. But if there is any asymmetry – if, for instance, the 'poor' who suffer relatively less under the income tax system than under the poll tax are induced to work much less whilst the 'rich' who lose relatively are induced to work very little more – the income effects could not be neglected and the net result would be income as well as substitution effects on the demand for leisure. This point would be all the more important if the poor (rich) were influenced not only by their own relative position under both tax formulae but also by the relative position of the rich (poor).

We have now dealt with most of the important issues in the comparison between poll taxes and proportional taxes. Before we move to the discussion of proportionate versus progressive taxes, however, it is worth pausing to consider the links between our arguments and those which have been used at various times in the past.

Reactions to taxes have sometimes been cast in terms of the concept of 'elasticity of demand for income in terms of effort'. The ideas behind this concept are exactly the same as those we have been discussing above. If one thinks of the net income per unit of effort as being reduced by taxation, then one has to ask whether the demand for income in terms of effort is elastic or inelastic. If it is elastic then one would expect less work to be done than before; if it is inelastic, one would expect more work to be done than before.

Now we can turn to the comparisons between proportional and progressive taxes. It will be convenient to treat the problem in much the same way as before – to begin with an individual who has a simple choice between working and not working and then to consider the complex cases of the more real world later.

First of all, we must compare a proportional tax with one which achieves progression by charging the various slices of income at successively higher rates. We saw before that the crux of the comparison between the poll tax and the proportional tax was to be found in differing effects on marginal net earnings. Now the essential difference between a proportional and a 'simple' progressive tax is that whereas in the former case both the average and marginal rates of tax are identical and remain unchanged whatever the income level, in the latter both rates increase with income and the marginal rate tends to increase faster than the average rate. Therefore, provided that people's reactions are much the same to a given change in income due to proportional or progressive taxes, one would expect the substitution effect to be much stronger in the case of progressive taxes and hence any tendency to reduce hours of work to be greater. And the more progressive the rate of tax the greater will be the marginal rate compared to the average rate and the greater would one expect this effect to be.

If one now turns to the sort of progression which comes from the combination of a minimum exemption limit and a proportional tax above the limit, the position is a little different, as in that case the marginal rate of tax diverges most from the average rate at the exemption limit. The substitution effect must obviously be stronger at this point in the income scale than it would be in the proportional tax case. Whether, however, it will be stronger than in the case of straight progression will depend on the proportion of the working population whose incomes are just about equal to the exemption limit, and whether their reactions to the large jump in the marginal rate, at that point, are so great as to outweigh the combined reactions of the whole population to the infinitely large number of infinitely small jumps implicit in the theoretical case of straight progression.

Finally, it should be observed that in the real world the complications of allowing for the threefold margin of choice and taking the reactions of a community (and not simply those of an individual) have to be taken into account as in the comparison between poll and proportional taxes. It must also be clearly understood that the supply of 'labour' can be affected by further education and training as well as by the number of hours worked. The analysis developed above can readily be applied, e.g. the substitution effect of the imposition of a proportional income tax will depend on the difference between the present value of the reduction in future net returns and that of the reduction in net earnings foregone by those undertaking further education.

2.2 *Income taxes, excise taxes and the supply of labour*

We now have to compare the effects of an income tax and an equal yield excise tax on labour's willingness to work.

The first point is that various complications result if the excise tax system applies only to consumers' goods. Let us assume to begin with that it embraces producers' goods as well, so that there is no question of exempting saving.

The second point to stress is that, in order to have a fair comparison between the two taxes we must assume an equal degree of progression in both cases, or, in other words (given the requirement of equal yield), the same marginal and average rates at each income level. This in turn implies that we are postulating a complicated set of excise taxes and not just a tax on one commodity, for it would normally be impossible to find a single commodity the consumption of which varied in such a regular way with income.

The traditional argument was that income taxes and excise taxes (in our wide sense), if constructed according to the same tax formula and if yielding the same revenue, would have exactly the same disincentive effects on the supply of labour, as the two marginal tax rates would be the same and the two average tax rates the same. In recent years, however, this conclusion has been challenged and so we must look at the arguments carefully. The essence of the problem is that if we can categorize commodities according to the extent to which they are substitutes for leisure in the eyes of consumers, it may be possible to arrange indirect taxes so that we have a smaller consumption of leisure than in the case of income tax. Ideally, we need to tax goods the demand for which is complementary with the demand for leisure, and subsidize those which are substitutes for leisure on the demand side. The results of taxing the first category (e.g. mid-week afternoon football matches or horse races) will be to reduce both the consumption of the commodity and the consumption of leisure; the results of subsidizing the second category (e.g. local commuter transport) will be to increase the consumption of the commodity but reduce the consumption of leisure. More formally, we can say that if the consumption of leisure is negatively elastic with respect to the prices of some commodities, then those commodities are the ones to tax.

It will be readily appreciated that we have here a proposition which belongs to the same family as the 'Ramsey rule' (i.e. when labour supplies are variable, then subject to various simplifying assumptions, tax rates should be inversely related to demand elasticities) described in Chapter 3. The argument for differentially high taxation of goods, the demand for which is complementary with the demand for leisure, is indeed very much in the mould of the optimal taxation school of thought, though it was discovered long before the recent upsurge of interest in this family of ideas.

There can be no question of the theoretical validity of the argument that the demand for leisure is likely to be more complementary with the demand for some commodities than with the demand for income in general. This can perhaps be seen most simply by considering the relevant alternatives. If taxation is on income in general, the only alternative 'commodity' is leisure and hence people will tend to consume more of it, but if taxation is on a limited range of goods people may consume more non-taxed goods and services rather than more leisure. The real question is how important we must rate these points. To begin with, there is *some* complementarity between the demand for income as a whole and the demand for leisure: it might be argued that higher incomes require more time both to think about how to spend them and to spend them. More important, one must re-emphasize the necessity of comparing like with like. A simple excise tax system might be sufficient to give us a low degree of progression, but with a low degree of progression the income tax disincentives are no great worry. To achieve a high degree of progression, we need a complex system of excise taxes on many commodities. Whether it would really be practicable to combine this with a system of taxing goods in relation to which the cross-elasticity of demand for leisure is negative, or even zero, is extremely doubtful, more especially when it is remembered that a number of the most likely candidates would be service industries which are particularly difficult to tax. Finally, it must be remembered that even though an indirect tax system of this kind may enable us to increase the supply of effort, so that we get nearer to the optimum mix of leisure and goods than we do with a progressive income tax, this achievement is at the expense of upsetting the optimum allocation of resources between other goods. In other words, one has a second-best situation where the removal of one impediment to optimal resource utilization does not necessarily mean that the end result is an overall improvement.

Now let us remove the assumption that the excise tax system covers producers' goods. In the simplest case, we are then faced with the contrast between an income tax and an expenditure tax. Assuming for the moment proportional tax rates in both cases and the rates adjusted to give equal yields, what will be the relative effects on the supply of work?

We shall soon discuss in detail the implications of adjusting expenditure tax rates so as to preserve the same yield as with an income tax system.[1] All we need say now is what is intuitively obvious, that when positive saving is taking place in a country the expenditure tax rate will have to be higher than the income tax rate if government revenue is not to fall, and when negative saving occurs the opposite will be true. With a proportional tax system and a society in which saving is normally positive, we should, therefore, expect to find that the terms on which a man can substitute present consumption for leisure will turn against present consumption at the margin when an expenditure tax is substituted. On the other hand, the terms on which leisure can be substituted for future consumption at the margin may or may not turn in favour of the latter depending on the ratio of saving to income, the rate of interest, the tax rate and the expected length of life of saving.[2] The final effect will, therefore, depend on a balancing of these considerations. If the demand for leisure is complementary with the demand for present consumption and substitutable with the demand for future consumption, work incentives may or may not be improved. But if the complementarity is between leisure and future consumption and the substitutability is between leisure and current consumption, work incentives will almost certainly be impaired. It is impossible to say for certain

[1] See below, pp. 83–4.

[2] *Ibid.*

what the net result will be, but there is some possibility that for the types of savings ratios and interest rates, etc. normally prevailing, work incentives may diminish.

A full analysis of these problems would really require us to combine together the notion of varying excise taxes on different commodities with the exemption of saving and to consider proportional and progressive taxes in all cases. But we have said sufficient to indicate the lines on which any such analysis should proceed.

One final point has to be made. It is often argued that income tax, especially in PAYE or withholding form, is a much more obvious and direct imposition than any simple excise tax and a fortiori than a series of excise taxes on different commodities. But this does not necessarily mean, as is sometimes thought, that income taxes must have more serious disincentive effects than excise taxes. It only means that they will have more effects. For although it is perfectly true that the substitution effect will be stronger in the income tax case, it will also follow that the income effect will be stronger too, and we cannot, therefore, deduce that the 'money illusion' of the type we postulate will necessarily turn the scales against the income tax.

2.3 *Transfers, other expenditures and the supply of labour*

First, let us take the comparison between transfers and subsidies. Transfers can obviously be thought of as a negative poll tax, at any rate in their simplest form, whereas subsidies are negative excise or sales taxes. An equal amount spent in each form will, therefore, have income effects which, subject to the caveats issued above, should more or less cancel out. The net effects would be the substitution effects of the subsidies; when an increase in expenditure is contemplated, for instance, the effect would be to cheapen goods relatively to leisure and therefore encourage more work in the subsidy case than in the transfer case, assuming substitutability between goods and leisure.

Second, we may compare lump sum transfers and public expenditures on goods and services. Equal amounts of expenditure in each direction will have similar income effects, and so the main question is whether substitution effects may differ. Obviously, there are grounds for thinking that people may respond more noticeably to changes in money incomings which they can spend as they please, than to changes in real incomings in the form of parks, schools, roads, etc. which have to be taken or left, but the ultimate answer will depend on the constituents of government expenditure. When government-provided goods are substitutes for leisure there is a greater likelihood that work incentives will increase than where they are complementary – in much the same way as excise taxes are likely to be more favourable than income taxes to work incentives when they are levied on goods which are complementary with leisure.

More generally, we can say that if revenue is raised in a given form – say, a proportional income tax, for simplicity – the combined effects of revenue raising and disbursement on work incentives will depend on the constituents of government expenditure. As a first approximation, income effects will cancel out and so the net effect will depend on substitution effects. When expenditure side substitution effects are important (e.g. if the revenue is used to subsidize wage goods and so increase the attractiveness of work at the margin) the net disincentive effect will be less than where they are not (e.g. transfer payments which are made irrespective of work effort). But it cannot be assumed that income effects always cancel out, e.g. if expenditure is confined to 'useless' items of which the population takes no cognisance, we are then left with nothing but the net impact on work incentives of the income and substitution effects of raising the income tax.[1]

Another comparison is between personal credits and personal allowances against income tax. If the same revenue is to be raised in both cases, then under a progressive income tax of the 'slice' variety we should find that poorer people would be better off under a flat rate credit system and richer people worse off. But it is impossible to say whether the net result would be an impairment of work incentives or not.

When transfers are not of the lump sum variety but are inversely related to the level of income, situations can arise where the implicit marginal tax rate on earnings (i.e. the loss in transfer income from working fractionally harder) can be extremely high. This is sometimes the case with state pension arrangements when it is stipulated that pensions will be reduced if the recipient continues to work; and it can easily arise with welfare payments, with potentially serious consequences on incentives to work, relatively to the lump sum transfer case.[2]

[1] For further discussion see A. R. Prest, 'The Taxable Capacity of a Country', in J. F. J. Toye (ed.), *Taxation and Economic Development* (Cass, 1978) and references cited, especially those relating to the work of C. S. Shoup.

[2] This subject is explored in detail in Chapter 14 below.

3 TAXATION AND THE SUPPLY OF SAVING

3.1 *Income taxes, expenditure taxes and the supply of saving*

We now turn to the relative effects of income and expenditure taxes on saving. We shall begin with the comparison between a proportional income tax applying to all types of income (including capital gains, etc.) and a tax which is proportional to consumption expenditure. Various side-issues such as the effects of progression in the tax structure, the implications of 'imperfections' of income taxes, etc. will be dealt with later.

A great deal has been written by economists in the past on the so-called 'double taxation of saving'. It has often been argued that an income tax (as compared to a lump sum tax) will tax savings when they are originally made and will also tax the fruits of those savings over the years. This is unjust, it is said, in that it amounts to taxing one stream of income twice over. Moreover, it has the effect of reducing saving below the level which might otherwise prevail and this will be a departure from an optimum position.

There are two distinct points here. First, it is perfectly possible to conceive of a lump sum tax which will offer greater incentives to saving than an income tax.[1] In so far as annual income is increasing through time by virtue of the interest on net saving, either the lump sum tax would have to be an increasing amount through time or the income tax rate a decreasing rate in order to yield the same revenue to the government in both cases. But this is a minor point. It is more important to emphasize that the identification of a lump sum with neutrality is not a matter capable of empirical verification. As we have emphasized before, it is impossible to vary the revenue collected from

[1] Pigou summarized the whole issue in this way. Given a tax rate of 100 x per cent, an interest rate 100 r per cent and saving for n years, a lump sum tax would take £x from a man whether he spent or saved £1. An income tax will take tax to the present value of £$[x + x(1 - x)] =$ £$x(2 - x)$ if £1 of income is permanently unconsumed and £x on £1 of unsaved income. If saving is for a limited period, the tax bite on £1 of income unspent for n years will be

$$£\left[x + x(1 - x)\left\{1 - \frac{1}{(1 + r)^n}\right\}\right]$$

as compared to £x on £1 of unsaved income. (*A Study in Public Finance*, Macmillan, London, 3rd edition, 1947, Ch. X.) Thus the differential between the income tax rates on spending and saving is relatively greater in the case of permanent than in that of temporary saving.

any one tax without simultaneously changing some other variables in the system. We shall therefore confine ourselves to the relative effects of lump sum taxes, income taxes and expenditure taxes on the ratio of saving to consumption, and eschew any considerations of ideal savings ratios or neutral tax systems with respect to savings ratios.

Turning to the income and expenditure taxes comparison, we shall start with the general case in which saving by an individual is taken to be for a limited period of time only. The case where saving is deemed to be in perpetuity will emerge in the course of our discussion.

It may be helpful to set out a numerical example. Suppose we take a man earning £4,000 a year and faced with the alternatives of an income tax of 50 per cent or an equivalent rate expenditure tax of 100 per cent.[1] It is assumed that £100 is saved in year 0 and £100 is dissaved in year *n* in either case. The rate of interest is taken as 5 per cent and the yield from saving is assumed to be entirely spent.

The relative positions may be set out as follows:

	Year 0			*Years 1 .... n−1*			*Year n*		
	Consumption	*Tax*	*Saving*	*Consumption*	*Tax*	*Saving*	*Consumption*	*Tax*	*Saving*
Income tax system	1900	2000	+100	2002½	2002½	0	2100	2000	−100
Expenditure tax system	1950	1950	+100	2002½	2002½	0	2050	2050	−100

In year 0 consumption will be 50 greater and tax 50 less under the expenditure tax system than under the income tax system. In years 1 .... *n*−1 the relative positions will be exactly the same, half of the interest income going in consumption and half in taxation. In year *n*, when dissaving takes place, consumption will be greater and tax less in the income tax than in the expenditure tax case.

It would therefore appear that an expenditure tax system gives a greater return to saving. Whereas in the income tax case the initial sacrifice of consumption only produces a net return of 2½ per cent per annum, in the expenditure case there is a net return of 5 per cent (i.e. £2.50 net income on £50 initial abstinence). The exact difference between the two cases can be seen to depend on the ruling rate of interest and the tax rate. The larger is either of these, the greater is the differential. If in the above example the rate of interest were 10 per cent, in the one case we should have a 10 per cent return and in the

[1] Cf. p. 48n.

other a 5 per cent return; if the income tax rate were 75 per cent (equivalent expenditure tax rate 300 per cent), the contrast would be 5 per cent as against $1\frac{1}{4}$ per cent. In other words, the taxpayer benefits by the annual yield on the amount of taxation which is deferred in the expenditure tax case.[1]

How much greater saving will be in one case rather than the other is essentially a problem of interest elasticity of savings. Those who believe that savings are highly elastic with respect to interest rates will expect a greater responsiveness to a given differential than those who believe savings to be interest inelastic.

We now come to an important point. Although, in the above example, the totals of tax collected for the whole period (years $0 \ldots . n$) and for the intermediate years $(1 \ldots . n-1)$ are the same in both cases, this is not so in either year 0 or year n considered alone. In the income tax case, it is 2,000 in each year; in the expenditure tax case it is 1,950 and 2,050 respectively. It can quickly be seen that a divergence must arise, given our assumptions of equivalent tax rates, in any year in which saving or dissaving takes place. Moreover, the more successful is an expenditure tax in promoting saving, the greater will be the discrepancy, e.g. if in year 0 savings were 200 in the expenditure tax case, the loss to the government would be 100 and not just 50 in that year. Therefore, it must be concluded that an equivalent rate expenditure tax will provide a stream of revenue which is worth less on ordinary discounting principles to the government than that yielded by the income tax.

So far we have considered the case of a single individual. Must the same conclusion hold for the whole community? If tax rates are proportional, it must hold for the community, as for any individual, that positive saving will make the expenditure tax yield smaller and negative saving will make it greater than that of an income tax. As the usual

[1] With an expenditure tax of 100 e per cent, £e is payable in tax if £1 is spent now; if £1 is saved and spent in year n, the present value of the tax bill will be

$$£\left[\frac{e}{(1+r)^n} + e(1 - \frac{1}{(1+r)^n})\right] = £e,$$

where 100 r per cent is the rate of interest. Therefore, the present value of the tax bill is the same whether £1 is spent or not; in the income tax case the present value of the tax bill was £x in respect of £1 of unsaved income and

$$£\left[x + x(1-x)\left\{1 - \frac{1}{(1+r)^n}\right\}\right]$$

in respect of £1 unspent for n years.

characteristic of modern economies is to have positive net personal saving every year, it seems a fair judgment that an equivalent rate expenditure tax will always produce less revenue than equivalent income tax.

The next step is to examine the consequences of increasing the expenditure tax rate to such a level that government revenue remains the same after the change-over. Let us assume to begin with that we consider the case of a single act of saving planned to last for a limited period of time. The effects of switching from an expenditure tax rate equivalent to the income tax rate to a higher one may be divided into substitution and income components. The substitution effects will be nil: at the margin the differential advantage to saving (as compared to the income tax case) will be neither greater nor less than with a lower rate of expenditure tax. The income effect of replacing an equivalent rate expenditure tax by an equivalent revenue expenditure tax is likely to mean reductions in both consumption and saving, as compared to the equivalent rate case. In general, we should still expect saving to be higher than in the income tax case, but how much higher depends on such factors as whether those who benefit most from the changes (i.e. those with the highest average ratios of saving to income) have high marginal propensities to save.

But this is all on the assumption of a known tax structure. Once we allow for the fact that people do not know the tax rates which will prevail at the date of dissaving, the expenditure tax loses some marks. Even if the probabilities that tax rates may rise or fall by year n are equal, a sort of risk premium must be allowed as an offset against the advantages of the expenditure tax in favour of saving. There is obviously nothing corresponding to this in the income tax case.

When saving is planned to last for ever, complications of this latter sort do not arise and the balance of advantage in favour of the expenditure tax, both before and after allowing for the change in the tax rate necessary to keep revenue unchanged, is much greater than in the case of saving for a limited period.[1]

[1] If we write 100 e' per cent for the equivalent revenue expenditure tax rate where $e' = x/[c(1 - x)]$, c being the fraction of Personal Income, net of tax payable in the income tax case, consumed in the expenditure tax case (cf. p. 49, n.2), the tax payable on £1 consumed now will be £e'. If £1 is saved for ever and the interest income is spent, the present value of the tax will be £e'; if interest income is saved, tax will be nil. In the income tax case (cf. p. 82n.) the present value of tax will be £x in respect of £1 of unsaved income and £$[x(2 - x)]$ in respect of £1 of permanently unconsumed income, irrespective of whether interest income is spent or saved.

It might now be asked whether the criterion of an equal tax yield is really the right one. Could it not be argued that the maintenance of the same level of social rather than government income is just as good if not better as a standard? If the combination of more private saving and less public saving which we have in the expenditure tax case in year 0 is sufficient to generate the same level of social income as in the income tax case, is not this a fair comparison? Obviously, such a principle cannot be a general one for assessing the relative merits of taxes. When we look at the allocative effects of income taxes and excise taxes, equal government yield seems a more appropriate criterion than equal social income. And if it is claimed that the criterion of equal social income is more appropriate in this particular case, then it could be argued that the effects of changes in saving of different types (and, via the implicit change in the national debt – if revenue is smaller in the expenditure tax case – in monetary conditions and interest rates) are complicated and elusive. It is not by any means easy to say what really is equivalent in this sense.

Finally, there is the fundamental consideration that if we do not postulate equal-yields we are not really comparing the effects of an income tax and an expenditure tax, but rather the effects of an income tax with the *joint* effects of an expenditure tax and some other change. If the expenditure tax yield is less than that of the income tax in any year, the other change in the system could in principle be an increase in other taxes, a reduction in expenditure or an increase in borrowing. In all these cases, it becomes impossible to disentangle the effects of this change from those due to the substitution of the expenditure tax for the income tax.

Our previous discussion of risk-bearing and incentives to work must now be recalled. The arguments in this section have been concerned with the division of a given amount of income between spending and saving. If, however, either because of greater incentives to take risks or greater incentives to work, the total of income is increased, we should have more saving even if the ratio of spending to saving were unchanged. In fact, as we have seen, there is not much reason for thinking that more risk-bearing would be undertaken with an expenditure tax and the probability is that *less* work would be done. It might well be the case therefore that the total level of output would be less and so even though the spending/saving ratio changed in favour of saving, the overall amount of saving might be less than in the income tax case. Irrespective of the most likely result in the real world, the general principle must be emphasized that we cannot reach any final verdict about the relative effects of expenditure and income taxation on saving without asking about the repercussions on total income as well as the division of any given income.

For our final topic, it is of interest to compare an income tax which excludes investment income with one which taxes all kinds of income.[1] If the same total yield is predicated, and hence tax rates have to be higher in the former case, what can be said about the likely effects on saving? One obvious result is that less tax will be paid in the former case by the propertied groups and therefore, in so far as their marginal propensity to save is higher than that of wage and salary earners, the level of saving will increase. Furthermore, the yield to new savings will be greater to the extent that future interest income is relieved of taxation. On both these grounds, income and substitution effects, one may find more saving and less consumption in the investment-income exempt case. Here again, further reactions on the willingness of different groups to work or on that of property owners to invest in more risky fashion may modify the general argument.

Whether a system of exempting investment income from tax will lead to more or less saving than an expenditure tax seems to depend on four main considerations. First, if saving is for a limited period only, the differential against saving found in the ordinary income tax case disappears for both alike; only in the limiting case when saving is meant to last for ever and when interest income is never spent, will the expenditure tax have an advantage over the income tax exempting investment income. Secondly, depending on whether the total of personal investment income is greater or less than the total of personal saving in any one year, there will need to be a larger or smaller change in the tax rate in the investment income exempt case, if we are to preserve equal revenue. In addition, the groups hit by the higher tax rates will not be identical: non-property-owners in one case, non-savers in the other. As a consequence, the reactions to work and to risk-taking may differ in the two cases. Thirdly, as those who benefit by the change are not identical in the two cases, the marginal propensity to save the benefits from the tax change may differ. Finally, in the expenditure tax case there is always the risk in the temporary saving case that the tax rate may change against a man by the time he dissaves; there is nothing comparable to this in the other case.

[1] See also p. 50 above.

3.2 *Income taxes, capital taxes and the supply of saving*

We must now survey the relative effects of income taxes and capital taxes on the supply of saving. First, we shall compare the relative effects of annual taxes on capital and taxes on investment income. Later we shall turn to the comparison between taxes on investment income and occasional levies on capital, whether in the form of death duties or once-for-all capital levies. We shall also ask how these conclusions are affected by taking variants of the main types of income and capital taxes. We assume that income includes all accruals such as those due to capital appreciation.

We have just seen some of the consequences of taxing investment income or exempting investment income from tax. As a first approximation we can say that annual taxes on capital are a fairly close substitute for taxes on investment income. Therefore, the comparison between the savings effects of raising a given sum by a capital tax and raising the same sum by a general income tax raises broadly the same issues as the exemption of investment income from income tax. In either case, we have to look at the savings implications of transferring some of the tax burdens from incomes from work to incomes from property, or vice versa.

If this is so, we can leave aside the more general question of annual taxes on capital as against annual income taxes and concentrate on the particular problem of the detailed merits, from a savings viewpoint, of annual taxes on capital as against taxes on investment income yielding the same sums of revenue. Initially, we assume proportional taxes in both cases.

It might be thought that if the average rate of return were 5 per cent per annum, we should have exactly similar results from a tax of 20 per cent on investment income and a 1 per cent tax on capital. There is, however, the important difference that owners of different types of capital assets will be treated very differently in the two cases, those with a higher than average return on capital paying greater taxes in the investment income tax than in the capital tax case and vice versa. It is also often argued that a tax on capital will strike at capital appreciation whereas a tax on investment income will not do so. This, however, is a matter of definition of income. If income is defined in the sense of including accruals of spending power, then a tax on investment income would strike at capital appreciation in much the same way as a tax on capital wealth.

Given these arguments, can it be said that one type of tax is more conducive to saving than another? The differences of substance are that the capital tax hits holdings of liquid assets and other non-income yielding forms of wealth more severely than a tax on investment income and that on the other hand (at any rate in the case where loss offsets are incomplete in the income tax case) it treats capital in risky enterprises relatively more leniently. If, therefore, potential savers intended to hold their acquisitions to wealth in the form of liquid funds, the capital tax would be a greater deterrent to saving than the equal-yield investment income tax. If on the other hand, potential dissaving is likely to be done from non-income yielding assets, a capital tax would diminish saving by its encouragement of dissaving, and conversely with investments in risky outlets.

We now ask how the analysis differs when progressive rather than proportional taxes are admitted. If investment incomes were in direct ratio to the size of capital assets it would in principle be possible to levy taxes of the same degree of progression in both cases, in the sense of mulcting the same amount from any one individual in either case. In practice, the lack of close correspondence between income and capital means that such a result would be unattainable and there would therefore be an indeterminate effect on the relative level of saving in the two cases. It is, of course, more likely that loss offsets will be incomplete with a progressive income tax and therefore inducements to put savings in risky enterprises correspondingly diminished.

Now we may inquire into the differing effects of equal-yield death duties and taxes on investment income and the supply of saving. To begin with we shall assume that death duties are levied according to the size of the testator's estate and that they are also levied on a proportional basis. There are two principal considerations here: the income (or wealth) effects and the substitution effects. The replacement of an annual tax on investment income by a death duty calculated to give an equal yield to the government would obviously have differing repercussions on the different age-groups in the community. Younger people would be exchanging a continuous series of small annual liabilities during both their own and their heirs' lifetime for uncertain but probably distant large liabilities on the death of themselves or their heirs; older people would be exchanging the prospect of a few small liabilities in their own lifetime (plus an infinite series of small liabilities during the lifetime of their successors) for the prospect of a large impost in the near future plus other large imposts as future generations pass away. No certain answer can be given about the net reactions of the whole community for they will depend on a complex of issues: the relative numbers of old and young, their relative levels of income and wealth, and their relative propensities to save out of marginal accessions to income and capital, this in turn depending on relative attitudes towards the interests of heirs. Therefore, no universal conclusion is possible, but if a guess had to be made it might well be that the increased saving of the young would not match the dissaving of the old and so the net effect of the change might be to reduce saving. On the other hand, the substitution of death duties for annual investment income taxation would add one powerful incentive to save: all that class of saving ('hump' saving) destined to be spent before death would not be subject to tax in the death duty case, whereas the annual income from it would be taxable in the investment income case. There are complications here about the appropriate tax rates to secure the same revenue in both cases, but it seems likely that the death duty system would in this respect discourage saving less than the income investment system tax. Perhaps the overall conclusion, bearing in mind the large amount of saving which is undertaken with the intention of subsequent spending in one's own lifetime, is that death duties are less inimical to saving than equal-yield investment income taxes. Consideration of the relative effects on risk-taking and incentives to work, and hence on total output and the amount available for division between saving and consumption, would seem to reinforce this conclusion.

Once we admit a progressive structure of death duties, we have to look at the comparison between duties levied at death on the estate of the testator and those levied according to the size of the bequest, or according to the size of the legatee's estate. It is often argued that death duties on the latter two bases are likely to be less inimical to saving, as the burden of duty can be reduced by the expedient of splitting an estate between a large number of beneficiaries. Reflection, however, will show that this will not necessarily be the case if we stick to our assumption of an equal-yield tax. Although a succession duty type of arrangement will, compared to the present system, reduce the amount of duty payable by an estate of a certain size split among a number of beneficiaries, it would presumably increase the amount of duty payable by an estate of the same size left to one beneficiary only. (It should be added that this would not necessarily follow if the normal death duty was not applicable to gifts inter vivos but the succession duty was so applicable.) Unless it can be shown that these reactions would be asymmetrical in some way, such an arrangement would not differentiate in favour of saving. However, there is one kind of asymmetry which may be important. Under the normal death duty systems no distinction is drawn between bequests to near and distant relatives. If a succession duty discriminates in favour of the former then it may well be that this arrangement would increase saving, in so far as people feel a stronger compunction to save for their wives' and children's benefit than for their second cousins' benefit.

Finally, we come to the comparison between the results of a capital levy and a death duty repeated at approximately thirty-year intervals. The first difference here is that one occurs during life, the other occurs after life, and possibly after one's son's life. Whereas a capital levy removes both the income from capital and the prestige and security of owning capital during one's lifetime, death duties will only affect one's family and not oneself in these respects. On these grounds it might be thought that a capital levy is more likely to impede saving than a regularly but infrequently occurring death duty. If, on the other hand, the capital levy is totally unexpected and if people are convinced that it is once-and-for-all, then it would in all probability lead to a greater annual flow of saving than would occur under a system of death duties.

3.3 *Income tax reliefs, subsidies and the level of company investment and saving*

Our discussion of the effects of various taxes on the supply of saving has so far been couched, explicitly or implicitly, in terms of the effects on personal saving. A good deal of this reasoning is applicable, mutatis mutandis, to company saving but, in addition, there are some other points to consider. Conversely, some of our reasoning (e.g. on death duties) has no relevance to company saving, or at any rate to saving by companies in which the directors do not own the greater part of the capital.

We have already looked into the considerations which determine the choice between risky and non-risky investments. We shall at a later stage consider how taxes can increase or diminish the level of investment relatively to the supply of saving. Therefore we need not concern ourselves with either of these topics here. Our job is rather to analyse how far tax inducements are likely to increase corporate saving.

Under this general heading two different issues are subsumed. First comes that of the inducement to save rather than distribute corporate profits. Second, we have that of the willingness to undertake new (physical) investment.

In respect of the first, much the same issues as those raised in our discussion of the relative effects of income taxes, expenditure taxes, etc. on personal saving are relevant. For instance, income taxes which differentiate against distribution either directly (e.g. higher rates of corporation or profits tax on distributed profits) or indirectly (e.g. taxes at some standard rate if the profits remain in the company's hands, and taxes at some higher rate applicable to the individual if they do not) will obviously swing companies in the direction of distributing their profits to a lesser extent than if such discrimination were non-existent. As we shall see later, there are some complications here, but for the moment no more need be said on this matter.

In the second case, the obvious comparison which springs to mind here is that between an income tax which discriminates in favour of capital formation and one which does not. One case of any such favouritism is when a firm is allowed to treat the whole of any capital expenditure as immediately deductible for income tax assessment purposes, but there are many half-way and even quarter-way houses. Another type of discrimination is the Investment Allowance which operated for some time in post-war Britain. Briefly, this had the effect of giving a subsidy to many types of capital expenditure.[1] Tax relief of this kind, even when associated with a higher tax rate (to maintain equal-yields between two forms of income taxes) will tend to encourage both the level and the rate of growth of investment. It does not follow that the increased profitability of investment will necessarily induce companies to save more; obviously enough, they may raise external finance instead. But in so far as company saving is motivated by specific expenditure objectives or in so far as firms follow working rules about the proportion of new capital expenditure which must be met from retained profits, the effects of tax relief on investment may be to generate some additional saving.

4 MINOR COMPARISONS

Our object now is rather different from that in the preceding sections of this chapter. Whereas previously we were concerned with detailed analysis of the relative effects of different kinds of taxes on the supply of labour and capital, we now simply try to enumerate some of the other less obvious ways in which taxes can affect the supply of resources available.

[1] Cf. p. 201.

In dealing with the supply of labour we concentrated on what we termed the 'flow' aspect. But plainly taxes, etc. can affect the 'stock' aspect. Income taxes which make generous allowances for children are more conducive to a high birth rate than those which do not. Government expenditures on old age pensions and welfare facilities are more likely to lower death rates than other forms of expenditure. Nor is the stock of labour influenced solely by the movements of birth and death rates. Income taxes and particularly highly progressive income taxes may, compared to equal-yield excise taxes, have important effects on migration from one country to another.

The substitution of an expenditure tax for an income tax in one country might also have effects on migration patterns. If no countervailing measures were taken, there would be a marked tendency for people who had accumulated capital under the expenditure tax regime to emigrate in order to dissave under an income tax regime; conversely, those living in an income tax country would not choose to emigrate to the expenditure tax country if they expected to be net dissavers of previously accumulated assets.

In the case of capital, we concentrated on the 'stock' aspect. Although the most important tax effects relate to that, there are other considerations. A system of depreciation allowances which is solely related to the number of years of use of a machine is obviously inferior in many respects to one which also reflects the degree of usage. The UK system of 'balancing allowances' which in effect enabled firms to write off the whole initial cost less scrap value of an asset when it was worn out and scrapped, even though this might be well in advance of its notional date of retirement, clearly had advantages compared to a rigid system of depreciation which cumulated with time and only with time. Similarly, a system of subsidizing investment such as that implied by the UK system of investment allowances, conferred greater benefits over any given period of time on those who utilized their machinery intensively and scrapped it frequently than those who did not.

Examples of these minor comparisons could easily be multiplied. Perhaps we have said sufficient to show the main sorts of ideas involved.

5

EQUITY

1 INTRODUCTION

Our task in this chapter is to examine the relative merits of different taxes and expenditures from the standpoint of equity. We begin with some preliminary consideration of the general meaning of equity and a brief discussion of the formidable problems of setting up the optimum or ideal situation. In section 2 we discuss equity in relation to the size distribution of income; and section 3 investigates other aspects of distribution. Throughout the emphasis will be on the differences between the equity effects of different taxes. Section 4 looks briefly at taxes and expenditures taken as a whole.

1.1 *The meaning of equity*

The abstract meaning of equity is a problem for the moral philosopher rather than the economist and we can do no more here than point out some of the relevant distinctions. Frequently, equity is identified with various other general criteria such as fairness, justice or avoidance of hardship, and linked with particular phenomena such as the distribution of income or property. Perhaps the simplest way of illuminating the general problem is to divide it into two main aspects: the treatment of people in like and unlike circumstances. Similar treatment of people in similar circumstances seems a fairly safe proposition. To argue otherwise would seem to offend all principles of justice, equity or any other variant of the general theme. Dissimilar treatment of people in dissimilar circumstances is a much more debatable proposition, however. Whether dissimilar circumstances justify any difference in tax treatment and if so, how much, is an issue of great magnitude and complexity.

Part of the difficulty is that there is no unique definition of dissimilar circumstances. It could obviously refer to incomes, or spending, or wealth, and to any of the various meanings which these concepts can in turn be given (e.g. income measured on an annual or a lifetime basis). As we have already seen and shall see in other connections, the concept of income is particularly treacherous. Nor is the combination of these criteria likely to be an easy solution. Two men might have very similar incomes but very unequal property at their disposal. How are we to weigh the similarity against the dissimilarity? There are other problems also. Even if we could agree to measure dissimilarity by reference to income only, we still have to decide what are to be taken as income units or groups of income units. Is a household of six people with a given level of income to be treated in the same way as a single person with the same income, and if not, how should the treatment differ?

It requires little thought to see that such considerations are likely to arise in virtually all questions of tax theory. Dissimilar circumstances are in fact the rule and exactly similar circumstances a most unlikely contingency. But even if dissimilarity of circumstances could be 'nailed' in some unique way, another problem of perhaps even greater complexity raises its head. How far should taxation be adjusted to take account of these dissimilarities? If we want to tax the rich but exempt the poor, where should the dividing line be drawn, at £750 a year, £1,000 a year, or some other figure? And how steep should be the progressiveness of taxation above whatever line is drawn?

Historically, there has been a number of attempts to grapple with this set of problems. The most important and most influential is the sacrifice theory associated with such great names as Mill, Sidgwick, Edgeworth and Pigou. Although the theory is no longer widely accepted today, no discussion of the principles of public finance would be complete without it.

1.2 *The sacrifice approach*

The sacrifice (or ability to pay) approach can be interpreted in a number of different ways. Certain basic assumptions are common to all interpretations, however, and it is important to specify these at the outset. The first is that there is no difficulty in identifying, or at any rate correlating, units of income with units of utility or satisfaction, i.e. we can pass easily from what may be thought of as objective or external standards to subjective or internal standards. This does not necessarily imply that income is the only determinant of utility but it does mean that it is the principal determinant. Secondly, it has to be postulated that the utility curve for income has a downward slope. As income increases total utility increases but at a decreasing rate, i.e. the *marginal* utility of income varies inversely with income. Thirdly, it is assumed that everyone's income utility function has exactly the same characteristics. As a consequence, we can think of the total utility of income at two income levels as differing by the same amount, irrespective of whether we are considering a single individual with different income levels at different points in time or two individuals with divergent incomes at the same point in time. Finally, in its most usual form, the theory has been applied to the revenue rather than the expenditure side of government. The traditional approach has been to assume a given level of expenditure, put aside the distribution of the benefits derived from that expenditure and discuss how the sacrifice involved in financing it should be apportioned.

Given all these assumptions – and of their validity we shall have something to say later – it is possible to set out some general principles of taxation. The first ('equal sacrifice') is that the sacrifice, or the number of units of utility extracted from each taxpayer, should be exactly the same. The second ('equi-proportional sacrifice') is that each individual should be required to forego the same fraction of his total utility. The third ('least aggregate sacrifice') is the principle of minimizing total sacrifice for the community. This is achieved if the *marginal* rather than the *total* sacrifice is the same for everyone. If it were not the same, then total sacrifice for the community could be reduced by reallocating the tax burden until this point were reached. The logical implication of this doctrine is that the utility remaining to everyone after tax rather than the utility taken away should be the same.

Each of these variants of sacrifice theory may result in a different tax formula. Provided that the marginal utility of income declines as income increases, the equi-proportional variant of the theory will generally (though not necessarily always) result in a progressive tax structure, whatever the rate of decline. But this will not be so with equal sacrifice. On that criterion, the marginal utility of income must decline more than proportionately as income increases, to justify progressive taxation. If the rate of decline is less than proportionate, regressive taxation would be required. If it is exactly proportionate, i.e. the curve is a rectangular hyperbola, proportional taxation is needed. Given the fact that the marginal utility of income declines at all, the least aggregate or minimum sacrifice formula leads logically to such a degree of progression that every taxpayer, and in some circumstances every person, is reduced to the same dead-pan level of equality. This can be seen if we simply reflect that, by virtue of the assumptions underlying the theory, any post-tax inequality of income would imply that marginal sacrifices were unequal. Equal marginal sacrifice implies, in the well-known phraseology of Pigou, 'lopping off the tops of all incomes above the minimum income and leaving everybody, after taxation, with equal incomes'.

Needless to say, there are many glosses on these various versions of sacrifice theory. Without considering these, and therefore with full recognition of the brevity of our summary of the theory, we can see that, given the initial assumptions, the sacrifice theory does provide us with some principles on which to base the treatment of people in dissimilar circumstances. It is important to note, however, that even in this rarefied atmosphere we have no really firm directive, as we can reach different conclusions according to the particular version of sacrifice theory we choose to select.

Today, many, if not most, economists would find themselves unable to accept all the premises on which sacrifice theory, in any of its forms, is based. There are some strong and powerful arguments why this should be so, but before we mention them, one apparent difficulty which is of no real consequence needs to be discussed. It might be imagined that, because sacrifice theories usually ignored the expenditure side and were developed as if taxation were purely confiscatory, this was a grave defect of reasoning. This is not so, however, as the same general ideas could in principle be applied to the expenditure side. If, for instance, we accept the ultimate logic of the minimum sacrifice variant and plump for complete equality of incomes after tax, there is no reason in principle why the calculations of 'tax' should not include offsets in the form of those government expenditures available for allocation to individual beneficiaries. In practice the statistical difficulties may be greater, but this is not an objection with which we are concerned at this moment.

The three central assumptions of sacrifice theory are the connection between units of income and units of satisfaction, the declining slope of the income-utility curve and the identical nature of the curve for all. It is extremely difficult to accept any of these with great confidence or in any more concrete form than the vaguest of generalities. Obviously, there are plenty of cases in which a greater income may not be accompanied by a decline in the marginal utility of that income. This may be because the appetite grows with what it feeds on or it may be that a larger income has disadvantages (e.g. it may be subject to greater fluctuations or it may be more indirect if it is in the form of undistributed profits of companies, imputed to individuals) not shared by a smaller income. Similarly, the comparability of satisfactions between individuals postulated by the third assumption does not commend itself today as an acceptable procedure. If introspection or intuition is the only means of demonstrating that two people with equal incomes derive equal satisfaction from them, most economists would not feel they could rely heavily on this line of approach. It seems reasonable to conclude that sacrifice is not only unmeasurable and incapable of quantification for any one individual but also not comparable as between individuals. With such fundamental objections it would seem to be impossible to accept these conclusions derived from the theories of sacrifice, even if these conclusions were to have a more definite form than has ever been the case.

1.3 *The optimal taxation approach*

The optimal taxation school, to which we have referred in previous chapters, has had quite a lot to say in recent years about taxation efficiency and vertical equity. Different members of the school have formulated a number of ideas but it seems reasonable to characterize them all as setting out an individual's utility function specifying his choice between goods and leisure and thus attempting to set up optimal tax schedules in such a way that social welfare would be at a maximum after tax had been collected. The social welfare function chosen might be of a Benthamite utilitarian type (maximizing the sum of individual utilities) or a Rawlsian type[1] (maximizing the utility of the worst off individual). The tax components might be primarily direct, primarily indirect, or a mixture of both, there being no presumption that direct taxes should be reserved for equity promotion and indirect for resource allocation, or vice versa. There has been some intensive examination of the properties of income taxes in this context with results (e.g. the undesirability of rising marginal rates and the case for linear or constant marginal rate income taxes together with an exemption below which negative taxes would apply) which clearly surprised some of the contributors to the debate themselves. Ingenious as many of these arguments are, however, it cannot be claimed that they have yet reached the stage of relevance for policy even in the areas where they have been developed. One obvious drawback to the constant marginal rate principle for personal income tax is the high rate which would be needed, given the necessity to make adequate provision for

[1] J. Rawls, *A Theory of Justice* (Harvard University Press, Cambridge, Mass., 1971).

minimum subsistence support. This obstacle has emerged in many studies into the feasibility of social dividend schemes and the like, as we shall see in Chapter 14. And there are a number of problems such as that of horizontal equity, where the contribution has been minimal so far – it might indeed be said that this particular problem has simply been eliminated by assuming identical utility functions in the usual exposition.

There is one other important point arising out of these arguments which it is convenient to note now: the case on broad equity grounds for imposing a proportionate tax on consumption rather than one on income. If it is thought that the appropriate objective is to interfere as little as possible with relative utility levels over people's lifetimes and that utility is a function of lifetime consumption, it can then be argued that a consumption tax has advantages over an income tax. If we take two contemporaries with no initial wealth and the same lifetime earnings pattern, one of whom will consume the whole of his income every year and the other save in earlier years and dissave in later years, it will then follow that under an income tax regime, but not under a consumption tax one, the latter is penalized relatively to the former in the sense that present values of tax bills are greater. It would, therefore, seem that there is a clear case in equity for preferring a consumption tax (or, for that matter, an income tax excluding property income) to an income tax. However, this argument does depend crucially on the assumptions, which many might not accept: that one should look at such matters on a lifetime basis and that a man's utility is a function of his lifetime consumption and nothing else. It should also be realized that the concept of a lifetime basis inevitably carries with it some implications for the integration of the tax treatment of gifts and bequests with that of consumption. Furthermore, many might regard as strange a concept of equity which reduced tax burdens for middle-aged savers and increased them for elderly dissavers.

1.4 *Other criteria*

Brief mention must be made of various other attempts to set up ideal patterns of tax equity. First, comes the so-called benefit theory. The essence of this argument is to liken the government to a business enterprise and argue that it should charge for the services it performs, as if they were goods in the market place. In effect, this is equivalent to saying that government receipts and expenditure should be distributionally neutral or, more accurately, should not distort the pattern of income distribution away from what it would be if, in some sense, the government were 'commercialized'. If, in fact, benefits rendered by governments are greater for richer people than for poorer people, taxation should, according to this theory, be on a progressive basis. But any such progression is designed to counteract the tendency to non-neutrality, rather than to treat people in dissimilar circumstances differently. If, for instance, it were thought that benefits were less for richer people than for poorer people, then taxation should be regressive on this principle.

Obviously, there are grave defects in any such theory. The most fundamental is that governments simply cannot be likened to business entities in all respects. It is precisely because defence, education, etc. cannot be left entirely to the free play of the market that we put them in government hands. Moreover, many of the benefits of this kind are communal rather than individual and just cannot be charged for in the same way as apples or oranges. And one of the functions of taxation is to redistribute income in a different way from that which would emerge from a purely market economy. To insist on charging for services rendered as if they were provided by private enterprise would therefore be directly at variance with the exact reasons why they are not entrusted to private enterprise. Although the benefit theory does have a role, particularly in local finance, it clearly cannot be the supreme guide in matters of tax equity.

Apart from the benefit theory, various other attempts have been made to state how unequally people in dissimilar circumstances should be treated. In the end, most of them can be reduced to some vague statement, such as what society considers equitable, sometimes (though not always) with reference to some more specific notion such as alleviation of hardship, inequalities of opportunity and so on. Most of these 'theories' really throw away the baby with the bath water – and perhaps even the bath-plug as well. To define equity as what is thought to be equitable is as circular a piece of reasoning as is likely to be found anywhere.

1.5 *Summary of equity principles*

We must conclude, therefore, that the meaning of equity remains nebulous. Although we can pay lip-service to the twin principles of equal treatment for people in like circumstances and unequal treatment in unlike cases, the attempts to pin these statements down have not been successful. Partly because unlike circumstances can take many different forms (income, wealth, etc.) and partly because we have no clear rules for determining how far correction of inequality should go, it is impossible to postulate any sort of optimum or ideal position to be used as a bench-mark. People have many varying characteristics. If we think of an individual as defined by a vector of characteristics it is not possible to compare vectors in terms of a scalar magnitude like a tax bill unless we also have a vector of the weights attached to the various characteristics. The need for such weights makes the value-loaded nature of equity explicit. Finally, it should be noted that even if any such bench-mark could be discerned, we should not necessarily have any guidance for the conduct of public finance so long as there were any non-fiscal routes (e.g. improved educational facilities, direct control of monopoly processes and all the other multifarious methods of government intervention) of reaching it.

In the remainder of this chapter we therefore concentrate on the much less ambitious task of analysing the relative distributional results of different taxes and expenditures rather than looking at their merits from the standpoint of an indefinable ideal. We concern ourselves principally with the effects on the distribution of income between different income groups. But we shall also pay some attention to the distribution of consumption and the distribution of property. Nor shall we neglect other aspects of distribution such as that between single people and families.

Before carrying on with our argument, however, we should pause to draw attention to the implications of our summary of the equity argument. If there is no theoretically solid basis for tax progression, it follows that the usual systems of progressive taxation and expenditure have no easily definable rationale. This does not justify us in proclaiming that they are in some sense wrong, but it does justify us in recognizing the underlying truth of the phrase 'the uneasy case for progressive taxation'.[1]

[1] An interesting argument, based on utility interdependence, has emerged in recent years. If we postulate that A is not only concerned with his own utility but also with that of B, then both may gain by a gift from A to B. If so, this brings distributional considerations within the usual Pareto-optimality framework. If redistribution can make some people better off without making anyone worse off, publicly organized transfers between income groups are just as necessary as, say, the public provision of social goods. Although this line of argument is relevant to redistribution in some circumstances, it is not clear that these are all that common. Mandatory redistribution (when the transfers are not acceptable to everyone) may well be a far more important phenomenon than voluntary redistribution (when the transfers are acceptable to everyone). See H. M. Hochman, and J. D. Rodgers, 'Pareto Optimal Redistribution', *American Economic Review*, September 1969, and comments by various writers in subsequent issues. These points are taken up in Chapter 14.

1.6 *Method of comparison*

In the previous chapters we have had two main methods of procedure. Wherever fruitful, we tried to analyse the net effects of, say, an equal increase in income tax and reduction in excise taxes on the allocation of resources and the supply of labour, etc. As an alternative, we set up the hypothesis of a non-distorting tax and asked how an equal-yield[1] income tax or expenditure tax, or whatever the case might be, would differ in its effects. In our analysis of the effects of different tax and expenditure structures on the distribution of income we shall follow the second type of procedure rather than the first. For this purpose, we need to have a standard of reference and the one we shall adopt is that of a distributionally neutral government tax or expenditure. To trace the distributional effects of, say, introducing or increasing an income tax, we shall assume that simultaneously another tax is reduced which of itself does nothing to alter the size distribution of income within the private sector of the economy. This is not a simple concept and we must pause for a moment to explain some of the ramifications. As with our previous reference standards, there is by definition no method of empirical investigation to find out what sort of tax would have the necessary properties, for it would be impossible to vary such a tax whilst holding all other government transactions constant. Quite apart from this, it can easily be seen that a simple concept such as a proportional income tax deemed to rest entirely on the factors of production on which it is levied, would not necessarily give us the right answer. We could not, for instance, assume that, if such a tax were reduced to zero and everyone's post-tax income increased in exactly the same proportion, the distributional effects of any progressive income tax which actually exists could easily be calculated. Even if we were confident that we could trace the various effects of the latter – and, as we shall shortly see, this is a very tall order – we could not set the resultant calculations of post-tax incomes against those obtaining in the hypothetical proportional tax case. This is because the pre-tax income distribution to which the hypothetical adjustments are made, cannot be taken to be identical with the actual pre-tax income distribution on which the progressive income tax operates. If a proportional income tax (that being, for the moment, our mental picture of a

[1] Richard Musgrave makes the point (*The Theory of Public Finance*, McGraw-Hill, New York, 1959, p. 212) that 'equal yield' can be interpreted in money or real terms and that the two will not necessarily be the same if one tax differs from another in its impact on the prices of government-purchased goods. No attempt is made here to deal with this point.

distributionally neutral tax) actually existed, we should expect to find a pre-tax income distribution different to that which actually rules in a world of non-neutral government taxes and expenditures.

The concept of an equal-yield distributionally neutral tax is therefore fraught with difficulty. Nevertheless, it is still superior to any other method of approach. Unless we are prepared to adopt this technique we are condemned to even less satisfactory alternatives. We might simply take the distributional effects of increasing a tax, but we should then really be tracing the joint effects of raising the tax and adding to the government surplus – and hence reducing the National Debt or making some similar monetary adjustment. Alternatively, we might look at the distributional effects of raising a tax and simultaneously raising expenditure; in this case the jointness of any consequences is even more obvious. Nor, finally, is the alternative of simply exploring the *net* effects of raising one tax and lowering another as fruitful in this part of public finance as it is at other points.

Various other points should be made. To concentrate on the distributional effects of taxes we shall assume that factors of production are in perfectly inelastic supply to the economy as a whole. Furthermore, we shall for the most part operate within the framework of a given share of the private sector in the national product, although this assumption will have to be modified in any comparison of the relative effects of government transfer payments and purchases of goods and services. Another point is that we shall not attempt to trace *all* distributional effects. The very fact that we talk about income 'groups' means that some of these effects will be swallowed up and netted out within the groups, and all the more so the greater the width of the groups. Even more important, we shall not draw any welfare conclusions from our analysis. We mark off the frontier quite clearly at the effects on the distribution of real income and do not attempt to probe further into the vast hinterland behind. Finally, we shall use the term 'incidence' to refer to the effects of taxes and expenditures on the size distribution of income in the private sector.

2 TAXES, EXPENDITURES AND THE DISTRIBUTION OF INCOME BY SIZE

2.1 *General considerations of incidence*

We saw in Chapter 2 that the notion of 'incidence' has had a number of different meanings historically. Today, most economists would confine the term to the effects of taxes and expenditures on the distribution of income as distinct from its size. But that still does not mean that the concept is a simple one.

First of all, a distinction has to be drawn between what one might call legal and economic answers. A lawyer might say, for instance, that an excise duty on domestic production of whisky is borne by the distiller in that he has the legal responsibility for paying over the tax to the authorities. But an economist would want to ask whether the tax is *shifted* in any way, forwards on to intermediaries or the ultimate consumer, or backwards on to suppliers of labour or other inputs to distilleries.

The same distinction holds on the expenditure side, e.g. a subsidy to employers in respect of their wages bill might or might not be shifted to employees depending on whether or not wages rose proportionately with the subsidy, and so the legal and economic assessments could easily diverge again.[1]

A second consideration is that one is basically concerned with changes in *relative* rather than *absolute* prices of products and factors. A's money income may increase more than B's but if the prices of the products A buys increase relatively more than those bought by B, A's overall position will deteriorate relatively to B. More generally, we can say that changes in the relative position of different groups will depend on three influences (a) changes in money income before tax; (b) changes in amounts deducted from money income by way of income tax or social security contributions; and (c) changes in prices of goods and services bought by different groups.[2] Any analysis which fails to centre on relative movements is unlikely to be helpful; and we neglect at our peril price movements in other factor markets or goods markets.

We can illustrate the principles involved by a simple example. Suppose that A and B are two individuals; A is a producer of x and a consumer of y, B is a producer of y and a consumer of x. The government is a consumer of both x and y in certain fixed proportions. The differential tax change will affect the distribution of real income between A and B not only by changes in personal tax liabilities but also by its effects on the prices of x and y. An increase in the price of x (that

[1] The terms 'formal' and 'effective' incidence are sometimes used in this context. See, for example, J. A. Kay and M. A. King, *The British Tax System* (Oxford University Press, 1978), Ch. 1. But this terminology has sometimes had a different meaning and so it seems best to avoid it.

[2] A distinction is often made between the sources side and the uses side. But the sources side operates by two separate means ((a) and (b) above) and it seems better to make this distinction explicit.

of *y* being unchanged) will raise the earnings of A and lower the real value of B's purchases and thus produce a redistribution of income on two counts, and a fortiori if the price of *y* falls. If we make the example more complicated by imagining that A sells a factor *m* which is used to make *x* and B sells a factor *n* which is used to make *y* and that both A and B are consumers of *x* as well as *y*, then the same principles can still be seen to hold. In this case A's change in real income will depend on the change in his pre-tax income (i.e. price of *m*), the change in his personal tax liability and the gains and losses due to price changes in *x* and *y*. Such examples are far too simple to be a picture of the real world, but they serve our purpose if they put us on guard against accepting naïve theories of the distributional effects of taxes.

A third consideration is that of ceteris paribus. In order to confine one's attention to the distributional changes of any given tax or expenditure measure one must try to isolate it. This means that one has to think in principle of some countervailing budgetary measure which both keeps the budget balance unchanged – and there are in turn a number of different ways of specifying what is involved in that – and is itself distributionally neutral. It is by no means easy to achieve any such objective but in principle that is what one must try to do.

Some other general principles might be noted more briefly.

(a) *Taxes on sellers or purchasers*. From the viewpoint of the economist (though not the lawyer) it is of no importance whether a tax is legally imposed on one side of the market or the other. The distributional effects of national insurance contributions, for instance, will tend to be the same whether imposed on employers or employees.

(b) *Elasticity considerations*. Tax or subsidy burdens tend to fall more heavily on the more inelastic side of the market. If supply is totally inelastic we expect suppliers to bear the whole of a tax; and consumers likewise if demand is totally inelastic. Conversely, if, say, supply is totally elastic (Figure 3.5(a)) all the tax falls on consumers. So we can say that tax burdens depend crucially on the degree of substitutability on the demand and supply sides.

Similarly, it is often argued that the supply of labour as a whole is inelastic and so the greater part of the burden of an income tax falls on those who sell labour. But this proposition is much less true when substitutability is, for instance, possible between overtime and leisure.

(c) *Taxes are borne by individuals*. All taxes must fall on individuals whether taxes are imposed initially on corporations or products or wealth; in the last resort it must be some group of individuals which suffers a relative deterioration in its economic position. It is entirely false to argue that 'corporation tax hits those who can best afford to pay – i.e. wealthy companies'. Such a tax may not be shifted and so fall on owners of capital. But it might also be shifted backward so that wages of workers rise less than would otherwise have been the case. Or it might be shifted forwards in the form of higher prices so that the burden falls on both workers and owners of capital.

One method of analysing these problems, due to Harberger,[1] has been very much in use in recent years. Assuming an economy consisting of two products and two factors, one starts from the proposition that a general tax on all expenditure is equivalent to a general tax on all incomes under certain assumptions. The products tax and the incomes tax can each be divided into two constituent taxes, one on each product and one on each factor. One can then sub-divide these four constituent taxes into taxes bearing on each of the factors used to produce such products. Given a matrix of this sort, and a limited amount of information about some of the taxes, one can then deduce incidence implications about all the others. So it follows that a small amount of information enables us to derive a wide range of conclusions about tax incidence. This type of analysis was originally developed in the context of corporation tax incidence but has been subsequently found to be of much wider application. Attempts of this kind to break away from the straitjacket of partial equilibrium analysis must clearly command the closest attention. Nevertheless, it must be remembered that there are some drastic simplifying assumptions in this particular approach (e.g. fixed factor supplies, closed economy, no economies of scale, perfectly competitive conditions), and so one should not run away with the idea that all incidence questions are settled for ever.

2.2 *Distributional effects of factor taxes*

How do these general principles apply in the case of a factor tax such as an income tax? Frequently, it is assumed that an income tax rests where it is put; if a 50 per cent tax is placed on those earning £2,000 a year and a 25 per cent tax on those earning £1,000 a year, then it is argued that this causes redistribution (as compared to a distributionally neutral tax) by virtue of the 'obvious' fact that those with higher incomes

[1] A. C. Harberger, 'The Incidence of the Corporation Income Tax', *Journal of Political Economy*, June 1962. For a simplified exposition see G. F. Break, *'The Incidence & Economic Effects of Taxation'* in A. S. Blinder *et al.*, *The Economics of Public Finance* (Brookings Institution, Washington DC, 1974).

pay proportionately and absolutely more than those with lower incomes.

This is far too simple a view. It may be easiest to grasp the possible fallacies involved if we examine the assumptions implicit in reasoning of this sort. This sort of view can only be justified by one of two extreme assumptions. It would hold true, if, first, the supply of each and every factor to each and every industry was perfectly inelastic. In such a case we could imagine that each factor continues to do exactly the same amount of 'work' in the same place, irrespective of the absolute or relative change in its money income. Secondly, if the demand for every product were conceived to be perfectly elastic we could again imagine that relative prices of all products and factors would remain unchanged, as any tendency for changes to occur would immediately set corrective forces in motion.

The assumptions have only to be set out in this naked form to realize how implausible they are. As we have seen in Chapter 3, even a proportional (and a fortiori a progressive) income tax will tend to push labour from unpleasant to pleasant industries or capital from risky to non-risky (in the case of incomplete loss offsets). Such movements will result in some price movements of some commodities and factors and hence it is most unlikely that the incidence of even a general income tax can be confined to the first or most obvious effects on post-tax personal incomes. Various other points such as the habits of unions of bargaining for 'take-home' pay and the fact that prices of goods and services may not be at the point of maximum profitability when the tax is imposed, may have even more direct effects on relative prices.

Two further points should be made. It is sometimes argued that a general non-discriminatory income tax would have no effects on relative prices of goods and factors. This could only be true if the tax were truly general and applied to all forms of reward as well as all forms of activity. It is precisely because there are various non-monetary types of reward (working in pleasant industries), and non-monetized types of activity (growing vegetables for oneself instead of selling them) that such a tax is a figment of the imagination and nothing more. It should be noted that an identical distribution of money income by size-groups in each industry would not be a sufficient condition for the distribution of real income to remain unchanged in the face of an income tax which in one way or another discriminates between the products of different industries. Although relative money rewards would be unchanged, the prices of goods consumed by the different income groups need not remain unchanged. Secondly, it should be noted that the initial direction of adjustment to an income tax tells us nothing about its incidence. If an income tax discriminates against one industry, whether because the factors in that industry earn higher monetary rewards than in others or because tax rates are higher in that industry, there may be no immediate reaction by entrepreneurs to raise prices. Nevertheless, if factors are encouraged to move from or discouraged from staying in that industry, prices will rise sooner or later relatively to those in other industries. And if demand and supply conditions are such that prices in the industry discriminated against do not themselves rise in absolute terms, there will nevertheless be distributional effects if other prices fall. It cannot be over-emphasized that a discussion which stops short at asking whether an income tax applying to one industry is shifted backwards or forwards in that industry tells us very little about the *overall* distributional effects.

2.3 *Distributional effects of product taxes*

The naïve assumption about such indirect taxes is that they raise the prices of taxed products, and the effect on income distribution is to be measured by the relative extent to which the taxed commodities are consumed by high and low income groups. Thus, if oysters are taxed and potatoes are untaxed and oysters are assumed to be consumed entirely by high income groups and potatoes by low income groups, it would be argued that such indirect taxes are 'borne' by high income groups.

Once again, such a conclusion would only hold under very restrictive assumptions. If the supply of a commodity is completely elastic or if demand is completely inelastic then its price will rise by the full amount of the tax. Even in this eventuality, however, it does not necessarily follow that the 'naïve' conclusion holds. Under our general assumption that an indirect tax structure is replacing a distributionally neutral tax structure, the likelihood is that (unless people's speed of reaction to the reduction of one tax and increase of the other is such that immediate adjustments are made to spending habits) there will be some lag in the changes of spending consequent on the tax changes, and therefore the general price level for all goods and services will tend to remain unchanged. But if the prices of taxed goods have risen absolutely and as a consequence spending on them has increased, this must imply that other prices have fallen. Therefore, confining oneself to the superficial results cannot possibly give a complete answer.

More generally we can say again that we have to look at changes in *relative* prices of products and factors. Whether the price of the taxed product is raised absolutely in the first instance is only the beginning of the analysis. If it is so raised, we shall obviously have distributional effects due to the fact that some commodity prices have risen relatively to others and that consumption patterns of different income groups are not identical. But we shall also tend to have a reduction in the volume of consumption of the taxed commodities, and a movement of factors from those industries into others. This will mean both reduced earnings for those factors with relative advantages in the production of taxed commodities and reduced prices of non-taxed commodities. If, on the other hand, prices of taxed commodities do not rise initially, factor earnings in these industries will be mulcted by the taxes; they will therefore move out, with much the same consequential effects as before on relative prices of goods and factors and income distribution. To revert to our example, we must consider not only the price of oysters but also the price of potatoes, and the changes in employment and earnings of oyster producers and potato growers as well as the likelihood of richer people buying oysters or poorer people producing them.

We can see, therefore, that the naïve view does not hold in the indirect tax case any more than in the direct tax case. Furthermore, knowledge of whether indirect taxes are shifted forward or not tells us very little about distribution. To quote R. A. Musgrave, 'the direction of adjustment does not determine incidence and it must not be confused with incidence'.

2.4 *Direct and indirect taxes*

We are now able to make a straight comparison between direct and indirect taxes instead of relating them separately to a reference standard. We have seen that the same general principles determine the distributional effects of either type of tax. In neither case is it sufficient to look at the obvious repercussions, and in neither case is the degree of forward or backward shifting the end of the analysis. In both cases, the crucial problem is the extent of relative price changes of goods and factors.

Seen in this light, it is apparent that there is no basic difference between the distributional effects of direct and indirect taxes, save that the latter exempt saving, assuming that they do not apply to capital goods. Even the exemption of saving does not necessarily mean that rich people are much better treated than poor people because of a higher average propensity to save. First, taxes on consumption will catch dissaving; so saving for a limited, as distinct from an indefinite, period only postpones tax liabilities; it does not eliminate them. Secondly, the precise extent to which savings/income ratios vary between income groups is not always straightforward. One must be careful about taking at face value cross-section family budget data which typically show the saving/income ratio as increasing with income. In so far as those classified as low income recipients consist of people with temporarily low incomes, one would expect savings to be run down in attempts to maintain previous living standards. Hence the recorded saving/income ratio for lower income groups will be less than the true one.

So, in principle, any particular scheme of redistribution which is considered desirable can be achieved by either direct taxation or indirect taxation. The precise method of achieving this end may differ in the two cases. With indirect taxes, one would expect the principal means of adjustment to be via prices of goods rather than factors, on the grounds that whereas there is a systematic relationship between budget patterns and income levels, there is less reason to believe that specific changes in relative factor returns will accrue specifically to high or low income brackets. Hence, in this case tax-induced changes in product prices are more likely to have important consequences for distribution than tax-induced changes in factor prices. With taxation of incomes, on the other hand, it is highly likely that there will be a systematic relationship between the size of income and the amount of the tax payment (and probably between type of industry and pattern of income distribution) but not nearly so likely that those commodities principally consumed by the rich will rise (or fall) in price relatively to those consumed by the poor. Therefore, it seems fair to say that with indirect taxes the main method of adjustment will be the prices in the goods market and with direct taxes the rewards in the factor market. But this differing path of adjustment does not in the least affect the general principle that we can attain any given redistribution either way.

This may be difficult to accept at first sight, but reflection will show that a direct tax which is passed on to the consumer may be just as regressive as any indirect tax. Similarly, an indirect tax which, for instance, causes factors to move out of a luxury industry catering for the rich alone into an industry catering for mass consumption, may be quite as progressive as any direct tax.

It must be emphasized that these are matters of high principle and not detailed practical policy. In any one particular case it may well be true that an indirect (or direct) tax is a better way of reaching a given objective. It may be impossible to levy direct taxes for administrative reasons, for instance. Alternatively, it may be, and in fact usually will be, impossible to grade indirect taxes so as to have a smoothly progressive system. One tax may also be infinitely superior to the other on allocative grounds. But points such as these should not blind us to the fundamental issues at stake in this particular context: that over a wide range direct and indirect taxes are alternative methods of achieving any particular redistribution of income on which the government of the day may be bent.

2.5 *Other tax comparisons*

The principles developed above apply in the round to the equity effects of other taxes. Social security taxes, licence duties and the like can all be analysed in terms of their price effects in goods and factor markets relatively to those of a distributionally neutral tax. This does not mean that it is easy to pin down distributional effects in these other cases. For instance, the precise way in which an employer payroll tax works its way through the system has been a matter of argument among economists for many years. To some extent the division of opinion has been due to emphasis on different time horizons with the main short-term effects being on product prices and the main long-term effects on factor prices. But there is also a more general point that the distributional effects of broad-based taxes such as those on payrolls or value added are likely to be more difficult to trace than, say, low-rate excise taxes on particular commodities.

One other class of taxation requires further examination. Those taxes which bring about a redistribution of the wealth of the private sector of the economy have somewhat different consequences for the redistribution of income. Whilst it is not necessarily true that taxes on capital directly produce changes in the distribution of private wealth, it is a reasonable approximation to think on these lines in the case of death duties and capital levies. We shall, therefore, look at the distributional effects of taxes such as death duties or capital levies relative to an equal-yield but distributionally neutral tax structure.

If capital taxes of this kind are met by the sale of assets by the tax-payers, several effects follow. First, the total of private wealth may be less than it otherwise would have been. Suppose we imagine private wealth to be, say, £25,000 million, positive annual personal saving under the distributionally neutral tax system to be £500 million, and negative saving nil. If the negative saving due to a capital levy is £500 million and positive saving is no greater than with the neutral tax then we have the result that personal wealth might conceivably have increased in one year from £25,000 million to £25,500 million with the distributionally neutral tax, but will not increase at all if this tax is replaced by a capital levy. There is a haziness about this argument which must be explicitly recognized. The difference as stated between the two cases would only hold on the assumption that the additional saving in the reference case would be matched by additional physical investment. If this were not so there would be a downward pressure on employment, prices and factor rewards. As, however, we are abstracting from such matters in this chapter, we shall assume that this saving is so matched by physical investment, and that, therefore, private wealth is smaller with the capital levy than in the reference case. This, it must be emphasized, is entirely dependent on the assumption that positive saving is no greater in the capital levy case than in the distributionally neutral case.

In the second place, the distribution of wealth may be different under the two-tax formulae. There can be no certainty about this, for if the assets sold to meet a capital levy are absorbed by people of similar capital status to that of the sellers, the distribution of wealth by size groups may not change much and perhaps not at all. And, in any case, the comparison is clouded by the different amounts of capital wealth in the two situations. Finally, a capital levy may produce a different structure of interest rates and yields on capital compared to that which would obtain in our standard case.

On the basis of this reasoning, one can see that a slight modification of our previous technique of analysing effects of taxes on distribution is necessary. Whereas previously we were content to analyse in terms of changes in goods and factor prices, we must now recognize that the concept of a factor 'price' is two-dimensional. The income accruing to an owner of property depends not only on the rate of return on the property but also on the amount of property at his disposal. Therefore, redistribution of income may come about either through changes in property holdings or in property yields. It can be seen that such considerations do not affect wages and salaries; tax measures cannot transfer the power to work or think from one owner of labour to another. The spread of skill and knowledge comes about as a result of an increase in the total rather than a redistribution of an existing stock. But because capital can be so transferred we must acknowledge that the relevant 'price' for distributional considerations is a two-dimensional one, covering both the amount of capital in a man's possession and the market rate of return on that capital.[1]

We must repeat that it is a simplification to treat these matters as if they were relevant only in the case of taxes on capital. Some taxes on capital (e.g. rates on houses) may cause no direct redistribution of private wealth; other taxes (e.g. highly progressive income taxes) may cause some direct redistribution of wealth in so far as they lead to a different volume of saving or dissaving from that which would have prevailed with a distributionally neutral tax structure. In such cases the arguments developed in this section would apply to these taxes too.

2.6 *Government expenditure*

We are now in a position to say something about the relative distributional effects of the various forms of government expenditure. We need not spend much time on the contrast between transfers to individuals and subsidies on goods and services. The considerations relevant to the contrast between direct and indirect taxes apply here in an exactly analogous manner: given the revenue of the government, we can compare the effects of these two types of expenditure either with one another or in relation to distributionally neutral expenditure, assuming always that we are comparing equal sums of expenditure throughout.

There is another comparison in this area of our inquiry which is not quite so straightforward. What are the effects of government expenditure on goods and services as compared with, say, an equal amount of distributionally neutral transfer payments? In the latter case, the share of the national product going to the private sector is unchanged: in the former, it is reduced by the amount of product absorbed by the government. It seems reasonable to argue that three considerations are relevant to the comparison. First, we have to ask whether the private sector share is more equally distributed in the case of government 'exhaustive' expenditure than in the transfer case. This is simply a matter of applying the principles already enunciated. Secondly, we have to ask whether the larger public sector which we have in the 'exhaustive' case is more evenly distributed than in the transfer case. This is in principle (and also in practice) a far more difficult problem as

[1] The discussion of tax capitalization (p. 64, above) should also be recalled in this context.

at this point we lose the help of the market and the pricing system. All we can do is to make some essentially arbitrary decision about the destination of the benefits of the public sector. Is government defence expenditure more or less beneficial to everyone to the same extent or is it of more benefit to those with property than to those without? Even in principle, there is no unique answer to a question of this kind.

Thirdly, we have to ask about the relative weights attached to redistribution in the private and public sectors. Suppose, for instance, that the public sector increases slightly in extent and the private sector decreases slightly, but that distribution in both sectors is in some sense unchanged. Can we then say that 'overall' distribution is unchanged or should we regard the situation as different in some way from the case of smaller public and larger private sectors? And, to complicate the example more, suppose that distribution in the private sector becomes more uneven but the opposite holds in the public sector, how are we then to weigh up the relative merits of transfer and 'exhaustive' expenditures?

This conundrum, or series of conundra, can be pin-pointed if we return to the examples of government educational expenditures. Suppose we imagine that the government can either pay over to parents sums of money earmarked in some way for expenditure on education, or that it can provide state schools. Leaving aside such welfare points as the amount of choice offered to parents in the two cases, what can we say of the relative distributional effects? In the case of transfers there will be a certain determinate redistribution of income in the private sector compared to that which would obtain with a distributionally neutral system. (In this particular case, there will clearly be redistribution between single persons and families, as well as between income groups.) In the case of state expenditure on schools, the real resources commanded by the private sector will be less (and those utilized in the public sector greater) and the distribution of benefits will in all probability be different in both the public and the private sectors from what they would have been in either the distributionally neutral or the educational transfers case. It should be noted that these problems are not really solved by ignoring the distribution in the public sector, and concentrating on that in the private sector and (usually implicitly) taking that as representative of the whole. Such a procedure is equivalent to assuming that distribution is really the same in both sectors. Unless we really believe that to be the case, a more critical attitude to these problems is necessary.

One final point should be made. In so far as the government makes payments to the private sector which are thought to increase its capital wealth rather than its income (e.g. lump sum compensation payments rather than an annual grant) the relevant variables are the change in the total of private wealth, its distribution among individuals and any changes in the rate of return of capital, just as in the comparison between the capital levy and the distributionally neutral tax.

3 OTHER CRITERIA OF DISTRIBUTION

Our analysis has so far been confined to the distribution of income by size-groups. It is time now to glance at some other aspects of distribution. We shall first consider the heads of the analysis relating to distribution of income from other viewpoints such as factor shares, and single people versus families, and then we shall pass to the use of consumption or wealth measures as alternatives to income.

3.1 *Distribution of income by factor shares*

The principles determining the effects of taxation on the distribution of income by factors are essentially similar to those determining the share by size-groups. Indeed, this must be so, for the way in which changes by size-groups come about is through the movement of labour and capital from one industry or occupation to another. It would be possible for a system of taxation to have no effects on distribution by size-groups whilst altering factor shares (or vice versa), but such a state of affairs is extremely improbable. We can say, therefore, as a general principle, that the effect of any given tax structure (relatively to a distributionally neutral structure) can be measured by its effects on relative prices in the product and factor markets. A tax which reduces earnings of labour relatively to those of capital, or which increases prices of goods consumed by labour relatively to those consumed by capitalists, will shift the share of income in favour of capital on either count. Without looking at both these processes, and computing the net effects, we are in no position to analyse the whole situation.

3.2 *Distribution between families of different size*

The recipients of income can be classified in many ways and the distribution by families of different size is selected simply to show the general principles involved in one other form of classification. There are a number of ways in which deliberate attempts can be made to discriminate by tax measures in favour of larger families: income tax reliefs, child benefit payments, subsidies to essential foodstuffs (consumed proportionately more by larger than smaller families), free school and health services, etc. In general, it seems fair to say that the redistributional effects of these efforts are probably simpler and less far-reaching than in our previous cases. We have argued that a progressive income tax may affect the relative position of richer people by causing changes in gross earnings, as factors are induced to move from one occupation to another, as well as by the direct change in the amount of richer people's incomes surrendered to the government. Such shifts of factors from one occupation to another would not seem to be nearly so important in the case of taxes discriminating by family size, as these will hit in the same way whatever the industry or occupation. Therefore, we should not expect changes in relative goods or factor prices to be so widespread in this case. It might be that some marriages will take place which would otherwise not have taken place but once again – apart from possible long-run consequences on the birth-rate – there would not appear to be any likely immediate effects on the relative prices of goods and factors. Subsidies on essentials are likely to be more complicated in their results as in most cases such subsidies are likely to favour low income groups as well as large families. However, even in this case we should expect the major reaction to come through the change in relative prices of goods rather than those of factors. It is not easy to see why subsidization of foodstuffs which may expand the size of agriculture and the foodstuffs processing industry relatively to other sectors should thereby cause any changes in pre-tax earnings of bachelors relatively to married men.

3.3 *The distribution of consumption*

Until now we have examined the relative effects of taxes on the distribution of income. There is obviously no reason why income should be the only touchstone and it is not difficult to produce cogent arguments for using consumption instead. It might, for instance, be argued that income is a very arbitrary concept at the best of times and that even if one agrees to include such items as capital gains, there are still some very awkward problems of adventitious gains such as gambling and gifts. Furthermore, it could be argued that the principal objective of taxation is to reduce the amount which people take out of the common pool rather than affect the amount they put into it. Therefore, it is said, a tax structure which aims at securing greater equality of spending rather than greater equality of disposable income is likely to be more satisfactory.

Arguments of this kind are not wholly convincing. There are obviously a large number of measures of inequality – income, consumption, wealth, the rate of change of income, etc. – between which the ultimate choice can only be made on a wide variety of grounds. The argument about a common pool seems to confuse ends and means; even though we grant that the principal economic objective of taxation is to restrict consumption, this does not mean that we have to accomplish it by taxation based on consumption, any more than that the limitation of wealth inequality must be accomplished only by taxes on wealth.

Therefore, the case for saying that the sole criterion of equality or inequality must be consumption or spending power is a weak one. But supposing for the moment we accept the argument and the further implicit argument that such equality is to be attained by taxation rather than by other means of government action such as educational or anti-monopoly measures. Let us now inquire into the relative effectiveness of a progressive tax on spending and a progressive income tax as methods of securing this objective.[1]

Before we can make the comparison, we must be clear about our definition of an income tax. Are we to take an all-inclusive tax embracing capital gains and adventitious receipts or are we to take a tax of the old British type which excluded such elements of income? Obviously, the strongest case for a spendings tax, as a means of reducing inequality, will be to compare it with the old British type of income tax. To the extent that our conclusions are unfavourable to a spendings tax, they will apply a fortiori if we compare it with an all-inclusive income tax. To the extent that they are favourable, they will be less so compared with the all-inclusive tax.

It seems fairly clear that a spendings tax is likely to be a more effective means of reducing consumption inequalities than an income tax. Whereas capital gains and adventitious receipts, whether spent or saved, will not be subject to income tax, they will be caught by an expenditure tax to the extent that they are spent. Similarly, dissaving out of accumulated capital will also be taxed in the latter case but not the former.

Unquestionably, therefore, the spendings tax has some advantage in

[1] Note that the comparison between effects of income and expenditure taxes is distinct from that on p. 99, where we were concerned with equity in the sense of equal treatment of people with equal endowments on a lifetime basis.

these matters. The real difficulty, however, is to know *how much* spending inequalities will be reduced thereby. Whilst the spendings tax does hit at some sources of inequality left untouched by an income tax, it leaves two – income in kind and consumption dressed up as business expenses – completely untouched.[1] The effectiveness of the spendings tax as a means of producing egalitarian consumption is very much dependent on the relative importance of these exceptions. It should not be thought that this is something which can easily be pinned down. There are a thousand and one ways in which the line between personal consumption and expenses of production may be difficult to draw, ranging from the more blatant devices such as using wives as secretaries on trips abroad to the transport of a child by car to school in the course of travelling to the office.

The basic difficulty is that personal consumption is not an easily definable concept. Not only is the distinction between personal consumption and expenses of production shadowy but that between consumption and saving is also fraught with snags. Is the purchase of a durable consumer good such as a car to be regarded as entirely an act of consumption or one of both consumption and saving? If the latter, how do we distinguish between the two components? One can sympathize with the urge to cast aside income as a suitable basis for taxation. By doing so, one dodges the thorny problems of deciding whether some kinds of receipts such as unspent capital gains are really income and saving or not. But one still has to grapple with the definition of consumption and to mark it off both from expenses of production and from personal saving. Although the first distinction has to be made if the income base is taken, the need for the latter only arises if we take consumption rather than income as a base.

A further point about the comparison of progressive income and expenditure taxes relates to fluctuations in income and expenditure over time. A progressive income tax obviously differentiates against incomes which fluctuate violently over the years but not against fluctuating consumption, whereas with an expenditure tax it is exactly the reverse. An income tax is hard on an author or playwright; an expenditure tax is hard on the man who chooses to be miserly for twenty years and then have a wild spending spree, compared to the man who

[1] In fact, the position may be worse than this. If the tax rate on consumption is higher under an expenditure tax than that implicit in an income tax (in order to secure equal revenue) the incentive to convert current personal into current business consumption will be *greater* in the expenditure tax case. Cf. A. R. Prest, 'The Structure and Reform of Direct Taxation', *Economic Journal*, June 1979.

maintains a steady level of consumption and saving, year in and year out. Therefore, it must be recognized that if we are judging the two taxes as methods of securing greater equality of consumption, the expenditure tax carries with it, whether we like it or not, the potentiality of greater equalization of consumption over time as well as between any two individuals or groups of individuals at any one time.

A device for mitigating some of these problems has recently been suggested by various people.[1] Assets would be divided into two categories, registered and unregistered. Whereas the purchase or sale of a registered asset would count as a deduction from or accession to the tax base, such would not be the case with unregistered assets. Whether or not the income from such assets should be liable to tax is a matter of some dispute among the participants to the discussion, depending on their relative attachment to equity and resource allocation principles. But the relevance of such a device for our purposes here is that abnormal expenditures can be met by drawing down unregistered assets without any tax penalty and so the disincentive inherent in a progressive expenditure tax against such outlays is removed. Many new difficulties arise, however, in devising and operating a system of this sort.[2]

3.4 *The distribution of wealth*

The distribution of wealth could also be a criterion by which effects of taxes are measured. The determinants of wealth distribution are many in number, the most obvious being inheritance, gifts and saving or dissaving out of income. It would be impossible to analyse all the ways in which different taxes affect even this small number of determinants. Instead we shall mainly concentrate, as in our consideration of the distribution of consumption, on one specific comparison in order to show the kinds of issues involved.

The particular comparison we intend to make is between duties levied on the estate of the deceased and duties levied on beneficiaries under a will. If we assume an equal yield of duty in the two cases, we seek to find whether there is any likelihood that one set of duties will lead to a more even distribution of property than the other. At first sight, one might argue that a succession type of duty would be bound to lead to a more widespread and even distribution of bequests, as this would appear to be a means of reducing liability to duty, if a progress-

[1] See, e.g., Meade Report, *op. cit.*, Ch. 9.

[2] See A. R. Prest, 'The Meade Committee Report', *British Tax Review*, No. 3, 1978.

ive system is in force. If, however, the same amount of revenue is to be raised from either system, the ultimate result is not quite so obvious, as it must depend on the precise arrangement of the succession duty. All the same, unless this duty were actually made regressive with the size of the bequest, we should still expect the initial conclusion to hold. Furthermore, in so far as gifts inter vivos would be more fully brought to account under a succession duty, even less consideration need be paid to the equal-yield complication.[1]

So much for the direct effects on inheritance. We have already discussed the more indirect effects of these two sorts of taxes on the supply of saving and we saw that on balance we might perhaps expect saving to be greater with the succession type of duty. This does not enable us to draw any firm conclusions about the distribution of wealth. But in so far – though only in so far – as there is any correlation between an individual's wealth and his annual saving, then it might be expected that this would be an offsetting factor to the greater equality of wealth brought about directly.

4 ALL TAXES AND EXPENDITURES

We have throughout concentrated on the relative effects of different kinds of taxes and expenditures on the distribution of income, consumption, etc. For our last topic, we glance briefly at the effects of the whole system of taxes and expenditure on the distribution of income.

Essentially the same principles apply in this case. We ask, in effect, how the distribution of incomes after taking all taxes and expenditure into account compares with that which would obtain under a distributionally neutral system. There is, however, some ambiguity about the meaning of a distributionally neutral system as this might mean *either* a system in which both the revenue and expenditure sides are distributionally neutral *or* one in which lack of neutrality on one side is exactly offset by non-neutrality (in the opposite direction) on the other.

Note that it is *not* a fruitful approach to ask how the distribution of incomes net of taxes and expenditures compares with the distribution of incomes in the absence of all taxes and expenditures for we should then be postulating a world in which government did not exist, which does not seem to be a very meaningful basis of comparison.

Although, in principle, the analysis simply brings together the sub-analyses for the individual taxes, there are many practical and, as some

[1] See Chapter 15, p. 409 for further discussion.

think, overwhelming statistical difficulties. It is extremely difficult to devise a means of measuring a distributionally neutral system, and, even if this is done, the assumptions needed for measuring the incidence of all taxes are far more heroic than those needed for considering marginal changes in taxation. The dangers of inconsistent assumptions about elasticities of supply and demand and about the overall flow of money payments are only too great even for the most wary. Similarly, the incidence of public goods expenditure raises difficult questions about whether it should be deemed to accrue equally to everyone or be weighted according to the inverse of the marginal utility of income to the different recipients. There are also further queries about whether one should be concerned purely with effects on the distribution of income or whether attempts should be made to measure changes in welfare. To go further into these matters would, however, be beyond the scope of a chapter concerned with Principles.[1]

[1] For further discussion, see A. R. Prest, 'Statistical Calculations of Tax Incidence', *Economica*, August 1955; and 'The Budget and Interpersonal Distribution', *Public Finance*, Pts. I and II, 1968.

6

INCOME STABILIZATION

1 THE THEORETICAL BACKGROUND

1.1 *Fiscal effects on unemployment*

In this chapter we discuss the ways in which taxation and expenditure may influence the aggregate level of economic activity. Section 1 starts with a theoretical discussion of the macroeconomic effects of taxation and expenditure, and then discusses in more detail the criteria whereby we judge the effectiveness of different fiscal measures. Section 2 discusses various practical considerations in both the short and long run.

The question underlying the analysis of this chapter is how the fiscal acts of government may influence the level of money national income, whether by their effects on the volume of output and employment, or on prices. Where we discuss fiscal affects on unemployment, therefore, we shall have little to say about frictional and structural unemployment, which have less connection with the overall level of economic activity. Nor shall we discuss in any detail the precise way in which fiscal policy affects the economy. For the most part we concern ourselves with the following more modest question: given that we have decided by how much we wish to change the level of money national income, which taxes or expenditures will do so most effectively? Our discussion will be further restricted by setting to one side the problems of uncertainty and of an open economy.[1]

Much of the discussion in this chapter will be based on the standard IS–LM model, an example of which is given in the Appendix to this chapter. The model makes a number of simplifying assumptions, the relaxation of which we shall discuss later. It is assumed first of all that fiscal operations do not change the distribution of income in any way. Secondly, it is assumed that spending on consumption and investment depends only on the level of disposable income, the rate of interest and exogenous factors. Thirdly, it is sums collected in taxation rather than

[1] For a more detailed treatment, see A. Peacock and G. K. Shaw, *The Economic Theory of Fiscal Policy* (Revised edition, Allen and Unwin, 1976).

tax rates which are deemed to remain unchanged when considering the effects of variations in government expenditure. Similarly, government spending is assumed to be unchanged whilst we consider the effect of variations in tax revenue. Fourthly, we assume a closed economy. Finally, it is assumed that the supply of labour to the economy as a whole is inelastic, so that changes in the level of taxation do not affect labour supply.

It should be noted that the model specified in the Appendix to this chapter does not commit the reader to any particular view about the relative merits and impacts of fiscal and monetary policy. In theory, the relative strengths of the two types of policy will depend on the precise interactions between the goods and money markets, in particular on the interest sensitivity of consumption and investment in the goods market, and the income and interest elasticity of the demand for money. It is not our purpose here to enter the debate as to whether fiscal or monetary policy is more effective at combating cyclical fluctuations. We content ourselves with the more limited aim of discussing the relative effectiveness of different types of fiscal policy. In doing so our only specific assumption about the monetary sector is that its various parameters are not such as entirely to offset the effects of fiscal policy on the level of economic activity. In other words we rule out the case of complete 'crowding out'. This means that we are assuming that the interest elasticity of the demand for money is greater than zero, and the income elasticity of the demand for money is less than infinite. From equation (11) in the Appendix it can be seen that these two restrictions are sufficient to ensure that the LM curve will not be vertical.

Let us now consider the theoretical effects of different types of fiscal policy in the general context of this model. Starting with government spending, it is necessary to make the crucial distinction between government expenditure on goods and services on the one hand, and transfer payments on the other. In the former case, the government is directly involved in spending itself, whereas in the latter it merely transfers money to individuals. The overall effect on the level of economic activity of direct government expenditure on goods and services is shown by the government spending multiplier, as given, for instance, by equation (17) in the Appendix. For given values of the monetary parameters, this multiplier will be larger the smaller are the marginal leakages from private spending.

The effect of a given volume of government transfers on the level of economic activity will be smaller than the effects of the same nominal expenditure on goods and services. At its simplest, this is because if the government spends £100 itself there will be both direct and multiplier spending effects, whereas if the same amount is transferred to individuals there will be only multiplier effects. Thus, an increase in transfer payments is analytically equivalent to a tax cut, and so the multiplier for transfer payments is the same size but of opposite sign to the tax multiplier.

For exactly the same reason, a reduction in taxation holding government expenditure constant will have a smaller impact than an equal increase in government expenditure on goods and services, as shown by equation (18) in the Appendix. In general, it makes little difference to the overall impact on GNP whether the government cuts taxes by £100, or increases transfer payments by £100. The two policies will generally have similar aggregate effects, which will usually be smaller than those of an additional £100 of government expenditure on goods and services.[1]

It follows that if the government increases taxes and transfer payments by the same amount, there will be no overall effect on the level of economic activity, but if the government raises taxes and expenditure on goods and services by an equal amount, there will be a small expansionary effect.

It is necessary to consider also the effects of different methods of financing a government deficit. A government can obtain current resources from the private sector either by taxation (as discussed above) or by borrowing. If we rule out borrowing from abroad, the government still has various ways of financing a deficit. At one extreme, it can borrow from the domestic non-bank private sector by selling bonds. At a first approximation this will leave the nominal supply of money unchanged, and so the government spending multiplier given by equation (17) in the Appendix will still apply; the nominal money stock remains constant, and so the expansionary impact of fiscal policy will be at least partly choked off by an increase in the interest rate.

At the other extreme, the government can borrow from the Bank of England. This is tantamount to increasing the nominal supply of money, and so the effect of increased government spending financed

[1] But all three multipliers will be about the same size if people regard government expenditure on goods and services as part of their incomes and therefore increase their saving. See Carl S. Shoup, *Public Finance* (Weidenfeld and Nicolson, 1969), pp. 563–64.

by an expansion of the money supply is given by the government spending multiplier (equation (17)) *plus* the money supply multiplier given by equation (19). The first of these multipliers shows the impact on real national income of an increase in government spending holding the supply of money constant; the second shows the effect of an increase in the supply of money, holding other things (including government spending) constant. In this case an expansionary fiscal policy is accompanied by an expansionary monetary policy and the overall effect is stronger than in the case where the government deficit is financed by bond sales.

These are the standard conclusions to be derived from a very simple model. It is worth discussing the effects of relaxing the assumptions made earlier. Since it would be an enormous task to do this in detail we shall do no more than indicate the modifications involved. First comes the assumption that no redistribution of income takes place. It is clearly unrealistic to assume that fiscal policy has no impact on the size distribution of income, but the real question for stabilization purposes is whether redistribution per se has any substantial macroeconomic implications. It can be argued that as income is redistributed, say from rich to poor, the ratio of consumption to income will rise by virtue of the empirical fact that in any one year the poor consume a larger proportion of their income than the rich. However, if it is only the *average* propensity to consume that changes with income the expansionary effect on economic activity of a redistribution from rich to poor will be smaller than if the *marginal* propensity increases with income.[1]

Other theories of aggregate consumption spending generally conclude that the macroeconomic effects of redistribution are likely to be small, though for different reasons. The relative income hypothesis[2] suggests that the savings ratio depends on people's position in the income hierarchy, an implication of which is that redistribution does not automatically produce a change in the flow of spending. The permanent income hypothesis[3] argues that the savings ratio is constant if income and consumption are both measured so as to exclude purely transitory components, and that any deviation of the savings ratio is

[1] The reader can verify from equation (16) in the Appendix to this chapter that $\partial Y/\partial a$ is smaller than $\partial Y/\partial b$.

[2] For an exposition of this theory, first put forward by Duesenberry, see any intermediate textbook of macroeconomics, for instance, G. Ackley, *Macroeconomic Theory* (Macmillan), Ch. 10.

[3] See, for instance, G. Ackley, *loc. cit.*, and M. Friedman, *A Theory of the Consumption Function* (Princeton University Press, 1957).

likely to be caused by transitory factors, which are unlikely to be related systematically to the distribution of income. The overall conclusion is that whichever explanation of aggregate consumption spending one chooses, the effects of redistribution on economic activity are unlikely to be large.

A completely different set of arguments about the impacts of redistribution runs as follows. In so far as fiscal measures produce a change in the relative shares of capital and labour there may be effects on the level of private investment. For instance, if the share of profits in national income decreases as a result of fiscal measures, we should expect to find *some* decline in the ability or willingness to invest on the part of the private sector. Thus, redistribution from capital to labour may have a contractionary impact.

The second assumption was that private spending depended on income, the interest rate and exogenous factors. This might not be so, firstly because spending may be related to the composition as well as the size of income. Suppose the government increased taxation and transfer payments by equal amounts, but there is an asymetry between the two sets of reactions of the private sector. In this case, the combined effect of the two changes need no longer be neutral, but might generate an increase or decrease in spending. Similarly, if government expenditure on old age homes reduced the need to save for old age, we should expect a different effect from that of, say, military spending. Secondly, spending may be a function of many variables other than income and the rate of interest, for instance, wealth. In so far as employment policy involves a government deficit and an addition to total government debt or the stock of money, this will alter the volume of liquid assets owned by the private sector and hence may have wealth effects on the level of private spending.

The fourth assumption was that tax yields rather than tax rates remain constant while government spending changes. If this assumption is removed we can see that the expansionary effects of government expenditure will be smaller than in the simple case. This can be shown in two different ways. First of all, as the relevant expenditure multipliers given in equations (17) and (18) in the Appendix to this chapter show, the multipliers will be smaller the greater are the marginal leakages from the circular flow of spending. Taxes related to spending are just such a marginal leakage and would, therefore, be expected to reduce the size of the expenditure multipliers. A second way of demonstrating the same effect is to note that in the case of an increase in government spending on goods and services, holding tax rates constant, the expansionary effects of the additional spending will partly be offset by the additional tax revenue resulting from the increase in income.

The next assumption was that of a closed economy. It would be a major task to explore all the ramifications of dropping this assumption. The essential point is that, in practice, imports have a substantial income elasticity. This means that part of any increase in aggregate income will be channelled into imports, and so will contract the level of domestic spending. For this reason, one would expect the impact of fiscal policy to be smaller in an open economy.

The last assumption was that of an inelastic supply of effort. We can best show the effect of relaxing this assumption by considering a proportional tax on earnings together with a lump-sum transfer to the individual of exactly the amount that is taxed away from him. In this way income effects are eliminated and, via the substitution effect, we should expect people to work less since the relative price of leisure has fallen. As a result, therefore, money national income will tend to fall despite the balancing of the extra taxation by extra transfer payments.

1.2 *Criteria of effectiveness of fiscal measures*

In this section we pass from the general ways in which fiscal policy influences the level of money national income to a more detailed examination of the criteria by which the various types of measure may be judged. Initially, we discuss the ingredients of successful counter-cyclical measures in a static context, before proceeding to some of the dynamic problems involved.

It is useful to start by remembering the distinction between the problems associated with cycle and trend. Since the war, most income fluctuations in the UK have been of a short-run cyclical nature, as distinct from long-run trends. It has often been argued that one should analyse cycle and trend together, and there are various theories showing how the two interact. But though, in practice, cycle and trend are inextricably linked, it is still useful to separate them, since different types of policies may well be involved in dealing with short-run and long-run problems. We start with short-run fluctuations, and return to long-run problems later.

Counter-cyclical fiscal weapons must possess three properties if they are to be successful, those of size, automaticity, and timing. The *size* of any fiscal measure is important. It might be thought that quadrupling a small expenditure should have much the same influence on the level of income as doubling a large one. But, in practice, there are obvious administrative problems. It is easier to plan, and much easier to implement, a 10 per cent addition to road building than, say, a ten-fold expansion of some minor government activity. On the revenue side, the position is even clearer. A tax which accounts for a large proportion of government revenue is likely to be more suitable as a means of increasing or decreasing revenues than a tax which brings in only a small percentage of the total. Income tax does well on this criterion, whilst motor vehicle licence duties do not.

The second criterion is that of *automaticity*. If there are two means of reducing tax receipts by, say, £500 million over the same period, one of which is automatic and the other requires administrative action, the former has obvious advantages on the grounds both of simplicity and economy, leaving aside any question of the desirability or otherwise of governmental discretionary powers. The qualification 'over the same period' should be noted. Much of the argument about the relative merits of 'built-in stabilizers' and policies which require administrative action hinges on whether one type of correction takes effect more quickly. Automatic machinery is not usually thought superior to manual methods if it operates at a much lower speed, and fiscal policy is no exception. For instance, if we have the choice of arranging our fiscal system in such a way that tax receipts will drop automatically by, say, £10 million for every £100 million drop in income or, alternatively, of arranging to make tax reductions of this magnitude when income begins to fall, the crucial point is whether the two policies would start to work at the same time and with the same intensity.

This leads straight to our third criterion, that of *timing*. In general terms, it is clear that the more it is possible to synchronize counter-cyclical fiscal policies with the movements of income they are designed to correct, the more effective they will be. There are three well-known reasons why timing may be inaccurate. First, the authorities may be slow to recognize the onset of slump or boom (the recognition lag); secondly, even when the need for counter-cyclical measures is recognized, there may be administrative or political delays in taking action (the executive lag); and thirdly, there may be delays before there are any effects on the economy (the operational lag).

It can easily be seen that these criteria shade into one another and may be in conflict. Although one tax has a bigger base on which to operate and thus satisfies the size criterion, it may be more difficult to vary quickly and thus earn fewer marks on timing. Similarly, if one arrangement of tax implies a more than proportionate fall in revenue for any given fall in income, but at the same time we think that by appropriate changes in tax rates it would be possible to produce the same absolute fall in revenue at an earlier point in the down-swing, automaticity clearly loses its merits. On the other hand, even perfect timing of something which results only in very small variations in revenue or expenditure may be of little help.

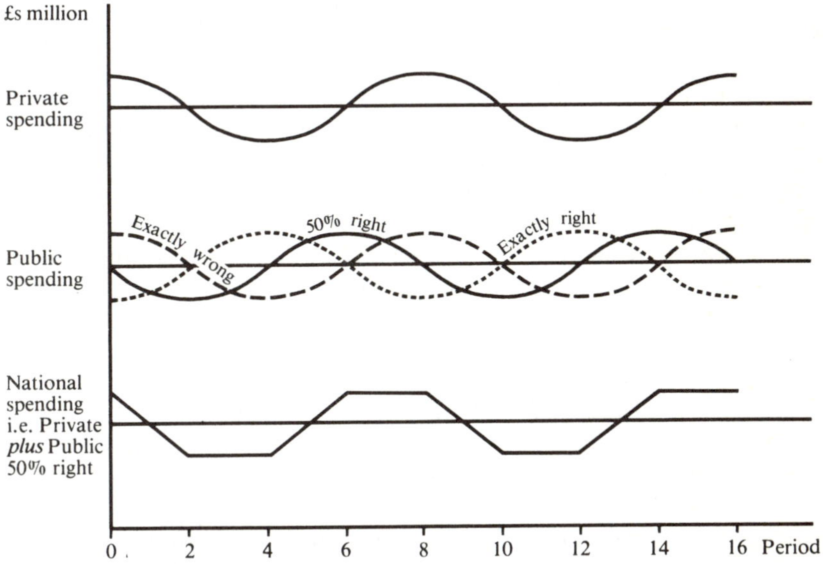

Figure 6.1 Stylized representation of the timing of policy

The issue of timing requires further amplification, since it raises issues of the dynamic impacts of fiscal policy. The underlying problem is that the right action at the wrong time may aggravate rather than alleviate the situation, and it has been argued that this has been exactly what post-war economic policy in the UK has done.[1]

Figure 6.1 illustrates the major dynamic issue in somewhat stylized

[1] See, for instance, J. C. R. Dow, *The Management of the British Economy, 1945–60* (Cambridge University Press, 1964). Also F. T. Blackaby (ed.), *British Economic Policy 1960–74* (Cambridge University Press, 1978), especially Chapter 14.

fashion. The top line shows a picture of the cyclical movements of income in an economy where no deliberate corrective action is taken and where there is no built-in stabilization. The second line shows a number of patterns of government corrective action according to whether timing is exactly right, exactly wrong, or half right. It is clear that the first type will tend to smooth out the cycle and that the second will tend to exaggerate it. What about the third type? At first sight, it might be argued that this intervention may be better than nothing. But the bottom line shows that this is not the case, for we now have a cycle in which the speed of transition from boom to slump and vice versa is much greater than before. Instead of four periods for the movement from peak to trough we now need only two periods, and correspondingly longer periods at the peak and in the trough. In more complex models with an explicit dynamic structure, it can be shown that such 'half right' policies can easily make the situation worse, and that the argument that 'any government counter-cyclical policy is better than nothing' is very dangerous. What is worse, these models show that government policy can increase not only the frequency of cyclical fluctuations (i.e. the duration of each cycle) but also their amplitude (i.e. the percentage excess of boom over slump).

2 PRACTICAL CONSIDERATIONS

2.1 *The relative merits of various fiscal measures as counter-cyclical devices*

This section starts by analysing the relative merits of different types of tax and expenditure as a means of counteracting short-run fluctuations in the level of national income, and then discusses briefly the possible influence of fiscal policies in the long run. We begin by considering various taxes, and then turn to the expenditure side.

(1) *Income tax* is a good starting point. From the point of view of size it obviously scores heavily. When personal income tax covers the greater part of the working population as well as non-workers such as retired people, even small variations in its yield are bound to have a substantial effect, which will be stronger the smaller are the number of exemptions from income tax, e.g. a tax which includes capital gains is better than one which does not.

As regards automaticity, the yield of a personal income tax will automatically fall in times of slump, quite apart from any deliberate change in tax rates. There are several reasons for this. First, revenues will decline because there will be a decline in taxable incomes. Some people will be unemployed; partnerships and sole traders may have negative incomes; capital losses may be experienced. A second, and completely separate point, is that with a progressive tax structure, tax receipts will tend to fall more than proportionately to incomes over the course of the cycle. This will obviously be the case for a tax structure in which marginal rates rise with income. But it will also be the case for a tax structure with a single rate of tax and tax-free allowances. For instance, suppose that an income tax allows people to earn £1,000 tax free, and taxes any income above this at 35 per cent. Then a person with an income of £2,000 would pay £350 in tax, and someone with an income of £4,000 would pay £1,050 in tax. If there is a boom and an individual's income doubles from £2,000 to £4,000, his tax bill will triple from £350 to £1,050, and if there is a slump and an individual's income halves from £4,000 to £2,000, then his tax bill will go down to one third of its previous level. These counter-cyclical effects operate a fortiori when marginal rates of tax rise with income. We therefore conclude that the more an income tax incorporates features of this kind the more it is likely to be a successful counter-cyclical device. When we turn to timing, another feature of modern income taxes is also in its favour. When a large part of tax is collected at source by some system of weekly withholding, it is, on the whole, likely to be more successful from the timing angle than if taxes are paid in arrears. It is possible to imagine cases in which this need not be so. In the early stages of the upswing it would be an advantage for taxes to be paid in arrears, as the disposable income available later in the cycle would be greater. In any case, if people pay in arrears and accumulate reserves to meet tax liabilities and adjust their reserves rapidly as their prospective liabilities change, the timing may still be good but it is obviously better if the adjustment is a direct one.

On the other hand, if automatic variation is judged insufficient, it is not easy in the UK to change the rates of tax quickly. As we shall see in Chapter 9, a formal budget session is required to change the rate of income tax, and this cannot be arranged at a moment's notice. And even after the budget, there is bound to be a gap of several weeks before the necessary arrangements can be made for the complicated changes in tax tables. Furthermore, once the tax year has started, though it is possible to lower tax rates, it is generally rather difficult to raise them. So in this respect there is an element of inflexibility in the personal income tax.

(2) *Taxation of company profits* can be summarized more quickly. The major point in its favour is that profits tend to fluctuate more than national income. On the other hand, the tax is proportional and not progressive. The fact that part of these taxes is collected in arrears[1] in the UK is not important as firms adjust their tax reserves in accordance with current profits. There are a variety of reasons why taxes on corporations may not gain high marks as counter-cyclical devices. If losses can only be carried forward, as is broadly the case in the UK, the reduction in tax liability at the time of the slump is not as great as if the losses can be carried back and refunds claimed on taxes paid in the past. For that matter, carrying forward will also reduce liability to tax in the upswing. Replacement cost depreciation is likely to imply a larger offset against profits in the boom, and hence a smaller amount of tax payable, than original cost depreciation. Much the same is true for LIFO ('last-in, first-out').[2] Therefore, the personal income tax should be rated as a better automatic stabilizer than a corporate profits tax.

(3) *Expenditure taxation.* The arguments over the merits of expenditure taxation as a counter-cyclical device are somewhat complex. If we accept the usual proposition that consumption tends to rise and fall less than proportionately to income, then a proportional expenditure tax will show smaller proportionate and absolute variations in yield over the course of the cycle than a proportional income tax. This proposition will hold irrespective of whether the expenditure tax rate is equivalent to the income tax rate or whether it is increased to produce the same yield as income tax. With progressive rates of tax we should expect the discrepancies to be even greater. So on this basis it might be thought that an expenditure tax should be rated below an income tax as a stabilizing device. Although it would have many of the virtues of the income tax, of size, automaticity and timing, it would not possess the same elasticity of yield.

This, however, is not the end of the story. It is clear that in a boom year a proportional income tax would produce a greater rise in tax revenues than a proportional expenditure tax. But, equally, it is likely that the expenditure tax would lead to a greater rise in private saving than the income tax. To the extent that the larger increase in tax revenues of the income tax is equal to the larger increase in saving of

[1] But not Advance Corporation Tax – see Chapter 9, p. 199.
[2] See Chapter 16, p. 423.

the expenditure tax, it can be argued that there is nothing to choose between the two types of tax from a counter-cyclical viewpoint.

But it is still necessary to dig deeper. It is true that during an upswing it is possible for increases in saving under an expenditure tax to match increases in tax revenues under an income tax. But the situation is not necessarily symmetrical with respect to a downswing, in which the revenues of an income tax would tend to fall more rapidly than those from an expenditure tax. But it is not obvious that in this case extra dissaving under the expenditure tax would match the decline in tax revenues under the income tax, both because it is often not possible for people to dissave in excess of their own capital resources, and because the people who save during an upswing may not be the ones who wish to dissave in a downswing.

Other points must also be made. To the extent that in practice private investment is strongly influenced by the availability of finance, it is also related to the rate of private saving. If this is the case, the increased private saving under an expenditure tax would generate a greater increase in investment than the increased tax revenues accruing to the government under an income tax. Thus the extra saving generated by an expenditure tax during a boom cannot be regarded as fulfilling the same automatic stabilizing functions as the increase in revenues under an income tax.

Finally, the assumption that larger private saving and lower taxation are equivalent to lower private saving and larger taxation ignores the monetary effects that budget surpluses and deficits can have. A larger deficit in the boom might give rise to an increase in the supply of money, which would tend to reduce interest rates and increase investment, thus partly nullifying the effects of any increase in private saving. Overall, therefore, an income tax will usually be superior to an expenditure tax as a counter-cyclical device.

(4) *Indirect taxes*. After the discussion of expenditure taxes, we can be fairly brief on the subject of indirect taxes. As regards size, indirect taxes earn good marks if they cover a wide variety of commodities and a large proportion of personal consumption. On automaticity, they will score better if taxes are arranged on an ad valorem basis, and if rates are highest on those goods with the greatest income elasticity of demand. If so, tax receipts will obviously fall more than proportionately to falls in income during a slump. As regards timing, the administrative problems of changing tax rates are on the whole not so formidable as with income tax, particularly if there is a low rate sales

tax or value-added tax applying across the board rather than a high rate of duty on a few commodities. The timing problem is complicated if people's expectations are such as to make their reactions to a change in the rate of tax perverse, i.e. if a tax cut induces the expectation of an even greater cut. On the whole, therefore, it is probably true that a network of indirect taxes is less effective as a counter-cyclical device than an income tax.

Under the general heading of indirect taxation, it is necessary also to discuss the effects of taxing investment as well as consumer goods. If this makes it possible to influence the rate of spending on investment as well as on consumption, the case for indirect taxation is greatly strengthened. There are two ways in which such a technique might work.

First, there could be indirect taxes or subsidies on investment goods in the same ways as on consumer goods. Secondly, there could be a system of allowing investment expenditure to be offset, or partially offset, against profits taxation in the way that investment allowances formerly operated in the UK. By this means, the spending of £1 on new investment brought in its train an allowance of, say, 20 per cent of that £1, which could be offset against current profits in addition to normal depreciation allowances. The system was thus analogous to one of subsidizing investment in some direct fashion. The initial allowance system which gives an inducement to investment by advancing depreciation allowances in time rather than by increasing their total size over the lifespan of an investment can be regarded as a poor relation of investment allowances.[1] The converse of investment grants and subsidies is the type of tax on capital goods which operated in Sweden from 1955 to 1957, and the converse of initial allowances is the type of deferred depreciation which operated in Canada in 1951.

Obviously, any tax system which can offset the flow of investment spending must be of crucial importance in counter-cyclical policies. And even though these devices relate only to fixed investment and not to inventory changes, they nevertheless apply to a large and very volatile fraction of total spending. There are, however, some drawbacks. It is not easy to see how this sort of system can be automatic. The discouragement of investment during a boom requires deliberate administrative interference to change the rate of investment allowance, etc. and is not something which takes place automatically. In fact, the automatic operation of an investment allowance would be the reverse of what is needed, in so far as a high level of investment in

[1] See Chapter 9, section 2.1 for a fuller description.

boom years would bring in train big offsets to profits, and hence reduce tax payable. Conversely, in the slump, tax charges would increase. Moreover, it is not clear that businessmen's reactions to changes in tax rates of this kind can possibly be quick enough to produce very sharp adjustments in the levels of expenditure, given the complicated nature of much modern equipment and the lengthy planning needed in many investment decisions.

(5) *Other tax changes*. Variations in national insurance contributions have sometimes been suggested as a counter-cyclical device. In the usual form, with no contributions payable by the unemployed, they contain some element of automaticity. However, to obtain any major change in revenue, variations in rates would be necessary, and even then the total contribution to the flow of spending might not be large, at any rate in the short run.

A further possibility is changes in taxes on capital, such as capital transfer tax. These obtain very few marks as counter-cyclical weapons. They are usually relatively unimportant in the amount of revenue they produce, and in any case are more likely to be paid out of capital than income, and also paid well in arrears. Nor can we expect very quick changes in revenue when the rates of tax are changed.

Although the discussion of tax changes has implicitly and sometimes explicitly dealt with expenditure items such as transfers and subsidies, which have the same general characteristics as various types of taxes, there are other types of expenditure as yet unconsidered.

(6) *Public works expenditure* is historically by far the most important form of counter-cyclical expenditure policy, involving spending on roads, bridges, and the like. Such expenditure has the great merit of having direct effects on spending as well as indirect effects, so that the full government spending multiplier (equation (17) in the Appendix to this chapter) applies and as a counter-cyclical device must therefore be considered superior to tax reductions or government transfer payments. On the other hand, there are other considerations relevant to the size and composition of the public sector. On allocative grounds one might not want more roads, and this consideration would have to be weighed against the argument that road building may be a quick way of reducing involuntary unemployment.

A second problem is that the organization of such expenditures is a difficult matter. It is not simply a question of having all the plans and blueprints for all the relevant agencies – local and semi-national as well as national – ready and available for instant action at the onset of a depression; it is also one of making sure that the plans are actually carried out sufficiently quickly to enlarge the stream of purchasing power when it is most needed. It is most unlikely that such priorities can earn high marks from a timing viewpoint.[1] Finally, even if the timing problem could be resolved, one must expect a narrow concentration of these expenditures on the construction industry. Given the specific nature of many inputs to that industry, this would not necessarily lead to rapid expansion of employment in the economy as a whole.

(7) *Other types of government expenditure*. There are a variety of devices that can be used. Amongst those used today are running a deficit on trading operations or adjustment of government stocks of materials. In some ways, such schemes have advantages over the traditional public works expenditures. They are likely to be more easy to introduce, more flexible, and to have more widespread effects on the economy than public works. It is also possible to introduce some element of automaticity into such schemes. Instructions could be given to a raw material authority to add to stocks if prices fell below a pre-determined level, or release them if prices rose above it. Similarly, profits of government trading organizations will tend to rise in good years and fall in a slump. These advantages, however, are largely theoretical and there is little empirical evidence about the effectiveness of such methods.

2.2 *The relative merits of various fiscal measures in the long run*

In the previous section we discussed the relative merits of different taxes in reducing cyclical movements about a static trend. We now discuss how these conclusions might be modified by long-run considerations of economic growth. Since this is still a largely uncharted area many conclusions can only be tentative. As a start it is helpful to make a number of distinctions. First of all, short-run cyclical fluctuations of the sort discussed previously should be distinguished from the long-run trend of actual output. The form of the relationship between these two is shown in Figure 6.2(a). Secondly, we have to distinguish between the long-run trend in actual output and the long-run trend in potential output, which is the hypothetical output that could be attained if all factors of production remained fully employed in the

[1] Some interesting data on US experience are to be found in S. J. Maisel, 'Varying Public Construction and Housing to Promote Economic Stability', in *Federal Expenditure Policy for Economic Growth and Stability* (Joint Economic Committee, Washington DC, 1958). It took some 7–8 years to disburse funds authorized under the Housing Act of 1949, the average lag between contract approval and expenditure alone being of the order of 2–3 years.

long run. Actual output will generally fall short of potential output, as illustrated in Figure 6.2(b).

This section starts with a discussion of the ways in which fiscal policy could reduce both short- and long-run deviations from the trend of potential output, and then goes on to discuss how fiscal policy might influence the rates of growth of both actual and potential output in the long run. These questions are not entirely distinct from one another, but it is useful to consider them separately.

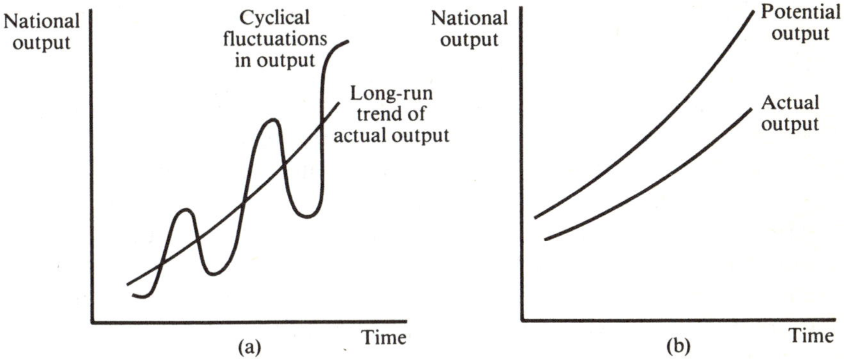

Figures 6.2(a) and (b) Examples of short- and long-run trends in output

Taking short-run cyclical deviations from the long-run trend of actual output, we can say that, broadly, the arguments developed above apply in exactly the same way as they did when there was no long-run growth. The criteria of size, timing and automaticity are relevant in both cases whether we think of cyclical fluctuations in vacuo or superimposed upon some trend line of growth. In one case it is a problem of matching saving with investment, and in the other of matching the rates of growth of saving and investment.

However, when account is taken of long-run economic growth, complications can be caused by the interaction of cycle and trend in that an increase in the long-run rate of growth of full-capacity output can lead to a reduction in cyclical fluctuations. It has been suggested that much of the cyclical character of British post-war economic history can be explained in terms of over-rapid increases in demand relative to the underlying rate of growth of potential output. When this occurs, actual output begins to rise faster than potential output, so that plant and equipment are over-utilized, the margin of spare capacity reduced, and bottlenecks occur. To the extent that this is an accurate picture of the post-war situation in Britain, it follows that if it were possible to increase the long-run rate of growth of potential output one ought to find short-term deviations less troublesome. In other words, it is possible that an increase in the underlying rate of growth could reduce short-run cyclical problems.

A completely different set of problems arises when we consider long-run deviations of actual from potential output. In particular, it is necessary to discuss the possibilities of long-run high unemployment, and of long-run inflation. Starting with unemployment, the requisite anti-inflation measures may be illustrated from the discussion of the 1930s and 1940s in connection with the 'stagnation thesis'. There was then a widespread belief that advanced capitalist societies would experience great difficulty in reducing the proportion of income saved to a level sufficiently low to achieve anything near full employment, given the likely reduction in the return to investment over the years. Although this view is no longer held widely today, some of the discussion about the appropriate fiscal measures and the way in which they differ from counter-cyclical measures is relevant, particularly in the years since 1973 when unemployment has been high.

The first point is that in the case of long-run unemployment, timing is of far less importance. In the case of short-run cyclical fluctuations, one of the great advantages of income tax is the speedy, and largely automatic, adjustment of its yield to changes in economic circumstances. This is of far less importance over the long period, and so the great advantages of income taxes are no longer so outstanding.

Another point on which there has been much discussion, especially in the USA, is whether government power to conquer these stagnationist tendencies is limited by debt considerations. Whilst counter-cyclical fiscal policy does not add to the level of National Debt, the increases in the slump being cancelled out (at least in principle) by reductions in the boom, over a long period of stagnation there would be a tendency for the National Debt to rise. It follows that the servicing of the debt may need additional taxes and this may have disadvantages such as work disincentives. The ramifications of this problem will not be discussed in any detail but, briefly, it can be said that a rising level of debt need not be an obstacle. First, provided there is no simultaneous problem with inflation, it is not unreasonable during a period of sustained unemployment to finance at least part of a budget deficit by expanding the supply of money, thus minimizing the additions to debt and interest charges. Secondly, interest charges on a growing volume of debt can themselves be financed by expanding the money supply. Thirdly, any increases in current revenues which are needed to meet the service of debt are less burdensome in a rapidly growing economy than in a stagnant one.

The problems of long-run inflation have been of vastly more importance in the post-war world. In this case, it can again be argued that timing and automaticity are rather less important. The principal argument is whether inflation arises primarily on the demand side or directly via cost increases. In so far as price increases are due to trade unions asking for higher wages rather than an increase in overall demand relative to supply, a policy of increasing the government surplus will be unavailing, and might make the situation worse. It could be argued that if trade unions watch the retail price index and the government raises indirect taxes to reduce the level of aggregate demand, thereby leading to an increase in the price index, this may actually intensify the cost push forces. Even though it can be argued that in the last resort all inflation can be traced back to the common denominator of an excess supply of money, it may nevertheless be the case that in the presence of structural phenomena such as increasing unionization we may have the nasty consequence that no one level of aggregate demand will simultaneously satisfy the needs both of restraining inflation and restraining unemployment.

Whether there does indeed exist any long-run trade-off between unemployment and inflation has been the subject of much debate. A pioneering article by A. W. Phillips in 1958[1] suggested that a trade-off did exist. Later work by Friedman and others[2] denies this, stating that it is not possible without accelerating inflation to reduce unemployment below its natural rate.[3] It is not our purpose here either to summarize the debate or to enter it as protagonists. Given the current state of knowledge, it is as well to be somewhat agnostic about the influence of fiscal policy on long-run inflation.

Partly in the light of such agnosticism it should be noted that the relative merits of automatic and discretionary adjustments have been discussed at some length in the long-run context. Arguments have been put forward in favour of fixed rules for increasing the stock of money at

[1] A. W. Phillips, 'The Relationship Between Unemployment and the Rate of Change of Money Wage Rates in the U.K., 1862–1957', *Economica*, Vol. 25, 1958.

[2] For an excellent summary of the debate see A. M. Marin, 'The Phillips Curve (Born 1958, Died?)', *Three Banks Review*, No. 96, December 1972.

[3] The natural rate of unemployment is the level of unemployment consistent with wage stability.

a given rate per annum or of changing government tax revenues along pre-determined lines rather than making ad hoc adjustments as occasion warranted. The main arguments have centred round the amount of discretion which the executive should have in economic matters and on the effect, or lack of it, of attempts at 'fine tuning' the economy.

Finally, we turn to a brief discussion of the ways in which fiscal policy might influence the long-run rates of growth of actual and potential output. The links between fiscal policy and economic growth are complex and far from a settled part of economic theory. The first point to note is that the elimination or alleviation of cyclical fluctuations may itself influence the rate of economic growth. It was suggested earlier that if the rate of growth could be increased, this might itself reduce cyclical fluctuations by reducing bottlenecks, etc. But the interaction between cycle and trend may also go in the opposite direction, inasmuch as alleviating the cycle might increase long-run growth. If the fear of slump is removed, it can be argued that businessmen will take a more optimistic view of future possibilities and plan capital expansion accordingly. Moreover, there will be less waste of capital due to unpredicted and unpredictable fluctuations. Therefore, even if fiscal measures had no direct influence on the rate of growth of actual or potential output, they could certainly influence them indirectly, and hence the various tax and expenditure devices discussed in the previous section can affect the rate of growth by this means, if by no other.

Turning to the ways in which fiscal measures might influence long-run growth rates directly, it is not possible to be very definite. We should start by noting that full capacity output is a multi-dimensional concept. It implies full (in some sense) usage of the existing stock of physical capital; full application of existing technical knowledge; full employment of the labour force seeking work; and so on. Now, at any given time the level of output which makes the fullest use of machinery is not necessarily the same as that which would give full employment to the labour force. In an advanced economy the full-employment ceiling at the top of the cycle is normally lower than the full-capacity ceiling of capital, in the sense that there is still unutilized capacity at full employment. In many less developed countries, we have the reverse situation: full utilization of capital equipment, technical knowledge and skill but under-utilization of the labour force. Similarly, the growth rate of full capital utilization output may diverge from that of full labour utilization output. Thus, the role of fiscal policy is not simply one of increasing the growth rate of, say, the stock of capital and of expenditures on technological training by the same percentage amount. Rather, it is one of varying the relative rates of growth of the constituent items so as to smooth out any disharmonies between them.

It is, therefore, impossible to generalize about the targets with which policy should be principally concerned at any one time. In some cases, it may be encouragement to people to enter the labour market in greater numbers or to work harder; in others, encouragement to the private sector to increase the rate of capital formation in plant and buildings. This means that the relative merits of different types of taxes and expenditures are relevant also in the context of long-run growth. For instance, if we are convinced that a proportional income tax is more likely than a progressive one to increase work effort, then this conclusion will carry over to a long-run situation in which we wish to increase work effort or employment because of the existence of excess capacity at full employment. On the other hand, if capital is the long-run bottleneck, and if we think that investment allowances or similar devices will increase the rate of capital formation more than a reduction in corporation tax producing the same loss in revenue to the government, then this tax can be used as a long-run instrument as well as a counter-cyclical one.

In practice, many fiscal measures will operate on both the long-run trend of potential output (i.e. the supply side) and on the rate of growth of demand. If tax action is taken to increase the rate of growth of private saving, this will obviously act not only on the rate of growth of income at which planned saving equals planned investment, but also, via the effects on the stock of capital, on the rate of growth of full-capacity output.

There is one important exception which can bring about increases in supply without necessarily affecting the level of demand. A change in government expenditure on goods and services can be divided into consumption and investment components. An increase in the investment component might be expected to increase the rate of growth of full-capacity output, while an increase in government current consumption might not. Whilst the composition of government expenditure on goods and services does not matter much in a counter-cyclical context, it does definitely matter in the context of long-run growth. It should be noted that 'consumption' and 'investment' have to be carefully defined. 'Investment', in the form of housing expenditure, might have little effect on the capacity growth rate, whereas 'consumption', in the form of expenditure on education, might have great effects, as has been shown by research in a number of countries.[1] More generally, taxes have to be judged by their resource-allocating and resource-creating effects, as well as by their merits as cyclical compensating devices, when dealing with the added complexities of the long run.

[1] See G. Becker, *Human Capital* (Columbia University Press, 1964) and also E. F. Denison, *Why Growth Rates Differ* (Brookings Institution, Washington DC, 1967).

APPENDIX TO CHAPTER 6: A SIMPLE MACROECONOMIC MODEL

1 THE MODEL

1.1. *The goods market*

$C = a + bY_D$	(consumption function)	(1)
$Y_D = Y - T$	(disposable income)	(2)
$I = g_0 - g_1 r$	(investment function)	(3)
$G = \overline{G}$	(government spending)	(4)
$Y = C + I + G$	(equilibrium condition)	(5)

1.2 *The money market*

$M_D = m_0 + m_1 Y - m_2 r$	(demand for money)	(6)
$M_S = \overline{M}/P$	(supply of money)	(7)
$M_D = M_S$	(equilibrium condition)	(8)

where: Y = real national income
C = aggregate consumption spending
I = aggregate investment spending
G = government spending
T = total tax bill
Y_D = disposable income
r = rate of interest
$\overline{M}$ = nominal stock of money
P = aggregate price level

In this model $\overline{G}$, T, $\overline{M}$ and P are treated as exogenous, and a, b, g_0, g_1, m_0, m_1, and m_2 are constants. The model deals only with the case of a closed economy.

2 THE IS AND LM CURVES

2.1 *The IS curve*

From (1) to (5):

$$Y = a + b(Y - T) + g_0 - g_1 r + \overline{G}$$

$$Y(1 - b) = a - bT + g_0 + \overline{G} - g_1 r$$

$$Y = \frac{a + g_0 + \overline{G} - bT}{1 - b} - \frac{g_1}{1 - b} r \tag{9}$$

$$= A + Br \tag{10}$$

where:

$$A = \frac{a + g_0 + \overline{G} - bT}{1 - b}$$

and

$$B = -\frac{g_1}{1 - b}$$

(9) is the IS curve showing the equilibrium value of Y in the goods market as a function of r and the goods market parameters, i.e.

$$Y = f(r, a, b, g_0, g_1, G, T).$$

2.2 *The LM curve*

From (6) to (8):

$$m_0 + m_1 Y - m_2 r = \overline{M}/P$$

$$m_1 Y = \overline{M}/P - m_0 + m_2 r$$

$$Y = \frac{\overline{M}/P - m_0}{m_1} + \frac{m_2}{m_1} r \tag{11}$$

$$= E + Fr \tag{12}$$

where:

$$E = \frac{\overline{M}/P - m_0}{m_1}$$

and

$$F = \frac{m_2}{m_1}$$

(11) is the LM curve showing the equilibrium value of Y in the money market as a function of r and the money market parameters, i.e.

$$Y = g(r, m_0, m_1, m_2, M, P).$$

3 EQUILIBRIUM IN THE GOODS AND MONEY MARKETS

3.1 *The general solution*

From (11):

$$m_2 r = m_0 + m_1 Y - \overline{M}/P \rightarrow r = \frac{m_0 - \overline{M}/P}{m_2} + \frac{m_1}{m_2} Y \qquad (13)$$

Thus:

$$r = J + HY \qquad (14)$$

where:

$$J = \frac{m_0 - \overline{M}/P}{m_2}$$

and

$$H = m_1/m_2$$

Substituting (14) into (10):

$$Y = A + B(J + HY) = A + BJ + BHY$$

Therefore,

$$Y(1 - BH) = A + BJ.$$

$$Y = \frac{A + BJ}{1 - BH} \qquad (15)$$

is the general solution to the IS–LM model.

3.2 *The specific solution*

From (15), (9), (10), (13) and (14):

$$Y = \frac{\dfrac{a + g_0 + \overline{G} - bT}{1 - b} + \left(\dfrac{-g_1}{1 - b}\right)\left(\dfrac{m_0 - \overline{M}/P}{m_2}\right)}{1 - \left(\dfrac{-g_1}{1 - b}\right)\left(\dfrac{m_1}{m_2}\right)}$$

$$= \frac{\dfrac{m_2(a + g_0 + \overline{G} - bT) + g_1(\overline{M}/P - m_0)}{(1 - b)m_2}}{\dfrac{m_2(1 - b) + g_1 m_1}{(1 - b)m_2}}$$

Thus:

$$Y = \frac{(a + g_0 + \overline{G} - bT)m_2 + g_1(\overline{M}/P - m_0)}{(1 - b)m_2 + g_1 m_1} \qquad (16)$$

is the equilibrium of both goods and money markets.

3.3. *Tax and expenditure multipliers*

The various multipliers are then simply the relevant derivatives of (16).

(a) The government spending multiplier is:

$$\frac{\partial Y}{\partial G} = \frac{m_2}{(1-b)m_2 + g_1 m_1}. \tag{17}$$

(b) The tax multiplier is:

$$\frac{\partial Y}{\partial T} = \frac{-bm_2}{(1-b)m_2 + g_1 m_1}. \tag{18}$$

(c) The money supply multiplier is:

$$\frac{\partial Y}{\partial M} = \frac{g_1 P}{(1-b)m_2 + g_1 m_1}. \tag{19}$$

7

ADMINISTRATIVE EFFICIENCY

1 THEORETICAL CONSIDERATIONS

1.1 *The meaning of administrative efficiency*

In this chapter we discuss administrative efficiency and compare the relative merits of different types of revenue and expenditure. Section 1 sets out the theoretical background by outlining the meaning of administrative efficiency, and in the light of this discussing what constitutes an ideal tax from an administrative point of view. Section 2 considers the relative administrative merits of different types of tax and expenditure. In section 3 we make an administrative case study of the possibility of introducing self-assessment for income tax into the UK.

Administrative efficiency implies the minimization of the real resources needed to administer any tax or expenditure. This is a matter of concern, since the costs of tax administration are true economic costs in the sense that resources not devoted to tax administration could be used for other types of public expenditure (e.g. building roads, or schools, or hospitals), or for increased private expenditure via reduced taxes.

The real resources used in the administration of any tax or expenditure include not only the absorption of goods and services by the public sector of the economy, but also those used in the private sector. For example, in the case of PAYE[1] in the UK or withholding in the USA, it is necessary to add to the cost of the services provided by government officials the expenditure of employers in administering their part of the system, and the time and trouble expended by the general body of taxpayers and their advisers.[2] We shall ignore the idea that the opportunity cost may be zero to some people, inasmuch as the time taken to

[1] Pay As You Earn (PAYE) is the UK system of withholding income tax on wage income. See Chapter 9, p. 195.

[2] One explicit estimate is that in 1970 the total cost of operating the system of direct personal taxes in the UK was some 4–7 times as great as public sector administrative costs. See C. T. Sandford, *Hidden Costs of Taxation* (Institute for Fiscal Studies, 1973), p. 44. Other rough estimates put the figure somewhat lower.

fill in the relevant forms may not be at the expense of productive activity. In other words, even if the principal result of people's efforts to complete their tax returns is a reduction in leisure, this is in itself an economic cost.

A further valuation point is that in discussing the administrative effort involved in different taxes or expenditure we shall assume the optimum known methods of administration. For example, we argue later in this chapter that income tax in the UK could be administered more cheaply with a system of self-assessment. The administrative costs of income tax will therefore be discussed on the assumption of the most up-to-date methods, including self-assessment, if that is, indeed, the cheapest method.

When discussing efficiency we try to compare the amount of goods and services absorbed in the administration of any one tax with that needed for the administration of another tax producing the same revenue, and similarly on the expenditure side. Two qualifications have to be made in any such comparison. First of all, comparisons of saving of real resources will always be rather vague, since the amount of resources necessary to administer a tax is an imprecise concept, even in principle. It might be possible to say that a certain minimum number of officials is necessary to assess liability to a particular tax, and to collect tax accordingly. But to translate the intentions of legislation into effective action and to prevent any evasion may require a large number of preventive officers. How large that number should be is, in the last resort, a matter of equity. To ensure that everyone pays *some* income tax may require an Inland Revenue department of size x; to ensure that everyone pays the *exact* amount which is his due, might require an administration of size z, where z is greater than x. To comply with popular feelings of fairness and to minimize dissatisfaction may require an administration of size y, where y is greater than x.

At first glance, the last measure seems to be the appropriate estimate of the administrative cost of any tax. But this need not be so. The magnitude $(y-x)$ measures the administrative machinery necessary to bring the administration of any tax up to a minimum acceptable standard of fairness. To measure this would require some assessment of what constitutes an acceptable degree of fairness, or a maximum possible degree of unfairness in the case of each tax. But there is no presumption that an 'equal' amount of fairness in respect of each tax (however defined) is socially desirable. Public reaction may be very different depending on the age and character of the tax, the degree to which its provisions are understood, the rates chargeable and so on. Thus, no very precise or rigorous criteria are possible in discussing the resources necessary to administer a tax, or in measures of the standards of tax administration.

The discussion of this chapter is restricted in a second sense. Whereas analysis of the relative advantages of various taxes from the viewpoint of equity or resource allocation can be generalized to all countries, this is much less true of the administrative advantages of various taxes and expenditure. Some general points can be made. Customs evasion is easier if a country has land frontiers rather than sea frontiers; income tax is more easily administered when the population is literate and keeps accounts or when peasant agriculture is unimportant; densely populated areas are less expensive per head of the population to administer than scattered communities. But it is not easy to push beyond generalities of this kind without introducing the specific background of a single country. To the extent necessary, discussion here will be rooted in UK institutions.

There are two areas related to tax administration which will not be discussed in any detail in this chapter. There is an obvious positive correlation between administrative costs and the size of the public sector. But the size of the public sector is a topic with major implications for the economy as a whole which dwarf purely administrative considerations.

Another subject left on one side is the extent and consequences of tax avoidance (i.e. legal methods of minimizing tax liabilities) and tax evasion (i.e. reducing tax liabilities by illegal methods). We shall not discuss these issues per se, but will refer to them when relevant.

1.2 *The ideal tax system*

This section sets out the characteristics of an ideal tax from an administrative point of view, and then discusses the administrative consequences of deviations from them. From an administrative viewpoint, the most important characteristic of an ideal tax is that it should apply to every member of a clearly defined category. Thus, a tax might be levied on every individual in the country on a certain date, or on every birth or death or marriage during a year. Such categories can generally be defined clearly, and so there are no difficulties in deciding whether any individual is exempt from the tax. It might, in principle, be possible to specify in a similar manner that every economic transaction within a certain period is liable to tax, but it is easy to see that here there is much more scope for argument. For example, decisions would have to be made about the distinction between gifts and transactions. Nor is classification simplified if the authorities aim at particular types of transactions (e.g. how does one give an exact definition of food or clothing?); or if they levy taxes on physical assets (e.g. if residential properties are taxed, are huts, caravans or tents included?).

A second characteristic of an ideal tax from an administrative point of view, is that equal amounts per head should be levied. It is obviously much easier to run a system under which everybody pays, say, £10 per head, than one in which the amount due varies according to economic circumstance. Similarly, if the amounts payable remain unchanged from one year to another the task of administration will be easier.

A third characteristic of an ideal administrative system would be emphasis on collecting small sums frequently rather than large ones infrequently. This may seem paradoxical inasmuch as *less* work would seem to be involved in collecting large sums infrequently. It is, however, an ancient principle of taxation stretching back to Adam Smith, that tax payments should meet the convenience of the taxpayer. Except where the *annual* tax payment is only a small fraction of *weekly* income this must mean tax payments on an instalment basis; otherwise the willing co-operation of taxpayers, so essential to the smooth running of the tax-collecting machinery, would not be forthcoming.

A fourth saving in administrative cost arises if the basic information for tax collection can be derived as a by-product of some other administrative process, for instance, a population census. At least one former British territory found that universal adult suffrage, the right to vote being dependent on the production of a tax receipt certificate, considerably reduced the cost of tax collection. Similarly, an income tax deduction system operated by employers is rendered both more acceptable and cheaper if it can be integrated with the machinery for wage payments.

The final desirable characteristic is that the costs of administration of a tax system should be reasonably constant over time. It might well cost less over the average of a period of years to collect a given annual tax by method A rather than method B. But if the costs of method A vary considerably from one year to another while those of method B do not change, the task of government budgeting is likely to be less burdensome in the case of B than of A. Hence, the total costs of tax collection and budgeting together may be less under B than A.

This description of the characteristics of the administrator's dream points out the various ways in which departures from the ideal may arise. First of all, the category to which a tax applies may not be clearly defined. We have already pointed out that the number of economic transactions is less easily defined than the number of people in a country. Similarly, if a tax is levied on all income recipients this immediately opens up for exploration the no-man's-land between income, capital, gifts and transfers. And if the tax is applied in such a way that everyone, with, say, less than £1,000 per annum is exempt, but everyone with higher income pays a fixed sum per annum, this raises a further problem inasmuch as it invites attempts to show that any one income is less than the minimum exemption level. These problems are intensified if we move from a poll tax to a proportional or progressive tax structure, where there is every inducement to the taxpayer to conceal part of his gross income or to claim more than his due allowance against that income. Either manoeuvre is likely to add to the expense of tax administration at both the public and private level. The same principle holds if we consider the transition from a uniform sales tax to one which differentiates between goods and services.

A related cause of departure from the ideal occurs when changes are made in tax rates, coverage, or allowances from one year to another. In so far as these changes are the results of the need to finance varying amounts of expenditure from one year to the next, the necessary additional administrative expense would be common to all taxes. But to the extent that the receipts from different types of tax fluctuate to a differing degree, one can draw a distinction between different taxes in respect of administrative costs of this kind. It would usually be the case that the introduction of an entirely new tax system must involve a considerable administrative effort initially (e.g. the introduction of PAYE in the UK in 1943). But, obviously, for comparative purposes some long-run average of administrative costs is the more appropriate concept.

Attempts to extract relatively large sums relatively infrequently from taxpayers have often led to discontent and heavy expenditure on collection. One of the great administrative advantages of PAYE is that tax demands stay in line with income during the year, and end-year adjustments are minimized. This is important for many people, e.g. those with very low incomes living a hand-to-mouth existence and those with very high incomes attracting rising marginal rates of tax. For exactly the same sort of reason it has proved impossible to implement suggestions for incorporating a variety of different rates of tax into the PAYE codes for the great mass of taxpayers, though a reduced rate band was re-introduced in the Budget of April, 1978. Even this feature increased the administrative costs of PAYE, and to introduce further rate bands except for a small number of people with high incomes would directly add to the work of preparing and operating the PAYE codes, and would indirectly cause further difficulty and work if the delay in introducing tables with upward rate revisions meant very heavy tax payments immediately after they came into operation. Finally, it should be added that PAYE does not have a monopoly of convenience to the taxpayer, as indirect taxation more or less automatically meets this criterion.

Another reason why any actual tax structure may not have optimum administrative properties may be found in the division of responsibility for administration. This responsibility can be shared in a number of ways. There might be choices between central and local administration, as with an income tax levied for local purposes, or between public and private administration, as in the case of income tax deduction at source. In all these cases the basic issues are the old and well-known ones. Delegation of authority may offer closer touch with the taxpayers; it may also avoid the diseconomies of any large-scale administrative organization. Against this, there is a greater danger of overlapping and duplication. So it is impossible to be dogmatic on this aspect of the subject. Finally, although in principle fluctuating administrative costs are undesirable, it is not easy to see that any one type of tax is more likely to be more objectionable in this respect than in any other. And these fluctuations, in any case, are likely to be dwarfed by other economic fluctuations. They will, therefore, be ignored.

2 THE RELATIVE MERITS OF DIFFERENT TYPES OF TAX AND EXPENDITURE

2.1 *Taxes*

We start by comparing the administrative merits of different types of tax, and then briefly discuss the expenditure side.

2.1.1 *Direct versus indirect taxation* Not a great deal can be said about the administrative costs of direct and indirect taxes without going into the details of particular taxes. However, a few general points can be made.

First comes the contention that for administrative reasons direct taxes cannot be levied on people with very low incomes. This is recognized in the UK by exempting those with very low incomes from tax; and PAYE cards do not have to be kept for employees earning less than a certain amount. As a result, a number of low-paid earners and others are outside the scope of income tax. On the other hand, in so far as people in this category consume goods subject to customs duty, excise duty or value-added tax they are not exempt from indirect taxes, at any rate on the assumption that some of the incidence of these taxes rests on consumers.

It is a time-honoured idea that this is the only feasible arrangement. But it is doubtful whether this remains true under modern conditions. PAYE revolutionized the machinery for tax assessment and collection from lower income groups. Before the Second World War there were only some four million income tax payers in the UK, whereas in recent years the number has been something over twenty million. Before 1914 it was thought impossible to apply income tax to wage-earners at all, whereas today they constitute the great bulk of taxpayers. The tax-credit proposals of the early 1970s would have increased the number of taxpayers further. It may be undesirable on equity grounds to collect income tax as well as indirect taxes from those with low incomes, and it may be impossible to arrange indirect taxes so that they do not hit the majority of low-income recipients. But these are different matters. When tax payments can be readily exacted by the Inland Revenue or Customs and Excise, the administrative argument for the latter does not seem conclusive.

Looking at the administrative advantages of direct and indirect taxes, a second general point of comparison concerns not the *size*, but the *kind* of income. When there are a large number of small independent producers, or when many are illiterate or incapable of keeping accounts, or when the subsistence and barter sections of the economy are important, it is obviously much more difficult to operate any system of income taxation other than a poll tax. In these cases, the administrative argument for some kinds of indirect tax – particularly those levied at a point of export from or import into the country – are very much stronger. On the other hand, some of the administrative arguments against income tax apply to purchase or sales taxes, barter transactions being an obvious case in point.

2.1.2 *Income versus capital taxation* Taxes on capital, whether levied only at death or on a recurrent annual basis, are likely to be more difficult to administer than taxes on income, mainly because in practice capital is more difficult to value. Most income is earned and its measurement presents no major difficulties of principle, at any rate in a world where valuations are not made of human capital and hence there are no problems of human depreciation or amortization. Similarly, when individual property income is taken to be the cash value of dividends and interest received and to exclude any capital gains, there is again no fundamental problem of valuation. The measurement of depreciation and obsolescence presents difficulties when we turn to corporate income, and there are many complications due to the admixture of various taxes (income tax and corporation tax) and differential rate bands of individual taxes. But it is generally accepted that the administrative complications are smaller than those of valuing capital assets.

The reasons for this are fairly apparent. First, the measurement of any capital asset requires, in principle, knowledge not only of the income currently derived from it, but also that expected in the future, together with a suitable rate of discount. When there is a wide market in assets (e.g. publicly quoted securities) there need be no undue difficulty about valuation. But it is a different matter in the case of, say, assets in a privately owned company.

A second difficulty in valuing capital is that whereas it is generally acceptable to leave out many forms of imputed income for income taxation purposes, the same is not true in the case of capital. The imputed income derived from the possession of Old Masters or jewellery is not normally included under income tax assessments, but most governments are reluctant to leave out the capital value of these assets when levying a capital tax or death duty. Even when there is a regular and ready market for such items, there will be various expenses of obtaining professional valuations. And when no regular market exists there may be all sorts of additional expenses, including those of appeals from the taxpayer.

A third problem is that fluctuations in capital values may be very much greater between any two years than fluctuations in income, and so there may be additional administrative costs in budgeting to keep tax revenues more or less constant.

The overall conclusion is that the traditional administrative prejudice against capital taxes is well founded when the alternative is an income tax on some forms of income. However, if an income tax were comprehensive and covered imputed income from capital assets and accrued income from capital gains (which implies a comparison of *two* sets of capital values each year) the difference might not be so great.

Finally, it is clear that death duties which require valuation of capital assets once a lifetime instead of each year as in the case of an annual capital tax, are administrativcly less troublesome, except inasmuch as occasional large payments are less convenient to taxpayers than regular small ones. Additionally, death duties which are related to the size of the bequest to a beneficiary (and a fortiori if the existing wealth of the beneficiary is also taken into account) rather than simply to the total estate of the deceased, are less acceptable from an administrative viewpoint.

2.1.3 *Income versus expenditure taxation* The discussion of the problems of valuing capital for tax purposes warns us that expenditure taxation, in the usual sense of taxing income *less* saving, is likely to encounter difficulties. This time it is a matter of measuring additions to the stock of assets rather than the stock itself. It is not our task to discuss in detail the complications of administering an expenditure tax, so we shall merely illustrate the types of administrative problem that arise.

(i) Business expenditure has to be separated from personal expenditure so that complications arise in the case of a small businessman who passes all his funds whether for production or consumption through one account. In that case, expenditure on consumption (which is taxable under an expenditure tax) has to be separated from expenditure on inputs (which is not). Difficulties are greater than with an income tax in this sort of case.

(ii) In the case of durable consumer goods it might be a case of hardship to treat expenditure as belonging entirely to the year of acquisition, particularly with a progressive expenditure tax. But 'spreading' provisions – and subsequent amendments if the asset is sold before the end of its 'life' – or amendments to the list of 'spreadable' assets would create enormous administrative problems.

(iii) Saving in the form of additions to cash-holdings, whether in note or deposit form, would present no real problem as it would be in people's interests to declare them. On the other hand, consumption financed by running down stocks of notes acquired *before* the tax was introduced would be difficult to check.

(iv) A particular problem is the distinction in practice between consumption and saving. If the acquisition of an asset is regarded as consumption, tax will be paid at the time of its acquisition but not at the time of its disposal; in the case of an act of saving the position is reversed. In the case of some assets (e.g. the purchase of a house) it is not obvious which treatment should apply. Arguments have been put forward for treating the acquisition of some assets as consumption, both on the grounds of administrative efficiency, and because the dissaving of these assets would make possible some degree of smoothing of year-to-year variations in taxable expenditure.[1]

(v) A further problem arises under an expenditure tax regime from the temptation to save up to the age of 65 whilst at work, partly at the expense of the revenue authorities, and then to emigrate to a country where there was no tax on expenditure out of saving. Administrative measures to prevent such action might be very costly, to say nothing of non-administrative considerations.

The amount of checking that an expenditure tax requires would almost certainly mean some departure from the traditional British system of *preventing* opportunities for fraud (Inland Revenue prosecutions were unknown before 1916), and a move nearer to the American technique of allowing people to take advantage of such opportunities but punishing them severely if they are caught.

A completely different consideration is the likely stability of tax revenues as between an income or expenditure tax. Unless the usual relationship of changes in saving to changes in income were modified by the introduction of an expenditure tax, consumption expenditure would tend to be more stable from one year to another than income. This is likely to be an aid to government budgeting, though less helpful as a counter-cyclical device. On the other hand, in so far as people do from time to time have inescapable heavy outlays (funerals, sickness, etc.) a tax system which bears more heavily in such years than others is less likely to satisfy the criterion of convenience to the taxpayer.

2.1.4 *Different types of indirect taxation* Chapter 19 discusses the administrative costs of different types of indirect taxes, and so not much need be said here. The principal question is whether taxes should

[1] This is the distinction between so-called 'registered' and 'unregistered' assets discussed in Chapter 5, p. 119. For further details see J. E. Meade, *Report, op. cit.* pp. 175–9. Also A. R. Prest, 'The Structure and Reform of Direct Taxation', *Economic Journal*, June 1979.

be levied at the manufacturing, wholesale or retail stage. On the one hand, there are far fewer manufacturers than wholesalers or retailers, and they will also tend to be better record-keepers. On the other hand, there are undoubtedly more difficulties in the definition of the appropriate tax base the further one moves away from the retail level. The second main issue is the range of goods which it is possible to tax; for instance, how far can one tax services? We shall return to these issues in some detail later.

2.1.5 *Central versus local taxation* The detailed arguments about local taxation will be found in Chapter 20; this section presents only a brief discussion of the administrative merits of centrally and locally organized tax systems. The main point relates to the identification of a clear-cut taxable category. In particular, the distinction between income received and income generated is very troublesome if one wishes to assess and collect an income tax at the local authority level. Quite apart from the fact that a shareholder may live in one area and draw all his income from another there are further complications such as the division of a firm's undistributed profits between the several local authorities in which it may have plants. Thus identification and confirmation of either income produced or income received in a local authority may present serious difficulties. And if very different rates were chargeable in the various areas there might be a strong inducement to emigrate from one to the other, which might entail even more administrative effort.

On the other hand, a tax on property is far easier to arrange. There is no difficulty whatever in saying whether a house or a field belongs to one local area or another. The contrast between the relative ease of local administration of a property tax and an income tax is an illustration of the general principle that one of the determinants of the administrative costs of any form of tax is whether or not it relates to an easily distinguishable category.

2.1.6 *Taxes versus charges* In the case of many government owned and operated public services, railways, roads, water supplies, education, etc. the choice has to be made between financing expenditure by fees charged to the users of the services, on the one hand, or by supplying the good or service free (or cheaply), and financing it out of general tax revenue, on the other. As we have seen, the major considerations are equity and allocative efficiency.

As a general principle, free supply paid for out of tax revenues will be possible only where demand is highly inelastic, or where it is rationed in some way.

Conversely, even if demand is elastic, fees should not be charged if there are social reasons why the public should consume large amounts of the commodity in question (e.g. education). However, from a narrowly administrative viewpoint one needs to consider the more general case, and therefore at this stage we ignore the fact that equity and efficiency principles may rule out some possibilities. We start by discussing some objections which are frequently raised to the charging of fees, and then consider some of the arguments against not charging them.

The basic arguments against charging fees frequently turn out not to be administrative. Consider, for instance, the supply of water to households. If industrial water consumption, and all consumption of gas and electricity, can be metered, it would seem feasible to do the same for domestic usage of water. This might not be done because of fears that under a metering system the amount of water used might be less than the social optimum. Similarly, private fee-paying education demonstrates that there is no strong administrative obstacle to the adoption of the fee-paying principle for public education.

Postal and transport facilities are usually arranged on a fee-paying basis, with the major exception of roads. The reason often given why charges are not usually made for road facilities is that the vehicle is privately owned whilst the road is publicly owned. But this argument seems rather weak. At both ports and airports the vehicles are owned by different authorities from those operating the land-based facilities. The real reason why charges are not made for public highway facilities is the difficulty of checking the amount of use made of any particular facility by any one individual. It is reasonably easy to ascertain when a ship uses a port or an aircraft an airfield, but an altogether different matter to say when a car enters or leaves a road. Although a tax on petrol will exact contributions roughly proportional to total road usage, it is more difficult to ascertain usage of roads which are particularly congested or particularly expensive to build or maintain. The contrast between American and British practice is interesting. The American expressways, parkways, etc. are roads with few intersections and entrances and exits and consequently tolls are easily collected. The British motorways, for a variety of reasons, are much less self-contained and so the expense of collecting tolls is prohibitive.

Overall, the *administrative* arguments against the fee-paying system are not very strong, except in the case of roads. What, then, are the consequences if fees are not charged? It is here that the distinction between commodities with elastic and inelastic demands becomes vitally important. It may well be that the demand for water is fairly inelastic, and that although some more might be used when free than if paid for, the difference in consumption is not enormous. Similar arguments could be made for such items as spectacles and dentistry. In contrast, the demand for municipal housing or railway services would be enormous if no charges were made, and so some other form of rationing would be necessary once any spare capacity was fully utilized. This obviously pushes up the administrative costs tremendously and should be rejected under normal conditions. From an administrative viewpoint, therefore, it is usually easier if charges are levied except in the case of certain commodities for which demand is inelastic.

The general conclusions of this section can be stated briefly. There are certain general principles to be followed if a tax is to be administratively acceptable. These are: (a) a readily identifiable body of taxpayers; (b) a simple structure of tax rates, allowances and the like; (c) a minimum amount of changing of rates and regulations; and (d) convenience to taxpayers. Although the traditional arguments in favour of direct taxation for small earners are not quite as strong as they seem, it can be concluded that the administrative case for income rather than capital or expenditure taxation seems fairly clear. As a natural corollary, it also follows that the task of tax administration is less the smaller the number of taxes. Many countries have suffered just as much from the multiplicity of taxes as from the complications of any one tax. It is said that in Italy some forty-three different taxes entered into the price of a cup of coffee early in the post-war period and in Australia, in the inter-war period, it was in principle possible for an individual to be subject to a number of different income taxes.

2.2 *Expenditure*

In this section we pose the parallel question to that asked on the revenue side, i.e. given a certain sum of money for spending by the government, which outlet or outlets will minimize administrative costs? But as soon as this question is put one can see that it is so vague as to be virtually unanswerable. The whole concept of what is an administrative cost on the expenditure side is rather nebulous. On the revenue side we saw that administrative costs could not be entirely separated from some notion of equity. This is true also on the expenditure side (e.g. the time and trouble caused to the administration and the ultimate beneficiary by complaints about unfair treatment of a child by an education authority). But in addition, on the expenditure side there is a formidable problem of disentangling administrative work from benefits. On the revenue side, the amount of revenue collected and the costs of collection are reasonably distinct things. But on the expenditure side, this may not be so at all. Especially in the case of services (e.g. military, education, health), it is fiendishly difficult to separate the administrative costs from the ultimate benefit.

In some cases it may be possible to demonstrate that a smaller number of civil servants could be capable of organizing a larger number of hospitals or schools without loss of 'quality' of service. Alternatively, it may be possible to show that arranging a contract to supply goods and services would be more economical than direct government provision. But the amount that can usefully be said in general terms is small. Furthermore, even if administrative costs could be disentangled, they would almost inevitably carry less weight on the expenditure than the revenue side. It is perfectly possible to conceive of a tax not being introduced, or being abandoned after introduction, because of the costs of collecting it, however admirable it may be on other grounds. But it is hard to believe, for instance, that supplementary benefit would be abandoned on the grounds that it takes 30,000 civil servants to administer it.

Nor is there much that can be said in general terms about 'extravagance' in government expenditure. 'Extravagance' in the sense of devoting relatively more expenditure to one sort of outlay than meets with the electorate's approval is of itself a problem of misallocating resources, equity, etc. rather than an administrative consideration. And from an administrative viewpoint 'extravagance' may be an indication of too little rather than too much administrative expenditure in the sense that the misallocation of resources might have been less had there been more civil servants and office staff in control. It does not seem appropriate to embark in detail on this topic.

One area where it is possible to say a little more is the relative administrative costs of grants and subsidies. Here the issues are rather more clear-cut and there is less difficulty in disentangling the cost of administration from the ultimate benefit. For instance, suppose we consider the relative costs of benefits to old age pensioners which take the form either of money grants or coupons for free (or cheap) electricity. In either case one needs careful scrutiny of the people entitled to benefit, and regulations about the exact circumstances in which they can draw benefit, for example, machinery to prevent relatives continuing to draw it after the death of the designated recipient, and so on. But fairly obviously in the case of coupons entitling the recipient to cheap electricity there are going to be additional costs. The sale of coupons by those requiring less heating may absorb time and energy on the part of themselves and intermediaries and there would have to be an apparatus for reimbursing the electricity supply authorities. On the basis of this illustration, and it does not seem unfair to generalize from it, it can be concluded that administrative as well as resource allocation arguments are likely to favour grants rather than subsidies, subject always to the assumption that there are no social reasons for encouraging consumption of any particular commodity.

Another field in which something can usually be said is the form taken by grants and subsidies. We shall discuss this at some length when dealing with local authorities, but we can point out some of the issues now. Grants for specific purposes to local authorities or to industry, can take the form either of a unit or a percentage grant. In the former case, payment might be made on the basis of, say, the number of children in school and in the latter on the basis of, say, 50 per cent of total expenditure on education. It is frequently argued that from an administrative viewpoint, unit grants are preferable on the grounds that in the case of subsidies the central authority must inevitably demand close and careful accounting by the local authority and that if half of the total expenditure is being met from other sources the local authority will not be encouraged to economize. The counter-arguments are fairly strong. Meeting a specified percentage of expenditure is a straight-forward idea, whilst precision about a 'unit' for grant purposes is far less easily attainable. If a local authority does have to meet a substantial fraction of expenditure, such as 50 per cent, the incentive to economize will still be strong, and if there are particular social virtues in promoting one line of expenditure, unit grants are clearly less acceptable. In conclusion, we can say that the general principles developed in the revenue discussions have some application on the expenditure side, but it is far less easy to come to any general conclusions.

3 A CASE STUDY: SELF-ASSESSMENT FOR INCOME TAX

3.1 *The Meaning of self-assessment*

In this section we give a case study of some of the practical considerations underlying tax administration by summarizing a recent study[1] of the possibility of introducing a system of self-assessment for income tax into the UK. Inevitably this discussion will not be applicable in its entirety in other countries with very different income tax systems and background conditions. Nevertheless, many of the questions raised are not specific to any particular tax system. We start by discussing the meaning of self-assessment for personal income tax as well as some related issues. We then outline the major arguments for and against self-assessment for income tax, and finally suggest some specific policy proposals.

It was said earlier that the costs of tax administration are true economic costs in the sense that tax administration uses resources which could otherwise be used for other purposes. The costs of collecting income tax in the UK are substantial. In 1977–8 the Inland Revenue employed about 85,000 people and spent a total of £425 million[2] on tax administration. Both the number of employees and administrative expenditure have risen sharply in recent years, and compare unfavourably with at any rate the public costs of tax administration in many other countries. This gives at least a prima facie reason for investigating the possibility that self-assessment could reduce administrative costs.[3]

Let us start by defining self-assessment as it applies in the case of personal income tax. It is useful to think of the administration of income tax as having two broad functions. *Primary* functions are those that are logically essential to the operation of income tax. They are:

(a) the calculation of total income;
(b) the calculation of total tax-free income;
(c) the calculation of total taxable income; and
(d) the calculation of tax due.

[1] N. A. Barr, S. R. James and A. R. Prest, *Self-Assessment for Income Tax* (Heinemann, 1977).

[2] Board of Inland Revenue, *121st Report*, Cmnd. 7473 (HMSO, 1979), paras 39 and 67.

[3] The Inland Revenue is not unaware of this – see, for instance, Board of Inland Revenue, *120th Report*, Cmnd. 7092 (HMSO, 1978), paras 85 to 91, and *PAYE – Possible Future Developments* (Inland Revenue, March 1979).

In contrast, *secondary* functions are not *logically* necessary for the administration of income tax, but are needed in practice as an aid to the primary functions. They are:

(a) withholding of tax at source on some kinds of income;
(b) official assistance to taxpayers; and
(c) checking and verification by the tax authorities of tax returns prepared by the taxpayer.

Self-assessment can then be defined as having two distinct features:

(1) the taxpayer rather than the tax administrator is responsible for the first three primary functions, the fourth being optional; and

(2) verification activities are carried out by the tax administration only on a sample of tax returns, though probably with an arithmetical check of all returns.

In other words, under a system of self-assessment it would be the taxpayer rather than the tax administrator who would be responsible for preparing tax returns and doing the necessary calculations.

In some ways this is a less radical proposal than it appears. First of all, most other industrialized countries have this sort of system for personal income tax. Secondly, there is already a considerable amount of self-assessment for various taxes in the UK. For example, value-added tax is self-assessed. The wealth tax proposals of the mid-1970s[1] generated considerable controversy both in the Select Committee and outside Parliament[2] but one of the few aspects of the tax on which there was no disagreement was that liability should be self-assessed. Capital transfer tax also contains significant elements of self-assessment; and there is already an element of self-assessment on the part of self-employed people in the UK.

Any discussion of self-assessment must involve a number of related issues. The most important of these are as follows:

(1) Simplification of tax allowances, making it easier for the taxpayer to understand the requirements of the new system.

(2) Non-cumulative withholding on wages and salaries: the main reason for withholding tax cumulatively[3] as is currently done in the UK is that it makes end-year adjustments infrequent. But once all taxpayers file an annual return assessing their own liability, end-year

[1] *Wealth Tax*, Cmnd. 5704 (HMSO, August 1974).

[2] *Select Committee on a Wealth Tax*, Session 1974–75, Volume I, *Report and Proceedings of the Committee*, HC 696–1 (HMSO, November 1975).

[3] Cumulative and non-cumulative withholding are explained in Ch. 9, p. 175. For the purposes of this discussion the key distinction is that under a cumulative system it is usually possible to withhold tax much more accurately during the course of the year than with a non-cumulative system.

adjustments become normal and natural, and so there is little cost, and large gains in other areas, from a switch to the non-cumulative withholding found in most other industrialized countries.

(3) Current year payment of tax on self-employment and similar income: if a taxpayer is responsible for his own tax affairs it is reasonable to ask him to make an estimate of his income for the current year and to make interim payments of tax on account. It should be noted that there is little to be gained here by way of administrative savings – the main argument is one of equity between wage earners and self-employed taxpayers in so far as tax payments tend to be delayed more in the latter case than in the former.

(4) Flexible marginal tax structures: once it is no longer necessary at all costs to avoid large numbers of end-year adjustments it becomes possible to have a variety of structures of rising marginal tax rates if one wishes to do so.

All these considerations enter our discussion at various points.

Before proceeding to a discussion of the pros and cons of self-assessment we should mention an important caveat. It is one thing to suggest that self-assessment offers scope for reducing the *public* costs of tax administration. But it will inevitably increase *private* costs to an unknown extent because of the additional cost to the taxpayer both in terms of his own time and effort and in paying for expert advice. There is an approximate analogy here to the comparison between self-service and non-self-service petrol stations. Self-service garages require fewer personnel; there may also be advantages for the motorist (e.g. shorter waiting times), but some disadvantages in that he has to do the bulk of the work himself. Self-assessment might lead to a decline in the total resources, public plus private, devoted to tax administration, but one cannot be certain about this; even if it did not, the loss might be mainly in terms of leisure foregone rather than other activities. The arguments below about the saving of administrative resources should be interpreted in this light.

3.2 *The arguments for and against self-assessment*

There are three major arguments in favour of self-assessment for personal income tax in the UK. These concern (a) the saving of resources; (b) increased equity and flexibility; and (c) increased taxpayer understanding. We discuss these in turn.

(1) *The saving of resources*. A strong prima facie argument for self-assessment is that in 1973 the Inland Revenue had four times as

many employees per taxpayer as the US Internal Revenue Service, and consequently administrative costs were 1.75 per cent of revenue collected for the Inland Revenue and only 0.48 per cent for the Internal Revenue Service. It could be argued that this is not the result of self-assessment per se, but arises because of the extensive use of computers in tax administration in the USA. But this argument is only a part of the story. The Inland Revenue has computerized one of its nine regions, and though this is more productive than the rest of the UK it is nowhere near as productive as the US tax authorities.

A similar comparison shows that in 1973 it cost $18 to process a tax return in the USA in comparison to £11 in the UK despite the fact that services cost more in the USA. The main cost saving in the USA arises from the extensive use of computers and also from the fact that in the USA taxpayers code themselves, and tax is withheld on a non-cumulative basis. It should be noted parenthetically that the Inland Revenue issues 25 million handwritten coding notices each year under the present UK system.

Two comments are necessary. First of all we should stress again that the argument outlined above refers to the saving of resources in the *public* sector. In economic terms the efficiency arguments as to the proper balance between public and private sector costs should centre on such issues as whether there are any substantial economies of scale in tax administration which can be exploited only by public administration, or whether people's tax affairs have become so complex that it is more efficient to treat each individually, thus implying greater private sector involvement. Secondly, we should note that these cost saving arguments refer primarily to wage earners rather than to recipients of other types of income. Wage earners, however, are the great bulk of taxpayers.

(2) *Equity and flexibility.* As regards equity, under the current system elements of the income of self-employed people in the UK are taxed in arrears, thus giving a considerable advantage to recipients of such incomes relative to wage earners. Under a system of self-assessment it would be possible to tax the self-employed on a current year basis using an estimate of their current income. This procedure which is used in many other countries including the USA and Canada, would increase equity as between the employed and the self-employed.

From the point of view of flexibility the key question is whether the UK should retain its complex withholding system which effectively requires a very inflexible tax structure to ensure that there are few end-year adjustments, or whether we should abandon the constraint of few end-year adjustments which would allow a much more flexible structure of income tax. For example, with self-assessment, end-year adjustments would be normal, and so it would be possible to abandon the long basic rate band, and replace it with any desired structure of marginal tax rates. At this stage we make no comment as to the desirability of increasing the number of marginal tax rates, but simply point out that self-assessment would remove the administrative barriers which have always prevented their introduction in the past.[1]

Similarly, under self-assessment it would be possible to subject short-term national insurance benefits to tax, as was the initial intention when the system was introduced in 1948. This proved to be impossible for administrative reasons under a cumulative withholding system and was therefore quickly abandoned. It is largely because such benefits are non-taxable that the possibilities arise of people being better off on national insurance benefits than earning, thus creating serious labour market distortions.

Self-assessment would also make the introduction of a local income tax much easier. According to the Inland Revenue[2] it would require an extra 12,000 employees to administer a local income tax under the present system. Under self-assessment the extra costs of a local income tax would be very small.

(3) *Increased taxpayer understanding*. It can be argued that self-assessment will force the taxpayer into a better understanding of the tax system. This is likely to be enhanced by the efforts that the tax authorities will have to make under self-assessment to educate the taxpaying public. This aspect has not only economic effects, narrowly defined, but also much broader implications for citizenship and democracy.

We turn now to the major arguments against self-assessment. These concern (a) the economic and social costs of the change; (b) the assertion that self-assessment will lower the quality of tax administration; and (c) that self-assessment leads to more inequity than the present system. We take these points in turn.

(1) *The costs of change*. From an economic point of view it may be argued that self-assessment involves high initial costs in replacing a

[1] For instance, one of the major criticisms of the tax-credit proposals was that they would be unable, for administrative reasons, to include a reduced rate band for those with low incomes. See N. Kaldor, 'A Critique of the Green Paper Proposals', in *Select Committee on Tax-Credit*, Vol. II, June 1973, and discussion in Chapter 9.

[2] See their evidence to *Local Government Finance*, Cmnd. 6453 (HMSO, 1976).

well-established system by a new one, or increases costs in the private sector, or entails new costs associated with end-year adjustments and a peak load of activity in both the public and private sectors. There is no doubt that the transition costs would be substantial, and that even when the new system was running smoothly there would be some aspects of the new system that were more costly than current arrangements.

An altogether different set of arguments arises with the possible social costs of a change to self-assessment. These, in general, do not carry a great deal of weight. Most of them stem from some notion of inertia, with an implied appeal to the 'We've been together now for thirty years . . .' principle. To the statement that an old system is a good one, one can reply that an outdated system is a bad one. Similarly, little weight need be given to arguments that the British public could not cope with self-assessment. Since the public in most other industrialized countries is able to do exactly that, it would be necessary to explain why the British are less capable than they are. Finally, to the statement that there is 'no demand for change' one needs simply to ask for evidence for this proposition.

(2) *Lower quality of administration*. There are two arguments here. The first is that self-assessment may have its administrative advantages, but it also has disadvantages. This, of course, is true. Under a system of self-assessment, for instance, almost every taxpayer must complete a tax return, in contrast to the present situation. This would mean a much larger peak in taxpayer and Inland Revenue activity than at present. These disadvantages have to be set against the advantages outlined above; a strong argument can be made for thinking that the balance will be positive.

A second reason why self-assessment is said to lower the quality of tax administration is that it requires obtrusive verification. Up to a point this is also true. If people are allowed to calculate their own tax liability then more checks will be necessary than at present, even though most tax would continue to be withheld at source. It is certainly the case that tax authorities in many other countries have greater powers than the Inland Revenue. This point can partially be countered by observing that in general law-abiding taxpayers would have little to fear from enforcement activities.

(3) *Greater inequity*. One argument is that self-assessed tax liabilities will be less exact than those calculated by the tax authorities, so that people in identical circumstances may pay different amounts of tax.

Such a system, it is said, will produce 'rough justice' rather than exact justice. Whether or not one accepts this charge depends largely on whether or not one believes exact justice to be a realistic possibility or merely a philosophical mirage.[1]

A second point under this heading is that there will be more tax evasion with self-assessment. The counter-argument is that this is most unlikely where tax on most incomes continues to be withheld at source, and where self-employment income continues to be closely examined.

3.3 *Specific proposals*

A possible set of proposals for introducing self-assessment into the UK is as follows.

(1) *Background.* As a preliminary to self-assessment one would have to start with a simplification of allowances and of the existing tax return. Extensive computerization, non-cumulative withholding and self-coding are also necessary, desirable, or both.

(2) *Timing*. Self-assessment, as defined earlier, would be introduced in stages, starting initially with the incomes of the self-employed, then extending to capital gains, and finally to employment income.

(3) *Outline of the system*. Self-employment income would be subject to taxation on a current basis, with estimated tax payable in instalments during the year. Every self-employed taxpayer would complete an annual return in which he calculated his net tax liability. Where tax was underpaid a remittance would be included with the return. This system would be extended to cover capital gains, and eventually employment income.

(4) *Verification*. There would be a computer check of the arithmetical and internal consistency of all returns; verification would be restricted to a sample of returns.

(5) *Taxpayer assistance.* Extensive public sector assistance would be offered to taxpayers initially. Private sector assistance would probably grow over time and develop new forms as self-assessment became more widespread.

In conclusion, we should observe that these details concern tax *administration* and not tax *policy*. One of the great advantages of self-assessment, as we have stressed, is precisely that it makes possible a much wider range of tax policies than can be achieved under present arrangements. For instance, the proposals outlined above are compat-

[1] See the discussion in Chapter 5, sections 1.1 and 1.5, of the difficulty in giving analytical content to the problem of unequal treatment of unequals.

ible with the tax-credit proposals of the early 1970s;[1] they also make possible any desired structure of marginal tax rates, and any desired treatment of a wife's income. As we shall see in the Policy section these are all issues about which there has been a considerable amount of public debate; it is issues such as these which illuminate the important link between administrative considerations and economic and social policy.

[1] For detailed discussion, see Chapter 9, pp. 196–7.

REFERENCES (PART I)

[*Note*. The following list is neither an exhaustive bibliography of all the sources drawn on in the text nor a comprehensive list of supplementary reading. It is meant to be something of both, listing the major works on the subjects dealt with in the text and indicating the directions in which those interested in reading further might go. Two further points should be noted. The references are to books, essays and articles wholly, or almost wholly, concerned with public finance and therefore no mention is made of, for instance, the classical treatises on general economics which are only incidentally concerned with this subject. The allocation of references to Part I, Part II, and Part III is inevitably rather arbitrary and the division between them should not be regarded as watertight.]

1. BOOKS, ETC.

A. *Mainly General*

Bird, R. M. and Head, J. G. (eds), *Modern Fiscal Issues* (Toronto University Press, 1972).

Blinder, A. S. and Solow, R. M. *et al.*, *The Economics of Public Finance* (Brookings Institution, Washington DC, 1974).

Brown, C. V. and Jackson, P. M., *Public Sector Economics* (Martin Robertson, Oxford, 1978).

Buchanan, J. M., *Fiscal Theory and Political Economy* (University of N. Carolina Press, Chapel Hill, 1960).

Buchanan, J. M. and Flowers, M. R., *The Public Finances*, fourth edition (Irwin, Homewood, Illinois, 1975).

Burkhead, J. and Miner J., *Public Expenditure* (Aldine, Chicago, 1971).

David, W. L. (ed.), *Public Finance, Planning and Economic Development* (Macmillan, London, 1973).

Due, J. F. and Friedlaender, A., *Government Finance: Economics of the Public Sector*, fifth edition (Irwin, Homewood, Illinois, 1973).

Feldstein, M. S. and Inman, R. P., *The Economics of Public Services* (Macmillan, London, 1977).

Harberger, A. C., *Taxation and Welfare* (Little Brown, Boston, 1974).

Harberger, A. C. and Bailey, M. J. (eds), *The Taxation of Income from Capital* (Brookings Institution, Washington DC, 1969).

Hicks, U. K., *Public Finance*, third edition (Nisbet, London and Cambridge University Press, Cambridge, 1968).
Houghton, R. W. (ed.), *Readings in Public Finance* (Penguin, London, 1970).
James, S. R. and Nobes, C., *The Economics of Taxation* (Philip Allan, Oxford, 1978).
Johansen, L., *Public Economics* (North-Holland, Amsterdam, 1965).
Kay, J. A. and King, M. A., *The British Tax System* (Oxford University Press, Oxford, 1978).
Margolis, J. and Guitton, H. (eds for International Economic Association), *Public Economics* (Macmillan, London, 1969), especially chapters by R. Dorfman, R. A. Musgrave and P. A. Samuelson.
Meade, J. E. *et al.*, *The Structure and Reform of Direct Taxation* (Institute for Fiscal Studies – Allen and Unwin, London, 1978).
Millward, R., *Public Expenditure Economics* (McGraw-Hill, London, 1971).
Musgrave, R. A., *The Theory of Public Finance* (McGraw-Hill, New York, 1959).
Musgrave, R. A. and Musgrave, P. B., *Public Finance in Theory and Practice*, second edition (McGraw-Hill, New York, 1976).
Musgrave, R. A. and Peacock, A. T. (eds for International Economic Association), *Classics in the Theory of Public Finance* (Macmillan, London, 1958).
Musgrave, R. A. and Shoup, C. S. (eds for American Economic Association), *Readings in the Economics of Taxation* (Allen and Unwin, London, 1959).
Pigou, A. C., *A Study in Public Finance*, third edition (Macmillan, London, 1947).
Rolph, E. R. and Break, G. F., *Public Finance* (Ronald Press Company, New York, 1961).
Shoup, C. S., *Public Finance* (Weidenfeld and Nicolson, London, 1969).
Shultz, W. J. and Harriss, C. Lowell, *American Public Finance*, eighth edition (Prentice Hall, Englewood Cliffs, New Jersey, 1965).
Smith, W. A. and Culbertson W., *Essays in Honor of R. A. Musgrave* (North-Holland, Amsterdam, 1976).
de Marco, A. de Viti, *First Principles of Public Finance* (Cape, London, 1936).
Williams, A., *Public Finance and Budgetary Policy* (Allen and Unwin, London, 1963).

B. *Mainly Specific*

Ando, A., Brown, E. C. and Friedlaender, A. F., *Studies in Economic Stabilization* (Brookings Institution, Washington DC, 1968).
Balopoulos, E. T., *Fiscal Policy Models of the British Economy* (North-Holland, Amsterdam, 1967).
Barr, N. A., James, S. R. and Prest, A. R., *Self-Assessment for Income Tax* (Institute for Fiscal Studies – Heinemann, London, 1977).
Bird, R. M., *Charging for Public Services* (Canadian Tax Foundation, Toronto, 1976).

Blueprints for Basic Tax Reform (U.S. Treasury, Washington DC, 1977).
Blum, W. J. and Kalven, H. Jnr., *The Uneasy Case for Progressive Taxation* (University of Chicago Press, Chicago, 1953).
Breton, A., *Economic Theory of Representative Government* (Macmillan, London, 1974).
Brittain, J. A., *The Payroll Tax for Social Security* (Brookings Institution, Washington DC, 1972).
Buchanan, J. M., *Public Goods* (Rand McNally, New York, 1968).
Buchanan, J. M., *Public Principles of Public Debt* (Irwin, Homewood, Illinois, 1958).
Downs, A., *Economic Theory of Democracy* (Harper, New York, 1957).
Edgeworth, F. Y., 'The Pure Theory of Taxation' in *Papers Relating to Political Economy*, Vol. II (Macmillan, London, 1925).
Fisher, I. and Fisher, H. W., *Constructive Income Taxation* (Harper, New York, 1942).
Friedman, M., 'The "Welfare" Effects of an Income Tax and an Excise Tax' and 'The Effects of a Full-Employment Policy on Economic Stability' in *Essays in Positive Economics* (University of Chicago Press, Chicago, 1953).
Goode, R., *The Corporation Income Tax* (John Wiley, New York, 1951).
Goode, R., *The Individual Income Tax*, second edition (Brookings Institution, Washington DC, 1976).
Hansen, B., *Fiscal Policy in Seven Countries* (OECD, Paris, 1969).
Head, J. G., *Public Goods and Public Welfare* (Duke University Press, Durham, N. Carolina, 1974).
Heller, W. *et. al.*, *Fiscal Policy for a Balanced Economy* (OECD, Paris, 1968).
Kaldor, N., *An Expenditure Tax* (Allen and Unwin, London, 1955).
Layard, R., *Cost-Benefit Analysis* (Penguin, Harmondsworth, 1972).
Lodin, S. V., *Progressive Expenditure Tax: An Alternative* (Liber Förlag, Stockholm, 1978).
Musgrave, R. A. (ed.), *Broad-Based Taxes: New Options and Sources* (Johns Hopkins, Baltimore, 1973).
Peacock, A. T. and Shaw, G. K., *The Economic Theory of Fiscal Policy*, second edition (Allen and Unwin, London, 1976).
Pechman, J. A. (ed.), *Setting National Priorities, The 1979 Budget* (Brookings Institution, Washington DC, 1978).
Recktenwald, H. C., *Tax Incidence and Income Redistribution* (Wayne State University Press, 1971).
Sandford, C. T., *The Hidden Costs of Taxation* (Institute for Fiscal Studies, London, 1973).
Seligman, E. R. A., *The Shifting and Incidence of Taxation*, fifth edition (Columbia University Press, New York, 1927).
Simons, H. C., *Personal Income Taxation* (University of Chicago Press, Chicago, 1938).

Smithies, A. and Butters, J. K. (eds for American Economic Association), *Readings in Fiscal Policy* (Allen and Unwin, London, 1955).

Stein, H., *The Fiscal Revolution in America* (University of Chicago Press, Chicago, 1969).

II. ARTICLES

Aaron, H. J. and McGuire, M. C., 'Benefits and Burdens of Government Expenditure', *Econometrica*, November 1970 and related articles in *Econometrica*, 1976.

Atkinson, A. B., 'How Progressive should Income Tax be?' in M. Parkin (ed.), *Essays on Modern Economics* (Longman, London, 1973).

Atkinson, A. B., 'Optimal Taxation and the Direct v Indirect Tax Controversy', *Canadian Journal of Economics*, November 1977.

Baumol, W. J. and Bradford, D., 'Optimal Departures from Marginal Cost Pricing', *American Economic Review*, 1970.

Buchanan, J. M., 'Public Finance and Public Choice', *National Tax Journal*, December 1975.

Corlett, W. J. and Hague, D. C., 'Complementarity and the Excess Burden of Taxation', *Review of Economic Studies*, 1953–4 (I).

Diamond, P. A. and Mirrlees, J. A., 'Optimal Taxation and Public Production', *American Economic Review*, March and June 1971.

Feldstein, M. S., 'The Effects of Taxation on Risk Taking', *Journal of Political Economy*, Sept.–Oct. 1969.

Harberger, A. C., 'The Incidence of the Corporate Income Tax', *Journal of Political Economy*, June 1962.

Hicks, U. K., 'The Terminology of Tax Analysis', *Economic Journal*, March 1946.

Hochman, H. M. and Rodgers, J. D., 'Pareto-Optimum Redistribution', *American Economic Review*, September 1969.

Little, I. M. D., 'Direct versus Indirect Taxes', *Economic Journal*, September 1951.

Mieszkowski, P. M., 'Tax Incidence Theory: The Effects of Taxes on the Distribution of Income', *Journal of Economic Literature*, December 1969.

Mieszkowski, P. M., 'The Property Tax: an Excise Tax or a Profits Tax?', *Journal of Public Economics*, April 1972.

Mirrlees, J. A., 'An Exploration in the Theory of Optimum Income Tax', *Review of Economic Studies*, April 1971.

Musgrave, R. A., 'Cost-Benefit Analysis and The Theory of Social Goods', *Journal of Economic Literature*, September 1969.

Musgrave, R. A. and Domar, E. D., 'Proportional Income Taxation and Risk-Bearing', *Quarterly Journal of Economics*, May 1954.

Phillips, A. W., 'Stabilization Policy in a Closed Economy,' *Economic Journal*, June 1954, and 'Stabilization Policy and the Time-Form of Lagged Responses', *Economic Journal*, June 1957.

Prest, A. R., 'The Expenditure Tax and Saving', *Economic Journal*, September 1959.

Prest, A. R., 'The Budget and Interpersonal Distribution', *Public Finance*, Pts. I and II, 1968.

Prest, A. R., 'Public Finance: Backward Area or New Frontier?', *Economica*, May 1973.

Prest, A. R. and Turvey, R., 'Cost-Benefit Analysis: a Survey', *Economic Journal*, December 1965.

Ramsey, F. P., 'A Contribution to the Theory of Taxation', *Economic Journal*, March 1927.

Robertson, D. H., 'The Colwyn Committee, The Income Tax and the Price Level', *Economic Journal*, December 1927.

Samuelson, P. A., 'The Pure Theory of Public Expenditures', *Review of Economics and Statistics*, November 1954; 'A Diagrammatic Exposition of a Theory of Public Expenditure', *Review of Economics and Statistics*, November 1955; and 'Aspects of Public Expenditure Theories', ibid., November 1958.

Sandmo, A., 'Optimal Taxation: an Introduction to the Literature', *Journal of Public Economics*, No. 6, 1976.

Shoup, C. S., 'The Theory and Background of the Value-Added Tax', *Proceedings of National Tax Association 1955* (Sacramento, California).

Shoup, C. S., 'Debt Financing and Future Generations', *Economic Journal*, December 1962.

Stiglitz, J. E., 'The Effects of Income, Wealth and Capital Gains Taxation on Risk-Taking', *Quarterly Journal of Economics*, May 1969.

Tobin, J., 'Liquidity Preference as Behaviour towards Risk', *Review of Economic Studies*, February 1958.

Whalley, J. E., 'A General Equilibrium Assessment of the 1973 UK Tax Reform', *Economica*, May 1975.

PART II
INSTITUTIONS

8

THE GOVERNMENT AS A WHOLE

1 INTRODUCTION

1.1 *General Government*

It may be helpful to set out the position of the government as a whole before we come to the details of central government (Chapter 9), national insurance and related expenditures (Chapter 10), and local authorities (Chapter 11).

We start by giving an outline picture of the government as a whole and draw attention to some of the matters of definition which have to be resolved in any such description. Subsequently, the expenditure and revenue sides will be discussed separately.

A simple outline of the main features of government finances in the UK in 1977 is given in Table 8.1. It can be seen that total revenue on current account was some £56,000 million, of which taxation in one form or another came to about £50,000 million. The major components of general revenue were income taxes (the most important single source) and the various indirect taxes. Together these made up nearly three-quarters of government revenue. National Insurance contributions are also a tax on income, although they are allocated to a separate fund. They made up about 17 per cent of government revenue, a considerably larger sum than the revenue raised directly by local authorities (though the latter also received substantial grants from central government which are netted out in this table). These revenue sources will be discussed in considerably greater detail in the following chapters.

The rest of the current account section of Table 8.1 gives a very broad breakdown of expenditure by level of government. It is vital at this stage to remember the distinction[1] between:

(a) government consumption of current goods and services, such as education and the National Health Service;[2] and

(b) total government current expenditure, including transfer payments such as subsidies.

[1] See Chapter 2 above, pp. 11–12.

[2] But leaving out capital formation such as the building of schools and hospitals.

It is important in any policy discussion to be clear about the definition of the government sector one is using. If the focus of interest is the proportion of GNP devoted to the satisfaction of public demand on current account, then the relevant concept is government consumption of current resources; but if one is interested in the impact of

Table 8.1

UK General Government Current and Capital Account, 1977 (£m)

Receipts		*Expenditure*	
I *Current account*			
General tax revenue		Goods and services	
central	35,541	central	17,275
local	5,194	local	11,846
National insurance		Transfer payments	
contributions		central	22,995
central	9,453	local	3,102
Other revenue:		Current surplus:	
central	2,641	central	–804
local	3,420	local	1,835
TOTAL	56,249	TOTAL	56,249
II *Capital account*			
Current surplus		Gross capital formation	
central	–804	central	1,410
local	1,835	local	3,531
Capital taxes		Transfers	
central	907	central	1,410
Financial deficit:		local	142
central	2,904		
local	1,651		
TOTAL	6,493	TOTAL	6,493
III *Financial transactions*			
Miscellaneous sources (net)		Financial deficit	
central	251	central	2,904
local	–91	local	1,651
Borrowing requirement		Net lending	
central	4,465	central	272
local	183	local	–19
TOTAL	4,808	TOTAL	4,808

Source: *National Income and Expenditure 1967–77* (HMSO, 1978).

taxation on incentives, it is more useful to look at the combined total of current consumption and transfer payments, or at total government revenue as a proportion of GNP. As we shall see in sections 2 and 3 of this chapter both of these concepts pose many questions of definition in practice.

Current expenditure on goods and services in 1977 amounted to some 53 per cent of the current account total of £55,000 million, the three most important items being military expenditure, the National Health Service, and education. Transfer payments amounted to some £26,000 million, about 47 per cent of the same total. The main components of this type of expenditure were state retirement pensions, unemployment and sickness benefits, supplementary benefits and interest on the national debt. Such payments to the personal sector are made by the central government both directly and through the National Insurance Fund, and also by local authorities. The various cash payments will be discussed in detail in Chapter 10.

Looking at current expenditure overall, it is noteworthy that in 1977 some 27 per cent was by local authorities, though they raised only 15 per cent or thereabouts of total revenue.

The second part of Table 8.1 summarizes the capital account of the various levels of government. Taxes on capital such as capital gains tax and capital transfer tax had only a small yield of £907 million. On the expenditure side the important point to note is that local authorities spent more than twice as much as the central government on capital formation. The largest items under this heading were housing, roads, education and the National Health Service.

The third part of the table shows how the deficits arising from the combined effects of Parts I and II fitted into the general picture of government borrowing and lending.

1.2 *Problems of definition*

One must start by clarifying the meaning of the government sector and deciding how to draw the boundaries. The first boundary is that between government and public corporations. The types of criteria which are relevant are whether day-to-day operations are possible independently of government administrative departments, and whether there are powers to borrow from the market and to hold reserves of funds. In fact, the bodies which satisfy these criteria in the UK are fairly easily distinguishable and do not in any case enter into the main corpus of government accounts. So this does not constitute any great difficulty.

Some problems arise in the differentiation of government from companies and from the personal sector. Grants are made, for instance, to the English Tourist Board. Ought its accounts to be consolidated with the Central Government or not? On the whole, it seems preferable to regard any such institutions, which are primarily commercial in character and not wholly dependent on government support, as part of the company sector. Similarly, grants are made to the universities and various learned societies, but nevertheless they possess sufficient independence of action to warrant inclusion in the personal rather than the government sector. On the other hand, there are a large number of grant-aided institutions (e.g. the Medical Research Council, the Atomic Energy Authority, the White Fish Authority) which do not appear to be sufficiently commercial in character or independent of detailed financial control to justify separation from the central government. In these cases it is better to consolidate their accounts with general government. These examples show that the dividing line is a very fine one. Nevertheless, it is one which has to be faced fully and squarely before the traditional accounts can be cast into a form suitable for integration.

Given the differentiation of government from non-government activity, there is one further general point to discuss. A distinction has to be drawn between government 'commercial' and government 'administrative' departments. The precise reasons for this will emerge shortly. In the meanwhile, are there any principles for making such a distinction? The types of points which seem to arise are whether the functions might be performed by a company, whether most of the transactions are with the private rather than the public sector of the economy, whether the organization aims at covering its costs, etc. If we take a fairly wide definition of this sort, then we have to include as 'commercial' not only such obvious candidates as the Mint, but also the Exports Credit Guarantee Department.

It will be seen from this discussion that the notion of General Government differs from that of the public sector as a whole in so far as the latter includes, for instance, various activities of public corporations. Until 1977 the *National Income Blue Book* concentrated most of its attention on the public sector in this wider sense, but since then it has confined its main tabulations to the narrower definition.

One must also ask whether the *Blue Book* data are the most suitable when looking at government generally. The answer is quite clearly 'yes'. Although there is an alternative means of giving a comprehensive account of the expenditure side in the annual *Public Expenditure White Paper*, this does not help us on the revenue side. And although there are other sets of accounts which do cover both revenue and expenditure at central or local level – and we shall draw on these in later chapters – they cannot readily be consolidated in such a way as to net out transactions (e.g. payments from central government to the National Insurance Fund or to local authorities) between different constituent components of government. Nor are they always cast in a form suitable for immediate usage, e.g. a rather elaborate process of reconciliation is necessary between the traditional Exchequer accounts and the *Blue Book* format.[1]

The next step is to relate these consolidated data to the national accounts. There are obviously two ways of doing this: by comparing government expenditure with national expenditure or by comparing government income with national income. In principle, one could also compare government value added with the national aggregate of value added or even government employment with total employment, but obviously the income and expenditure comparisons are much more relevant in considerations of public finance. We shall therefore concentrate exclusively on these two measures.

2 GOVERNMENT EXPENDITURE AND NATIONAL EXPENDITURE

National expenditure is usually classified under the headings of final expenditure on current goods and services, domestic capital formation, and overseas investment. Our task is to estimate the size of the government component under each of these heads, so that we then know the proportion of total output absorbed by the government.

The first point is that we must exclude current expenditure of government commercial organizations from the total of government current expenditure. The reason for this is straightforward: if the government buys factor services for subsequent re-sale to the public it is acting as an intermediary and not as a final consumer. To include such expenditure as part of government consumption would in fact duplicate what is in any case going to appear as personal consumption.

[1] See, for example, *Financial Statement and Budget Report 1978–79* (HMSO, April 1978), Table 15.

This is the reason why we found it necessary to emphasize the importance of the distinction between government administrative and commercial departments. If, for instance, a publicly owned airport is treated as a government commercial enterprise, all the operating expenses are excluded from the total of government expenditure. If, on the other hand, it is thought of as an administrative department, these expenses are not so excluded. This leads on, however, to a further difficulty. In this particular case, as in a number of others, various receipts (landing fees, etc. in this instance) are associated with the provision of the service. If an expenditure is ruled non-commercial, should it be taken as gross or net of such receipts? This is another difficult problem, but the relevant criterion seems to be that if the receipts are to be treated as negative expenditure, they must be tied in very closely with the expenditure of a Department and must be a more or less inevitable accompaniment to that expenditure. If these conditions are satisfied, expenditure should be reckoned net of such receipts, otherwise no deduction should be made.

Another point about trading or commercial activities of the government is the treatment of their capital expenditure. This obviously does not duplicate expenditure by another sector and therefore must be included in the total of government spending.

The other major principle in the definition of government expenditure is that, if we are to compare it with a national total, we must exclude all unilateral payments – subsidies, grants – and all financial transactions on capital account, such as payments to sinking funds to amortise debt or loan repayments. Obviously none of these outpayments *directly* involves the use of real resources and they must not be included in this total of government expenditure.

If we extract data from the 1978 *National Income Blue Book* and *Balance of Payments Pink Book* on these principles we find the 1977 pattern as shown on p. 183.

These figures need a few words of amplification. Government current and capital expenditure follow the lines indicated. Net government foreign investment, etc. is the difference between identifiable government services and interest expenditure abroad and similar receipts from abroad. The fact that it was negative in 1977 implies that government expenditure abroad was greater than government 'sales' abroad and thereby the drain of government on real resources available was pro tanto reduced, at any rate in the short run (see Table 8.2).

Table 8.2

Government Expenditure and National Expenditure, UK, 1977 (£m)

	Government	*National*
Current expenditure at market prices	29,121	112,651
Gross domestic capital formation at market prices	4,889	26,717
Net foreign investment, etc. at market prices	−1,473	1,530
TOTAL	32,537	140,898

Total government expenditure = 23 per cent of GNP (at market prices).

The figure of 23 per cent only applies with the definitions we have used. If public corporation capital formation were included in the government sector, the ratio would be 26 per cent rather than 23 per cent. If expenditure, both government and national, were taken at factor cost instead of at market prices, the percentage would be greater since the average rate of indirect taxation (net of subsidies) is greater in respect of goods consumed by the private than the public sector. If a narrow rather than a wide definition of government commercial activities were adopted, the percentage would be raised again. For in that case *some* current expenditure (even if the gross expenditure is partially offset by miscellaneous receipts) would count as being that of the government. On the other hand, if the activities of the government in supplying police, justice, roads, etc. were regarded as a form of intermediate rather than final output, this would have the effect of reducing the ratio since there would be an equal absolute reduction in both government and national expenditure.

So it can readily be seen that there is no unique figure, on which all can agree, of the proportion of national resources absorbed by the public sector. And in so far as there are various activities which for one reason or another are not taken fully into account in GNP data we have yet another reason for treating government/national expenditure ratios with caution. Nor would it be correct to assume that these various corrective factors remain the same over time or between countries; so one cannot make expenditure ratio comparisons with impunity.

3 GOVERNMENT REVENUE AND NATIONAL INCOME

We now change the focus of attention from the absorption of resources by government to the proportion of national income that passes through its hands.

One might think at first that the concept of the ratio of government revenue to national income is unambiguous. If one takes the total of current receipts from Table 8.1 and adds the item capital taxation we find that revenue thus defined was some 40 per cent of GNP at market prices in 1977. This ratio is in fact frequently computed, although sometimes on a slightly different basis, and one regularly finds it quoted as evidence of the weight of the tax burden in the UK. Those who wish to emphasize what they consider to be a high level of taxation will contrast the ratio with the lower figures prevalent before World War II or even in some years since then. Those who maintain that the scale of taxation is not inordinate will compare this ratio with that found in other OECD countries and point out that the UK usually comes about one-third or one-half way down among the seventeen countries for which comparisons are usually made.[1]

A major difficulty with such computations is that no distinction is made between larger tax proceeds corresponding to larger government purchases of goods and services, and larger tax proceeds corresponding to larger transfer payments and other non-exhaustive expenditures. Intuitively, it would seem that the economic significance of these two reasons for increases in revenue is very different, and that for some purposes it is important to distinguish between them.

In fact, the more we look at the revenue ratio the more complex the whole issue becomes. We saw, in our discussion of Expenditure, that one of the problems of defining Expenditure was whether to take it gross or net of associated fees. Once we begin to look at the definitions of Revenue from this sort of viewpoint, the whole matter bristles with difficulties. Not only do we ask ourself 'is this item positive revenue or negative expenditure?' but in addition we must face the complementary question 'is that item positive expenditure or negative revenue?'. In this latter category a large number of decisions have to be taken. Many subsidies and grants could be argued about. For instance, the changeover from investment grants to initial allowances in 1971 had the effect of reducing the crude revenue/GNP ratio. Conversely, the

[1] See, for instance, *Economic Trends*, December 1977 and December 1978 for recent illustrations.

switch from income tax child allowances to child benefit in the late 1970s increases the ratio. And why should the interest on the National Debt be regarded as expenditure rather than as an offset to revenue, i.e. as if it were a prior charge to be met before reckoning net revenue? It seems fair to say, after considering such points as this, that the purely accounting problems are much more formidable on the revenue than on the expenditure side. Although the definition of expenditure on goods and services, which is essentially all we need for the expenditure comparisons, has its pitfalls, those encountered in differentiating between revenue and non-exhaustive expenditure are much more numerous. Since a satisfactory revenue comparison involves the solution of both sorts of problems, it is clearly much harder to achieve.

Even if the accounting difficulties could be satisfactorily resolved, we are by no means out of the wood if we want to pursue the revenue side. It is usual to argue that one should include the trading profits of government enterprises in the revenue total. But if one once admits trading enterprises into the picture at all, what is the logic of including their net profits rather than their gross receipts? Suppose we consider the operations of the National Savings Bank. Some of the receipts are used to pay the wages of Post Office clerks, some to meet the salaries of the Civil Servants at headquarters and, if there is a surplus over working expenditure, some can be thought of as available to pay, say, the salaries of Treasury officials. The usual way of reckoning government revenue is to include the last of these three categories but not the others. But if we are seeking *the* definition of revenue, is there any logic in this procedure? On the other hand, it can be maintained that net profits is too wide rather than too narrow a concept. If we want a measure of revenue which reflects the coercive, as distinct from the commercial, role of government there is a case for saying that one should only include elements of excess profits arising from commercial operations.

Then there is the nasty question of the 'inflation tax'. In so far as a government relieves people of discretionary purchasing power by financing its expenditure through new credit creation or by inflicting real capital losses on holders of existing government debt, why should one distinguish between this form of taxation and that conventionally listed as such in the national accounts (including an element which also comes about as a result of inflation, i.e. when exemption levels and rate band starting points of progressive income taxes are not indexed with price changes)?

We may conclude therefore that the most appropriate measure of government revenue is by no means easy to settle. At the same time it should not be thought that this is a good reason for abandoning the quest and simply concentrating on the expenditure side. It is of some importance to know 'that part of the flow of incomes which is compulsorily diverted by governments and so is not at the direct disposal of the citizenry taken as a whole'.[1] In other words, the ratio of government revenue to some national aggregate is very closely tied to questions about the extent of the sector where non-market considerations prevail. But the problems of making such calculations should not be under-estimated. Quite apart from those of defining revenue the appropriate measure of a national aggregate is a matter for contention. One series of arguments is about the relative merits of conventional aggregates – GNP verses GDP, the market price versus the factor cost base, and so on. Another[2] is whether one cannot justify some more unconventional aggregate which corresponds more closely to the stream of purchasing power from which tax demands are met, e.g. personal income plus personal capital gains together with pre-tax profits of corporations (less dividends paid) and (taxable) trading surpluses of public authorities. Such a concept would correspond far more closely to the aggregate income of the whole body of taxpayers than do the conventional national accounts aggregates.

So there are a large number of conceptual queries in any revenue side calculations. And even when calculations are made one must beware of biases in time-series or cross-section comparisons arising from differential understatement of GNP, due to, for instance, the difficulty of ascertaining the true incomes of small firms or traders. Nor should one over-state the gains likely to come from such calculations. They are not an unambiguous indicator of the degree of government intervention in an economy, for instance. Nevertheless, despite all the limitations, such calculations when carefully made can throw light on some important aspects of governmental activities.

[1] See A. R. Prest, 'Government Revenue, the National Income and All That', in R. M. Bird and J. G. Head (eds), *Modern Fiscal Issues* (University of Toronto Press, 1972), p. 139. For further discussion see A. R. Prest, 'Public Activities in Perspective: A Critical Survey', International Institute of Public Finance, *Secular Trends of the Public Sector*, 1976 *Conference Proceedings* (Cujas, Paris, 1978).

[2] *Ibid.*

9

THE CENTRAL GOVERNMENT

1 AN OVERVIEW OF CENTRAL REVENUE AND EXPENDITURE

This chapter starts with some background issues, and then looks in some detail in section 2 at the major sources of central government revenue. Section 3 discusses the Parliamentary procedures for authorizing and controlling expenditure. Details of the Budget of June 1979 are given in the Appendix to this chapter.

We start by outlining the structure of Central Government accounts and look briefly at the major sources of revenue and expenditure as classified in the *Financial Statement and Budget Report*. The first major distinction is between Revenue and Expenditure items on the one hand and the National Loans Fund on the other. We start with Revenue and Expenditure, and return to the National Loans Fund later. The distinction between the two categories is not that between current and capital transactions, since all central government physical capital expenditure comes under the former heading. Broadly, the National Loans Fund is concerned with changes in the central government's financial assets and liabilities. Revenue and Expenditure items deal with all other transactions.

Table 9.1 sets out the main items of expenditure in 1978/79, amounting to an estimated total of £51,378 million. This figure should not be regarded as the total 'turnover' of the central government and its agencies, but only as the expenditure of the central core of administrative departments. The figure excludes expenditure by the National Insurance Fund and a number of trading and commercial departments, a subject to which we return later.

In discussing central government expenditure, a distinction has to be made between *Supply expenditure* and *Consolidated Fund expenditure*. The distinction between the two is largely historical and more one of procedure than of the type of expenditure involved under either head. The point will be discussed further in section 3 which outlines Parliamentary procedure. Table 9.1 shows the breakdown of central government expenditure into its Supply and Consolidated Fund components. Defence constitutes some 15 per cent of Supply expenditure and Civil 85 per cent. Civil expenditure can be divided into administration (items II, IX, XIII, XIV, XV), making 13 per cent of the total, economic (III, IV, VI) 12 per cent, social (VII, XI, XII) 39 per cent and miscellaneous (VIII, X, XVII) 36 per cent.

Table 9.1

UK Central Government Expenditure, 1978/79 (est.) (£m)

Supply Services			46,178
I	Defence	6,886	
II	Overseas services	1,062	
III	Agriculture, Fisheries and Forestry	535	
IV	Trade, industry and employment	3,039	
VI	Roads and transport	1,266	
VII	Housing	2,618	
VIII	Other environmental services	299	
IX	Law, order and protective services	1,249	
X	Education and libraries, science and arts	1,740	
XI	Health and personal social services	6,163	
XII	Social Security	6,683	
XIII	Other public services	1,071	
XIV	Common services	1,157	
XV	Northern Ireland	592	
XVII	Rate Support Grant, financial transactions, etc.	7,968	
	Allowance for price changes (rounded)	2,400	
	Supplementary provision (net)	1,450	
Consolidated Fund Standing Services			5,200
	National Debt (transfer to National Loan Fund)	3,160	
	Northern Ireland – share of taxes, etc.	786	
	Payments to EEC, etc.	1,237	
	Other services	17	
TOTAL			51,378

Source: *UK Financial Statement and Budget Report 1978/79* (HMSO, 1978).

Table 9.2 puts these current expenditures into their historical perspective, and shows that they have increased over 300 times since 1913/14 and nearly 60 times since 1938/39. This is a much larger increase than the rate of growth of population or the general rise in prices over the period, or even of the two combined, and shows how

Table 9.2

UK Central Government Expenditure, 1913–14, 1938–39 and 1978–79

	1913/14		*1938/39*		*1978/79*	
	£m	%	£m	%	£m	%
National Debt	25	14	231	25	6,400	12
Defence	77	44	272	29	6,886	13
Other	73	42	424	46	41,332	75
Total	175	100	927	100	54,618	100

Sources: UK *Financial Statement* (1914/15) and (1939/40), *63rd Statistical Abstract* for the UK, Cd. 8448 (HMSO, 1917), and UK *Financial Statement and Budget Report 1978/79, op. cit.*
Note: The total for 1978/79 differs from that given in Table 9.1 in that total costs of servicing the National Debt are included and not simply the transfers to the National Loans Fund (see below, p. 213).

much greater is the extent of government involvement in the economy today. Several points are noteworthy. First, defence expenditure as a proportion of total expenditure has fallen dramatically, from 44 per cent in 1913/14 to 13 per cent in 1978/79. Secondly, though the absolute magnitude of the National Debt has increased enormously from £800 million in 1913/14 to £40,000 million in 1976,[1] both the National Debt as a percentage of GNP and the percentage of total expenditure attributable to debt service has declined. The corollary of these two features is, of course, the expansion of Other expenditure; this is primarily social expenditure (about £30 million in 1913/14 and about £15,000 million today) but there has also been a large increase in economic expenditure, from a negligible amount in 1913/14 to just below £5,000 million today.

The main features of central government revenue are shown in Table 9.3. Apart from relatively minor miscellaneous receipts, most central government revenue is collected by the Inland Revenue (£24,860 million in 1978/79) and Customs and Excise (£13,750 million in 1978/79). Broadly speaking the Inland Revenue collects taxes on income and capital, while Customs and Excise collects indirect taxes.

[1]The size of the National Debt, like many economic variables, is somewhat elusive – see for instance, C. V. Downton, 'The Trend of the National Debt in Relation to National Income', *Bank of England Quarterly Bulletin*, Vol. 17, No. 3, September 1977.

Before discussing the precise meaning and coverage of the individual taxes, Table 9.4 gives a brief historical perspective. We see that the importance of the Customs and Excise Department has declined somewhat relative to that of the Inland Revenue over the past 60 years or so, essentially reflecting the increasing importance of income taxes as a source of government revenue.

Table 9.3

UK Central Government Revenue, 1978/79 (est.) (£m)

Inland Revenue		24,860
Income tax	19,310	
Surtax	15	
Corporation tax	4,170	
Petroleum revenue tax	170	
Capital gains tax	375	
Development land tax	10	
Estate duty	50	
Capital transfer tax	320	
Stamp duties	440	
Customs and Excise		13,750
Motor Vehicles		1,120
Miscellaneous Receipts		1,541
National Insurance Surcharge		1,475
TOTAL		42,746

Source: UK *Financial Statement and Budget Report, 1978/79, op. cit.*
Note: Customs and Excise total includes duties and levies payable to the EEC.

Table 9.4

UK Central Government Revenue, 1913/14, 1938/39 and 1978/79 (est.) (£m)

	1913/14	1938/39	1978/79 (est.)
Inland Revenue	88	520	24,860
Customs and Excise	76	341	13,750
Miscellaneous	10	66	4,136
TOTAL	174	927	42,746

Source: UK *Financial Statement* (1914/15), (1939/40) and (1978/79).

2 CENTRAL GOVERNMENT REVENUE

2.1 *Inland Revenue*

2.1.1 *Income tax* In this part of the chapter we discuss government revenue in terms of the main tax agencies. Section 2.1 discusses the Inland Revenue, section 2.2 Customs and Excise, and section 2.3 outlines briefly various other central government financial sources. Discussion of the revenues of the National Insurance Fund is postponed until Chapter 10. The various taxes collected by the Inland Revenue are discussed in some detail under four main headings, (a) personal income tax, (b) capital gains tax, (c) corporation tax, and (d) the various other taxes collected by the Inland Revenue.

Since income tax is much the most important responsibility of the Inland Revenue, we start with an historical overview before proceeding to its current institutions and administration. The tax started its current life in 1842, when it was introduced by Peel. However, Peel's legislation was based largely on that operating during the Napoleonic Wars, and particularly on the Income Tax Act of 1806. The first income tax in this country was introduced by Pitt in 1799 and (with a temporary abolition after the Peace of Amiens) lasted until 1816. Research has shown clearly that the major features of this legislation were due to Pitt and his, therefore, must be the credit for the tax legislation of 1842. To trace the development of income tax through the nineteenth and twentieth centuries would require a volume in itself, and so we make historical references only where they are helpful in explaining the present system. For present purposes, we need to discuss (a) the historical definition of income as relevant for tax purposes, and (b) income historically exempted from tax.

Income tax in the UK has always applied in principle very broadly, i.e. both to income originating within the UK and to income accruing to inhabitants of the UK. Thus, not only is the foreign recipient of dividends from Britain subject to tax, but so is the British recipient of dividends from overseas. Such a wide range of application was of little consequence historically when British tax rates were low and foreign income taxes virtually non-existent. But in recent years doubts and difficulties have arisen which we shall discuss in Chapter 18.

The definition of income relevant for income tax is the result of a long process of legal and administrative amendments to the list of items specified by Pitt. The process has been ad hoc rather than based on any broad theoretical principles, and this is not the place to comment in any detail. Historically, income was regarded as arising for tax purposes only if an actual receipt, either in money or in kind, took place. The only major exception to this generalization was the imputed value of the flow of services arising from owner-occupied property which was thought to be too obvious a benefit to an individual to escape tax. In contrast, this general principle was the basis for the exclusion from tax of capital gains, and it was this point on which the sharpest division of opinion arose.

In fact, the position on these two issues has now been completely reversed; the imputed rent from owner-occupied property is no longer subject to tax while, on the other hand, capital gains have been gathered into the tax net. The taxation of capital gains will be taken up in some detail below.

So much for the principles underlying the definition of income potentially liable for tax. In practice such income has been historically identified by means of a classification going back to Pitt's day. The basis was *Schedules* introduced in 1803. Schedule A referred to the net annual value of income from the ownership of land, buildings and other hereditaments.[1] Schedule B covered income arising from the occupation of land other than dwelling houses or buildings used for a trade or business. In the past this included farmers, but they were transferred to Schedule D during the last war and since then Schedule B has been little more than a museum piece covering sporting rights, commercial woodland, etc. Schedule C relates to interest from certain securities from UK and overseas governments, where payments are made in Britain. Schedules D and E are the most important. Schedule D covers the profits of trade, businesses and professions and certain other income including interest on loans and income from abroad. In contrast to virtually all other types of income, tax is assessed on the basis of the preceding year's income.[2] Schedule E covers income from offices, employment or pensions. In very broad terms, Schedule D relates to the income from self-employment, while Schedule E relates to employment income and pensions. In terms of the income covered, Schedule E is by far the largest. In 1965 another schedule (Schedule F) was added as a consequence of the introduction of corporation tax on

[1] After the abolition of owner-occupier taxation in 1963, the remaining items of income under Schedule A were transferred to Schedule D, though there was a subsequent resuscitation of Schedule A in a minor way.

[2] Though an Inland Revenue study in 1978 was not unsympathetic to the idea of switching the taxation of Schedule D income on to a current-year basis.

company profits (until then income tax covered companies as well as individuals). This schedule was the basis for collection of income tax at source on company dividends, and will be discussed below.

Just as the income assessable for tax is identified by means of definite categories, there are also clearly defined categories of exempt income. The most important are the investment income of charities, hospitals, etc. disability pensions to members of the Armed Forces, interest from certain UK securities payable to persons not ordinarily resident in the UK, and interest on certain types of small savings.

Until 1973 there was also a system of levying *surtax*. Although not as venerable as income tax, it had nevertheless been in existence since the famous Lloyd George People's Budget of 1909. The precise operation of the tax was complex, but the main object was to tax a small number of higher incomes at progressively higher tax rates. However, the linkage to the income tax system was awkward and it operated in a very different way (e.g. tax payments were always in arrears), and it was therefore decided to combine income tax and surtax into a new system of *unified tax* from April 1973. This tax contains a *basic rate* of tax and *higher rates*.

With this brief historical background in mind we can now turn to the current state of income tax. This is most usefully done by outlining (a) the income normally regarded as tax free, (b) the tax rates that are applied to taxable income, (c) the relative treatment of earned and investment income, and (d) various benefits for children which are, in practice, an integral part of the income tax system. These are discussed in turn.

The allowances made in computing taxable income are set out below (all data refer to 1978/79):

Personal:

Single person	£985
Married couple	£1,535
Wife's earned income allowance	£985
Additional personal allowance (for those with single-handed responsibility for children)	£550

Miscellaneous:

Allowances for old age, housekeeper, dependant relative, mortgage interest, life assurance premia.[1]

[1] From April 1979 life assurance premia have been paid on a net of tax basis in that whereas previously an individual was given an allowance against basic rate tax of 16½ per cent of sums paid, he now simply pays 82½ per cent of the premia formerly due, but gets no tax relief.

In addition to these standard allowances, the expenses of earning an income are in principle allowable as deductions, although the precise working of the regulations is complex, and depends on whether the income is earned under Schedule D or E. In general, the regulations under Schedule E are tighter than those under Schedule D.

The structure of marginal tax rates for 1978/79 was as shown in Table 9.5.

Table 9.5

Marginal Rates of Income Tax, UK, 1978/79

Taxable income slice (£s)	*Tax rate (%)*
0– 750	25
751– 8,000	33
8,001– 9,000	40
9,001–10,000	45
10,001–11,000	50
11,001–12,500	55
12,501–14,000	60
14,001–16,000	65
16,001–18,500	70
18,501–24,000	75
Over 24,000	83

Two features of the rate structure are noteworthy. First, the 33 per cent, or basic rate, covers a very wide range of income. This has long been a feature of the UK system, largely because it greatly simplifies the taxation of all secondary sources of income (e.g. the wages of a second earner in the family, or dividend or interest receipts). The second noteworthy feature is that in comparison to most other countries the marginal tax rates at the top of the income scale are very high.[1]

For many years before 1973 special relief was given for earned income. This was a somewhat curious system implying that the normal situation was to be in receipt of unearned income, special treatment being given if income happened to be earned. With the introduction of unified tax in 1973, this concept was abandoned and the opposite one

[1] In 1976 the only countries with top marginal tax rates at or above the UK level were Algeria, Egypt and Tanzania, see A. R. Prest, 'What is Wrong with the UK Tax System?', in *The State of Taxation* (IEA, 1977).

was introduced, i.e. the rate structure shown above applies if income is earned or if unearned income does not exceed some specified amount, but if unearned income exceeds this amount (or, in the case of discretionary and accumulating trusts, all income received) an investment income surcharge is levied. The limits above which unearned income is subject to the investment income surcharge have changed from time to time. In 1978/79, the surcharge was 10 per cent for investment income between £1,701 and £2,250 per year and 15 per cent for investment income in excess of this, save that for people aged 65 or over the limits were £2,501 and £3,000, respectively. In computing tax liabilities when incomes are partly earned and partly unearned, the general principle is that, as far as possible, allowances have to be offset against earned income.

The preceding paragraphs have outlined the structure of income tax per se. But in addition, it is important to remember certain benefits for children which, though not strictly part of the income tax system, are, nevertheless, closely related to it. In the past as well as the income tax allowances for children (called child tax allowances), there were also family allowances payable in respect of any children after the first. These were weekly cash payments to the mother of the child, which were taxable. The combined effect of child tax allowances and family allowances was somewhat complex and the system has been phased out. Since April 1979 child tax allowances and family allowances have been replaced by child benefit, which is a weekly cash payment to the mother in respect of all children including the first child, and is tax free.[1] We shall discuss child benefit further in our discussion of social security in Chapter 10.

We turn now briefly to the administration of income tax. The cornerstone of the system ever since Pitt's day, has been the insistence on collection at source. In the case of wage- and salary-earners (Schedule E) this is effected by the system of PAYE. Under this system employers deduct tax cumulatively so that the tax deducted in any week or month does not depend solely on the pay of that week or month, but takes account of total pay received and tax deducted since the start of the tax year.[2] This ensures that tax payments broadly match income tax liability at each pay day. Although this can lead to sudden

[1] Child tax allowances have been retained for British children living abroad and not entitled to child benefit. For further discussion see Chapter 10, section 3.1.

[2] For a more detailed discussion see N. A. Barr, S. R. James and A. R. Prest, *Self-Assessment for Income Tax, op. cit.*, pp. 25–31.

increases in tax payments or sudden refunds if a person's income suddenly deviates from its normal level, it has the great advantage of collecting revenue easily and preventing the vast majority of wage- and salary-earners from ending the tax year with any arrears or excesses of tax payments. Although there were rough-and-ready attempts to match tax payments with liabilities before the introduction of PAYE in 1943, it is only since then that the system can be said to have worked well. Moreover, the administrative simplifications which have been introduced since then have made it a matter of routine operation for employers, employees and the Inland Revenue, though there have been considerable difficulties in keeping up with inflationary changes in recent years.[1]

Although PAYE is now the major instrument for deduction of tax at source, the general principle of source deduction has traditionally applied to most other forms of income as well. As we have mentioned, tax is in effect deducted at source from company dividends before they are paid out to shareholders;[2] similarly, mineral royalties, income charged under Schedule C and interest and dividends payable by overseas companies through agents in the UK are all subject to tax deductions before payment. Indeed, only miscellaneous payments such as fees are left substantially uncovered by the source deduction system. It follows therefore that a very large fraction of total income is taxed by a method which is both easy to administer (e.g. the number of people from whom the Revenue collects tax is greatly reduced) and difficult to evade.

The size of the income tax net in the UK can best be appreciated by noting that over 20 million tax units (husbands and wives normally being treated as one tax unit) pay tax out of a population of some 56 million.

Before leaving the subject of income tax we should mention briefly a major reform which, had it been enacted, would have changed in a fundamental way the structure of income tax, and for that matter also the system of national insurance and its associated welfare schemes.

[1] As an example of these difficulties see N. A. Barr, 'PAYE Codes in 1977–1978', *British Tax Review*, No. 6, 1977. For a more official review of PAYE, see Board of Inland Revenue, 120th *Report*, Cmnd. 7092 (HMSO, 1970), Ch. 5, 'The Future of the PAYE System'; also *PAYE – Possible Future Developments* (Inland Revenue, March 1979).

[2] As we shall see shortly (p. 199), tax is not deducted as such from dividends before they are paid, but tax-credit arrangements give much the same result. The shareholder is taxed on the aggregate of the cash dividend and the tax credit, but as the tax credit satisfies the basic rate tax, a basic rate taxpayer has no further tax to pay.

Under the tax-credit proposals[1] of 1972 those covered by the scheme would have received weekly tax credits at the proposed rates of £4 per week for a single adult, £6 per couple, and £2 per child, and would have been taxed at a basic rate of 30 per cent on all income, except that those with the highest income would have continued to pay higher rate tax. The main groups excluded from the scheme were to have been the self-employed, and those earning less than one-quarter of national average earnings (those receiving national insurance benefits would have been covered). Under these proposals, which were essentially a negative income tax scheme, people with low income would have received a tax-credit which was greater than their tax liability, and so their take-home pay would have been greater than their gross pay.

This is not the place to discuss in any detail the changes in PAYE that the tax-credit system would have brought about. The major change would have been the move to a non-cumulative system of withholding. This would have been possible because the vast majority of people would have paid a basic rate of tax on all their income. Accompanying this would have been a number of technical changes to enable non-cumulative withholding to be accurate, such as the paying of life assurance premia on a net-of-tax basis. In addition, national insurance sickness and unemployment benefits would have become taxable, but would also have had credits attached. The questions of non-cumulative withholding, and the taxation of short-term national insurance benefits were discussed in Chapter 7. We shall return to some of the more general issues raised by negative income taxation in Chapter 14.

2.1.2 *Capital gains tax* Capital gains tax made its first appearance in the UK with the introduction of a speculative gains tax in 1962, under which short-term gains were subject to the individual's marginal rate of income tax and surtax. In 1965 a much more comprehensive system was introduced. For individuals, short-term gains (i.e. gains realized on assets held for less than 12 months) were subject to the appropriate rate of income tax and surtax; long-term gains were taxed either at 30 per cent or, if more favourable to the taxpayer, at his marginal rate of income tax and surtax in respect of half of his gains up to a maximum of £5,000 and the whole of his gains in excess of £5,000. The short- and

[1] See, for example, *Proposals for a Tax-Credit System*, Cmnd. 5116, October 1972; Select Committee on Tax-Credit, Session 1972/73, *Report and Proceedings*, HC 341–I, 341–II, 341–III (HMSO, 1973); also A. R. Prest, 'Proposals for a Tax-Credit System', *British Tax Review*, No. 1, 1973, and N. A. Barr and J. F. H. Roper, 'Tax-Credits: An Optimistic Appraisal', *Three Banks Review*, No. 101, March 1974.

long-term taxes were mutually exclusive in that no single gain could be subjected to tax under both heads. Short-term losses could be offset against short-term gains, and long-term losses against long-term gains, but there was no provision for offsetting long against short, or vice versa. As for companies, no distinction was drawn between short- and long-term gains, all being treated as part of company profits and taxed accordingly. There were some provisions whereby shareholders in unit and investment trusts were allowed personal tax relief on capital gains tax paid by the trusts. No such provisions existed for shareholders in other companies.

This system applied to a very wide range of capital gains, the most important exceptions now being UK government and government guaranteed stocks held for more than twelve months, motor vehicles, gambling winnings, owner-occupied principal residences and chattels (if worth less than £2,000). A 'rollover' provision applied to business assets sold at a profit but subsequently replaced. Capital gains of charities and pension funds were exempt but those on assets disposed of by gift or death if above a certain limit were not.

Since 1970 there have been considerable changes. First, experience showed that the administrative burden of collecting taxes on very small capital gains was not worth the effort; accordingly, there is now in effect an exemption in respect of the first £1,000 of gains in a year, with the next £4,000 being charged at 15 per cent, the next £4,500 being charged at 50 per cent and the balance charged at 30 per cent. The purpose of the 50 per cent rate is to bring the average rate of tax up to 30 per cent for gains of £9,500. So large gains are taxed at a flat 30 per cent. Secondly, the distinction between short- and long-term gains tax has been abolished, and all gains are now subject to long-term tax only. The only remaining vestige of the former distinction is that gains on government stocks are taxable if they are held for less than a year, but exempt if held for longer. Thirdly, the liability to capital gains tax at death (or in respect of certain gifts, inter vivos, such as to national institutions) was extinguished. Fourthly, the provisions designed to integrate the liabilities of unit or investment trusts and those of their shareholders were simplified and further liberalized. Fifthly, as we shall see shortly, the rate of taxation of company capital gains was, in effect, brought into line with the normal rate for individuals of 30 per cent. Finally, since 1978 there has been a rollover relief which applies when someone makes a gift of business assets. The effect is that the donor is not liable to capital gains tax, but the donee will be liable on a disposal of the assets. We shall return to some of these matters in Chapters 13 and 16.

Gains from land development have had a complex history. Between 1967 and 1970 they were subject to a special betterment levy, and from 1970 to 1974 to long-term capital gains tax. From 1974 to 1976 certain gains arising from the disposal of land and buildings were taxed as income. From 1976 land gains have been subject to Development Land Tax, which will be discussed later.

2.1.3 *Corporation tax* The historical background of corporation tax is somewhat complex. Before 1937 there was no special system of taxing companies in the UK. They were subject to income tax at the standard rate on undistributed profits and were also required to withhold tax at the standard rate on distributions and account to the Inland Revenue for it; shareholders paying tax at the standard rate had no further obligation, while those paying higher or lower rates paid additional sums or received refunds. Between 1937 and 1965 companies were required also to pay additional tax on the whole of their profits, distributed and undistributed, but defined so as to exclude interest on borrowed money; the profits tax rate at the end of the period was 15 per cent.

This system was superseded by corporation tax. From 1966 companies were no longer subject to income tax or profits tax but to corporation tax (at 40 per cent initially) on the whole of their profits. In addition, income tax had to be deducted at the standard rate from dividends (Schedule F), with subsequent adjustments for low or high income shareholders.

In 1973 the system was changed again; while retaining the name corporation tax the principle of *imputation* was introduced. The essence of the 1973 system is a partial set-off, or imputation, of company taxation against personal taxation. In other words, part of the corporation tax paid by a company on its distributed profits is allowed to the individual shareholder as a credit against his income tax liability. For the basic rate of income tax of 33 per cent operating in 1978/79, this works as follows: the company pays corporation tax (at 52 per cent in 1978/79) on the whole of its profits, but in two parts. First, when a dividend is paid out it pays advance corporation tax (ACT) at a rate equal to 33/67 of the dividend. Secondly, mainstream corporation tax is computed on the basis of 52 per cent of the profits for an accounting period *less* ACT on distributions.

An example may help to show the way the system works. Suppose a company wishes to distribute a dividend of £67. The ACT on this dividend is 33/67 of £67, or £33. So the company sends £67 to its shareholder and £33 to the Inland Revenue. At the end of the accounting period the company calculates its profit, and pays the government corporation tax at a rate of 52 per cent of this profit, *minus* the ACT that it has already paid. From the viewpoint of the shareholder, the system works in the following way. His gross receipts are the dividend of £67 *plus* the ACT paid by the corporation of £33. His gross dividend is therefore £100, which is the basis for income tax. If the shareholder's liability is at the basic rate (33 per cent in 1978/79) there is no additional payment due, as the ACT already paid (£33) is given as a credit against income tax liability. Non-taxable shareholders can claim payment of the £33, and higher rate taxpayers have to pay at a rate equal to the difference between their marginal rate and the basic rate.

We shall have quite a lot to say about the imputation system in Part III (especially Chapter 17) and so will not discuss it further now. But two other points about company taxation need to be made. First, capital gains made by companies were taxed at the normal level of corporation tax until 1973, without any relief for capital gains tax liabilities of shareholders (apart from unit and investment trusts). Since 1973, only a proportion of company capital gains are taxable thereby making the effective rate 30 per cent, the same as that for individuals. Secondly, small companies are given preferential treatment: where profits were less than £50,000 per year in the financial year 1977 income was taxed at a reduced rate of corporation tax of 42 per cent, and there was also a tapering concession on profits in the £50,000 to £85,000 range; and again, only a proportion of capital gains are taxed.

Having discussed how company profits are taxed, it is necessary also to outline what exactly constitutes corporate profits for the purposes of corporation tax. Starting from a crude definition of profit as the difference between total revenue (i.e. turnover) and total costs, no problem arises so long as both revenue and costs relate to current rather than to capital items. Thus, for instance, the costs of hiring labour and buying raw materials are deductible for tax purposes and so are interest charges on debt. However, a problem arises in the case of capital inputs such as buildings or machinery. All the expenditure on such items can take place in a single year, but the flow of services arising from them takes place over several years. The question, therefore, is how rapidly the tax authorities allow such items to be offset against tax. The various concessions for company investment are discussed below.

In addition to normal wear and tear allowances, British companies have enjoyed a variety of concessions since World War II.

(a) *Initial allowances* were first introduced in 1945. They enable a firm to write off a given percentage of the cost of a capital asset in the year of acquisition in addition to the normal wear and tear due for that year. This initial allowance in the first year is compensated by smaller allowances in succeeding years, so that no more than the original cost is written off over the life of the equipment.

(b) *Investment allowances* were first introduced in 1954. In this case, the special allowance in the year of acquisition of the capital equipment is a net addition to the total of allowances granted over the life of the equipment, e.g. if the investment allowance is 20 per cent, the total allowances over the life-span are 120 per cent, the normal wear and tear allowance being granted every year.

(c) *Free depreciation* was first introduced in 1963, and allowed firms to write off the original cost of capital equipment over any time period and without any pre-determined rules.

(d) *Investment grants* were first introduced in 1966. They were a straight subsidy on the purchase of new plant and machinery by the manufacturing, extractive and construction industries. Rates varied over time and depended on geographical location; the administration was in the hands of the department responsible for industry rather than the Inland Revenue; and the basis for depreciation was capital cost *less* the cash grant. Initial allowances were available for assets not qualifying for investment grants.

In 1971 investment grants disappeared and initial allowances were restored, only to have a resurrection of grants, albeit in somewhat different form in 1972. Given this history any description may well be out of date by the time this appears in print, but a summary of the situation in early 1979 is as follows. There was a 100 per cent first year allowance for all investment in plant, machinery (other than motor cars) and aircraft, and free depreciation for new ships. New industrial buildings were granted an initial allowance of 50 per cent plus 4 per cent per annum; new hotel buildings received an initial allowance of 20 per cent plus 4 per cent per annum; and new agricultural buildings an allowance of 20 per cent plus 10 per cent per annum. There were also initial and annual allowances for mining works. Thus most industrial investment enjoyed accelerated depreciation. There was also a variety of special cash grants to certain types of investments in certain regions of the country.

Stock relief: since 1974 there has existed an entirely new type of tax relief, which is best explained in a slightly roundabout way. Business profits for tax purposes are calculated broadly as

$$\text{profit} = \text{value of output} - \text{cost of inputs.}$$

Output can be used in two ways: (a) as sales, and (b) as additions to stock. Thus,

$$\text{value of output} = \text{value of sales} + \text{change in the value of stock.}$$

The last term can be positive (if stocks increase) or negative (if they are drawn down), and can be extended to cover stocks of inputs as well as stocks of output. More explicitly,

$$\text{change in the value of stock} = \text{value of closing stock} - \text{value of opening stock.}$$

So company profits can be calculated as

$$\text{profit} = \text{value of sales} - \text{cost of inputs} + (\text{value of closing stock} - \text{value of opening stock}).$$

Now, if stock in volume terms remains constant then the change in physical stock is zero and the term in brackets should also be zero. This will be so when prices are constant, in which case, if opening and closing stocks are identical, so is their value.

But if prices rise over the accounting period the money value of a given volume of stock will be greater at the end of the period than at the beginning, and so the term in brackets will be positive and hence 'profits' higher even if physical stock is unchanged. This problem became acute after 1973 when rates of inflation rose sharply and as a result, company profits as measured for tax purposes and hence also for tax liabilities were artificially inflated by rising prices.

Concern with the problem has various dimensions. In 1974 the Government appointed an Inflation Accounting Committee (the Sandilands Committee) to look into financial reporting under inflation. The Committee's report was published in 1975[1] and has been the subject of heated discussion (see Chapters 13 and 16, below).

[1] *Report of the Inflation Accounting Committee*, Cmnd. 6225 (HMSO, 1975).

But in 1974 companies were already facing severe liquidity problems as a result of inflationary stock increases and so the Chancellor acted in advance of any agreement on methods of inflation accounting. *Stock relief* was introduced in November 1974, backdated to 1973. Under this scheme companies could deduct for tax purposes the excess of the change in the book value of stocks over 10 per cent of gross trading profits; in other words the maximum taxable profit resulting from any increase in the value of stock was 10 per cent of gross trading profit. The figure of 10 per cent was chosen as a rough average for the economy as a whole of the increase in profit not attributable to inflationary increases in the value of stock. In 1976 the figure was raised to 15 per cent of trading profit after depreciation allowances, with the idea of making the concession more beneficial to those firms with heavy capital investment programmes.[1] In 1978 steps were taken to convert these tax deferrals into permanent tax reductions. We shall return to these matters in Chapter 16.

2.1.4 *Other Inland Revenue taxes* We start with death duties and capital transfer tax, and then proceed to stamp duties, petroleum revenue tax, and development land tax.

Death duties in one form or another can be traced back to 1694, though the estate duty of modern times originated in 1894. This tax, which was phased out after 1974, charged tax at a progressive rate on the total value of a person's estate at death. Gifts, inter-vivos, were taxable if made within seven years of death, the valuation of the gift being progressively reduced in the case of gifts made more than four years before death. Gifts to certain types of institution (e.g. the British Museum) were exempt under all circumstances; gifts to charities were exempt if under £50,000, or if made more than one year before death.

Capital transfer tax, first announced on 26 March 1974, was introduced in the Finance Act 1975 and took effect from 26 March 1974 for transfers, inter-vivos, and from 12 March 1975 for death transfers. The tax is chargeable on a cumulative basis on an individual's lifetime transfers plus his estate at death. In principle the tax is similar to the combination of an estate duty and a gift tax. The operation of capital transfer tax is best described by outlining (a) those transfers which are exempt from the tax, and (b) the tax rate otherwise applicable.

[1] Under both schemes relief was recovered when stock values fell over a period of account. The amount of the recovery was the lesser of the actual fall in value or the total relief allowed, and unrecovered, for earlier periods.

The following types of transfer are exempt from capital transfer tax:

(i) transfers between husband and wife in life and on death;[1]

(ii) transfers made by an individual in any one tax year up to a value of £2,000 plus the amount by which the transfers set against this exemption in the previous year fall short of £2,000;

(iii) Outright gifts to any one individual in any one tax year up to a value of £100;

(iv) transfers made out of an individual's income after tax, as part of normal expenditure;

(v) transfers up to certain limits made as a wedding gift;

(vi) a variety of other transfers, such as the maintenance of a former spouse, or of a child in full-time education, or of a dependent relative; transfers to charities and to certain bodies concerned with the preservation of the national heritage; and the transfer of certain works of art subject to undertakings about the provision of access to the public.

The rates of tax applicable are progressively higher on successive slices of the cumulative total of chargeable transfers, with a lower scale of rates for lifetime transfers up to the value of £310,000 than for transfers on death. Under both scales the first £25,000 of transfers is tax free; the rates on the remainder of lifetime transfers rise from 5 per cent on the slice between £25,000 and £30,000 to 75 per cent on the excess over about £2 million, as shown in Table 9.6. The rates on transfers at death differ in as much as the marginal rates rise more sharply for transfers up to £160,000, and more slowly for transfers between £160,000 and £510,000.

Relief is given to businesses, including farmers; under certain circumstances the value of a business can be reduced by 50 per cent for capital transfer tax purposes. There are also special reliefs in respect of agricultural property transferred by full-time working farmers and of growing timber transferred on death.

Finally, we should turn briefly to the complex question of the treatment of trusts under capital transfer tax.[2] For this purpose it is necessary to distinguish between two types of trust. Where an interest in possession exists in the settled property (i.e. where the trust is in favour of named beneficiaries) the person entitled to the interest is treated as though he owned the capital and the taxation consequences are largely the same as if he owned the property himself. On the other hand, where no such interest in possession exists (i.e. where the trustee has discre-

[1] Provided that the recipient spouse is domiciled in the UK.

[2] For a useful introduction to the subject of trusts, see Meade, *op. cit.*, Chapter 19.

tion as to who benefits from the trust) then the settlement is treated as a separate entity, with its own independent cumulation. Capital transfer tax is charged when property leaves the settlement, or if an interest in possession arises; tax is also charged every ten years (at 30 per cent of the normal rate of tax).

Table 9.6

Capital Transfer Tax Rates, UK, 1978/79

<table>
<tr><th>Slice of chargeable transfer (£000s)</th><th>Lifetime transfers tax rate (%)</th><th>Transfers on death tax rate (%)</th></tr>
<tr><td>0–25</td><td>0</td><td>0</td></tr>
<tr><td>25–30</td><td>5</td><td>10</td></tr>
<tr><td>30–35</td><td>7½</td><td>15</td></tr>
<tr><td>25–40</td><td>10</td><td>20</td></tr>
<tr><td>40–50</td><td>12½</td><td>25</td></tr>
<tr><td>50–60</td><td>15</td><td>30</td></tr>
<tr><td>60–70</td><td>17½</td><td>35</td></tr>
<tr><td>70–90</td><td>20</td><td>40</td></tr>
<tr><td>90–110</td><td>22½</td><td>45</td></tr>
<tr><td>110–130</td><td>27½</td><td>50</td></tr>
<tr><td>130–160</td><td>35</td><td>55</td></tr>
<tr><td>160–210</td><td>42½</td><td rowspan="4">60</td></tr>
<tr><td>210–260</td><td>50</td></tr>
<tr><td>260–310</td><td>55</td></tr>
<tr><td>310–510</td><td>60</td></tr>
<tr><td>510–1010</td><td>65</td><td>65</td></tr>
<tr><td>1010–2010</td><td>70</td><td>70</td></tr>
<tr><td>Over 2010</td><td>75</td><td>75</td></tr>
</table>

Stamp duties, like death duties, have a long history stretching back to the seventeenth century, but in their present form they date from the Stamp Act of 1891 and subsequent amending legislation. The main duties now are: ad valorem duties on the transfer of property (e.g. the sale of houses and land whose sale price exceeds £15,000, and of shares); capital duty payable in respect of chargeable transactions by capital companies as defined by the 1973 Finance Act; and duties on life insurance policies. The first is by far the most important and accounts for some 90 per cent of total yield. There are also a number of minor imposts which are not worth listing in detail.

Wealth tax: a type of tax on capital which exists in other countries is in the form of an annual tax on an individual's net worth. In the mid-1970s there was considerable discussion about introducing such a tax in the UK, though so far there has been no legislation.

Petroleum Taxation: a special system of royalties and taxation of profits has been created by successive Acts and regulations to deal with the extraction of North Sea oil and gas, of which the most recent are the Oil Taxation Act of 1975 and the Petroleum Submarine Pipelines Act 1975. The avowed object of the system is to ensure the UK maximum benefits from its own energy resources, while leaving producing companies an adequate return. The system consists of three elements; (a) Royalty, (b) Petroleum Revenue Tax, and (c) Corporation Tax, levied in that order.

Royalty is 12½ per cent of the landed value of the oil less, for First (1964) to Fourth (1971–2) Round Licences only, the cost of conveying the oil ashore and of initial treatment (not refining). In addition, the Secretary of State is empowered at his discretion, with the consent of the Treasury, to refund royalties free of petroleum revenue tax and corporation tax in whole or in part to enable a licensee to develop or continue production from a field if the licensee would not otherwise do so because the field did not satisfy normal commercial criteria.

Petroleum revenue tax is chargeable on each field separately at a rate of 45 per cent of the net income from the field, defined as the gross revenue from the field *minus* royalties and operating costs (excluding interest payments). The tax applied from 13 November 1974, though capital expenditure incurred earlier is allowed against it. The Government announced in August 1978 its intention to raise the rate of petroleum revenue tax from 45 to 60 per cent as from 1 January 1979.

Three main additional allowances are available against petroleum revenue tax.

(a) No tax need be paid until the net revenue received exceeds the capital spent on exploration and development plus an 'uplift' of 75 per cent on most of this expenditure (to be reduced to 35 per cent from August 1978 under the Government's proposals) which in part compensates the companies for the fact that interest payments are not allowed against petroleum revenue tax. This is intended to help companies to recover their capital early in the life of a field, thus increasing the net-of-tax return to the companies at that time. The 175 per cent capital allowance (135 per cent under the Government's proposals) can be spread over several years if a company so desires. A group may also set-off against its profits on an operative field abortive exploration expenditure elsewhere in the North Sea. This is the only significant exception to the 'field-by-field' nature of the tax.

(b) A tax-free allowance is available to set against petroleum revenue tax liability after account has been taken of all other deductions equivalent to the money value of one million tons of production per year up to a cumulative maximum of 10 million tons per field (to be reduced to ½ million metric tonnes with a maximum of 5 million tonnes under the Government's proposals). There is no carry forward or backward of this allowance.

Thus the petroleum revenue tax regime operating in late 1978 was a 45 per cent rate, 75 per cent uplift and one million long tons oil allowance. The Government proposed to change this to a 60 per cent rate, 35 per cent uplift, and ½ million metric tonnes oil allowance. As of March 1979 it was intended that these changes be implemented in the main 1979 Finance Bill.[1]

(c) Finally, a 'safeguard' provision restricts the total petroleum revenue tax charge to not more than 80 per cent of the amount by which net income exceeds 30 per cent of total capital expenditure on the field to date. Thus, if capital expenditure was £100 and net income (as defined above) was £50, the maximum petroleum revenue tax payable would be 80 per cent of the difference between £50 and £30 (30 per cent of capital expenditure) – i.e. £16. If the net income is less than this proportion of capital expenditure, no petroleum revenue tax is payable. This provision was designed principally to offer protection to the licensees against a fall in the price of oil relative to other prices.

Corporation tax – ring fence: in calculating profits for corporation tax purposes, operating costs, ro63lties and petroleum revenue tax are deducted. To protect its revenues, the Government has erected a so-called 'ring fence' around North Sea oil operations. This means, in effect, that the oil companies cannot set-off against their oil profits any losses or capital allowances on their non-oil activities elsewhere in the UK or from their oil activities outside the UK. This ring fence came into operation for most purposes on 11 July 1974.

Development land tax, which was introduced by the Development Land Tax Act 1976, was envisaged as the first part of a more wide-ranging scheme for the control of land development. The tax is

[1] See Appendix to Chapter 9.

imposed on development value realized from the disposal of an interest in land. It is also charged when development value is realized on the commencement of a project of material development. It replaces the development gains charge under which certain capital gains were taxed as income. The tax is complex and we shall describe it only in the broadest outline.

In general, development land tax is levied on the difference between disposal proceeds (which in the case of a project of material development are taken as the market value of the interest with permission to carry out that development) and a base value (which may be related either to the value of the interest in its current use or to the cost of its acquisition, together with expenditure on certain improvements). With some exceptions the tax applies to development value realized on disposals made on or after 1 August 1976. The rate of development land tax is 80 per cent; but the first £10,000 of development value realized in any financial year is exempt and the next £150,000 realized in any financial year up to and including that ending on 31 March 1980 is charged at 66⅔ per cent.

There are several major exemptions to development land tax. First, the tax applies only to developments involving a potential change of land use or redevelopment; where no such change occurs, capital gains tax applies. Secondly, the sale by an owner-occupier of his principal residence is exempt. Finally, tax is not charged where an interest in land is passed on as an outright gift or on death. In this case capital transfer tax will normally apply.

2.2 *Customs and Excise*

The taxes collected by Customs and Excise can be dealt with more briefly than those administered by the Inland Revenue. At first sight it might be thought that the most useful distinction would be that between the customs component and excise component of these taxes. In fact, customs duties in the UK are levied for two fundamentally different reasons: (a) to protect British and latterly EEC producers, and (b) to raise revenue (in conjunction with comparable excise duties). In what follows we therefore make the distinction between protective duties, consisting of some customs duties, and revenue duties, consisting of excise duties and the remaining customs duties. Though this distinction can be a trifle blurred at times, it is probably the most useful.

Looking first at protective duties it is worth noting that although customs duties date back to the time of King John, the present protective duties are of comparatively recent origin. The first imposition came in 1915 with a 33⅓ per cent duty on a limited range of goods. These duties were modified and extended during the 1920s and 1930s, both in the form of specific Acts like the Safeguarding of Industry Act of 1921 and in the Import Duties Act 1932 (adding a general ad valorem duty) and in various Finance Acts to protect specific commodities such as silk and hops. The broad effect of this legislation, which was consolidated by the Import Duties Act of 1958, can be summarized by saying that it provided for the imposition of an import duty unless otherwise exempted; this was a decisive change of principle from the earlier attempts at protecting individual commodities. Since 1945, however, the various tariff negotiations under the General Agreement on Tariffs and Trade have resulted in reductions of duty or at least agreements not to increase them. Since entry into the EEC in 1973, the Common External Tariff of the Community has gradually replaced the earlier tariff structure. Import levies on foodstuffs were also adopted. In 1977/78 the yield from customs duties and EEC agricultural levies was £860 million, or about 2½ per cent of the value of all imports. Import duties and levies are paid to the EEC under the European Communities Act 1972 and a refund is made to the UK Government to cover collection costs.

The most important individual excise tax is the tobacco tax, which was expected to yield about £2,450 million in 1978/79. Duty used to be charged by weight of the leaf tobacco before manufacture, but since 1976 when the tobacco products duty, which is charged on the finished product, was introduced, part of the duty on cigarettes has been an ad valorem charge on the retail price. At the same time provision was made to alter by Order the rates of the new duty by up to 10 per cent in either direction. Phasing out of the old customs revenue duty was completed at the end of 1977 as part of a programme of tax harmonization with the EEC.

Duties on alcohol and alcoholic drinks were expected to bring in some £2,400 million in 1978/79. The excise duties on spirits, beer, imported wine, made-wine (formerly British wine) and cider contribute to the total. Before accession to the EEC customs revenue duties gave a preference to Commonwealth products, but since final adoption of the common customs tariff of the EEC only EEC products are exempt from protective import duties and the excise duties are applied to all products irrespective of origin.

The third important group of excise duties is composed of the taxes on light and heavy hydrocarbon oils, which are charged alike on home produced and imported oils, and which were expected to yield about £2,500 million in 1978/79. About two-thirds of this total derived from the duty on light oils (mostly petrol) and of the third contributed by heavy oils, most is for diesel fuel. The system of duties is complex, reliefs of various kinds being given for miscellaneous purposes. Revenue from indigenous oil production is also derived from the petroleum revenue tax administered by the Inland Revenue, the proceeds of which will become increasingly important as more North Sea oil is brought ashore.[1]

The three main groups of duties were expected to yield £7,350 million in 1978/79; more than half of the total revenue collected by Customs and Excise. Other duties can be quickly described. The main betting duties in 1978/79 were *pool betting duty* of 4 per cent on the stake money on pool betting and fixed-odds coupon betting (mainly the football pools), and *general betting duty* of 7½ per cent on most bets other than on-course bets. There are also various duties on gaming machines and certain gaming premises. Various miscellaneous duties such as those on matches and mechanical lighters are too unimportant to justify description.

Purchase tax was a major tax until 1973. It was levied at a wholesale level on a fairly narrow range of domestically consumed goods, and did not apply to any services. There was more than one rate of tax, with the idea of differentiating between more and less necessary items of consumption. In its last year of operation, 1972/73, it yielded some £1,400 million. There remains a vestige of this tax, *car tax*, of 10 per cent on the wholesale value of a new car. This was introduced from 1 April 1973 in order to prevent any substantial reduction in the tax on cars.

Value added tax (VAT) was introduced on 1 April 1973 in place of purchase tax.[2] This tax, which is a post-war development, was first operated in the mid-1950s in France. Since then it has spread to many countries and is a key element in the finances of the EEC countries and of the Community itself.

[1] See pp. 206–7.

[2] And also of *Selective Employment Tax* which was imposed on labour employed in the non-manufacturing part of the economy. The tax was in operation from 1966 to 1973; its effects have been analysed by W. B. Reddaway, *Effects of the Selective Employment Tax* (*First Report*, HMSO, 1970; *Final Report*, Cambridge University Press, 1973).

There was also an associated feature, the *Regional Employment Premium*, a system of subsidizing labour employed in manufacturing establishments in Development Areas.

As we have seen,[1] a value added tax can in principle approximate to a tax on income or on consumption, depending on the precise computation of value added. UK legislation, like that in other European countries, allows the cost of capital inputs to be deducted, and so, in effect, we have a tax on consumption rather than income. The main difference from a retail sales tax is in the method of collection. Two points are noteworthy. First, by its very nature a Value Added Tax is a multi-stage tax, being collected at all the different stages in the production process and not just at the final stage, as with a retail sales tax. Secondly, tax liability is computed by the 'tax from tax' method. Liability for any transaction is based on 'output tax' (i.e. the tax certified as having been paid on the total value of sales) *minus* 'input tax' (i.e. tax certified as having been paid on purchases). In other words, tax liability on value added is computed indirectly by deducting input tax from output tax. The great advantage of this method is the self-policing element in tax collection; it is clearly to the advantage of anyone paying input tax to obtain written evidence of this fact. This more or less compels the previous stage of production to declare the amount, which from its point of view is an output tax, to the tax authorities. Mass evasion under such a system is not easy.

Another feature of the UK system is that it is on a 'destination' rather than an 'origin' basis, i.e. imports are taxable but exports not so. This is another standard feature in Europe.

As regards the coverage of the tax we need to discuss both (a) the range of activities to which the tax applies, and (b) the rates of tax applicable to such activities. The general principle for coverage is that anyone engaging in business activities is within the scope of the tax unless specifically exempted. The tax covers a very wide range of transactions, services as well as goods, second-hand goods as well as new ones, hire purchase and imputed sales as well as supplies for cash. There are two very different kinds of exemptions. First, traders with sales of taxable items totalling less than a certain amount (£10,000 per annum in 1978/79) are, subject to small qualifications, exempt if they so wish. Secondly, various activities are specifically exempt. This means that they are outside the tax net altogether, e.g. postal services provided by the GPO, betting (already taxed under other legislation), various financial activities (insurance, banking, stock-exchange jobbing), and the greater part of education and health provision. There are disadvantages as well as advantages of being exempt; output is not

[1] See pp. 48–50.

taxable but any tax on inputs has to be borne by the purchaser (i.e. he cannot claim back his input tax).

Turning to the rates of tax, taxable supplies may be liable to tax at the standard rate (8 per cent in 1978/79), at the higher rate (12½ per cent in 1978/79), or zero-rated. Zero rating is different from exemption in as much as not only is there no liability for tax on outputs, but any element of input tax paid at previous stages can be reclaimed. It is thus possible to de-tax output of a particular commodity completely. Examples are exports, most food for human consumption, domestic fuel and light, most types of passenger transport, and housing. Inevitably, the border line between the 12½ per cent rate, the 8 per cent rate, the zero rate and exemptions is bound to be arbitrary and there are some well-publicized examples, e.g. take-away food is zero-rated while restaurant meals are not.

A few other points should be mentioned about the UK system of VAT. The number of collecting points is some 1¼ million, much greater than the 70,000 or so under purchase tax. This has necessitated a large administrative staff of around 12,000[1] to run the system. The yield in 1978/79 was estimated to be some £4,775 million. The tax is collected in arrears (three-monthly is the standard basis).

As we shall discuss in some detail in Chapter 19, VAT also has major EEC implications. Since entry into the EEC the UK Government, with other Member States, has agreed to a measure of structural harmonization of VAT systems. This is contained in the EEC Sixth Council Directive on value added tax, which came into force for the UK on 1 January 1978. It entailed very little change in our existing system.

Since 1 January 1979 Member States which have implemented the Sixth Directive are committed to pay into the EEC Budget Community 'own resources' a sum equivalent to the proceeds of levying a notional tax rate of up to 1 per cent of the harmonized tax base agreed under the Directive. In practice the sum is calculated in this way, but is paid out of the Consolidated Fund, and thus has no direct effect on VAT receipts.

The *Regulator* system was introduced in 1961. Under this system the Treasury has power to raise or lower the rates of the main excise duties and VAT to a maximum in any one year of 10 per cent and 25 per cent, respectively, of existing rates, and subject to Parliamentary approval within a given time. These provisions introduced an important element of flexibility.

[1] The figure is an estimate for 1977/78, see *Hansard*, Col. 950, 16 May 1978.

2.3 *Other central government financial sources*

To complete our description of the individual taxes we need to mention briefly those not coming under the Inland Revenue or Customs and Excise. Driving licences and motor vehicle licences are issued by the Driver and Vehicle Licensing Centre at Swansea. An annual charge known as *vehicle excise duty*, which is administered by the Department of the Environment, is levied at different rates on different vehicles. The annual charge for cars in 1978 was £50, though in early 1979 it became government policy to abolish this charge gradually and replace it with an increased petrol duty designed to yield the same revenue.

The national insurance surcharge is a major departure from previous tradition, inasmuch as it is, in essence, a payroll tax. Its estimated yield in 1978/79 was about £1,775 million.[1] We shall not pursue the matter in this chapter, but will discuss it in some detail in Chapter 10.[2]

The *Miscellaneous* component in Table 9.3 (£1,541 million in 1978/79) is composed of a wide variety of items, such as radio and television licences, various elements of interest payments, and loans repayments.

This completes our discussion of the Revenue and Expenditure items shown in Tables 9.1 and 9.3. Our remaining task is to survey the National Loans Fund, the main components of which are shown in Table 9.7. The receipts of the National Loans Fund come from two sources. The first, amounting to £3,240 million, consisted of the interest on previous loans, together with such items as the profits of the Issue Department of the Bank of England. The second item of receipts, amounting to £3,160 million, is simply an out payment from the Consolidated Fund.[3] Expenditure by the National Loans Fund consists of the service of the National Debt (including management costs), amounting to £6,400 million in 1978/79, and various loans. These loans are to the nationalized industries and, in 1978/79, particularly to local authorities, to whom some £1,123 million was lent.

The relation between the Revenue and Expenditure items covered by the Consolidated Fund on the one hand, and the National Loans Fund on the other, is shown in Table 9.8. The combined deficit of the Consolidated Fund (estimated at £8,632 million in 1978/79), and that of the National Loans Fund (estimated at £1,240 million in 1978/79),

[1] This is higher than the figure in Table 9.3 because of a post-budgetary increase in the rate of surcharge.

[2] See pp. 233–4.

[3] The Consolidated Fund contains all Central Government current account receipts, as listed in Table 9.3.

Table 9.7

UK Central Government National Loans Fund, 1978/79 (est.) (£m)

Receipts		*Payments*		
Interest, etc.	3,240	Service of National Debt		6,400
Receipts from Consolidated Fund	3,160	Loans (net)		1,240
		Nationalized industries and other public corporations	21	
		Local authorities	1,123	
		Other	96	
TOTAL	6,400	TOTAL		7,640

Source: *UK Financial Statement and Budget Report, 1978/79.*

Table 9.8

Summary of Central Government Transactions, 1978/79 (est.) (£m)

Consolidated Fund	
Total revenue (Table 9.3)	42,746
Total expenditure (Table 9.1)	51,378
Deficit	−8,632
National Loans Fund	
Consolidated Fund deficit (as above)	−8,632
Other transactions	
receipts (Table 9.7)	+6,400
payments (Table 9.7)	−7,640
Total Net Borrowing by National Loans Fund	−9,872
Other funds and accounts (net)	+1,935
Central Government Borrowing Requirement	−7,937

Source: *UK Financial Statement and Budget Report, 1978/79.*

together with certain other miscellaneous items, make up the Central Government Borrowing Requirement, estimated for 1978/79 at £7,937 million. This figure is the major component of the Public Sector Borrowing Requirement (PSBR), which is widely regarded as one of the key variables of macroeconomic control. As we saw in Chapter 6, a government can obtain current resources from the private sector either by taxation or by borrowing. The two major sources of borrowing are from the public (usually through the sale of various sorts of government bonds), or from the Bank of England, mainly through expansion of the money supply. The PSBR shows the excess of intended spending by all levels of the public sector combined over current tax revenues, which will have to be financed by such borrowing.[1]

3 PARLIAMENTARY PROCEDURE

3.1 *Revenue and expenditure*

In this section we summarize the Parliamentary procedures for the control of expenditure and the raising of revenue, and in section 3.2 their pros and cons.

Parliamentary control of expenditure derives mainly from the way in which the government plans and controls its own expenditure, so that the present system is designed more to meet the government's than Parliament's needs. At present there are three main systems: (a) the public expenditure survey (PESC); (b) the supply estimates; and (c) cash limits. We discuss these in turn, and then look at procedures connected with the Appropriation Account and the Consolidated Fund Standing Services.

(1) *The public expenditure survey*: in any one year public expenditure is determined largely by decisions made some time earlier. Public spending is planned for five years by the government on the basis of its strategy and its assumptions about the growth of available resources, and of changes in relative prices. The latter change is measured by the *relative price effect* which takes account of the fact that the prices of commodities bought by public authorities tend to rise faster than prices generally. There are two reasons for this. First, throughout the economy the price of labour tends to rise faster than the general price level (i.e. real earnings increase); and secondly, public expenditure has a higher average direct labour content than does activity in the private

[1] For a wide-ranging critique see T. S. Ward and R. R. Neild, *The Measurement and Reform of Budgetary Policy* (Heinemann, 1978).

sector. On average the relative price effect adds some 0.6 per cent per year to total public expenditure.[1]

Plans for future spending are published annually around the end of the year in the public expenditure White Paper together with a brief commentary on medium-term prospects for the economy, and sometimes projections of future revenue.

Each White Paper sets out the government's expenditure plans at constant prices for 15 main programmes covering all public expenditure over a period of four years, with year 1 being the year in which the White Paper is published.[2] The plans for year 2 are comparatively firm, those for later years less so. The plans are arranged both by programme and by spending authority. In addition there is a breakdown between (a) expenditure using up real resources, (b) those which are merely transfers, and (c) those which involve changes on capital account.

The White Paper which sets out the government's decisions is normally debated by Parliament but its spending plans do not need specific Parliamentary approval. Indeed, it was designed in 1961 as a Government planning mechanism rather than a Parliamentary one, and the regular series of White Papers did not start until 1969.[3] From Parliament's viewpoint its main value is in the information it gives about the government's medium-term spending plans in the light of its assessment of future economic trends. This is very different from the information needed for any detailed scrutiny of expenditure.

(2) *The supply estimates* have a long history and have traditionally been the most important means of Parliamentary control. We should note from the start that though the terms 'estimate' and 'supply estimate' continue to be used for historical reasons, the word 'estimate' is not used in its ordinary sense. A supply estimate is not in any sense a prediction of future expenditure, but much more a management limit beyond which the Treasury will not authorize expenditure. Actual expenditure could be lower (because of under-spending) or higher (because of the later adoption of a supplementary estimate).

[1] See *Public Expenditure White Papers, Handbook on Methodology* (HMSO, 1972), paras. 68–71, and P. M. Rees and F. P. Thompson, 'The Relative Price Effect in Public Expenditure: Its Nature and Method of Calculation', *Statistical News*, No. 18 (HMSO, August 1972).

[2] See, for instance, *The Government's Expenditure Plans 1979/80 to 1982/83*, Cmnd. 7439 (HMSO, 1979).

[3] The origin of the Public Expenditure Survey is to be found in the Plowden Committee Report, *Control of Public Expenditure*, Cmnd. 1432 (HMSO, 1961). For the changes in 1969 see the Green Paper, *Public Expenditure: A New Presentation*, Cmnd. 4107 (HMSO, 1969), and also First Report, Select Committee on Procedure, Session 1968/69, *Scrutiny of Public Expenditure and Administration*, HC 410 (HMSO, 1969).

Year 2 of the public expenditure plans ties in with the supply estimates for the financial year subsequent to that in which the White Paper is published, but the supply estimates are valued at different prices and use different conventions. The formal starting point of the process is a request from the Treasury in October each year asking Departments to prepare estimates for the coming financial year. After argument and counter-argument between the Treasury and the departments, the resulting estimates are introduced into Parliament in February of each year. Civil estimates (i.e. those relating to civil departments) are traditionally introduced by the Financial Secretary to the Treasury and the Defence estimates by the minister concerned.

The civil estimates are grouped according to *classes*, *votes*, and *sub-heads*. Classes refer to broad categories of expenditure such as roads and transport, housing, and social security. There were 15 classes in 1978/79 as listed under supply services in Table 9.1. Within each class, expenditure is divided into between 4 and 26 votes, one for each major type of expenditure within the class. Thus, education and libraries, science and arts (Class X) has 26 votes, covering education, libraries, the research councils, and various museums. Each vote is divided into sub-heads which itemize expenditure in detail, distinguishing salaries from other expenditure. An alternative classification of expenditure on National Accounts principles is also given.

Formerly, the supply estimates were discussed by the *Select Committee on Estimates*, an all-party Committee sitting in detailed judgment on various items of expenditure. Since 1971 this body has been superseded by the *Select Committee on Expenditure*, a larger body with more widely ranging functions inasmuch as it is closely concerned not just with the details of central government, but with public expenditure as a whole. It also has a number of extremely active sub-committees which have clashed with officials on a number of occasions – e.g. the Trade and Industry Sub-Committee on the subject of Concorde costings.

After discussion of the estimates, usually around July, an *Appropriation Act* is passed which divides up the sum authorized by the Estimates and allocates it specifically to each vote. Certain characteristics of the discussion should be noted. First, only members of the government have the power to propose an estimate and no one at all can propose an increase in an estimate which has already been submitted. This is obviously of immense importance as a deterrent to graft. Secondly, the supply debates are never completed by 31 March, the end of the financial year, and unless action was taken Departments would run out of funds at that time. Therefore, special provision is made by passing the *Consolidated Fund Act* which authorizes lump-sum advances to tide Departments over the interim. Another function of the Consolidated Fund Act is to approve Supplementary Estimates relating to the Expenditure of the year just ended.

Though in years gone by debates on the supply estimates were the main method of Parliamentary control, this is no longer really the case both because little debating time is now accorded supply, and because the form of the estimates does not lend itself to Parliamentary scrutiny. Historically, the estimates were discussed by a Committee of the Whole House on 29 supply days, but latterly these have come to be days when the Opposition has general debates; expenditure is now discussed by the House as such, and over a smaller number of days. There could, in principle, be a debate on the details of the Appropriation Act when it is a Bill, but this is not done on the technical ground that the Bill is founded upon supply resolutions already passed by the House. Thus, there is little debate on the Estimates.

Nor, as we have said, would debate on the estimates be very helpful, because of their form. Since 1974 the Supply estimates have been grouped in the same 15 classes of programme as those in the White Paper to make it easier to relate the two documents, but they are on a different price basis. Estimate prices do not relate to a specific date, but are generally those ruling in the autumn before publication of the Estimates. The only comparative figures given for each vote in estimates are the corresponding sums voted for the previous year expressed in previous year prices. No indication is given of the likely out-turn for the previous year, nor are any actual out-turn figures given for the year before that. Nor is there any analysis of changes between the years to show whether they are due to price changes or quantity changes.

The overwhelming conclusion is that estimates, in their present form, are of little use as an instrument of Parliamentary scrutiny or control since they do not set out the basic information needed to show whether the expenditure is justified. Nor is this information available anywhere else. In addition, the number of estimate heads has been reduced over the years by the Treasury, despite the dramatic increase in the scale of government operations. After allowing for inflation, the average size of a vote in 1978 was almost 100 times larger than a century earlier.[1]

(3) *Cash limits* are the newest element of the present system. They were introduced in 1976 at a time when there was rapid inflation.[2] Even in times of modest inflation the Supply estimates do not give a good indication of the amount of money likely to be spent during the year. This is because the estimates are generally calculated at the price levels prevailing when they are prepared, taking account only of pay increases known at the time. Supplementary estimates were therefore needed to cover price increases, and for most services were regularly provided. So for the most part the estimates did not operate as a direct control on the amount of cash spent. When inflation gathered pace, and particularly when the prices of different goods and services rose at different rates, they become an even poorer indicator of the volume of spending during the year.

Cash limits incorporate the government's inflation factors for the coming year and hence limit the amount of money to be spent. They are not submitted to Parliament for approval, but are simply published by the Treasury with the Budget in March or April of each year. They show the amount of cash the government proposes to spend on certain services, taking into account both the planned volume of expenditure shown in the public expenditure White Paper and expected increases in prices and wages. In all the limits cover some 60 per cent of central government expenditure (including the rate support grant and loans to nationalized industries) in the ensuing financial year. Once fixed, the limits can be revised only as the result of a specific policy decision to change the level of provision of a particular service.

Cash limits are applied to expenditures grouped into 'blocks' designed to be large enough to provide spending authorities with scope for finding the most economical and effective way of carrying out their programmes within the limits, while at the same time ensuring financial control. The limits represent the maximum amount which the government proposes should be spent on the services comprised in each block during the coming financial year. In general no block is the responsibility of more than one department. Some blocks include expenditure which is not within the definition of public expenditure used in the

[1] This fact, together with much of the information in this section, is drawn from Fourteenth Report from the Expenditure Committee, Session 1977–78, *Financial Accountability to Parliament*, HC 661 (HMSO, 1978).

[2] See *Cash Limits on Public Expenditure*, Cmnd. 6440 (HMSO, 1976).

public expenditure White Paper, and others include elements of expenditure which do not conform to the categories covered by votes, but which for control purposes are grouped with closely related voted expenditures. In other words, just as there is no simple relationship between categories in the White Paper and in the Supply estimates, nor is there any simple relationship between either of these two and the cash limit blocks.

Since Local Authorities have their own sources of income (mainly rates), cash limits cannot be applied to them directly. Instead, a limit is placed on the amount of financial assistance provided to local authorities by the Central government through the rate support grant and supplementary grants. Similarly, in the case of nationalized industries a limit is placed not on their total expenditure but on loans and grants issued to them.

Most of the areas excluded from cash limits are those which are demand determined (e.g. social security benefits). The items to be excluded are decided by the government without the need for Parliamentary approval.

There is no doubt that the imposition of cash limits helped to control total expenditure, but there are several disadvantages. First, Parliament has no say in the level of the limits. Secondly, the volume of expenditure in real terms may be too high or too low if the government's estimate of the rate of inflation is too high or low, respectively; finally, there is some evidence suggesting that anxiety to prevent over-spending cash limits can lead to under-spending.

We turn now to the *Appropriation Accounts*. Payments authorized under the Consolidated Fund Act and the Appropriation Act are made by the *Paymaster General*, whose function it is to meet the bills of the various departments and scrutinize all out-payments to ensure that they correspond with what has been authorized. All these payments are subsequently checked by the *Comptroller and Auditor General*, an appointee of the Crown who is removable only by a petition of *both* Houses of Parliament. He is thus in an immensely powerful position to carry out his task of verifying that payments made by the Paymaster General correspond to votes as specified in the Appropriation Act.

At the end of each financial year the Appropriation Accounts are prepared, showing the actual out-turn of expenditure for each vote. They are prefaced by a report from the Comptroller and Auditor General, and are published in the January after the end of the relevant financial year (i.e. more than nine months after the end of the period to which they relate, which is long by modern standards). The Accounts give reasons for the main changes, but there is no attempt to explain why any total is different from the estimates in terms of price and volume changes. Nor is there any information about how far the main objectives of the department's programmes have in fact been achieved.

In constructing the Appropriation Accounts, the Comptroller and Auditor General receives aid from the *Committee of Public Accounts*, a body with mandatory rather than advisory authority, which examines the Appropriation Accounts and has the power to interrogate the Accounting Officers of Departments and make them explain their actions. At the same time its function is basically to check the legality rather than the wastefulness of expenditure and therefore its role as a guardian against waste should not be unduly emphasized.

This, then, is the essence (though by no means the totality) of the Parliamentary procedure for supply. Before passing on to the revenue side, we should mention briefly the *Consolidated Fund standing services* procedure. This is vastly simpler since it deals with payments which Parliament has authorized by statute once and for all and hence requires little detailed scrutiny. Such payments, listed in Table 9.1, cover items like payments from the Consolidated Fund to the National Loans Fund (see Table 9.7) for servicing the national debt, and payments to Northern Ireland and the European Communities of agreed shares of certain revenues. Such expenditures are authorized by the House by means of a *financial resolution* without any lengthy or detailed discussion.

On the Revenue side the procedure can be summarized more quickly. The keystone is the Chancellor's Budget Speech usually in March or April. By tradition, he sets out the financial events of the preceding year, and gives his general appraisal of the economic situation and his forecasts for the coming year, including his proposals for meeting the cost of the estimates currently before the House. The revenue proposals are subsequently discussed at length[1] by the *Committee of Ways and Means*, a Committee of the Whole House. As is the case with the Supply estimates, there are various rules controlling the discussion, e.g. no Member can propose increases in taxation. The upshot of these deliberations is the *Finance Act*, which is essentially the Budget's revenue proposals in legal dress, and as modified by the

[1] Changes in commodity taxes are usually brought into effect immediately and dealt with by formal legislation later.

course of the discussion in Committee of Ways and Means. The Finance Act is normally passed in July of each year.

Borrowing is sanctioned by a resolution of the Committee of Ways and Means authorizing the Treasury to make an issue of stock. Statutory authority for any such action is usually given in the next Consolidated Fund Act or Appropriation Act. A final feature of Revenue procedure must also be mentioned. This is the inviolable principle that all receipts must be paid into the Consolidated Fund of the Exchequer (which was established in 1787 as 'a fund into which shall flow every stream of the revenue and from whence shall issue the supply for every public service'). Many detailed devices have been evolved over the years by the Customs and Excise and the Inland Revenue departments to prevent fraud within the departments and to ensure that this practice is always observed.

3.2 *Pros and cons*

The preceding section gives a basis for an evaluation of Parliamentary financial control. The first feature is that it is grounded in tradition. Many of the procedural changes and devices were evolved a long time ago (e.g. the Department of Exchequer and Audit, presided over by the Comptroller and Auditor General, and the Public Accounts Committee date back to the 1860s) and are by now well-tried instruments of control. Consequently, it is not surprising that the British system is excellent for dealing with the traditional problems which it was designed to meet, specifically the problems of dishonesty, and of unauthorized spending.

As regards checks against dishonesty, whichever link in the chain one considers – taxpayer, tax collector, other civil servants, Member of Parliament or Minister – there is some very effective device to prevent fraud. The single Exchequer account, into or from which all receipts and payments flow, the impossibility of any proposal for an increase in an Estimate from the floor of the House, and the separation of the function of the Inspector of Taxes responsible for income tax *assessments* from those of the Collector of Taxes responsible for tax *collection* – all these and many other devices make it possible to claim that the British system offers greater safeguards against dishonesty than most other countries, and more indeed than was the case in Britain itself at, say, the end of the eighteenth century.

The other traditional difficulty with which the British system copes well is unauthorized spending by individual departments. The detailed presentation of the estimates, the scrutiny of the Paymaster General and Comptroller General, the necessity for Treasury approval in order to use unspent balances under one sub-head[1] to meet an excess under another, and the checks imposed by the investigations of the Select Committee on Expenditure and the Public Accounts Committee, all play their part in making departments adhere to Parliamentary decisions on expenditure.

But, as we have seen, other aspects of British public financial control have been less than totally successful. The very fact that the British system succeeds in coping with these traditional difficulties raises doubts as to whether it is so well adapted to dealing with new problems, both those brought about by increased complexity, and those that result from the increased size and scope of public financial activity. In the post-war years there has been a vast expansion of the traditional functions of Parliament, and in addition the nature of government has become more technical and complex. This is partly a matter of individual objects of expenditure (e.g. defence) becoming less readily comprehensible by the layman, and partly that the processes of expenditure (e.g. grants to Local Authorities) have themselves become more complex. Thus, we saw above that neither the public expenditure survey nor the supply estimates make possible detailed Parliamentary scrutiny or control. And while cash limits do at least roughly control expenditure, they again are not debated by Parliament. Furthermore, none of these three methods of expenditure control divide expenditure into the same categories or use the same prices.

A different though related point is an almost total failure to consider revenue and expenditure decisions together. Thus, it is difficult for debate to focus on the opportunity cost of additional expenditure in terms, say, of raising the basic rate of income tax.

Problems have also arisen in some of the newer types of state activity, in particular the nationalized industries. The old techniques cannot apply here; by necessity the traditional accounting system and conventions of the Exchequer are inapplicable to great industries running, or supposed to be running, on commercial principles. Clearly, it is impossible for Parliament to control the day-to-day running of these enterprises. And the record of the two major committees – on public accounts and expenditure – have been somewhat mixed in this respect. Various attempts were made in the immediate post-war years to set up a special committee of the House specifically to review the

[1] In the case of defence estimates the Treasury can sanction a transfer from one vote to another.

operations of the industry, but considerable difficulty was experienced in agreeing on suitable terms of reference for such a body. Then in December 1956 a Select Committee on Nationalized Industries was set up, charged with the responsibility of examining the reports and accounts of the nationalized industries. It has issued a number of reports on particular industries and also devoted a great deal of time to the general principles involved.[1] In addition, there have been some important White Papers setting out general government policy.[2]

As a result of the obvious deficiencies in Parliamentary (as opposed to government) control and scrutiny of expenditure various reforms have been proposed. In 1978 the Treasury suggested that the three main expenditure systems (the public expenditure survey, the supply estimates, and cash limits) could be reduced to two by merging the Supply estimates and cash limits. Specifically, the Treasury proposal examined by the Expenditure Committee[3] made two suggestions.

(a) The structure of votes and cash limits should be aligned wherever possible and subsequently reflected in the layout of the Appropriation Accounts. Thus, blocks of expenditure which are cash-limited would cover exactly the same services as the corresponding votes (which would have to be restructured to coincide); and expenditure which was not cash-limited would be in separate votes.

(b) Supply estimates should be presented on the same price basis as that used to set cash limits, namely estimated out-turn prices (i.e. prices as they are expected to be when the expenditure takes place). Thus, estimates would reflect as far as possible the full expected cost of the services they covered.

While these are rather limited proposals they do offer advantages: Parliament would have a voice in the setting of cash limits; the vote system would be at least partly rationalized; and with fewer supplementary estimates and no separate cash limit document Parliament would be able to devote more time to the Supply estimates themselves.

However, it has been suggested that these changes are too limited

[1] *First Report Select Committee on Nationalised Industries*, 1967/68, Vols. I, II, III, H. of C. 371–1, 371–2, 371–3 (HMSO, 1968).

[2] *The Financial and Economic Obligations of the Nationalised Industries*, Cmnd. 1337 (HMSO, 1961); *Nationalised Industries: a Review of Economic and Financial Objectives*, Cmnd. 3437 (HMSO, 1967); and *The Nationalised Industries*, Cmnd. 7131 (HMSO, 1978).

[3] HC 661, *op. cit.* (HMSO, 1978).

and that more radical measures are needed.[1] Ideally a system of public accounting should provide information on three things:

(i) whether expenditure has been properly authorized;
(ii) how efficient is the management of government; and
(iii) how effective is expenditure – i.e. the extent to which spending meets its objectives and produces results.

At present the information presented to Parliament satisfies only category (i), and so various changes have been proposed. They start with suggested improvements in the public expenditure White Paper, but the bulk of the changes concern the estimates. It is suggested that these should show:

(i) actual expenditure for the year immediately preceding;
(ii) estimated out-turn for the current year;
(iii) the budgeted expenditure for the forthcoming year, much as in the present estimates, but giving more Vote heads and separating cash limited from non-cash-limited items; and
(iv) price and volume changes of (iii) against (ii). Assumptions about price changes should be made explicit, and proposed volume changes related to any new legislation that influences them.

It was also proposed that the Appropriation Accounts should be presented in comparable format and should show how far any significant differences between Estimate and out-turn were due to price or volume changes and the reason for such changes.[2]

A much more modest reform from the US may well be useful, whether or not the reforms described above are ever put into effect. *Tax Expenditures* refer not to explicit government expenditures, but to revenues forgone by the government in the form of tax deductions. Thus, it is argued, if the government forgoes revenue of £500 million by allowing mortgage interest payments to be deductible for income tax purposes, this is just as much an expenditure as an explicit £500 million subsidy to public sector housing. Since the mid-1970s the US Budget has contained detailed information on tax expenditures in the US.[3]

[1] *Ibid.* For a more general critique of existing arrangements see T. Higgins, 'Parliamentary Control of Public Expenditure – A Backbench Revolt', *National Westminster Quarterly Review*, August 1978.

[2] This suggestion was rejected by the Treasury, see 'Treasury Opposes Spending Linkage', *Financial Times*, 12 December 1978.

[3] See, for instance, *Budget of the United States Government: Special Analyses, Fiscal Year 1980*, Special Analysis G (Washington DC, 1979). For a British investigation see J. R. M. Willis and P. J. W. Hardwick, *Tax Expenditures in the United Kingdom* (Heinemann, 1978). See also *The Government's Expenditure Plans 1978/80 to 1982/83, op. cit.*

APPENDIX TO CHAPTER 9

This Appendix summarises the major provisions of the June 1979 Budget. We start with the main tax changes, following the order of Chapter 9, section 2, and then discuss the uprating of social security benefits announced during the budget debate. All data are drawn from the *Financial Statement and Budget Report 1979–80*, and the House of Commons *Official Report* (Hansard), 12 and 13 June 1979, which should be consulted for further details.

The overall effect of the various changes was: forecast central government revenue for 1979/80 of £51 billion (the 1978/79 outturn was £43 billion); and estimated expenditure was £59 billion (£51 billion in 1978/79). The public sector borrowing requirement was estimated to fall from £9.2 billion in 1978/79 to £8.3 billion in 1979/80.

It was proposed to increase the *income tax* personal allowances from £985 to £1165 (single person) and from £1535 to £1815 (married couple); the additional personal allowance was raised from £550 to £650. The age allowance was increased from £1300 to £1540 (single) and from £2075 to £2455 (married).

The first £750 of taxable income continued to be taxed at a reduced rate of 25 per cent. The basic rate was reduced from 33 per cent to 30 per cent, and the basic rate band increased by £2,000 to £9,250. The higher rates of tax above 60 per cent were abolished, and the width of the remaining higher rate bands increased. The structure of rates proposed in the budget was therefore as follows:

BAND OF TAXABLE INCOME	TAX RATE	BAND OF TAXABLE INCOME	TAX RATE
£	%	£	%
0– 750	25	15,001–20,000	50
751–10,000	30	20,001–25,000	55
10,001–12,000	40	over £25,000	60
12,001–15,000	45		

It was proposed that the investment income surcharge should be levied at a single rate of 15 per cent (abolishing the former reduced rate of 10 per cent), with a threshold of £5,000 for all taxpayers (replacing the differential threshold for people over retirement age).

Capital gains tax was to be carefully re-examined with special reference to the impact of inflation on gains.

The rate of *corporation tax* remained at 52 per cent and the reduced rate for small companies at 42 per cent. The lower and upper limits for the 'small company' rate of corporation tax were raised from £50,000 to £60,000 and £85,000 to £100,000, respectively. The rate of Advance Corporation Tax was set at 3/7ths of any distribution to correspond with the new 30 per cent basic rate of income tax.

Stock relief was retained in broadly its existing form except that the profit restriction in calculating the amount of stock relief was reduced from 15 to 10 per cent. It was also proposed to write off the balance of stock relief still outstanding for 1973–74 and 1974–75. It was stated that the whole question of business taxation under inflationary conditions was to be reviewed.

It was proposed to extend various transitional reliefs for discretionary trusts under *capital transfer tax*. There were no other specific proposals to change the tax, which was to be covered by the same thorough study as capital gains tax. It was proposed to change the rate of *petroleum revenue tax*, the uplift and the oil allowance as set out on page 207. It was proposed to reduce the rate of *development land tax* from 80 to 60 per cent, and to increase the annual exemption from £10,000 to £50,000.

There were no proposals to change the *excise duties* on alcohol. Those on tobacco were subject to a technical change with no effect on the price of tobacco products. The hydrocarbon oil duties on almost all types of oil products were increased.

The standard rate of *value added tax* was increased from 8 to 15 per cent; the 12½ per cent rate of value added tax was abolished and the goods and services previously subject to it charged at the new standard rate of 15 per cent.

Vehicle excise duties were unchanged, but further study was to be made of the idea that they might be phased out and replaced by higher excise duties on petrol.

The national insurance surcharge remained at 3½ per cent.

It was announced in the Budget debate that the main *national insurance benefits* listed in Table 10.4, and related social security benefits, would be uprated from 12 November 1979. The new rates of benefit are given in House of Commons *Official Report*, 13 June 1979, cols. 453–8. Most benefits were increased by rather more than expected. As an example, the basic retirement pension for a single person was expected to increase by some £2.50, from £19.50 per week to about £22 per week; instead it was uprated by £3.80 to £23.30 per week (and from £31.20 to £37.30 per week for a married couple). Other benefits were similarly uprated.

One major change in the system (as opposed to changes in the rates of benefit) was foreshadowed. It was proposed to introduce legislation to tie the statutory uprating of pensions to changes in prices rather than to the larger of price and earnings increases.

10

THE NATIONAL INSURANCE FUND AND RELATED EXPENDITURES

1 AN OVERVIEW OF THE NATIONAL INSURANCE FUND

1.1 *Revenue of the National Insurance Fund*

In the last chapter we discussed the revenues of the Consolidated Fund. To complete the picture of the financial structure of central government it is necessary to set alongside it the *National Insurance Fund*, which we discuss in this chapter in some detail both because of its size and because of the scope of national insurance and related benefits.

On the revenue side the relation between the two funds is fairly straightforward. As we shall see shortly, the revenue of the National Insurance Fund is derived from a small number of clearly defined sources, the main ones being national insurance contributions, a grant from the Consolidated Fund and interest receipts on its accumulated reserves. Virtually all other central government revenues go into the Consolidated Fund.

On the expenditure side matters are considerably more complicated. Broadly speaking, benefits paid from the National Insurance Fund are those payable on the basis of a national insurance contributions record, such as unemployment or sickness benefits, whilst similar benefits paid from the Consolidated Fund are generally awarded on the basis of other criteria such as income level (e.g. supplementary benefit) or the number of children in the family (e.g. child benefit).

From a purely financial point of view, since we have already discussed the Consolidated Fund, it would be necessary to talk only about the National Insurance Fund. In fact, our discussion on the expenditure side will be much more wide-ranging for two reasons. First, in Chapter 14 we shall be discussing income support in some detail, for which a working knowledge of the various cash benefits will be necessary; and secondly because in practice there are so many linkages and interactions between national insurance benefits and other cash benefits that it is essential to discuss them together.

We therefore start this chapter with a description in section 1 of the revenue of the National Insurance Fund, and then proceed to a detailed discussion of national insurance contributions and a brief review of the Fund's expenditures. Section 2 describes the main national insurance benefits (paid out of the National Insurance Fund) together with some non-contributory benefits paid out of the Consolidated Fund which have the same objectives as national insurance (e.g. pensions for the over 80s). Section 3 then looks at the remaining cash benefits which are paid from the Cosolidated Fund.

The present system of national insurance goes back to 1948. There were originally three funds, the National Insurance Fund, the National Insurance (Reserve) Fund, and the Industrial Injuries Fund, but since April 1975 they have been merged into one. The current account of the National Insurance Fund for 1977 is given in Table 10.1. The major sources of revenue which we shall discuss in greater detail are from various classes of insured persons, from a grant from the central government, and from interest receipts.

In 1977 employer contributions came to £5,133 million. Individuals pay different contributions according to, among other things, their employment status. Employees' contributions amounted to £3,200 million, and the contributions of self-employed people to £267 million. Altogether individuals paid £3,483 million in national insurance contributions.

The second major source of revenue of the National Insurance Fund was a central government contribution of £1,585 million. The details of this contribution are somewhat complex but, in essence, the National Insurance Fund received a supplement from the Consolidated Fund equal to 18 per cent of its revenue from contributions from insured persons on the assumption that there was no contracting out.[1]

In the past the National Insurance Fund typically did not have a large or long-term surplus, but recently this has changed. The interest item of £336 million in 1977 shown in Table 10.1 is the interest on a recently accumulated surplus of some £4,000 million. The size of the surplus has led to heated debate about the proper role of the Fund, though a surplus of some sort (though not necessarily of this magnitude) is desirable for a number of reasons. First, there is a need for working capital to bridge any short-term imbalances, and to fund the various

[1] The details of contracting out are discussed below, p. 243.

Table 10.1

Current Account of the National Insurance Fund, UK, 1977 (£m)

Revenue		
Employers' contributions		5,133
Contributions from insured persons		
Employees' contributions	3,200	
Contributions from self-employed persons	267	
Contributions from non-employed persons	16	3,483
Grants from Central Government		1,585
Interest		336
Payments in lieu of graduated contributions		12
Total revenue		10,549
Expenditure		
Current grants to personal sector		
Retirement pensions	6,403	
Widows' benefits and guardians' allowances	472	
Unemployment benefit	635	
Sickness benefit	608	
Invalidity benefit	703	
Maternity benefit	92	
Death grant	16	
Injury benefit	50	
Disablement benefit	195	
Industrial death benefit	29	9,203
Current surplus		899
Other		447
Total expenditure		10,549

Source: *National Income and Expenditure,* 1967–77, Table 7.4.

agencies that actually pay out the benefits. A surplus of £4,000 million represents about 17 weeks' outgoings for the Fund. Secondly, it has been said that the new state retirement pension scheme[1] will require a growing increase in contribution rates which could at least partly be cushioned by drawing down an accumulated surplus. Finally, the surplus, being for the most part held in various forms of government debt, has been helpful with the Public Sector Borrowing Requirement. It is the latter aspect that has drawn a certain amount of political fire.

The total receipts of the Fund in 1977 were £10,549 million, over 20 per cent of total central government revenue, and larger than any other single source of revenue except income tax. This revenue does not go through the same Parliamentary procedure as other central government revenue. The annual contribution review is debated in Parliament and so is the uprating review. Issues such as the accumulated surplus or the extent of uprating of benefits may be challenged on these occasions.

1.2 *National Insurance Contributions*

Before discussing the expenditure of the National Insurance Fund we should explain in some detail the way in which national insurance contributions are collected, especially as there have been considerable changes over the past twenty years. When the present scheme started in 1948 it followed the original Beveridge concept of flat-rate contributions giving entitlement to flat-rate benefits. In the words of the Beveridge Report,

> Every person ... will pay a single security contribution by a stamp on a single insurance document each week ...
>
> Unemployment benefit, disability benefit [and] retirement pension after a transition period ... will be at the same rate irrespective of previous earnings.[2]

Thus, from 1948 onwards all insured persons were required to stick a national insurance stamp on their national insurance card each week. The cost of the stamp varied by age, sex, marital status, and employment status, and rose steadily over the years.

In the 1950s it was increasingly felt that the flat-rate state retirement pension was inadequate, and should be supplemented by an earnings-related pension. So, from 1961 employees, except those with very low earnings, were generally required to pay a graduated contribution in

[1]. Described in section 2.2, below.

[2] *Social Insurance and Allied Services* (The Beveridge Report), Cmd. 6404 (HMSO, 1942), p. 10.

addition to the stamp. These two contributions, the weekly stamp and, for certain employees, the graduated contribution, existed side by side until April 1975 when the entire system of national insurance contributions was revised.

Under the present arrangements almost anyone over school-leaving age and under normal retiring age, who is at work is liable to pay national insurance contributions. For the purposes of national insurance there are three types of contribution, those for employed persons, those for self-employed, and those for non-employed, as summarized in Table 10.2.

Table 10.2

National Insurance Contribution Rates, 1979/80

CLASS 1	– employed persons who earn over £19.50 per week	6½ per cent of all earnings up to £135 per week. Employers pay 10 per cent of the same amount (plus 3½ per cent national insurance surcharge)
CLASS 2	– self-employed persons with profits in excess of £1,050 per year	Flat-rate payment of £2.10 per week
CLASS 3	– non-employed persons (voluntary contributions)	Flat rate contribution of £2.00 per week
CLASS 4	– self-employed persons	5 per cent of profits or gains between £2,250 and £7,000 per year

(1) *Employed persons* (i.e. most wage and salary earners): Class 1 national insurance contributions are paid in respect of employed persons. These involve contributions by both employee and employer, and since 1975 both contributions have been earnings-related. Between 1975 and 1978 there were transitional complications, which we shall ignore, and concentrate on the fully fledged system that has been in operation since April 1978.

In 1979–80 the employee's basic contribution was 6½ per cent of his or her earnings up to the *upper earnings limit* (£135 per week in 1979/80), with various exceptions. The first is that those with incomes below the *lower earnings limit* (£19.50 per week in 1979/80) do not have to pay any contribution. Secondly, those who have contracted out of the State earnings-related pensions scheme[1] pay the full Class 1 contribution only up to the lower earnings limit, thereafter paying 4 per cent up to the upper earnings limit. The minimum contribution payable for any year to be regarded as a full contribution year for national insurance purposes is the contribution due on 50 times the lower earnings limit. Persons receiving unemployment or sickness benefits, if they would otherwise fall below the minimum contribution for the year, are credited with the basic national insurance contribution (i.e. no contribution is paid, but future benefits are awarded as though a contribution of 6½ per cent of the lower earnings limit had been paid). In the past married women could opt out of the bulk of their national insurance contribution (thereby losing entitlement to most benefits), but this option is no longer available to women entering national insurance, or re-entering it after a gap of two years or more.

It should be noted, parenthetically, that unlike income tax, and unlike most other national insurance contributions, the income limit for Class 1 contributions operates on a week-by-week basis. For instance, a person who earned £19.60 per week in 1979 for half the year, and £19 per week for the other half would be required to pay contributions in the weeks in which he earned £19.60, even though his average for the year was less than £19.50, per week. These contributions will not be refunded. This is in striking contrast to the way in which income tax would operate in a similar situation.

The basic employer Class 1 contribution in 1979/80 was 10 per cent of the employee's gross weekly earnings up to the upper earnings limit. But no contribution is payable for employees with earnings below the lower earnings limit.[2] In the case of the employer contribution, as we saw in Chapter 9, there is the added complication of the *employers' national insurance surcharge*, a levy of 3½ per cent of the employee's earnings, on top of the 10 per cent employer Class 1 contribution, bringing the total employer contribution to 13½ per cent.

The revenue from the employers' national insurance surcharge does not go into the National Insurance Fund, but into the Consolidated Fund. The levy is regarded as an additional source of government revenue, which is collected as a surcharge on national insurance contributions purely for administrative convenience. It is, in effect, a

[1] The details of contracting out are discussed below, see p. 243.
[2] The upper and lower earnings limits are described on p. 232.

payroll tax, and was introduced as a temporary measure at a rate of 2 per cent during the economic crisis of October 1976. After the Budget of April 1978 the rate was raised to 3½ per cent. The tax was estimated to yield £1,474 million in 1978/79, and now that the tax has been introduced it is likely to prove as temporary as the introduction of income tax. There are a variety of sound arguments that can be used to support such a payroll tax, and we do not criticize the principle as such. What can be said, though, is that the tax was introduced as a crisis measure, and was preceded by no public discussion and followed by virtually no Parliamentary debate. There can be no doubt that this is not an ideal way in which to introduce a major tax reform.

Both the employee and employer Class 1 contributions are collected through the PAYE mechanism, as is the employer's national insurance surcharge. These contributions help to pay for the employee's unemployment and sickness benefit, for his retirement pension, and for a variety of other national insurance benefits, discussed in more detail below. In addition, part of the contribution is channelled to the National Health Service. Part of the employer's contribution goes into the Redundancy Fund and the Maternity Pay Fund.[1]

(2) *The self-employed* pay both Class 2 and Class 4 national insurance contributions. The Class 2 contribution in 1979/80 was at a flat-rate of £2.10 per week.

Class 4 contributions in 1979/80 were levied at a rate of 5 per cent of a self-employed person's profits between £2,250 and £7,000 per year.

The Class 2 contribution is collected in the form of a weekly stamp, as of old, while the Class 4 contribution is collected by the Inland Revenue as part of the assessment for income tax of income under Schedule D.

These contributions do not entitle a self-employed person to as large a range of benefits as are available to an employee. There is no unemployment benefit, nor any earnings-related sickness benefit, nor any earnings-related component of the national insurance retirement pension. Nor is there any entitlement to redundancy pay.

The rules for people who are both employed and self-employed are somewhat complex, and we shall not describe them here. The principle

[1] Employers have an obligation in certain circumstances to make payments for redundancy and maternity leave. The cost of these payments is met partly by the employer directly, and partly from the relevant national fund to which the employer contributes.

is that a person who is both employed and self-employed is potentially liable to pay Class 1, Class 2, and Class 4 contributions subject to a ceiling on total contributions in any one year.

(3) *The non-employed*, broadly speaking, are those who are not members of the labour force, such as students or married women who are not currently working. Such people, if they wish to maintain an unbroken contributions record, have the option of paying Class 3 contributions, at a flat rate in 1979/80 of £2.00 per week.[1] The payment of Class 3 contributions does not entitle the individual to any immediate benefits, but may enhance entitlement to benefit in the future.

Thus, virtually all adult workers and a substantial number of the non-employed pay national insurance contributions which are paid into the National Insurance Fund rather than the Consolidated Fund. Formally, therefore, national insurance is a contributory scheme. But, as we shall see in Chapter 14, the contributory principle has been so eroded from Beveridge's original scheme that it can today legitimately be doubted whether this is any longer the case in fact.

1.3 *Expenditure on National Insurance and other benefits*

The expenditure of the National Insurance Fund is shown in Table 10.1. Apart from a surplus of £899 million, and certain other items, mainly administrative, the bulk of the expenditure of the Fund, as one would expect, is on cash benefits to the various classes of insured person. By far the largest expenditure is on retirement pensions, amounting in 1977 to £6,403 million, nearly 70 per cent of all national insurance benefits. It should be noted that this figure does not include State pensions outside the scope of national insurance, such as war pensions, and pensions to the over 80s who retired too soon after 1948 to be entitled to an ordinary national insurance pension.

After retirement pensions the largest benefits are for unemployment, sickness, invalidity, and widowhood; expenditure on these four together was £2,418 million in 1977, over 25 per cent of total national insurance benefits. The figure includes both the flat-rate and earnings-related unemployment, sickness and invalidity benefits.[2]

[1] Women looking after young children are normally able to avoid breaks in their contributions record without paying Class 3 contributions because they receive home responsibility protection; see p. 241.

[2] These schemes are discussed in more detail on pp. 245–7, below.

Expenditure on the remaining national insurance benefits came to £854 million, covering both the cradle (maternity benefits) and the grave (the death grant), and a variety of other circumstances such as industrial injury. Finally, the bulk of the Other category is the current expenditure on goods and services of the Fund; these are mainly the costs of administration.

In concluding this brief review of the National Insurance Fund two general points should be noted. The first, as we have already seen, is the magnitude of the financial operations involved. In effect we have a third estate alongside the Inland Revenue and Customs and Excise. The second is that this revenue does not go through the normal budgetary procedure of central government. Although administered by the Department of Health and Social Security the accounts of the National Insurance Fund are kept quite separate from the normal Estimates and Appropriation Accounts. Changes in the rates of contributions or benefit may be announced in Parliament separately from the Budget and are debated on separate occasions. The annual accounts do not form part of the Appropriation Accounts, though public expenditure controls apply as much to national insurance benefits as to other areas of government spending.[1]

Before looking at national insurance benefits in greater detail it may be helpful to give a brief survey of cash benefits generally. In this chapter and those following we shall use the term 'social security' to refer to state cash benefits generally. Broadly speaking, social security benefits fall into two categories: (a) benefits paid out of the National Insurance Fund, which are available only to those with an appropriate contributions record, and (b) various non-contributory benefits which are available independent of a person's contributions, paid out of the Consolidated Fund. The various social security benefits, and the expenditure on each are shown in Figure 10.1 and Table 10.3. Looking at them together we see that total expenditure on social security benefits in 1977 was £12,437 million. Some 75 per cent of this was on national insurance benefits, as we have already seen. In addition, benefits amounting to £3,234 million were distributed on a non-contributory basis. By far the largest expenditure under this heading was £1,750 million on supplementary benefit, which is available to everybody with income and wealth below certain limits. Expenditure on child benefit was £805 million. Other payments under this category

[1] National insurance benefits are covered by PESC control, as discussed in Chapter 9, section 3.

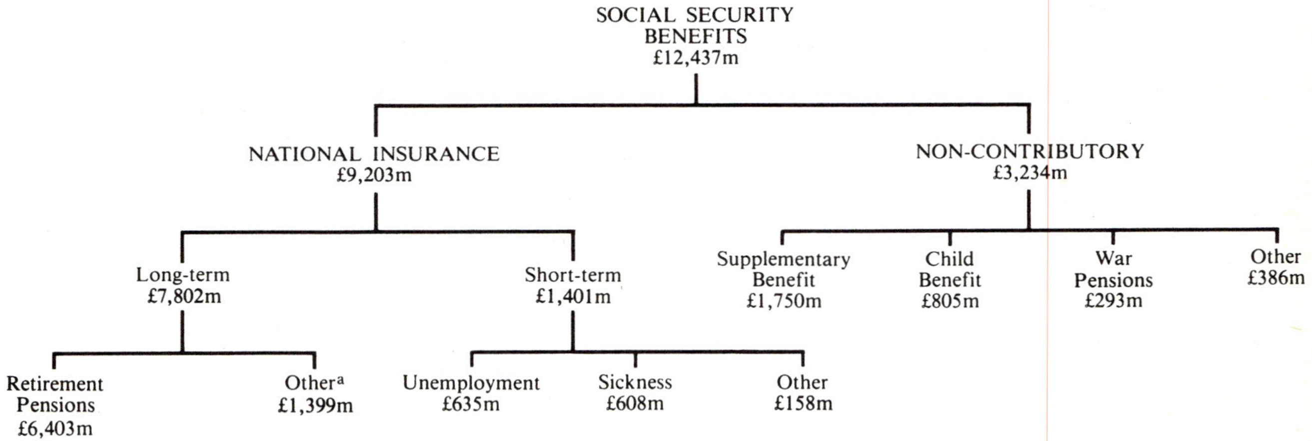

Source: *National Income and Expenditure, 1967–77*, Tables 7.1 and 7.4.

Notes: [a] Other benefits are: widows' benefits, and invalidity, disablement and industrial death benefits.

Figure 10.1 Outline of expenditure on cash benefits, UK, 1977 are war pensions and service grants amounting to £293 million, and various other non-contributory benefits, such as family income supplement, amounting to £386 million.[1]

Other grants to the personal sector (e.g. grants to universities and colleges) amounted to £1,926 million in 1977. Total transfer payments by the central government thus consist of grants to the personal sector, shown in Table 10.3, together with interest on the National Debt and subsidies.

Table 10.3

Central Government Current Grants to the Personal Sector, UK, 1977 (£m)

Social security benefits		
National insurance benefits	9,203	
Supplementary benefits	1,750	
Family allowance/child benefit	805	
War pensions and service grants	293	
Other non-contributory benefits	386	12,437
Other grants to the personal sector		1,926
		14,363

Source: *National Income and Expenditure 1967–77*, Table 7.1.

All these payments have grown considerably over the years. Between 1955/56 and 1975/76 *real* expenditure on retirement pensions rose from £1,401 million to £4,791 million, and for the remaining national insurance benefits from £650 million to £2,021 million. Supplementary benefit payments rose from £370 million to £1,187 million, and expenditure on other non-contributory benefits from £633 million to £943 million.[2] Total real expenditure on social security has thus risen from £3,054 million in 1955/56 to £8,942 million in 1975/76, nearly a three-fold increase. Between 1971/72 and 1975/76 real expenditure on social security per head of population rose by approximately 25 per cent.[3]

[1] We shall discuss child benefit and family income supplement in section 3.

[2] All figures are in 1975/76 prices. For further details see Department of Health and Social Security, *Annual Report 1976*, Cmnd. 6931 (HMSO, 1977), Chapter 2.

[3] *Ibid.*, p. 15.

2 NATIONAL INSURANCE BENEFITS

2.1 *A brief history of National Insurance*

In this section we discuss in some detail the main national insurance benefits, together with some non-contributory benefits fulfilling essentially the same purpose. We start with a brief historical review; section 2.2 discusses state retirement and widow's pensions, and non-contributory pensions for the over-80s; in section 2.3 we look at unemployment, sickness and invalidity benefits, and in section 2.4 survey briefly the remaining national insurance benefits.

The historical development of national insurance in the UK can very broadly be divided into four periods: (a) before the twentieth century; (b) the twentieth century up to 1948, prior to the system resulting from the Beveridge Report of 1942; (c) the Beveridge system (1948–65); and (d) the modified Beveridge system (post-1965).

Probably the starting point for state involvement in the relief of destitution came with the Poor Law Statute, 1601. In the three centuries that followed the spirit underlying the Poor Law was that the condition of the poor was due to their own laziness and improvidence. During the twentieth century, and particularly since the Report of the Royal Commission on the Poor Laws and Relief of Distress 1909, there has been a movement away from this view and towards the idea of compulsory insurance and assistance on a national basis. This view has been strengthened by the perception that industrial society does not distribute its rewards anything like equally, or necessarily in proportion to effort, and by the mass unemployment of the 1920s and 1930s which could in no way be attributed to the laziness of the unemployed.

The first major departure from the Poor Law was the Old Age Pensions Act 1908, which enabled people aged 70 or over to receive a weekly pension subject to a means test, but without the stigma of poor relief. This act was closely followed by two contributory schemes of insurance against ill-health and unemployment under the National Insurance Act 1911, which provided for the payment of cash benefits in the event of sickness, disablement and maternity, and for certain medical benefits. The Act provided, inter alia, for a limited scheme of compulsory unemployment insurance provision for certain classes of worker.

In the years that followed, both schemes were extended. The

original health insurance scheme was enlarged both by increasing the number of people covered and by the passage of the Widows', Orphans' and Old Age Contributory Pensions Act 1925, which provided the first national scheme of contributory pensions, and was extended by a further Act in 1929. The scheme for health insurance was administered through a large number of friendly societies, trade unions, industrial societies, etc.; the contributory pension scheme was administered by the relevant government department. The unemployment insurance scheme was managed by the Ministry of Labour through the employment exchanges.

The health insurance scheme (including pension provision) and unemployment insurance were considerable advances on the old Poor Law, but they had a number of serious disadvantages. The schemes lacked co-ordination, were far from universal in scope, and contained certain inequalities in the benefits provided.[1]

Partly as a result of these deficiencies the entire structure of National Insurance was reviewed in the Beveridge Report of 1942,[2] whose recommendations formed the basis of the National Insurance Act 1946. This chapter together with Chapter 14 outlines and analyses the structure of insurance created by the 1946 Act and subsequent legislation. Under the Act a comprehensive, unified and compulsory system of insurance against loss of income by interruption of earnings was introduced.

In 1965 all enactments from 1946 to 1964 were consolidated in the National Insurance Act 1965. The National Insurance Act 1966 introduced earnings-related short-term benefits, and the National Insurance Act 1971, introduced invalidity benefits for the long-term sick. The Social Security Act 1975, consolidated all previous national insurance legislation and made major changes in the system of national insurance contributions, and the Social Security Pensions Act 1975, enacted a major overhaul of the state pension scheme. These pieces of legislation will be described in this chapter and analysed in Chapter 14.

2.2 *National Insurance Retirement and Widows' Pensions*

As we have seen, state retirement pensions go back to 1908. We shall review the arrangements in force since 1948, with particular emphasis

[1] For a detailed analysis of the development and the pros and cons of National Insurance prior to 1948 see B. B. Gilbert, *The Evolution of National Insurance in Great Britain* (Michael Joseph, 1973), and *Social Insurance and Allied Services* (The Beveridge Report), *op. cit.*

[2] *Social Insurance and Allied Services*, *op. cit.*

on the provisions of the Social Security Pensions Act 1975, which define current arrangements.

In July 1948, as a result of the Beveridge Report, the basic state pension was set at £1.30 per week for a single person and £2.10 for a married couple. Under the arrangements then prevailing flat-rate contributions gave entitlement to flat-rate benefits, and apart from periodic increases in the rates of contribution and benefit, these arrangements continued through the 1950s. In 1961 an earnings-related national insurance contribution was levied in addition to the flat-rate contribution, specifically to pay for an earnings-related retirement pension.

There were substantial changes in these arrangements with the passing of the 1975 Social Security Pensions Act, and since this is one of the most important pieces of social security legislation since the National Insurance Act 1946, it is worthwhile explaining its major provisions in some detail. We have already seen how the individual's social security contribution, most of which is for the state retirement pension, is levied. To qualify for a full pension under the 1975 Act an individual must generally have paid contributions to the new scheme for at least 20 years, and either to the new scheme or its predecessor for at least 49 years (men) or 44 years (women).[1]

Where a person fails to meet this requirement a retirement pension will be awarded on a sliding scale. But in sharp contrast to previous legislation, years spent by a parent at home looking after children will not in general result in a loss of pension. The idea behind this *home responsibility protection* is that pension entitlement should not be substantially affected if a person spends several years looking after young children. Thus, a woman who drops out of the labour force for 15 years to look after her children will have to work for only 29 years (i.e. 44 *minus* 15) to qualify for a full retirement pension.

On the benefits side the major provisions of the 1975 Act may be summarized as follows:[2]

(1) The weekly pension is earnings-related and consists of two components, which we shall call the *basic component* (which is flat-rate) and the *additional component* (which is earnings-related).

(2) The basic component for a single person is equal to the lower

[1] To qualify for a full retirement pension, a person cannot have more than one year of non-contribution for every decade or part decade of his or her working life, defined as 16–65 (men), 16–60 (women).

[2] Examples will be given below, p. 243.

earnings limit, which is set at about one-quarter of national average earnings (£19.50 from November 1978).[1] For earnings below this, the basic component is reduced pound for pound with earnings.

(3) The additional component for a person with a full contributions record reflects the individual's earnings at the rate of 25p of pension per pound of earnings between the lower earnings limit and a ceiling set at the upper earnings limit.

(4) The pension will be based on the individual's best 20 years of earnings, thus improving pension rates by allowing years in which earnings were low to be left out of account.

(5) The same pension formula applies to men and women, though pensionable age is 65 for men and 60 for women.

(6) The scheme will reach full maturity after 20 years. For each year of contribution the contributor will earn entitlement to pension rights equal to $1\frac{1}{4}$ per cent of the excess of his earnings (or the ceiling, whichever is the lower) over the lower earnings limit. Thus, a person who has contributed for 20 years will receive 25 per cent (i.e. $20\times1\frac{1}{4}$ per cent) of the relevant earnings.

(7) A man receives an increase in his pension if he is married. However, if his wife has been working and has built up a pension entitlement greater than this, then instead of the husband's increase the wife will receive the full pension to which she is entitled on the basis of her earnings. In the case of a pensioner couple with two contribution records the surviving spouse will receive the basic pension plus *both* additional components, subject to the latter not exceeding the maximum which could have been earned by a single person.

(8) The basic component will be uprated each year in line with the increase in average earnings or the increase in prices, whichever is the greater. The earnings-related component will be protected in two ways. First, the earnings on which the individual's pension is calculated will be revalued in line with the general movement of earnings from the year in which they were received up to the last tax year before entitlement to pension arises. Thus, the earnings-related pension, when it is first awarded, will be based on the 20 years in which the individual's *real* earnings were highest. Secondly, the earnings-related component, once in payment, will be uprated each year in line with increases in the price level.

(9) The pensions of people who continue working beyond pension-

[1] The actual calculations are done on an annual basis, but achieve the same effect as the (simpler) weekly description in the text.

able age will be increased by 7½ per cent (in real terms) for each year that the pension is forgone.

(10) As with the old graduated pension scheme, it remains possible for members of approved occupational pension schemes (i.e. private schemes) to contract out of the earnings-related component of the State scheme, though membership of the basic component is compulsory. People who contract out will rely on an occupational scheme for a part of their pension, and for this reason minimum standards must be met if their members are to be allowed to contract out of the State scheme. Occupational pensions are required to bear a minimum relationship to final salary, or average salary expressed in real terms, and to contain a minimum accrual rate and minimum provision for widows and dependants. A crucial feature of the new system is that once a pension is awarded under an approved occupational scheme the State will uprate the guaranteed minimum pension (i.e. the pension which an individual with an identical earnings record would have received under the State scheme) in line with changes in the price level each year. Thus, in striking contrast to all previous experience, the State is agreeing to inflation-proof the guaranteed minimum pension paid under approved pension schemes. We shall return to this point in Chapter 14.

Let us take a specific example of the way that the scheme will work at maturity (but assuming 1979 data for simplicity). Suppose someone retires with a full contribution record, and with average earnings over his best 20 years of £80 per week (the 1979 weekly average). If he were single he would receive a basic pension of £19.50 per week plus one-quarter of the excess of his average earnings (£80) over the base level (£19.50). His earnings-related pension would therefore be £15.13 per week and the total pension £34.63.[1]

People who continue to earn more than small amounts after pensionable age are more or less forced to defer retirement. In 1979 up to £45 per week could be earned without affecting entitlement to

[1] Contributions for the earnings-related component have been calculated since April 1978, and during the transition period from 1978 to 1998 matters will be somewhat more complicated. Suppose the same person were to retire in 1988. Since he has contributed to the scheme for only 10 years the earnings-related component of his retirement pension would not be 25 per cent of (£80–£19.50), but only 12½ per cent, or £7.56. Such a person would probably also have earned entitlement to the old graduated pension. All this assumes that he retired at the age of 65. If, however, he had deferred retirement till 70 (possibly in order to earn higher benefits) the situation would yet again be different. Pension entitlement is increased by 7½ per cent for each complete year of deferral of retirement, and so if the individual has deferred for five years his pension under the new scheme (but not his graduated pension) will be increased by 37½ per cent (i.e. 5×7½ per cent). In this case, the individual will receive a weekly pension of £37.21 (i.e. (£19.50+£7.56)×1.375), plus his graduated pension.

pension. But a man under 70 (or woman under 65) lost 50p of pension for every £1 earned between £45 and £49 per week, and lost pension pound for pound with earnings thereafter. For those with average or higher incomes who worked up to five years after the normal retiring age deferral was thus largely involuntary.

In 1979 the basic retirement pension for a single individual was £19.50. In the same year the level of long-term supplementary benefit was £19.90 plus rent, and so a pensioner receiving only the basic state pension was eligible also for supplementary benefit. One of the main purposes of the new scheme is to reduce the numbers receiving both retirement pensions and long-term supplementary benefit, which historically has been a serious problem. At the end of 1977 out of 8.4 million national insurance retirement pensioners some 2.1 million also received supplementary pension.

We have already discussed the pension provision for the surviving spouse when both are of pensionable age. But there is national insurance provision also for a wife who is below pensionable age when her husband dies. There are three types of benefit for widows: widow's allowance, widowed mother's allowance, and widow's pension.

(1) *Widow's allowance.* This benefit, for which most widows are eligible, is payable at a rate of £27.30 (in 1979) per week for the 26 weeks immediately following the husband's death, to a widow who is under 60 when her husband dies, or if over that age, if her husband was not a retirement pensioner. There may be additional payments if the widow has dependant children at a rate of £5.35 per child plus child benefit. As well as the basic widow's allowance an earnings-related supplement may also be payable, based on her late husband's earnings, and calculated in broadly the same way as the earnings-related supplement to unemployment and sickness benefit, described above, though without the limit on total benefit of 85 per cent of reckonable weekly earnings applied to some other benefits. Widow's allowance is payable only if the husband had an appropriate contributions record.

(2) *Widowed mother's allowance* is payable to a widow with at least one qualifying child under 19 when her widow's allowance ends after 26 weeks. The benefit is payable at the rate of £19.50 per week (in 1979), plus the same benefit per child as those paid with widow's allowance. As with the widow's allowance, the benefit will be paid only where the husband had an appropriate contributions record, but the contribution conditions are more stringent in the case of the widowed mother's allowance.

(3) *Widow's pension* is payable to:

(i) a widow after the termination of her widow's allowance, if she is not eligible for widowed mother's allowance and was over the age of 40 when her husband died, and

(ii) a widow after she ceases to be entitled to a widowed mother's allowance if she is then over the age of 40. The pension is payable at a rate of £19.50 per week (in 1979) if the widow is aged 50 or over, and at a reduced rate if she is between 40 and 50. The contribution conditions for widow's pension are the same as those for the widowed mother's allowance.

In addition to these national insurance pensions there is also the *non-contributory pension for people over 80.* This is intended primarily for people who retired too soon after 1948 to have built up an adequate national insurance record. Anyone who is 80 or over and is not receiving a national insurance retirement pension, or who is receiving one at a low rate, may qualify for a non-contributory retirement pension of £11.70 per week (in 1979) for a single person and £7.05 for a married woman. As its name implies this is not a national insurance benefit, and is paid out of the Consolidated Fund.[1]

2.3 *Unemployment, sickness, and invalidity benefits*

Under the National Insurance Act 1946 benefits were provided to protect an individual in the case of temporary interruption of work due to unemployment or sickness. At the beginning, as with retirement pensions, these benefits were flat-rate, but in 1966 earnings-related supplements were introduced, payable automatically to many people entitled to unemployment or sickness benefit.

For a single individual with a full contributions record the flat-rate unemployment and sickness benefit from November 1978 was £15.75 per week. The flat-rate unemployment benefit is payable for up to one year; the flat-rate sickness benefit is payable for up to 28 weeks, and thereafter the individual is eligible for invalidity benefit.[2] An individual claiming unemployment benefit must be willing and able to work; claims for sickness benefit must be accompanied by a doctor's certificate.

Earnings-related supplement is payable for only six months, starting on the 13th day of the period of interruption of work. In 1979 if

[1] For further details of pensions, other contributory schemes and child benefit, see *Guide to Contributory Benefits and Child Benefit* (Child Poverty Action Group, London, published annually).

[2] See below, p. 246.

reckonable weekly earnings were between £15 and £30 the supplement was calculated as one-third of the amount over £15. For earnings over £30 there was an additional 15 per cent of the amount between £30 and £105. Reckonable weekly earnings are normally calculated by dividing by 50 the individual's total earnings in the last complete income tax year before the period of interruption of employment. The earnings-related supplement is paid in addition to the flat-rate benefit so long as total benefit does not exceed 85 per cent of reckonable weekly earnings. The maximum supplement payable to an individual earning £105 per week in 1979 was thus $33\frac{1}{3}$ per cent×(£30–£15) plus 15 per cent (£105–£30)=£16.25, and so the maximum unemployment or sickness benefit for an individual was £32 per week.

As with retirement pensions, there is, in practice, a link between unemployment and short-term supplementary benefit inasmuch as after a year at the latest an unemployed person will become dependent on supplementary benefit.[1] If an individual has received benefits for the maximum time permissible, he must then find employment for at least 13 weeks at a minimum of 16 hours per week to requalify for benefit.

The contribution conditions for unemployment and sickness benefit are somewhat complex, and it is best to approach them indirectly. We saw earlier that a minimum annual contribution based on 50 times the lower earnings limit is necessary if a year is to count as a full contributions year. To qualify for full unemployment or sickness benefit an individual has to have paid a contribution of at least this amount in the complete tax year preceding the calendar year in which the interruption of employment occurred. In 1977/78 the lower earnings limit was £15 per week and the employee Class 1 contributions rate was $5\frac{3}{4}$ per cent. Thus, someone earning £15 per week would have paid a Class 1 contribution of £0.86 per week, or £43.12 over 50 weeks. Therefore, to qualify for full unemployment or sickness benefits in 1979 an individual had to have paid at least £43.12 in national insurance contributions in the previous tax year. Where contributions fall short of this level but exceed half, benefit is paid on a sliding scale.

Since 1971 coverage has been extended in a number of ways to people suffering from long-term illness. *Invalidity benefit* replaces

[1] A person who is sick is less likely to become dependent on supplementary benefit since after six months of sickness benefits and earnings-related supplement he will normally be eligible for invalidity benefit, as discussed below.

sickness benefit after 28 weeks, and so may be regarded as a long-term sickness benefit. In 1979 it consisted of a weekly pension of £19.50. In addition, for those whose incapacity began more than five years before pensionable age an *invalidity allowance* is payable. The allowance varies according to the age at which incapacity began and the benefit is payable up to age 70 (65 for women). A person is eligible for invalidity benefit if he or she has previously been receiving sickness benefit, so that, in effect, the contribution conditions are the same as for sickness benefit.

In 1975 *non-contributory invalidity pension* was introduced, payable to those who do not qualify for invalidity benefit. Married women may also qualify for the pension provided they are incapable of performing normal household duties. The pension is payable without any income test to people who are incapable of work and have been so for at least 28 weeks. As its name implies the pension is not a national insurance benefit, and is paid out of the Consolidated Fund.

There exist a variety of other non-contributory benefits for the disabled. The two most important are the *attendance allowance* and the *mobility allowance.* The attendance allowance is a benefit paid in respect of people who require frequent prolonged or continual assistance or supervision. The benefit is not taxable, nor is it taken into account in assessing other benefits.

The mobility allowance is a benefit for people who are unable or virtually unable to walk, but are able to go out and so make use of the allowance. The allowance is taxable, but is not taken into account in assessing other benefits.

The *help with travel to work scheme* helps a disabled person to meet the high cost of travel to work where he or she is unable to use public transport. The *invalid care allowance* is a benefit for people of working age who stay at home to care for a severely disabled relative.

From Table 10.1 the total cost of these benefits in 1977 was £635 million for unemployment benefit, £608 million for sickness benefit, and £703 million for invalidity benefit (but excluding those benefits paid from the Consolidated Fund).[1]

[1] For further details of these arrangements see *Guide to the Social Services, 1978* (MacDonald Evans, 1978), pp. 140–153; *Guide to Contributory Benefits and Child Benefit, op. cit.; National Welfare Benefits Handbook* (Child Poverty Action Group, published annually). For the rates of benefit, both current and historic, see *Social Security Statistics* (HMSO, annually). For up-to-date information, see also FBI (*Family Benefits and Pensions*) and HBI (*Help for Handicapped People*) available from DHSS and Post Offices.

2.4 *Other National Insurance Benefits*

We saw in Table 10.4 that retirement and widow's pensions, unemployment, sickness and invalidity benefits together made up about 90 per cent of direct national insurance disbursements. The remaining 10 per cent of national insurance payments comprise a wide variety of different benefits, outlined briefly in this section, and summarized in Table 10.4 together with the other benefits.

Table 10.4

The Main National Insurance Benefit Rates in October 1979 (£s per week)

Retirement benefits	
Basic state retirement pension	
single person	19.50
married couple	31.20
Graduated pension	earnings-related
Earnings-related component of state pension	earnings-related
Non-contributory retirement pension for people over 80:	
single person	11.70
married woman	7.05
Widow's benefit	
Widow's allowance (first 26 weeks of widowhood)	27.30
Widowed mother's allowance	19.50
Widow's pension	19.50
Unemployment and sickness benefits	
Basic unemployment and sickness benefit	
single person	15.75
married woman	11.70
Earnings-related supplement	earnings-related
Invalidity benefits	
Invalidity benefit	19.50
Invalidity allowance (in addition to invalidity benefit)	1.30–4.15
Non-contributory invalidity pension	11.70
Maternity benefits	
Maternity grant	25.00
Maternity allowance	15.75

Table 10.4—*continued*

Death benefits	
Death grant for an adult	30.00
Death grant for persons under 18	9–22.50
Industrial injuries benefits	
Injury benefit	18.50
Earnings-related supplement for injury benefit	earnings-related
Disablement benefit (100 per cent rate)	31.90
Death benefit	
first 26 weeks	27.30
thereafter for spouse who is disabled, elderly, or looking after children	20.05
otherwise	5.85
Miscellaneous benefits	
Child's special allowance (excluding child benefit)	5.35
Guardian's allowance (excluding child benefit)	5.35
Increases for dependants (main benefits only)	
Retirement	
wife or other adult	11.70
each child (excluding child benefit)	5.35
Unemployment and sickness	
wife or other adult	9.75
each child (excluding child benefit)	0.85
Widow's children	
each child (excluding child benefit)	5.35

Source: *Hansard*, 12 April 1978.
Note: Benefits are normally uprated in November each year.

(1) *Maternity*. There are two maternity benefits, the *maternity grant* and the *maternity allowance*. The maternity grant is a once-and-for-all payment of £25 intended to help with the general expenses of having a baby. In cases of multiple births a grant may be paid for each child. The grant is payable on either the woman's own contributions or on those of her husband, provided that one of them satisfies the contribution conditions. In contrast, the maternity allowance is a weekly payment to a working mother, and is payable only on the basis of her own

insurance record. For a woman with a full contribution record it is normally paid for 18 weeks, beginning 11 weeks before the expected week of confinement, but it cannot be paid for any period in which the claimant does paid work. In addition to the standard allowance there is an earnings-related supplement, which in certain circumstances can be increased to cover dependants. The total cost of the benefit in 1977, from Table 10.1, was £92 million.

(2) *Death*. A death grant is normally payable on the death of a contributor, or a contributor's spouse or child. For an adult covered by a full contributions record the death grant is £30, normally payable to the person responsible for meeting the cost of the funeral. The original intention was that the grant should be sufficient to pay for a simple funeral, though inflation has almost entirely eroded its ability to do so. Total expenditure on the death grant in 1977 (see Table 10.1) was a mere £16 million.

(3) *Industrial injury benefit* applies, broadly speaking, to all employed earners, i.e. those paying Class 1 national insurance contributions, though there are extensions to cover certain other cases such as unpaid apprentices. There are three types of benefit payable for personal injury as a result of an industrial accident.

(a) *Injury benefit* is payable for no more than 26 weeks to any person who is incapable of work as a result of an industrial accident or a prescribed industrial disease. Additional benefit is payable for a wife, or other adult dependant, and for children, as with sickness benefit. An earnings-related supplement may also be paid to an individual in receipt of injury benefit calculated in the same way as that for unemployment and sickness benefit, and subject to the same contribution conditions.

(b) *Industrial disablement benefit*: injury benefit is payable only to a person entirely unable to work (whether temporarily or permanently) and for no more than 26 weeks. In contrast, industrial disablement benefit is payable (i) for the entire duration of any disablement, whether temporary or permanent, and (ii) whether or not the disablement prevents the person from working at all. The benefit is payable when injury benefit ceases, or from three days after the accident if there was no incapacity for work. Industrial disablement benefit will be paid to any individual who, as a result of an industrial accident or disease, suffers a loss of physical or mental faculty; the amount of benefit will vary with the degree of disability.

The extent and period of disablement is assessed by an independent medical board. Comparison is made with a normal person of the same age and sex, and no account is taken of whether or not the injury has caused loss of earning power.[1] A weekly pension is awarded in the light of the assessment as to the degree of disablement, the amount varying in 1979 from £31.90 per week for a person judged to be totally disabled, to £6.38 for someone judged to be 20 per cent disabled. Where the extent of the disablement is assessed at less than 20 per cent, disablement benefit is normally paid in a lump sum which depends on the period and degree of disablement, and will not normally exceed £2,120.

There are a variety of additional payments which may be made to a person in receipt of industrial disablement benefit. These cover people who are unemployable, cases of special hardship, and cases of exceptionally severe disablement where the beneficiary requires constant attention.[2]

(c) *Death benefits*: when a man is killed in an industrial accident or dies from an industrial disease, his widow will receive a pension of £27.30 per week (in 1979) for the first 26 weeks after the death. Thereafter, his widow receives a pension of £20.05 per week, provided that (i) she is also entitled to an allowance for a child, or (ii) that at the time of his death she was over the age of 50, or (iii) that at the time of his death she was permanently incapable of self-support. Widows who have drawn a pension of £20.05 per week may continue to do so when their children are no longer eligible for the child allowance if they are over 40. Otherwise, the pension is £5.85 per week. All these benefits are paid for life, or until the widow remarries, at which time she will receive a gratuity equal to 52 times the weekly pension she was receiving. Where the insured person was a married woman, her widower is entitled to a pension for life at the rate of £20.05 per week provided that he was being wholly or mainly maintained by his wife and is permanently incapable of self-support.

(4) *Miscellaneous benefits*. Two additional national insurance benefits specifically concern children.

(a) *Child's special allowance* is a benefit for a woman whose marriage has been dissolved or annulled and who has not since remarried. It is payable on the death of her former husband if she has a child to whose

[1] A person whose earning power has been reduced may apply for a special hardship allowance in addition to the industrial disablement benefit.

[2] Details of these additional payments may be found in *Guide to the Social Services, op. cit.*, Ch. 41, and *Guide to Contributory Benefits and Child Benefit, op. cit.*

support he was previously contributing at least 25p a week. The allowance is £5.35 per week for each child, with child benefit (but not child benefit increase)[1] being paid in addition.

(b) *Guardian's allowance*: if the parents of a child are dead, and at least one of them satisfied a nationality or residence condition, then anyone who looks after a child as part of his or her family and receives child benefit for the child may qualify for a guardian's allowance. The guardian's allowance has the same value as the child's special allowance. In certain circumstances the allowance can be awarded on the death of only one parent, where the parents had previously been divorced, or where the surviving parent cannot be traced or is serving a long term of imprisonment.

(5) *Increases for dependants*. The level of many of the benefits mentioned above may be increased where the beneficiary has dependants whom he or she supports. These additional benefits are generally available both for adult dependants, and dependent children. In the case of dependent children, child benefit is normally payable in addition to the increases for dependants listed in Table 10.4, though the child benefit increase is, in general, available only to the recipients of short-term benefits.

The level of all these benefits is reviewed at least once a year. In the case of national insurance benefits, the method of uprating is prescribed by law. The other benefits are raised on an ad hoc basis, and most of them are increased annually. A rare exception is the death grant, which was set at £20 in 1949, raised to £25 in 1958 and to its present level of £30 in 1967. As this sum is clearly unrealistic, the 'cradle to grave' claim of the welfare state should, perhaps, be amended to 'cradle to deathbed'.

We have already mentioned that there exist interrelationships between the increases payable for child dependants, and child benefit payments. Similarly, there is a relationship between national insurance benefits generally, and supplementary benefit. This arises because many national benefits are set at a level below that of the comparable supplementary benefit rate, so that many people whose sole source of income is from national insurance are eligible also for supplementary benefit. In the next section we outline the mechanism whereby many people receive both national insurance benefits and supplementary benefit.

[1] See p. 254 below.

3 BENEFITS OTHER THAN NATIONAL INSURANCE

3.1 *Child benefit*

Having now discussed the major national insurance and related benefits we turn in this section to a variety of other benefits, all paid from the Consolidated Fund. By far the most important of these are child benefit and supplementary benefit.

Since child benefit has been in operation for only a short while it is useful to review the historical background. Until April 1977 there were two distinct forms of financial assistance to families with children. First, the threshold for income tax liability was higher for families with children by virtue of *child tax allowances*. In 1976/77 a family was allowed an extra £300 per year of tax-free income in respect of a child under 11 years old, £335 per year for each child between 11–16, and £365 per year for each child over 16. These child tax allowances (like any tax-free income) were more valuable the higher a person's marginal rate of tax; the £300 allowance for a child under 11 was worth nothing to a family below the tax threshold, £105 in tax saved to a family paying the then basic rate of 35 per cent, and £210 in saved tax to a family facing a 70 per cent marginal rate of tax.

Up to April 1977 a completely separate form of assistance to families with children was *family allowances*, first introduced into Great Britain in 1946 following a long period of discussion. In 1976/77 they were payable at the rate of £1.50 per week for the second and subsequent children in any family. Unlike the child tax allowances which were usually granted to the father, family allowances were payable on a weekly basis specifically to the mother. The main complication with family allowance was that they were taxed in two ways. First, they were taxable as earned income and, secondly, from the late 1960s, they were subject to 'clawback'. The effect of clawback was to reduce by £52 per year the child tax allowance applicable to any child for whom a family allowance was paid. The combined effect of these two forms of tax was to make family allowance worth less the higher a family's income and, in the case of families facing the top marginal rates, to make it worthwhile not to claim it at all.

Up to April 1977, therefore, the position for a typical family was that the father received the child tax allowances, which would be worth more the higher the family's income, and the mother would receive the family allowances, which would be worth less the higher the family's income. This system has now been entirely replaced[1] by the much simpler *child benefit*, which has been fully in operation since April 1979. In April 1977 child benefit for all children in the family, including the first, replaced family allowances, and child tax allowances were progressively replaced by higher child benefit. There is no need to dwell on these transitional arrangements, and the following paragraphs describe the child benefit system as it has operated since April 1979.

Child benefit is a tax-free, weekly payment in respect of each child in the family. From April 1979 it was payable at a rate of £4 per child per week. Child benefit is not a national insurance benefit; the payments are administered by the Department of Health and Social Security.

For child benefit purposes a child is someone living in the UK and under the age of 16, or under 19 if receiving full-time education. The benefit is payable to the person responsible for a child, and this can be either someone with whom the child is living, or someone who contributes to the support of a child living elsewhere. When a child lives with both parents the mother has title to the benefit.

Some single parents who receive child benefit are eligible also for *child benefit increase*. From November 1978 this has been payable at a rate of £2 per week for the first or only child. The increase has to be claimed separately from child benefit. In principle, all single parents are eligible for a child benefit increase, but entitlement is withdrawn if the parent is already in receipt of certain long-term national insurance benefits such as a child's special allowance, guardian's allowance, or benefits for the dependent children of widows or retirement pensioners.[1]

In contrast to the combination of child tax allowances and family allowances, child benefit is administratively much less cumbersome, and is worth the same to everyone, irrespective of their income.[2] The benefit is part of a gradual trend towards standardizing the benefits payable in respect of children under different schemes of income support. Table 10.3 shows that expenditure on the benefit in 1977 was £805 million.

[1] Except where a UK taxpayer has a dependent child who is living outside the UK.

[2] These and other benefits were discussed on pp. 251–2, above. For further details see *Guide to Contributory Benefits and Child Benefit, op. cit.*

[3] The relative treatment by income of families of different sizes is discussed in Chapter 13, section 2.

3.2 *Supplementary benefit*
Supplementary benefit is paid to individuals and families when all else fails. It is therefore not surprising, as Table 10.3 shows, that expenditure on supplementary benefit in 1977 was £1,750 million; this was larger than expenditure on any other benefit except the national insurance retirement pension. The numbers involved are also large. In February 1978 there were just over 3 million persons in receipt of supplementary benefit, of whom some four-fifths were either pensioners (1.7 million) or unemployed (667,000). There is a great deal of confusion about supplementary benefit, in part because of its emotive nature. But much of the confusion arises because of the genuine complexities of the scheme. Where a benefit is designed to supplement people's incomes, there are bound to be complicated questions about the interactions of supplementary benefit and other sources of an individual's or family's income. We shall therefore start with a description of the benefit, before proceeding to a more detailed discussion.

Poor Law legislation finally ended in 1948 when it was replaced by the National Assistance Act 1948. The National Assistance Board took over from local authorities the responsibility for meeting the financial needs of people with insufficient resources. In 1966 the National Assistance Board was abolished, and the Supplementary Benefits Commission was established within what was later to become the Department of Health and Social Security to award (a) *supplementary pensions* to those over pension age and (b) *supplementary allowances* to those under pension age.

Supplementary benefit may be paid to anyone aged 16 or over. Benefit is calculated by setting *requirements* against *resources*. If the latter are less than the former, the difference between the two is paid as benefit. Requirements are calculated as:

(i) *the weekly scale rates*, as laid down by Parliament,
(ii) *rent addition* for weekly housing expenses, and
(iii) *exceptional circumstances addition* for special needs such as heating or diet.

Resources include national insurance benefits, child benefit, any maintenance payments, and any other income, of which certain small items can be 'disregarded'. In special circumstances *exceptional needs payments* may be made. These are lump-sum grants to meet particular needs such as clothing, furniture, fuel bills, etc. Supplementary benefit also acts as a 'passport' to other benefits, such as free prescriptions, free dental treatment, and free school meals.[1]

We shall discuss supplementary benefit in some detail under three main headings: eligibility, the basic benefit, and additional benefit.

(1) *Eligibility*. Anyone aged 16 or over who is not in full-time work may be eligible for supplementary benefit, whether or not he or she has a national insurance record. A person receiving a national insurance benefit may also be eligible for supplementary benefit. A person working part-time may be eligible, but benefits are not normally payable for people in full-time work. For those under pensionable age the Supplementary Benefits Commission has the power to make the right to benefit conditional on registering for work. This rule is not applied in the case of the sick, single parents of children under 16, and blind people not used to working outside the home. Certain other groups may not be required to register for work, or to register only quarterly, depending on the circumstances.

(2) *The basic benefit*. The determination of the amount of supplementary benefit in any particular case rests on two considerations: (a) how much benefit is awarded to a family with no other income, and (b) how this benefit is affected by any income the family does have. These correspond to the 'requirements' and 'resources' aspects of the administration of supplementary benefit. We discuss these in turn.

(a) *Benefit levels for those with no income*: the requirements element of supplementary benefit is the amount that an individual or family is considered to need to live on, and will include (i) a weekly living allowance, and (ii) a rent allowance. A weekly living allowance is calculated according to scale rates laid down by law, which vary according to the numbers and ages of any dependants. The scale rates for 1979 are shown in Table 10.5. There are two scales, the ordinary and the long-term. The long-term rate is paid to people receiving a supplementary pension, and also to those who have been receiving a supplementary allowance for two years either continuously or in periods not separated by more than 13 weeks, during which they have not been required to register for work. Persons aged 80 and over receive an additional 25p per week (50p if both husband and wife are 80 or over). The ordinary scale rate for 1979 varied from £12.45 per week for a single non-householder to £52.30 per week

[1] For details of supplementary benefit and a variety of other non-contributory benefits see *National Welfare Benefits Handbook, op. cit.*

for a family of five containing three teenage children. A higher rate of benefit is payable where the householder or a dependant is blind.

Table 10.5

Supplementary Benefit Scale Rates, 1979

<table>
<tr><th>Ordinary scale</th><th>Ordinary rate
£s per week</th><th>Long-term rate
£s per week</th></tr>
<tr><td>Husband and wife</td><td>25.25</td><td>31.55</td></tr>
<tr><td>Single householder</td><td>15.55</td><td>19.90</td></tr>
<tr><td>Any other person aged:</td><td></td><td></td></tr>
<tr><td>18 and over</td><td>12.45</td><td>15.95</td></tr>
<tr><td>16–17</td><td colspan="2">9.55</td></tr>
<tr><td>13–15</td><td colspan="2">7.95</td></tr>
<tr><td>11–12</td><td colspan="2">6.55</td></tr>
<tr><td>5–10</td><td colspan="2">5.30</td></tr>
<tr><td>Under 5</td><td colspan="2">4.40</td></tr>
<tr><td>Blind scale</td><td></td><td></td></tr>
<tr><td>Husband and wife</td><td></td><td></td></tr>
<tr><td>If one of them is blind</td><td>26.50</td><td>32.80</td></tr>
<tr><td>If both of them are blind</td><td>27.30</td><td>33.60</td></tr>
<tr><td>Any other blind person aged:</td><td></td><td></td></tr>
<tr><td>18 and over</td><td>16.80</td><td>21.15</td></tr>
<tr><td>16–17</td><td>10.45</td><td>10.45</td></tr>
</table>

Source: *Hansard*, 12 April 1978.
Note: Child benefit and child benefit increase are, in effect, deducted from the above rates; see p. 258.

The rent allowance will work in different ways depending on whether the recipient of benefit is a tenant or an owner-occupier. The rent and all rates of a tenant are normally met in full. If the lease or tenancy agreement makes the tenant responsible for repairs the recipient of supplementary benefit also receives a standard allowance of 76p per week. The Supplementary Benefits Commission has the power to meet only that part of the rent which it considers reasonable. It has the discretion also to pay a lower rate of benefit to anyone who is classified as a non-householder. Under the law a non-householder receives a lower rate, and a standard rent addition which was £1.45 in

1979. The law does not define 'non-householder', so problems can arise in cases where living arrangements are fluid, such as squatters, people sharing flats, and people living with relatives.

In the case of owner-occupiers the law states that the rent addition should cover rates, ground rent, and mortgage interest payments, plus an allowance for repairs and insurance, but no capital repayments. Again, the Supplementary Benefits Commission has the power to meet only that part of the interest payment which is considered reasonable. In addition to mortgage interest payments, rates, and ground rent, an allowance of £55.30 per year is made to cover repairs and house insurance.

We can thus summarize the requirements aspect of supplementary benefit by saying that a typical couple with no other income will receive a weekly benefit determined from the ordinary scale rate, plus a rent allowance.

(b) *The treatment of income*: in general, a family will receive a lower level of benefit if it has other sources of income. The resources element calculates how much income a family has for the purposes of supplementary benefit. The underlying principle is that all income is included in a family's resources unless it is specifically 'disregarded'. The main disregards are for earnings. For a single parent the first £6 per week of net earnings from part-time work are not counted. For others the first £4 net per week are not counted for those who are not required to register for work (£2 per week for people who are required to register). In addition, the first £4 of a wife's net earnings are ignored, and so are most earnings of a child under 16. An important point is that 'net' earnings for the purposes of supplementary benefit means earnings after tax and national insurance contributions and after allowing for all reasonable expenses of work, including fares and child-minding costs. The ability to deduct these expenses is in striking contrast to the rules applicable for tax purposes to Schedule E income, and is another example of the discrepancies between the different constituents of the overall tax picture in this country. There are a variety of other disregards for income like education maintenance allowances, maternity and death grants, and the first £4 of most other types of income. Disregards apart, *all* income including child benefit and national insurance benefits are included in a family's resources.[1]

In addition, any capital the individual or family owns may affect entitlement to benefit. The value of an owner-occupied house is

[1] Attendance allowances and mobility allowances are not so included.

entirely ignored. Other capital, including savings, redundancy payments and some tax rebates are dealt with in the following way: capital of less than £1,250 is ignored; for any capital of £1,250 or more any actual income it produces is ignored, but income is imputed at the rate of 25p per week per complete £50 of capital above £1,200, and this amount is added to any other income for the purposes of calculating the family's resources. The implied interest rate is ½ per cent per week or just under 30 per cent per year on a compound basis.[1] This discrepancy in the relative treatment of earnings and imputed income from capital is analogous to the application of the investment income surcharge in the case of income tax.

An individual's or family's benefit is calculated as the difference between its requirements and its resources. If requirements are estimated at £30 plus rent, and resources are estimated as £20 per week, then the individual or family will receive supplementary benefit at a rate of £10 per week plus rent. Thus, at the margin an extra pound of resources costs £1 of benefits, in economic terms a 100 per cent implicit tax rate. What this means is that the implicit tax on disregarded income is 0 per cent, and on all other income including most national insurance benefits is 100 per cent. Supplementary benefit can therefore be thought of as 'topping up' family income from whatever source to bring it up to a basic minimum. We shall return to these matters in greater detail in Chapter 14.

(3) *Additional benefits*. While many of the actions of the Supplementary Benefits Commission are prescribed by law, the authorities also have considerable discretion. To explain which activities are laid down by law, and which are the result of discretionary rules, is a major study in itself, and we shall do no more than touch on the issue. The main area of discretion concerns additional payments to individuals or families whose specific circumstances warrant them. There are two types of discretionary payments, *exceptional circumstances additions*, which are weekly payments, and *exceptional needs payments*, which are once-and-for-all payments for specific contingencies. The exceptional circumstances additions are payable on a weekly basis in cases like special diets which are necessary on medical grounds, and for which a

[1] For further details of the calculation of the requirements and resources elements of supplementary benefit see the following:

National Welfare Benefits Handbook, op. cit.; The Law Relating to Supplementary Benefits and Family Income Supplement (HMSO); *Supplementary Benefit Handbook* (HMSO, 1977); and A. Lynes, *Penguin Guide to Supplementary Benefits* (Penguin, second edition, 1974).

doctor's certificate can be produced. The additional payment is 95p per week in most cases, but can be as high as £2.25 per week for serious medical conditions. Exceptional circumstances additions can be paid also for extra heating and for a variety of smaller items such as especially heavy laundry expenses in cases of illness or infirmity, telephone charges for a housebound person living alone, and fares for a regular visit to a relative in hospital, to name but a few. These payments may be made in a very wide variety of circumstances and it is precisely for this reason that they are discretionary. Equally though, much dissatisfaction and argument can arise where a claimant feels that he or she has unjustifiably been turned down for additional benefit.

Recipients of supplementary benefit can also receive exceptional needs payments. These are discretionary lump-sum grants. There is no legal limit to how much can be paid or when they can be paid except that the need must be 'exceptional' and the authorities must consider it reasonable to make an exceptional needs payment in the circumstances. As with exceptional circumstances additions the authorities have a wide degree of discretion. Payments may be made in certain circumstances for clothes; to replace bedding and household equipment; in very exceptional circumstances to pay fuel debts if the claimant is threatened with disconnection; to replace or repair broken heating appliances; to contribute to the cost of any clothing or tools needed when starting a new job; and for a variety of other once-and-for-all expenses such as help with the funeral expenses of a close relative if the claimant cannot meet the bill from his own resources or from money left by the deceased.[1]

Additionally, supplementary benefit acts as a 'passport' to a variety of other benefits such as free prescriptions, free dental treatment, spectacles under the National Health Service, free welfare milk and vitamins for pre-school children and expectant mothers, free school meals and hospital fares. We shall refer to these in the next section.

3.3 *Other non-contributory benefits*

Finally we turn to a miscellany of remaining benefits the main characteristics of which are their multiplicity and complexity. Some are administered nationally by the Department of Health and Social Security, others locally; and those administered locally can be subdivided into those over which local authorities have a broad measure of

[1] For further details of exceptional circumstances additions and exceptional needs payments see *National Welfare Benefits Handbook, op. cit.*

discretion, and those over which they do not. Local Authority finance is properly the subject of the next chapter, but it will give a better overall picture of income support in the UK if we discuss all cash awards together.

The benefits outlined below are only a very partial listing described in the broadest detail, since their practical operation is complex and constantly changing.[1]

(1) *Family income supplement* is payable to families (including one-parent families) with low incomes where the head of the family is normally engaged in full-time paid work, and where there is at least one dependent child. Under the Family Income Supplements Act 1970 the administration of the benefit is in the hands of the Supplementary Benefits Commission. It is payable to families whose normal gross weekly income is below a prescribed amount determined by Parliament. In 1979 the prescribed amount was £46 for a one-child family, increasing by £4 for each additional child. The weekly amount payable is half the difference between a family's gross income and the prescribed amount, subject to a maximum payment of £10.50 for a one-child family, and increasing by £1 for each child.[2]

In the case of a married couple, or a man and woman living together, it is the man who must be in full-time work and it is he who must make the claim. Full-time work for the purposes of family income supplement is at least 30 hours per week (24 hours for a single-parent family). An award will normally be made for 52 weeks, and once made will not be affected by any change of circumstances during that period. Families receiving family income supplement are automatically entitled to the same variety of additional benefits as those receiving supplementary benefit.

(2) *Rent rebates.*

(3) *Rent allowances* (unfurnished tenants).

(4) *Rent allowances* (furnished).

(5) *Rate rebates*.

Rent rebates are awarded to council tenants, and rent allowances to tenants in the private sector. Rate rebates are awarded to householders responsible for paying the rates. The amount of benefit generally will depend on the claimant's gross income (including that of his or her

[1] For details of these various benefits see *National Welfare Benefits Handbook, op. cit.*, and *Means Tested Benefits* (National Consumer Council, 1977), Appendix 2.

[2] The interested reader in search of details will find a very compendious account in *National Welfare Benefits Handbook, op. cit.*, and *Means Tested Benefits, op. cit.*

spouse), the size of the household, and the amount of rent and rates. The benefit will generally be larger the lower is family income and the higher are the rent and rates. The benefits are not normally available to families in receipt of supplementary benefit.

Other schemes range over educational benefits (e.g. free school meals, clothing grants); health benefits (e.g. free prescriptions, free welfare milk and vitamins); benefits for the disabled and handicapped (e.g. the fares to work scheme); employment and job-training benefits; help for the elderly (e.g. meals on wheels); legal aid; and help for the homeless. In all there are almost fifty schemes of this sort. The interested reader is referred to the footnote on p. 261.

This concludes our survey of the various national insurance and non-contributory benefits. We shall return to some of the policy issues they raise in Chapter 14.

11

THE LOCAL AUTHORITIES

1 INTRODUCTION

It may be useful to begin by distinguishing between the different types of local authorities and their respective functions. In England and Wales (as Scotland and Northern Ireland are rather different in local authority matters, some of our discussions will not apply to them) the major distinction was for many years between two-tier and single-tier authorities. In the two-tier case, the upper tier consisted of counties and the lower one took various forms: municipal boroughs or urban district councils or rural district councils. Broadly speaking, the division of functions was such that the share of the county was progressively greater the smaller and less important were the lower tier authorities. The single-tier authorities (county boroughs) combined the functions of the components of the two-tier authorities. The lowest rung of the administrative ladder was made up of several thousand parish councils. London was regarded as being in a category of its own, with a two-tier system consisting since 1965 of the Greater London Council and thirty-two boroughs plus the City of London.

Since 1 April 1974 there has been a radical change in the numbers, structure and functions of local authorities in England and Wales. The upshot is that with the sole exception of the Isles of Scilly there is now a two-tier system throughout, consisting of fifty-three counties and 369 districts (excluding London). Within this structure there is a further differentiation in that six of the counties covering large conurbations (e.g. Merseyside, Greater Manchester) are designated as metropolitan counties; and the thirty-six districts controlled by them are called metropolitan districts. The division of functions between county and district differs as between the metropolitan areas and the rest; in the metropolitan areas the districts have more responsibilities (e.g. education, personal social services, libraries) than in the latter. The consequence is that metropolitan districts and non-metropolitan counties predominate in their respective areas.[1] The overall result of the reduc-

[1] Proposals were afoot early in 1979 for the transfer of some powers from non-metropolitan counties to the larger districts inside them.

tion in numbers of authorities (from some 1,400 to just over 400) was a strengthening of functions of counties relative to the large cities (e.g. in respect of planning). Parish councils survive in the new structure, sometimes taking the place of the higher level status formerly enjoyed by many small towns; and there are new community councils in Wales.

There has been a parallel set of changes in Scotland, except that it dates from 1975 and there is no metropolitan and non-metropolitan distinction. Northern Ireland has single-tier all-purpose authorities only.

2 THE REVENUE AND EXPENDITURE PICTURE

2.1 *Expenditure*

We follow roughly the same line of approach as with the Central Government, taking expenditure first, then revenue and finally procedure. The emphasis is somewhat different, however, with, for instance, proportionately less time being spent on the discussion of financial procedure. It is also necessary for statistical reasons to confine discussion to the last available completed accounts rather than the estimates for a forthcoming year. Table 11.1 shows local authority expenditure in the UK in 1977.

Table 11.1

UK Local Authority Expenditure, 1977 (£m)

Current (excluding trading)		16,165
Education	5,618	
Other social expenditure	1,619	
Public works and services	1,477	
Debt interest	3,130	
Other	4,321	
Capital (including trading)		3,654
Housing	1,995	
Public works and services	427	
Education	536	
Other (including trading)	573	
Grants and loans	123	

Source: *National Income Blue Book* (HMSO, 1978).
Note: The provisional figure for the total current expenditure for 1978 was £17,458m.

No time need be wasted explaining the meaning of the individual items; 'Other social expenditure' includes such items as personal social services. 'Public works and services' covers roads, street lighting, fire services, etc.; 'Other' is a miscellaneous category embracing administration, police, justice, etc. In the *capital* group, 'Public works and services' has much the same meaning as above.

Table 11.2

UK Local Authority Expenditure: 1913/14 and 1938/39 (£m)

	1913/14		*1938/39*	
Current (excluding trading)		122		386
Education	36		118	
Health	9		86	
Roads	23		68	
Other	54		114	
Capital (excluding trading)		25		172
Housing	Nil		67	
Roads	4		16	
Trading	5		37	
Other	16		52	

Sources: *Statistical Abstracts of the UK.*

It may be worth spending a moment or two saying why the *current* group should exclude 'trading' and the *capital* group include it. By 'trading' is meant not only the usual local authority enterprises including housing management and repairs, but the more unusual ones such as the municipal wash-house at Manchester or the telephone system at Hull. The reason for excluding current expenditure is that we need to be in a position to be able to add together all government expenditures to compare them with national expenditure and outlay. As governmental trading expenditure is not a final demand on the resources of a country, but is an intermediate step towards satisfying consumer demands, it would be double-counting to include it under both the local government heading and the personal consumption sector. On the other hand, local authority capital expenditure on trading services is not duplicated in the same way and therefore should not be excluded from the total. In other words the treatment here has to tie in with that in Chapter 8.

Roughly comparable historical data on local authority expenditure may help to pinpoint the more significant features of Table 11.1. The first point from Table 11.2 is the growth in local authority expenditure, though it should be noted that the percentage increase since 1913/14 is far less than in the case of the Central Government. Secondly, there have been changes in the relative importance of capital and current expenditure; this is principally due to the development of municipal house-building. Education has grown in importance relative to total current expenditure but health has declined, particularly since the inauguration of the national Health Service in 1948, and changes in organization in 1974. Finally, the importance of trading other than housing in the capital sector has diminished in recent years (in 1977 it accounted for only £102m) since the nationalization of various industries such as gas and electricity where local authorities were formerly prominent.

Table 11.3

UK Local Authority Revenue, 1977 (£m)

Current		18,000
Rates	5,194	
Grants	9,370	
Trading surplus (gross)	143	
Rent, interest, etc.	3,293	
Capital		3,654
Surplus from current account	1,835	
Capital grants	187	
Net borrowing:		
Central Government	1,380	
Other	185	
Other transactions	67	

Source: *National Income Blue Book* (HMSO, 1978).
Notes: (1) Trading surplus and rent are before depreciation.
(2) The provisional figure for total current receipts in 1978 was £19,483m.

2.2. *Revenue*

Turning to the revenue side, the main items are set out in Table 11.3. The noteworthy features are the importance of self-financing relative to borrowing in the capital account and the excess of revenue from grants over that from rates in the current account. The historical data of Table 11.4 help us to fill out this picture in respect of the current account.

Table 11.4

UK Local Authority Current Revenue, 1913/14 and 1938/39 (£m)

	1913/14	*1938/39*
Rates	82	215
Grants (current)	27	164
Trading (net)	3	–30
Other	9	49
TOTAL	121	398

Source: *Statistical Abstracts of the UK.*

The outstanding point historically is the changing relative importance of rates and Central Government grants. Whereas rates were 68 per cent of current revenue in 1913/14, the percentage fell to 54 per cent in 1938/39 and to 29 per cent in 1977. This has been due partly to the slow growth of revenue from rates and partly to the large increase in grants from the Central Government. It will be convenient to summarize the main characteristics of these two sources of revenue before discussing the other features of Tables 11.3 and 11.4.

Rates on occupiers of land and buildings are an ancient tax linking directly with the Poor Rate of the seventeenth century and, more indirectly, with even older taxes. Rates in their modern form are paid on the 'rateable value' of property which is, in principle, equal to the yearly rent which would be acceptable to both landlord and tenant, on the assumption that the latter pays for insurance, repairs to the property and maintenance generally.

It should be noted that if a property is unoccupied then it does not command any rent and historically no demand for rates could be made during any such period.[1] The exact amount payable for an occupied property depends not only on the rateable value but also on the rate in the pound charged by the local authority. Whereas the former changes infrequently (in principle there is a quinquennial revaluation but in practice the intervals between valuations are longer), the latter is likely to change annually in accordance with estimated expenditure and the yield from other sources of revenue. The rate poundage is calculated by dividing the yield of a penny rate in the area into the total sum to be raised. Suppose, for example, the amount needed is £360,000 and the

[1] Since 1967 local authorities have had limited powers to charge rates on unoccupied properties. These powers were extended in 1974.

total rateable value for an area is £480,000. A penny rate would then produce £4,800 and by dividing this sum into £360,000, we find that the rate has to be £0.75.

Since the Local Government Act of 1948, the responsibility for assessing rateable values in England and Wales has rested with the valuation department of the Inland Revenue. So, today there is a centralized responsibility for assessment instead of purely local arrangements. The rate poundage is, of course, fixed locally. It should be noted that county councils are not rating authorities and they finance themselves by making demands (known as 'precepts') on the districts in their area. The component units of the lower tier therefore levy rates both to finance their own expenditure and to meet the demands of the upper tier.

Although the basic principle of rateable values is that they should correspond to rents, there have been many concessions over the years. The most important example of de-rating is that of agricultural land and buildings which for many years have been fully de-rated. Charities are 50 per cent de-rated; and so is industry in Scotland. Crown properties are not rateable in law but the distinction there is a purely formal one in that they make equivalent contributions in lieu. Until recent years all types of property in a given area were charged at the same rate poundage, but since April 1967 there has been a differential element in that domestic ratepayers are now charged at a lower rate than non-domestic. In addition, further concessions ('rate rebates') are made to people below specified income levels, taking account of numbers of children and other family circumstances.[1]

Central Government grants have a shorter history than local rates. The first grant recognizable as such appeared in 1831 when an allocation of £90 a year was made to Berwick Corporation for the repair of Berwick Bridge. There was a gradual extension of grants for different purposes in the course of the nineteenth century until they reached something like 14 per cent of local revenue by 1888. In that year, an attempt was made to introduce a system of assigned revenues, whereby specific revenues of the Central Government (e.g. 40 per cent of probate duties) were earmarked for local authorities. This did not prove a very successful innovation and, in effect, the system of making specific grants to Local Authorities for specific purposes continued. The next major landmark was the Local Government Act of 1929. This had three main sections: the first dealt with a reorganization of

[1] See Chapter 10, section 3.3 for details.

functions among Local Authorities, the second with de-rating of agriculture and industry, and the third with the grant system. In the last, the main departure from previous practice was the introduction of a *block grant* in the place of a number of specific grants. This block grant was not tied to specific types of expenditure but was allocated according to various indicators of the resources and needs of local authorities such as the number of children, the level of employment, the number of inhabitants per mile of road and so on. This was a revolutionary notion and although World War II prevented its full implementation, the principles behind it are now widely known and accepted. The Local Government Act of 1948 introduced the *exchequer equalization grant* which, although substantially different in detail from the block grant of 1929, embodied the same general principles of differentiating between richer and poorer local authorities. The next major change was in 1958. The exchequer equalization grant was renamed a *rate deficiency grant* and modified once again in detail. At the same time a new *general grant* was introduced in place of a large number of the specific grants.

In 1967, there was another major change in that a new *rate support grant* was introduced with three major components: a *resources* element taking over from the rate deficiency grant, a *needs* element taking over from the general grant, and a new *domestic* element. Further changes were made in each of these components as a result of the Local Government Act 1974. The resources element is about 30 per cent of the total and the needs and domestic elements 60 and 10 per cent respectively.

The idea behind the *resources* element is that additional help should be given to authorities with relatively small resources. A national standard rateable value per head of the population is computed for the country as a whole. If any individual local authority has a rateable value per head less than the national standard, it receives a grant on the basis of the shortfall in rateable value per head multiplied by its poundage. In other words the government acts as a ghost ratepayer. On the other hand, those authorities (mainly in London) with rateable values per head above the standard do not have to pay any 'tax' to the Central Government.

The *needs* element is based on a complex formula designed to compensate authorities according to needs. The basic ingredient is population, but numbers of old people, numbers of children and housing factors also count. The precise basis is liable to change from year to year. At one time there was a negative element in the computation, whereby reductions were made on the basis of the product of a given rate in the pound; this ceased with the changeover from the general grant.

The third element – the *domestic* one – is that provision has been made for reimbursing local authorities in respect of rate reductions for domestic ratepayers (of the order of 25–30 per cent of what rate bills would otherwise have been); and for partial reductions in the case of mixed hereditaments. The rate support grant is determined every year in advance. The projected sum for England and Wales for 1979/80 was £7,258m; the resources element accounted for £2,137m, the needs element for £4,434m, and the domestic element for £687m.

So much for an account of the grants which are not related to particular items of local authority expenditure. These account for about 90 per cent of the total, the remaining ones being either specific (e.g. 50 per cent of expenditure on police) or supplementary (largely for transport purposes). The main difference between the specific and supplementary categories is that the former is open-ended with no formal overall total set by the government, whereas the latter is not so.

The remaining sources of local authority revenue need not take up much time. Trading surplus comes from trading operations. The rent figure is the net difference between rents received (plus various subsidies relating to housing) and the costs of management, repairs and the like. It must be fully understood that the subsidy payment from central government for housing is of the order of £1,000m p.a., i.e. of the same order of magnitude as the total of specific and supplementary grants.

The receipts on capital account are fairly straightforward. The capital grants are not really an additional species of grant but should be thought of as mainly corresponding to specific grants. The net borrowing item calls for a little more explanation. Local authorities can borrow[1] on their own account or from a Central Government agency, the Public Works Loans Board. In the decade after 1945 there was a strong emphasis on the latter type of borrowing, but then there was a reversal of policy and much smaller sums were available from this source during the next decade. Subsequently, policy changed again and we now have an intermediate position. Other borrowing may take a large number of forms ranging from inter-authority borrowing and

[1] But only for capital purposes, very short-term situations aside.

sums placed on deposit by individuals, to bonds and stocks issued in the market or borrowing in foreign currencies.

To summarize the revenue position, it can be seen that local authorities are more dependent on grants from the centre than was formerly the case. The principal reason is that the yield from rates has failed to rise concurrently with Local Authority expenditure and, in the absence of any new local taxes, this has inevitably meant that the balance has had to be found from grants. Two historical explanations of the slow rise in the yield from rates have been the existence of rent control on domestic property and the de-rating of industry and agriculture in the 1920s. As a result there have not only been direct reductions in the yield of rates but it has also become harder to rate other types of property on a true basis. The system of relief to domestic rate-payers introduced in 1967 is evidence of this.

Although the decline in rates is the major phenomenon, local authorities have been progressively deprived of one possible further source of revenue. The nationalization of gas and electricity meant the end of local authorities in these fields and hence the loss of trading profits from these enterprises. However, since there is little evidence historically that these activities were on balance very remunerative, their loss was less important from the viewpoint of revenue than from that of power and prestige. It may also be that there will be some alleviation on this front in the future in that local authorities have two new sources of revenue from the mid-1970s – a share in the proceeds of the national development land tax[1] and a system of local lotteries.

The obvious question which arises from these considerations is the sorts of reforms which are necessary in local authority finances, but this would lead us into questions of policy with which we are not yet concerned. We shall discuss this topic in detail in Chapter 20.

3 ADMINISTRATIVE PROCEDURES

The final topic for discussion is the procedural arrangements for local authority revenues and expenditures. There are two main topics:[2] the determination of the total amount of grant each year and the mechanics of the local authority budgeting process.

[1] See Chapter 9, section 2.1.4, for details.

[2] We do not discuss here the many ways, formal and informal, in which local authorities are subject to Central Government control, but it may be noted that the controls over capital expenditure and borrowing are particularly stringent. A system of cash limits control was also imposed in the mid-1970s. (See Chapter 9, section 3.1.)

Although there is an annual charade in which it is pretended that the grants total is determined by applying a certain percentage to a certain aggregate total of local authority expenditure, both the percentage rates and the total are liable to adjustment depending on the in-fighting between central and local authority representatives. The central government largely calls the tune on specific and supplementary grants and the domestic element of the rate support grant. The division of the remainder of the rate support grant between needs and resources is essentially an iterative process aimed at causing the least offence to the least number of local authorities.[1]

Although grants for a given financial year are determined initially in the preceding November, increases – subject to the controls on cash limits – may be made for subsequent changes in pay and prices. Finally, there is nothing as simple as paying each type of grant to each tier of authority direct. In England and Wales the needs element is paid only to non-metropolitan counties and metropolitan districts (including London boroughs); the resources element is paid only to districts, metropolitan or non-metropolitan. So there has to be a 'pass-through' element for both of the main ingredients of the rate support grant.

Turning to the mechanics of local authority budgeting, the cycle of events is that in January of each year, or thereabouts, estimates of expenditure for the forthcoming financial year starting on 1 April are prepared by each local authority department, in conjunction with the council treasurer. It should be noted that deficit budgeting is not one of the permissible options. These estimates are presented to the finance committee of the local authority. This committee sifts the estimates on the basis of both their intrinsic merits and their revenue implications. They are then transmitted in March to the 'budget' meeting of the authority for approval and for the fixing of the rate poundage for the forthcoming year. The responsibility for the general control and checking of revenue and expenditure throughout the year is shared by the finance committee, the council treasurer, and the relevant departmental committee. After the end of the year, the accounts are subject to audit. It is at this point that a most important figure appears – the District Auditor – who to some extent fills the same role at the local level as the Comptroller and Auditor General at the central level. The district auditor is a civil servant and therefore completely independent

[1] See *Local Government Finance*, Report of the Committee of Enquiry, Cmnd. 6453 (HMSO, 1976); and also A. R. Prest, *Inter-Governmental Financial Relations in the UK*, Research Monograph No. 23 (Australian National University, Canberra, 1978).

of the local authorities among which he works. He performs the normal functions of any commercial auditor, but also sees that local authorities do not exceed their statutory powers in any way. What gives him his very special measure of authority, however, is his power to disallow illegal expenditure and surcharge it to the members of the council responsible. This is an extremely powerful weapon and the use of it, or the threat to use it, is sufficient to make even the most fearless members of the most important local authorities tread warily.

APPENDIX TO PART II: THE PUBLIC FINANCES OF THE US

The aim here is to present a very brief sketch of the US system of public finance, mainly with the intention of pointing out some contrasts with the UK and providing some sort of foundation for the parallels we shall draw in the discussion of policy in Part III. We start by taking the consolidated figures of revenue and expenditure at all government levels in the US and putting them into perspective by reference to the national income. Then, we indicate the relative importance of the different components in the consolidated total. Subsequently, we examine the main constituents of the Federal part in rather more detail. Finally, we say a little about Federal revenue and expenditure procedure.

The first point to make is that the US is a different political animal from the UK in that it has a Federal constitution. This must never be forgotten in any discussion of revenue and expenditure problems, since it colours every single aspect of them. It comes up straightaway when we begin to look at the size of consolidated government revenues and expenditures, as we have to integrate the three layers of government – Federal, state and local – for this purpose. In 1977 the consolidated total of all government expenditures was $622 billion, some $394 billion of this being in respect of goods and services. The consolidated revenue total was $603 billion.[1]

If we calculate the ratio of government expenditure on goods and services to GNP in the same way as with the UK,[2] we find that it was 21 per cent for the US in 1977. This was of the same order of magnitude as the corresponding figures in the UK. If we take the ratio of government revenue to GNP, we find that it was 32 per cent. But all the warnings in Chapter 8 about the meaning of such a figure must be remembered.

As in the UK, there has been an increase in the ratio of government expenditure on goods and services to GNP over the last fifty years, the 1938 ratio for the US being some 15 per cent. In that country, as in the

[1] Data are all from *Survey of Current Business*, unless otherwise indicated.

[2] Cf. Chapter 8, section 2.

UK, it seems to be a matter of popular belief that this percentage has risen to an even greater extent that it actually has.

The relative importance of the Federal and the state and local components of revenue and expenditure are set out in Table A.1.

Table A.1

US Government Revenue and Expenditure, 1977 ($ billion)

Revenue		*Expenditure*	
Federal			
Personal	169	Goods and services	145
Corporate profits	61	Transfer payments	173
Indirect	25	Grants-in-aid	67
Social insurance contributions	119	Net interest payments	29
		Net subsidies (i.e. subsidies *minus* profits of government enterprises)	8
TOTAL	374	TOTAL	422
State and local			
Personal	57	Goods and services	249
Corporate profits	10	Transfer payments	30
Indirect	140	Net interest payments	−6
Social insurance	22	Profits of government	
Federal grants-in-aid	67	enterprises	−6
TOTAL	296	TOTAL	267

Source: *Survey of Current Business, July, 1978.*

It can be seen that today the Federal Government outweighs the state and local governments in importance, whichever measure we choose. On the revenue side, the Federal Government raises over 60 per cent more revenue than all the state and local governments combined, if we exclude from the latter, as we must, the 'revenue' derived from Federal grants-in-aid. On the expenditure side, the position is much the same, although, it should be noted, Federal expenditure on goods and services is not nearly as important, relative to state and local expenditure, as is its expenditure on transfer payments.

This supremacy of the Federal government is a relatively recent phenomenon. If we go back to 1913 we find that the state and local governments raised more than 75 per cent of total revenue at that time, and in 1938, although the proportion had fallen, the amount was still well over half the total. There has been a similar trend on the expenditure side.

Most of our remaining discussion on the US public finances will relate to the Federal level, but before starting it may be worthwhile skimming very rapidly over some of the most important aspects of State and local finances. There are, of course, fifty states, but the number of local taxing jurisdictions is over a hundred thousand. Consequently, it is not surprising that the local authorities as a whole are more important fiscally than the states. Local governments raise much the same revenue from their own sources as the states, but because of the grant system, spend considerably more.[1] The states rely mainly on sales taxes, licences and income taxes for their own revenue, the local authorities largely on property taxes with some help from utility revenues and the like. On the expenditure side, the division of functions is such that the main items of state expenditure are highways, education, hospitals and welfare, whilst at the local level education is much more important and highways less so. The 'purely local' types of expenditure – fire, sanitation, etc. – are of course administered entirely at the local level.[2] However, there is so much diversity that no simple generalizations are really justified.

The main constituents of Federal expenditure in 1977 were goods and services, and transfer payments. Under the former heading, by far and away the most important item was defence expenditure, which accounted for some two-thirds of the total. The transfer payments included a wide variety of items, but much the most important were social security payments and veterans' benefits. Grants-in-aid are grants to state governments for a number of purposes and according to a number of formulae, and net interest payments are simply the excess of interest payments on Federal debt over receipts on loans. Net subsidies include a number of items, the most important being housing. As compared to 1938, the most important change, which dwarfs everything else, is the growth in the relative importance of the defence budget.

On the revenue side of the Federal budget, we must spend a little more time. The personal heading in Table A.1 consists almost entirely

[1] *Governmental Finances* (Department of Commerce, Bureau of the Census, Washington, DC) (annual); and Tax Foundation, *Facts and Figures on Government Finances* (Washington DC) (annual).
[2] *Ibid.*

of personal income taxes, but estate and gift taxes account for some $7 billion of the total. The corporate profits tax needs no immediate explanation. Indirect taxes cover excise taxes and customs duties, the former accounting for the major part of the receipts. Social security contributions are self-explanatory. Historically, these ratios were very different. Immediately before 1913, customs and excise revenues accounted for about 95 per cent of the total and personal income tax was non-existent. Even in 1939, customs and excise revenues were some 37 per cent of the total, corporation profits tax 22 per cent and personal income taxes only 20 per cent.[1] The emergence of the personal income tax to a position of dominance over the last fifty years has, if anything, been even more marked in the US than the UK.

Personal income tax in the US started in its modern form in 1913. The first point to make is that there has always been a complete divorce between income taxation of persons and of corporations in the US; the personal income tax has not applied at all to corporations nor the corporation tax to persons. We shall say more about this when we come to the corporation income tax; we mention the point now to give preliminary warning.

The concept of *gross income* in the US is broadly comparable to that in the UK except for the treatment of gambling winnings (included in the US), social security benefits, interest on state and local bonds and the first $100 of any dividends (excluded in the US). Persons, individual traders and partnerships are all caught up in the personal income tax net.

The transition from *gross income* to *adjusted gross income* involves deductions for business expenses, certain types of pension contributions, alimony and so on, which again are comparable to those in the UK in general principle.

The next concept is that of Net Income and this may be derived in one of two ways from *adjusted gross income* at the option of the taxpayer. First, there is the alternative of what used to be called a standard deduction (but was re-named a zero bracket amount in 1978) of $2,300 for a single person and $3,400 for a married couple in 1979. Secondly, the taxpayer may itemize his claims for deductions in respect of charitable and political contributions, interest on personal loans, most state and local taxes, losses through theft, certain medical expenses, union subscriptions, expenses of work (e.g. tools, clothing) and alimony payments. The effect of these regulations is that in

[1] *Annual Report of the Secretary of the Treasury on The State of Finances* (Washington DC, 1941).

practice small- and middle-income recipients take the zero bracket amount and large income recipients more frequently claim the itemized deductions. (Some low income recipients are further helped by the earned income credit calculated on the basis of 10 per cent up to $5,000 of income but phased out in such wise that no one with an income of more than $10,000 in 1979 benefited from it.) It should be emphasized at this point that this is one respect in which US personal income tax regulations are most at variance with those in the UK. Apart from the (much more restricted) charitable contributions, working expenses, deductions for working abroad and the very limited relief for contributions to professional societies, there is nothing comparable in the UK to the expense deductions in the US.

We then move from net income to taxable income as a result of exemptions. These were $1,000 in 1979 for each person living in a family. There is no differentiation between children and adults, nor between children of different ages, but there are some special provisions in the shape of additional credits as well as exemptions for, e.g. retired people. Here again, therefore, there are substantial differences from UK practice.

Marginal tax rates depend on family circumstances, there being 16 rates for single people and 15 for married couples in 1979. For a single person, they ranged from 14 per cent on the first $1,100 of taxable income to 70 per cent[1] if over $108,300. (Married couples filing joint returns faced the same range of marginal rates but spread out over a wider range of incomes so that, for example, the 70 per cent rate only applied to incomes over $215,400.)[2] This pattern of differing rate schedules (other schedules apply to married couples filing separate returns and to unmarried heads of households) was introduced in 1969 as a substitute for the former system whereby married couples could split taxable income in half and then pay twice the tax payable on each component half. Although tax liabilities for single people may now be as much as 20 per cent above those for a married couple with the same income, the differentiation in favour of the latter is considerably less than before. Other points should also be noted. First, there is a complicated provision for ensuring that a minimum amount of tax is payable, even by those who claim very large deductions. Second, capital gains are treated in a different way to other income. A distinction is drawn

[1] The maximum rate on earned income is restricted to 50 per cent. This in effect favours high earned relatively to high unearned income.

[2] Again, with a maximum rate of 50 per cent on earned income.

between short-term gains and losses. Net short-term gains are taxed as ordinary income. Net long-term gains are taxed at a maximum rate of 28 per cent. If there are net short-term gains and net long-term losses, the latter are deductible from the former in the assessment of taxable income. If there are net short-term losses and net long-term gains, the former are deductible from the latter. If the sum of all losses exceeds the sum of all gains, whether short or long, the excess is deductible from current income up to the extent of $3,000 or from ordinary income of the following years until exhausted.[2] Capital gains taxes on assets transferred by gift or bequest are deferred until the recipients sell the assets. Finally, there is no automatic correction of exemptions, bracket starting points and the like for inflation as in some other countries.

A system of *withholding* applies to wages and salaries, but it does not operate on a cumulative basis, like PAYE, and so there is not the same exact correspondence between tax liabilities and payments at any one time. In fact the great majority of taxpayers over-pay tax during the year and receive a refund subsequently. People not in receipt of wages and salaries are required to file declarations of estimated income and pay tax in quarterly instalments if their income is above a minimum level. Self-assessment is therefore an integral part of the US system. At the same time, it seems fair to say that the principle of deduction at source is not nearly so well established in the US as it is in the UK, e.g. there is nothing comparable to the UK system of withholding tax on equity dividends and debenture interest. This is no doubt the reason why a so much larger fraction of income of this sort has in the past escaped the tax net in the US than in the UK.

In summary, personal income tax in the US differs in a number of major ways from income tax in the UK but in general coverage – some 80 million or more assessments in the US and 20 million or more in the UK – they are similar. And as a revenue-raiser the personal income tax is relatively more important to the Federal Government of the US than it is to the Central Government of the UK.

The *corporate profits tax* in the US brings in some $61 billion of tax per annum. The computation of business profits follows the same general principles as in the UK but there are substantial differences of detail in the operation of depreciation and depletion allowances. In

[1] Gains on owner-occupied houses are exempt from tax, if another house is bought within eighteen months at a price not less than that at which the old one was sold. There are further concessions to old people in this respect.

respect of depreciable assets, the traditional method was always that of straight line depreciation.[1] Since 1954, however, two alternatives have been allowed, the diminishing balance method[2] familiar in the UK and the 'sum of the years-digits method',[3] both of which enable assets to be depreciated more rapidly in the early years of life. Since 1962 reductions have been made in assumed lengths of life of capital equipment. Also a tax credit of 10 per cent (maximum rate) is allowed against purchases of new machinery and equipment and some other assets for use in the US; it should be emphasized that this measure differs from the UK system in permitting an offset against tax otherwise payable, rather than a deduction before tax liabilities are computed. In respect of depletion of natural resources (and these are defined to cover sand, gravel and oyster shells as well as all the traditional resources such as oil) the US, despite some cutbacks in 1969, is incomparably more generous than the UK.[4] The LIFO (last-in-first-out) treatment of inventories is more common in the US than in the UK. But as in the UK there is no generalized adjustment on profits for inflation.

Once net profits are computed the rate of corporate profits tax, except for small businesses, was 46 per cent in 1979. This rate applies to distributed and undistributed profits alike and no credit is allowable to shareholders against their personal income liability on dividends. Whether and to what extent this sort of arrangement constitutes 'double taxation' is a subject we shall take up in Chapter 17. The provisions for corporations trading abroad are more liberal than those in the UK despite some restrictions imposed over the years.

The system of *estate and gifts* taxation was overhauled in 1976 so that there is now more uniformity in the treatment of the two types of transfers. The nominal tax rate structure, ranging from 18 per cent on the first \$10,000 to 70 per cent on the excess over \$5 million, is the same in both cases. There is also a uniform credit (\$30,000 in 1977 and rising to \$47,700 in 1981) which can be taken against tax liabilities under either or both heads. Nevertheless, there are differences between the two. The most important is that the estate tax is payable on a gross figure (i.e. the amount transferred plus the amount paid in

[1] i.e. an equal percentage of the purchase price of the asset each year.

[2] i.e. an equal percentage of the written-down value of the asset each year.

[3] i.e. a different fraction of the purchase price each year, the denominator being related to the total length of life of the property and the numerator to the number of years of life remaining. For example, if the estimated length of life is five years the denominator will be 15 (5+4+3+2+1), the fraction is initially $\frac{5}{15}$ and subsequently $\frac{4}{15}$, $\frac{3}{15}$, $\frac{2}{15}$ and $\frac{1}{15}$.

[4] This generosity extends to individuals and partnerships as well as corporations.

tax) whereas the gift tax base excludes tax paid. It follows that although the nominal rate structure is the same, the effective tax rate on gifts is less than that on estates, with the obvious incentive to make gifts in life rather than at death. Deductions also differ under the two heads: the surviving spouse deduction under the estate tax is the higher of $250,000 or half the estate, whereas the basic amount allowed for gifts between spouses is $100,000 (though higher in certain cases). There are further complications with gift tax in that each spouse can claim a $3,000 exclusion each year for each gift to each donee; and there is also a cumulation principle embedded so that the relevant tax rate in any one year depends on the totality of amounts given away since 1932. A further difference is that credits are given against state estate tax liability but not against state gift tax liability. Gifts are held to be in contemplation of death, and hence taxable at the estate duty rather than the gift tax rate if made within three years of death. Gifts to charities are excluded from the base for both estate and gift tax but there was some tightening of provisions relating to trusts in 1976 so as to reduce generation skipping problems.

It can easily be seen from this summary that estate taxes are not nearly such an impost as they are in the UK, even if allowance is made for differences in private wealth per head.[1]

Customs and Excise duties account for a much smaller fraction of Federal Government revenue than of Central Government revenue in the UK, partly due to substantial reductions in the post-war period. There are taxes at manufacturing level on liquor, tobacco, motor fuel, telephones and various other minor imposts. Of the total, alcoholic beverages, and motor fuel are the two main components, accounting between them for more than half of the receipts. All excise taxes on gasoline and diesel fuel and half the taxes on motor vehicles and parts collected by the Federal Government are specifically earmarked for road development.

Social insurance contributions relate to receipts in respect of old age, survivors', disability and health insurance and of unemployment insurance. In the former case, tax (including a hospital component) was levied in 1978 at the rate of 12.1 per cent (6.05 per cent on both employer and employee) on the first $17,700 of employee income.[2] The total contribution rose in 1979 to 12.26 per cent on the first

[1] See Chapter 13, p. 302, for an explanation of the principle involved here.

[2] Self-employed people pay at a rate intermediate between that of the employee and the employee plus employer.

$22,900 of income with the prospect of further substantial rises in the 1980s. Today most of the workforce, apart from those under government retirement systems, is covered by this legislation. It should be added that benefits are related to average earnings during employment, although not proportionately.

Unemployment insurance is less comprehensive, less uniform and more in the hands of the various states. In 1978 the basic Federal tax was a tax on employers normally equal to 3.4 per cent of the first $6,000 of the wages of each worker, but credits of as much as 2.7 per cent are allowed against this in respect of payroll taxes paid under state unemployment insurance laws. The normal effective rate of Federal tax is therefore of the order of 0.7 per cent on the first $6,000 of wages.

It is not possible here to provide more than the most sketchy survey of budgetary procedure at the Federal level in the US. But it may serve to highlight some of the differences of the system from that in the UK.

The *formulation* of the budget is the general responsibility of the administration and the particular task of the Office of Management and Budget in consultation, of course, with various agencies and the President's Council of Economic Advisers. The initial work starts in the late spring of each year and is completed by the end of the calendar year. At that time, the Treasury's revenue estimates become available and the budget for the fiscal year commencing on the following 1st October is transmitted by the President to the Congress early in January.[1] The procedure for *authorization* by the Legislature of these proposals is very different from that in the UK. The expenditure proposals are examined in detail by the Appropriations Committee (and its various sub-committees) of the House, and a final version is agreed upon which may be very different from that originally proposed. A similar process takes place in the Senate and the views of the two legislative bodies have to be resolved in compromise Bills for transmission to the President. It should be noted that there is no single consolidated Bill for appropriations corresponding to the Appropriations Act in the UK, but a whole series of Bills. Similarly, on the revenue side, tax proposals are considered by the Ways and Means Committee and sub-committees of the House and the Finance Committee and sub-committees of the Senate, and final compromises reached. Until recent times there was no effective linkage between

[1] In 1968, as a result of the Report of the President's Commission on Budget Concepts (Washington DC, October 1967) a new form of budget presentation was adopted, providing for a more complete coverage than previously.

revenue and expenditure considerations. But in 1974 a new Congressional Budget Office was established with Budget Committees in both Houses, and there is now a much better procedure for controlling total expenditure and formulating revenue and expenditure policy jointly – and a much more explicit one than that in the UK.

At the *implementation* stage, the Legislature maintains a closer interest than is found in the UK and the Appropriations subcommittees liaise with the spending agencies. Finally, at the *postmortem* stage, there is a sharing of responsibility between the Legislature and the Executive. The Appropriations Committees and subcommittees together with the General Accounting Office check and audit past expenditures on behalf of Congress. The Office of Management and Budget has some responsibility for reviewing past performances on behalf of the Executive.

The system is so radically different from the UK that it is not really possible to compare them. Perhaps the most outstanding points of difference are the power of the Legislature to modify and even reverse the Executive's proposals (a budget is never passed in the form in which it is introduced, as is more or less the case in the UK), the much less tightly knit legislative procedure in the US (e.g. the absence of a single Appropriation Act) and the very much smaller role of the Treasury, relative to other departments, in that country.

REFERENCES (PART II)[1]

I. BOOKS, ETC.

Beer, S. H., *Treasury Control* (Oxford University Press, Oxford, 1965).

Bridges, Lord, *The Treasury* (Allen and Unwin, 1964).

Child Poverty Action Group, *Guide to Contributory Benefits and Child Benefit* (London, annual).

Child Poverty Action Group, *National Welfare Benefits Handbook* (London, annual).

Family Welfare Association, *Guide to the Social Services* (MacDonald Evans, London, 1978).

Goldman, Sir S., *The Developing System of Public Expenditure, Management and Control* (HMSO, 1973).

Heclo, H. E. and Wildavsky, A., *The Private Government of Public Money* (Macmillan, London, 1974).

Hepworth, N. P., *The Finance of Local Government*, third edition (Allen and Unwin, London, 1976).

Hicks, U. K., *British Public Finances 1880/1952* (Home University Library, Oxford University Press, Oxford, 1954).

Johnstone, D., *A Tax Shall be Charged* (HMSO, London, 1975).

Maxwell, J. A. and Aronson, R., *Financing State and Local Governments*, third edition (Brookings Institution, Washington DC, 1977).

Musgrave, R. A., *Fiscal Systems* (Yale University Press, New Haven, 1969).

Normanton, E. L., *The Accountability and Audit of Governments* (Manchester University Press, Manchester, 1966).

Peacock, A. T. and Wiseman, J., *The Growth of Public Expenditure in the UK*, second edition (Allen and Unwin, London, 1967).

Pechman, J. A., *Federal Tax Policy*, third edition (Brookings Institution, Washington DC, 1977).

Prest, A. R., *Intergovernmental Financial Relations in the UK*, Research Monograph 23 (Centre for Research on Federal Financial Relations, Canberra, 1978).

Recktenwald, H. C. (ed.), *Secular Trends of the Public Sector* (International Institute of Public Finance, Cujas, Paris, 1978).

Sabine, B. E. V., *British Budgets in Peace and War, 1932–45* (Allen and Unwin, London, 1970).

[1] See introductory note to References (Part I) on p. 170.

Schultze, C. L., *The Politics and Economics of Public Spending* (Brookings Institution, Washington YDC, 1968).
Shehab, F., *Progressive Taxation* (Oxford University Press, Oxford, 1953).
Whiteman, P. C. and Milne, D. C., *Whiteman and Wheatcroft on Income Tax* (Sweet and Maxwell, London, 1976).

II. ARTICLES

Barr, N. A., 'Labour's Pension Plan – a Lost Opportunity?', *British Tax Review*, Nos. 2 and 3, 1975.
Clark, C., 'Public Finance and Changes in the Value of Money', *Economic Journal*, December 1945.
Prest, A. R., 'Government Revenue and the National Income', *Public Finance*, 1951.
Prest, A. R., 'Government Revenue, the National Income and All That', in Bird, R. M. and Head, J. G., *Modern Fiscal Issues* (*op. cit.*).
Prest, A. R., 'On the Distinction between Direct and Indirect Taxation', in David, W. L., *Public Finance, Planning and Economic Development* (*op. cit.*).

III. OFFICIAL PUBLICATIONS

A. *United Kingdom* (all HMSO, London).

Appropriation Accounts (annual).
Better Pensions, Cmnd. 5713 (1974).
Capital Transfer Tax, Cmnd. 5705 (1974).
Cash Limits on Public Expenditure, Cmnd. 6440 (1976).
Central Office of Information, *The New British System of Taxation* (Reference Pamphlet No. 112, 1977).
Central Statistical Office, *National Income Statistics: Sources and Methods* (1968).
Department of Health and Social Security, *Annual Report.*
Development Land Tax, Cmnd. 6195 (1975).
Estimates, Civil and Defence, etc. (annual).
Finance Accounts of the UK (annual).
Finance Act (annual).
Financial Statement and Budget Report (annual).
Future Shape of Local Government Finance, Cmnd. 4741 (1971).
The Government's Expenditure Plans 1979–80 to 1982–83, Cmnd. 7439 (1979).

Inland Revenue Statistics (annual).
Industrial and Regional Development, Cmnd. 4942 (1972).
Investment Incentives, Cmnd. 4516 (1970).
Land, Cmnd. 5730 (1974).
Local Government Act, 1972.
Local Government Act, 1974.
Local Government Finance, Report of the Committee of Enquiry, Cmnd. 6453 (1976).
Local Government Financial Statistics (annual).
National Income and Expenditure Blue Book (annual).
National Insurance Fund Accounts (annual).
Proposals for a Tax-Credit System, Cmnd. 5116 (1972).
Public Expenditure: a New Presentation, Cmnd. 4017 (April 1969).
Public Expenditure White Papers, Handbook on Methodology (1972).
Reform of Corporation Tax, Cmnd. 4630 (1971).
Reform of Corporation Tax, Cmnd. 4955 (1972).
Reform of Personal Direct Taxation, Cmnd. 4653 (1971).
Reports from Select Committee on Procedure (annual).
Report of Commissioners of Customs and Excise (annual).
Report of Commissioners of Inland Revenue (annual).
Reports of Committee on Public Accounts (annual).
Reports of Expenditure Committee (annual).
Report from Select Committee on Corporation Tax, HC 622 (1971).
Reports of Select Committee on Nationalized Industries (*Reports and Accounts*) (annual).
Report and Proceedings of Select Committee on Tax-Credit, HC 341 (1973).
Review of Value Added Tax, Cmnd. 7415 (1978).
Social Security Act, 1975.
Taxation of Capital Gains, Cmnd. 2645 (1965).
Taxation of Capital on Death, Cmnd. 4930 (1972).
Value Added Tax, Cmnd. 4621 (1971).
Value Added Tax, Cmnd. 4929 (1972).
Wealth Tax, Cmnd. 5704 (1974).

B. *United States* (All US Government Printing Office, Washington DC).

Annual Report, Secretary of Treasury.
Budget of US Government for Fiscal Year (annual).
Governmental Finances (annual).
Joint Economic Committee, *Analysis and Evaluation of Public Expenditures: The PPB System.*
Report of President's Commission on Budget Concepts (1967).
Survey of Current Business – Annual July (National Income) issue.
Your Federal Income Tax (US Treasury – annual).

PART III

POLICY

12

INTRODUCTION TO POLICY DISCUSSION

Discussion of public financial policy can in principle take two different forms. At one end of the scale, one can attempt to draw up a blueprint for the overall reform of the revenue and expenditure system. Any such blueprint must consider the relative importance of the various ends served by the revenue-expenditure system, the way in which individual taxes and expenditures contribute to these ends and the co-ordination of these individual contributory elements. Among the nearest foreign approaches of the post-war years to this sort of blueprint have been the proposals of Shoup in Japan, Kaldor in India, Musgrave in Colombia and those of the Carter Commission for Canada.[1] The words 'nearest approaches' should be stressed; none did in fact cover the whole of the suggested area, although the Carter Commission in particular went a good deal of the way towards it. In this country the most ambitious attempt was that of the Meade Committee[2] but despite the width of its vision and the challenging nature of many of its proposals, the subject-matter was essentially direct taxation with relatively little discussion of indirect taxation or of expenditure.

The other extreme is to discuss the reform of individual taxes or expenditures without reference to one another, without necessarily attempting to cover the whole field and without much consideration of the overall effect on the economic system. Examples of this are so common that it is hardly worth mentioning them, but a typical case would be to argue for the inclusion of capital gains as part of income for tax purposes without linking this with any discussion of the system of taxing undistributed profits of companies.

We shall attempt to steer a mid-course between these two approaches. We shall not attempt to cover all the policy issues current in the UK today, nor shall we make any systematic attempt to work out the exact revenue implications of our ideas. On the other hand, we

[1] *Report on Japanese Taxation.* Shoup Mission (GHQ, SCAP, Tokyo, 1949); N. Kaldor, *Indian Tax Reform* (Dept. of Economic Affairs, Ministry of Finance, India, 1956); R. A. Musgrave and M. Gillis, *Fiscal Reform for Colombia* (Harvard Law School, Cambridge, Mass., 1971); *Report of Royal Commission on Taxation* (Carter Commission), (Queen's Printer, Ottawa, 1966).

[2] *Report, op. cit.*

shall attempt to keep more than one ball in the air when it seems especially necessary to do so and, in particular, when dealing with the interacting issues involved in capital gains taxation, depreciation and inventory policy and company taxation. We shall also aim at a unity of method, in so far as we shall stick as closely as possible in all our discussions to the relative merits of different ways of raising the same sum in taxation or of spending the same amount of revenue.

Steering an intermediate course always involves the risk of losing sight of both shores rather than keeping one in sight. But there are two reasons why such an approach seems justified here. The first is simply the limitation of space which rules out comprehensive discussion. The second is that this is not an attempt to solve the immediate fiscal problems of a country or present a ready-made quantitative programme for a political party. Our object is rather to demonstrate how the analytical principles set out in Part I can be used to develop one's thoughts about some of the problems facing the UK over the next few years. We are not concerned simply with those issues which demand immediate solution but with those to which attention will have to be directed over the medium period, say, the next ten years or so. This will involve some of the issues of tax harmonization and co-ordination arising out of Britain's entry into the EEC. Nor shall we be limited by any consideration of what is politically practical, in the sense of what any specific political party is likely to do. Our intention is to apply economic and not political principles to the issues we discuss; if this is labelled 'academic' we shall take that as a compliment rather than an insult.

We shall deal successively with the following topics. First, we have two chapters dealing with personal income taxation and social security issues. We examine in succession the progressiveness of the tax structure, the relative treatment of individuals and families, the differential taxation of earned and investment income, capital gains taxation, indexation of income taxation and the arguments for and against the expenditure tax. Then we look at various conceptual matters arising in welfare programmes, negative income taxation, major national insurance issues, non-contributory cash benefits and benefits in kind. Next comes a chapter on personal capital taxation. After exploring general principles, the taxation of capital transfers and of wealth are examined in detail, with some conclusions on appropriate UK policy in these areas. We then have two chapters exclusively devoted to company taxation: the first is concerned with the definition of taxable profits and the establishment of appropriate measurements of depreciation and the like in the face of inflation or the need to bolster capital formation; the second deals with the case for and the methods of integrating corporate and personal taxation. The next chapter is also largely, though not quite exclusively, concerned with corporations in that we then turn to the taxation of overseas income; the main weight of the chapter is on the prevention of over-taxation, taking account of EEC as well as purely UK considerations, but some attention is also paid to the tax problems raised by multinational company transfer pricing practices. The last two chapters deal successively with the main problems of indirect taxation (and most particularly with VAT harmonization inside the EEC), and with the principles of local authority finance and possible reform in the grants and rating systems.

It will be obvious from this catalogue that we do not set out to discuss issues of Policy in a comprehensive fashion. Although Chapter 14 ('Income Distribution and the Welfare State') is concerned with a number of issues arising from social security and related expenditures, we do not pretend to give as much coverage to the expenditure as to the revenue side. Nor, for instance, do we embark on any appraisal of stabilization policy in this country, the finances of devolution or the pricing and investment policy of public corporations and similar bodies. One simply cannot cover all topics of this kind within the space available. And given that constraint, it seemed best in terms of general economic principles to concentrate on those matters on which we might have a comparative advantage.

It must be emphasized that the distinction between Principles, Description and Policy is not rigid. There have already been instances in Parts I and II where we have strayed into the Policy field (e.g. reform of the central government financial mechanism). There will be instances in Part III where we have to push Principles further before, or even after, reaching Policy conclusions. It is not thought necessary to apologize for this: economics is, after all, one subject and there are no watertight divisions between its component parts. But Part III does differ very clearly from Part I in two important respects, which have been mentioned earlier[1] but may be recalled at this stage. First, this Part is inevitably directed towards the problems of one specific country, the UK – this was, incidentally, another principle of selection of topics – but the arguments are illustrated by references to other

[1] Cf. p. 6.

countries, and in particular the US and the EEC. It is hoped that this Part will therefore have some relevance to other countries. Second, the level of argument is on the whole more difficult than that in Part I, or for that matter Part II. This is inevitable. It is always much more difficult to achieve a satisfying blend of theory and practice than to discuss either in isolation.

13

PERSONAL INCOME TAXATION

1 PROGRESSIVENESS OF THE TAX STRUCTURE

1.1 *The current structure of income tax in the UK*

This chapter discusses some of the major policy issues in the taxation of personal incomes, where income tax is defined broadly to cover not only the taxation of wages and salaries and the like, but also the deduction of tax on company dividends at source (or any equivalent procedure) and the mixed incomes of sole traders and partnerships. We analyse six aspects of the present system: first, the degree of progression in the present system (discussed in section 1); then the relative treatment of single persons and families (section 2), the relative treatment of earned income and investment income (section 3), the taxation of capital gains (section 4), and indexation (section 5). Finally, in section 6, we draw together from other chapters some of the major theoretical and practical arguments about expenditure taxation.

These topics are not independent of one another. For instance, the most appropriate treatment of families depends on the imputation of income to a non-working spouse, which takes us straight back to the progressiveness of the system. Another important question in thinking about family taxation is the extent to which supplementary income comes from work as distinct from capital – and this obviously connects the second and third topics. We shall try to bring out these and other interconnections as we proceed.

Nor are these topics anything like exhaustive. There are many other issues – the treatment of old people (perhaps, in view of likely trends in population structure, this subject has received less attention than it deserves), the question of income averaging, and so on. We shall not deal with these topics – partly because of limitations of space and partly because some of them were exhaustively treated by the Royal Commission[1] – but this does not suggest that they are unimportant.[2]

[1] Royal Commission on the Taxation of Profit and Income, *First Report*, Cmd. 8761 (HMSO, 1953), *Second Report*, Cmd. 9105 (HMSO, 1954), *Final Report*, Cmd. 9476 (HMSO, 1955).

[2] A more general discussion of the current system of income tax is contained in J. E. Meade, *Report*, *op. cit.*, Chapter 2.

Section 1 is organized as follows: after dealing with some conceptual issues we discuss the degree of progressiveness of income tax in the UK; we then make some comparisons with other times and places; finally we make a brief critique of the present situation.

In thinking about the progressiveness of any particular tax there are a number of important background points which should be borne in mind, and we deal with these first.

(1) *The limitations of analysing one tax in isolation.* It is as well to recall that it can be highly misleading to look at the progressiveness of any part of the system of taxation or expenditure in isolation. For instance, if income tax were highly progressive but the revenue used mainly to subsidize the production of Rolls-Royces or the import of mink coats, the overall effect could be regressive. On the other hand, a proportional income tax whose proceeds were used to provide benefits mainly for the poor would provide an overall progressive effect. The succeeding discussion of the progressiveness of the UK income tax should therefore be seen solely as a discussion of the progressiveness of personal income tax and *not* of the progressiveness of the system as a whole.

(2) *The relevance of tax incidence.* As we have seen earlier,[1] the incidence of any tax will generally be shared between the buyer and the seller, so that, in principle, income tax could be borne entirely by the income recipient, or entirely by the income payer, or could be shared between the two. Obviously the progressiveness of the tax structure will be very different depending on which outcome occurs. About the only thing that can be said with any certainty about the incidence of income tax is that we do not really know what it is.

(3) *The definition of progressivity.* Before proceeding further we should define with some precision what we mean by 'progressiveness'. A tax structure is said to be progressive if tax liability, T, as a proportion of income, Y, rises as income rises – i.e. a tax is progressive if T/Y increases as Y rises. Examples of progressive tax functions are shown in Figures 13.1 (a) and (b). Figure 13.1 (b) is, broadly, the US tax function, with marginal rates rising fairly smoothly with income. Thus, in the USA, income tax starts at a rate of 14 per cent and rises in 2 or 3 per cent steps for small increases in taxable income.

Figure 13.1 (a) is an approximation of the UK situation. As we shall see below (see, for instance, Table 13.1) a tax function of this type is also progressive. A common misapprehension about the UK system is

[1] See Chapter 5, section 2.1.

that 'we do not have a progressive tax structure because almost everyone pays the same tax rate'. This statement is quite simply wrong. While it is true that most people face the same marginal rate of tax, this is not the same thing as saying that tax payments are proportional to income. A tax structure is progressive if marginal tax rates rise with income, and the UK system does just that (and did so even before the reintroduction of a 25 per cent reduced rate band in 1978), since it has a 0 per cent rate followed by a basic rate of 33 per cent. Any system which has a tax-free allowance (equivalent to a 0 per cent tax rate) followed by a positive rate of tax, will be progressive,[1] as the centre column of Table 13.1 shows.

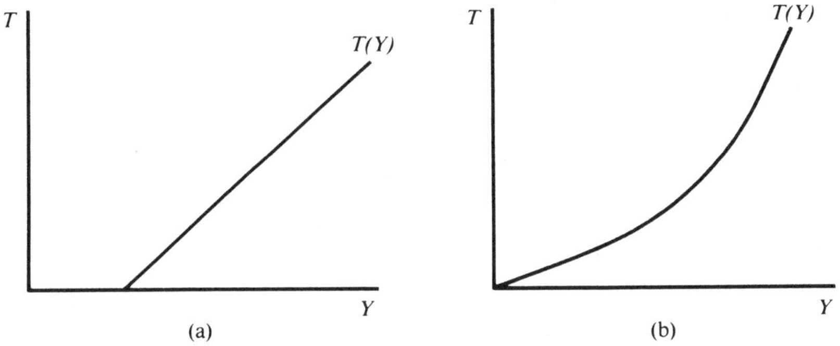

Figure 13.1 *Stylized examples of two progressive tax functions*

(4) *The relevance of progressivity.* We discussed this in the Principles section. There we saw that the major impacts of the degree of progressivity of personal income tax were on the supply of labour and capital to the economy and on the size distribution of income.[2] The literature on optimal taxation discussed in Chapters 3, 4 and 5 deals with a number of these aspects. The discussion of self-assessment for income tax (Chapter 7) is not concerned with the principles of progressivity but the administrative method of achieving any desired degree of progressiveness. The following discussion focuses mainly on the incentive and equity aspects of progressivity.

(5) *The 'correct' degree of progressivity.* Despite considerable effort there is still no generally accepted theory which tells us what is the 'correct' distribution of income or wealth. Quite apart from not

[1] Though this does not preclude discussion of whether the degree of progressivity is the 'right' one.
[2] See Chapters 4 and 5.

knowing the target at which we should aim our arrows, we may also know very little about the course of their flight. We have already said (Chapter 5) that the effects of direct taxes on the size distribution of income depend on a complex process of change of product and factor prices about which we are unlikely to know very much. And even though, for any given distribution of income, we can say somewhat more about the efficient allocation of resources and the responsiveness of labour supply to changes in an income tax, any attempt in practice to trace the exact effects of any particular tax change meets formidable obstacles, such as the distinction between the short- and long-run period elasticities of supply and demand for factors of production.[1]

To sum up the story so far, we have said (a) that the progressiveness of the system as a whole is not the same as the progressiveness of income tax; (b) that the progressiveness of income tax will depend on the incidence of the tax, about which we know very little; and (c) that although we have a workable definition of progressiveness narrowly defined, and accept its importance, we are not able to say anything definitive about how progressive the tax 'should' be or, in practice, to say a great deal about the efficiency impact of any particular tax change.

However, it is not terribly helpful simply to observe that there is little that we can say. In practice, governments have to construct systems of income taxation, and these structures have to be progressive (or proportional or regressive), so it is important to try to form some judgment of the facts. The first task is to outline the exact form of the progression of personal income tax in the UK. We start by discussing the case of a single individual, on the assumption that the whole of his or her income is earned. The position for 1978/79 is shown in Charts 13.1 (a) and (b) and in Table 13.1. Starting with a tax-free allowance of £985, the effective rate of tax rose from under 1 per cent on £1,000 to about 75 per cent on an income of £100,000. The marginal tax rate rose from zero to 25 per cent at £985, for the first £750 of taxable income, and then rose to the basic rate of 33 per cent for taxable income over £750 and under £8,000. Thereafter the marginal rate on earned income rose in steps, usually of 5 per cent, to a top rate of 83 per cent, on taxable income in excess of £24,000. If unearned income was in excess of £2,250 (£3,000 if aged 65 or over), an additional 15 per

[1] That this rapidly becomes rather a complex matter can be seen, for instance, in D. Laidler, *Introduction to Microeconomics*, Chapters 17 and 18.

cent tax was levied, thus raising the top marginal rate to 98 per cent. In other words, the marginal net reward at this level was 2 per cent, i.e. 100 per cent *minus* 98 per cent. A one per cent reduction in the marginal rate of tax would therefore raise the marginal net reward to investment income by no less than 50 per cent (i.e. from 2 per cent to 3 per cent).

Table 13.1

Single person liability to income tax, UK, 1978/79

Income (£s)	*Effective tax rate* (%)	*Marginal tax rate* (%)
500	0	0
1,000	0.4	25
2,000	13.7	33
4,000	23.4	33
5,000	25.3	33
6,000	26.6	33
7,500	27.9	33
10,000	29.9	40
12,500	33.7	50
15,000	37.8	60
20,000	43.6	75
25,000	51.4	83
50,000	67.2	83
100,000	75.1	83

Source: *Financial Statement and Budget Report, 1978/79.*
Note: Income all earned.

Chart 13.1 (a) shows clearly that one of these steps – that for the 33 per cent basic rate – is particularly broad. There is no reason in principle why this should be so, but as we explained above[1] this arrangement is more or less essential to the administrative feasibility of the cumulative withholding feature of the current PAYE system. The question whether such an arrangement would be desirable in the absence of administrative reasons is a large one, though the view has often been expressed that the marginal tax rates should rise more smoothly with a larger number of steps, and hence smaller jumps in the marginal rate. There is no prima facie reason why one system should

[1] See Chapter 7.

Chart 13.1a Marginal and effective rates of tax
Single person, UK 1978/9
Income range £0–£8,500

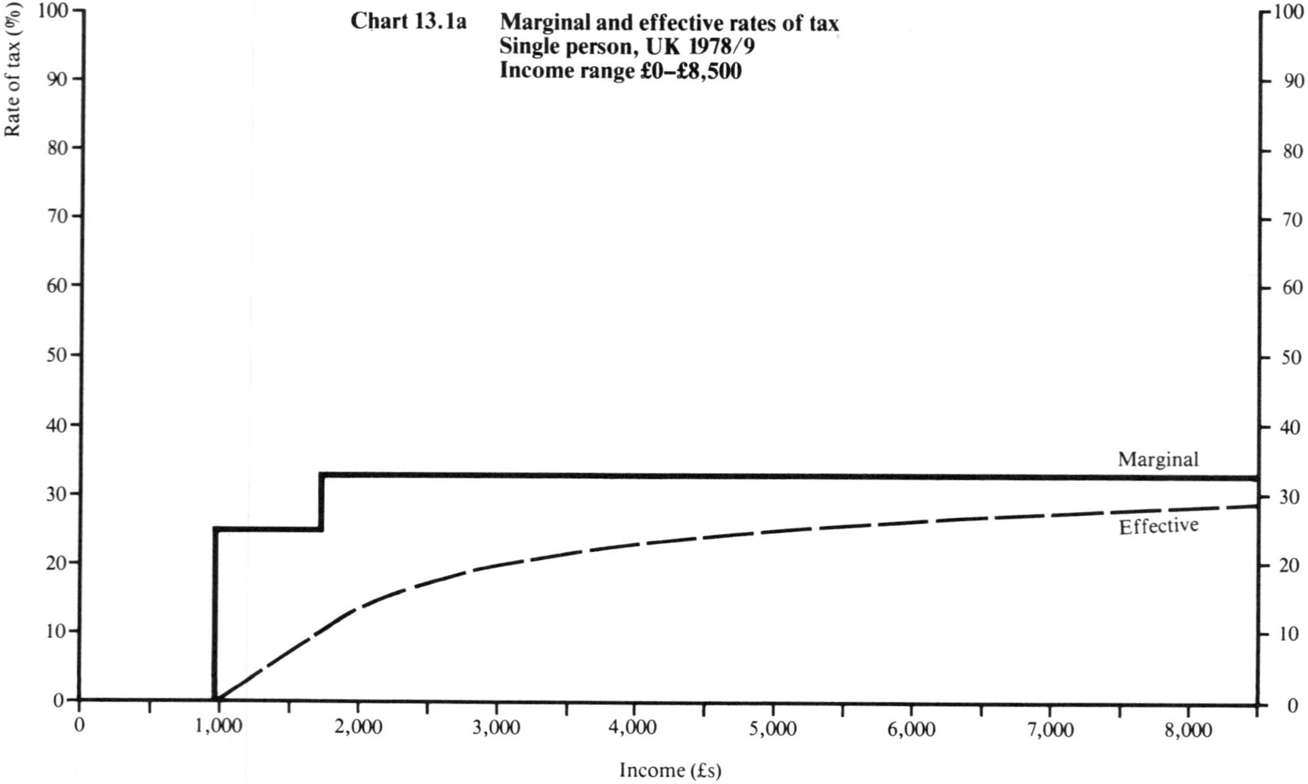

Chart 13.1b Marginal and effective rates of tax
Single person, UK 1978/9
Income range £8,000–£50,000

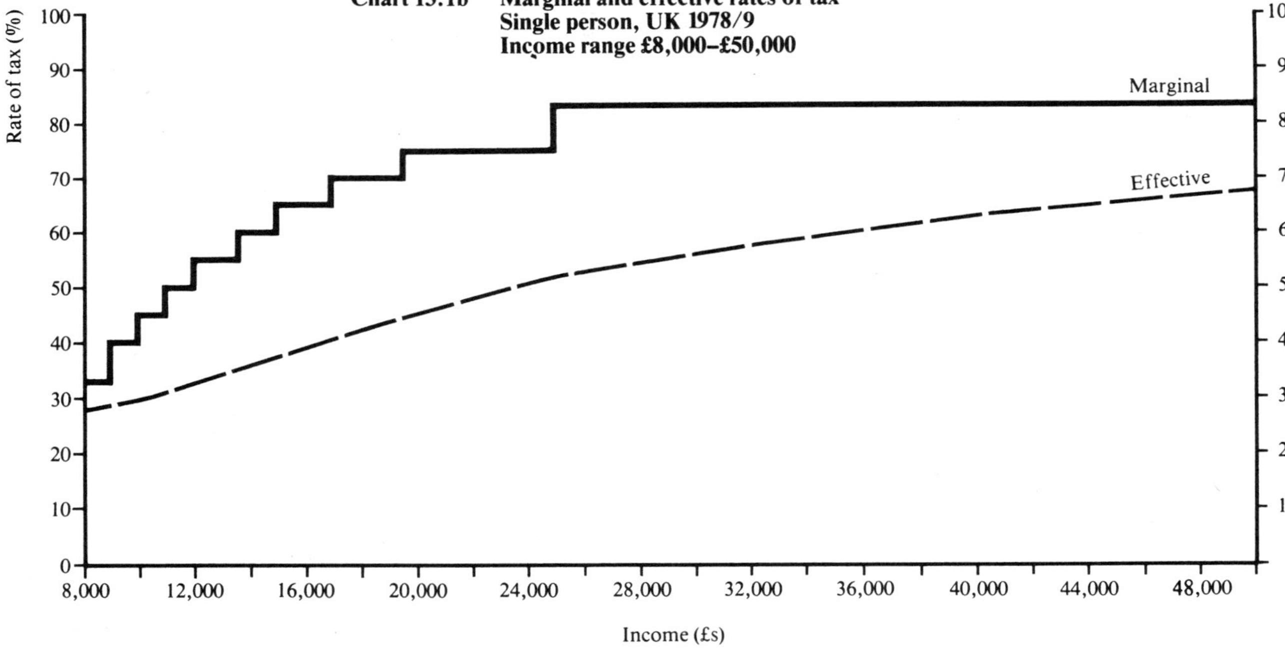

offer less incentive than the other, though other efficiency aspects are brought out in the optimal income-tax literature discussed earlier.[1]

Table 13.1 and Charts 13.1(a) and (b) tell us the percentage of income liable to tax at different income levels,[2] but this does not mean that we have a clear picture of the 'burden' of taxation. For this we need to know also about the number of income recipients in each range of income. If there is a great concentration of income in the middle ranges of the income distribution, the meaning of the effective rates is very different from what it would be if there were a large number of people at either extreme. For instance, a 100 per cent marginal tax rate on incomes in excess of £500,000 would be irrelevant if there were no incomes as high as this.

Table 13.2 therefore shows the percentage tax liability of each quintile of income recipient and each quintile of income. As we might expect on a priori grounds, the bottom 20 per cent of income recipients pay a lower rate of tax than the bottom 20 per cent of incomes. This is because the lowest 20 per cent of recipients receive considerably less than 20 per cent of total personal income, and with a progressive tax structure this means that they pay a lower proportion of their incomes in tax. Correspondingly, the highest quintile of income recipients pays a lower tax rate than the highest quintile of incomes. As the definition of an income recipient is so nebulous, the more meaningful tabulation is that by amounts of income; but both are important. Thus, we find that the lowest quintile of income pays an effective tax rate of only 14.8 per cent (which is something of an overestimate for the reasons explained in the notes to Table 13.2); the middle three quintiles pay between 19 and 23 per cent of their incomes in tax, while the highest quintile attracts an effective rate of tax of 32½ per cent. It should be emphasized that these calculations reflect all the tax allowances to which the various income groups are entitled, as well as the rates of tax and the size distribution of income before tax.

The other two columns of Table 13.2 use the same basic data for a different purpose. Instead of showing the effective tax rates applicable to each quintile, we can show their relative contributions to the total yield of income tax. We see, for instance, that around 30 per cent of tax is collected from the highest quintile of incomes and some 18 per cent

[1] See Chapters 3 and 5.

[2] Although Table 13.1 and Charts 13.1(a) and (b) refer to single individuals only, the same general features are found with families. The principal difference is that the additional allowances mean higher starting points at which income tax becomes payable.

Table 13.2

Income tax payments by quintile of recipients and quintile of incomes, UK, 1976/77

Quintile	*Classification by quintiles of recipients*[a]		*Classification by quintiles of income*[a]	
	Percentage of income paid in tax	*Tax paid as percentage of total tax paid*	*Percentage of income paid in tax*	*Tax paid as percentage of total tax paid*
Lowest	10.5[b]	3.5	14.8[b]	13.5
Second	17.1	9.4	19.6	17.9
Third	19.5	15.4	28.8	18.7
Fourth	20.5	22.0	22.3	20.3
Highest	27.5	49.7	32.5	29.6

Source: *Inland Revenue Statistics*, 1976, Table 29 (HMSO, 1977).
Notes: [a] Figures derived from sample survey, and conform to income tax definitions of income and numbers (e.g. long-term gains excluded, short-term capital gains included, husband and wife count as one recipient).

[b] Data exclude incomes below £735 and all non-taxable income. The percentage of income paid in tax for the lowest quintile would be lower than shown above if such income were included. The point can be illustrated with data from *National Income and Expenditure, 1967–77*, *op. cit.*, Table 4.8.

[c] Data interpolated as necessary.

from the second quintile. Even more striking, the highest quintile of income recipients pay half of the total income tax bill, while the lowest three quintiles pay little more than one-quarter of it.

It should be stressed that so far we have simply analysed the *statistical* implications of the present income tax rates and allowances when applied to the present structure of incomes in the UK. We have not drawn any deductions about the 'true' distribution of tax burdens.

1.2 *Some comparisons*

It is helpful to give these matters some perspective by comparing the present situation with the USA, and also briefly with pre-war days. At some risk of belabouring the point, it should be stressed that we are not in any way comparing the overall progressiveness of different systems but simply looking at the systems of income tax.

When comparing marginal and effective tax rates in different countries it is obviously necessary to adjust for differences in the nominal value of money. The obvious way of doing this is simply to use the sterling/dollar exchange rate. But this leaves out differences in real income in the two countries, and so for the present purposes it is more useful to look at the difference in money income per head,[1] which will reflect differences both in the price level and in the level of real income. We therefore compare the marginal and effective rates of personal income tax in the two countries on the assumption that personal income per head (in dollar terms) in the USA is about 3⅓ times greater than in the UK (in sterling terms) – e.g. that a UK income of £1,000 is approximately equivalent to an income in the US of $3,333 dollars.[2]

Charts 13.2 (a) and (b) and 13.3 (a) and (b) on pages 304 to 307 give the comparisons of marginal and effective rates for single individuals (including those for 1938/39, calculated in a similar way to those for the USA). They show that in the UK today the effective rates of tax are both considerably higher and start at a considerably lower level of equivalent income than was the case in 1938/39. The comparison with the USA today is similar, though the difference is less marked. The same is true also for marginal rates – that at nearly all levels of income the current UK rates are higher than those for the USA currently and the UK before the war. The overall conclusion is that the structure of income tax in this country is more progressive today than in either of the other two cases.

How valid are these comparisons? Correcting for the differences in personal money income rather than simply for differences in prices is the more interesting comparison (e.g. for discussing incentives to migration from the UK to the USA, or for analysing the effects of personal income taxation on labour supply). Yet clearly such comparisons have their limitations. For a start they show only the application of published tax rates to incomes assessed for tax. If incomes assessed for tax diverge from 'true' incomes to differing extents for the years and countries compared, this causes problems; and to the extent that the divergence varies systematically with income the charts may be misleading. It must be emphasized that, for comparative purposes, under-assessment does not matter, only the extent to which under-assessment varies across income groups.

[1] The most unambiguous and straightforward figure is personal income per head of the working population. This abstracts from the problem of changes in definition of taxable income and the numbers subject to tax.

[2] Personal income in the USA in 1977 was $1,536,700 million and the workforce 90.5 million (*Federal Reserve Bulletin*), giving an average income of about $17,000, compared to about £5,000 in the UK.

In the case of the USA we have to ask whether the definition of taxable income is similar to that in the UK. First of all, it is possible to correct roughly for the deductions permitted in the US tax system (which have no counterpart in the UK) by adjusting downward the nominal US tax rate to take account of the zero bracket amount.[1] Next comes the question of the relative importance, at corresponding income levels, of untaxed or partly taxed income (mainly capital gains and business expenses) for the two countries. Though there is no exact answer, there is no evidence of any substantial difference in this respect between the two countries. It should be pointed out that our choice of deflator puts the UK tax rates in a favourable light relative to those in the USA. By comparing personal incomes we compare the tax rates on an income in the UK of £2,000 with one in the US of $6,667. If we were simply to use the official exchange rate, we would compare a UK income of £2,000 with a US income of around $4,000, which would greatly increase the extent to which UK tax rates exceeded those in the USA.

Comparisons such as these are possible only between tax structures which are broadly similar. For many countries it is not possible to compare the progressiveness of income tax even in the crude way we have done. For instance, countries like France have considerably lower rates of income tax than the UK, but have payroll taxes of the order of 30 per cent. As we have seen, such taxes can be paid by the employee (in the form of lower wages), by the employer (in the form of lower profits), or by employees and employers generally (if the tax is passed on in the form of higher prices). It is therefore meaningless simply to look at the narrowly defined nominal structure of income tax in France without making some assumption about the incidence of the payroll tax.

Though our comparisons have sidestepped such difficulties, it is still insufficient to compare tax rates alone. Quite apart from the difficulties already discussed, no cognisance has been taken of relative income distributions over time or across countries. For a better picture we must return to our analysis of income tax liability by quintile of income and of recipients.

Table 13.3 shows these calculations for the USA. For all quintiles of income the UK has higher effective tax rates, which confirms the

[1] In fact, the upper income groups normally gain more than the lower income groups from the deduction system. This means that in comparing US and UK tax rates we should remember that the higher income groups in the US are taxed less heavily than the preceding charts suggest.

Chart 13.2a Marginal rates of tax, UK 1938/9, UK 1977/8, USA 1977
Single person
Income range £0–£8,500 (UK 1977/8)

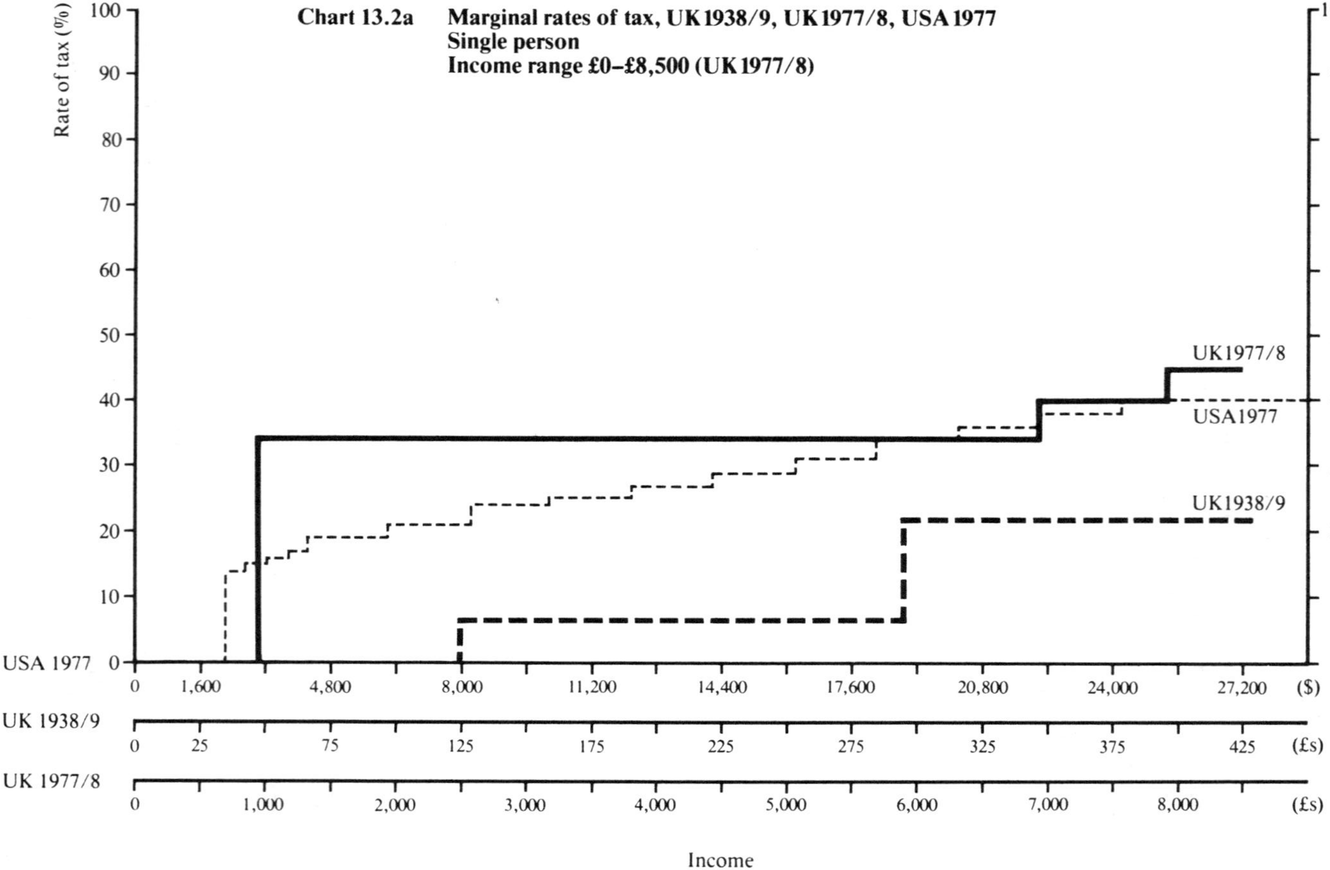

Chart 13.2b Marginal rates of tax, UK1938/9, UK1977/8, USA1977
Single person
Income range £8,000–£50,000 (UK1977/8)

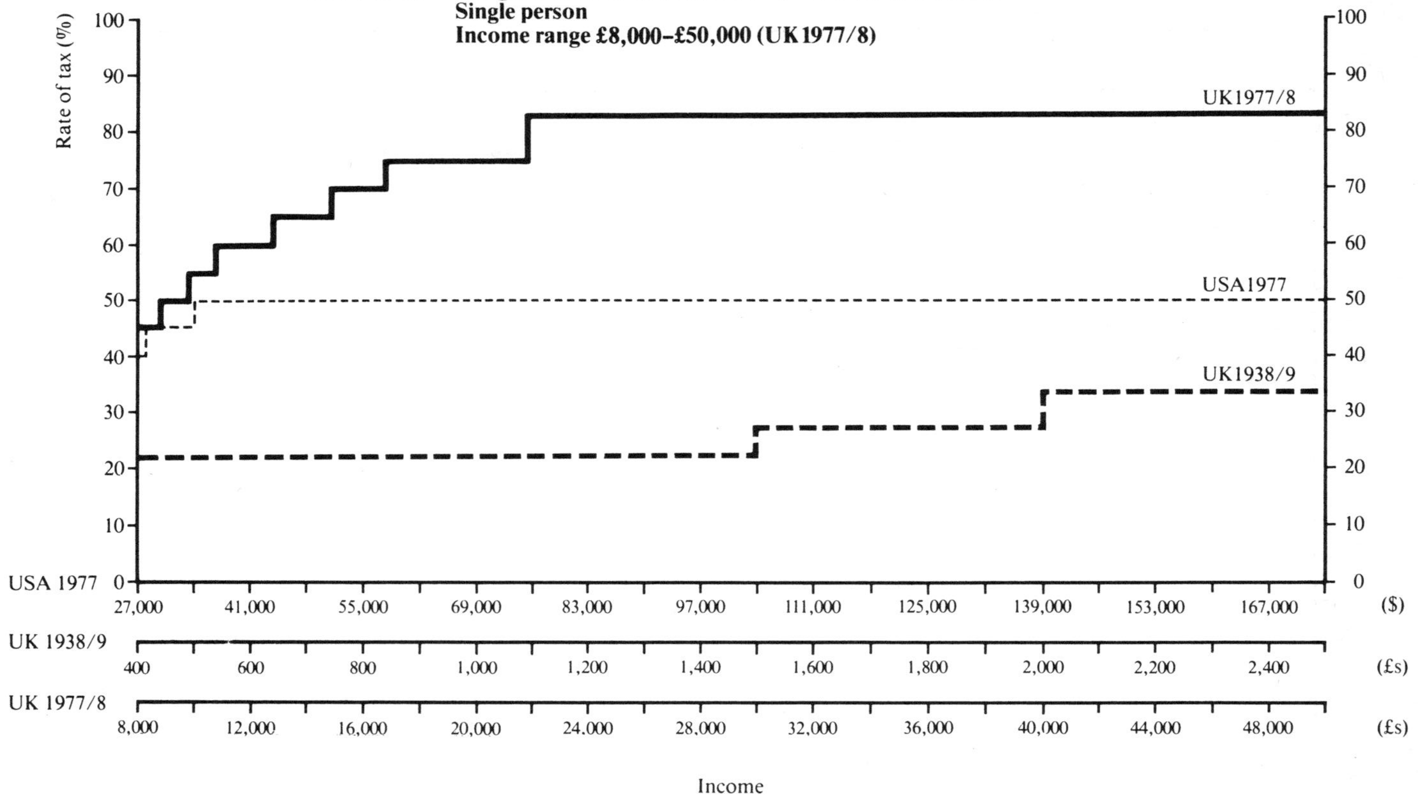

Chart 13.3a **Effective rates of tax, UK1938/9, UK1977/8, USA1977**
Single person
Income range £0–£8,500 (UK1977/8)

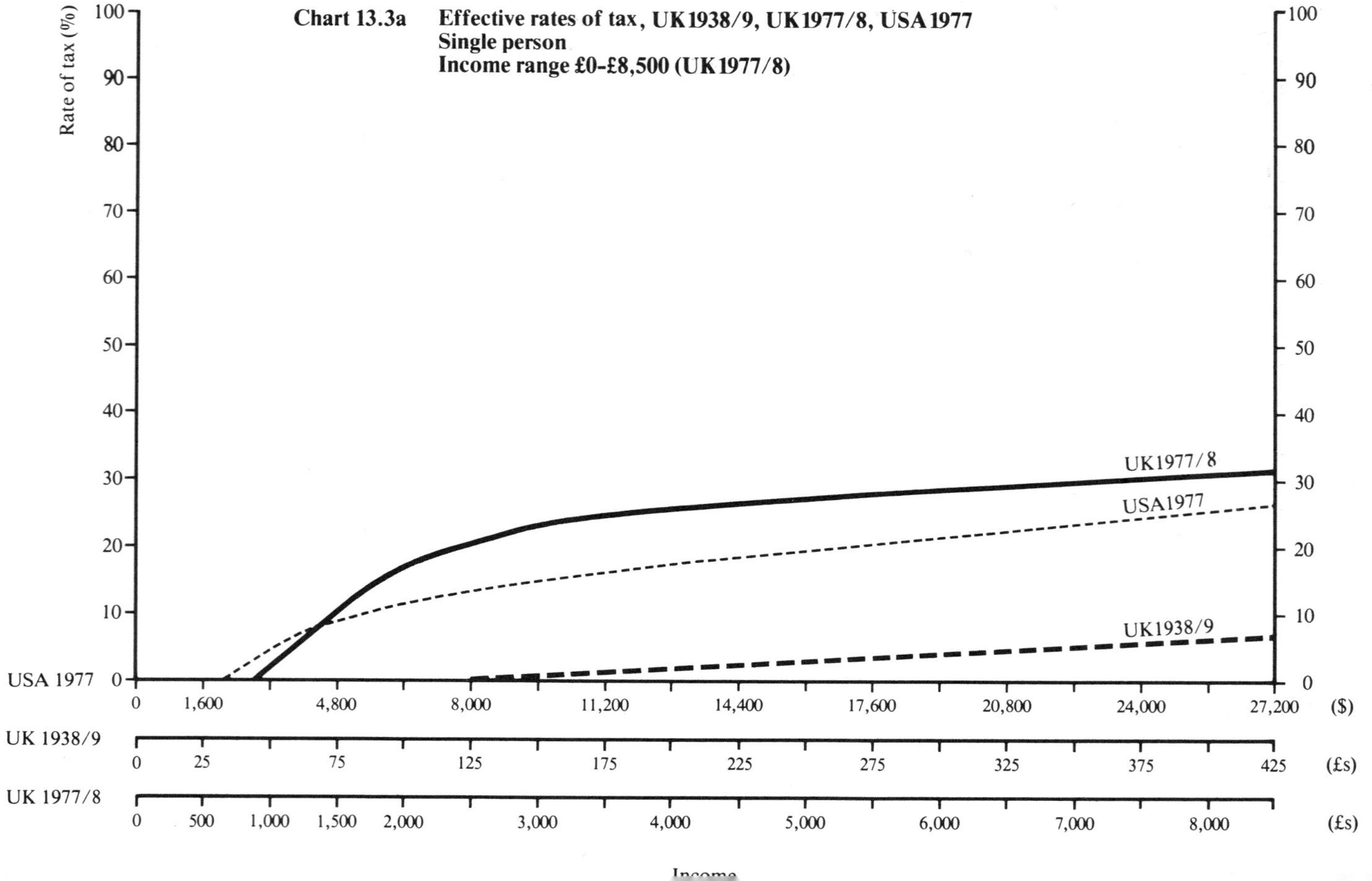

Chart 13.3b Effective rates of tax, UK1938/9, UK1977/8, USA1977
Single person
Income range £8,000–£50,000 (UK1977/8)

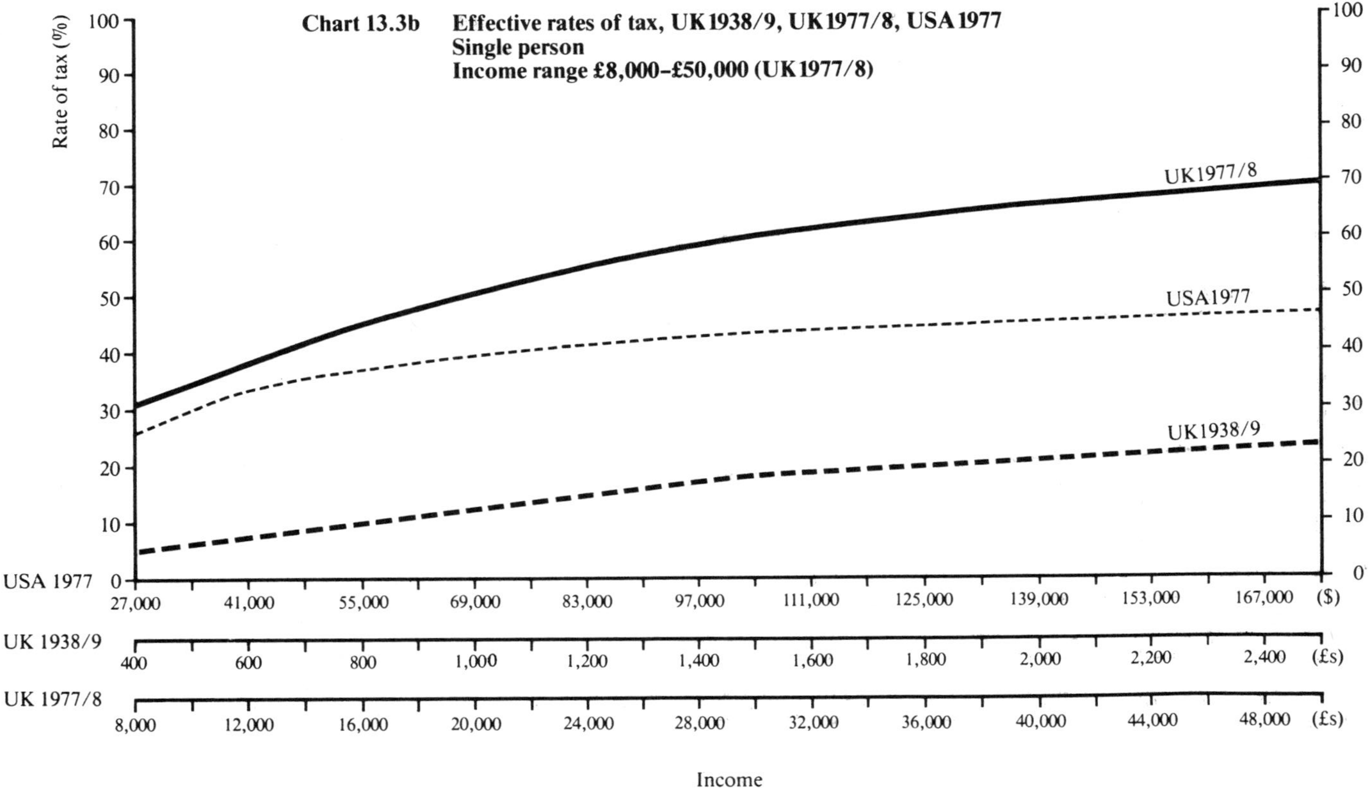

impression derived from the charts. The lowest 60 per cent of incomes in the USA pay on average less than 5 per cent of their incomes in tax, which is little more than one-third of the UK figure.[1] As for contributions to total tax, giving a rough measure of progressivity, there is a substantial degree of similarity between the two countries, especially for the classification by incomes.

Table 13.3

Income tax payments by quintile of recipients and quintile of incomes, USA, 1975

Quintile	*Classification by quintiles of recipients*		*Classification by quintiles of income*	
	Percentage of income paid in tax	*Tax paid as percentage of total tax*	*Percentage of income paid in tax*	*Tax paid as percentage of total tax*
Lowest	0.5	0.1	5.8	8.8
Second	4.6	3.0	10.2	15.6
Third	8.7	10.3	11.8	18.1
Fourth	11.1	21.4	14.3	21.7
Highest	17.7	65.2	23.5	35.8

Source: US Treasury, *Statistics of Income, Individual Returns, 1975* (Washington DC, 1978).
Note: The income concept is that of Adjusted Gross Income. This corresponds roughly to Personal Income, with certain omissions such as social security benefits; it also includes one-half of long-term capital gains.

Are there any reasons for thinking that differences of definition of income may invalidate these comparisons? The most important differences of definition relate to social security payments (which are partially included in the definition of taxable income in the UK and are excluded in the USA) and long-term capital gains (partially included in the definition of taxable income in the USA, but excluded in the UK). But the absolute magnitude of such differences is small relative to the size of taxable income as a whole. For instance, Table 9.3 shows the estimated yield of capital gains tax in the UK in 1978/79 as £375 million, a trivial amount in comparison to the total yield of income tax of £24,860 million. Even if all capital gains were attributed to the highest quintile, the overall picture would remain essentially

[1] But see the important caveat contained in the notes on Table 13.2.

unchanged. There are many other queries that can be raised (e.g. in relation to the amount of income disguised as business expenses), but again there is little reason to think that this would substantially modify the conclusions derived from comparing Tables 13.2 and 13.3. In summary these showed higher tax burdens at all income levels in the UK, but very similar contributions by the different quintiles of income to the total tax bill in the two countries.

1.3 *The effects of income tax in the UK*

We start this section by summarizing empirical work on the effects of taxation on work effort, and then discuss possible interpretations of the results. Next we investigate other possible ill-effects of high rates of taxation, and finally mention briefly the alternatives.

(1) *The effects of taxation on work effort.* On the basis of the theoretical discussion in Chapter 4 it can be argued that high marginal rates of tax (up to 83 per cent on earned income in 1978/79) will have strong repercussions on incentives to work. In theory the effect of taxation on work effort will depend on the relative strengths of the income and substitution effects, and for that reason there has been a substantial amount of empirical work over the years. Early work relied on attitude surveys in which workers were asked about their responses to actual or hypothetical changes in tax rates. One of the first of these was organized by the Royal Commission in the mid-1950s, covering operative and supervisory grades engaged in productive employment and capable of varying their output per hour or their number of hours per week; Break's work[1] in the later 1950s was on similar lines, but concentrated on a sample of 306 self-employed accountants and solicitors; his work was subsequently brought up to date.[2] More recently a major study was conducted by Brown and Levin.[3] What these surveys sought was an indication of the supply elasticity of work effort with respect to its net wage. If taxation is a strong disincentive the elasticity will be high (since a tax increase is equivalent to a reduction in the net wage). In this case the substitution effect of cheaper leisure would dominate the income effect of lower post-tax

[1] G. F. Break, 'Effects of Taxation on Incentives', *British Tax Review*, June 1957, and 'Income Taxes and Incentives to Work', *American Economic Review*, September 1957.

[2] D. B. Fields and W. T. Stanbury, 'Incentives, Disincentives and the Income Tax: Further Empirical Evidence', *Public Finance*, No. 3, 1970; and 'Income Taxes and Incentives to Work: Some Additional Empirical Evidence', *American Economic Review*, June 1971.

[3] C. V. Brown and E. Levin, 'The Effects of Income Taxation on Overtime: The Results of a National Survey', *Economic Journal*, Vol. 84, No. 336, December 1974.

income. If taxation were not a disincentive we would observe a low labour supply elasticity.

The findings of these surveys have tended to confirm one another. The main result was that relatively few people really understood how they were affected by income tax, but in general few people thought that their actions were much affected by it. Thus at least for workers facing the basic rate of income tax, the supply elasticity was fairly low, and taxation was not a substantial disincentive. For those with higher incomes, paying the higher rates of income tax, the evidence was rather more mixed, but gave at least some indication that the higher rates of tax, though a labour supply disincentive, were not a very strong one.

More recently there has been a substantial amount of econometric investigation, especially in the USA, into the determinants of labour supply. One of the main studies, by Hall,[1] broadly confirmed the results of the attitude surveys that the supply elasticity of primary workers was low, so that no serious question of disincentives arose. Other studies have tended to confirm the general tenor of Hall's results. But an important exception, found by Hall and others in the USA and confirmed by Greenhalgh[2] in the UK, concerned secondary workers (broadly speaking, people who are not permanent members of the labour force, such as teenagers, married women, and people past retiring age). Unlike the survey work which concentrated on primary workers only, the econometric work investigated secondary workers separately and found the supply elasticity to be substantial. There is thus strong evidence suggesting that high rates of tax can be a substantial disincentive for secondary workers.

(2) *Possible interpretations of the empirical results.* Having outlined the available empirical evidence we need to discuss what conclusions, if any, may be drawn. It was common to disbelieve the results of surveys on the grounds that most workers had little understanding of their true tax position, and tended in any case to rationalize their answers to questions of this kind (e.g. the under-reporting of expenditure on alcohol and tobacco in the Family Expenditure Survey). This kind of reasoning is speculative at the best of times, and certainly holds little water now that the survey results have been largely corroborated by econometric investigation.

[1] R. E. Hall, 'Wages, Income and Hours of Work in the U.S. Labor Force', in G. Cain and H. Watts, *Income Maintenance and Labor Supply: Econometric Studies* (Markham, 1973).

[2] C. Greenhalgh, 'A Labour Supply Function for Married Women in Great Britain', *Economica*, Vol. 44, No. 175, August 1977.

A second explanation of the absence of disincentives is simply to say that the income effect of high tax rates offsets the disincentive effects of the substitution effect. A special case of this argument would be the assertion that the substitution effect is small since people work mainly for non-monetary considerations. This argument is unexceptionable as far as it goes; but at the same time one should not place too much reliance on such a proposition since long-run elasticities of factor demand and supply tend to be greater than short-run ones. It is necessary also to be careful about what we mean by ceteris paribus. For instance, if we are discussing the effects of high rates of taxation on those with high incomes, it is not enough to look at the income and substitution effects of the well-off. If they are worse off because of a tax increase then someone else must be better-off, either through increased government spending or through the reduction of some other tax. It can be argued that if high rates of tax are used to finance transfers to lower income groups the income effect in favour of work effort for the well-off is likely, at least in part, to be offset by the unfavourable income effect on the work effort of the recipient group.

A third, and completely different, explanation of the absence of major labour supply disincentives runs on tax avoidance lines.[1] The argument here is that it is too simple to confine one's analysis to the published structure of tax rates – that one needs to consider also people's incentives to avoid taxation by increasing the proportion of their income in non-taxable form. This can be done in a variety of subtle ways, as any businessman, accountant or tax lawyer well knows. The incentives to shift to jobs offering expense allowances rather than higher salary, or the incentive to take more of one's payment in non-taxable income, or the incentive to pursue a corporate identity rather than remain a partnership or sole trader are only three out of many well-known devices. Thus it might well be true in some crude physical sense that there is no effect of high marginal rates on work effort, but this is so only because people take action to avoid the highest rates of tax, and so the actual rate of tax is less than the apparent rate. There is no systematic evidence that this actually happens; it is simply an hypothesis consistent with the factual data of such surveys as we have, and with the general observation that tax

[1] We should perhaps remind ourselves that tax *evasion* is illegal. Tax *avoidance* is the reduction of one's tax bill by legitimate means (e.g. by buying a house and so qualifying for mortgage interest relief).

avoidance has become a major industry. The process may be carried further by tax evasion, moonlighting, etc.

(3) *Other possible effects of high tax rates.* At this stage it might be argued that since taxation does not appear to be a major disincentive at least for primary workers, possibly because the highest rates of tax can be avoided, there is nothing to worry about. As an efficiency argument, this states that since the total level of output is not substantially effected there is no problem; in terms of equity the argument says that there is no need to think that the rich are being unduly taxed, because they are able to avoid the worst effects of the tax system.

Though these arguments seem plausible at first glance we regard them both as completely false. High tax rates can have ill-effects in terms of both efficiency and equity quite independent of any effects on work effort. There are two additional efficiency impacts. The first, and less important, is that tax avoidance is costly in resources, since it takes up the time and money of skilled people whose efforts would better be directed to more productive ends. To say this is unimportant is equivalent to saying that it does not matter if students throw knives at their teachers since their teachers normally manage to dodge out of the way. This does not appear to be a very strong argument.

The second efficiency argument is more important; to say that high tax rates have no adverse effects if they leave the total volume of output unaffected is false because it overlooks the effect of taxation on the *composition* of that output. The essential point is that we get a different product mix through the shifting of factors trying to minimize tax liabilities from that which we would have in the absence of high marginal tax rates (but assuming an equal tax take in some hypothetically innocuous form). Thus the company director may get lavish entertainment expenses and the employee free luncheon vouchers. The fact that luncheon vouchers are sometimes found selling for cash is evidence that people are receiving income in a form they would not choose. In theoretical terms high marginal tax rates can bring about a deadweight welfare loss, even while leaving real GNP unaffected.

Such tendencies to tax avoidance may be slow and hard to discover, but they are important precisely because they are not obvious. Steps will always be taken to deal with blatant tax avoidance; it is the most imperceptible that are likely to be the most persistent.

There are also equity arguments against the proposition that high tax rates have no costs if labour supply is unaffected. The first is that if those with high incomes are able to avoid the highest rates of tax we are no longer able to talk with any confidence about the redistributive effects of the tax system. If it is possible to avoid the higher rates of tax then the picture of a steep rate of progression is a false one, and there would be no need to get upset about the mulcting of the rich. But this overlooks two points. First, the progressive rate structure will strike unevenly, inasmuch as some people are better able than others to avoid its strongest impact, and this is inherently inequitable. Second, what the argument is really saying is that the system works by its faults. The upper income groups continue to work 'hard' precisely because the tax rates which apply in principle do not apply in practice.

A second equity argument concerns the yield of the highest rates of tax. Not only do they yield little revenue because of tax avoidance and the small number of people to whom they apply; but doubts have been expressed about whether their yield is positive at all. It has been argued that an increase in the top rate of tax from (say) 80 to 90 per cent will not increase tax revenues but will actually decrease them by increasing tax avoidance. In particular, one form of tax avoidance is emigration. And if very high marginal rates of tax make people emigrate (e.g. various highly paid sportsmen and pop stars), then it is indeed possible that, by leading to a reduction of the tax base, high tax rates actually *reduce* the proceeds of income tax – in other words the elasticity of the tax yield becomes negative.

The emigration argument is highlighted by comparing the UK rates with the maximum marginal rates, and the levels of income at which they apply, in other countries. Western European and North American countries are usually content with maximum rates which are less than ours (e.g. 50 per cent for earned income in the USA and 43 per cent in Canada at a Federal level). Even when the income tax rates of lower-tier authorities are added, the contrast is still very marked. And usually these rates are not reached until much higher levels of income than those at which the top rates are applied in the UK.

The conclusion is that even if they have no adverse effects on the total volume of output there are strong arguments against very high marginal tax rates: the strongest arguments concern the deadweight welfare loss via effects on the *composition* of output, and the possibility that the yield of the top rates is negative. Additionally, resources are 'wasted' in avoidance activities, and inequity results when some people can avoid the highest rates more easily than others.

(4) *Possible alternatives*. None of this is meant to suggest a plea for the abandonment of a high degree of progression. All we suggest is that

it makes little sense to pretend to do what we are not doing and are not likely to do. If it is decided that the present state of affairs is not satisfactory there are in principle two solutions: (a) to tighten up the system so that the nominal rate structure applies in practice, and (b) to reduce somewhat the higher rates of tax on the grounds that in practice their effect is very limited. This might be accompanied by expanding the tax base by reducing allowances and deductions, and possibly taxing certain types of imputed income.

Taking these arguments in turn, it would, in principle, be possible to tighten all loopholes by cutting down expense allowances, withdrawing earned income treatment of some types of Schedule D income, and so on. Undoubtedly there are loopholes in existing legislation which need to be plugged, and no doubt others will be found in the future which will require similar treatment. But to proceed from there to a system of control sufficiently detailed to make the top rates of income tax *really* effective is likely to require a degree of control which would be both very expensive to administer, and very frightening in its political implications.

The alternative is to give up the pretence that we can enforce in a uniform way tax rates of up to 98 per cent. How far the process of redistribution should go is a value judgment, and no one can say which is the 'right' distribution, even if we could measure it. But it is difficult to argue for a system which strikes more effectively at some people than at others with the same income. It can be argued that it is much more inequitable to have a highly progressive system working haphazardly than an apparently less progressive system working more uniformly and effectively. If we adopt the course of reducing the very highest rates of tax it may be necessary very slightly to increase the rates on lower incomes to obtain the same revenue. But, to the extent that these high rates may have a negative yield for the reasons already described, a decrease in the top rates of tax may, in fact, enable a *reduction* of the rates on lower levels of income.

Even if this were not the case, there are other possibilities such as a slight increase in Value Added Tax. We shall refer to these as we proceed, but for the time being we conclude by repeating that there are serious doubts on both equity and efficiency grounds about the highest rates of income tax.[1]

[1] Similar issues arise in the case of the high implicit taxation imposed by the withdrawal of income-related benefits. These form part of a broader discussion of the poverty trap in Chapter 14, section 4.

2 THE RELATIVE TREATMENT OF INDIVIDUALS AND FAMILIES

2.1 *Basic Principles*

So far, we have discussed the subject of progression broadly, as if all family units were alike, even though family structures and their tax treatment entered implicitly into some of the tables. In this section we discuss explicitly the tax treatment of different-sized families in the context of a progressive income tax. Section 2.1 discusses some underlying principles, first for persons and couples with no children, and then for families with children. Section 2.2 looks at the present British system.[1]

In discussing the tax treatment of households of different sizes and characteristics we must start by asking what it is that we are trying to achieve. In principle, we are reaching towards some notion of horizontal equity; traditionally this has called for the 'equal treatment of equals', where equality is measured in terms of money income and is subject to adjustment for the number of dependants and various other characteristics. This concept has been criticized in recent years on grounds both of logic and of practicality. As an alternative, Feldstein[2] defines horizontal equity as a situation in which all individuals face the same tax schedules *provided* that they have the same tastes and abilities (i.e. the same utility functions). In this case people of equal income not only pay the same tax but also forgo the same utility. In contrast, if individuals have different utility functions then horizontal equity, requiring equal loss of utility, can be attained only by charging people with the same income different amounts of tax. This is clearly impracticable.

Despite these difficulties, most recent work on the subject continues to use the traditional definition of horizontal equity, both on the grounds that individuals' utility functions probably do not differ substantially, and, less implausibly, that any differences in utility functions are not substantially related to income. If we accept as a definition of horizontal equity in this context a situation where individuals with similar income and family circumstances pay the same amount of tax,

[1] Throughout this section the terms 'family' and 'household' are used synonymously and with the same meaning as the more precise but less felicitous 'tax unit'. A 'housewife' is a married person of either sex without paid employment, who works in the home.

[2] See Martin S. Feldstein, 'On the Theory of Tax Reform', *Journal of Public Economics*, Vol. 6, 1976.

we need next to ask what this might mean in practice. Two major aims are:

Desideratum 1: tax liability should be unaffected by marital status, i.e. there should be no financial reward or penalty for marriage, and

Desideratum 2: families with equal incomes should pay the same taxes.

These and a number of other criteria are listed in Meade.[1]

Bearing in mind these aims, with which few would disagree, we turn now to a discussion of the various principles of taxation which have existed at various times in different countries. We do so on the assumption that the tax structure in question is a progressive one. The two major principles of taxation that exist are (a) the *Individual* basis and (b) the *Aggregation*, or *Unit*, basis. The Individual basis, as its name suggests, simply taxes individuals on their own income, with no regard whatever for their family circumstances. Thus tax liability depends on one's income, and on nothing else. The Aggregation principle starts from a notion of income sharing. In its extreme form, Aggregation treats the entire family as though it were a single individual, aggregates family income, and taxes it as heavily as a single individual with the same income. We shall refer to this as the 'pure' system of Aggregation. The 'modified' system of Aggregation, while still working from a notion of income pooling, recognizes that the taxable capacity of a family with a given income will generally be smaller than that of a single individual with the same income. Probably the most important type of modified Aggregation is the so-called 'quotient' system, whose operation we shall outline shortly.

What are the pros and cons of these principles? Four advantages have been claimed for the Individual system. The first is that a person's tax bill is independent of his or her marital status; taxation is thus neutral with respect to marriage. This accords with Desideratum 1.

A second advantage claimed rests on some notion of the independence of the individual, and on the idea that individuals' tax liabilities should depend on their own earnings and circumstances, and should be independent of the earnings and circumstances of others, even those in the same family. But this argument is almost certainly an overstatement. The fundamental interdependence of a great many living arrangements has to be acknowledged. The wife of the wealthy businessman, who has zero current income because she stays at home to manage the servants, is fundamentally different from a blind

[1] J. E. Meade, *Report*, *op. cit.*, Chapter 18.

beggar-lady, and so it is highly dubious to argue that each should be taxed as an isolated individual, and that each, with zero current income, should pay no tax.

A third argument which is sometimes put forward for the Individual basis of taxation rests on the premise that a married man with a non-working wife should pay the same tax as a single man with identical income (i.e. no tax concessions should be granted to married men). This means that two people living off a given income pay the same tax as a single individual living off that income. It has been suggested that this can be justified by taking account of the imputed value of the services of the non-working spouse. This proposition cannot be entirely dismissed; indeed, some calculations show that the imputed value of housewives' services may often be large relative to money incomes of husbands.[1] The main weakness with this line of argument is that there is unlikely to be a systematic relationship between the imputed value of a wife's services and the income of her husband. In particular, it is not obvious that the value of these imputed services will be higher for a wife whose husband has a high money income. Therefore, not too much should be made of this claimed advantage.

As well as the equity claims of the Individual basis outlined above, there is also an efficiency argument which asserts that a move from an Aggregate to an Individual basis will encourage work effort. This is because such a move will generally reduce the marginal rate of tax (leading to a substitution effect in favour of work effort); but if the yield of the tax is to remain constant, the average rate of tax will have to be raised (leading to an income effect in favour of work effort by both wife and husband). If, in addition, the husband loses any married man's allowance[2] in the switch to an Individual basis, there will be a further income effect encouraging the husband to work more.

The disadvantages of the Individual basis are threefold and serious. While the Individual basis makes tax neutral with respect to marriage (Desideratum 1), it will, nevertheless, result in a situation where a married couple's tax bill will depend on the relative income of husband and wife. Thus, a couple with all its income received by one partner will pay more tax than a couple with an equal joint income, half received by each partner. This violates Desideratum 2. The second criticism is that the Individual basis ignores the fact that households and families really exist and ignores the fact that the needs and characteristics of a

[1] Colin Clark, 'The Economics of Housework', *Oxford Bulletin of Statistics*, May 1958.

[2] The UK married man's allowance is described in Chapter 9, page 193.

household differ fundamentally from those of a single person. This leads to a host of anomalies, not least of which are those just mentioned. Finally, using an Individual basis it is often difficult to apportion investment income in a satisfactory way between spouses.

Turning now to the Aggregation basis in its pure form, the major advantage here is precisely that it rectifies the anomalies described in the preceding paragraph – namely that if all household income is aggregated and then taxed as though it were received by a single person, then households with equal income will pay equal amounts of tax (Desideratum 2). But to offset this undoubted advantage, it fails to comply with Desideratum 1, since we now have a situation where the tax system is no longer neutral with respect to marriage. With full aggregation a married couple both of whom work will pay more tax than two working unmarried individuals with the same total income, and this tax penalty upon marriage increases the smaller the divergence between the earnings of husband and wife, and the more progressive is the tax system.

Such a tax penalty raises problems far wider than the simple issue of economic equity, and has been a political football for many years. In recognition of this, many countries modify their Aggregation system so as to minimize, or remove, the tax penalty on marriage. The most explicit way of doing so is the Quotient system, under which a married couple with a total income of (say) £5,000 (irrespective of the proportions in which this is earned by the husband and wife) will pay the same amount of tax as two single individuals each earning £2,500. It can be verified that under such a system two individuals each earning (say) £2,500 will suffer no tax penalty if they marry, and if their total income of £5,000 is earned in unequal proportions then they will receive a tax bonus upon marriage. The quotient system thus avoids tax penalties on marriage, and makes tax liability for a couple independent of the relative earnings of husband and wife (Desideratum 2). But it does so only by introducing the disadvantage that the tax system is no longer neutral towards marriage, except as a special case.

A second major disadvantage of the quotient system is that its underlying premise is rather dubious. It is just not true that a couple in which the husband earns £8,000 and the wife nothing is no better off than one in which each partner earns £4,000. This is because there are formidable costs to earning income. These costs embrace not merely travel costs and the value of the leisure foregone, but also the foregone value of the services of the non-working spouse (e.g. the costs, both social and domestic, of 'latch-key' children). Furthermore, the two-earner household would find it difficult to raise its income substantially since both members are working. This is less likely to be the case with a one-earner couple. Under the quotient system the one-earner couple not only enjoys the untaxed benefits of a considerable amount of psychic income, but also a tax advantage relative to single people. This generosity to non-working wives has efficiency implications as well as equity ones; there is a substantial labour supply disincentive hidden in the fact that under the quotient system every pound that the wife earns is subject to the couple's marginal rate. Thus the wife could face high marginal tax rates from the first. It can be argued that the disadvantages are a high price to pay to avoid any tax penalty upon marriage.

Returning to our two Desiderata (one, that tax should be neutral with respect to marriage and, two, that equal-income couples should be equally taxed), we have now reached a position where any application of the Individual basis or the Aggregation basis will achieve at best one of these. The truth, in fact, is even worse than this; the two characteristics are inherently in conflict, as under a progressive tax system *any* structure that is neutral with respect to marriage will not treat equal-income couples equally. Once we recognize that this is inescapable under a progressive system it is worthwhile exploring the characteristics of the quotient system in somewhat more detail. Suppose we have a married couple, Dan who earns £5,000 and Doris who stays at home, and two single individuals (Eric and Ernie) each earning £2,500 per annum. With aggregation under a progressive tax system, Dan and Doris will pay more tax than Eric and Ernie, and one might argue that this is equitable since Dan and Doris have the higher total (i.e. money plus imputed) income. Under a pure quotient system Dan and Doris would pay exactly the same tax as Eric and Ernie, and *less* tax than Eric and Ernie would pay together if they had unequal earnings. The quotient system in general thus *subsidizes* imputed income. The argument would be further complicated if Eric and Ernie's income was from investment, so that they were both able to enjoy their leisure at home.

There are thus considerable equity problems raised by the quotient system. In practice, it is noteworthy that when it was used for married couples in the USA it was found necessary to apply it not only to married couples but also to unmarried heads of households, and to make special provisions for the first two years of widowhood and widowerhood. The astonishingly large bonus to marriage for upper-income groups implicit in the system was also the subject of much comment.

The overall conclusion is that with a progressive tax structure both the Individual basis and the Aggregation basis (in whatever form) will result in anomalies, and that which set of anomalies is disliked less is largely a matter of social choice. The only escape route is to abandon the idea of a progressive income tax structure. With a proportional tax none of the problems arise – the Individual and Aggregate Bases boil down to the same thing, and both conform with Desiderata 1 and 2. For this reason, among others, various people have suggested a move to proportional income taxation.

To conclude this section we should say a few words about the tax treatment of children. Suppose, initially, that they have no income of their own. The Individual basis of taxation in its pure form implies that the decision to have a child rather than, say, a hi-fi system or a sports car, is a matter of choice for the individual or couple, and that therefore the allowances for families with children should be no greater than for those without. There are a number of objections to such a statement, but the most compelling is that even if justice were done in this way between parents with and without children, injustice might well be done to the children themselves. Thus the Individual basis must be regarded as untenable where children are concerned.[1] On the other hand, there is no overriding reason to go to the opposite extreme and accept the full quotient system for children. We saw that the quotient system raised issues of principle which centred largely on the treatment of imputed income as between married couples and 'unmarried' couples with the same total income. Such arguments do not apply in the case of children.

So some tax concessions are clearly necessary in respect of children, but their amount relative to those for adults and relative to the income of the taxpayer, is very much a matter of social and population policy. If one believes that birth rates are affected by current incomes, one could encourage the birth rate with higher tax remissions, and upper income group birth rates by correlating the tax remissions with income of the parent.

How do children's earnings affect these conclusions? If there is any unearned income, the obvious answer is to aggregate it with the income of the parents. The majority of the Royal Commission almost tied themselves in knots arguing this proposition, but the Minority's insist-

[1] See also the discussion of adult equivalences in Chapter 14, section 1.2.

ence upon it[1] seems absolutely right. Whatever the amount and extent of relief to be given to children, the separation of their unearned income from the rest of the family was totally unjustified.[2] With earned income, however, it seems reasonable to assume that in most cases the 'adult' children should be regarded as separate tax units, and therefore their income should not be aggregated with that of the parents with whom they lodge, but should be taxed separately.

2.2 *The present British system*

2.2.1 *Tax burdens for families of different sizes* Having discussed the principles underlying the taxation of families, we now examine how far the present British system conforms to them. With some rather limited exceptions, such as earning wives in upper income families, the general principle in the UK has always been to insist on Aggregation (so that the husbands and wives are treated as a single unit with a single income), but to make allowances for greater family responsibilities. In some European countries (e.g. France) the quotient system is used.[3]

From 1948 to 1969 the US system was in effect a half-way house between the British and the French, the quotient system being applicable to wives but not to children; but since 1969 the quotient element has largely disappeared in favour of differential rate schedules with higher rates for single people than for married couples.

The tax and expenditure treatment in the UK of families with different numbers of children is illustrated in Table 13.4. Taking the single person's allowance in 1978/79 as 100, the married man's allowance was 156 and total allowances increased with family size so that a three-child family with two parents had an allowance of 307 and a single parent family with three children an allowance of 355.[4]

Several points are worth noticing about this table. First of all, there has been a widening of differentials between family sizes in recent

[1] Cmd. 9105, P. 77ff.

[2] The controversy still rages: in 1969 unearned income of children under 18 living at home was aggregated with that of their parents: from 1972 it was disaggregated. The possibility of re-instituting aggregation has been raised.

[3] To illustrate the quotient system, if one takes a husband, wife and two children and the children are counted as half units, the tax payable by the family would be three times that payable by a single individual with an income equal to one-third that of the family; with progressive tax rates this treatment is obviously more favourable to the family than the British system.

[4] The tax treatment of children is an aspect of the more general problem of adult equivalents discussed in Chapter 14. See also Chapter 10, section 3.1.

years, as part of an explicit government policy to aid families. A second and related point is the emergence in recent years of higher relative benefits for one-parent families. The higher tax allowances and the child benefit increase for single-parent families seem to be based on some sort of notion that these families have a lower imputed income than those with two parents, and so should pay less tax. Finally, it should be noted that the differentials are very much less than in the US where each member of the family normally receives the same exemption, thereby making the index number 200 for a married couple and 500 for a three-child family.

Table 13.4

Index numbers of income tax allowances and child benefit, UK, 1978/79

Single Person	100	
Married Couple	156	
	Two parents	*Single parent*
One-child family (child aged 11–16)	206	222
Two-child family (children aged under 11 and 11–16)	253	285
Three-child family (children aged under 11, 11–16 and over 16)	307	355

Notes: (1) Computations include child benefit and child benefit increase (i.e. the higher rate of child benefit paid to some single-parent families) converted to equivalent tax allowances at a 33 per cent tax rate, but exclude welfare payments such as family income supplement. The age-differentiated tax allowances for children were phased out from April 1979.

(2) As noted in Chapter 9, section 2.1, persons with single-handed responsibility for children receive a higher income tax allowance than other single people.

However, a tabulation of personal allowances for income tax and child benefit is not sufficient to tell the full story when the tax system is progressive. We need to consider various additional benefits for families with children, such as family income supplement, and also to see how these change at different levels of income. The story in this respect is somewhat complicated. To recapitulate, there was until 1975 an income tax allowance in respect of children (called child tax allowance), together with family allowances for all children in the family other than the first.[1] Family allowances were weekly cash payments to the mother of the child, and were taxable. Since April 1979 a new system has been in operation, whereby child tax allowances and family allowances have been replaced by child benefit, a weekly, tax-free cash payment to mothers of all children including the first. The new system was phased in between 1976 and 1979, with child benefit gradually increasing and the child tax allowances gradually being phased out. In addition family income supplement (FIS) is available for low-income families with children. As we saw in Chapter 10, FIS is a weekly cash payment to families with a working head, where the payments rise with the number of children and fall with family income.

We can estimate the effects of these various allowances in two stages. Firstly, one can compute the tax saving of a family relative to a single individual at different income levels. This can be done simply by estimating how much better off a family of given size and income is compared to a situation where no tax allowances, child benefit, etc. are available. The results are given in Table 13.5. It can be seen that in 1978/79 at a very low level of income couples without children derived virtually no benefit relative to single individuals from the various allowances; but the same was not true of married couples with families, since child benefit and FIS, being cash payments rather than tax-free allowances, were received in full, even by those below the tax threshold. What also emerges clearly is the decline in the position of families with children relative to single individuals and childless couples as income increases. This is true both for two-parent and single-parent families.

Table 13.5

Index numbers of gains from tax allowances and various benefits, UK, 1978/79

Level of earnings (£s)	*Single person*	*Married couple*	*Two parents*		*Single parent*	
			2 children	*3 children*	*2 children*	*3 children*
1,000	100	102	343	396	375	444
2,000	100	156	328	414	361	462
5,000	100	156	253	307	285	355

Note: Computations include income tax allowances, child benefit, child benefit increase, and family income supplement. Incomes are assumed to be earned by the husband in the two-parent case. Children are aged under 11 and 11–16 in the two-children case, and under 11, 11–16 and over 16 in the three-child case.

[1] See Chapter 10, section 3.1.

Table 13.6

Net tax liabilities by income and family size, UK, 1978/79 (£s)

Level of Earnings	*Single person*	*Married couple*	*Two parents 2 children*	*Two parents 3 children*	*Single parent 2 children*	*Single parent 3 children*
1,000	4	0	−785	−957	−889	−1113
2,000	275	116	−426	−691	−530	− 847
3,000	605	423	107	−67	3	− 223
4,000	935	753	437	263	333	107
6,000	1595	1413	1097	923	993	767
10,000	2987	2760	2433	2247	2323	2091
20,000	8716	8681	8277	8042	8173	7886

Note: As Table 13.5.

The second stage of estimation is to compute how actual tax liabilities, positive or negative, change for one size of family relative to another as income increases. Table 13.6 shows that at low income levels child benefit, FIS, etc. sufficed to make the net position of the family much better than that of single individuals or childless married couples. But in relative terms this differential declined dramatically as incomes increased, so that the effective tax rate at high income levels hardly varied with family size. This was partly the result of the replacement of child tax allowances by child benefit, and raises the very real question of whether the relative treatment of smaller and larger families at high income levels is equitable.

Another, though rather different, point can be found in the calculations underlying Table 13.6. This is the fact that at an income of £2,000 families with two and three children both paid income tax and were in receipt of FIS. We shall see more of such overlaps between the tax and benefit systems in the next chapter.

2.2.2 *The tax treatment of wives' incomes* So far we have concentrated mainly on the relative tax burden in the UK of families of different size and composition, and with different incomes. We turn now to an entirely different aspect of the tax treatment of families – the tax treatment of wives' incomes. Since this has been the subject of increasing controversy and acrimony in recent years it is worthwhile giving a brief historical sketch. At some risk of over-simplification, a man's wife at various times historically has been regarded as part of his property, and hence regarded as no more able to have income in her own right than, say, his cattle. If one starts from this premise, the Aggregation basis is the obvious way to treat the joint income of husband and wife. Over the past hundred years, legislation has increasingly reflected the changed position of women both within marriage and in society, though the Aggregation basis has remained largely unaltered.

The situation today is that the income of husband and wife will normally be aggregated for tax purposes, and where a tax return has to be submitted it will normally be a joint return, containing the incomes of both husband and wife, and completed by the husband. Married couples have the option of deviating from this arrangement in one of two ways. Under *separate assessment* each partner will complete his or her own tax return, and each will have his or her own dealings with the Inland Revenue. This arrangement affects who writes to whom about what, but in no way alters a couple's tax liability. In contrast, under *separate taxation* husband and wife will be taxed on their earnings as though they were two single individuals. In this case the husband will lose his married man's allowance, and receive only the single person's allowance while the wife will receive the same tax-free allowance as before. Thus low-income couples will lose by choosing this option (since they lose tax-free income equivalent to the difference between the married man's and single person's allowances). A high-income couple will gain, inasmuch as less of their total income will be subject to the higher rates of tax. Whether or not it is to a couple's financial advantage to opt for this election will depend on the relative strength of these two factors.

While separate assessment and separate taxation have gone some way towards removing a wife's dependent status, there is one major caveat – namely that the two options apply only to a wife's *earned* income. A wife's investment income continues to be aggregated with her husband's income, and he is liable for the tax on it.

There can be all sorts of complaints in principle about such a system. But in addition there have been many complaints in recent years about the day-to-day operation of income tax as it affects wives. Since these have generated a considerable amount of heat and not much light, it might be useful to outline the major criticisms. Most complaints seem to have fallen under two heads, which we might call 'paperwork' criticisms and 'money' criticisms. Paperwork criticisms are complaints about the way the system operates, rather than about how much tax is charged to each partner. There are three main complaints under this head. The first concerns the Inland Revenue's insistence that income tax forms, and related correspondence, should be filled in by the husband, hence the instructions, until quite recently, that 'if you are a married woman living with your husband, he should complete this form as if it were addressed to him'. A second, though related, complaint concerns the Inland Revenue's reluctance to correspond with wives about their own tax affairs, and to write instead to the husband. This generated a situation where a wife would write to the Inland Revenue about the taxation of her earnings, and the reply would be addressed to the husband. As a result of public pressure it was announced in Parliament in 1978 that these two administrative practices would be abandoned.

A third 'paperwork' criticism is rather more serious. This concerns the difficulty of maintaining financial privacy within marriage. Since separate assessment and separate taxation are not applicable to a wife's investment income, these should appear on her husband's tax return. This makes it difficult for a wife to keep from her husband the extent of her investment income and hence, by implication, the value of the assets generating this income. Even in simple cases like a small savings account held by the wife, the interest from the account will be taxed via a change in the *husband's* tax code. As of 1979 this practice still continues.

The 'money' complaints refer to the impact of the operation of income tax on the relative tax bill of husband and wife. The major complaint was that where a couple are taxed jointly, any tax rebate which is due on the wife's income will normally be paid to the husband. This was generally the case even with a wife's *earned* income, except where such a rebate could be dealt with by a change in her tax code. This system, which derives directly from the historical notion of a wife as part of her husband's property, was abandoned for a wife's earned income in 1978 as a result of public pressure and several newspaper campaigns. The system still applies, however, to a wife's investment income.

A second complaint concerns the allocation of various tax-free deductions such as those for mortgage interest payments to the husband, even though the payments are being made by the wife. This applies where the house is in the husband's name, where it is jointly owned, and even where it is in the wife's sole name. As of 1979 this practice continues.

A third area of complaint which cost people money in the form of higher tax bills concerned various of the minor personal allowances, such as those for a housekeeper, for a daughter's services, and for a child-minder/housekeeper for unmarried people. In the past the housekeeper allowance was applicable only for a female housekeeper and the daughter's services allowance, as its name implied, only for a daughter, and the 'child-minder' allowance could be claimed only for a female relative. These restrictions were lifted in 1978, and where such allowances are available for a helper of any sort they now apply irrespective of whether the helper is male or female.[1]

There is one anomaly in this area which can work to the wife's advantage. We shall use the 1978/79 personal allowances of £985 for a single person, £1,535 for a married man, and £985 for the married woman's allowance as an example. Suppose we have a married couple both of whom work. Between them they can earn £2,520 of tax-free income, consisting of the £1,535 married man's allowance, and £985 wife's earned income allowance. If the wife ceases to work, their joint tax-free income will be £1,535, equal to the married man's allowance. In contrast, if the husband stops working, and the wife is the only earner, total tax-free income will be £2,520. The explanation is as follows: the first £985 of the wife's income can be set off against her married woman's allowance. But a married woman's income is not really hers but her husband's for tax purposes, and so any income that she earns in excess of £985 can be offset against *his* married man's allowance. This result follows entirely logically from the initial premise that a married woman's income belongs to her husband for tax purposes, and results in the somewhat curious anomaly that if a family has only one earner, it is to the family's advantage for this to be the wife.[2]

It can readily be seen that all the anomalies discussed above follow fairly directly from the Aggregation basis of taxing families, which itself is a direct consequence of an historical view of wives as part of their husband's property. A strong case can be made for abandoning the idea of Aggregation in today's changed circumstances and social attitudes, and there are many who urge a switch to an Individual basis at least for earned income. We saw in the preceding section that this would have the advantage of treating all individuals equally, and of

[1] This point is stressed in the Inland Revenue leaflet FA 1 (1978), which explains the Finance Act 1978.

[2] A rather more detailed analysis of the tax treatment of married women's income may be found in *Income Tax and Sex Discrimination*, published by the Equal Opportunities Commission, 1978.

creating a tax system that was neutral with respect to marriage. However, we also saw that it would lead to the unhappy result if applied strictly that married couples with equal incomes could pay different amounts in tax depending on the relative earnings of husband and wife. Unless we abandon the progressive taxation of income, any basis of taxation of single people and married couples will create its own set of anomalies. It is up to the electorate to decide which set of anomalies it dislikes least – and in today's climate of opinion it might well be the case that an Individual basis is more appropriate. But this is clearly a major change of principle, not just cosmetic tinkering and so should not be undertaken casually or hastily. The government announced in 1978 that these matters were under active consideration, and it is to be hoped that any resulting proposals will be extremely carefully thought out, especially with regard to investment income.

The overall conclusion is that there are no easy answers as to an appropriate working definition of horizontal equity. We have already seen that the two ideal properties of tax neutrality towards marriage and equal tax payments by married couples with equal incomes are almost inherently in conflict. The Aggregation basis will satisfy the latter, but violates the former and can easily discriminate against married women. The Individual basis is neutral with respect to marriage, and hence in its treatment of married women, but can treat single-earner families (particularly those with children) rather harshly.

An entirely different set of problems emerges when one investigates the relative treatment of families with different numbers of children at different income levels. It can be argued that the British system of treating large poor families generously but being very parsimonious at higher income levels may not be ideal. It is clear that there are few simple answers.

3 EARNED AND INVESTMENT INCOME

3.1 *A brief historical background*

In this section we discuss the relative tax treatment of earned and unearned income. After a brief historical overview we discuss in turn the arguments for and against taxing unearned[1] income more heavily than earned.

[1] Henceforth referred to by its technical name of investment income.

Although discussed from the very beginning,[1] differential treatment of earned and investment income was not introduced into British tax law until 1907. From then until 1920 a higher rate of tax applied to investment income than to earned income. In 1920 this method was abolished on the recommendation of the Royal Commission of that year, and a new system, which lasted until 1973, was introduced. The essential feature was that a special deduction, calculated as a fraction of earned income, was allowed in computing taxable income. This, in effect, resulted in investment income being taxed at a higher rate than earnings. For many years this deduction was applicable only in the case of income tax and not surtax, but latterly it had a wider range. However, this system in turn ran into various difficulties. Since 1973 we have had the investment income surcharge, under which unearned incomes above a certain limit pay additional tax.[2]

The relative treatment of earned and investment income varies considerably from one country to another. In the USA there is less discrimination between the two types of income than in the UK. There is nothing corresponding to the old British earned income relief or to the new investment income surcharge. Both earned and investment incomes are subject to the same schedule of marginal rates, the only discrimination being that the maximum rate of tax on earned income is 50 per cent, compared to 70 per cent on investment income. On the other hand, the interest on state and local bonds, for example, is exempt from tax and this, together with some under-reporting of interest and dividends, in practice makes for some concessions.[3] Canada completely reverses the position by effectively allowing the first $1,000 of unearned income to be tax-free.

3.2 *Reasons for discrimination*

In this section we outline the arguments traditionally put forward for differentiation in favour of earned income. But before we do so we need to anticipate some later arguments. We shall take the position

[1] Pitt made his own position unambiguously clear in 1799: 'to think of taxing these species of income on a different rate would be to attempt what the nature of society will not admit' (quoted by F. Shehab, *Progressive Taxation* (Oxford, 1953), p. 49).

[2] See Chapter 9, section 2.1.

[3] Holland and Kahn ('Comparisons of Personal and Taxable Income', in *Federal Tax Policy for Economic Growth and Stability* (Washington DC, 1955)) found that 87 per cent of dividends but only 39 per cent of interest receipts were reported in 1952. But the position has improved somewhat since then, especially since the reporting of dividends, interest, etc. has been mandatory on their payers. See also Joseph A. Pechman, *Federal Tax Policy*, third edition (The Brookings Institution, Washington DC, 1977), Chapter 4.

that there is a strong case either for taxing undistributed profits, or the adoption of a capital gains tax, or a combination of the two in order to tax investment income more comprehensively, and in the following analysis we assume that one of these courses has been adopted. If neither is adopted the argument for differentiation in favour of earned income is that much stronger.

The arguments traditionally put forward for favouring earned income are (a) the alleged precariousness of earnings, (b) the costs of earning income, and (c) the advantages conferred upon the owner of capital. We shall look at these propositions in turn.

(1) *The precariousness argument.* The usual argument for differentiation in favour of earned income is that it is more 'precarious' than unearned. There seem to be several different meanings to this idea. The first is that an individual can earn an income only for a maximum number of years, whereas unearned income (at any rate from government securities) can be expected to last indefinitely. The second meaning is that the dispersion of earned income may be greater than that of investment income. Income from earnings may cease before retiring age, due to disability or death; it may be interrupted by sickness; and fluctuations in earnings even for healthy people may be greater than fluctuations in income from, say, government bonds. These points are clearly most relevant when the tax structure is progressive.

How are we to assess these arguments? In the case of the limited length of life argument it is not at all clear that there is any case for differentiation. This is simply because if an income of a given amount lasts for a shorter period than another of the same amount it is also taxed for a shorter period. As J. S. Mill[1] put it:

> When it is said that a temporary income ought to be taxed less than a permanent one, the reply is irresistible, that it is taxed less; for the income which lasts only ten years, pays the tax only ten years, while that which lasts for ever pays for ever.

Furthermore, if there is any argument for differentiating between perpetual investment income and earned income simply because of the differences in the length of life, then there is also an argument for differentiating between perpetual investment income and investment income liable to cease through commercial failure. From an equity standpoint the Mill argument would seem to apply here too. In fact, for

[1] *Principles of Political Economy* (Ashley Edition), p. 811.

reasons connected with the allocation of capital between different uses,[1] we might want some differentiation, but such an efficiency consideration is not relevant to any argument about the equity of taxing earned and investment income alike.

To the assertion that earnings may have a higher variance than investment income, a possible counter-argument is the increased stability of earnings that trades unions are said to bring about. Finally, if a somewhat different point is put forward – that an earner has to save for his old age whereas a property owner does not – the answer is that the many concessions to saving for superannuation purposes today largely take care of this problem. In addition one needs to know whether the property owner has accumulated his property out of earned income. If so, it could be said that his need to save now is less because he started earlier.[2]

(2) *The costs of earning argument.* This argument in favour of differentiation stresses the costs of earning a living compared to those of living on property. There are two separate points here. The first, as discussed in section 2 of this chapter, is that there are real costs of physical and mental effort in earning a living, and these do not or need not arise with investment incomes. The second is that earned income is in large part the return to investment in training and education, and if no tax relief on this capital formation is allowed, there should be a differential rate of tax on earned income.

Considerable doubts can be raised about the 'wear and tear' of earning a living. If the 'real cost' of working is to be included in the definition of income, then so also should job satisfaction be added to income. But whatever one's views on these philosophical issues there is no reason to believe that the 'real cost' is correlated with the size of earned income. One could just as easily argue for a flat-rate allowance for earned income on this account. The education and training costs argument is more persuasive. Obviously, one of the reasons (though not the only one) why people incur the expense of training is to earn higher incomes, both money and non-money. Therefore, it can be

[1] e.g. if A has £1,000 in government bonds yielding 4 per cent and therefore bringing in £40 per annum, whereas B has £800 invested in an industrial debenture which, solely because of doubts about its longevity, yields 5 per cent and therefore an income of £40, it might be argued that a proportional income tax will be equitable as between A and B but will tend to encourage B to divert some of his assets into government securities, on the usual risk argument (see page 44). This could be avoided by a differential income tax or a uniform capital tax, but at the expense of being inequitable as far as the taxation of income is concerned.

[2] See G. F. Break and R. Turvey, *Studies in Greek Taxation (Athens, 1964), pp. 124—6 for further discussion.*

argued, an investment for these purposes should either be written off at the time it is made or amortized during its useful life, and if neither of these is possible an earned income relief is a reasonable substitute. As we shall see later,[1] the tax treatment of depreciation raises some awkward questions. The main reason for having a liberal depreciation system for physical capital is to encourage capital formation. Few will challenge the proposition that greater investment in education and training is in general desirable. But the application of a blanket earned income relief system makes no distinction between high incomes due to innate natural ability (e.g. a footballer) and high incomes due to intensive training, and so does not seem an ideal instrument for achieving this end. There is no more reason for allowing amortization in the case of natural gifts than there is in the case of the exploitation of natural resources.

(3) *The advantage of capital argument.* The third argument for discrimination states that the possession of capital conveys advantages over and above the mere fact that if people possess capital they are in a better position to spend in excess of annual income than people who possess no capital, but there are perhaps also rather vaguer notions of the psychic income derivable from the mere fact of possessing capital.

This argument is not particularly strong. It is true that the possession of non-human property allows greater opportunity for spending, but an earned income relief compensates for this only very imperfectly. It will differentiate between an earner and an investor, each with the same income. But it will not differentiate at all between two property owners each with the same income but with different amounts of capital. It is precisely the difference in the amounts of capital in people's ownership which is the key issue here. Thus a device which discriminates according to income must be somewhat rough and ready.

3.3 *Reasons against discrimination*

There are two major efficiency arguments put forward against taxing investment income more heavily, the 'savings' argument and the 'risk' argument.

(1) *The savings argument* concerns the encouragement of savings. For a given yield of income tax, the abandonment of differentiation in favour of earned income would obviously reduce the rate applicable to investment income. This would be desirable if (a) the current system

[1] See Chapter 16.

discriminates against savings, and if (b) the supply of savings is elastic with respect to yield, and if (c) additional savings lead to an increase in the rate of economic growth. We have already looked into the issues underlying the first two links in this chain, about both of which it is hard to be definite. The third link is even more contentious, so that the adoption of this argument is as much a matter of personal belief as of positive economics.

(2) *The risk argument* asserts that the lower rates of taxation on investment income will have beneficial effects on the distribution of capital resources, ensuring that risky industries are not starved of funds. This is the standard argument which we have already discussed.[1]

These are the opposing arguments. How, if at all, do we resolve them? We saw that the strongest argument for differentiating against property income lies in the reserve power of property. The strongest argument against differentiation is the effect on the incentive to save. This seems to suggest that the right sort of solution might be to abandon discrimination against investment income, which in any case does not deal very well with the reserve power argument, and to rely on capital taxation in one form or another. This would have the advantage of hitting at what is really important in this context, the amount of capital in a person's possession. However, this brings us to a whole series of further issues which it is more convenient to leave to Chapter 15.

Finally, there is the argument that it is inequitable to tax more heavily the return to accumulated as opposed to inherited capital, inasmuch as the lifetime income tax bill of a person who saves will be higher than that of a person who does not. This point is taken up in more detail in Chapter 15.

4 CAPITAL GAINS TAXATION

4.1 *The relation of capital gains to income*

The discussion of this section is divided into three parts. First we ask the theoretical question whether, and in what sense, capital gains can be regarded as part of an individual's income. Next, in the light of our discussion, we ask whether there is a good case for taxing capital gains. Finally, we give a brief assessment of capital gains taxation in the UK.

[1] See Chapter 3, section 3.3.4.

The traditional approach to the question whether or not capital gains are part of an individual's income is to distinguish three main types of capital gain, (a) those due to increases in the rate of interest, (b) those due to price changes, and (c) 'pure' capital gains.

(1) *Capital gains corresponding to a fall in the interest rate.* Supposing we have capital gains which exactly match a fall in interest rates. Should these be regarded as part of income or not? There are two views. On the one hand, holders of bonds are now better off than they were on capital account. On the other hand, none of the capital gains can be spent without reducing the flow of future income.

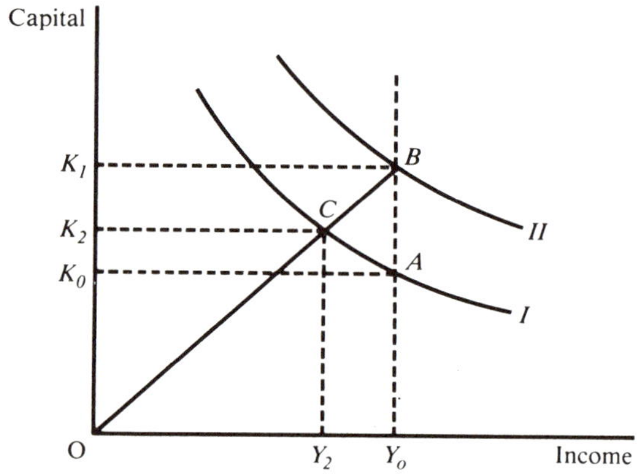

Figure 13.2 Income and capital gains

The answer to this question depends on people's preferences between income and capital. After interest rates fall, part of the capital asset may be sold, and hence one may end up with less income but more capital than before the change in interest rates. If in this situation the individual feels indifferent between the two combinations, one can say that some part of his capital gain can be regarded as income. Figure 13.2, originally due to Paish,[1] illustrates this point clearly. In the initial situation, shown by point *A*, the individual has OY_0 of income, and OK_0 of capital, and is on indifference curve *I*. A fall in the interest rate from OY_0/OK_0 to OY_0/OK_1 will carry him to point *B* on indifference curve *II*. If he then spends part of his capital he can be thought of as

[1] F. W. Paish, 'Capital Value and Income' in *Post-War Financial Problems and Other Essays* (Macmillan, 1950).

moving along the ray *OB*. At point *C* he will again be on indifference curve *I*. It is thus possible for the individual to spend part of the capital gain, K_1–K_2, without reducing his utility.

The conclusion is that where a capital gain is caused by a decrease in the rate of interest, part of it, but not all of it, can be regarded as income.

(2) *Capital gains corresponding to general price rises.* Where the value of a capital asset increases exactly in line with increases in the general price level, the key point is that both the income flow and the value of the asset increase in money terms but not in real terms. In terms of Figure 13.2, money capital gains represent a movement from *C* to *B*. If a price deflator is used, there is a return to point *C*. Since, in real terms, one starts and finishes at point *C*, there seems to be no reason whatever for regarding the change in nominal capital values as part of real income. If some sort of relief is given to bond holders for a fall in the real value of their assets, then it is not unreasonable to give relief against inflation also to the holders of equities.

(3) *'Pure' capital gains.* This is the case where capital gains occur in the absence of a general rise in prices or a general fall in the interest rate, or where gains exceed those resulting from any changes in prices and interest rates. We start with gains that occur with certainty, and then progress to uncertain gains. Capital gains that occur with certainty, such as a growth in value of a savings certificate or a dated stock, require little discussion. The appreciation is a substitute for annual interest payments and quite clearly should be regarded as part of an individual's annual income.

Uncertain gains are not so straightforward. Consider a shareholding at the beginning of 1979 which promises an annual yield of £50. If we capitalize at 5 per cent, this gives a value of £1,000. However, suppose that at the beginning of 1980 the income prospect for some reason has now become £100. On the same basis of capitalization, the value will now be £2,000. Two views may be put forward about the change in capital value during 1979.

First, one could argue that at the beginning of 1980 it would be possible to spend half one's capital and still be as well off as one thought one was at the beginning of 1979. In this case the capital gain is clearly part of one's income.

Against this, one might argue that the valuation in 1979 was wrong, and simply a consequence of imperfect foresight. In that case, one has not received an addition to one's income, but simply improved the accuracy of the valuation of one's assets. Under this argument capital gains would not be part of one's income.

The solution lies between these extremes. If in fact we agree at the beginning of 1980 that the valuation for 1979 was wrong, then it must follow *either* that the estimates of capital value for 1979, and hence of income for 1978, was wrong, or that the estimate of capital value for 1978 and hence the income for 1977 was wrong – and so on. Therefore revising one's estimates of the value of the capital asset does not enable us to deny that capital gains represent income during *some* period, though we are not able, necessarily, to say *which* period.

While this approach gets us some way, it does not get to the heart of the matter which really hinges on the definition of income. The two most enduring definitions of income are (a) the Hicks definition and (b) the Haig-Simons definition.[1]

(1) *The Hicks definition.* With deceptive simplicity, this defines a person's income as 'the maximum value which he can consume during a week, and still expect to be as well off at the end of the week as he was at the beginning'.[2]

While this definition of income is unassailable in principle it is, unfortunately, totally unworkable in practice for the accountant or tax inspector. The obvious difficulty lies in the word 'expect'. It is not possible for other people to work out what a taxpayer expects, let alone whether such expectations are reasonable or not. So it is not possible in this case to move from the *concept* of income to the *measurement* of income. And for practical purposes such as taxation, ease of measurement of income is crucial. Tax officials have to work with verifiable facts and hence have to consider not what one could *expect* to consume over a period, but what one could *actually* consume while maintaining a constant net worth. This brings us to the second definition of income, frequently used in North America in relation to tax matters.

(2) *The Haig-Simons definition.* This defines income as the total of an individual's consumption expenditure at market prices *plus* the change, positive or negative, in the net value of his property rights in any given period.[3]

[1] Using Meade's terminology, these are definitions B and A of income, respectively. See *Report*, *op. cit.*, pp. 30–33.

[2] J. R. Hicks, *Value and Capital* (Oxford University Press, 1939), p. 172.

[3] See H. Simons, *Personal Income Taxation* (Chicago, 1938); W. S. Vickrey, *Agenda for Progressive Taxation* (Ronald Press, New York, 1947); and R. M. Haig, 'The Concept of Income – Economic and Legal Aspects', in R. M. Haig (ed.), *The Federal Income Tax* (Columbia University Press, 1921).

This is very different from the Hicks definition. If in any year a person does better than he expects (a premium bond win, or an unexpected inheritance), his income will be higher on a Haig-Simons definition than on a Hicks definition inasmuch as his actual consumption, though not his expected or sustainable long-run consumption, can be higher. Conversely, in an unexpectedly bad year the Hicks definition of income will be higher than the Haig-Simons one. In many ways, the Hicks definition is closer to permanent income, and the Haig-Simons definition to current income.

What light do these definitions of income shed on the question of whether capital gains should be treated as income or not? Both definitions rule out capital gains due to price increases. Under the Hicks definition any other capital gain should be treated as part of income unless the consumption of the capital gain would reduce the expected flow of future income. Thus 'pure' capital gains should be treated as income in the Hicks sense, as might part of those associated with a decrease in the rate of interest.

Under the Haig-Simons definition it is obvious that all capital gains in excess of increases in the general price level, whatever their cause and nature, and whatever changes in expectations they bring about, should be regarded as the income of the period in which they accrue, and taxed just like any other income. At its simplest, if an individual improves his position, taking consumption and net assets together, his taxable income has increased, and the traditional distinction between income and capital gains is irrelevant.

Attractively simple as the Haig-Simons definition appears in principle, it leads to a number of problems in practice. The first is that capital gains are liable to be discontinuous and volatile, so that with a progressive tax system unless there were some system of averaging there would be tax discrimination over time relative to less volatile forms of income. Another problem is the treatment of unrealized gains. If gains are taxed only when they are realized, and unrealized gains remain untaxed, there is a strong temptation for people to remain 'locked-in' to existing assets. Proposals to tax unrealized gains have a habit of floundering before reaching the statute book.[1] And although it is possible to catch unrealized gains in respect of assets transferred from one owner to another (whether by gift inter-vivos or at death), the

[1] As in the case of the Canadian proposals of 1969. The main reason seems to have been the fear that people would be forced to liquidate assets to pay tax, i.e. the reverse of the lock-in argument. Cf. J. G. Head, 'Canadian Tax Reform and Participatory Democracy', *Finanzarchiv*, 1972, No. 1.

advantages of tax deferral up to the time of transfer still remain.[1] A third problem concerns the effect of inflation. Under a pure Haig-Simons definition, all measures of income and capital gains should be adjusted for changes in the price level. This raises broad issues of how to adjust income tax for inflation, which will be discussed in the next section.

There is one final result of the pure Haig-Simons definition which though not anomalous in logic is likely to appear strange in the eyes of many people. This can best be shown by example. Consider a millionaire whose million pounds is invested at 10 per cent, yielding an annual flow of £100,000 in interest. Suppose the market rate of interest rises from 10 per cent to $11\frac{1}{9}$ per cent, so that the capital value of his investment falls to £900,000. He has now made a capital loss of £100,000, but his annual income continues to be £100,000. But in the year of the change of the interest rate his income on a Haig-Simons definition is zero, since the capital loss exactly offsets the interest income payment. In such a year the millionaire would pay no income tax.

The conclusion of this section is that the Hicks definition is analytically pure, but unworkable in practice, while the Haig-Simons definition, though workable in practice, can create a variety of difficulties.

4.2 *The arguments for and against a capital gains tax*

We turn now from the problems of relating capital gains to income, to arguments about the appropriate rate of tax for such gains. The major arguments concern (a) stabilization, (b) allocation, (c) the supply of savings, (d) equity and (e) administration, each of which will be discussed in turn. We shall assume throughout that we are comparing the effects of raising revenues this way with those of raising an equivalent sum from an income tax which does not apply to capital gains, but which otherwise has a similar progressive structure.

(1) *Stabilization.* There are two major questions here: the first is whether the yield of capital gains taxation is likely to fluctuate more widely than the yield of income tax. The answer here is a qualified yes.

[1] An investigation in the US showed that unrealized gains were very much more important than realized over the period of 1948–64. This showed also that if capital gains are included, the personal income time series is much more volatile. See K. B. Bhatia, 'Accrued Capital Gains, Personal Income and Saving in the US, 1948/64', *Review of Income and Wealth*, December 1970.

The yield of capital gains tax in the UK has fluctuated in recent years from £139 million in 1970/71 to a high of £387 million in 1975/76. Its estimated yield in 1978/79 was £375 million. Any estimates of the yield depend on a variety of assumptions about the operation of the tax, but all that we are interested in at present is the *dispersion* of the yield rather than whether the estimated mean yield is correct. In the USA there was a reduction in the yield of capital gains tax from plus $576 million to minus $89 million between 1928 and 1931, whilst other personal income tax receipts fell only from $588 million to $335 million over the same period. Between 1936 and 1938, the contrast was between the change from $177 million to $12 million for capital gains tax and from $1,043 million to $753 million for income tax.[1] It might be argued that these were exceptional years, but exceptional years have an awkward habit of recurring.

The second question we have to ask is whether such swings in the yield of capital gains tax move in a counter-cyclical way? On the whole, this would appear to be the case, as capital gains are more likely in the upswing than in the downswing. On the other hand, to the extent that interest rates tighten in boom years, capital losses on that account may run the wrong way. However, this mainly counter-cyclical result can be vitiated by delays in collection, which would be particularly important if the system allowed for any sort of averaging. Overall, we may say that an income tax which includes capital gains in its base will probably, though not decisively, have better counter-cyclical properties than an equal revenue income tax which does not include capital gains.

(2) *The allocation of resources.* The major question here is the effects of a capital gains tax on willingness to invest capital in risky enterprises. As we have seen,[2] it does not follow that an income tax which includes capital gains and losses differentiates more against risky enterprises than one which does not. But it is clear that the rewards for some kinds of risk-taking do take the form of capital appreciation rather than income. Thus, the willingness of businessmen to develop enterprises whose rewards are partly in the form of capital gains and partly in the form of income is likely to be less when the tax base includes realized capital gains, even when allowance is made for the opportunity to offset capital losses. This argument suggests that there may be a decline in risk-taking. But the argument is considerably

[1] L. Seltzer *The Nature and Tax Treatment of Capital Gains and Losses* (NBER, 1951).

[2] See Chapter 3, section 3.3.

weaker in cases where the elasticity of supply of capital is low. Thus, for instance, a tax on gains in the capital values of urban land sites will not have very serious effects, as the supply of such sites in any given area is fixed.

Obviously one cannot be dogmatic on matters as broad as these; but it is significant that the minority of the Royal Commission on Taxation, who could hardly be accused of soft-heartedness in such matters, conceded that the elasticity of supply of risk-bearing was such that it would be impossible to tax capital gains as though they were ordinary income. In general, this is in line with the conclusions emerging from a Hicks definition of income, but runs counter to the application of a Haig-Simons definition.

One final point should be mentioned. It is sometimes argued that the 'locked-in' problem in the USA (i.e. the fact that people hold on to assets whose capital values have increased solely because of the accumulated tax liability) is caused by the exemption from tax of capital gains held until death. This is obviously not so; it is always worthwhile to defer tax for as long as possible, so any system of realized, as distinct from accrued, capital gains taxation must face this as a likely consequence in the capital markets.

(3) *The supply of savings.* The question here is the elasticity of savings with respect to its net rate of return. More specifically, we need to ask how far saving is responsive to rates of return at all, and how much regard is paid to returns in the form of capital gains rather than ordinary income. We need to ask also whether people with a high average propensity to save will attach particular importance to capital appreciation. These are all matters on which empirical evidence is inconclusive.[1] Beyond posing the question, therefore, we can say little beyond the platitudinous remark that capital gains tax is likely, at least to some extent, to have an adverse effect on savings.

(4) *Equity arguments.* The equity argument is the strongest one for a capital gains tax. At its most basic, if capital gains are regarded as income, whether wholly or in part, the failure to include them in the tax base means that some taxpayers are receiving a gift at the expense of others. In addition, capital gains are not distributed randomly, but accrue more to the 'rich' than to the 'poor', both because the rich own more capital per head and because they are more likely to place it in

[1] But see J. A. Pechman (editor), *The Expenditure Tax* (Brookings Institution, Washington DC, 1979).

investments which pay part of their return in the form of capital appreciation.[1]

This argument is a strong one. But we should not draw from it the conclusion that the taxation of capital gains raises no equity problems. First of all, any tax capable of practicable application must be applied when gains are realized rather than when they accrue; it may be possible to mitigate this by some sort of averaging device, or by subjecting capital gains to a lower rate of tax than other income. But we should not deceive ourselves that by this system we are taxing incomes of any given period with any precision. Second, if the tax is applied to all capital gains, whatever their cause, there are serious doubts about whether some of these gains should really be regarded as income, for the reasons discussed above. While it is true that greater equity can be achieved by taxing capital gains than by exempting them, it is nevertheless the case that no tax is conceivable which will be really capable of hitting at capital gains of all kinds.

A final equity argument is that through the long-term operation of market forces the capital gains tax might be passed forward via the effects on the supply of capital to risky industries, and therefore will not really be borne by those for whom it was intended. This may be true, but it is impossible to say how true, and is an argument that can be applied equally to almost any other tax. It is therefore not a very strong argument against capital gains tax.

(5) *Administration.* Probably the greatest difficulty caused by a capital gains tax is that of administering it. There seems little doubt that the taxation of capital gains in the USA is the subject of more acrimony and more time consumption by officials and taxpayers than any part of the income tax code. It has been said that the size of the US tax code could be halved if capital gains were simply treated as ordinary income, rather than entitled to a 60 per cent exemption. The problems are really twofold – those of introducing the tax in the first place and those of continuing the operation of an existing tax. The costs of continuing a system of capital gains taxation are high enough,[2] but those of introducing the tax are considerable. The initial difficulties are most formidable in the case of unquoted securities and other assets without a readily ascertained market value. Quoted securities and many types of real estate obviously are much easier to deal with. Once people have

[1] This point was verified empirically for the USA by L. Seltzer, *op. cit.*, Chapter V.

[2] See C. T. Sandford, *Hidden Costs of Taxation* (Institute for Fiscal Studies, London, 1973), especially Chapter 7.

become used to the operation of the tax the whole system can doubtless run much more smoothly. But even so its costs are substantial.

4.3 *A brief assessment of capital gains taxation in the UK*

As we saw in Chapter 9, the UK has had a fully-fledged capital gains tax since 1965. The position in early 1979 was that the normal rate of tax on capital gains is 30 per cent for both individuals and companies, but it could be considerably lower for many people. The tax is levied on realizations and on many gifts, but not at death. The yield has risen over the years from around £16 million in 1967/68 to £375 million in 1978/79.

Changes over the years have reduced some of the early difficulties. The same normal rate of tax on capital gains is applied to both companies and individuals; inter-relations between the taxes on capital gains made by unit or investment trusts and their shareholders have been streamlined; and the exemption of gains of less than £1,000 per annum has helped administration. But the introduction of development land tax in 1976 greatly complicated the taxation of development gains, and created the usual problems of definition where different taxes apply to related activities.

Many problems still remain. First, there is the possible disincentive to risk-taking. As we have said, this is an area in which one should not be too definite, but it is fair to ask whether it is appropriate to tax all capital gains at the same rate irrespective of the length of time for which assets are held. A second problem concerns the dangers of 'lock-in', which are somewhat greater when there is no capital gains tax at death. Third, equity aspects raise such issues as the rates of tax on capital gains compared to that on other types of income, and the correction of nominal capital gains to allow for inflation.

The exemption at death is the easiest subject. The abandonment of 'constructive realization' at death in 1971 was a retrograde step and cannot really be defended. It was argued at the time that taxation of capital gains at death had produced very little revenue after allowing for consequential effects on estate duty receipts. But this was far from being a conclusive argument, as the temptation to hold on to assets until death is clearly less in the situation where they are taxable at death than one where they are not.

One way of tackling the incentives and inflation problems simultaneously would be to copy the Swedish device of a tapering rate of capital gains tax, which varies inversely with the length of time for which the asset has been held. (For administrative simplicity one might adopt the logically equivalent practice of varying the proportion of the gain on which the tax is levied.) Under such a system it might be appropriate to tax short-term gains on assets held for less than a year at ordinary income tax rates. A good tax structure would not have a large discrepancy between the short-term rate and the starting long-term rate, otherwise there would be problems of people holding appreciated assets for 366 days if 365 days were the dividing line; the rate could fall to zero after, say, a period of seven years. There are various complications: the long-term rate should not fall linearly with the length of holding period, but relatively slowly at first and more rapidly later; it would be necessary to specify rules about loss carry-forwards, e.g. that an unrelieved loss in any year should be carried forward on the assumption that it 'belongs' to the loss-making stock which has been held for the shortest, rather than the longest, period. It would also be necessary to allow people an option to be taxed at the marginal rate of income tax rather than the flat-rate of capital gains tax, to avoid hardship to those with small incomes. Such a system could be a practical way of tackling the twin evils of risk disincentives and paper gains.

If one did not wish to make such a drastic change, there are other possibilities. One would be to adjust the valuation of capital assets in accordance with the price index, as discussed in the next section, and estimate capital gains with reference to such an adjusted base. If this is done, one must ask also whether it is appropriate to have a maximum tax rate on capital gains which in 1978 was less than one-third of that on investment income (i.e. 30 per cent as opposed to 98 per cent), in comparison to North America where the ratio is two-fifths (e.g. 28 per cent and 70 per cent in the USA).[1]

If an inflation adjustment is incorporated, it can be argued that there is a case for taxing capital gains under ordinary income tax.[2] There is no simple answer to such a proposition. It depends, for instance, on whether capital losses can be offset only against capital gains (as in the UK) or can be offset against other forms of income (as is possible up to $3,000 in the USA).[3] If net losses from any one year can be carried forward only against future gains, this implies that an individual's gains tend to be taxed earlier in his life, and so effectively at higher rates than

[1] In striking contrast, Australia has no capital gains tax at all.

[2] Cf. J. Helliwell, 'The Taxation of Capital Gains', *Canadian Journal of Economics*, 1969, No. 2.

[3] Cf. A. B. Atkinson, *Unequal Shares*, *op. cit.*, pp. 161–6 for the view that not only should capital gains be taxed as ordinary income (with some averaging) but also that capital losses could only be offset against capital gains. Substantial arguments can be raised against such a proposition.

his losses.[1] So one could justify a lower rate of tax when this restriction on losses applies.

Finally, we must state a general proposition, and one to which we shall return later. It is quite impossible to discuss the appropriate taxation of capital gains in isolation from that of company profits taxation. It has been well known for a long time that there is a close relationship between capital gains and profit retentions.[2] It therefore follows that the whole issue of capital gains is likely to be less important the more the taxation of companies induces dividend payments rather than retentions. A rounded view necessitates consideration of capital gains and company taxation simultaneously; neither can be properly judged on its own.

5 INDEXATION

The ill-effects of inflation are many and well known; they concern equity (e.g. arbitrary redistribution between lenders and borrowers) and efficiency (e.g. the transactions costs of inflation, and the distortion of inter-temporal decisions). The distortions of the tax system caused by inflation are an important part of these costs; this section outlines the major ones and discusses what, if anything, can be done about them. The issues involved are discussed under the subheads of: the ill-effects of inflation on taxation, the definition of indexation, the ways in which indexation might be applied, and problems with indexation.

(1) *The ill-effects of inflation on taxation* concern fiscal drag, the definition of income, and differential lags in taxation. We discuss these in turn.[3]

(a) *Fiscal drag.* The essence of the problem is that with a progressive income tax structure inflation will result in more and more taxpayers paying part of their incomes at higher and higher tax rates unless the starting points for each rate band are raised in line with changes in the price level. The problem arises also with taxes like capital transfer tax

[1] In so far as an individual's income increases through time and becomes liable to higher marginal tax rates, this may be a factor working the other way.

[2] Cf. O. Harkavy, 'The Relation Between Retained Earnings and Common Stock Prices for Large Limited Corporations', *Journal of Finance*, September 1953.

[3] For a fuller discussion of the effects of inflation on taxation, see David R. Morgan, *Over Taxation by Inflation*, Hobart Paper 72, IEA, 1977; H. J. Aaron, *Inflation and the Income Tax* (The Brookings Institution, Washington DC, 1976); and the Mathews Committee Report, *Inflation and Taxation* (Canberra, 1975).

which is progressive on a cumulative lifetime basis. In other words inflation increases the real burden of any progressive direct tax.

The same forces work in the other direction for those indirect taxes whose magnitude is fixed in nominal terms. For instance, inflation will steadily reduce the real value of a tax of (say) 50 pence per bottle of wine. Since the commodities on which high taxes are placed usually have a low price elasticity of demand, this decline in their relative price will reduce the real yield of the tax imposed upon them. Thus a further effect of fiscal drag is to alter the relative importance of direct and indirect taxation so as to make direct taxation relatively more important.

The overall result is that inflation produces major changes in tax burdens as between different taxpayers which were not anticipated at the time the rate structure was fixed. Such considerations have led a number of countries, including Canada, Denmark, Holland and Sweden, to introduce indexation of their personal income tax in recent years.

(b) *The definition of income.* We have already hinted at this issue in the previous section when we discussed whether capital gains should be treated as income, and concluded that no gain arising solely from an increase in the general price level should be regarded as part of income. It can similarly be argued that only interest receipts in excess of the rate of inflation should be treated as income for tax purposes. Thus £1,000 invested at 10 per cent has a yield of £100; but if the rate of inflation is 7 per cent then a person could consume only £30 without making himself worse off in the future. Thus only £30 (i.e. the *real* as opposed to the *nominal* interest receipt) should be regarded as income.[1]

In the absence of such adjustments, inflation thus extends the income tax base beyond what should really be treated as income. We should be clear that this problem is analytically distinct from fiscal drag, and could occur even in its absence (e.g. if the tax structure were proportional).

Similar arguments can be raised about physical assets. Fixed assets like plant and machinery raise problems of whether depreciation should be on a current cost or historical cost basis. Assets like stocks raise the sort of problems discussed in Chapter 9, which gave rise to the introduction of stock relief.

(c) *Differential lags in taxation* can occur where one type of income

[1] Some further aspects of inflation and the definition of income are discussed in Chapter 16, section 3.

(e.g. Schedule E income) is taxed on a current basis while another (e.g. Schedule D) is often taxed in arrears. Clearly it is to the taxpayer's advantage to delay payment as long as possible, and the value to him of a given delay will be greater the higher is the rate of inflation. The 'concession' can be thought of as arising either from the right to pay tax in depreciated currency, or as an interest-free loan from the government.

It is not the delay which causes inequity, but the fact that the length of the delay is different for different people. The result is that differential delays in tax payment result in marked inequity during times of rapid inflation. This can occur independently of either of the other two ill-effects of inflation.

(2) *What is indexation?* The principle of indexation is deceptively simple. All it does is to adjust nominal magnitudes for changes in the value of any sensible index. The choice of index will depend on the purpose at hand. It may be appropriate to use a price index, making an appropriate choice between the retail price index, the pensioner index, or an index of the prices of capital goods;[1] or it may be better to use average earnings (pre- or post-tax) or changes in the level of GNP. Still other indices would be appropriate for other purposes.

Misunderstandings about indexation are common. An argument against indexation is that it 'substitutes today's arithmetic for tomorrow's judgement'. This is not strictly true. If, for instance, the personal allowances for income tax were tied to the retail price index this would stop the Chancellor changing the value of the personal allowances as much as he (or Parliament) liked. But he would still be able to make tax increases explicit, rather than allow inflation to do the job for him. So it is false to imagine that indexation restricts freedom of action in any way.

(3) *How might indexation be applied?* This is best discussed by considering separately the various taxes. Though this chapter is concerned mainly with personal income taxation, corporation tax is mentioned briefly; this is necessary because of the many links between corporate and personal taxation, which are discussed in detail in Chapter 17.

(a) *Income tax.* As we saw earlier in this chapter, the real burden of income tax has risen substantially since 1938/39, reflecting the increased scope of government activity. In real terms there has been a fall in the value both of the tax threshold and of the starting points of

[1] See Chapter 16 for a more detailed discussion of the impact of inflation on corporation tax.

the rate bands, which became particularly severe in the years after 1972. The combined effect of inflation and stringent budgets shows up dramatically in Table 13.7. Between 1972 and 1978 the single person's allowance rose from £591 to £985, an increase of 67 per cent. But over the same period prices more than doubled, so that in real terms the allowance fell from £591 to £428 – 72 per cent of its former value. To have achieved the same real value in 1978 as in 1972, the allowance would have had to be £1,360.

Table 13.7

Personal allowances adjusted for inflation, single person, UK, 1972/73–1977/78

Year	*Personal allowance (current £s)*	*Retail price index (1972 = 100)*	*Real value of personal allowances (1972 £s)*	*Index number for real personal allowances*
1972/73	591[a]	100	591	100
1973/74	595	109	546	92
1974/75	625	127	492	83
1975/76	675	157	430	73
1976/77	735	183	402	68
1977/78	945	212	446	75
1978/79	985	230	428	72

Source: *Financial Statement and Budget Report*, various years, and *Monthly Digest of Statistics*, various years.
Note: [a] *The* figure for 1972/73 has been adjusted to take account of the introduction of the unified tax in 1973/74.

Until 1977 the value of the personal allowances was changed by the Chancellor on an ad hoc basis. But during debate on the 1977 Finance Bill backbenchers forced on the government an amendment which tied the real value of the main personal allowances to changes in the retail price index. It is not clear how much effect this amendment will have in the long run; for instance, the increases in personal allowances in the October 1977 'mini-budget' were announced as 'advance payments' of the increases required by indexation and due the following April. This illustrates the point made earlier, that indexation does not remove administrative discretion.

Other countries such as Canada, Denmark, Holland and Sweden have tied their tax thresholds and the starting points of their rate bands to changes in the retail price index. There are no compelling reasons, administrative or otherwise, why this could not be done in the UK.

(b) *Corporation tax.* As we saw in Chapter 9, the effects of inflation on corporation tax were felt most acutely in the inflationary increase in the value of stocks. The proper treatment of such increases is analogous to the arguments about the treatment of capital gains which are attributable solely to general increases in the price level, and could, in principle, be dealt with by taxing as profit only that fraction of stock gains which exceed increases in the price level. In fact, as we saw in Chapter 9, tax relief was given in a much simpler way, which allowed an average measure of relief to all firms, rather than being tailored to the individual circumstances of each firm.

Other than stock relief the only element of corporation tax which is adjusted from time to time to take account of inflation is the profit limits for small companies taxed at the lower rate of corporation tax. These are not indexed, but there is no reason in principle why they should not be. We return to these questions in some detail in Chapter 16.

The general issue of the presentation of financial accounts in the context of inflation was the subject of a Committee of Enquiry into Inflation Accounting which reported in 1975.[1] The issues involved are complex, and the controversy aroused by the Report suggests that the area is something of a minefield which one would do well to avoid.[2] The main problem of principle concerns the question of how widespread the coverage of indexation of corporate accounts should be – for instance whether a company's monetary assets and liabilities should be indexed as well as more obvious items like the value of plant, machinery and stocks.

(c) *Capital gains tax* in the UK still applies to both nominal and real gains, though the government has agreed to consider whether some relief might be given for inflationary gains. On the face of it the indexation of capital gains appears simple. Suppose, for instance, that an asset was bought for £1,000 and sold five years later for £5,000. The nominal gain is £4,000. If prices had doubled over the period then the

[1]*Report of the Inflation Accounting Committee* (the Sandilands Committee), Cmnd. 6225 (HMSO, 1975).

[2]For detailed discussion of the Sandilands Report, see J. A. Kay, 'Inflation Accounting – A Review Article', *Economic Journal*, Vol. 87, No. 346, June 1977. For a more general discussion, see H. J. Aaron, *Inflation and the Income Tax*, *op. cit.*

revalued purchase price is £2,000, and the real gain is only £3,000. But if the initial purchase price had been £3,000 the revalued purchase price would be £6,000, and indexation would convert a nominal gain of £2,000 into a loss of £1,000. To administer such a system the government would simply publish an appropriate price index relative to which asset values would be measured. Such a system might be considered as an alternative to the tapering provisions described in the previous section, whereby capital gains were taxed less heavily the longer the asset had been held. This method would not be without its administrative difficulties, however.

(d) *Unearned income and debts.* One major problem with indexing capital gains as described in the previous paragraph is that we cannot just leave matters there, since inflation results in an over-statement not only of capital gains but also of other types of unearned income such as the interest on bank and building society deposits. As we saw earlier,[1] the real interest receipts on savings of £1,000 with an interest rate of 10 per cent and an inflation rate of 7 per cent are £30, and it is only this which should be regarded as taxable income. It is manifestly inequitable to index capital gains without indexing interest income; one should not be indexed unless both are.

But, again, we cannot leave matters here. If interest receipts are to be indexed for tax purposes, then so must interest payments. In the example above it would not be equitable to tax the saver only on his £30 real return, but to allow a person borrowing £1,000 at 10 per cent to deduct for tax purposes the whole of his £100 interest payment. This suggests that interest payments as well as interest receipts should be indexed for tax purposes. In a year with an inflation rate of 15 per cent this would mean that a person with a £1,000 mortgage paying a 10 per cent nominal rate of interest would be paying a real rate of minus 5 per cent. Applied strictly, indexation would require not a tax deduction of £100, but one of *minus* £50. In other words the person would be taxed as though he had an interest *receipt* of £50. Clearly indexation of interest flows, to say nothing of the indexation of capital gains and losses, could not be applied quickly to a housing market which has capitalized the heavy implicit subsidy on mortgages.[2]

The overall conclusion is that it is difficult to have 'bits' of indexation – either one has none, or one has to index most of the tax system and capital market. This is not per se an argument against indexation –

[1] Page 345.
[2] See also Chapter 16, section 3.3.

merely a caution that the subject is complex and interrelated with other variables, and should therefore be introduced only after careful thought.

(e) *Social security benefits* is one area in which indexation has existed de facto for many years, and de jure since 1973. Until 1973 most of the major social security benefits moved broadly in line with pre-tax average earnings; since then long-term benefits such as pensions have in principle been tied to changes in the level of pre-tax earnings, while short-term benefits such as unemployment and sickness benefit have been tied to changes in the price level. In practice there have been complications which we shall discuss in Chapter 14. Nevertheless it is true to say that social security benefits have to all intents and purposes been indexed for at least 30 years.

(4) *Problems.* Needless to say, indexation raises a host of problems, both of principle, and of a practical nature, and we will sketch out only the most important of these.

(a) *The coverage of indexation.* As we saw above, if one wishes to index capital gains one is more or less forced to index interest receipts as well, and this forces one to index interest payments as well. To have a little indexation is almost as difficult as to be slightly pregnant. The choice of how far indexation should proceed will depend in part on what we are trying to achieve, which brings us to the controversy of whether indexation merely moderates the *effects* of inflation (which it certainly does), or whether it will also help to moderate the inflation itself. In other words, does indexation help us to live with inflation, or does it cure it? Those who claim that indexation would reduce the rate of inflation base their arguments on models which include inflationary expectations, and assert that wage settlements are influenced by the expected rate of inflation. Thus indexation of wages will mean that low settlements can be reached (since the real value of the increase will be protected by indexation); and if price increases are influenced by wage increases, then reduced wage settlements will bring about reduced rates of price increase. This type of argument is used to bolster the claim that indexation can reduce inflation. As yet the issue has not been settled.[1]

(b) *The choice of price index.* This is a completely different problem to those discussed above. The most obvious candidate as the basis of indexation is the general index of retail prices. But it has two disadvantages. First, it includes indirect taxes, so that an increase in the rate of

[1] For further discussion see R. A. Jackman and K. Klappholz, *Taming the Tiger* (IEA, 1975).

VAT will raise the retail price index and thus lead to a reduction in the nominal level of income tax. Thus attempts to increase revenue from indirect taxation would partially be offset by reductions in the yield of direct taxation.

A similar problem arises if there is a change in the terms of trade. Increases in the price of imported goods such as food would lead to income tax reductions in the UK. This is inappropriate because changes in the terms of trade require a reduction in domestic living standards, and tax reductions are not exactly a good way of achieving this.

The price of gross domestic product at factor cost (the GDP deflator) excludes indirect taxes and imported goods and services, and so avoids the problems of the retail price index. But it includes not only the prices of goods and services bought by individuals for consumption purposes, but also the prices of investment goods and government services. Nevertheless it might well be the best index of general price movements.

For some purposes it may be more appropriate to use average earnings as an index, as is done already for some social security benefits, though there are various technical problems with doing so in a widespread way.[1] It may well be the case that any general system of indexation would involve the use of several indices.

(c) *Time lags.* A final problem is that lags occur between price movements and the construction of the price index, and between the appearance of the index and its application to tax brackets and social security payments. The provisional increases in income tax personal allowances applying between April 1979 and April 1980 were based on price movements to December 1978 – i.e. an average lag of about nine months. This does not matter as long as inflation is at fairly low or steady rates, but would be highly undesirable during times of high or rapidly changing rates of inflation. It would be highly desirable either to reduce the lag in constructing price indices, or to achieve a similar result by making provisional estimates of the relevant indices.

6 EXPENDITURE TAXATION

6.1 *The arguments in principle*

We deal with various aspects of expenditure taxation in a number of chapters throughout the book, but it may be helpful to pull the

[1] See A. R. Prest, 'Inflation and the Public Finances', *Three Banks Review*, March 1973.

arguments together at this point given the topicality of the subject. The arguments in favour of expenditure as a tax base rather than income go back many years,[1] and have recently been revived by the Meade Committee and others.[2]

The main questions of principle discussed earlier related to (a) the supply of capital (i.e. the supply of saving), including the question of risk-taking,[3] (b) the supply of labour,[4] (c) stabilization,[5] and (d) equity.[6] These arguments are summarized in Table 13.8, from which it can be seen that the pros and cons are by no means cut and dried.

6.2 *Some practical considerations*

On the practical aspects we have already encountered a number of problems. We mentioned five in Chapter 7:[7] the separation of business from personal expenditure; the time allocation of expenditure on durable consumer goods; the policing of expenditure out of cash holdings built up in income tax days; the dividing line between acts of consumption and of saving; and the problem of emigration by people with assets accumulated tax-free under an expenditure tax regime.

A number of other questions will be raised in later chapters. One is the integration of capital taxation with expenditure taxation;[8] another is the case for a flow of funds corporation tax;[9] and another is the treatment of investment income to and from abroad.[10] Many of these problems are formidable and it would be most unwise to minimize them. In particular, one must not make the mistake of comparing a brand-new, barnacle-free expenditure tax with the income tax as we know it. If past experience in tax matters is any guide at all it is only too likely that an expenditure tax arrangement would soon have its own set of barnacles clinging to it. The very fact that it is so difficult to rid the income tax of its unwanted excrescences should warn us that this is a game one cannot hope to win.

A further set of considerations is whether any advantages that even a pure expenditure tax may have in principle will be much of an advantage as a matter of practice. For instance, we saw in Chapter 3[11] that an

[1] See, for instance, N. Kaldor, *An Expenditure Tax* (Allen and Unwin, 1955).

[2] J. E. Meade, *Report*, *op. cit.*; J. A. Kay and M. A. King, *The British Tax System* (Oxford University Press, 1978); US Department of the Treasury, *Blueprints for Basic Tax Reform* (Washington DC, 1977); and S. V. Lodin, *Progressive Expenditure Taxation – An Alternative* (Liber Förlag, Stockholm, 1978).

[3] Chapter 3, section 3.3, and Chapter 4, section 3.1.

[4] Chapter 4, section 2.2.

[5] Chapter 6, section 2.1.

[6] Chapter 5, section 3.3.

[7] Section 2.1.

[8] Chapter 15, section 2.1

[9] Chapter 16, section 5, and Chapter 18, section 4.2.

[10] Chapter 18, section 3.

[11] Section 3.

Table 13.8

Comparison in principle of income and expenditure taxation

THE SUPPLY OF CAPITAL (1) Capital market distortions (pp. 49–50)	An expenditure tax (ET) together with a flow-of-funds basis for taxing corporations will not distort the marginal returns to saving and investment. In that respect, an ET is superior to income tax (IT) as it is usually applied.
(2) The supply of saving (pp. 82–7)	There will be more saving under an ET to the extent that saving is interest-elastic. Whether this is an argument in favour of an ET depends on whether any increase in savings ultimately leads to an increase in real income per head.
(3) Risk-taking (pp. 48–9)	A proportional IT may be more favourable to risk-taking than an ET if full loss-offsets exist.
THE SUPPLY OF LABOUR (pp. 79–80)	An ET may lead to more or less labour being supplied. When comparing an ET with an equi-yield IT there will be no income effect. The substitution effect will work against labour supply in the ET case where leisure is exchanged for current consumption, but the ultimate effect will depend also on the terms on which an individual can exchange present for future consumption.
STABILIZATION (pp. 32–3)	Income tax is likely to be the better counter-cyclical weapon because its yield is more elastic with respect to fluctuations in national income. But the opposite may be the case if tax changes are thought to be only temporary.

EQUITY (pp. 99 and 117–19)	Both taxes are equally good from the viewpoint of vertical equity. Which is superior in terms of horizontal equity is the subject of much argument.

expenditure tax can reduce capital market distortions by equalizing rates of return to savers and investors. But it is necessary as a practical matter to ask also how important quantitatively are the resultant welfare gains. It is not unfair to observe that completely different types of capital market distortions might be even more important (e.g. the fact that access to borrowing is much easier for some than for others; and for some is impossible).

Nor should one underestimate the very serious transitional problems of the changeover – problems for both taxpayers and government – and be content with an analysis concentrating on the long-run situation. Indeed it can be argued that the transitional problems are so formidable that one would find it hard to make the change at all, in the sense that people would be tempted to accumulate funds before the changeover date, and then be able to utilize them without any tax penalty afterwards.

At the same time, one must recognize that if anything like a full-blooded expenditure tax could be brought into operation there would be many administrative advantages as well as disadvantages. Some other taxes such as capital gains tax and corporation tax could go, at any rate for domestic transactions; indexation would be very much easier in that one would not have to worry about excessive taxation of investment income or the tax treatment of capital gains or losses; and many other simplifications (e.g. the tax treatment of trusts) would be possible.

But it is quite clear that we are not likely to see an expenditure tax in the UK in the near future, if only for the reason that the Inland Revenue has made it clear that no major policy changes can be implemented before the income tax system is fully computerized in a few years' time.[1] In the meantime there is plenty of room for honourable and well-informed people to differ over the desirability of expenditure taxation, though less room for differences about the formidable administrative difficulties involved.

[1] Board of Inland Revenue, *121st Report*, Cmnd. 7475 (HMSO, February 1979), pp. 29–30.

14

INCOME REDISTRIBUTION AND THE WELFARE STATE

1 BACKGROUND ISSUES

1.1 *Conceptual issues*

This chapter follows on from the discussion in Chapter 13 of the progressiveness of income tax by analysing some of the main policy issues arising from what is loosely referred to as the 'welfare state'. After some background issues in section 1, our discussion centres on cash redistribution via taxation (section 2), via national insurance (section 3), and via non-contributory benefits (section 4). In section 5 we look briefly at benefits in kind. It should be clear from the breadth of these topics that we shall do no more than lay out the major issues, with no pretence of giving a complete treatment. Reference will be made to more specialized literature as we proceed.

In this section we start with some conceptual issues (section 1.1); we then discuss problems in the definition and measurement of poverty (section 1.2); section 1.3 discusses some of the issues raised by the 'cash versus kind' debate.

At the start of Chapter 13 we stressed the danger of analysing one tax in isolation, and the consequent need to think of the system as a whole. We also emphasized that the (usually unknown) incidence of any tax limited our ability to say much about its distributional effects. These two warnings apply with equal weight here. Clearly, a benefit which is paid mainly to those with low incomes will be much more progressive if paid for out of taxation on the rich, than if it is financed, for instance, by the national insurance contributions of the poor themselves. On the question of incidence too, we face problems similar to those discussed in Chapter 13. We do not know, for instance, whether income support schemes such as family income supplement result in the poor receiving lower wages; nor do we know whether the employer national insurance contribution is passed back to the employee, in part or in full, in lower wages.

A final conceptual point concerns the distinction between poverty and inequality. Poverty refers to the absolute or relative standard of living of the lowest x per cent of the population, whilst inequality refers to the overall degree of disparity in income level between the lowest x per cent and the average or the highest x per cent. In terms of Figure 14.1, which shows a stylized income distribution, poverty is greater the larger is the shaded area, and inequality is greater the greater the degree of dispersion of the income distribution. Thus inequality is greater with the income distribution shown by the dotted line than that shown by the continuous line in Figure 14.1.

In discussing income redistribution it is important to be clear whether it is poverty or inequality which is the focus of attention. Some policies can reduce both poverty and inequality, but it is possible, at least in principle, that policies to reduce one might increase the other. As we saw in Chapter 13, the highest rates of income tax raised little revenue, and are therefore of little use in reducing poverty directly. There is still an equity argument supporting these high rates on the grounds that they reduce inequality. But if it is true that they create disincentives which reduce output below what it would otherwise be, then these high tax rates may actually make poverty worse. Whether or not this is actually the case is an unanswered empirical question; we are not saying that high tax rates will aggravate poverty, but simply point out the possibility that they might do so.

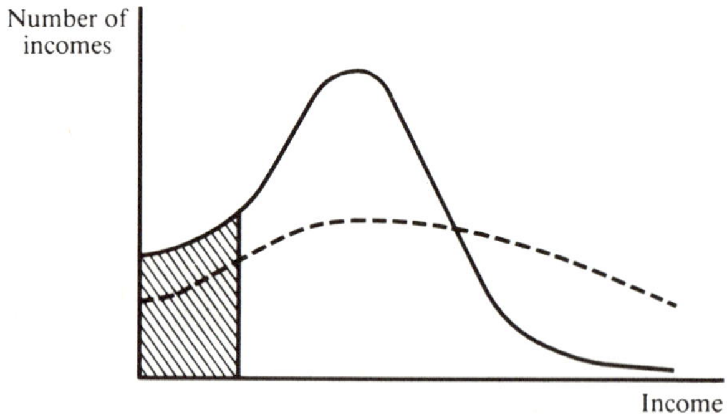

Figure 14.1 Stylized income distributions

1.2 *Problems in the definition and measurement of poverty*

There are two major questions in discussing poverty: (a) how do we define poverty, and (b), given our definition of poverty, how do we measure its extent. In this section we discuss these questions in turn, and then briefly describe how the question has been answered in the UK since 1948.

The notion of poverty clearly carries with it some idea of deficiency. In principle, we should like to measure poverty in terms of utility, and to define someone as poor if their utility is below some minimum level. Since this raises insuperable measurement problems we have to turn to observable variables such as consumption or income. The difficulty with using actual consumption as a measure of poverty is that it does not enable us to distinguish between those who have low consumption because it is all they can afford on the one hand, and the rich ascetic on the other. So, for practical reasons, poverty is usually defined in terms of income, which gives a measure of a person's power to consume.

As usual, when talking about income, we have to ask whether we are talking about money income only, or whether non-money income is to be included. If we omit non-money income then we are ignoring factors like job satisfaction and the value of leisure. These two items may not be crucial for the poor, but job *dissatisfaction* and factors like bad housing might make the poor in reality even poorer if poverty is defined in terms of income including non-money income. Even if we limit ourselves for practical reasons to a narrow definition of poverty in terms of money income, there still exists a variety of conceptual problems.

(1) *Is poverty absolute or relative?* On an absolute definition a person is poor if he cannot afford to keep himself alive and healthy. Early studies[1] tried to define poverty 'objectively' by reference to the nutritional requirements of an average person, and the cheapest ways of fulfilling these. There are serious objections to this procedure on both practical and philosophical grounds. In practical terms, people have different nutritional requirements even if one leaves aside special diets for medical reasons, and so it is not possible to formulate any universally applicable standard. Even if one could, it would not be reasonable to expect people to fill these requirements at minimum cost – to quote a student essay, 'People are not walking linear programmes'. Philosophically, the idea of an absolute definition of poverty stems

[1] The classic early studies are B. Seebohm Rowntree, *Poverty: A Study of Town Life* (Longmans, 1901) and Charles Booth, *Life and Labour of the People of London* (London, 1892). For a later follow-up, see B. Seebohm Rowntree, *Poverty and Progress: A Second Social Survey of York* (Longmans, 1941). For a modern assessment, see Asa Briggs, *Social Thought and Social Action: A study of the Work of Seebohm Rowntree, 1871–1954* (Longmans, 1961).

from historical times when most people lived close to a subsistence level, where it was natural to define poverty in terms of a subsistence level of consumption; but this is out of place when (at least in the developed countries) people live well above a subsistence level, and where the concept of deprivation is applied not only to physical matters but to emotional and cultural ones as well.

This brings us to relative poverty. Under this definition, with deceptive simplicity, a person is defined as poor if he or she feels poor. Poverty is thus defined relative to the standards of society in which one lives, inasmuch as a person living close to a subsistence level will not feel particularly poor if the same is true of everyone else, but would feel poor if he lived, for instance, in the UK. If poverty is defined as an absolute concept, the poverty line will remain fixed in real terms at a subsistence level, whereas with a relative definition the real value of the poverty line will tend to rise with living standards generally.

(2) *What is the unit whose income is being measured?* This question was foreshadowed by the discussion in Chapter 13 of different ways of taxing families. In the present context there are two aspects to the problem – whom does one include in the family unit, and how do we treat children for the purposes of defining a poverty line? The problem of the definition of the family unit may be summarized as follows. Suppose we have a family consisting of father, mother, two children and granny, whose sole source of income is £5,000 per year earned by the father. If granny is included in the family unit, and the poverty line for a family of five is £2,500, then there is no problem of poverty since an income of £5,000 for five people is above the poverty line. But if granny is regarded as a separate unit then she will count as poor since she has no income of her own. Thus, the narrower the definition of the unit whose income is being measured the greater the incidence of poverty. At its extreme, if everybody were assessed individually then well over half the population would be poor since very few children have any income of their own. On the other hand, the broader the definition of the income unit the fewer the people who will be defined as poor; if an extended family definition is used, then nobody would be counted as poor so long as there were a rich relative somewhere in the family.

The problem is more intractable than it seems. At its heart lies the notion of income sharing. If a group of four people has an income of £5,000 all earned by one person, then no one will be poor if the income is shared, and three of them will be poor if it is not. So what really matters is the extent to which income is shared. But in practice we cannot observe this, and so income units have to be defined on the basis of observable facts such as whether or not two people are married. Take the case of a man and a woman with two children. From the observed fact that the man and the woman are married we draw the inference that he is sharing his income with his wife and children. But it is just as possible for a married man to keep most of his income for himself as it is for an unmarried man to support lavishly the woman with whom he lives, and their children. If we could observe income sharing there would be no difficulty in defining income units. Difficulties arise precisely because we cannot.

A completely different problem concerns the weighting of dependants. If the poverty line for a single person is 100, then should the poverty line for a couple (whether married or not) be 200, or less than 200? And should an extra 100 be added for each child, or less than 100; and should the amount paid per child be related to his or her age?

Answers to such questions come from the more general one of comparing the standard of living of families of different sizes and composition. Families with the same standard of living are said to have 'equivalent' incomes, from which can be derived equivalence scales which say, for instance, that a family consisting of a man, wife and two children has an 'adult equivalent' of 2½, meaning that the family needs an income of 2½ times that of a single person to have an 'equivalent' standard of living.

Like many other apparently simple questions, that of adult equivalence is extraordinarily difficult. The first set of problems is conceptual, and hinges on the meaning of the term 'standard of living'. This can be defined either (a) in terms of the family's material standard of living (i.e. their consumption), or (b) in terms of utility. Whichever way one answers the question, one has then to face a set of intractable operational problems.

If equivalence is defined in terms of consumption levels the problem is that families of different types and incomes will tend to consume different bundles of commodities. Young people will spend more on household goods and less on social life after marriage; in middle age people spend their money on (for instance) cars and foreign travel; as pensioners they may be concerned more with warmth and a colour television. When families of different types have different expenditure patterns it is not possible to measure precisely the extent to which their wants are satisfied, and hence equivalence scales, without drastic simplifying assumptions.

The problem is even more intractable when equivalence is defined in terms of utility, for the familiar reason that utility cannot be measured. Consider the case of children. The assumption that a child is (say) one half of an equivalent adult implies that a married couple with an income of £*X* will be worse off measured in terms of their material standard of living if they do have a child than if they do not. But if they have a child by choice, then it can be argued that in *utility* terms they are *better* off. In such circumstances it is not possible to compare standards of living without resort to cardinal utility – clearly not a practical possibility.

The conclusion is that, conceptually, equivalence scales cannot adequately capture reality without taking account of varied consumption patterns and utility differences – and cannot, as a practical measure, take account of either. Thus there is no definitive measure of adult equivalence.[1]

(3) *Over what time period is income measured?* Though simple to explain, this problem, too, has no ready answer. Consider a salesman who earns £100 per week in commission but receives no wage; in a given year he works 50 weeks, earning £5,000, and in the remaining two weeks due to illness he earns nothing. If his income is measured over a year he is not poor, but on a weekly basis he is poor for two weeks of the year. As another example, though the student grant is set at about the same weekly level as the basic State retirement pension, students are not generally regarded as a poverty stricken group, though pensioners are. This can be justified by the fact that students' incomes will usually be considerably higher in the future, whereas pensioners' incomes will not. So it is appropriate to take a long-run definition of income when defining a poverty line for students. But in other circumstances the answer could be completely different. For example, if a student with no family or relatives to help him, and no job with which to support himself, applies for supplementary benefit during the summer vacation it would not be very helpful to refuse him benefit on the grounds that he has a high expected lifetime income. So, for the

[1]The major studies in this area are: S. J. Prais and H. S. Houthakker, *The Analysis of Family Budgets* (Cambridge, 1955); B. Singh and A. L. Nagar, 'Determination of Consumer Unit Scales', *Econometrica*, 41, March 1973; and J. L. Nicholson, 'Appraisal of Different Methods of Estimating Equivalence Scales and Their Results', *Review of Income and Wealth*, Series 22, No. 1, March 1976.

purposes of awarding supplementary benefit, the relevant definition of income is usually short run.

We have now discussed three problems in defining poverty – the absolute or relative definition, the choice of an income unit, and the choice of a time period. It is quite clear that none of them has any unambiguously correct answer, and so any definition of poverty will be arbitrary. The definition of poverty, like the definition of what constitutes a 'fair' distribution of income, is more a matter of social and political conviction than of positive economics.

Let us suppose that a definition of poverty, say the long-term supplementary benefit scale rate, has been reached by some unknown process. One can then ask how many people are poor in terms of that definition. Even this simple question cannot be answered readily. It is not possible to use the number of people in receipt of supplementary benefit as an estimate of the poor population, since not everyone who is eligible for benefit receives it. In other words, the take-up rate for supplementary benefit, and for most other benefits, is less than 100 per cent. If we knew the take-up rate, it would be a simple matter to scale up the number receiving supplementary benefit to an estimate of the total number of poor people; unfortunately, though much work has gone into estimating take-up rates,[1] our knowledge is still very limited. So on this definition the number of poor people in the UK is larger than the number in receipt of supplementary benefit (just over 3 million in 1978), but we do not know how much greater.

Nor is much help available from Inland Revenue figures. As we saw in Chapter 9, the Inland Revenue knows very little about people with incomes below the tax threshold. When estimating poverty, these are the very people in whom we are interested. As a result, estimates of the number of poor people have to be constructed from data derived from sample surveys.[2]

Even if we had a good idea of the number of people below any given poverty line this would still give at best only a partial picture. It is not our purpose here to discuss the various measures of poverty and inequality that have been put forward,[3] but an example will illustrate

[1] See, for instance, *Means Tested Benefits* (National Consumer Council, 1977), Chapter 3; *Report of the Supplementary Benefits Commission for 1977* (HMSO, 1978), Table 5.3; and Supplementary Benefits Commission Discussion Paper No. 7, *Take-Up of Supplementary Benefits* (HMSO, 1978).

[2] For a summary of various results, see A. B. Atkinson, *The Economics of Inequality* (Oxford University Press, 1973), page 194.

[3] For a discussion of measures of inequality, see A. B. Atkinson, *ibid*., Chapters 1 and 2, and A. B. Atkinson (ed.), *Wealth, Income and Inequality* (Penguin, 1973).

the point. Suppose the poverty line is £2,000 per year and there are 2,000 poor people, of whom 1,000 have an income of £1,900 and the rest an income of £1,000. Clearly there is less poverty than if all of the 2,000 people had an income of £1,000 – yet a mere head count does not show this. Furthermore, by spending £100,000 a government can raise all incomes of £1,900 to £2,000, thus at a stroke reducing the number of poor people by half. Yet in doing so it will not have helped the really poor at all.

What we have said so far is that it is not possible either to define poverty, or to measure it in any satisfactory way. This, however, is a very academic conclusion, and governments, whilst well aware of such conceptual impasses, do not have the luxury of avoiding them. So we conclude this section by outlining the answers that successive governments have given in the UK since 1948. If poverty had been regarded as an absolute concept the poverty line today, as represented, for instance, by the long-term supplementary benefit scale rate, would have about the same real value in real terms as in 1948; in other words, the benefit would simply have been uprated in line with price changes. In fact, most benefits have kept pace at least with changes in pre-tax earnings, thus showing that in practice poverty has been regarded as a relative concept. For instance, between 1948 and 1976 the long-term supplementary benefit scale rate rose in nominal terms by 950 per cent and average earnings by 895 per cent.

The definition of the income unit has been slightly broader than that used for income tax purposes. For instance, a man and a woman living together, but not married, will be treated as single people for income tax purposes. For the purpose of many cash benefits people living together will be regarded as a single income unit, irrespective of their marital status.[1]

This brings us to the question of the poverty line for families of different sizes. In practice, the poverty line for a single individual has been set at about 20 per cent of pre-tax average earnings; for a married couple the figure is around 30 per cent and for a family of four between 40 and 50 per cent. Thus if the poverty line for a single person is 100, for a married couple it will be 150 and for a family of four 200. These are the adult equivalences used in calculating the poverty line.

[1] The treatment of cohabitation has always generated a great deal of heat and not very much light. For further discussion of this problem area, see R. Lister, *National Welfare Benefits Handbook* (Child Poverty Action Group, 1977) and A. Lynes, *Penguin Guide to Supplementary Benefits* (Penguin, second edition, 1974).

1.3 *Cash versus kind*

We discussed in Chapter 3 some of the economic justifications for government intervention. Most of the reasons put forward, such as externalities, public goods and increasing returns to scale, were efficiency arguments. But the government may also wish to intervene for equity reasons, primarily to redistribute income or wealth. There are two fundamental ways in which the State can make the poor better off. First, it can increase their real purchasing power, either by transferring tax revenues to those with low incomes who then make their purchases at market prices or by subsidizing the prices of the goods they buy.

Second, the State can transfer some commodities directly to those with low incomes at a zero (or notional) price in quantities determined by the State. The crucial policy question that has to be asked is why it is that the State redistributes some 'necessities' directly, such as health care and education, but not others like food or clothing.

A variety of answers can be given to such questions. There are those who support State allocation of certain commodities on the basis that on human and ethical grounds they should be excluded from the usual economic calculus.[1] Our discussion in this chapter is much narrower, as we discuss only the *economic* reasons for different methods of state intervention. In broad terms there are two economic justifications for redistribution in kind. One relates to the characteristics of the good being redistributed, and the other to the characteristics of the utility functions of the 'rich' who pay taxes and the 'poor' who receive benefits. We discuss these in turn.

Characteristics of the good: the essence of the argument here is that if a good conforms to the so-called 'invisible hand' assumptions then market allocation is likely to be more efficient than State allocation. But if in the case of a particular commodity the assumptions do not hold then it is necessary to examine the extent to which the commodity fits or does not fit the neo-classical archetype, and then to decide what type of State intervention might be justified.

The major neo-classical assumptions are (a) that the consumer will have perfect knowledge both about prices and about the nature of the product; (b) that there will be perfect competition; and (c) that there will be no market failures such as externalities or public

[1]For a particularly cogent argument for this view see, for instance, R. M. Titmuss, *The Gift Relationship* (Penguin, 1970).

goods. If one or more of these assumptions is flagrantly inappropriate to a particular good, it is then necessary to ask what type of state intervention, if any, is justified. There are three major types of State intervention:

(i)Regulation: e.g. hygiene laws for the sale of food, laws preventing those without qualifications from practising medicine, and consumer protection generally;

(ii) Subsidy: e.g. to passenger transport;

(iii) Provision: e.g. the National Health Service.

Taking food as an example, the 'invisible hand' assumptions are not substantially violated. By and large, consumers have a good idea of the price of different food products and a reasonable idea of their flavour and nutritional value; at least at a retail level the sale of food is competitive; and no substantial market failures arise in the production or consumption of food. The only violation is that people generally do not have perfect knowledge about the ingredients of processed foods, or the conditions under which they were produced. State regulation is sufficient intervention to deal with this, by requiring ingredients to be printed on packaging, and by the enforcement of a variety of hygiene laws. In economic terms such legislation increases the consumer's knowledge to the point where he can make a rational decision.

The case of health care is very different, inasmuch as most of the 'invisible hand' assumptions are violated, giving considerable justification for a variety of different types of state intervention. We shall discuss the case of health care in considerably more detail in section 5.

Characteristics of people's utility functions: the essence of this argument is that if the utility functions of rich and poor are interrelated, both rich and poor may prefer redistribution in kind to redistribution in cash. In addition, redistribution in kind may be the only way of redistributing to children.

The standard neo-classical utility function shows the utility of the rich, U_R, as

$$U_R = f(Y_R)$$

where Y_R is the income of the rich. Note that utility depends only on the individual's income, and on nothing else. Similarly, the utility of the poor will depend only on their income, so that

$$U_P = f(Y_P)$$

where U_P is the utility of a poor man, and Y_P his income. But now suppose that the utility of the rich man is reduced by the knowledge of the poverty of the poor man. In that case the income of the poor man will enter his utility function so that

$$U_R = f(Y_R, Y_P)$$

In this case cash redistribution from rich to poor may raise the utility of both the rich and the poor man. Such redistribution would unambiguously increase the utility of the poor man; it would increase the utility of the rich man inasmuch as he would enjoy the reduced poverty of the poor man, but would reduce his utility by reducing his own income. Redistribution will continue as long as the utility gain to the rich man outweighs the utility loss; formally it will continue so long as

$$\frac{\partial U_R}{\partial Y_P} > \left|\frac{\partial U_R}{\partial Y_R}\right|$$

where the first derivative is the utility gain to the rich man resulting from the increase in the income of the poor man, and the second expression is the utility loss of the rich man resulting from the decline in his own income. An argument such as this can justify cash redistribution.[1]

But it may be the case that the rich care more about the way in which poverty manifests itself than in poverty *per se*. As a specific case, suppose the connection between rich and poor is not an income externality, but a consumption externality. In this case the rich man is concerned not with the low *income* of the poor man, but with his low level of *consumption*. In practice, the rich are concerned not only with the *level* of consumption of the poor, but also with *what* the poor consume. The rich derive utility from seeing the poor feeding and clothing themselves and their children, but derive disutility from seeing (or imagining) the poor consuming 'inappropriate' goods such as alcohol. In this case,

$$U_R = f(Y_R, G_P, B_P)$$

where U_R and Y_R are before, and G_P and B_P are respectively 'good' and 'bad' consumption by the poor ('good' and 'bad' for these purposes being defined by the rich). The utility of the rich increases with G_P and decreases with B_P.

In this situation the rich man would be unlikely to favour cash redistribution, for fear that the poor man would consume the 'wrong' goods and so reduce his utility. He will, however, be prepared to

[1] For a fuller exposition of this analysis, see H. Hochman and J. Rodgers, 'Pareto Optimal Distribution', *American Economic Review*, Vol. LIX, No. 4, 1969; also the Comments by P. A. Meyer and J. J. Shipley, R. A. Musgrave, and R. S. Goldfarb, and the Reply by H. Hochman and J. Rodgers, *ibid*., Vol. LX, No. 5, December 1970. See also p. 101n.

redistribute in kind, making sure that the commodities redistributed in kind are the 'good' sort. Redistribution will continue as long as

$$\frac{\partial U_R}{\partial G_P} > \left|\frac{\partial U_R}{\partial Y_R}\right|$$

where the first expression is the increase in the utility of the rich resulting from the consumption by the poor of 'good' commodities, and the second expression is the rich man's utility loss resulting from the reduction in his own income.

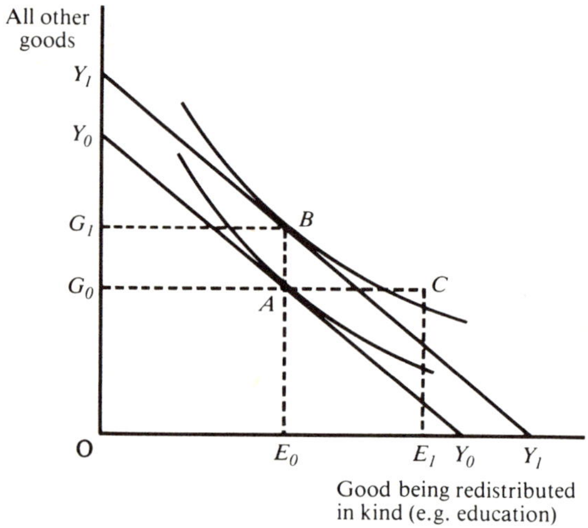

Figure 14.2 Redistribution in kind

Merit goods are commodities imposed on individuals independent of their tastes. The analysis of the previous paragraphs 'explains' the existence of merit goods. Consider the example of education, as illustrated in Figure 14.2. Suppose a family has money income as shown by the budget line Y_0Y_0 and purchases all its goods at market prices. It would then choose a point such as A, consuming E_0 of education and G_0 of other goods. Let us now suppose that people are given two choices. First, they could be given sufficient cash to shift their budget line to Y_1Y_1. In this case we assume that they will move to a point like B and consume the same amount of education as before, E_0, and an increased quantity of goods, G_1. Alternatively, they could receive additional education E_1 minus E_0, at a zero price as a non-transferable transfer in kind, thus moving them to point *C*. If the poor were rational they would prefer the in-kind transfer to the cash redistribution, since *C* is on a higher indifference curve than *B*. The rich, too, might prefer the in-kind transfer, even though it costs more than the cash transfer, since they fear a utility loss if the poor spent a cash transfer on 'bad' goods. So the rich, too, might prefer point *C* to point *B*, and so both rich and poor might prefer redistribution in kind to redistribution in cash.

There are thus two entirely separate economic arguments that can be used to support redistribution in kind, based, respectively, on the characteristics of the good, and those of people's utility functions. It should be stressed that these are narrow economic arguments based on technical considerations, and in no way dependent on political beliefs. In making policy decisions both technical and political arguments have to be taken into account.

2 TAXATION AND REDISTRIBUTION

2.1 *Negative income taxes*

Many solutions of the poverty problem have been put forward. Almost all fall under three main heads, advocating increased redistribution via:

(a) Extension of the tax system to include income subsidies as well as positive taxation. Prominent among these are various schemes of negative income tax, discussed in this section;

(b) Extension of the national insurance system to cover larger classes of beneficiaries, and to pay higher benefits. Prominent among these are the 'New Beveridge' proposals in the Meade Committee *Report* and elsewhere, to which we shall refer in the next two sections; and

(c) Extension of the current system of non-contributory benefits; we shall discuss these in section 4.

One of the most frequently advocated ways of raising the income of the poor is via schemes that guarantee everyone a basic minimum income. These schemes frequently involve a greater or lesser integration of direct taxation and social security. All of them can be described and analysed under the generic name of 'negative income tax'. We start this section by describing what is meant by negative income tax, and then turn to a general discussion of the advantages and disadvantages of such schemes. In section 2.2 we outline briefly one possible way in which a negative income tax might advantageously be introduced into the UK, and discuss briefly an alternative strategy for income redistribution. A common thread in this and succeeding sections is that there are no easy solutions to the problem of poverty in any country like the UK, which has a relatively large number of people with low incomes and a relatively small number of people with high incomes. This is not to be taken as an argument against redistribution, but as an observation that increased redistribution is unlikely to be brought about without an awareness of the difficulties involved.

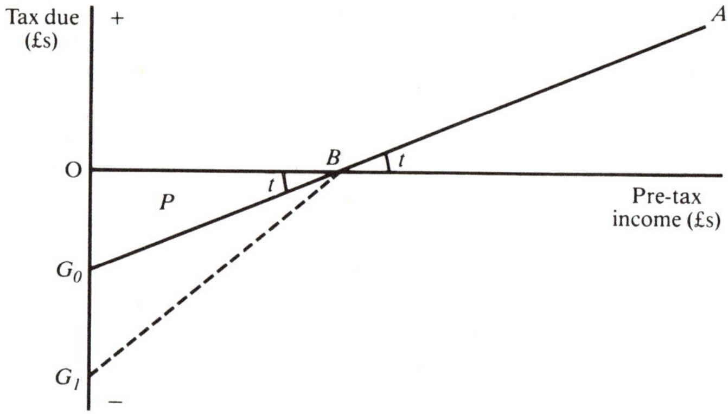

Figure 14.3 Simple negative income tax schemes

A simplified version of the current UK income tax system is shown in Figure 14.3 by the line *OBA*. In this system an individual is allowed to earn £*OB* tax free, and any income above this is taxed at a rate of *t* per cent. For the time being suppose $B = £1{,}000$ and $t = 35$ per cent. The simplest scheme of negative income tax would work as follows: if an individual's income is above £1,000 he pays a tax of (say) 35 per cent of the excess of his income over £1,000; if his income is below £1,000, he *receives* 35 per cent of the shortfall of his income below £1,000. Thus someone with an income of £1,200 would pay tax at a rate of 35 per cent on £200, or £70, while an individual with an income of £800 would *receive* £70. Such a system is shown in Figure 14.3 by the line G_0BA. It is, in principle, perfectly possible for a negative income tax to have different tax rates above and below the breakeven income, *OB*. Such a tax function is shown by the line G_1BA; if the tax rate below the breakeven income is 50 per cent, then an individual with an income of £1,200 will pay tax of £70 as before, but an individual with an income of £800 will now receive 50 per cent of the shortfall below £1,000, i.e. £100. The system is extended to larger families by having a higher breakeven income.

The simplest negative income tax will have only one tax rate, and can be represented algebraically by relating the individual's tax bill, T, which can be positive or negative, to his income, Y, in the following way:

$$T = t(Y - B)$$

where t is the tax rate applied above and below the breakeven level of income, B. This is the system shown by the line G_0BA in Figure 14.3.

It is often more useful to think of such a scheme in a different way. Continuing with our example of a single tax rate of 35 per cent, an individual with an income of zero will receive an income subsidy of 35 per cent of the shortfall of his income below £1,000 – in other words he will receive £350; this is the amount OG_0 in Figure 14.3. It should readily be apparent that it would be entirely equivalent to pay everybody £350 and then tax all their other income at 35 per cent. This result follows simply from the equation above. Multiplying out the brackets, we obtain the individual's tax bill as

$$T = tY - G$$

where $G = tB$ is the income subsidy given to everybody, and the individual then pays tax at a rate, t, on the whole of his income, Y. Similarly, an individual could be given a larger guaranteed amount, say OG_1 in Figure 14.3, and then pay a 50 per cent tax on the first £B of his income and a 35 per cent tax on the remainder. A scheme such as this, which gives everyone a tax-free lump sum and then taxes any other income, goes under the generic name of a *social dividend scheme*. What we have shown is that there is an exact equivalence between social dividend schemes and negative income taxes. Such schemes have been given a variety of other names such as minimum income guarantees, reverse income tax, and guaranteed minimum income schemes. Analytically, they are all identical. All have three crucial parameters, the size of the payment to an individual with no other income, G, the breakeven level of income at which an individual's net tax liability is zero, B, and the tax structure that applies to any income which the individual receives. In the case of a system with a single tax rate, t, any two of these parameters completely characterize the scheme. Consider, for instance, the system given by the line G_0BA in Figure 14.3. Thought of as a negative income tax, we know the breakeven level of income, B, and the tax rate, t, from which we can calculate the benefit payable to someone with no income, $G_0 = tB$. Looked at as a social dividend, we know that an individual receives G_0 to start with, and then pays tax at the rate t on any other income that he receives; it is thus obvious that the breakeven income $B = G_0/t$.

More has probably been written about the possibilities of negative income tax than about any other proposed reform of income support; in discussing the pros and cons here, we shall give only the barest outlines of the debate. We have already seen that tax-free allowances under a progressive income tax are worth more the higher is a person's income. The first distributional advantage of a negative income tax is that it pays the same benefit to everyone.

A second advantage is rather more controversial. Various schemes have been put forward[1] advocating that social security should be wholly or substantially abolished and replaced by a negative income tax which guarantees everybody a level of income about equal to the supplementary benefit level. Some of these schemes have made rather exaggerated claims for the efficacy of negative income tax as substantially solving the problem of poverty. Others, such as the discussion in the Meade Committee *Report*, have been very carefully thought out and are much more circumspect in their claims. From Figure 14.3 it is clear that with a negative income tax, low-income claimants will benefit by an amount related to the triangle P. The crucial question is by how much they would be helped.

The essence of the arguments against negative income tax is (a) that any scheme that redistributes substantial amounts of income would either be very costly and/or would require very high tax rates, and (b) that negative income tax is not necessarily a very strong redistributor of income. Let us take the cost points first. For illustrative purposes we can think of two types of negative income tax, the first giving a small guaranteed income, like OG_0 in Figure 14.3 and the second giving a much higher guaranteed income, such as OG_1. If we opt for the first type, of which the tax-credit proposals mentioned in Chapter 9 are an example, then the cost is not high, and no high tax rates are necessary to finance the scheme. But, as the guaranteed income is low, no substantial help is given to the poor, and a variety of additional social security benefits will still be necessary.

So if we wish negative income tax to solve these problems on its own, we have to give a high guaranteed income such as OG_1. But if we do

[1] See, for instance, A. Christopher *et al.*, *Policy for Poverty* (IEA Research Monograph no. 20, 1970).

this, given the size distribution of income in the UK, then either the scheme will be very expensive in terms of other public expenditure foregone, or it will be necessary to levy a very high rate of tax to pay for it. At present the average rate of income tax and national insurance contributions (i.e. income tax and national insurance contributions as a percentage of total personal income) is approximately 20 per cent. Calculations for the UK in 1972 suggested that to finance a negative income tax sufficiently large to enable abolition of other social security benefits, would require an income tax burden of two or three times this amount.[1] The disincentives this might create, especially in the labour market, were discussed in Chapter 13 (section 1.3).

Not only would any major negative income tax be very costly, but it is not clear that it would redistribute income very strongly in the UK. This is for two reasons. First, as the guaranteed income is increased, the average rate of tax has to be raised to finance it. Second, there are substantial numbers of people in the UK with low incomes and relatively few with very high incomes, and so the tax increase necessary to finance an increase in the guaranteed income will fall substantially on those with low and average incomes, thus clawing back a substantial proportion of the benefit to the poor of the higher guaranteed income.[2]

The overall conclusion is that negative income taxes in no way offer a complete solution to the problems of low incomes, though as we shall see in the next section, they may be helpful for a variety of other reasons.

2.2 *Possible reforms*

There are two ways out of this rather gloomy conclusion. One is to retain the idea of a negative income tax, but to make it a small one and combine it with other schemes for raising the incomes of the poor; the second is the New Beveridge type of proposal which abandons the idea of a negative income tax, and instead concentrates on raising the level of national insurance and related benefits.

Since a small negative income tax will not solve the problem of poverty on its own, it can be justified only if it can make other redistributive schemes more effective. One way in which this might be achieved is via the tax-credit proposals, an outline of which was given in

[1] N. A. Barr, 'The Costs of Negative Income Tax' in *Select Committee on Tax-Credit*, Vol. III, Appendices to Minutes of Evidence, HC 341–III, 1973.

[2] See N. A. Barr, 'Negative Income Taxation and the Redistribution of Income', *Oxford Bulletin of Economics and Statistics*, Volume 37, No. 1, February 1975, as corrected in Volume 38, No. 2, May 1976.

Chapter 9. These proposals suggested weekly tax-credits in 1972 of £4 per single adult, £6 per married couple, and £2 per child, and income to be taxable from the first pound onwards. Such a scheme can be characterized by the line G_0BA in Figure 14.3, where the amount OG_0 is the weekly tax credit for the individual or family. The scheme, however, excluded the self-employed and those earning less than one quarter of the national average on the grounds that the self-employed are taxed in half-yearly instalments, and so have no weekly liability against which to offset the weekly credits, and because the very poor almost certainly already received some sort of income support and so it would merely have complicated the administration of cash assistance if they had received, for instance, some of their income as a tax credit and the rest as supplementary benefit. The estimated cost of the tax-credit proposals in the early 1970s was about £1,300 million. But the additional cost of making the scheme universal would have been only £112 million plus the cost of additional administration.[1]

The relevance of these facts today is their suggestion that a universal tax credit scheme (which is really just a negative income tax of the sort described above) is financially feasible if the tax-credits are chosen to supplement existing schemes of income support rather than to supplant them. How useful would such a scheme be? We saw in the preceding section that one of the major difficulties in identifying and counting the poor is the fact that the Inland Revenue knows nothing about them. One of the key features of a universal tax credit scheme is not that it would redistribute income strongly (which it would not, because the level of tax credits would have to be low), but that for the first time it would bring the whole population under the Inland Revenue umbrella. There would thus be one scheme covering the whole population, to which various other selective schemes could be attached for different groups of the population. The idea, in other words, would be to use a universal negative income tax not to *solve* the problem of poverty, but to enhance the effectiveness of more limited schemes designed specifically to help the poor.

It has been suggested[2] that a scheme of this sort would enable a substantial degree of rationalization of the large number of national insurance and non-contributory benefits outlined in Chapter 10. Further, it would make possible the use of computers to search out

[1] *Select Committee on Tax Credit*, H. C. 341–II, 1973–74, Volume II, page 424.

[2] See, for instance, N. A. Barr and J. F. H. Roper, 'Tax Credits: An Optimistic Appraisal', *Three Banks Review*, No. 101, March 1974.

individuals or families potentially eligible for benefit, and the calculation of the appropriate level of benefits for those who were eligible. While a major change like this could be carried out only after extensive preparatory work, it should be noted that almost all the ingredients exist individually, although they have never been mixed together in the manner described here. Finally, although the tax-credit scheme itself was shelved, it should be noted that the replacement of child tax allowances and family allowances by child benefit is very much a step towards tax-credits.[1]

Another line of reform is the New Beveridge proposals, the most recent outline of which was contained in the Meade Committee *Report*.[2] This scheme dispenses altogether with a negative income tax and concentrates on raising the level of existing benefits. While a large negative income tax would cover everybody with one scheme, and would give high benefits on the basis of the single criterion of low income, the New Beveridge approach involves a more selective system with a variety of selective benefits for different groups of people. We shall return to the issue of universal versus selective benefits in section 4, when we discuss categorical and non-categorical schemes of income support.

3 NATIONAL INSURANCE

3.1 *Why have national insurance at all?*

This section examines the rationale and *modus operandi* of those benefits which are paid only if an individual has an appropriate insurance record. Section 3.1 asks what economic justification there is for compulsory national insurance, particularly in the cases of unemployment and sickness. Section 3.2 examines the principles underlying State pension schemes, and section 3.3 looks in some detail at the pros and cons of the present State pension system. We start by outlining the efficiency arguments for national insurance, before proceeding to some broader issues.

The economic justification for national insurance breaks down into three separate questions: (1) why do people insure voluntarily at all, (2) under what circumstances should the State compel people to insure, and (3) why should the State provide the insurance itself?

[1] The payment of life assurance premiums net of tax from April 1979 onwards is a similar such step.
[2] J. E. Meade, *Report*, *op cit.*, Chapter 13.

(1) *Why do people insure voluntarily at all?* The short answer is that if a person is risk-averse (i.e. if his utility function exhibits diminishing marginal utility of income), then uncertainty per se causes him disutility and he will be prepared to pay a positive price for certainty. This argument is illustrated formally in Figure 14.4 which shows that for a risk-averter successive increases in income bring successively smaller increases in utility. Suppose an individual faces two possible outcomes,

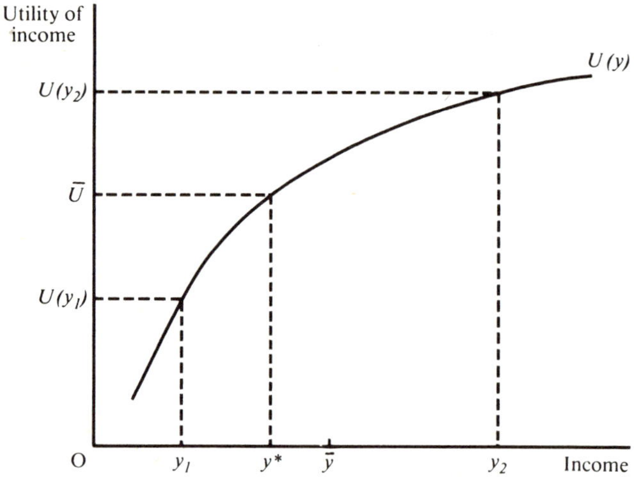

Figure 14.4 Utility of income for a risk-averter

a 'good' outcome, y_2, yielding utility $U(y_2)$, and a 'bad' outcome, y_1, yielding $U(y_1)$, which occur with probabilities p_2 and p_1. The expected value of the individual's income, $E(y)$, is then

$$E(y) = \bar{y} = p_1 y_1 + p_2 y_2$$

and his expected utility, $E(U)$ is

$$E(U) = \bar{U} = p_1 U(y_1) + p_2 U(y_2)$$

If the probabilities are each equal to one half, the individual's expected income would simply be the average of the two possible outcomes, y_1 and y_2, shown in Figure 14.4 as $\bar{y}$. Similarly his expected utility would be the average of the utilities of the two possible outcomes, $U(y_1)$ and $U(y_2)$, shown as $\bar{U}$. We can now show how much a rational individual would be prepared to pay for certainty. In Figure 14.4, the individual knows that he will receive an income either of y_1 or y_2. He knows that one outcome will occur, but not which, and he also knows that his expected income is $\bar{y}$, and his expected utility $\bar{U}$. From the diagram we can see that the individual can obtain a level of utility $\bar{U}$ in two different ways, *either* as the expected utility he derives from the two uncertain outcomes, y_1 and y_2, yielding an expected income of $\bar{y}$, *or* from a certain but lower income of y^*. A rational individual will be indifferent between an expected income of $\bar{y}$ and a certain income of y^*. He will therefore prefer an income of, say, $(y^* + 1)$ with certainty to an expected income of $\bar{y}$, and will therefore be prepared to pay up to $(\bar{y} - y^*)$ to insure.[1]

These sorts of consideration underlie the voluntary purchase by individuals of insurance against burglary, or against any financial loss from cancelling a holiday for medical reasons, and the like. Since these decisions are typically left to the individual's discretion, why cannot the individual be allowed to make similar decisions over insurance against loss of income due to unemployment, sickness or old age? This brings us to our second question.

(2) *Why does the State compel people to insure?* The short answer is that where an individual bears all the costs of his actions the efficiency grounds for State compulsion are limited: but this situation can change as soon as an individual imposes costs on others. Formally, this is the issue of externalities again.[2] It can be argued that an individual should be allowed to make his own decisions about whether or not he insures against income loss due to unemployment, sickness, or old age, and to bear the consequences if he fails to insure adequately. If a person does not insure his belongings and is burgled, he is normally left to suffer the consequences himself. Similarly, one could argue that if a person fails to insure against unemployment and then loses his job and starves to death as a consequence, then all that has happened is that he has made a voluntary decision and borne the consequences of that decision himself.

If people took the same attitude towards the loss through theft of an uninsured Picasso and the loss of life through starvation of a man and his family through failure to insure against unemployment, then national insurance could indeed be voluntary. But as an empirical observation people do not regard these two types of loss as equivalent; since the death by starvation of uninsured people imposes heavy

[1] These arguments are developed more fully in D. Laidler, *Introduction to Microeconomics* (Philip Allan, 1974), Chapter 9, and M. Friedman and L. Savage, 'The Utility Analysis of Choices Involving Risk', *Journal of Political Economy*, 1948, reprinted in *AEA Readings in Price Theory*.

[2] The argument could also be framed in terms of merit goods, as discussed in Chapter 3, section 2 and on p. 366.

psychic costs on others, we make sure that such people always receive some sort of income support.

Compulsory national insurance can therefore be justified on the grounds that failure to insure imposes costs not only on the individual himself, but also on others, either in the form of psychic costs if the uninsured individual starves, or in the form of the financial costs of ensuring that he does not starve. There is an exact analogy here with car insurance. Individuals who drive cars are compelled to take out insurance precisely because an uninsured motorist involved in an accident will usually impose costs on others. Quite correctly, the legal compulsion in this case applies only to third-party damage (i.e. only to damage to *other* people); motorists are not compelled to take out insurance against their own financial losses. Though in this country the State compels motorists to insure, it does not provide insurance itself, but merely requires insurance with an approved private agency. This brings us to the third question.

(3) *Why does the State provide national insurance rather than compel private insurance?* The answer to this question lies in the technical conditions for the feasibility of private insurance. We saw above that given the two possible events y_1 and y_2, the expected outcome $\bar{y}$ depended crucially on the probabilities p_1 and p_2. To make the example more concrete, suppose that there is a probability of one in one hundred that one's house will be burgled and that if it is burgled £1,000 worth of possessions will be lost. A potential loss of £1,000 is faced with a probability of 1 per cent, and so the expected loss in any given year is £10. If large numbers of other people face an identical situation, an insurance company, ignoring administrative costs, could expect to make a profit by charging a premium of £11 or £12 per year. In broad terms this is the way that private insurance works. For this to be possible, however, the probability of the insured event occurring has to have two characteristics: (a) it has to be known or estimable, and (b) it has to be exogenous in the sense that it cannot be altered substantially by the individual, by the insurance company or by government action. The probability of being burgled can be estimated from police records of the number of burglaries recorded in the area where one lives; and that probability might alter slowly over time as society becomes more lawless or as police protection improves, but it cannot be substantially altered by the behaviour of the individual or the insurance company. Hence private burglary insurance is possible.

Let us now consider individually the major national insurance benefits. The average probability of an individual being unemployed is well known; it is simply the aggregate unemployment rate for the economy as a whole. But unless one believes that there is a natural rate of unemployment which is completely unalterable, the entire thrust of macroeconomics for at least forty years assures us that the unemployment rate is not exogenous. This being the case, it is not possible to predict unemployment rates, and so private unemployment insurance could not operate, and the task falls to government. It is noteworthy that there are no substantial private unemployment insurance schemes anywhere in the world.

Turning to sick pay insurance, the situation is somewhat different. Again, the probability of an individual becoming ill can be estimated. Furthermore, the probability can be regarded as exogenous, in the sense that it cannot readily be altered. The probability may change from year to year, e.g. it will be higher in a winter with a large 'flu epidemic. But this does not make private insurance impossible, because such events are themselves exogenous. The provision of a sick pay insurance scheme by the State can therefore be justified in efficiency terms only by arguing that there are economies of scale to be derived from running it alongside unemployment insurance. It should be noted that in many countries, including the UK, it is possible to take out private sick pay insurance.

In the case of pensions, as we shall see in the next section, the major problem with private pension schemes is that they cannot provide insurance against inflation without State assistance. This again is a technical problem with insurance which can be regarded as a justification for State provision of pensions.

The efficiency arguments for national insurance thus rest on externality arguments justifying State compulsion, and technical failure in the insurance market justifying State provision of the major benefits, though with a somewhat weaker argument for sick pay insurance than for other schemes.

Over the years there has been much confusion about the purposes of national insurance. From an economic point of view, one can think of it either

(a) as a device to correct a market failure; this is the efficiency argument which we have just discussed, or

(b) as a device to redistribute incomes; this is largely an equity argument.

More broadly, social historians argue whether national insurance was introduced by the middle classes to protect the poor from their own improvidence (this view follows the philosophy of the old Poor Laws), or whether it was done more for the equity motives discussed earlier in this Chapter. Gilbert argues for the latter view, when he states that the evolution of national insurance

> ... proceeded also from a new awareness among those of the upper classes who were in daily contact with the poor that the old assumptions about poverty simply were not true. All of the poor were not lazy and improvident. Industrial society clearly did not distribute its rewards equally, or according to effort.[1]

Translated into economic terms, the misfortunes of the poor, whether caused by their own improvidence, by misfortune or by broader reasons, imposed an externality upon the middle classes. As we saw in section 1, such an argument can be used to explain redistribution from the rich to the poor; and as we have just seen, technical problems in the insurance market can justify compulsion. There are thus very good arguments for thinking of national insurance both as a technical device to deal with market failure and as a redistributive device. But one should be very clear that the two cases are argued on very different grounds.

In practice, the two arguments have not always been properly distinguished. In the UK both are recognized, so that it arouses little comment when the State not only provides pensions because of technical failures in the pensions market, but also redistributes from rich to poor within the State pension scheme; we shall return to this in some detail in the next section. But in the USA the arguments for the social security pension scheme are couched much more on efficiency grounds. Nevertheless, the basic social security retirement pension in the USA can be earned in as little as ten years, which constitutes a considerable redistribution from long- to short-term contributors. That such redistribution arouses a considerable amount of controversy is due to the fact that the basic rationale for social security in the USA has never been made explicit.[2] It is to the rationale of State pension schemes that we now turn.

[1] B. Gilbert, *The Evolution of National Insurance in Great Britain* (Michael Joseph, 1973), p. 13.

[2] For a detailed discussion of these issues in a US context, see Alicia H. Munnell, *The Future of Social Security* (The Brookings Institution, Washington DC, 1977). See also Appendix to Part II for a brief discussion of the US social security system.

3.2 *Financing retirement pensions*

3.2.1 *Methods of financing pensions schemes* We start by outlining different ways of financing pensions schemes and reviewing their pros and cons, and then turn to a discussion of some equity issues. These form a background to section 3.3 which evaluates the current State pension scheme.

The economic function of pensions is to transfer consumption over time. From the viewpoint of the individual, what he wishes to do is to consume less than he produces during his working years in order that he may continue to consume once he has retired. Pensions are thus a mechanism for transforming current consumption into future consumption. The two major ways of organizing this are by 'funded' schemes and 'pay-as-you-go' schemes.

A pension is said to be '*funded*' or 'money buying' if the contributions of the members of a pension fund (frequently run in the private sector by insurance companies) are invested in a variety of financial assets the return on which is credited to its members. Such a fund has at all times sufficient reserves to pay all future pension claims as they fall due and the pension of any individual will be based on the sum of his past contributions. From an economic point of view, the process is little different from putting a proportion of one's earnings into a bank deposit account throughout one's working life.

At the time that an individual retires the pension fund will be holding all his past contributions together with the interest and dividends earned on them. This usually amounts to a large sum which is converted into an annuity.[1] The annuity is then the individual's pension.

There are two major implications of funded schemes of this sort. First, they will always have sufficient reserves to pay all outstanding future liabilities. This is because an individual's entitlement is simply his past contributions plus the interest earned on them. A second implication, which follows from the first, is that an average individual

[1] An annuity is a monthly or annual payment by the insurance company to the individual for the rest of his life given to him in exchange for a lump-sum payment. It is essentially a bet between the individual and the insurance company. If the individual dies shortly after agreeing to exchange his lump sum for an annual income payment, then the insurance company wins; if the individual lives to a ripe old age, he wins. This is another example of risk-averse individuals being prepared to pay a positive price to buy certainty. While there is no need in principle for an individual to buy an annuity with his lump sum (he could just live off his capital), in practice he will do so in the UK both because most people prefer certainty, and because the Inland Revenue will allow as a tax deduction only contributions to pension funds which compel the individual to convert at least three-quarters of his lump sum into an annuity.

or a generation as a whole gets out of a funded scheme no more than it has put in. The funding principle itself has a venerable antiquity. Macaulay, writing in 1848, stated that

> there can be no greater error than to imagine that the device of meeting the exigencies of the state by loans was imported into our island by William the Third. What really dates from his reign is not the system of borrowing, but the system of funding. From a period of immemorial antiquity it has been the practice of every English government to contract debts. What the Revolution introduced was the practice of honestly paying them.[1]

We shall return shortly to other implications of funding.

Macaulay notwithstanding, the State today has no need to accumulate reserve funds in anticipation of future pension claims, but has the option of taxing the working population to pay the pensions of the retired generation. Such *pay-as-you-go* methods form the basis of almost all State pension schemes today.

The major implication of the pay-as-you-go system is that it relaxes the constraint that the benefits received by any generation must be matched by its own contributions. As was shown by Samuelson,[2] with a pay-as-you-go scheme it is in principle possible for *every* generation to receive more in pensions than it paid in contributions, provided that real income rises steadily; this is likely to occur either when there is technological progress and/or when there is steady population growth.

We turn now to the pros and cons of the two methods of finance. The main advantages of pay-as-you-go schemes are that they are generally able to increase the value of pensions in payment not only in line with prices (so as to counteract the effects of inflation), but also in real terms so as to allow pensioners to share in economic growth occurring after their retirement. These points are illustrated in simplified fashion in Table 14.1. In period 1 the total income of the workforce is £1,000, so that a pension contribution rate of 10 per cent yields £100. Now suppose that by period 2 prices and earnings have risen by 100 per cent. A contribution of 10 per cent now yields £200, which has a real value of £100 at the old price level. In other words, a pay-as-you-go scheme with a 10 per cent contribution rate has maintained the real value of pensions in the face of inflation. Now suppose that instead of

[1] Thomas Babington Macaulay, *The History of England from the Accession of James the Second* (Longmans, 1864), Vol. 1, pp. 137–8.

[2] See P. A. Samuelson, 'An Exact Consumption-Loan Model of Interest with or without the Social Contrivance of Money', *Journal of Political Economy*, 1958.

inflation there is economic growth, so that earnings rise to £2,000 while prices remain at their original level. In this case the 10 per cent contribution rate has a yield of £200, with a real value of £200. Thus the pay-as-you-go scheme has made it possible to double the real value of pensions.

A third advantage of pay-as-you-go schemes is that full pension rights can be built up very quickly. This is because pensions are paid not by one's own previous contributions but by the contributions of the current workforce.

Table 14.1

Stylized effect of inflation and growth on a pay-as-you-go pension scheme

	Period 1	*Period 2 (Inflation)*	*Period 2 (Growth)*
(1) Total income of workforce	£1,000	£2,000	£2,000
(2) Price index	100	200	100
(3) Pension contribution rate	10%	10%	10%
(4) Available for pensions	£100	£200	£200
(5) Real value of pensions [(= line (4) ÷ line (2)) × 100]	£100	£100	£200

Against these undoubted advantages must be offset the major disadvantage[1] of pay-as-you-go finance – the fact that it is very sensitive to any change in the age structure of the population which reduces the working population relative to the number of dependants. Thus, increased longevity will increase the number of pensioners and prolonged education by young people will reduce the size of the workforce. Yet more striking, a lowering of the retirement age cuts both ways, simultaneously reducing the workforce and increasing the number of pensioners. Finally, any large 'bulge' in the birth rate can have a disastrous effect on the ratio of workers to pensioners. For instance, there was a large bulge in the birth rate in 1948. At the moment, this is an asset since these people are about thirty years old and this makes for a large labour force. But when this group reaches retirement age, around the year 2010, there will be a rapid increase in the number of pensioners, creating financial problems

[1] It is sometimes said that another major disadvantage of pay-as-you-go finance is that it makes pensioners dependent on the future workforce. Whilst this is true, not dissimilar problems arise with funding. See p. 382–3, below.

for pay-as-you-go schemes. A similar problem exists in the USA and in many of the countries of Western Europe. The effect on the age distribution of the population of a bulge in the birth rate is rather like an ostrich swallowing an orange.

Turning now to funded schemes, their disadvantages tend to mirror the advantages of pay-as-you-go schemes. As regards inflation, we need to distinguish (a) pensions in build-up, when contributions are still being paid, and (b) pensions in payment. Funded schemes generally can cope with inflation occurring during the build-up of pension rights, and with a given rate of *anticipated* inflation once the pension is in payment. But funded schemes are generally unable to cope with unanticipated inflation occurring once pensions are in payment. The reason for this is not difficult to understand. An average pensioner under a funded scheme has built up during his working life a capital amount consisting of his contributions and the interest earned on them. Let us suppose that on retirement this amounts to £50,000. He then exchanges this for an annuity paying, say, £5,000 per year. If he is a representative member of his generation, then all he can receive over his lifetime is the sum total of his £50,000 of contributions plus the interest they attract. If inflation occurs after his retirement it will reduce the real purchasing power of his pension, and there is very little that the pension fund can do about it.[1]

In principle, an individual can insure against any uncertainty. We saw in the previous section how private insurance works in the case of, say, burglary. But it is not possible for private insurance companies to offer inflation insurance, both because the future inflation rate is very hard to predict, and because it is most certainly not exogenous. Thus, again, we have a failure in the private insurance market and it is this argument which is an efficiency justification for State pension provision.

For very similar reasons it is not possible for funded schemes substantially to increase the real value of pensions in payment in line with economic growth that occurs after a pensioner's retirement. Finally, it takes a long time to build up full pension rights in a funded scheme because it takes an individual many years of contribution to build up a lump sum sufficiently large to pay him an annuity which will support him fully in retirement.

Against these disadvantages, it is often claimed that funded schemes have the major advantage of being insensitive to changes in the size of

[1] Unless the rate of interest is *always* sufficiently high to offset the effects of inflation.

the workforce relative to the number of pensioners. This claim is made because funded schemes accumulate sufficient resources so as always to have sufficient to pay the pensions of all their contributors. This is so because all that the average contributor receives is his own past contributions plus interest. Now it is certainly the case that a funded scheme has always on hand sufficient *money* to pay all outstanding *money* claims against it. As such it is a highly efficient device for transferring money over time. But we have already said that the economic function of pension schemes is to transfer *consumption* over time. And funded schemes are not a safe way of doing this, since we have already seen that they are unable to guarantee the real value of pensions in the face of unanticipated inflation after the pension is in payment.[1] It can be argued that if there are a large number of pensioners and therefore a large accumulation of pension funds, then any sharp decline in the size of the workforce can result in demand inflation as the large number of pensioners dissave out of their accumulated funds. If this is the case, then funded schemes, like pay-as-you-go schemes, are sensitive to demographic change.[2]

One final issue between pay-as-you-go and funded schemes concerns the level of aggregate saving. It has been argued that total saving will be higher with a funded scheme and that this might lead via increased investment to a larger capital stock, and to higher rates of economic growth. While such arguments cannot be faulted on logical grounds, their truth is ultimately an empirical question about matters which are little understood.[3] At this stage one has to be agnostic about the issue.

3.2.2 *Equity issues* One of the major results to emerge from the preceding discussion is that with a pay-as-you-go scheme it is possible for a generation as a whole to receive more in pensions than the sum of its own past contributions, thus making possible redistribution between generations. In this section we discuss redistribution *within* a generation.

The most obvious way in which this can occur is between the rich and poor. If everybody's benefits are strictly proportional to their own past

[1] An individual cannot guarantee the safety of his pension even by burying a crock of gold at the bottom of his garden. The State can always expropriate the gold either directly or by a wealth tax, or by engineering inflation and imposing a non-indexed capital gains tax on an accruals basis.

[2] See N. A. Barr, 'Myths my Grandpa Taught Me', *Three Banks Review*, December 1979.

[3] See, for instance, Martin S. Feldstein, 'Social Security, Induced Retirement and Aggregate Capital Accumulation', *Journal of Political Economy*, Vol. 82, No. 5, September 1974.

contributions, as is the case under a funded regime, then no redistribution takes place. But in many State schemes, including the current UK scheme, people who have low incomes, and hence pay low national insurance contributions, receive more pension per pound of contribution than people with higher incomes. This type of redistribution from rich to poor will be discussed further in the next section.

Another important type of redistribution is between men and women. The following statements of fact all refer to the UK.

(1) The normal retiring age for men is 65, at which age a man has a life expectancy of 77. The average man is thus retired for 12 years.

(2) The normal retiring age for women is 60, at which age women have a life expectancy of 80. This means that the average woman is retired for 20 years.

(3) It is therefore $20/12 = 1\frac{2}{3}$ times as expensive to provide a given weekly pension for a woman as for a man.

(4) If men and women pay equal contributions and receive equal weekly benefits then there is a subsidy from men to women. Since women live longer than men, abolishing the differential retirement age would reduce the subsidy, but would not eliminate it.

What are the policy implications of these facts? One answer would be to make women pay higher pension contributions in the same way that teenagers pay higher car insurance premiums because they are poorer risks. However, it is not difficult to defend a position of equal contributions for equal benefits. The most compelling argument is to say that any insurance scheme will involve redistribution from one group to another. Burglary insurance will redistribute from those with fewer than average burglaries to those with more than average burglaries. And any pension scheme will redistribute from the short lived to the long lived. This means that there will be redistribution from men to women, from smokers to non-smokers, from those with poor medical histories to those from healthy families, and so on. This being the case, it can be argued that as a matter of general policy one should recognize the fact of a subsidy from men to women, but having recognized it simply to leave it at that. More simply, the UK could follow most other countries and have the same retiring age for men and women.

3.3 *Critique of the current State pension scheme*

As we saw in Chapter 10, all national insurance contributions are paid into the National Insurance Fund, from which all benefits are paid. The State pension scheme is thus explicitly organized on a pay-as-you-go basis, and therefore has the advantages and disadvantages normally associated with pay-as-you-go schemes. Since 1948, the basic State pension has not only kept pace with inflation, but also with economic growth.

But as a pay-as-you-go scheme the State pension scheme is also sensitive to demographic change. The bulge in the birth rate of 1948 was followed by a more minor one in the mid 1960s, since when the birth rate has steadily declined. This means that in the years after 2025 there will be a very large number of pensioners and, on present evidence, only a small workforce to support them. A similar situation seems likely in the USA and in several countries of Western Europe, and thought is already being given to what solutions, if any, exist.

Turning from issues of finance to considerations of redistribution, the details of the contribution conditions and benefits of the current State pension scheme were outlined in Chapter 10. These imply that there will be considerable redistribution from rich to poor in any generation. This can be seen most clearly by ignoring for a moment the earnings-related component of the State pension. A contribution rate of 6½ per cent means that a person with a weekly income of £20 will pay £1.30 per week in contributions, and someone earning £100 will pay £6.50. If all that each receives is the basic State pension of £19.50 per week, then the rich person is paying five times as much for his pension as the poor man. Put another way, it means that the poor man is getting five times as much pension per pound of contribution. The existence of the earnings-related part of the pension ensures that this redistribution from rich to poor is not quite as strong as appears in our example. But it is still the case that those with low incomes will receive a pension that is a larger percentage of their previous earnings than will the better off.[1]

Thus there is one type of redistribution embodied in the contributions and benefit formulae. In addition, as we saw in Chapter 10, the National Insurance Fund receives an 18 per cent addition to its income from contributions directly from central government revenues, and to the extent that these are raised from progressive taxation this again implies redistribution from rich to poor. And since men and women pay identical contributions and receive identical weekly benefits, there is also redistribution from men to women.

Such redistribution, together with a large number of credits such as those for people at home looking after young children, and those who

[1] The same is true of the federal social security retirement pension in the US. See Appendix to Part II.

are unemployed or sick, means that the current pension scheme represents a considerable erosion of the original Beveridge principle that benefits be matched by contributions. As we saw earlier, the original intention was that everybody would pay the same contribution (the weekly stamp) and would receive the same benefit, so that there would have been no redistribution at all from rich to poor within a generation (assuming, e.g., equal life expectancy). In fact, the original proposals were for a funded scheme, which would also have ruled out redistribution between generations. The present scheme has moved so far from the original concept that some people have argued that it is not really a contributory scheme at all any more, but more of a tax/transfer scheme. They justify this argument by pointing out that men who continue to work once they have turned 65 (60 in the case of women) and who earn substantial amounts rapidly lose entitlement to their national insurance pension until they turn 70 (65 for women). The State, in effect, is applying a means test to the national insurance pension, which could never occur in a fully contributory scheme such as a private funded pension. Whether this is an advantage or a disadvantage is debatable.[1]

4 NON-CONTRIBUTORY CASH BENEFITS

4.1 *Criteria for evaluating income support schemes*

We turn now to some of the major policy issues raised by supplementary benefit and the other non-contributory schemes discussed in Chapter 10. This section discusses various economic criteria in terms of which such schemes may be judged; section 4.2 discusses the effectiveness of supplementary benefit in terms of these criteria; and section 4.3 discusses one of the major problems arising when there are not one, but many schemes of income support.

One of the major distinctions between different types of income support schemes is whether they are *categorical* or *non-categorical*. Categorical schemes are based on the assumption that people can be sorted into groups according to the cause of their poverty, and an anti-poverty programme instituted for each group. Hence we have supplementary benefits for families with no wage-earner and FIS for families with a low wage-earner.

[1] For a more detailed evaluation of the current state pension scheme, see N. A. Barr, 'Labour's Pension Plan – A Lost Opportunity?', *British Tax Review*, Nos. 2 & 3, 1975.

There are two major assumptions underlying the categorical approach:

(1) That the world consists of those who are self-supporting and those who are not, the two categories being mutually exclusive and exhaustive;

(2) That those who cannot support themselves can be classified into groups.

It is assumed that most people will be self-supporting either through work or through insurance against loss of income through unemployment, sickness or old age. Historically it was thought that there would be very few people who would not be self-supporting in one of these ways, and that these few could be categorized into, for instance, the disabled, widows with young children, the blind, and so on.

Underlying this approach is the old puritanical idea that it is unworthy to be poor, unless one has some 'good' reason. Historically, the 'worthy' poor consisted of people like widows with young children, where the breadwinner had been killed in an industrial accident, or the disabled. Such thinking lay behind the old Poor Law and also permeated much of the 1930s New Deal legislation in the USA. Given this viewpoint it was natural to construct one programme for each 'worthy' cause of poverty. The Beveridge Report, though much less restrictive in its attitude towards 'reasonable' causes of loss of income, distinguished eight causes of poverty, of which the major ones were unemployment, disability, retirement, widowhood, physical disease, and funeral expenses.[1]

In contrast, non-categorical schemes like negative income tax regard income as a spectrum; i.e. there are the self-supporting, the very poor, whom the state has to support almost completely, and then a large number of people in between. The philosophy underlying such schemes regards people as many and diverse, as are the causes of poverty, and so classification is made only in terms of need.

In assessing the effectiveness of any scheme of income support, whether categorical or non-categorical, three criteria can usefully be applied.

(1) *The level of support*; does the scheme ensure a socially acceptable standard of living for those who need assistance? This in turn raises two further questions:

(a) Is the scheme effective in dealing with poverty for an individual family?

[1] *Social Insurance and Allied Services* (The Beveridge Report), *op. cit.*, pp. 124–5.

(b) How much does the scheme redistribute between families?

(2) *The focus of support*; does the scheme give cash where it is needed and not where it is not needed? This again raises two additional questions:

(a) What are the marginal tax rates imposed by the scheme?[1]

(b) What are the effects of the scheme on work effort?

(3) *The cost of support*: is the cost of the scheme within the resources of the economy? It cannot be over-stressed that what we are talking about is not money, but resources. If schemes of income support create serious labour supply disincentives, this can reduce the goods and services produced in a year, which is the main reason for worrying about incentives. Discussion of the cost of any scheme has to include both the cost of the benefits received by the poor, and the costs of administering the scheme which, as we shall see in the next section, can be substantial.

4.2 *Supplementary benefit*

The institutions of supplementary benefit were discussed in Chapter 10. We start here by reviewing these institutions in terms of the criteria we have just outlined. We shall then be in a position to make a critique of the economic impacts of supplementary benefit. Finally, we discuss some of the major social and administrative criticisms currently being made about the scheme.

Starting with the *level* of supplementary benefit, the scale rates for 1979 are given in Table 10.5. As we saw in section 1.2, the scale rate has more or less kept pace with average pre-tax earnings since 1948, and hence has risen more rapidly than post-tax earnings.

One of the great unknowns about supplementary benefit is what proportion of people eligible for benefit actually apply. It is clear that so-called 'take-up rates' are less than 100 per cent. On the demand side this is because an unknown number of people do not apply for benefit because they feel stigmatized, either by the receipt of the benefit per se, or by the investigations necessary to establish eligibility. On the supply side it is possible that not everyone who applies for benefit and is eligible actually receives benefit. As a result take-up rates are less than 100 per cent. But there exists little hard evidence as to their size, though there is a strong presumption that the larger the benefit to

[1] If a family in receipt of benefits earns some extra income it will frequently lose some or all of its benefit. This is an implicit tax which can have labour supply effects. We shall return to these issues extensively in the following two sections. See also Chapter 10, section 3.2.

which a person is potentially entitled, the higher the take-up rate.[1] To an unknown extent, therefore, take-up rates of less than one interfere with the effectiveness of supplementary benefit as a means of bringing everyone's income up to an acceptable minimum.

On the *focus* of supplementary benefit the question is whether it gives benefit to those who need it, but withholds it from those who do not. This will depend on how rapidly a family loses benefit as its income increases. As we saw in Chapter 10, families on supplementary benefit are allowed to receive or earn a certain amount (between £2 and £6 per week) without affecting their entitlement to benefit. But once these disregards have been used up, the family will lose £1 for every £1 of extra income. This, in effect, imposes a 100 per cent implicit tax on families, and thus focuses benefits very sharply indeed.

It is worthwhile to show formally the budget constraint of an individual or family receiving supplementary benefit. This is done in Figure 14.5, which shows the combination of leisure and income available to an individual who starts with an initial endowment of 24 hours of leisure per day, shown as point *b* on the diagram. The line *ab* shows the individual's earning opportunities.[2] Suppose now a scheme is introduced under which a person's income will never be allowed to fall below an amount *0c*. This is shown by the line *cde*. An individual choosing 24 hours of leisure will now receive an income of *0c* = *be*. If he works, the first £4 (say) of his net earnings will be disregarded, and so his income rises above the supplementary benefit level. This is shown by the line *eg*. But once his disregards have been used up, he will lose £1 of supplementary benefit for every £1 he earns, and so his net income will increase no further. This is shown by the dotted line *fg*.

The budget line facing the individual is thus *afge*. The horizontal section *fg* shows that over the range of earnings where the individual loses £1 of benefit for every £1 he earns, his net income remains stationary. This is equivalent to an implicit marginal tax rate of 100 per cent in the sense that any extra earnings are 'taxed away' by the loss of supplementary benefit. This is important not only because it makes it difficult for families on supplementary benefit to raise their net disposable income, but also because it removes all financial incentive to work. If people work solely to earn money, then the budget constraint in

[1] See *Means Tested Benefits*, *op. cit.*, Chapter 3; *Report of the Supplementary Benefits Commission for 1977*, *op. cit.*; *Take-Up of Supplementary Benefits*, *op. cit.*

[2] Those not familiar with this construction will find it in any intermediate textbook on microeconomics. See, for instance, D. Laidler, *Introduction to Microeconomics*, *op. cit.*, Chapter 7.

Figure 14.5 collapses to the two segments *af* and *ge*, since at point *g* the individual will have the same income as at point *f*, but with more leisure. Thus no one who works only for money will choose a point on the line segment *fg*. If a person receives £32 per week in supplementary benefit which he loses pound for pound with any earnings above £4 per week, then the line *fg* will cover earnings from £4 to at least £36 per week. This very strong labour supply disincentive is the price one pays for focusing benefits sharply on those in need.

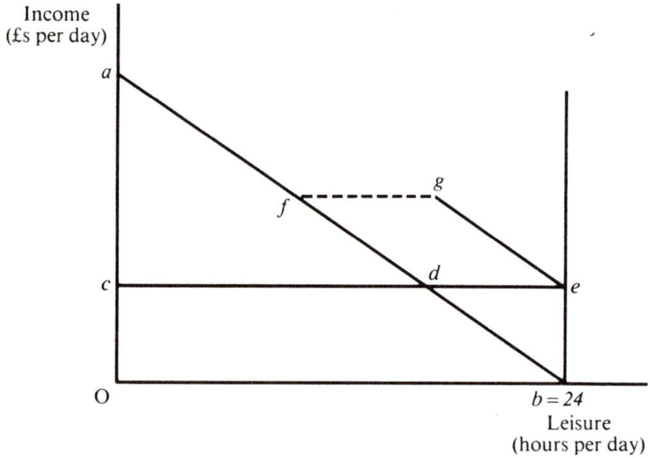

Figure 14.5 Stylized representation of supplementary benefit

This labour supply disincentive is one of the major economic criticisms of supplementary benefit. Looking at Figure 14.5 it is clear that any individual who works only for money will chose to be either on the line segment *af*, earning all his income and receiving no supplementary benefit (i.e. being completely self-sufficient), or will choose a point on the line *ge*. This means that he will be earning £4 per week or less and hence will be almost completely dependent on the State. Thus, by its very construction, supplementary benefit almost forces people into one of two extreme categories, that of being fully self-supporting or that of being almost completely dependent on the State. There is no real provision in the scheme for the working poor who are intermediate between the two extremes. There must be a substantial number of people who, though not able to be fully self-sufficient, may be able to make a contribution to supporting themselves. It is possible that these people are never apparent because the supplementary benefit system almost forces them into full dependence. To some extent this is conjecture, since one can only guess at the number of the working poor – the true number would become evident only if a scheme existed which enabled work and welfare to be combined easily.

The sad conclusion is that the very fact of focusing benefits sharply on those in need brings about one of the worst features of the supplementary benefit system – its tendency to be strongly divisive between the self-supporting and the dependent.

Our final criterion is that of *cost*, which was shown for supplementary benefit and various other forms of income support in Table 10.3. The number of people in receipt of supplementary benefit has now risen to about 3 million. In addition, benefits have kept pace with pre-tax earnings. For both reasons the cost of supplementary benefit has risen sharply over the years. And as the amount actually finding its way into the hands of the poor has increased, so have administrative costs. When the current national insurance scheme was started in 1948, it was thought that eventually almost everyone would be self-supporting either through work or through national insurance. Supplementary Benefit (then called National Assistance) was envisaged as a residual scheme for a very small number of people. A recent report[1] suggests that the tailor-made service (a little extra for coal here, a special grant for clothes there) which was designed for a small number of people cannot any longer be administered effectively when there are 3 million claimants receiving benefit in any single week. This has meant, for instance, that the number of officials required to administer supplementary benefit has risen from about 12,000 in 1966 to some 30,000 in 1978.

It has been argued that there could be considerable cost saving by simplifying the present scheme. This could be done by having fewer rates of benefit, simpler rules for assessing a claimant's resources, and by limiting discretionary lump-sum payments to truly exceptional cases like fire and floods. Some support for simplification arises from the fact that one-third of new awards for benefit granted each year are discontinued within a month. Thus there might well be a role for a simple short-term scheme with no frills and with very much simpler administrative procedures.

It is fairly clear that both the labour supply disincentives inherent in

[1] *Social Assistance: A Review of the Supplementary Benefit Scheme in Great Britain* (Department of Health and Social Security, July 1978).

supplementary benefit and the administrative complexity of the scheme derive from the view prevailing when national assistance was instituted that the scheme would be relevant only to a small number of people in a limited number of categories. Any major reform of the scheme would have to take today's changed circumstances into account. The same is true about changes in attitude, for instance over the role of married women. We discussed in Chapter 13 how these changes have aroused criticisms of the structure and administration of income tax. Similar criticisms have been raised over the structure of supplementary benefit.[1]

4.3 *The poverty trap*

We saw in the preceding section that supplementary benefit imposes an implicit marginal tax rate of 100 per cent. Implicit tax rates are embodied in any scheme which withdraws benefits as income rises. For instance, family income supplement pays a benefit of one half of the difference between family income and a benchmark level of income, as outlined in Chapter 10, and so embodies a 50 per cent tax rate. Similarly, a family will generally receive 12½ pence less in rent rebate if its income is £1 higher, an implicit tax rate of 12½ per cent. Similar tax rates are embodied in rate rebates, free prescriptions, free school meals and so on. If a family is on supplementary benefit and earns an extra £1, it could lose £1 in supplementary benefit. But a similar phenomenon can occur for a family which is not on supplementary benefit. In principle, to take an extreme case, a family earning an extra £1 per week could lose 33 pence in income tax, 6½ pence in national insurance contributions, 50 pence in withdrawn family income supplement, 12½ pence in lost rent rebate, and 3 pence in lost rate rebate. Thus an extra £1 in earnings has cost a total £1.05 in taxes and lost benefits, and the situation could be even worse if the family lost its entitlement to free prescriptions and free school meals. Thus tax rates of over 100 per cent can arise when a family receives benefit from more than one scheme. The so-called 'poverty trap' arises when such rates approach or exceed 100 per cent, and such rates have been documented for the UK.[2]

The ill-effects of such tax rates are two-fold. First, they make it very hard, if not impossible, for the poor to raise their net income. As we

[1] *Ibid.*, Chapter 11.

[2] See for instance, A. R. Prest, *Social Benefits and Tax Rates* (Institute of Economic Affairs, 1970), and D. Piachaud, 'Poverty and Taxation', *Political Quarterly*, 41, January 1971.

saw in Figure 14.5 illustrating the case of supplementary benefit, over the range of hours *fg*, extra work will not increase net income at all. Thus an implicit marginal tax rate of 100 per cent locks a family into poverty. The second ill-effect, as we saw in the last section, is that these high tax rates bring about a strong substitution effect against work effort and so are likely to be a potent labour supply disincentive.

Fortunately, a number of factors mitigate the worst impacts of the poverty trap. The most important of these are (a) the increasingly widespread tendency to award benefits for fixed periods, and (b) the fact that most benefits are uprated annually. Let us take the case of fixed period awards first. Family income supplement is granted on the basis of 5 weeks' pay slips and the award is made for 12 months, irrespective of intervening changes in income. Thus if a family is awarded £2 a week, it will receive a book of 52 vouchers for £2 each, which can be encashed week by week. In addition, as we saw in Chapter 10, family income supplement is a 'passport' to other benefits such as free school meals and free prescriptions, so that these too are awarded for a full year.

The main reason why benefits are awarded for a full year is undoubtedly the administrative convenience of not having to reassess people each time their income changes. This administrative practice has a substantial impact on implicit marginal tax rates, since any increase in earnings which occurs during an award period will not result in any immediate loss of benefit and so, at least in the short run, the marginal tax rate will be zero. And even if an increase in earnings is permanent, so that the next year's benefits are assessed on the basis of a higher income, any tax which is not paid at the time of the increase in earnings but only later, is likely to be at least partly discounted, and hence is likely to have less of a disincentive. In addition, as we shall see, benefits may well have been uprated by the end of the award period, and this might well take most of the sting out of reassessment. The moral of the story is to highlight the economic impact of administrative practice. It is quite possible that the economic consequences of the changes were not foreseen at the time they were made, and the fact that they have proved to be beneficial is largely fortuitous.

In our example above, we stated that a family earning an extra £1 could lose £1.05 in benefit. We now have to reinterpret this figure. It is certainly the case that if we compare family A with an income of £*n* with family B with an income of £($n + 1$) then family B will receive £1.05 less in benefit than family A. Thus the high implicit tax rates apply on a *cross-section* basis. However, what we are really interested in is the impact on family A's benefits of an increase in its earnings of £1. This is a *time-series* question, and as we have seen, the result of fixed period awards is that an increase in earnings will frequently lead to no loss of benefit, at least in the short run.

Thus fixed-period awards can mitigate the worst of the poverty trap. Furthermore, though uprating has not been a legal requirement, we have seen that in practice most non-contributory benefits have tended to rise broadly in line with average earnings. And since these upratings have been annual in recent years, reassessment at the end of an award period will generally be on the basis of uprated benefit structures. This further mitigates at least the nominal impact of the poverty trap.

An altogether different approach to the problem of the poverty trap is to be found in the 'New Beveridge' proposals advocated most recently in the Meade Committee *Report*.[1] The essence of these proposals is that benefits should generally be paid at a flat rate of not less than a subsistence level (i.e. at or above the relevant supplementary benefit scale rate). Implicit in such proposals is a rejection of means-tested benefits as far as possible.

The specific proposals in the Meade *Report* were that all social security benefits and the income tax threshold should be at the level of supplementary benefit; that there should be a home responsibility payment for wives with children; and that there should be a standard cash benefit for all children irrespective of the employment status of the parents. All benefits except the last were to be taxable, and many means-tested benefits would be phased out.

This type of approach raises a number of questions. First, the flat-rate nature of the benefits flies in the face of the increased tendency to make most national insurance benefits earnings-related. Second, there is the problem of which benefits are tied to the long-term supplementary benefit rate and which to the short-term. Third, there is the question of which means-tested benefits are to be phased out, and how. It is not our purpose here to make a detailed critique of this type of proposal,[2] but simply to relate it to the issue of the poverty trap.

There are really two arguments. The first is that since benefits are all at least at the level of supplementary benefit no one receiving full national insurance benefits would need supplementary benefit, hence

[1] J. E. Meade, *op. cit.*, pp. 276 *et seq.*
[2] But see the article by A. R. Prest in *Economic Journal*, *op cit.*

eliminating the application of the 100 per cent tax rate inherent in that scheme. The poverty trap would thus be alleviated by greatly reducing the number of people on supplementary benefit.

The second strand is that benefits are given by category of person (e.g. unemployed, sick, retired), rather than by the level of their income. In essence, the proposal is to give categorical benefits to certain classes of people, whose benefit will not be affected by any change in income, but only by a move into another category. Thus, someone who is unemployed and receiving unemployment benefit may change category from unemployed to employed, and hence lose his entire unemployment benefit on finding a job. This does not remove the problem of the poverty trap so much as redirect it, by concentrating the entire tax effect on the change of category of the persons receiving benefit.[1] These cases, in the main, would be people currently receiving national health insurance benefit.

Thus proposals of this sort would reduce the worst impact of the poverty trap partly by reducing numbers in receipt of supplementary benefit and partly by concentrating the rest of the withdrawal of benefit to a change in category of the recipient.

5 BENEFITS IN KIND

The two most important benefits in kind are health care and education. Since there is much more controversy over how health care should be allocated we limit ourselves to this topic, and take the example of the National Health Service to illustrate the question of provision in cash versus kind.

In 1977 total expenditure on the National Health Service amounted to £5,734 million. We do not propose to discuss here the structure or administration of this giant undertaking,[2] but continue in somewhat greater detail the discussion in section 1.3 of the economic justifications for the provision by the State of commodities such as health care. The question we are really asking is: what is the most effective way of organizing health care? We shall start with efficiency considerations and then proceed to some equity arguments.

Our starting point is the proposition made in section 1.3 that a

[1] For an analysis of schemes like this, see G. Akerlof, 'The Economics of Tagging', *American Economic Review*, March 1978.

[2] For details of the structure and administration of the National Health Service, see, for instance, M. Brown, *Introduction to Social Administration in Britain* (Hutchinson, 1977), Chapter 3.

market allocation of health care will be efficient only if various familiar assumptions are fulfilled. The main ones mentioned there were (a) perfect knowledge, (b) perfect competition and (c) no market failures. We discuss these in turn in the context of health care and if any assumption fails, then we discuss which type of State intervention (regulation, subsidy or provision) may be appropriate. Such efficiency arguments are important; 'social concern' is not the only relevant consideration. Resources devoted to health care cannot be used for schools or old age pensions. If we build another kidney machine there is less available for cancer research. The problem of opportunity cost exists as much for health care as for any other activity. So we cannot simply say that efficiency implies the best possible system of health care. This definition stresses the benefits but ignores the costs. The 'best' system is when we spend the whole of GNP on health care, and clearly this would not be optimal. In principle what we seek for health care is what we seek for any other commodity – namely that output at which marginal social value equals marginal social cost.[1] The question we ask here is the extent to which a market allocation would or would not achieve this result.

In theory, the market's efficiency as an allocative device depends, among other assumptions, on perfect knowledge. In practice, very few people have perfect knowledge about anything, but in many cases they have a fairly good idea both about the nature of the product and about its price. For instance, people generally have a broad knowledge of the characteristics of food, e.g. what constitutes a balanced diet, which foods have a high protein content, etc. But in the case of health care, most people know very little about the nature of the good. First, the consumer knows little about the use and effectiveness of most medical techniques, and the little he does learn generally comes from his doctor (i.e. the supplier). And even if the patient does learn about the efficacy of a treatment it is rarely of much future use, since many types of medical care (e.g. setting a broken leg) are not usually repeated on the same patient. Similar arguments (e.g. knowledge mainly from the supplier, infrequent purchase) can be applied, for instance, to cars and hi-fi. But in these cases it is usually possible to buy information (*Which*?, AA car tests, and so on). In the case of health care one frequently does not have time to seek the information (e.g. after a car accident), and this is often compounded by one doctor's reluctance

[1]For an excellent simple discussion of these points, see J. Le Grand and R. Robinson, *The Economics of Social Problems* (Macmillan, 1976), Chapters 1 and 2.

to comment on another's advice. Finally, even if teaching facilities existed, medicine is a technical subject and there is a limit to what the consumer could understand without himself becoming a doctor.

It is therefore reasonable to conclude that the consumer has highly imperfect knowledge of the nature of the product. Furthermore, his knowledge of the price of health care is little better. Not only do we not know what a particular type of treatment 'should' cost, but since medical care is not usually repeated we cannot even learn.

There is another argument that concerns the lack of perfect knowledge. It is also sometimes argued that health care is expensive and people cannot predict when they will need it; hence the State should provide health care services. This argument, as it stands, is false – as we saw in section 3.1, insurance exists precisely to deal with such uncertainties. So uncertainty justifies State intervention only if there is some reason why the private insurance market will not work.

A great deal has been written about the problems of private health insurance.[1] There are two major arguments. First, as we saw in section 3.1, private insurance can work only when the probability of occurrence of the insured event is exogenous. This is so in some cases of health care; for instance, the probability of breaking a leg or suffering a kidney complaint may reasonably be so regarded. But much health care is delivered by general practitioners, and the decision to go and see one's GP is most certainly not exogenous. Nor (for the most part) are such phenomena as pregnancy. For this reason many private medical insurance policies will not cover visits to a GP, nor the costs of a normal pregnancy (though they will frequently cover the costs of any complications). The name 'moral hazard' is given to this situation where the probability of the insured event occurring is largely in the hands of the person who is insured. An altogether different problem with private medical insurance is its inability to cope with the congenitally and chronically ill.

Health care thus totally fails to accord with the assumption of perfect knowledge. In part this can be dealt with by regulation – e.g. the State does not allow people to practise medicine unless they have what the state regards as an appropriate training. But the absence of knowledge,

[1]A pioneering article in this area is K. J. Arrow, 'The Welfare Economics of Medical Care', *American Economic Review*, Vol. 53, 1963, pp. 941–73, reprinted in M. H. Cooper and A. J. Culyer (eds.), *Health Economics* (Penguin, 1973). The latter reference also contains articles by A. J. Culyer and C. M. Lindsay bearing on the same issues.

and the fact that the ordinary consumer is in no position to acquire it for himself, is also one of the strongest efficiency arguments for the State provision of health care.

The other two assumptions required for the theoretical efficiency of the market mechanism can be dealt with more quickly. The role of perfect competition is to drive down costs and profits, and to enhance consumer choice. There are very few countries in which health care is competitive, and it is very arguable whether in this case such competition is desirable. On the one hand, hospitals may compete with each other to install the latest medical technology, but, on the other hand, the desire to reduce costs may reduce the quality of medical care. And the additional argument that competition can increase the range of consumer choice, is vitiated by the doubts already mentioned about whether consumers have sufficient knowledge to make a good choice. These arguments again justify at a minimum State regulation, but can also be used to buttress state provision.

The major market failure in the case of health care is the externality that can arise via the treatment of communicable diseases. A person who pays for a polio vaccination benefits not only himself, but also those people who cannot now catch polio from him. It is a familiar proposition that such externalities may justify subsidies for certain types of health care, but it is certainly not a justification for state provision.

There are equity as well as efficiency arguments against market provision. It is often argued that the State should provide health care because the poor would otherwise not be able to afford it. As it stands this is false. If the *only* problem were that of low income, one could simply increase the income of the poor and let them buy health care on the open market in the same way, for instance, as pensioners buy food. But, as we saw in section 1.3, the rich may be more prepared to redistribute to the poor by distributing 'good' consumption to them directly. Hence it may be politically easier to redistribute in kind than in cash and so both rich and poor might prefer in-kind provision. A second equity argument is that the difficulties with market provision discussed above might apply more acutely to the poor.

An altogether different equity argument concerns the role of giving. It has been argued that the doctor/patient relationship should not be thought of as an economic one.[1] This, like the assertion that children are not economic commodities to be bought and sold on the open

[1]See, for instance, R. M. Titmuss, *The Gift Relationship*, *op. cit*.

market, is fundamentally a moral judgement, and as such no one can claim a monopoly of wisdom.

So we are left with equity considerations, which are primarily value judgements, and an efficiency question which in practice asks which method of allocating health care is the least inefficient. Recent work by Culyer has attempted to bring these strands together.[1] He argues that the market misallocates health care for the reasons outlined above: he then asserts that the National Health Service almost certainly also misallocates, mainly because it has no clearly defined objective. According to Culyer, the appropriate objective for the National Health Service is to allocate health care on the basis of need – and much of his argument is concerned with providing an operational definition of 'need'. One way of doing this, he suggests, is to define an index of need in terms of factors such as time already spent waiting for treatment, and urgency based on the level of the patient's health (i.e. how ill), its rate of change (i.e. how rapidly the condition is deteriorating) and the number of his or her dependants. Factors to be considered in defining need, and their relative weights, should, he argues, be determined, say, by Parliament, and not by the profession alone. The concern of doctors should be to *evaluate* need on the basis of the criteria already laid down. This would introduce elements of public choice into health care.

[1]A. J. Culyer, *Need and the National Health Service* (Martin Robinson, 1976).

15

PERSONAL CAPITAL TAXATION

1 GENERAL PRINCIPLES

1.1 *Introduction*

We saw in Chapter 13 that the arguments for differential taxation of investment income were distinctly weak, the main difference between those living on earned and investment income being the reserve power of the property possessed by the latter, with this in turn being a pointer to some form of capital taxation rather than differential income taxation. We now have to ask whether this or any other argument is sufficiently strong to justify the special taxation of capital and, if so, what form or forms it should take.

Before embarking on our enquiries, it is worth noting that both the UK and the USA have made radical changes in their system of taxing personal capital during the 1970s and in no sense are we saddled with arrangements which have not been modified for many years. Indeed, the magnitude of the changes in the UK in 1975[1] might be thought by many people to be an impediment to further far-reaching changes in the immediate future.

The arguments for personal capital taxation will be examined in general terms in this section. Section 2 will deal with taxes on capital transfers and section 3 with taxes on wealth. Policy implications are discussed in section 4.

1.2 *The reserve power argument*

The proposition here is that a man with £50,000 of earned income does not have as large a taxable capacity as a man with capital of £1 million on which he gets a return of 5 per cent, or to use Kaldor's vivid illustration,[2] a beggar and a gold hoarder may each have zero current income but their capacity for bearing tax is not the same. Income taxation, whether differentiating between earned and investment income or not, does not place differing tax burdens on people with the

[1] See Chapter 9, Section 2.1.4 for details.

[2] *Indian Tax Reform*, *op. cit.*, p. 20.

same amount of investment income but different amounts of capital and so cannot be said to deal with this argument in any direct way.

At first sight this proposition is extremely plausible but before swallowing it hook, line and sinker one must look a little more closely at the reasons why different people may possess different amounts of capital. Suppose we take two contemporaries each with the same lifetime pattern of earnings from work. At any given point in the life cycle, one man may have more non-human capital in his possession than the other for one or more of three reasons: inheritance, accumulation and net capital gains. Suppose we now push the argument further and assume that appropriate taxes are levied on inheritances and net capital gains. There is scope for argument about the meaning of 'appropriate' but to take a well-known position, let it be assumed that the income tax system is of a Haig-Simons type providing for full taxation at marginal income tax rates of inheritances[1] and capital gains. In this eventuality, the reserve power argument for capital taxation can relate only to the second of the three reasons for possessing non-human capital, i.e. accumulation. But then one has to stand back and ask whether such a proposition is really acceptable. If individual A never saves during his lifetime but his contemporary B decides to save for a period of years, then it will follow that the usual income tax system will in any event impose a heavier tax burden in present value terms on B than on A.[2] It is not at all obvious why, in addition to this additional income tax burden, any impost on B's capital is justified. Indeed, it could be persuasively argued that such an impost would be grossly inequitable. And even if one took an expenditure tax world in which savers were not penalized relatively to spenders, it is still very difficult to see the equity of imposing a special tax on own-accumulation in order to cope with reserve power.

In practice, inheritances are not caught for income tax at all and capital gains are often taxed lightly, though there are some reservations on the latter proposition, given the usual absence of indexation. The effects of inheritance in contributing to possession of wealth have been studied by many people. One proposition is that the UK wealth statistics do demonstrate the possession of large capital sums by some

[1] The argument implies taxation of capital transfers at doneer level without any reduction in the donor's income tax liabilities. See H. Simons, *Personal Income Taxation* (University of Chicago Press, 1938), Chapter VI.

[2] Cf. pp. 82 ff. above.

young people,[1] and it is very hard to explain this other than by inheritance. Various studies have been made in recent years of the relationship between fortunes inherited and fortunes left at death;[2] the general conclusion has been that, as in the 1920s at the time of a similar investigation by Wedgwood, there is a strong correlation between amounts left by fathers and sons – with the implication that inheritance plays a role in either wealth or wealth-making capacity or both.[3]

The upshot is that one is on firmer ground in advocating some form of capital taxation as a supplement to income taxation, in the context of inherited wealth[4] (and perhaps also capital gains) than in that of accumulated wealth. Although inherited wealth would be caught by an annual tax on all capital this would seem to be an inefficient method of proceeding in that no distinction would be made between inheritance and accumulation. The presumption must be that if one is primarily concerned with limiting the size of inheritances, it is much better to tackle them by some system of taxing capital transfers directly.

So the proposition that the reserve power argument justifies a general capital tax, as distinct from inheritance[5] taxation, is by no means as clear-cut as is sometimes maintained.

1.3 *Other arguments for capital taxation*

However, this does not exhaust the claims for general wealth taxation and we must now look at other arguments which have been put forward. First, we shall take those for levying some form of capital taxation *as well as* the usual sort of income tax, i.e. the sort which excludes capital transfers and perhaps only taxes capital gains in a rough and ready way. Second, we examine those arguments favouring the imposition of a wealth tax *in partial substitution* for the income tax.

In the first category, we have the whole gamut of propositions that

[1] See A. B. Atkinson, *Unequal Shares* (Allen Lane, 1972), Chapter 3.

[2] See C. D. Harbury, 'Inheritance in the Distribution of Personal Wealth,' *Economic Journal*, December 1962; C. D. Harbury and P. C. McMahon, 'Inheritance and the Characteristics of Top Wealth Leavers in Britain', *Economic Journal*, Sept. 1973; and C. D. Harbury and D. M. Hitchens, 'The Inheritances of Top Wealth Leavers', *Economic Journal*, June 1976.

[3] Note that one cannot exclude the possibility that it may be the inheritance of ability, knowhow or just contacts from the earlier generation which is the major determinant of the wealth of the present generation.

[4] But see G. Tullock, 'Inheritance Justified', *Journal of Law and Economics*, October 1971.

[5] E.g. 'The ownership of wealth, . . . adds to the economic resources of a taxpayer so that the person who has wealth as well as income of a given size necessarily has a greater taxable capacity than one who has only income of that size.' *Wealth Tax*, Cmnd. 5704 (HMSO, August 1974), p. iii.

wealth is very unequally distributed, that such inequality is unacceptable and that capital taxation is the most effective way of diminishing it. This set of propositions calls for several observations. The first is that the interpretation of wealth statistics is fraught with difficulty;[1] and that in any event judgment about inequality is a highly subjective matter. It can also be argued that there has been some tendency for the distribution of wealth in the UK to become less unequal over time whether measured by percentage shares of total wealth of given quintile groups or by Gini coefficients.[2] But even if one thinks that it is an appropriate object of policy to aim at reductions in the inequality of wealth, the choice of policy instrument for such a purpose is not a foregone conclusion. One question is whether taxation is the appropriate technique at all; there are good reasons for arguing that the acquisition of more skill and training and the breaking down of restrictive barriers may be a better means of generating a more equal distribution of wealth. And if in the end one does plump for taxation measures, one has to ask whether an annual tax on wealth is a better instrument than taxes on capital transfers, bearing in mind the dubious equity credentials of the former[3] and their likely relative effects on saving.[4]

It is often argued that the imposition of an annual capital tax will help in the administration of income tax by providing cross-checks on income tax returns. One can accept this argument as it stands but it would nevertheless be incorrect to jump to any conclusion that there would be administrative advantages in supplementing the income tax with a capital tax rather than with a capital transfer tax. The latter would be less helpful in the process of cross-checking income tax returns but would in itself be far easier to administer than an annual capital tax, not so much because the number of assessments each year would necessarily be very different (that would depend on the relative coverage of the two taxes) but rather because a once-for-all valuation

[1] E.g. one would not expect a sizeable section of the population – all those under age 30, say – to own much capital and hence the distribution of wealth among the *whole* as distinct from the *adult* population is always likely to appear uneven whatever the precise statistical measure of inequality.

[2] See e.g. Royal Commission on Income and Wealth, *Third Report on the Standing Reference*. Report No. 5, Cmnd. 6999 (HMSO, November 1977), p. 76.

[3] See p. 401 above.

[4] See Chapter 4, section 3.2, for the argument that taxes at death (though not necessarily taxes on gifts inter-vivos) are less inimical to saving than an annual tax on capital. There are also other ways in which once for all transfer taxes are likely to have differing impacts to annual capital taxes, e.g. that the very act of transfer shows that a donor no longer has need of his assets. Cf. C. S. Shoup, *Federal Estate and Gift Taxes* (Brookings Institution, Washington, DC, 1966), p. 101.

at death is a far easier matter than the annual revaluation of assets necessary for an annual capital tax. Data on *public* administration costs are necessarily only part of the picture but it has been authoritatively stated[1] that they would amount to something like 6 per cent of tax yield, a far higher figure than one encounters with say personal income tax or value added tax.

Now we come to the second category of arguments for capital taxation, i.e. those favouring it as a partial replacement of income tax rather than simply as an addition to it.

The most general point here is the favourable effects on the disposition of wealth among different kinds of capital assets, compared to those likely to result from an equal-yield income tax. One point is that, on the assumption that the tax base excludes human capital, there would be a tendency to direct more resources into education and training and less into physical capital. Although, as we have seen, there is no finality in the arguments about the relative scope for extending investment in one direction relatively to the other, there is at least a presumption that human capital accumulation has had less than its due share of limelight in the past. So many would judge this an important virtue of a net-worth tax. As for physical capital formation, it is a well-known proposition that a capital tax tends to be neutral between risky and non-risky sources of income and between liquid and non-liquid assets. Therefore, we should expect to find a greater willingness to invest in risky assets than in the income tax case – at least on the assumption that loss offsets are not fully possible in the latter case. We should also expect to find less demand for liquid assets, with possible effects on the level of interest rates.

It will be noted that the preceding paragraph explicitly referred to taxation of net worth: this was quite deliberate in that any asset distribution advantages of partial replacement of income taxation by capital taxation could only be expected in the case of annual taxes on capital rather than inheritance taxation. At the same time the risky investment argument should not be overdone. For one thing, individuals are directly responsible for only a small proportion of physical capital formation in the UK and so one is mainly concerned with the choice between financial assets. In the latter case, it is by no means always true that the substitution of a capital tax for an income tax would have sensible results: it would, for instance, have tended to

[1] *Select Committee on a Wealth Tax*, HC 696 I-IV (HMSO November 1975). The tax rate structure assumed is of crucial importance for such calculations.

encourage the purchase of steel shares relatively to, say, those of computer firms in the early 1960s in the UK. In other words, one may have a low price/earnings ratio for stocks affected by political considerations and a high price/earnings ratio for stocks with low current dividends but expected high future dividends.

Sometimes it is agreed that net worth taxation might be preferable to income taxation from a work incentive viewpoint. To illustrate,[1] an income tax of 110 per cent would give an obvious incentive to suppress income. But the same yield, and for that matter similar distributional effects, could be obtained from a net worth tax of 9 per cent and an income tax of 50 per cent if the yield on capital were 15 per cent, whilst leaving substantial incentives to earn additional income. But there are some dangers here. Even if the combination of net worth and income taxes left substantial incentives at the margin to earn income for the purpose of current consumption, those whose principal motive for additional effort was the prospect of more current saving, or future consumption, would be much more adversely affected.[2]

Another argument for income tax replacement is that under inflationary conditions it is very hard to measure investment income satisfactorily and so the abolition of income tax on investment income, capital gains tax and stamp duties and their replacement by annual capital taxation would be preferable.[3] But these proposals are not very convincing. First, it is admittedly not easy to correct income taxation properly for inflation but it is not impossible, and to ditch the principle of similar taxation of people in similar circumstances on this account is a very drastic step. Second, there would be immense difficulties of administration – partly in terms of the numbers who would need to be assessed for wealth tax each year and partly in terms of integrating the domestic wealth tax with the foreign income taxation of investment income to or from abroad. So one cannot really feel that this is a rewarding path to follow.

1.4 *Conclusions*

One has to distinguish between the different reasons why people own very differing amounts of non-human capital. The arguments against capital derived from inheritance and perhaps also capital gains, are stronger than those against capital derived from accumulation.

[1] Cf. *Report on Japanese Taxation* (SCAP, Tokyo, 1949).

[2] See p. 79, above.

[3] See J. S. Flemming and I. M. D. Little, *Why We Need a Wealth Tax* (Methuen, 1974).

Although this consideration as such does not automatically lead to the inference that the main reliance should be on transfer taxation rather than on wealth taxation, it points in that direction. And none of the other arguments in favour of wealth taxation is sufficiently weighty to alter this conclusion.

2 TAXATION OF CAPITAL TRANSFERS

2.1 *The integration argument*

The idea of including gifts and bequests in the income tax system was put forward by Henry Simons some fifty years ago, as already mentioned.[1] To make any such system effective one is driven to the inclusion of such transfers in the income of the donee, but without any corresponding deduction from the income of the donor. For deductions at donor level would clearly not add to the taxable capacity of the two individuals taken together, except in so far as the donee's marginal income tax rate exceeded the donor's. On the other hand, most people have felt somewhat uneasy about the implication that transfers could be thought of as part of either consumption or saving of the donor. Furthermore, it has generally been agreed that averaging provisions of some sort[2] would be inescapable if the whole of gifts and bequests received were to be included as part of income subject to progressive tax rates. In so far as one attaches importance to relating the taxation of any particular gift or bequest to gifts and bequests made in previous years (the lifetime cumulation principle being the best-known example), there is still another reason why one may want to have a system of taxing gifts and bequests which is separate from the income tax system.

Suppose we now imagine that there is a personal expenditure tax in being. Would one still argue for separate taxation of gifts and bequests?

It should first of all be noted that the parallel with the income tax case is not exact. Whereas the integrated approach would always (minimum exemption levels apart) mean that both donor and donee would pay tax in the income tax case, this would not be so with the expenditure tax. In that case, the donor would always include the gift as

[1] See p. 401, above.

[2] See Meade Committee *Report*, *op. cit.*, pp. 137–40 for a discussion of different methods of averaging.

part of his expenditure but the donee would not suffer any additional tax liability so long as he did not run down the assets he received either for the purpose of additional consumption or additional transfers to others.

There has been a sharp division of opinion recently on whether to integrate gifts and bequests into an expenditure system. The Meade Committee on the whole argued against[1] on the grounds that expenditure averaging would then be necessary and that integration would make it impossible to apply the lifetime cumulation principle. On the other hand, Kay and King (themselves members of the Meade Committee) have subsequently argued in favour of an integrated system[2] on the grounds that this would widen the expenditure tax base and be an effective means of taxing owner-occupiers of houses.[3] They also maintained that the averaging problem was not a serious one in that donors could make gifts in years which suited them and (unlike the income tax case) donees would not be automatically taxed in the year of receipt.

Despite much recent discussion it is unlikely that an expenditure tax will be introduced soon, if at all, and so we shall not spend long on this debate. But it does seem worth making the point that it is not as easy as all that for donors to choose the date of making gifts. No one to our knowledge has yet developed a reliable system of forecasting the dates of deaths of individuals; nor are most people likely to feel that they can safely part with all their assets during their lifetime. So it is not clear that the need for averaging would be eliminated. There are also such further points as the greater flexibility in defining the appropriate family unit if one has a separate transfer tax. It is not axiomatic that the same definition is appropriate for 'ordinary' income and for gifts and bequests, but it is very hard to avoid that if one has an integrated system. There are also some formidable problems of integrating gifts and estates taxation into expenditure taxation if the latter applies only to a small fraction of the population.[4] Nor is there any easy way of taxing gifts at different rates to bequests in the integrated approach.

[1] *Op. cit.*, p. 513.

[2] *Op. cit.*, pp. 170–2.

[3] On the grounds that if the value of houses passed from one generation to the next were part of a progressive expenditure tax system, this would be an effective means of cutting down the concessions which owner-occupiers have won over the years.

[4] See A. R. Prest, 'Expenditure Tax Implementation' in *Annual Conference Proceedings*, Canadian Tax Foundation (Toronto, 1979).

Our conclusion is therefore that, whether one has an income tax or an expenditure tax system, the separate taxation of gifts and bequests is preferable to an integrated approach.

2.2 *Separate taxation*

If one is to have a separate system of taxing transfers, the first decision is on the *relative treatment of gifts and bequests*. As far as tax rates are concerned, there are arguments for and against making tax rates lower for gifts than bequests. On the one hand, lower rates are likely to encourage gifts inter-vivos relatively to transfers at death and this may well help the general aim of wealth redistribution. At least it will encourage redistribution between generations, if not between families. On the other hand, once one has different rates horrible problems arise of defining gifts in contemplation of death (so that the duty on bequests is not subject to wholesale avoidance, e.g. by death-bed gifts). On the whole, there does seem to be something to be said for encouraging gifts in life and so this would suggest a lower rate structure in that case. But it is important to maintain a reasonable relationship between the two rate structures, as is only too well illustrated by the history of the UK before 1975, when a highly progressive estate duty was allied to a zero tax on gifts made more than seven years before death. It should also be understood that harmonization of rate structures implies a consistent basis of reckoning the size of a transfer; in this respect the present UK system which bases tax on the sum of the amount transferred and the tax paid in the case of both bequests and gifts is internally far more consistent than the US Federal system which takes the gross figure, including the tax due, for bequests, but the net figure, excluding tax due, for gifts.

Another question of importance is the extent to which successive gifts, or gifts and bequests, are looked at together. One has a wide series of choices. At one extreme, one can take the whole series of gifts and bequests made (or received) over a man's lifetime, cumulate them over time and determine the relevant rate of tax on any one occasion by reference to the cumulated total received to date. Such a system becomes more complicated if one has different rate structures for gifts and bequests but not insuperably so. Alternatively, one can provide for integration over shorter periods – say ten years – if one does not wish to go as far as lifetime cumulation. There are some fairly obvious pros and cons: indexation of bracket limits in the face of inflation obviously involves one in more complexities if one has a lifetime basis rather than a shorter period. On the other hand, the lifetime principle is more likely to appeal to those anxious to curtail inheritance severely, as distinct from making it more difficult. One's judgement can go either way, but what really is important is that gifts should not be cumulated in isolation from bequests. It would make a mockery of any notion of integration to support any idea of that sort.

One other point might be made. Even if one has a system of aggregating gifts and bequests over time it would still be possible to achieve the same result as if one had separate rate schedules in the two cases by having a common rate structure but allowing interest on sums given away before death, the relevant amount being computed at the time of death.

We now consider the vexed question of *taxes on donors versus taxes on donees*. This has long been a matter of varying practices in different countries and conflicting opinions in all. For instance, the donee principle was favoured before the 1894 estate duty was introduced in this country; and for fifty-five years after that we had elements of donee as well as donor taxation. On the whole, Anglo-Saxon countries have tended to favour donor-based taxes and Continental countries donee-based ones.

As far as incentives to work, invest, save, etc., are concerned there is probably not much to choose between the two taxes. There is just one point of general principle. The arguments are sometimes cast in the form that in the donor-based case one should look at the reaction of the donor, whereas in the donee-based case one should look at those of the donee. This is fallacious. With both taxes, one must look at the combined reactions of both donor and donee if one is to have an overall picture; to do less must result in an incomplete one.

The most important consideration is that donee taxes are likely to be superior from an equity point of view. At its simplest, the proposition is that if one applies a progressive structure to donees, this will have both an immediate wealth effect in reducing tax burdens on multi-beneficiary transfers and a longer run substitution effect, encouraging the division of transfers among large, rather than small, numbers of beneficiaries. It is further assumed that this will make wealth distribution more equal – though in fact the major effect may be to redistribute down the generations (e.g. to grandchildren) inside any one family rather than between unrelated families. At a more refined level of analysis, allowance is made for the revenue effects; higher tax rates will be needed than in the donor-based case even if the pattern of division remains the same as before and yet higher rates if more fragmentation takes place – on the assumption that one is trying to raise the same revenue in both cases.[1]

Unfortunately, there are complications which are not always recognized. The first is that even if the rate structure were the same under the donor regime, we could easily have a situation where widows were treated relatively worse than grandchildren – in the sense that there is likely to be an inverse relationship between the number of beneficiaries from an estate and the degree of consanguinity. Therefore one might very well find that whereas an estate left wholly to the widow continues to pay the same amount of tax as under the old system, one which is distributed among several grandchildren pays less tax. In fact, the likely result is even worse than this. If, as we have argued, the tax rate relating to any given capital sum has to be higher under the new system than under the old, the widow who is the sole beneficiary will pay a higher absolute amount of tax than previously. So this really would be a case of adding injury to insult! Nor is it easy to dodge this outcome by incorporating an element of consanguinity relief into a donee-based tax. For it then becomes a difficult exercise to maintain the revenue yield, as much the greater part of transfers goes to immediate relatives; so if their tax burden is lightened by a concession of this kind, it becomes hard to find alternative victims.

Another nasty case is when there are descendants with very different needs. One son who is a financial genius may need very little support from his father's estate; another who is mentally deficient may need much more. Whereas a donor system allows a given total to be divided between such a progeny in whatever way is thought most appropriate without affecting the tax bill, this is not so with any simple donee tax.

A further problem with donee taxation is that there appears to be some correlation between the size of estates and the number of beneficiaries.[2] So the result of switching to the alternative system

[1]If it is said that one can accept the loss of revenue which would come from carrying over the present rate structure to an inheritance basis, then one must ask why the same loss cannot be accepted in the donor duty case – and whether the correct comparison should not be between the inheritance tax with the present (donor duty) rate structure and the donor duty with a new, lower rate structure.

[2]'The smaller the fortune, the larger the percentage of those who left all to their wives or husbands' (G. Z. Fijalkowsky-Bereday, 'The Equalising Effects of the Death Duties', *Oxford Economic Papers*, June 1950). For recent confirmation see Royal Commission on the Distribution of Income and Wealth, *Third Report on the Standing Reference*, Report No. 5, Cmnd. 6999, (HMSO 1977), p. 170. See also E. G. Horsman, 'Inheritance in England and Wales: The Evidence Provided by Wills', *Oxford Economic Papers*, November 1978.

would be to shift some of the tax burden from upper to lower wealth groups, if the progressiveness of the rate structure remained unchanged. No doubt this could be largely taken care of by an appropriate reconstruction of the rate structure but even so one might end up with some recipients of small bequests paying more tax than before.

These are formidable drawbacks to the substitution of a donee-based tax for a donor-based tax. Much as one may like the principle of encouraging a greater degree of estate splitting and much as one may think the donee principle has related advantages (e.g. the greater ease of relating the tax burden to the existing wealth of the recipient), one must recognize that the equity arguments are far from clear-cut.

So far we have said nothing about the administrative aspects. The main point here is that the administrative load of a donee-based tax would be greater, simply because tax would have to be raised from more people than before. One would not expect administrative costs to increase proportionately to the number of taxpayers but even so the additional burden would inevitably be substantial.[1] There are also some particular problems which would be awkward, especially in the trust area. Some of the most ardent devotees of donee based taxes have had qualms, or at least had to think very hard on these matters.[2] It is also significant and relevant that trusts have traditionally played a much larger role in Anglo-Saxon countries than in the Continental ones where inheritance taxation has been most prominent.

So once again, the arguments do not all go one way and one should be extremely wary about being too dogmatic on the choice between donor and donee based taxes.

We alluded to the possibility of relating tax rates to the degree of consanguinity between donor and donee. Another suggestion to be found in the literature is that the *age differential* between donor and donee should be a determinant of the tax bill.[3] The general principle is that the greater the excess of the donor's age over that of the donee the greater should be the tax bill, with the idea of minimizing the tax

[1] It was estimated in *Taxation of Capital on Death*, Cmnd. 4930 (HMSO, 1972) that the simplest form of inheritance tax would involve an additional 200 (20 per cent) official staff as a minimum, quite apart from additional work for executors and the like.

[2] Thus in a detailed survey of donee taxation on a cumulative basis it was stated: 'Trusts present a peculiarly intractable solution and no wholly satisfactory solution has presented itself.' (C. T. Sandford, J. R. M. Willis and D. J. Ironside, *An Accessions Tax*, Institute for Fiscal Studies, 1973.) And see the Meade *Report*, *op. cit.*, especially pp. 329–30 and 348–9 for the sorts of complications encountered in fitting trusts into the form of progressive transfer tax which it favours.

[3] See, for instance, W. Vickrey, *Agenda for Progressive Taxation* (Ronald Press, New York, 1947) and Meade *Report*, *op. cit.*, Chapter 15.

avoidance which can take place by 'generation skipping' (e.g. gifts direct from grandfather to grandsons rather than via sons attract one tax bill only and not two).

Age difference could be taken into account with either a donor or donee based tax though it is more usually associated with the latter; and the rationale is self-evident. Nevertheless, it is not a device which has found favour in practice with tax administrations, and for some fairly obvious reasons. One soon finds that any attempt to formulate the idea into a workable scheme results in a whole series of complications.[1] And even then one is left with awkward problems such as the ascertainment of accurate ages (e.g. if one of the parties to the transaction resides abroad); what is to be done if the donee's age exceeds that of the donor; and how one copes if one of the parties to the transaction is an institution, e.g. gifts by individuals to homes for stray dogs. All in all, one must conclude that this is not a very promising approach.

On the *rate structure* of transfer taxation, one must obviously strike a balance between the general aims of reducing disparities in reserve power and in the distribution of personal capital and the harmful effects of making the rate structure too progressive (disincentives to save, avoidance devices – emigration and the like – and sheer evasion). Reasonable men can reasonably disagree on how to strike the balance and so it would be silly to be dogmatic about it. But one or two particular points are worth noting. The more tightly one tries to restrict the ability to transmit non-human capital from one generation to another, the more will people try to secure wealth transmission in other forms. One may be able to penalize rich men from handing over real estate or securities to their children; but it is somewhat paradoxical if the consequence is the use of such assets to educate such children in the most expensive way possible. Another contentious subject is whether special relief should be given in respect of the transfer of particular assets – small businesses, firms and the like. Debate rapidly gets heated on this subject, as the purists cry out that any such concessions can only too easily defeat the whole purpose of transfer taxes, whilst the pragmatists argue in favour of enabling some enterprises to stay in the same family ownership from generation to generation. One particular point should be noted. It really is no answer on the part of the purists to say that capital markets should be improved so as to help small businesses finance themselves more easily rather than rely on transfer tax concessions. The deficiencies of capital markets in providing finance for small

[1] See below, pp. 413–14.

businesses have been recognized for at least half a century, without any one yet finding a satisfactory set of solutions. One other point remains to be made. If a transfer tax is being considered as a supplement to an expenditure tax rather than an income tax, one must beware that stiff transfer taxation may negate one of the reasons for substituting an expenditure tax for an income tax. We saw earlier[1] that the introduction of an expenditure tax would remove the bias against long-lived saving relatively to short-lived which is inherent in the income tax case. But in so far as transfers and transfer taxes are more associated with long-lived than short-lived saving, bias would reappear.

There are many *other features* of transfer taxation which would need extensive discussion in a comprehensive treatment. The definition of the tax unit is one: there are arguments both for and against an individual basis and often there is some compromise, such as the present UK position where the individual is the taxable unit but transfers between spouses are exempt. Another major subject is the scope of the tax coverage: whether it refers to people resident, ordinarily resident or domiciled in the UK or some wider group; and whether it refers to all assets located in the UK (or only those owned by certain categories of people), and whether it covers some assets located abroad.[2] And whatever one does in the transfer tax area in the UK, one needs extensive legislation relating to the different kinds of trusts found in the country. Finally, transfers to charities raise many questions.

All these latter matters are discussed in detail in the Meade *Report*[3] and it may be useful to conclude this section with a brief account of the main proposal made therein with respect to transfer taxation. It was proposed to introduce a progressive annual wealth and accession tax (PAWAT) which had two components, a positive one and a negative one. The positive element was to be arrived at by levying a tax on the donee which would depend on the size of the gift, the cumulative total of gifts received during the donee's lifetime and the excess of a notional high age (say, 85), over the donee's actual age. This positive element

[1] See p. 82, above.

[2] Thus the UK capital transfer tax applies to all assets, wherever located, if the donor is domiciled or deemed to be domiciled in this country; and to all assets located in this country regardless of domicile of the donor. 'Deemed domicile' in turn covers such cases as domicile in the UK during the three years prior to 10 December 1974 (when the detailed proposals were first announced) or residence in the UK in at least 17 of the preceeding 20 years or changes of domicile from the UK to the Channel Islands or the Isle of Man since that date.

[3] *Op. cit.*, Chapter 15.

could be thought of as an annual tax on wealth transmitted but paid as a lump sum at the date of transmission, the appropriate multiplier being given by the age factor.

A negative element would appear when any donor who had previously paid an element of positive tax in turn transmitted capital to someone else – this negative amount in turn depending on the size of the gift, the difference between age 85 and the donor's age and some tax rate related to his previous accessions of wealth. So the net yield of the tax in any one year would depend on the difference between the positive and negative elements.

A system of this sort would have many implications. To illustrate, it could be organized in such a way as to encourage early transfers of *inherited* wealth but it would be difficult to avoid discouragement of early giving of *accumulated* wealth.[1] But it will be obvious from our previous remarks that we should find it difficult to support a system which embraces the donee, lifetime accumulation and age difference principles so wholeheartedly, quite apart from the very serious reservations one must have about the administrative implications of such a formidably complex set of arrangements.[2]

3 WEALTH TAXATION

3.1 *Introduction*

We took the view earlier that the case for taxing wealth as such was less clear-cut and less compelling than that for taxing wealth transfers. Nevertheless, this does not rule out a secondary role for wealth taxation. Many countries (e.g. the Scandinavian ones) have had wealth taxes for many years[3] as well as some form of capital transfer taxation. The Meade Committee[4] thought that wealth taxation might have a role to play, particularly in the context of a proportional form of transfer taxation. Finally, one must be aware that the TUC and the Labour Party have had leanings in this direction for many years. In fact the

[1] In the first case, the difference in the multiplier applied to the positive and negative components is greater, the higher the ages of the two parties concerned; moreover, the relevant tax rate for the donee may be less, the lower his age. In the second case there is only a positive tax component and the amount will be less the older the donee, quite apart from the advantages of deferral to the donor.

[2] See A. R. Prest, 'The Meade Committee Report', *British Tax Review*, Number 3, 1978.

[3] There are records of capital taxes in 1571 and in 1613 to ransom the city of Alvsborg from the Danes. See M. Norr *et al.*, *Taxation in Sweden* (Harvard Law School International Program in Taxation, Little Brown & Co., Boston, 1959), Chapter 14.

[4] *Op. cit.*, Chapter 16.

1974 Labour Government declared that it intended to introduce such a tax[1] and was only deflected from its course after the Report of a Parliamentary Select Committee.[2] And the TUC has continued to argue the case right up to the time of writing.[3]

3.2 *Key questions*

There are four major groups of questions to be raised if one is contemplating the introduction of a wealth tax – the people to be included, the assets to be covered, the rate structure and the administrative machinery.

On the *people* included, one must first of all decide on an exemption limit. It has usually been argued that any such tax could not be applied effectively to large numbers of people and so the sort of exemption limit often advocated in the UK is about £100,000.[4] In thinking about the types of people to be covered the usual kind of thought has been that one should keep in step with the capital transfer tax system, so that whatever decisions taken with respect to the inclusion of people resident, ordinarily resident or domiciled would apply in the wealth tax case too. Similarly, it has been maintained that any such tax would apply to assets held in trust as well as in unfettered individual ownership. On the other hand, the case for parallel definitions of the tax unit for both types of tax has not been so uniformly accepted. Thus, as we have seen, the Labour Government's capital transfer tax of 1975 provided for individual liability in that case, but with no tax liability for transfers between spouses; on the other hand the 1974 wealth tax Green Paper[5] quite specifically left open the alternatives of taxing separately or aggregating assets of husbands and wives, though it was insistent that children's wealth should be aggregated with parental.

On *asset* coverage, much the same point about geographical location (e.g. whether to include assets of foreigners located in the UK) applies as with the definition of people to be subject to tax: keep in step with the transfer tax rules. As for different types of asset, the usual argument has been to start from an all-inclusive definition and then consider whether there was a pressing case for any exemptions. The most heated arguments have related to small businesses, farms and woodlands, art treas-

[1] See *Wealth Tax*, Cmnd. 5704 (HMSO, August 1974).

[2] See *Select Committee on a Wealth Tax*, HC. 696 I–IV, *op. cit.*

[3] E.g. TUC, *Annual Review* (London, 1978).

[4] In 1973 this would have meant a total of 110,000 taxpayers, assuming that wealth of husband and wife was not aggregated, HC, 694–IV, *op. cit.*, Appendix 124.

[5] Cmnd. 5704, *op. cit.*

ures, houses and household chattels and pension rights. We shall come back to some of these later but it might be noted straightaway that one cannot look to capital transfer taxation rules for any guidance on the inclusion and valuation of pension rights.

The *rate structure* is obviously linked to the previous questions about exemption limits and (if progressive) the aggregation of wealth of married couples. It also must depend on the transfer tax rate structures (e.g. the Meade Committee was prepared to support a wealth tax with a proportional, but not a progressive, transfer tax rate structure) and on whether the wealth tax is a substitute for or a complement to the investment income surcharge.

A frequent suggestion has been a spread of rates from 1.0 per cent (at, say, £100,000) to 2.5 per cent (or possibly 5 per cent) at £5 millions. But these figures are no more than crude illustrations and one cannot give flesh and blood to any ideas about the rate structure without settling all the questions already mentioned. Whatever the precise solution, the case for applying indexation to exemption and bracket limits is unanswerable.

On wealth tax *administration*, all commentators have been aware of the enormous valuation tangles which could so easily arise if steps were not taken to avoid them. So various mitigating suggestions have often been made, such as periodic rather than annual valuations and self-assessment of capital value and tax liability, etc.

3.3 *Major difficulties*

That the introduction and implementation of a wealth tax could hardly take place without friction is borne out by the experiences of the 1975 Select Committee.[1] Four volumes of statements, evidence, discussions and memoranda totalling some 2,000 pages in all appeared. Of this total the *joint* report of the Committee occupied precisely two paragraphs, as it was only found possible to produce a series of minority reports – in fact five in all. The contents of the minority reports differed enormously from tongue-in-cheek proposals which were obviously meant to discredit the whole idea to fundamentalist egalitarian drum-beating without even a semblance of economic analysis.[2]

The catalogue of problems is so lengthy that we shall have to be highly selective in illustrating them. Let us take three of the matters

[1] HC. 696, *op. cit.*

[2] For discussion, see A. R. Prest, 'The Select Committee on a Wealth Tax', *British Tax Review*, No. 1, 1976.

discussed by the Meade Committee: pensions, housing and household chattels.

The Committee declared categorically that it would include pension rights and seemed perfectly happy with the proposition that a table of 88 columns would cover the majority of cases. But as an illustration of the difficulties of trying to cover pension rights before they are taken up, one might refer to the Government Actuary's evidence to the Select Committee[1] that a 30-year-old man's rights to an indexed pension of £1,000 payable from age 60 plus a lump sum of £3,000 at that time could be given a present value ranging from £580 at one extreme to £60,190 at the other, depending on a fairly restricted set of assumptions about the interest rate, the tax rate and the inflation rate.

We have here a situation where whatever is done lands one in trouble. If all pension rights are included, there are extraordinarily difficult valuation problems; and if only pensions rights of those drawing them or entitled to draw them are included, one immediately introduces discrimination against elderly people; and if one leaves them out entirely, there is discrimination between people with and without substantial pension rights.

On housing the Committee hoped to take a short cut by seizing on a proposal made by the Layfield Committee[2] for adopting capital values of residential property as the future basis for local rates. But quite apart from whether this proposal will ever be adopted it is clear that it would not serve the Committee's purposes as the Layfield proposals were for capital valuations which would reflect the benefits of *occupation* rather than of *ownership*. Thus a short leasehold and a freehold property comparable in other respects would have the same valuation for rating purposes; but it would be utterly inappropriate to attach identical valuations to them for wealth tax purposes. In other words, if one does want to include house ownership in the wealth tax coverage, and it is very hard to see good reasons for omitting it, there is no alternative to special valuations on a fairly regular basis.

On chattels,[3] the Committee suggested a limit of £1,000 for individual items. This would obviously include a large number of cars and one cannot think that to be desirable. On the other hand, the

[1] HC. 696, I–IV, *op. cit.*, Appendix 143.

[2] Cmnd. 6453, *op. cit.*, 1976.

[3] Although we do not here discuss the valuation of works of art, it might be noted that the Select Committee (*op. cit.*, Appendix 44) asked well-known art dealers for their valuation of specific works of art – and received very varying answers, differing by a factor of 20 to 1 in one case (presumably a guide on which art dealers one should approach for sales and which for purchases, if nothing else).

Government's 1974 Green Paper suggested that each wealth taxpayer might be allowed an exemption of one car – presumably a sales drive for Rolls-Royce or other high-priced vehicles.

3.4 *Summary*

Overall, the more one inspects the wealth tax at close quarters the more one is inclined to shy away from it. Neither on grounds of principle nor of practicability does it have an obvious appeal. And if the question is asked, how is it that it works successfully in other countries, one must take leave to ask whether it does. One observation is that many wealth items (e.g. pension rights) are not covered; another is that highly conventional valuations are often accepted for those items (e.g. owner-occupied houses) which are included; and the third is that revenue contributions from the tax are exiguously small.[1]

4 POLICY FOR THE UK

Any newcomer to these matters might be forgiven for adopting either of two extreme attitudes: *either* that after the sweat of remodelling the whole system of capital transfer taxation in this country as recently as 1975, the first really major overhaul for eighty years, the new system should be left to run itself in for many years without any major amendments; *or* that the demonstrable advantages of accessions taxation and wealth taxation are such that no time at all should be lost in implementing either or both proposals.

A more judicious approach than either of the above might be to study the actual working of capital transfer tax in some detail and try to judge the extent to which it is fulfilling its purposes – whether the rate structure needs amendment, whether the list of special treatments is too long or too short, and so on. Inevitably, it will take some time before sufficient information is available to come to any reasonably firm conclusions. But it would seem much wiser to wait until that is possible than to clamour for immediate action on the lines of the latest brainwave. This is in no sense a plea for keeping the status quo at all costs; there may well be a case for substantial changes, but until the necessary experience has been gained with the new format it is extremely hard to judge whether there is one or not.

One change could be made immediately, however, and that is to

[1] E.g. Sweden, 0.7 per cent of all revenue, Germany 1.3 per cent. See C. T. Sandford, J. R. M. Willis and D. J. Ironside, *An Annual Wealth Tax* (Institute for Fiscal Studies, 1975).

introduce indexation of the bracket limits and the various exemptions in capital transfer tax. There is no excuse of any sort whatever for leaving this to the administrative discretion of ministers and civil servants. No doubt there can be plenty of arguments about the inappropriateness of any single price index one chooses to name. They should be firmly squashed and a decision taken to use the retail price index without further ado.

16

COMPANY TAXATION – THE DEFINITION OF PROFITS

1 INTRODUCTION

There are many problems of great interest in the formulation of any policy for taxing companies. We cannot possibly deal with them all and so we shall concentrate on three. In this chapter we shall discuss the decisions on income definition which must be made before profits are assessed for taxation and, in the next, the appropriate form and rate of company taxation and its integration, partial or otherwise, with personal income taxation. In the following chapter various international aspects will be considered. Obviously these three chapters, and indeed Chapters 13 and 15, are interrelated; the harshness of treatment under the one heading must influence policy under the other. But everything cannot be discussed simultaneously and it seems logical to take the computation of profits first, and then to discuss the rate of taxation, provided that we recognize the interdependence of all these subjects as we proceed.

Proceeding on the assumption, which we shall reconsider later, that we do want to tax the profits of corporations in some direct fashion, we first of all review, in section 2, what we might take as the appropriate computation of profits in the absence of persistent inflation. In section 3 we take into account the three main modifications when inflation is endemic: the measurement of depreciation of fixed assets, the necessary adjustments for inventories and changes in the real value of monetary assets and liabilities. In section 4 we look at the range and characteristics of adjustments to profits implied by various measures aimed at encouraging fixed capital formation; finally, section 5 is specifically concerned with the UK situation.

2 THE CORPORATION INCOME TAX (NO PERSISTENT INFLATION)

It is usual to distinguish three major areas of controversy in deciding on the appropriate base for the taxation of corporate income: the measurement of depreciation of fixed assets, the measurement of inventory profits and the treatment of capital gains and losses. Each of these will be discussed on its own initially but we conclude by examining some of the interrelations.

2.1 *The depreciation of fixed assets*

A number of questions can be raised about the appropriate measurement of depreciation of fixed assets. First, it is often said that the list of items for which wear and tear allowances are granted against profits by the Inland Revenue is incomplete. For instance, no allowances are given in respect of the depreciation of the great majority of non-industrial buildings. Second, it is frequently alleged that the period over which the Inland Revenue decrees that particular capital assets may be expected to last is often too long, i.e. that capital equipment is likely to be replaced before the date laid down by the revenue authorities. Thirdly, the time-pattern of the allowances granted is frequently criticized. In the UK the traditional pattern for plant and machinery was the diminishing balance method, which allows the same percentage rate of write-off each year but applies it to a diminishing balance, e.g. if the allowance rate is 10 per cent, in the first year of life the sum allowed on a capital expenditure of £100 is £10, in the second year £9 (i.e. 10 per cent of £90), in the third year £8.1 (i.e. 10 per cent of £81), etc. The straight-line method by which an equal absolute amount is written off each year applies to buildings in the UK, and as we have seen,[1] is in widespread use in the US.

In fact, the first problem, though important for some individual industries, is a fairly marginal one for the economy as a whole and was made less so after the introduction of depletion allowances for minerals in the UK in 1963 and depreciation on hotel buildings in 1978. The second problem was largely taken care of by the traditional system of balancing allowances which enabled a firm to recover for tax purposes the difference between the written-down value of an asset and its sale value when the asset was disposed of. The word 'largely' should be noted: the balancing allowance is less favourable to a firm than a system which correctly anticipates the life of capital equipment, in that some of the allowances due to it are deferred in time and hence worth less in terms of present value. But it should also be noted that, as we shall see later,[2] the problem was alleviated by major changes in the

[1] Cf. Appendix to Part II.

[2] See p. 441.

1971 and 1972 Budgets which introduced faster write-offs for many assets. These changes were also highly relevant to the third item mentioned above. So by and large none of these issues can be said to be strikingly important today.

Another argument is that the use of original cost depreciation allowances will give a false picture of profits in times of rising or falling prices and may therefore exaggerate fluctuations in income and output. In the boom, businessmen will think that, profits being so much greater, they should increase their rate of capital investment; dividend outpayments will be greater and hence consumption will be greater; trade unions will be tempted to press for higher wages when they see high profit figures, and conversely in the slump.

It is not difficult to pick holes in this chain of arguments. First of all, larger assessed profits in the boom will mean larger tax payments which, if government expenditure remains unchanged, will be a deflationary offset. Second, businessmen are surely sufficiently shrewd to realize that a high rate of return on old capital does not necessarily presage a high rate of return on newer, more expensive capital. Third, we know that many business firms deliberately step up their depreciation allocations in good times, even though allowances for tax purposes remain unchanged: as a consequence, one cannot assume that dividend payments will increase proportionately or anything like proportionately to net profits as assessed for tax purposes. So it seems fair to conclude, with the Royal Commission on Taxation, that this general problem 'appeared to us to rest mainly in imagination'.[1]

2.2 *The valuation of inventories*

Turning to inventories, the essential point is that under the usual FIFO ('first-in-first-out') system allowed by the Inland Revenue in this country, the increase in the money value of stocks over an accounting period is counted as an element of taxable profit, irrespective of whether it represents an increase in the physical volume of stocks held or simply a rise in the price level.[2] Conversely, if prices fall over a year the reduction in the value of stocks is reflected in taxable profits too; in fact, in this case a further concession is normally made in that if the market price of any items of stock at the end of the accounting year is less than that at which they were bought, the end-year value can be computed on the former basis. If prices rise during the next accounting

[1] Cmd. 9474, p. 112.
[2] See Chapter 9, section 2.1.3 for detailed illustrations.

period, assessable profits will be pro tanto greater than they would be if no concession were made, and so the value of the concession is limited, but none the less the deferment of tax is a valuable concession.

A number of reforms to the FIFO system have been suggested, but by far the most important is the proposal for LIFO ('last-in-first-out') accounting as is allowed in the USA (if also followed for financial reporting). The essence of this system is that stocks should be deemed to be used up in the reverse order to that in which they were bought. If, therefore, the volume of stocks is the same at the beginning and end of the accounting period there will be no inventory profit recorded over the year, however much prices rise. If, however, the volume of stocks increases over the year LIFO does not provide complete protection against the taxation of inventory profits. If an amount of stock equal to the increase in volume between the opening and closing dates of the period was bought at the opening date prices, LIFO will still prevent inventory profits from arising. If, however, purchases at opening-date prices are less in volume than the increase in quantity over the year, LIFO will only give partial protection against inventory profit taxation. Although there are a number of other methods of valuing stock in terms of constant prices at the beginning and end of a period, we can concentrate here on the FIFO versus LIFO arguments, as they exemplify all the main issues of principle as well as being the two most important alternatives.

If inventory profits are purely transient events, being offset more or less from one year to another by inventory losses, they are of no serious consequence. In fact, it could well be argued that the present (FIFO) system, which involves larger profits in times of rising prices than any system of valuing opening and closing stocks in terms of constant prices, is likely to have the better counter-cyclical properties. Firms pay higher taxes when they can best afford them and lower taxes when they are most pressed; conversely, the government receives higher taxes when they are most necessary. It might, of course, be true that a partial alternative to higher taxation in the upswing would be greater corporate or personal saving – but this is no more than a partial alternative. But if we have a situation of persistent inflation we cannot shrug off the problems as easily, as we shall see in the next section.

2.3 *Capital gains and losses*

The third major question of principle is whether capital gains and losses should in general be considered to be part of the profits of a corporation. We are now back to the same sorts of questions as those raised in relation to personal income tax in Chapter 13. If one argues by analogy from the measurement of social income, one would not include them; but if one accepts the premises of the comprehensive income tax as applying to corporations one would include them. In fact, the usual practise is to include them but tax at a lower rate than other income – a compromise without any theoretical justification but with obvious attractions to legislators.

2.4 *Interrelations*

Turning to interrelations between capital gains questions and fixed asset and inventory treatment, it is instructive to look at an argument by Kaldor[1] that the erosion of capital equipment through time and usage can be thought of as a gradually accruing capital loss. On this basis, it can be argued that in strict logic there is no general ground for giving any depreciation allowances whatever to business firms. If capital gains are completely exempt from taxation, there is no case for compensating for capital losses at all. If, on the other hand, capital gains are taxed as they are realized, allowances should be given for capital losses as they are realized,[2] but not as under the usual system, more or less as they accrue. Only under a system which taxed capital gains as they accrued would it be reasonable to spread depreciation allowances over the life of the equipment so as to recoup original cost by the date of retirement of the asset. As we never have such a system of taxing capital gains, then it would follow that there is no case for the usual cost depreciation system. However, most analysts have not been willing to carry through their logic as far as this.

If we approach the measurements of profits from the social angle, some system of eliminating inventory profits due to price changes seems to be called for; if, on the other hand, we think that all capital gains should be fully taxed, then the present system achieves just that. If prices of inventories rise in the course of a year and a manufacturer raises the price of his finished products, he will make capital gains in respect of those inventories purchased before the rise in prices.[3] This is

[1] *Indian Tax Reform*, *op. cit.*, pp. 72 ff.

[2] If, exceptionally, capital equipment were disposed of at a higher price than its original cost to the firm, the difference would then be taxable as a realized capital gain, *op. cit.*, p. 79.

[3] If, in the short run, the manufacturer does not raise prices of finished products as material costs rise, the profit figure for tax purposes and hence the amount of tax paid will tend to remain unchanged, the increased value of inventories being offset by greater working costs.

the issue, and the argument about whether in reality the stocks bought first are used up first, or vice versa, is just a red herring.

We have clearly not exhausted all matters relating to 'true economic' depreciation or to the appropriate treatment of inventories, or the relation of either of these two taxes to the taxation of capital gains, but the main questions arising in the taxation of corporation profits in the absence of persistent inflation have at least been aired.

3 THE CORPORATION INCOME TAX (PERSISTENT INFLATION)

We have now to reconsider the measurement of depreciation of fixed assets, the treatment of inventory profits and more general matters of capital gains taxation, when we allow for the possibility of persistent inflation.

3.1 *The depreciation of fixed assets*

If we approach the definition of business income from that of social income there seems to be some case for saying that the replacement cost basis for depreciation is the right one. Social income can be taken as the flow of goods and services which can be consumed without running down the nation's stock of capital. The national capital can in turn be thought of as remaining intact if the aggregate discounted value of the flow of services expected from it is the same at the end of a year as at the beginning of a year, after making sure that the calculation of expected returns is in terms of common prices and interest rates and that any changes, up or down, of a windfall character are left on one side. Although the calculation of depreciation on a replacement cost basis does not give any exact correspondence with this theoretical concept, the degree of correspondence is obviously far greater in times of changing prices than if the original cost basis is used. On this basis, we conclude that there is some theoretical case for replacement cost depreciation in the determination of business income.

Suppose we now approach the question from a different angle, the viewpoint of the ordinary shareholders in a firm. If inflation develops after a piece of capital equipment is installed, there must be a tendency for a rise in the price of the product made by the capital equipment and hence of the value of that equipment, as well as a rise in the price of new equipment of the same sort. Either the increase in demand for the products of firms will tend to bid up the prices of new capital equipment used by them, or the rise in the price of new capital equipment will itself tend to force up the prices of products. In both cases there will be an increase in the value of old as well as a rise in the price of new equipment. Of course, the proposition is only a very general one and all sorts of short-term influences (e.g price control over public utilities) may obscure its influence. But the influence will be at work whether or not there is any surface indication that it is at work. If this point is accepted, an important conclusion follows. Any increase in the value of existing equipment during a period of inflation will mean that capital gains are being made by the owners as their assets gradually increase in value. If therefore any policy is adopted of allowing depreciation to be claimed on an exact replacement cost basis, this is tantamount to exempting accrued gains of this kind from taxation. If the original cost system is adhered to, these capital gains are subject to the full weight of profits and income taxes. If an alternative policy is adopted, such as the variation of depreciation allowances in accordance with some general index number of prices, it is only real capital gains in the sense of the gains made by the owners of any one firm after correcting for the general change in the value of money which are taxed. Of these three lines of policy, the third would seem the most correct one to pursue.

Another argument is that a firm will not have sufficient funds to replace capital equipment in times of rising prices, unless depreciation is on a replacement cost basis. This view has often been put forward but it need not detain us long, as it can easily be seen to have no general validity. The central weakness is that the argument need not hold when net investment is taking place. Suppose we imagine a machine with a ten-year life purchased in year 0 for £100 and assume depreciation to be on a straight line basis. Imagine that an additional machine of exactly the same kind is purchased with the aid of new funds in year 5. Then in year 10, if there has been no change in the prices of these machines, the common depreciation fund will have accumulated £150 and there will therefore be £50 to spare over and above what is needed for the replacement of the first machine. Suppose that another machine is also bought out of new funds in year 10, so that the total stock rises to three machines. Then by parity of reasoning the amount in the depreciation fund in year 15 will be £100 greater than is needed for replacement purposes. Thus it can easily be seen that with a continuously growing stock of capital there will always be funds to spare if prices remain unchanged. Therefore it must follow that if prices of re-equipment do in fact rise, depreciation funds will only become inadequate if the outflow due to the price rise is more than sufficient to offset the inflow due to net investment.[1]

This is the central point about this argument, but in addition it must be remembered that there is no holy writ that replacement of capital equipment can be met only from accumulated depreciation funds. There are many other funds (e.g. past or current undistributed profits) which would have to be exhausted before it could be deduced that inadequate depreciation accounting would mean failure to replace capital equipment. Nor is there any empirical evidence in the post-war period to justify this notion of insufficiency of funds for replacement needs.[2]

Even though the insufficiency of funds argument is not convincing it clearly is the case that replacement cost depreciation based on changes in the general price level is more satisfactory conceptually than original cost depreciation or replacement cost depreciation based on asset prices. This is not to say that inflation adjustment cannot be solved by other very different means, a subject to which we shall return later. But replacement cost is one way of coping with the issue.

3.2 *The valuation of inventories*

As we have seen, a LIFO system will under some circumstances eliminate inventory profits due to rising prices. But it will not always do so, depending on such matters as the rate of turnover of stocks per annum, the distribution of stock purchases over time, the rate of price rise per annum and the smoothness or jerkiness of the price rise through the year. Nor does the LIFO principle offer any help in distinguishing between inventory profits corresponding to the rise in the general price level and profits in excess of that rise. As we saw with fixed assets, this distinction is important as one's objective should be to de-tax only gains which correspond to general price rises rather than gains in excess of such rises.

These obvious drawbacks with the LIFO system have led to many

[1] Cf. A. R. Prest, 'Replacement Cost Depreciation', *Accounting Research*, July, 1950 (reprinted in R. H. Parker and G. C. Harcourt (eds), *Readings in the Concept and Measurement of Income* (Cambridge University Press, 1969). A more comprehensive discussion of these matters is to be found in E. D. Domar, 'Depreciation, Replacement and Growth', *Economic Journal*, March 1953 (reprinted in *Essays in the Theory of Economic Growth* (Oxford University Press, 1957)).

[2] E.g. The Richardson Committee (*Report of Committee on Turnover Taxation* Cmnd. 2300 (HMSO, 1964), pp. 44 and 89) showed that after 1958 the (adjusted) total of annual allowances was actually higher than that for capital consumption.

suggestions over the years about the precise way in which inventory profits corresponding to the rise in the general price level should be eliminated from the tax base. The usual proposal is that one should apply a general price correction factor to some level of stocks (e.g. stocks at beginning-, mid- or end-year) and allow a deduction of this amount against inventory profits as usually computed. But it is easy to see that there is plenty of scope for argument about the precise way the adjustment should be made.[1] As we saw in Chapter 9, the rough and ready solution of deferring tax in respect of inventory gains exceeding a certain proportion of pre-tax profits has been adopted in the UK since 1974. It would only be by coincidence that this relief scheme would meet the criteria for correct adjustment. Nevertheless, it is an example of a scheme which can be made operational and does provide a measure of rough justice.

3.3 *Net monetary assets and liabilities*[2]

We now come to the most difficult and controversial item in profits adjustment in the face of inflation: changes in the real value of net monetary assets and liabilities. The general idea here is simply that even if nominal values of assets and liabilities remain unchanged, real capital gains will be made by firms which are net debtors and real capital losses by those which are net creditors. If the objective is to include all real capital gains and losses in the corporation tax base, there is just as much of a case for including any gains and losses of this sort as those relating to fixed assets and inventories, or, for that matter, real changes in the value of equity holdings (as discussed in Chapter 13).

Although the general principle is not too difficult to state, the detailed application is far from simple. To begin with, one cannot apply the concept to corporations in isolation. It would be quite invidious not to apply it to unincorporated businesses. But if one applies it to all business transactions, why should not personal capital gains and losses, whether arising from monetary relationships with the private or the public sector, also be adjusted in the same way? Once one starts to go down the road of including real losses and gains from monetary assets and liabilities one has to make corrections right across the board and

[1] See, for instance, Chapter 1 of H. J. Aaron (ed.), *Inflation and the Income Tax* (Brookings Institution, Washington DC, 1976); and Chapter XIV of the Mathews Committee Report on *Inflation and Taxation* (Canberra, 1975).

[1] See also Chapter 13, section 5.

not just to a few selected transactions or a few selected assets and liabilities.

The sort of problem which arises in detailed application can be illustrated in the following way. Suppose that someone makes a loan of £1,000, and the pre-tax return is £100, or 10 per cent. Let the tax rate be 50 per cent, so that the after-tax rate of return is 5 per cent. The loan would then be worth £1,050 at the end of a year. But now suppose that prices rise by 10 per cent during the year, implying a real capital loss of £100 to the lender and hence a substantial overall loss in real terms if there is no tax offset for the capital loss (and, for that matter, only a zero real rate of return even if tax offsets are possible). We can easily see that to maintain the lender's position intact in real terms, a pre-tax return of 21 per cent and full capital loss offset against tax will be needed. The end result would then be an after-tax income of £105 and a tax offset of £50 (in respect of £100 capital loss), making a total at the end of the year of £1155 i.e. a sum which in real terms is equal to the £1,050 which would have prevailed in the absence of inflation. Putting the point about rates of return algebraically, we can say that they must rise by a factor representing not just price inflation but also the decline in the real value of debt. We shall require that[1]

$$r = i(1 + \dot{p}) + \dot{p}$$

where r is the new interest rate, i is the old interest rate and $\dot{p}$ is the rate of price increase.

So a net return of 15.5 per cent is needed to compensate for a 10 per cent price rise if the original return was 5 per cent.

4 STIMULATION OF FIXED CAPITAL FORMATION

4.1 *Alternative methods*

Stimulation can take several forms. The first is to adjust wear and tear allowances wholly or partially to a replacement cost basis. The second is some form of accelerated depreciation which permits the advancement in time of the usual depreciation allowances. The third is the abolition of the regulations for spreading depreciation allowances over time according to predetermined rules. The fourth is the encouragement of investment by special subsidy. Although

[1] See H. J. Aaron, *ibid.*, and 'Inflation and the Income Tax', *American Economic Review*, May 1976, for a modern exposition. Irving Fisher (*Appreciation and Interest*, Macmillan, New York, 1896) made essentially the same argument.

the fourth method does not involve a change in the depreciation system, we discuss it here as it is one of the methods much in fashion since World War II.

It goes without saying that our comparison between the various methods will be based on the assumption that the amount of the tax concession per annum is assumed to be the same in each case. We are therefore looking at the comparative effects of concessions given in any one of these forms rather than taking a reduction in the rate of taxation of profits by a similar amount as our norm. But we shall none the less look at this latter possibility as well.

4.2 *The replacement cost system*

As already indicated, there are several different ways of adjusting original cost wear and tear allowances to a replacement cost basis. First, one might have a common price index of some sort for all the fixed assets entitled to wear and tear allowances, and adjust the total amount recoverable over the life of each asset according to the price rise since its purchase. Second, one might have a series of price indices for different broad types of assets. Third, one might have a system whereby one only granted additional allowances according to the extent to which the rate of price rise for any particular asset had been greater than the general price rise, and one presumably reduced the normal allowances to those firms experiencing a less than average price rise in respect of their capital equipment. Last, one might have a system which only allowed adjustments for a price change in respect of the written down value of an asset, i.e. if an asset originally costing £100 had been written down to £20 before prices changed and then prices doubled, the total amount given over the life of the asset in wear and tear plus balancing allowances would be £120.

We shall concentrate on the second of these possible meanings as exemplifying most of the issues involved. But we shall refer to the other variants as necessary. We shall also assume initially that we are dealing with a world of rising prices.

The first point is the obvious one that the absolute benefit of any reform will be greater to the firm with the greater amount of capital equipment, as measured by replacement value. It might also be thought that firms with more durable capital equipment will gain relatively more from a reform of this kind on the grounds that such equipment will tend to have a greater average age and therefore be likely to benefit more from the introduction of the replacement cost basis. This need not be so, however. If one thinks of two firms spending equal amounts on capital investment at the same time, one going for long-lived and the other for short-lived equipment, then it can be seen that the annual amount of depreciation will be less in the former than in the latter case, and hence on that score the annual benefit from the introduction of a replacement cost system will be less.

The next point is that the introduction of replacement cost allowances would confer a relatively greater benefit on those firms earning a low rate of return on their capital. If we imagine two firms with identical capital assets and with the same ratio of fixed to total capital, the *amount* of profit relieved of tax would be the same in both cases, quite irrespective of whether the total profit earned (and hence, in this case, the rate of return on capital) were greater in one case than the other. Is it desirable to boost the lower rate of return relatively more? One's inclination is to say that it is *not* desirable, but reservations must obviously be made if high profit rates are the result of monopoly rather than superior efficiency.

Inside any one industry, the introduction of replacement cost depreciation would be of greatest benefit to those firms with the oldest assets, at any rate on the assumption that prices had moved upwards continuously. It does not necessarily follow that those firms with the oldest assets are the least efficient or least dynamic in an industry, but there is obviously some presumption that they may be. As a minimum, one cannot say that the replacement cost system earns many good marks in this respect.

Finally, it can easily be seen that as between two firms, each with the same (replacement) value of capital, but one having a much larger ratio of fixed equipment to inventories than the other, the annual amount of the benefit will be greater in the first case and (on the assumption of an equal rate of return to capital whether in fixed or inventory form) the percentage of annual profits relieved of tax is also greater in the first case.

There are various practical problems in the introduction and operation of any such system (e.g. the choice of price index, knowledge of the cost of acquisition, etc.), but we shall not examine them here at all as they are so obvious and well known.

The next point we shall examine is the variant of the replacement cost system which would permit additional allowances only when the increase in the cost of capital equipment used by any one firm is greater than the general rise in prices, however measured. Here again there are the practical problems of sorting out the price rise for the many types of capital equipment which one firm may use, but they need not detain us. A concession on these lines would in effect wipe out any liability to tax on capital gains on fixed assets in times of inflation. But there is no general principle which would lead us to believe that those firms suffering the greatest rises in the prices of capital assets, and hence the greatest liability to capital gains tax, should be the ones most in need of encouragement to invest. The greater than average price rise might indicate less than average elasticity of supply of that type of capital equipment. Moreover, this type of proposal would imply a *reduction* in original cost allowances for those firms whose equipment prices have risen less than the rise in general prices.

A point must be made about the fourth variant of the replacement cost system, i.e. the adjustment of the written-down value of an asset. It is sometimes argued that this system will not produce sufficient depreciation funds to meet the cost of replacement. This does not necessarily follow. If a firm has a number of machines and the age-distribution is rectangular in shape (e.g. ten machines each lasting ten years and one being replaced every year), the addition to the depreciation fund in respect of all its machines will be sufficient to meet replacement outgoings in any one year (e.g. if the machines originally cost £100 each and then prices double, the funds available for the first machine due to be replaced at the new price level will be £200 – the sum of all depreciation allowances for that year – and not just the sum of £90 accumulated at the old price level and £20 at the new in respect of that one machine). It can be seen therefore that the correspondence between the precise form of the replacement cost allowance and the funds available for replacement depends on the general financial structure of industry. The larger the size of the financial unit, and hence the more close to rectangular the pattern of depreciation of assets, the more likely it is that the modified form of replacement cost will be sufficient.

Finally, we have constructed all our arguments about replacement cost up to this point on the assumption that we are operating in a world of rising prices. Clearly, as a long-term trend this assumption is the most realistic, but we must nevertheless ask how this system will operate under conditions of falling prices. Obviously, tax bills would be larger than under a system of original cost depreciation and so the system would be quite useless as a stimulus to investment. Unless, therefore, one thinks that periods of falling prices are likely to be so rare in future years as to be of negligible importance, this is a fundamental drawback to the replacement cost system, when we are looking at its merits as an investment stimulus.

To conclude, therefore, we may say that a replacement cost system will in a period of rising prices offer greater incentives to capital formation, but that these incentives will be distributed somewhat haphazardly among the more and less needy. In a period of falling prices, the system would offer less incentive to capital formation than the original cost method.

4.3 *Accelerated depreciation*

The essence of accelerated depreciation is simply the advancement through time of the wear and tear allowances to which a firm is normally entitled. The form which this has taken in Britain in the post-war period has been initial allowances which, as we saw in Chapter 9, were a means of enabling firms to claim a larger slice of their entitlement to allowances in the year of installation of a machine, at the direct expense of allowances in subsequent years. The total allowed remained at 100 per cent of the initial cost. In principle, it is not necessary that accelerated depreciation should take precisely this form (e.g. in some former British territories pioneer industry relief laws have taken the form of allowing new capital costs to be written off over a five-year period, at the rate of 20 per cent of initial cost per annum; in the US there have been special provisions on rather similar lines for capital expenditure incurred in the production of defence goods, and a variety of other means of hastening depreciation allowances in respect of the generality of capital expenditure),[1] but it will be convenient for us to keep our eyes fixed mainly on British experience none the less.

The most obvious advantage of accelerated depreciation is that taxpayers get the benefit of compound interest on sums involved: the present value of, say, £40 in the first year of a machine's life and £60 spread on a declining balance or straight line basis over the remaining nine years – if it lives ten years – is obviously greater than £100 recouped over ten years by either the declining balance method or the straight line method. Indeed, it has often been stated that initial allowances amount to a 'temporary, interest-free loan'. This is an understatement, however. The notion of a loan involves the idea of repayment, but there is no *necessary* repayment (e.g. if a business fails soon after claiming an initial allowance) involved in the system.

[1] See Appendix to Part II.

'Interest-free' means vastly different things to a company like ICI and the local greengrocer who claims an initial allowance for his delivery van. Nor is the notion of 'temporary' very illuminating; if in fact a firm is replacing its capital equipment evenly through time, the date of repayment will be postponed indefinitely, quite apart from the further advantages gained when it is adding to its stock of capital equipment. It seems more reasonable to characterize initial allowances as amounting to a free gift if sufficient income is earned to repay them, a larger gift if the business continues to grow, and a growing gift if the business grows at an increasing rate.[1]

Initial allowances can take and have taken a variety of different forms. It may help to sort out their inherent characteristics if we take first of all the limiting case where they amount to 100 per cent of cost, thus replacing the usual wear and tear allowances completely. We can return later to the variants.

The first point is that 100 per cent initial allowances give relief at the time when it is likely to be needed most, i.e. when new capital equipment is being installed and so are an effective alternative means of correcting for the inadequacy of original cost depreciation in times of persistent inflation. Although the correspondence between need and relief is not exact – if only because of the time lag between outlay on capital equipment and the subsequent tax remission – it must nevertheless be an enlargement of the borrowing power of a firm. As we have already seen, this enlargement is greater the higher the rate of net investment, and therefore this is a point at which the properties of the initial allowance system diverge markedly from those of the replacement cost system. The benefit now depends on the ratio of net investment to profits rather than the ratio of the stock of fixed capital to profits in the replacement cost case. Second, initial allowances will increase the willingness to undertake new capital formation and will remove the discrimination against more risky investment inherent in any income tax system in which loss offset provisions are, for one reason or another, incomplete.

Suppose we imagine that the return before tax but after depreciation on a moderately risky investment is 6 per cent and that on a really risky investment 8 per cent. If an income tax of 25 per cent is imposed, the net return is reduced to 4½ per cent in the first case and 6 per cent in the second. Neither the moderately nor the extremely risky investment will now be made; but the shortfall in the required return is greater in

[1] Cf. L. Johansen, *Public Economics*, *op. cit.*, pp. 251–6 for further discussion.

the latter case. But now suppose that instead of the usual depreciation system any new capital expenditure is immediately deductible from profits assessed for tax and that profits are large enough to absorb the charge. In both cases there will now be an immediate tax-saving, which will depend on the cost of the new capital equipment and the tax rate. If the new capital equipment costs £100 (and the tax rate is 25 per cent), there will be an immediate tax-saving of £25 as a result of the change of system. Therefore the effective cost of the new investment is £75 and not £100, but the net yields after tax can be taken as £4.50 and £6 respectively.[1] In the moderately risky case this will represent a return of 6 per cent (i.e. $\frac{4\cdot15}{75}$ × 100 per cent); in the extremely risky case 8 per cent (i.e. $\frac{6}{75}$ × 100 per cent). Hence it can be seen that the substitution of 100 per cent initial allowances for the usual wear and tear allowances restores the pre-tax position and abolishes the discrimination against the more risky investment implicit in many systems of taxing incomes and profits.[2] In effect a system whereby government shares in profits when firms are successful but also shares in costs when they are investing amounts to what is from an ex-ante viewpoint a zero-rate tax system.[3]

A few other characteristics of initial allowances are obvious, but must be set down explicitly. In so far as a larger volume of investment takes place in boom years than normal or slump years, the reduction in taxable profits will be greater in boom years than it would be with replacement cost allowances. Therefore the system will have less built-in flexibility than it would on the replacement cost basis.[4] Furthermore, adherence to 100 per cent initial allowances would certainly have odd effects on firms' accounts, and in the case of some traders and partnerships, the fluctuations of income and hence expos-

[1] The precise result is more complex than that shown in the example, as allowances must be made for changes in pre-tax income and for the disappearance of the wear and tear allowances formerly available. The end result is the same, however; cf. R. A. Musgrave, *op. cit.*, pp. 336–46 and also J. Heller and K. M. Kauffman, *Tax Incentives for Industry in Less Developed Countries* (Harvard Law School, Cambridge, Mass., 1963). The type of company tax is also relevant. If initial allowances are given against a non-integrated corporation tax (e.g. the UK, 1965/73), tax relief will be confined to that tax only and will not extend to income tax levied on shareholders; with the imputation system (the UK since 1973), which in effect incorporates basic rate personal income tax, relief is given on a wider basis.

[2] The same proposition holds for the type of value added tax which exempts capital expenditure from the tax base. Cf. p. 50.

[3] See E. Cary Brown, 'Business-Income Taxation and Investment Incentives', in *Income, Employment and Public Policy*, Essays in Honor of Alvin H. Hansen (New York, 1948).

[4] How much less depends on whether the increased profits after tax result in larger retained gross earnings or larger profit distributions.

ure to the rigours of progressive taxation would be unquestionably greater.

There are many possible variants of the 100 per cent initial allowance system, and all we can do here is to list them and discuss some of the salient characteristics. One variant is to confine the allowances to *net* capital formation only, another is allowances of less than 100 per cent, another is allowances varying between different industries and different assets. All these variants possess the same general characteristics as in the limiting case; obviously their distorting effects on profits may be less and their inducements to invest may be less, but we need not enlarge on these minutiae. Perhaps the major point about these sorts of schemes is that, from the viewpoint of the private sector, they are much more uncertain in their operation. Businessmen in the UK have complained bitterly about the frequent changes in the system in the post-war period. Indeed, it can readily be seen that if changes in the system of allowances are very frequent, they may actually be destabilizing. If the government increases allowances in the hope of stimulating investment, businessmen may curtail their investment plans in the hope that there will be a still greater allowance available in the near future.

Perhaps the final point to emphasize about accelerated depreciation is the reverse of this point – the flexibility as far as the government is concerned. Not only can the engine be stopped but it can also be put into reverse, in the sense that allowances can be deferred as well as accelerated through time. Thus at the time of the Korean boom a system of deferred depreciation was introduced in Canada in the hope of checking investment. Although it was not in operation sufficiently long to draw any firm conclusions about its practical merits, it is another instance of the large variety of ways in which accelerated depreciation can be adapted to the needs of an economy.

In general, we can conclude that an 'equal-concessions' system of initial allowances is superior to a replacement cost system, even in a period of rising prices, by virtue of the fact that it concentrates relief on two of the most important determinants of investment – the liquidity position of firms and the willingness to take risks. For similar reasons, it is also superior to a system of cutting down the rate of profits taxation in such a way as to give the same total benefit to industry.[1]

[1] A cut in profits taxation can make investment less profitable if there are very liberal depreciation provisions, investment allowances, etc. For instance, the allowances on plant and equipment investment in the UK in 1965 were such that the post-tax rate of return was higher than the pre-tax rate

4.4 *Free depreciation*

We refer under this heading to the system by which the revenue authorities allow firms to write off original costs as they please. This was the system in operation in Sweden for a number of years; it has also operated in the UK in respect of particular assets in particular industries at different times.[1] The general characteristics of this system are fairly straightforward. On the one hand, in so far as it leads to much faster writing off than would be the case with the usual system of wear and tear allowances, it approximates to the 100 per cent initial allowance system. On the other hand, it may not lead to more speedy writing off but simply to a different distribution of depreciation allocations through time, which might or might not make for effective interest concessions to firms.

The great advantage of this system is precisely that it allows firms to please themselves in these matters. This clearly has most important political implications but we are not principally concerned with those. The economic advantage is that it does allow firms to put more aside in years of high profits if they so choose. Although this would in many cases seem to be an accounting rather than an economic advantage, various witnesses before the 1955 Royal Commission laid great emphasis on it. As the Commission itself pointed out, however, there are two major difficulties with this system. The authorities must inevitably have less knowledge of and control over the yield of tax than in the other cases we have examined. Second (and this is common to the 100 per cent initial allowance system too), the authorities no longer have the power to influence investment decisions by variations in allowance. How much power they should possess in this regard is, of course, a matter of high principle, but one which the Royal Commission preferred not to discuss in detail.

4.5 *Investment allowances*

Investment allowances, as they worked at one time in the UK, were simply a combination of original cost depreciation with an outright

(cf.NEDO, *Investment Appraisal*, HMSO, 1965). So if, for instance, the tax rate on profits had been cut down to zero, investment would have been less profitable.

A similar situation has arisen in Development Areas in the UK since 1972. The combination of 100 per cent initial allowances and special grants for some types of capital equipment has led to post-tax and post-concessions profits exceeding pre-tax profits – in some cases, enormously so. See p. 442 n.

[1]Although the system in the UK since 1972 has frequently been labelled free depreciation, this is really a misnomer.

subsidy on investment. In effect, therefore, they possessed the characteristics of initial allowances in an accentuated form, the present value of, say, £20 at the time of installation of a new machine costing £100 *plus* the usual wear and tear allowances being greater than the present value of £20 *plus* the diminished wear and tear allowances inherent in the initial cost system. They made for increased ability and willingness to invest relatively to the ordinary reducing balance system of wear and tear, and they made for increased willingness to invest relatively to the initial allowance system – but not increased ability, if the rate of allowance was the same in the two cases. Finally, it should be noted that, in contrast to initial allowances,[1] investment allowances were fairly neutral between short- and long-lived capital equipment. So if the two types of allowance were so fixed as to give the same incentives for equipment of average life, we should expect investment allowances to be relatively more favourable for short- and initial allowances for long-lived equipment.

At one time it was thought that investment allowances were a major investment stimulant, e.g. it was often said that the UK investment boom of 1955 could be attributed to the introduction of investment allowances in the previous year. In subsequent years, however, there was much more scepticism on this subject. Various enquiries[2] among businessmen all seemed to suggest that investment allowances had very little influence on decisions to invest. On the other hand, it was noteworthy that when the corporation tax was introduced in 1965, one of the criticisms levelled against it was that it would reduce the value of investment allowances and hence cut the level of investment. And although the Chancellor cast doubts on the efficiency of such allowances in his Budget speech of 1965, it was not very long afterwards that he himself introduced free depreciation for the shipping industry.[3]

[1] See p. 440.

[2] See, e.g., *Report of Committee on Turnover Taxation*, Cmnd. 2300 (HMSO, 1964); R. R. Neild, 'Replacement Policy', *National Institute Review*, November 1964; D. C. Corner and Alan Williams, 'The Sensitivity of Business to Initial and Investment Allowances', *Economica*, February 1965; NEDC, *Investment in Machine Tools* (HMSO, 1965). For later discussion, see M. A. King, 'Taxation and Investment Incentives', *Journal of Public Economics*, 1, 1972.

[3] Although there is a good deal of disagreement in the USA about the precise effects of tax concessions on capital investment, there seems to be agreement that the influence was not negligible (see the different views expressed in G. Fromm, *Tax Incentives and Capital Spending*, Brookings Institution, Washington DC, 1971). But see R. Eisner and P. J. Lawler, 'Tax Policy and Investment: an Analysis of Survey Responses', *American Economic Review*, March 1975, for further qualification.

4.6 *Investment grants*

Between 1966 and 1970, there was a general system of investment grants in this country; and although this was abolished in 1970 in favour of initial allowances, it returned again for certain types of investment in Development Areas in 1972. Under this system, grants are no longer tied to profitability or tax rate levels, being identical for every firm with identical capital expenditure; they may (1966/70) or may not (1972 onwards) entail that the total for depreciation purposes is original expenditure *net* of investment grants; although the degree of discrimination between industries and geographical areas need not be greater than with accelerated depreciation or investment allowances, this has in fact been the case in the UK to date.

The benefits claimed for this system are that it is more open, more easily understood and also that relief is given at the time when investment takes place, so that firms with potentially great but low current profits can benefit. The disadvantages are that whereas tax-related concessions can be administered as part of the tax system, investment grants need an additional administrative organization; and that grants may well be given to firms which are perennial loss-makers.

4.7 *Conclusions on investment stimulation*

We have argued in general terms that some relief over and above the usual wear and tear allowances is justifiable. The *amount* of relief cannot be prescribed in any general way, simply because it is dependent on the other tax policies of government (and especially the taxation of business profits), the extent to which it is currently desirable to encourage saving and risk-taking, and the likely effects of tax relief at any given time on the attitudes of businessmen. On the *form* of relief perhaps one can be rather more definite. Our study of the attributes of the various possible measures must lead us to the general conclusion that additional depreciation in one form or another is likely to be superior in its effects on attitudes to risk-taking and the provision of finance for investment to a system of replacement cost depreciation.

Among the various means of augmenting depreciation allowances, we have to choose between initial allowances, free depreciation, investment allowances and investment grants. In fact, the choice is more complicated as, quite apart from combinations of these measures, there are variants such as investment credits on the US pattern (where the allowance is a credit against tax rather than a deduction from pre-tax profits) or substitution of a value added or payroll tax for a corporate profits tax. To take free depreciation first, there is the very real objection that the government has less control over the tax yield and over the pattern of investment. While one must sympathize with the contrary plea by businessmen that they never know where they are when initial or investment allowances are liable to vary from one year to the next, one must nevertheless recognize that tax policy must adapt itself to the uncertainties of the world. If the rates of allowances were fixed for ever and ever, some other facet of government policy would need to change as the general economic conditions of society change. On the choice between initial and investment allowances, a good deal could be said. Investment allowances have greater incentive effects per pound of revenue loss, but are fairly neutral between short- and long-lived capital goods. If it were thought that there is a correlation between length of life and riskiness of investment, this must reinforce the case in favour of initial allowances which give relatively greater help to long-lived than short-lived equipment – in that the period of tax deferral is longer in the former case. Whatever the pros and cons of these arguments, the prospects of the relative size of initial and investment allowances varying between industries or different types of assets according to the whims of different Chancellors, or what is more likely, the pressure mounted by interested parties is not a pleasing one. It needs little imagination to see the special pleading and intriguing to which the authorities would lay themselves open in these circumstances.

We might also ask about the merits of investment credits and outright subsidies on capital equipment, relatively to investment allowances. In one respect, the two former devices closely resemble one another. Whereas a given investment allowance leads to the same percentage reduction in the tax bill whatever the tax rate of the recipient, the other two confer a relatively greater benefit on firms paying lower tax rates. But the resemblance between outright gains or subsidies on investment and credits against tax in respect of investment is only partial. For the former confers benefits on firms when they are making no profits or even when they are making losses; whereas investment credits and investment allowances are only of immediate value to firms making profits – in other cases, they can only help to reduce future tax liabilities.

Obviously there are arguments both ways here. The old investment allowance system undoubtedly conferred unnecessarily large benefits on partnerships and sole traders operating in the higher surtax ranges. On the other hand, the investment grant system runs the obvious risk of being far too liberal to inefficient firms.

5 THE UK SITUATION

It is easy enough to pick holes in the UK structure of corporation tax in the light of the discussion of general principles. Even if there were no problem of persistent inflation, to start with the simplest case, the appropriate treatment of capital gains raises afresh some of the difficult questions already considered in Chapter 13.

Taking the adjustment for inflation next, the UK has a system of initial allowances (as set out in Chapter 9) which effectively takes care of depreciation adjustments for inflation in the case of plant and machinery but operates somewhat haphazardly in other cases. With inventories we have the rough and ready system of inventory adjustment introduced in 1974 (see Chapter 9 for details), which again provides inflation protection in many cases but not necessarily in all. But we have no system whatever of assessing the change in the real value of net monetary liabilities (assets) and adjusting capital gains (losses) accordingly. This latter deficiency is in turn linked with the lack of adjustment of personal capital gains and losses for inflation. It may well be that a fully-fledged system of inflation adjustment for taxation purposes is unlikely in the absence of similar adjustments for financial reporting,[1] but at least it should be clearly understood how arbitrary are the results of the present system with, for instance, relatively little liability to corporation tax on the part of those firms with heavy capital spending programmes or large inventory adjustments, but with substantial tax liabilities remaining for, say, financial institutions unable to claim much in respect of fixed asset expenditure or inventory adjustments but also not being in a position to obtain relief on real capital losses due to holding monetary assets in times of inflation.

In similar vein, one can point to what appear to be very arbitrary distinctions in the methods of promoting capital formation. It may be possible to justify the higher rate of initial allowances for plant and equipment (100 per cent) than that for industrial buildings (50 per

[1]So far progress on that front has been very limited, despite a vast amount of discussion. For the views of an official committee, see *Inflation Accounting* (Sandilands Committee Report), Cmnd. 6225 (HMSO, 1975); for a survey of this and related literature, see J. A. Kay, 'Inflation Accounting – a Review Article', *Economic Journal*, June 1977.

cent) on the grounds that initial allowances at a given rate are relatively more favourable to long-lived than short-lived assets. It may also be possible to justify grants in development areas over and above the standard initial allowances (e.g. 20 per cent for plant and machinery; see Chapter 9) on the grounds of regional policy, even though the end-result is that post-tax post-grant rates of return exceed those prevailing in the absence of taxes and grants.[1]

What is more difficult to justify, however, is the bias introduced by allowing corporations *both* to receive accelerated depreciation *and* to exclude interest payments from the tax base.[2] This can be seen very readily if we think of a corporation financing a substantial part of its machinery expenditure programme from borrowing, the interest on which is deductible for corporation tax but still being able to claim the same amount in initial allowances against profits on equity capital as if the whole of capital expenditure were financed by the latter means.[3]

Some investigators[4] have taken the view that these anachronisms in the present system are so great that the corporation tax in the UK should operate on a flow-of-funds basis. The general idea here is that corporations should be taxed on the difference over the course of the year between total cash inflows from the sale of goods and services and total cash outflows on the purchase of goods and services, making no distinction between current and capital transactions. The end-result would be that all expenditures on capital assets would be deductible in the year they are made but no interest payments would be so deductible. It is claimed that such a system would be far more rational than the present one; and would also bypass all the inflation adjustments discussed earlier. It would also be a natural accompaniment to a personal expenditure tax calculated on a cash-flow basis.

The generalization of the writing-off of capital investment in the year in which it takes place means that ex-ante the rate of corporate profits taxation would be zero and the post-tax rate of return on all corporate investment would be equal to the pre-tax rate of return; though this does not mean a zero rate of tax on an ex-post basis for all

[1] Thus an incorporated enterprise with a 10 per cent return before tax, and paying corporation tax at 50 per cent but receiving 100 per cent initial allowances and a separate grant equal to 20 per cent of capital investment would enjoy a post-tax post-benefit return of 16.7 per cent; an unincorporated enterprise paying tax at 75 per cent but otherwise in the same position would find its post-tax post-benefit rate of return to be 50 per cent!

[2] Cf. M. A. King, 'Taxation, Corporate Financial Policy and the Cost of Capital', *Journal of Public Economics*, 4, 1975.

[3] For further discussion, see Meade *Report*, *op. cit.*, pp. 230ff.

[4] *Ibid.*, Chapter 12; and J. A. Kay and M. A. King, *op. cit.*, Chapters 11 and 12.

profits in that, for instance, some firms will do better than originally expected and earn intra-marginal rents from their operations. However, there are many problems with any such flow-of-funds proposal. One is the appropriate way of treating financial institutions;[2] another is the relationship between corporations and the personal sector, both in the sense of the need to treat incorporated and unincorporated businesses in broadly similar ways and of crediting corporation tax, in whole or in part, against personal income tax; there is also the formidable problem of harmonizing proposals of this kind with those emanating from the EEC.[3] Nor must we forget the hackneyed but unsolved question of corporation tax incidence.[4]

So all in all it would seem that this bold plan of reforms is unlikely to come into effect in the foreseeable future and we are much more likely to be left with the present hotchpotch series of arrangements for a long time to come.

[1] Kay and King, *op. cit.*, p. 201.
[2] Meade *Report*, *op. cit.*, p. 240.
[3] *Ibid.*, p. 249.
[4] See Chapter 17, section 2.

17

COMPANY TAXATION – CORPORATE AND PERSONAL TAX INTEGRATION

1 INTRODUCTION

1.1 *Outline*

We have already described the mechanism of the British system of taxing corporate profits in Chapter 9 and we need only repeat that the effect is to tax all profits at a flat rate (52 per cent in 1978/9), gross up dividends to shareholders by a factor (33/67 in 1978/9) and tax the grossed-up dividends to personal income tax but allow a credit (equal to the grossing-up) against this liability. The net effect is that the credit exactly offsets personal income tax liabilities of those taxable at the basic rate; higher rate taxpayers are called on for additional payments and anyone not liable to basic rate tax receives a refund.

Our aim in this chapter is a limited one. We are not going to call into question the whole basis of assessment for company and personal taxation, and discuss such questions as the desirability of excluding, e.g. advertising and selling costs from admissible expenditure in the one case or that of saving/dissaving in the other. Nor shall we discuss the workings of petroleum revenue tax. We shall simply take the present system of profits assessment (subject to any modifications necessary on the basis of the preceding chapter) and discuss the appropriate principles of taxing such assessments. We shall start by looking at the fundamental reasons for company taxation; section 2 is devoted to the incidence of such taxation and section 3 to the possible forms which this taxation can take; finally there is an appraisal of the present position in the UK.

1.2 *Fundamental reasons for the insufficiency of personal income taxation*

The first reason for levying a corporation tax in addition to personal income tax might be that a company is a distinct organization from its shareholders, that it has some reality and existence on its own account. On this basis, it could be argued that taxation of companies should be entirely distinct from taxation of individual shareholders and that no cognizance need be taken of one tax in levying the other. It would not seem that this view can really be maintained through thick and thin: the way in which companies developed historically in the UK, and the ramifications of the tax treatment of inter-corporate dividends and the personal tax avoidance provisions in respect of close companies (effectively these prevent any divorce of corporate from personal tax liabilities in such cases), all point the other way. A second argument for a company tax rests on the benefit principle. Companies acquire very definite legal privileges through incorporation and therefore they should pay for these privileges. This would seem to be a weak argument, however. There is no easy means of measuring the cost of these privileges to society or the value of them to the firm concerned, but even if there were it seems highly unlikely that they would be proportional to profits and hence suitably paid for by a tax on profits. This argument can therefore be put on one side.

A third argument is that company profits taxation is a means of discriminating against unearned income. We have already seen[1] that the case for such discrimination is by no means straightforward. But even if one is persuaded of the justice of the end, the case for a tax on corporate profits as the means is pretty weak. The essential point is that this is only a way of catching equity and preference dividends and so leaves all other forms of unearned income, such as rent and interest, untouched. Nor do various other propositions such as taxation of corporations for anti-monopoly reasons carry any more conviction when analysed.

Leaving on one side the problems arising from the taxation of international investment income flows, to which we shall return in Chapter 18, the basic reason for company taxation is to preserve equity between the company shareholder class and others. If the only form of income taxation were personal income taxation, then the benefits from undistributed profits would be largely free of tax. They would not be entirely free of tax in that any dividends ultimately paid out of the additional earnings generated by the undistributed profits would be caught for tax. Similarly, if personal income taxation includes realized capital gains there would again be a likelihood of additional tax liability in the future. For although the general connection between the annual amount of undistributed profits and the rate of growth of the value of business capital assets is only a rough one, and the particular connection between the income held back from distribution to an individual shareholder and the capital gains he enjoys rougher still, there can be

[1] Chapter 13, section 3.

no doubt that there is an association between the two things. But these two possibilities of liability to future tax are clearly insufficient to compensate for the avoidance of personal income tax liability at the time profits are undistributed, simply for the reason that they are future tax liabilities – and, moreover, liabilities which may conceivably not arise for many years, and perhaps not at all if capital gains are not realized before death. If personal income taxation has to be supplemented in one way or another for this basic equity reason, an attempt must be made to minimize any resultant resource misallocation. In particular, we shall have to look extremely closely at the consequences of various corrective devices for the allocation of funds in capital markets. Whether the corrective device takes the form of a special tax on undistributed profits or not, this must be a fundamental consideration.

At this point we must face up to the connection between this argument and that in the previous chapter for granting accelerated depreciation. It might well be asked why one need have these complications: if one proposal is for greater taxation of companies and the other is for less, why not simply dispense with both? The answer is fairly obvious. Even if the total of tax collected were the same (and this need not necessarily be the case), whether one has both undistributed profits taxation and accelerated depreciation or whether one has neither, the distribution of the tax burden between firms (and hence between shareholders) would not be the same in the two cases. The combination of the two proposals results in relatively more favourable treatment of those companies with the higher rate of net investment than would be the case in its absence. That is the case for having this particular combination of tax proposals.

2 THE INCIDENCE OF CORPORATION TAXES

Before going further, we must bring out into the open an assumption upon which the discussion above was implicitly based. In saying that in the absence of taxation of corporate undistributed profits the shareholder class would benefit unduly, we assumed that, in some sense or other, the burden of any such tax would rest on them. Many people have argued, however, that this is not so and that impositions or increases of taxes on profits of companies are largely, if not wholly, passed on to the consumers of their products. We must therefore examine this argument in some detail.

It is necessary first of all to narrow down the issue as far as possible. We are not concerned now with the problems of long-period adjustment (e.g. via effects of income or profits taxes on risk-bearing), which we examined in Chapter 3. The present proposition is that even in the short period an imposition or increase in company profits taxation can cause a general rise in prices. It is usually assumed in the argument that purely macroeconomic considerations can be left on one side so that one hypothesizes that the increase in income taxation is accompanied by some notional reduction in lump-sum taxes and that the monetary system is sufficiently accommodating not to impede any movements of general prices. It is also recognized that there will tend to be movements of relative prices of products made by different enterprises depending on the particular form of the profits tax (e.g. a tax on undistributed company profits will have different effects to a tax on all company profits; and any special tax on company profits may mean differentiation between corporate and non-corporate enterprises), but these are not the main centre of interest and so will not be considered further here.

The traditional argument[1] was that in conditions of perfect competition every firm would already be maximizing its profits and so an imposition or increase of profits taxation would not induce any firm to make immediate changes in its pricing or output policy. Hence it was concluded that in the short run the burden of any such tax would rest on the firm itself and not on its customers. This argument was sometimes reinforced by appeals to the monetary situation, with the proposition that if this was sufficiently tight, a general rise was impossible anyway.

In recent years, this traditional argument has been challenged on a variety of grounds. To illustrate,[2] if one thinks that the economy is much more oligopolistic than competitive, it can be argued that an increase in profits tax acts as a catalyst enabling firms to break out from the dead-centre position in which they are afraid to shift prices upwards or downwards. Another point is that if firms aim at maximizing sales subject to a profits constraint, a profits tax can lead to price rises. Arguments of this kind have usually been coupled, explicitly or implicitly, with the proposition that one could not assume sufficient

[1] Cf. the summary of the Colwyn Committee position on p. 47 above.

[2] See R. A. Musgrave, *The Theory of Public Finance*, *op. cit.*, pp. 278 ff., for fuller discussion. Also N. Kaldor, 'A Memorandum on the Value Added Tax', *Essays on Economic Policy*, Vol. 1 (Duckworth, 1964).

rigidity in the supply of money or the velocity of circulation to rule out a general increase in prices if firms were aiming at it.

It is unlikely that such opposing views will be settled without much more extensive empirical research than has yet been undertaken – and perhaps not even then. In the meantime, the following points may be made. Although some investigations in the USA[1] point towards some forward shifting of the US corporation tax, these findings are certainly not universally accepted,[2] and so the subject is far from closed in that country.

The opportunities to pass on tax increases in this way are likely to be much less in an export-oriented economy of the UK type than in the USA. Econometric evidence seems to support this view as did that collected by the Richardson Committee in the early 1960s.[3] So in all the circumstances it seems fair to say that the burden of company profits taxation in the UK is likely to rest with companies in large measure. Before proceeding, however, it may be worth sketching in the conclusions which would follow if the shifting forward school of thought were correct. In this case, the arguments for company profits taxes disappear altogether as they would then amount to nothing more than a differential sales tax, the effective tax rate depending on the ratio of profits (or undistributed profits, if that is the tax base) to turnover. It would clearly be preferable on general grounds to have a non-discriminatory tax such as a flat-rate retail sales tax or a value added tax in their place. We shall return to the choice between these different possibilities when we come to the general subject of outlay taxes in Chapter 19.[4]

[1] M. Krzyzaniak and R. A. Musgrave, *The Shifting of the Corporation Income Tax* (John Hopkins Press, Baltimore, 1963).

[2] See e.g. Richard Goode, 'Rates of Return, Income Shares and Corporation Tax Incidence' in M. Krzyzaniak (ed.), *Effects of Corporate Income Tax* (Wayne State University Press, 1966); and R. J. Gordon, 'Incidence of Corporate Income Tax', *American Economic Review*, September 1967. Two more recent papers (W. H. Oakland, 'Corporate Earnings and Tax Shifting in US Manufacturing, 1930/68', *Review of Economics and Statistics*, August 1972, and R. Dusansky, 'The Short-run Shifting of the Corporation Income Tax in the US', *Oxford Economic Papers*, November 1972) each using much the same data arrived at diametrically opposite conclusions.

[3] See J. M. Davis, 'An Aggregate Time Series Analysis of the Short-Run Shifting of the UK Company Tax', *Oxford Economic Papers*, July 1972; and 'The Krzyzaniak-Musgrave Model – Some Further Comments', *Kyklos*, 1973, Fasc 2. See also *Report of Committee on Turnover Taxation*, Cmnd. 2300 (HMSO 1964).

[4] There was a good deal of discussion in the UK in the early 1960s about substituting a turnover tax for company profits taxation. Some of the arguments, and in particular the claim that such a change would help exports, rested on the assumption that profits taxation was passed forward to consumers. It was therefore contended that if all UK producers were relieved of company profits taxation and a value added tax were levied on domestic sales only, this would give a net inducement to sell in foreign

3 ALTERNATIVE FORMS OF COMPANY TAXATION

We now return to the main thread of the argument – that shareholders would pay too little tax if they were only liable to personal income tax and realized capital gains taxes. The next step is to survey the possible alternative remedies and their merits. We shall start with a general comparison between a tax on total company profits and one on undistributed profits; then deal successively with various crediting devices, the treatment of companies as if they were unincorporated businesses and the taxation of capital gains as they accrue. We shall need to have in mind various considerations: the possible danger of over-taxing as well as under-taxing shareholders; the effects on savings and the working of capital markets as well as general administrative aspects. We shall assume that the combined yield from corporation tax, personal income tax on dividends and related capital gains taxation will be the same in each case. It would obviously not make sense to insist on equal yield from a tax on total company profits and one which was, say, confined to undistributed profits in that the amount of tax obtained from the other sources would be likely to differ in the two cases. We simply have to consider a number of closely related taxes together.

3.1 *Taxation of all profits versus taxation of retained profits*

How does a system of taxing all company profits, taking no cognizance of personal income tax liabilities on dividends or capital gains, compare with one of taxing retentions only?

From the equity standpoint, the arguments are quite decisively in favour of a tax on undistributed rather than total profits. The former would obviously tend to promote the distribution of a larger percentage of profits, and hence a larger proportion of incomes would be subject to tax at the marginal rate appropriate to the individual concerned. How important this is obviously depends on whether there is any effective system of taxing capital gains. If there is no system at all or only a partial system the argument is very strong indeed, and even if there is a system, the coincidence of tax raised by this means with the benefits derived from undistributed profits is so uncertain as to leave a

rather than domestic markets. These arguments were criticized on the grounds that the combined effect of abolishing company profits taxation and introducing a value added tax would be to increase the domestic price level (i.e. the relief on profit taxation would not itself lead to any reduction in prices and the imposition of the value added tax would lead to an increase) thus counteracting any stimulus to exports. See *Report of Committee on Turnover Taxation* (*op. cit.*) and also symposium of articles by D. K. Stout, A. R. Prest and G. S. A. Wheatcroft *British Tax Review*, September/October 1963; also NEDO, *Value-Added Tax* (HMSO, 1969).

strong case on equity grounds for encouraging greater distribution out of profits. It should be emphasized that it is the impetus to greater distributions which is crucial, as only by this means can one avoid the inequity due to rich shareholders paying too little tax and poor shareholders too much. Whereas equity *between* the shareholder class as a whole and the rest of the community can be obtained by a variety of imposts on companies, whether on retained or on total profits, equity *within* the shareholding class is critically dependent on the extent to which profits are forced out to shareholders. So the equity advantages of taxing undistributed rather than total profits depend on their differing effects on the ratio of retentions to total profits.

How would a flat-rate profits tax affect the level of saving and investment compared to an undistributed profits tax? There are many complex arguments here and we cannot do more than point to the relevant headings. To start with, there are three different propositions which have to be distinguished: the effect on total saving, the effect on total investment and the 'quality' of additional saving and investment, the last of these bringing in issues of resource allocation as well as the supply of resources.

One's instinctive reaction is that the substitution of a flat-rate tax on all profits for one on undistributed profits is likely to increase company saving. The substitution effects of such a change are likely to favour retentions rather than dividend distributions and so are the income redistribution effects. It is sometimes argued that eventual liability to tax on additional capital gains in the greater retentions case will weaken the substitution effect; but when one takes into account such factors as the futurity and uncertainty of any such liabilities and the possibility of immediate relief from gains tax liabilities in so far as share prices fall currently as a result of dividend curtailment, this line of argument does not carry great conviction. On the income effects side, it is clearly true that some companies benefit relatively to others from the tax substitution; those who benefit will be disposed to increase both retentions and distributions whereas those who lose may be reluctant to cut their dividends and so make their retentions carry the burden. But one would not expect this to be more than a short-run result and as earnings grow over time firms in such a situation are likely to add to their retentions much more than to their dividends.

So the general result is likely to be an increase in company saving. But the overall effect on private saving will depend on what happens to the personal saving component. Here there are a number of crosscurrents, e.g. in so far as dividends paid out to insurance companies over the years are lower than they otherwise would have been, it may simply be that bonuses on life policies are reduced accordingly. There will also be direct reactions of individual savers to their level of dividends or the market value of their shares, but these are likely to be of such a complex character that no firm conclusions can be drawn about magnitude or direction in our present state of knowledge.

Even after allowing for any adverse reactions on personal saving, it is likely that private saving as a whole will be greater.[1] As a consequence, total investment in the economy can also rise, ceteris paribus, without getting into inflationary difficulties. This is an advantage of taxing total, rather than undistributed, profits which many have thought to be quite decisive. To go fully into these arguments would be outside our scope, but we must nevertheless make some observations on them. The first is that there is no settled body of opinion about the optimum percentage of GNP which should be devoted to saving and investment, rather than consumption, at any given time. Many people have devoted a great deal of thought to both the theoretical aspects[2] and, more recently, the empirical aspects (e.g. the historical contribution of investment in physical capital to the growth rate of an economy)[3] but it seems safe to say that this part of economics is still very much in a state of flux. Secondly, quite apart from arguments about what total saving should be at any given time, there are further problems about the particular uses to which saving may be put. One point is that if private saving increases more than private investment as a result of this type of profits tax, it would, ceteris paribus, be necessary to increase public expenditure on goods and services to avoid a fall in total output and employment; and some would regard any such increase in importance of the public sector as undesirable. The likelihood of an excess of private saving over investment is most difficult to forecast in the present state of our ignorance about what limits investment. If the main limitation is, in some sense or other, a shortage of readily available funds one might expect the barriers to private investment to be much lower after the tax change; but if a sine qua non of additional

[1] But see M. S. Feldstein and G. Fane, 'Taxes, Corporate Dividend Policy and Personal Savings. The British Post-War Experience', *Review of Economics and Statistics*, November 1973, for the view that this is not likely to happen.

[2] See, e.g., R. A. and P. B. Musgrave, *Public Finance in Theory and Practice*, *op. cit.*, Chapter 22.

[3] See, e.g., E. F. Denison, *Why Growth Rates Differ* (Brookings Institution, Washington DC, 1967).

investment is the payment of a large share of incremental profits as dividends to shareholders, the tax change may not be wholly favourable.

A subject on which it is possible to be rather more definite is the effect of the tax change on the composition or 'quality' of investment in the private sector. The central point here is that in the undistributed profits tax case the market would have a much greater say in the disposition of capital funds. This raises matters such as the importance one attaches to the freedom of choice of the ultimate owners of capital, one's views about their comparative ability to judge the most profitable outlets for capital (including the outlet of holding it in cash form rather than financing capital formation) and the respective costs of working the machinery of the capital market and self-financing. These are major policy issues which need a chapter, if not a book, to themselves. Here we shall be completely Draconian and simply state that we think that the balance of the argument is quite clearly on the side of market decisions. The strongest apparent argument against this is the relative costs of the two systems; for there can be no doubt that the capital market machinery is likely to be more expensive to operate than self-financing, and particularly so for smaller size firms. But this strength is to some degree apparent rather than real. It would in all probability be less costly in terms of real resources if it were illegal for the British motor industry to produce more than one type of car. But it would be generally agreed that such a restriction would be undesirable none the less. In so far as there is strength in the argument, it points to the need for improving the machinery of the capital market rather than cutting down the flow of funds to it.

A more subtle point is the proposition that those firms with the largest undistributed profit ratios are likely to be the most go-ahead growing elements in the economy. These will be hit relatively more by an undistributed profits tax than by a flat-rate tax; so it can be argued that for this reason the undistributed profits tax is relatively more inimical to growth. This argument is two-edged however. The most rapidly growing firms are likely to earn a greater return on their capital than others. Therefore the change from a flat-rate profits tax to an undistributed profits tax would imply a smaller percentage increase in the share of growing firms in the total tax burden than if percentage earnings on capital were equal to or less than those of stagnant firms. Any net impediments to growth which remained would tend to disappear in so far as larger distributions were made and more financing from the market took place; for there can be no doubt that such a development would be more favourable to the growing than to the stagnant firms.

This leads to another point of great importance. Emphasis on self-financing undoubtedly makes life easier for old-established firms and more difficult for new firms. The height of the threshold which a new firm has to surmount is unquestionably made greater if the common pool of funds on which it can draw is diminished. This is not necessarily the same thing as saying that monopolistic tendencies in any one industry are increased; it may still be feasible for an old-established firm in one industry to branch out into another. But the bias against new firms is quite unmistakable.

An investigation into some of these matters produced some important findings.[1] It was found in a regression of the rate of change of pre-tax earnings on (lagged) retentions and asset size for thirteen groups of British companies, that only in the case of one group was the sign of the regression coefficient for ploughback positive and significant, i.e. in the vast majority of cases there was no evidence to show that retained profits significantly influenced the growth of earnings. Of course, as the author was at great pains to point out, too much weight should not be put on these results. But they are the best we have; and it seems fair to say that the ball is now and has been for some years in the court of those who think there is a close dependence of growth on retentions to produce some evidence in support of their case.

One last point relating to company retentions is that in so far as there is a tendency for undistributed profits to increase relatively more than total profits in boom years and diminish relatively more in slump years, undistributed profits have an advantage over total profits as a tax base from the viewpoint of counter-cyclical policy.

We now come to the manifold considerations of administration. Unquestionably the simpler tax to administer is the flat-rate profits tax. This is not so much because it is more difficult to assess undistributed rather than total profits in any one year, but rather that difficulties arise when distributions exceed earnings in any one year. In that case there is an element of negative tax and this inevitably complicates matters.

[1] I. M. D. Little, 'Higgledy-Piggledy Growth', *Oxford Bulletin of Statistics*, November 1962. See also W. J. Baumol, P. Heim, B. G. Malkiel and R. E. Quandt, 'Earnings Retention, New Capital and the Growth of the Firm', *Review of Economics and Statistics*, November 1970; and G. Whittington, 'The Profitability of Retained Earnings', *ibid.*, May 1972. For a recent investigation, see D. G. McFettridge, 'The Efficiency Implications of Earnings Retention', *ibid.*, May 1978.

However, this difficulty should not be exaggerated. It would be incorrect to assume that the difficulties would be as great as those associated with the operation of the two-level profits tax (with a higher rate on distributed profits) in the UK between 1947 and 1958. In that case the problem was that if a firm distributed more in dividends than earnings, it had to face the withdrawal of 'non-distribution' relief, i.e. it had in effect to pay back the tax of which it had been relieved when the profits now distributed had originally been put to reserve. As a firm can never be sure that it will not have to distribute more than it earns in any one year, it can never be sure of its ultimate tax liabilities, and can never therefore have a fixed basis for its future planning or for the preparation of its accounts and reports to shareholders.

A tax on undistributed profits would not meet the same difficulties. If profits distribution is greater than earnings in any one year, this would entitle a firm to a refund of tax which could in principle be effected by a process of carrying back or carrying forward. It might be desirable from the government's point of view, e.g. estimation of likely revenue in any one year, to insist on carrying forward rather than back, but whichever way this process worked, a firm's estimate of its financial position would always be a minimum and not a maximum one. Although a firm may on occasions be more or less obliged to pay out more than it earns in a year, the number of times when it will be *obliged* to pay out less than earnings (and hence, with an undistributed profits tax, incur a greater liability to tax than it would wish) will be relatively few. There might well have to be limits on the power of a firm to claim tax relief in the event of liquidation but this would be the case anyway if the carryforward rule prevailed.

There is another and different aspect of the whole matter. On various occasions, we have stressed the interdependence of the systems of company and personal income taxation. To some extent it is a matter for choice whether we try for greater equity by forcing out more undistributed profits to their owners or by imposing a capital gains tax. If, therefore, we decide on an undistributed profits tax, the need for a capital gains tax is far less than if we have a flat-rate profits tax. Even if it is impossible to do without a capital gains tax altogether in the former case, it might well be possible to get by with some rough and ready system. It can therefore be argued that the right comparison of administrative difficulties ought to be based on the cost of running an undistributed profits tax (*plus* perhaps a rough and ready capital gains tax of some form) against that of running a flat-rate profits tax *plus* a refined capital gains tax. Seen in this light the administrative advantages of a flat-rate profits tax are not nearly so great.[1]

To summarize, we can say that equity objectives are more likely to be achieved if profit retentions are very low; but this would imply some sort of penal tax on undistributed profits. Whilst the savings disadvantages of such a tax are not as great as sometimes argued, a forcing out tax on these lines is not a likely prospect. The effects on capital markets would be extremely drastic. Therefore we need to think of measures which make total shareholder tax liability greater than it would be if there were only personal income (and capital gains) taxes but at the same time make for greater distribution ratios than would prevail if one simply taxed all company profits independently of personal income and capital gains taxes.

3.2 *Dividend paid credits*

With a dividend paid credit (or split-rate) system, corporation tax liabilities are reduced in respect of dividends paid out to shareholders. A full crediting system would imply a zero rate of corporation tax on dividends paid out, whilst keeping a positive rate on retentions; this system has been used in Greece, for example. A partial crediting system implies a lower rate of corporation tax on dividends than on retentions; for some years West Germany had a system of taxing the former at 15 per cent and the latter at 51 per cent and a similar arrangement was proposed for the UK in the early 1970s.[2]

The characteristics of this approach can best be seen by taking the limiting case of zero corporation tax on distributions; in that case, we have a tax at corporate level on retentions and a tax at shareholder level on distributions. If the former is chosen so as to be equivalent to the weighted marginal rate of personal tax for the shareholder class taken as a whole, then (ignoring, for simplicity, any possible liabilities to future capital gains taxation) there will be no undue advantages in retention rather than distribution.

[1] We shall have something to say a little later about different forms of company taxation in the context of the EEC, see p. 462.

[2] Cf. *Reform of Corporation Tax*, Cmnd. 4630 (HMSO, March 1971). The proposal was that undistributed profits should be taxed at 50 per cent corporation tax and distributed profits at 20 per cent. With basic rate personal income tax at 30 per cent, profits of 200 and retentions of 30, one would then have had the following situation: retentions 30, dividends (net of personal tax) 70, personal tax 30, corporation tax 70 (i.e. 100 on the basis of 50 per cent of total profits of 200 *less* 30 distribution relief on the basis of 30 per cent of dividend before personal income tax, of 100).

Equity will be achieved between the shareholding class taken as a whole and the rest of the community, though not between rich and poor shareholders in so far as the former are under-taxed and the latter over-taxed by the application of a uniform rate on retained profits.[1] Precisely what should be the appropriate rate of tax on undistributed profits is a matter for some discussion. The traditional belief was that it would be higher than the basic (then standard) rate of income tax on the grounds that shareholders were by and large rich people. But given the large and rapidly growing holdings of ordinary shares by life assurance companies, pension funds, unit trusts, etc.[2] representing very often (though not always) lower income earnings, this view is much more open to challenge today.

A system of partial crediting, such as proposed in the UK in 1971, would have had somewhat different characteristics. Whilst the total tax bite on retentions and on distributions would have been the same for basic rate taxpayers (i.e. 50 per cent corporation tax in the first case and 20 per cent corporation tax *plus* 30 per cent income tax in the second) and thus retention encouragement low, incomes from shareholdings would have been taxed at higher rates than those from other sources. Whereas a wage-earner with a taxable income of, say, £2,500 would have paid tax at 30 per cent, a shareholder with the same income would have paid income tax at this rate and an element of corporation tax as well.[3]

It might well be asked whether such differential treatment can be justified on economic as distinct from political grounds. The usual investment income argument is clearly not relevant: this would at the most justify differential treatment of *all* forms of investment income.

A slightly more plausible proposition is that if some sort of differentiation against dividend income was introduced in the past, it would have been capitalized in share prices in the past; as the then owners would have absorbed the whole of the tax burden, its removal now would confer uncovenanted benefits on present equity holders. Another proposition is that in so far as corporation taxes are partially

[1] Cf. C. E. McClure Jr., 'The Case for Integrating the Income Taxes', *National Tax Journal*, September 1975, for further discussion.

[2] According to the Royal Commission on Income Distribution and Wealth (*Income from Companies and its Distribution*, Report No. 2, Cmnd 6172 (HMSO, 1975), p. 18) over the average of 1969–73 only 50 per cent of ordinary shares in UK companies were held by persons, executors and trustees; and insurance companies, pensions funds and unit trusts held 16.9 per cent, 14.6 per cent and 4.1 per cent respectively.

[3] And even more if income were high enough to be subject to the investment income surcharge. Cf. Chapter 9, section 2.1.1.

passed forward, the net burden of such taxes on distributions and hence the differential tax treatment of shareholders, may approximate to zero.[1] Whether such a proposition holds in any particular case is obviously a matter for detailed study.

3.3 *Dividend received credits*

A dividend received credit (or imputation) system tackles the problem of integrating corporation and personal income taxes from the other end. Instead of giving relief to distributions at the corporate level, credits are given against personal income tax liabilities. Obviously, the general effect of encouraging distributions (compared to the non-integrated case) will be similar to the dividend paid credit; but the details differ.

Once again, we can draw a distinction between full and partial crediting systems. In the former case (e.g. the effective UK position before 1937), the dividend paid to a shareholder is grossed up in accordance with the amount of tax paid at company level, and the shareholder is then taxed to personal income tax on this gross amount but allowed a credit equal to the company tax.[2] In other words, the total tax on distributions is no higher than what would be imposed on the same level of income from other sources; and, in still other words, a company could declare a (gross) dividend equal to its total profits and still meet its tax liabilities without drawing on reserves. In the partial crediting system, the procedure is exactly the same but the grossing-up factor on distributions (and hence the credit against personal income tax) is not sufficient to remove all the weight of corporation tax from dividend recipients. Thus in setting up the UK 1973 system, a grossing-up factor and a credit of 3/7 of dividends was provided for: therefore an outpayment of 70 would gross up to 100 and a credit of 30 exactly offset personal tax liabilities (at basic rate) – but at a 50 per cent rate of corporation tax this meant that shareholders would in effect only be relieved of part of that burden. In other words, under this kind of system dividend income recipients pay tax at a higher rate than people with similar incomes from other sources; and a company cannot

[1] Cf. A. R. Prest, 'The Select Committee on Corporation Tax', *British Tax Review*, Jan/Feb. 1972, pp. 18–19.

[2] Taking total profits as 200, undistributed profits before tax as 60, and company tax and personal tax rates as 50 per cent, we should have the following position: undistributed profits after tax 30, company tax on undistributed profits 30, grossed up dividend 140 (net dividend 70, company tax 70) and personal income tax nil, i.e. 70 personal income tax exactly offset by a credit of 70 in respect of company tax.

pay a (gross) dividend equal to total profits and still meet its tax liabilities without drawing on reserves.[1]

It is essential that the personal tax liability and the corporation tax credit should relate to a *grossed-up* dividend; and it is also essential that in so far as any one individual is due to pay income tax at a higher (or lower) rate than the basic one he should be called on to pay the excess tax (or receive a refund). Crediting systems which do not observe these principles are liable to be unsatisfactory (e.g.Canada used to have a system of crediting 20 per cent of dividend payments against tax liabilities; but this was no help to those on low incomes below the tax threshold).

It is easy to see that as far as purely domestic profits and domestic shareholders are concerned, the split rate and imputation systems are very similar in their effects. A full crediting system could, under either approach, be arranged so that the rate of tax on retentions is equal to the weighted marginal rate of personal income tax on dividend recipients as a class; a partial system can produce equality between the rate on retentions and that on distributions subject to tax at the basic rate, even though shareholders pay more tax in toto than others with the same income level.[2] The only difference of note is that in the split rate case part of the immediate tax bill is corporation tax and part income tax; whereas (ignoring higher rate taxpayers) it is all corporation tax in the latter case. In so far as one thinks that corporation taxes are likely to be passed forward, shareholders would be treated a little more lightly in the second case than the first, ceteris paribus.

When there are foreign and not just domestic shareholders, the basic similarity of the two crediting systems no longer holds. We shall come to this subject in more detail later[2] but the basic point is that if relief is given at the corporate level all shareholders of such companies will benefit whoever and wherever they are; but if relief is given in respect of personal income tax, it can then be restricted to those within that tax net, if so desired.

[1] With total profits 200, a corporation tax of 50 per cent and a personal tax of 30 per cent, the maximum dividend payment would be 100: grossing up by 3/7 gives us 143 and personal tax on this at 30 per cent would be 43, i.e. only 43 of the 100 paid in corporation tax can be offset against personal income tax. See also Chapter 9, section 2.1.3.

[2] With profits of 200, retention of 30, corporation tax at 50 per cent, personal income tax at 30 per cent and a grossing-up factor of 3/7 we have the following: undistributed profits after tax 30, corporation tax 100, dividend paid out 70 (implying grossed-up dividend 100, personal income tax liability 30, credit for corporation tax 30). In other words, the tax total is 100, exactly the same as in the dividend paid credit case (cf. p. 453).

[3] Cf. p. 475.

3.4 *Taxing corporations like unincorporated businesses*

In many ways, the most logical way of treating companies is to impute undistributed profits to shareholders in proportion to their share of total equity capital, and then tax actual plus imputed dividend incomes at the appropriate marginal rate. This would immediately dispose of any unfairness whether between shareholders as a class and the rest of the community or between individual shareholders. It would also fit into the general pre-war tradition that undistributed profits should be subject to some rate of personal income tax rather than an entirely different levy, and into the particular tradition of treating close corporations (i.e. companies effectively controlled by not more than five persons) in some circumstances as if they were partnerships, and hence liable to pay higher rate tax on all profits, whether distributed or not.

It is often argued that this solution is completely impracticable, but it is not easy to see why this should be so. Companies have the necessary machinery for allocating dividends to individual shareholders, and there is no obvious reason why exactly the same methods cannot be used for imputing retained earnings to individual shareholders. What is true is that rich shareholders would then have greater incentives not to declare their dividends for higher rate tax, in that they would thereby avoid such tax on their aliquot share of retained earnings as well as on dividends received. How important this would be in practice requires detailed investigation, but it should be noted that even if it did take place the net result, as compared to the present system, would be that some rich men would escape all higher rate tax instead of all rich men escaping some. Another argument is that under this system rich men holding shares in companies distributing only small fractions of their earnings might find themselves faced with a tax bill in excess of their cash receipts. This would presumably lead either to pressure on such firms to distribute a larger share of earnings, or to the sale by rich men of their holdings in such firms. Either of these may be thought undesirable at first sight. But it must be realized that rich men's shareholdings in such companies are not always purely coincidental; the shares may have been bought on the expectation of large percentage retentions, or the interests of the rich shareholders may have been influential in securing such retentions. Therefore it cannot be automatically assumed that all such results of subjecting imputed earnings to higher rate tax would be harmful.

From the equity side therefore there is quite a lot to be said for this system, and the usual administrative arguments against it are not conclusive. Perhaps the strongest objection is that with this system the Government no longer has the power to tax company profits at a different rate from personal incomes. Our overall assessment must therefore depend on the weight we attach to this point as well as the equity and administration arguments.

Perhaps a suitable compromise might be to suggest the extension of this system from close corporations to 'less close' corporations or perhaps even to all private companies. This would mean an extension of existing practice rather than a radical departure from it. It would lead to some new differentials (e.g. between rich shareholders in private and public companies) but it would strike at the cases where the worst inequities of the present system are to be found. Whether this system is adopted for private companies, as distinct from subjecting them to the same kind of profits tax as public companies, is in the last resort a matter of how much importance we attach to rooting out inequities in the tax system, and whether there are any special grounds (such as the imperfections of the capital market which may make it less easy for private than for public companies to raise funds relatively to the risks involved) for not fully pursuing such a policy.[1]

3.5 *Taxation of accrued capital gains*

It is often argued that if capital gains could be taxed on an accruals rather than a realization basis, one would not need to supplement personal income taxation in any of the ways outlined above. In so far as undistributed profits lead to capital appreciation this is caught for tax straight away and the benefits of tax deferment inherent in capital gains taxation on a realization basis disappear. Even in this case, however, there may be some inequity depending on how much public recognition or evaluation of gains lags behind the retention of profits which generate them. And even though there may be some elements of capital gains taxation on an accruals basis in original cost depreciation systems,[2] it is generally agreed that a comprehensive accruals basis

[1] It should be noted that the Carter Commission, *op. cit.*, came down in favour of taxing corporations on the basis of imputed allocations of profits to shareholders. If this approach were adopted it would be necessary to write up the base value of an individual's assets for capital gains tax purposes by the size of his share in retained profits; otherwise there would be tax duplication. For further discussion of these and related issues, see M. Feldstein and D. Frisch, 'Corporate Tax Integration: the Estimated Effects on Capital Accumulation and Tax Distribution of Two Integration Proposals', *National Tax Journal*, March 1977.

[2] See p. 425.

would be very difficult to administer. The one substantial proposal on these lines in recent years[1] came to nothing.

4 THE CHOICE OF CORPORATION TAX IN THE UK

4.1 *The issues*

From a purely domestic angle, it could be said that the arguments have not been finally resolved in favour of the imputation system. As there have been dividend controls for the greater part of the time since it was introduced it is not possible to come to any certain conclusion, one way or the other, about the relative effects in practice of a partial crediting system and a separate system on the working of the capital markets and the supply of funds to the corporate sector. The combined effect of low corporate rates of return before tax, accelerated depreciation and inventory profits inflation adjustment have also meant that the amounts of mainstream tax have been cut to very low levels.[2] Nevertheless, there are those who would still argue for the separate system on grounds of general principle.[3]

On the other hand, it would not seem that there is much support left for a split-rate system. Although the Inland Revenue had a marked initial preference for the split-rate system on administrative grounds,[4] it would seem that the device of ACT, whereby sufficient corporation tax is collected at the time a dividend is paid to offset basic rate income tax liabilities,[5] satisfied their main fears. Further protective devices such as that which limits ACT to 30 per cent of profits in any accounting period (or, putting it the other way round, insists on a 20 per cent mainstream liability) will clearly act as a limitation on the size of distributions relatively to profits.[6]

[1] In *Proposals for Tax Reform* (Queen's Printer, Ottawa, November 1969), the Canadian government suggested that half of the capital gains on widely held Canadian corporation shares should be taxed in the usual kind of way but that in addition unrealized gains should be taxed on an accruals basis every five years.

[2] See Kay and King, *op. cit.*, Chapter 11 for further discussion.

[3] E.g. S. Surrey, 'Reflections on "Integration" of Corporate and Individual Income Taxes', *National Tax Journal*, September 1975. See also the Chancellor's 1976 Budget Speech (Hansard, Commons, 6 April 1976, col. 249).

[4] See Report from *Select Committee on Corporation Tax*, session 1970/71, HC. 622 (HMSO, November 1971).

[5] As a corollary, there is no danger of non-taxpayers, who are entitled to refunds, receiving refunds not covered by UK tax revenues.

[6] This rule means that if profits are 200, the maximum distribution for which ACT at 3/7 is allowed is 140, i.e. for any larger figure ACT would be more than 30 per cent (and mainstream liability less

In fact, the purely domestic issues are overshadowed by EEC considerations in this case. After many years of discussions a draft directive appeared in 1975 endorsing the imputation system and embodying the concept of tax credits for shareholders against corporation tax as the standard for EEC countries. As the proposals do not imply any radical reforms in the UK system, we postpone discussion of the details of the directive until the next chapter and simply note now that the general form of the tax is no longer a matter of dispute in the UK.

Two other matters which have given rise to much discussion are the treatment of close companies and of small companies.

As for *close* companies (i.e. broadly speaking, those controlled by five or fewer participants or by directors), matters have improved very considerably compared to the position in the late 1960s. This is partly an automatic result of the move towards a more integrated corporate-personal tax structure; when retentions are a means of avoiding *all* payment of income tax the temptation to enlarge them is obviously greater than when it is only *higher rate* income tax at stake – and this is precisely the difference between the post-1965 arrangements on the one hand and the imputation or split-rate systems on the other. The second reason why the whole close company issue is much less troublesome is that restrictions on distributions were very considerably lightened in recent years. As for *small* companies which are often, though not necessarily, also close companies, it has often been argued that a form of corporation tax which is broadly neutral between distribution and non-distribution is not appropriate in their case, precisely because they are so dependent on retained profits to finance their activities. It was announced in 1972 that the new corporation tax would be cut to 40 per cent for companies with annual profits of less than £15,000, with tapering relief to those in the £15,000 – £25,000 range. This was estimated to affect some 350,000 companies. By 1978 the figures had been revised so that a rate of 42 per cent applied to companies with profits up to £50,000 and tapering relief up to £85,000. Whether this is the ideal way of proceeding might be argued (e.g. it has often been maintained that the simplest device is to offer small companies a choice between treatment as corporations or as partnerships), but it can at any rate be argued that the reduction in the rate of

than 20 per cent) of 200. An alternative way of describing the restriction is to say that distribution plus ACT at 3/7 cannot absorb more than a company's taxable income. If larger distributions are in fact declared, surplus ACT can be carried back two years or, alternatively, carried forward.

corporation tax will have beneficial effects on the willingness to incorporate as well as the supply of finance.[1]

4.2 *Conclusions*

We have discussed the reasons why personal income taxation plus taxes on capital gains realizations are insufficient on their own. There are pros and cons for non-integrated and integrated personal and corporate tax systems. The recent British move towards integration is to be welcomed for a variety of reasons. But the final conclusion must be to reiterate that one can never divorce the subject of company taxation from that of personal income taxes on dividends and capital gains taxes on share disposals.

[1] For further discussion of this whole subject, see *Small Firms: Report of Committee of Inquiry on Small Firms*, Cmnd. 4811 (HMSO, 1971).

18

THE TAXATION OF OVERSEAS INCOME

1 THE ISSUES

1.1 *Introduction*

'Double taxation' is a banner which is frequently waved, with cries of righteous indignation, in tax discussions. The reasons are twofold: partly that there are a number of different ways in which so-called double taxation can take place, or can be made to appear to take place, and partly that it is so easy to wax eloquent on the apparently harsh resultant injustice. We shall confine ourselves here to one particular way in which double taxation may occur, i.e. when personal or corporate income comes under the jurisdiction of more than one national tax authority. Although related problems occur when, for instance, the Federal and the State governments in a federally administered country both claim to tax income, we shall only refer to this aspect of the problem incidentally and more or less by way of illustration. Similarly, there are analogous issues arising when different administrations lay claim to capital transfer taxes on the same assets (e.g because in one case the assets are located in its territory and in another because they belong to its residents). But these also will be outside our scope.

There is also the opposite problem to that of 'double taxation' – when business firms, pre-eminently multinational corporations, are able to arrange their affairs so as to generate an unwarranted proportion of their profits in countries which levy taxation at low (or zero) rates. This raises very different issues to those which concern us most and we cannot hope to discuss them fully here. However, at the end of the chapter we shall give an indication of the main issues arising in this context.

We deal with various background issues first and then come to underlying principles in section 2. Sections 3 and 4 are devoted to policy issues in the UK and EEC respectively; and section 5 to problems of transfers principally within multinational corporations.

1.2 *The UK position*

Within the income category, it is convenient to distinguish between that which is derived from the possession of property abroad and that resulting from working abroad. Income from property can in turn be divided into that which accrues directly to persons (e.g. dividends from companies located abroad, rents on real estate, etc.) and that received by companies from abroad (e.g. dividends paid by subsidiaries to parents). Income from work abroad arises in such cases as consultancy charges by engineers, fees to surgeons performing operations abroad, etc.

The legal position in the UK is extremely complicated in these matters and it would be quite impossible to discuss it in detail in this book. We must, however, try to summarize the broad outlines of the position and ask the indulgence of the legalistically minded if they feel that too many of the fine points are slurred over.

Income tax law and custom in the UK start from the presumption that the tax net should stretch over both income arising within the boundaries of the UK and income accruing to the residents of the UK. Moreover, the term 'residents' is widely defined to include people who may, in fact, live abroad for part of the year. The historical explanation, if not justification, of this apparent greediness of the authorities is that the convention arose in the days when tax rates were low and when relatively few other countries taxed incomes directly.

In the practical application of these rules a number of concessions have been made. The most important stem from the double taxation agreements which have been made with many countries since 1945, when the first (that with the US) was signed. The most usual feature of these agreements has been that the UK forgoes its right to tax at the full rate all the profits earned by a British company operating overseas. When a British company has a subsidiary *located*, *managed* and *controlled* abroad, no UK tax is payable on its profits if they are retained abroad. When profits are remitted to the UK by such independent subsidiaries, and in the case of *all* profits earned abroad by the parent company or British-controlled subsidiaries, agencies, branches, etc., credit is allowed for the foreign tax paid. It is important to note that such taxation is not just allowed as a deductible item from assessable profits but is treated as an offset to any UK tax liability. Furthermore, crediting of foreign income taxes, whether at central or local level, is given unilaterally against UK liabilities if no treaty exists.

The other main principle enshrined in the double taxation agreements has been, in a sense, the reverse of that just outlined. Whilst in the case of company profits the country of origin is deemed to have the prior right of taxation, in the case of incomes accruing to individuals a measure of exemption from tax is often allowed in the country of origin. Thus dividends paid by US companies to British stockholders are only subject to US withholding tax at the rate of 15 per cent. In the case of some British Government stocks (e.g $5\frac{1}{2}$ per cent Funding Stock 1982/4) the principle is extended further. Foreign holders of these stocks are automatically exempt from deduction of UK tax and do not have to go through the paraphernalia of claiming tax credits from their own Government.

Relief is given in various other ways. UK residents who worked abroad temporarily were taxed until 1974, not on their total foreign earnings, but on the amounts remitted to this country after meeting necessary expenses abroad. There were also special classes of UK residents (e.g. those resident but not domiciled here) to whom this remittance basis applied even in respect of other categories of income. But since 1974 the remittance basis concessions have been much attenuated so that for instance, UK residents working abroad for short periods pay UK tax on 75 per cent of their foreign earnings (assuming they are domiciled in the UK).

1.3 *Questions arising*

The principal complaint which arose in the 1950s about these rules and regulations was that undistributed profits of overseas operating subsidiaries of UK companies were not relieved of UK tax. As we have seen, the position historically was that they were only relieved if the subsidiary satisfied some stringent requirements about local (overseas) control. It must be noted that there was no real argument about *dividends* remitted to the UK, whether to individuals or to companies; it was generally accepted that no relief could be claimed for them over and above that provided in the Double Taxation Relief Agreements and some quarters thought even this too liberal. Other complaints were that the Double Taxation Relief Agreements worked harshly in detail, e.g. whilst credit was given for foreign income taxes, none was given if any particular country chose to levy an export tax instead of or in addition to the income tax. Another point, of which a lot was made, was that if a developing country chose to reduce its tax rate in the hope of attracting foreign capital, this simply resulted in a present to the UK tax authorities, as it automatically added to the amount of tax they received. Exactly the same result followed if, instead of reducing its tax rate, the overseas territory gave relief in the form of more liberal depreciation than that allowed in the UK. Finally, it was added that many other developed countries provided relief against tax on income derived from overseas and therefore, in some sense or other, this was an argument why the UK should do so too.

There were two major sets of legislation bearing on these matters. In the 1957 Finance Act, it was provided that a company registered in the UK but trading abroad could, under certain conditions, be designated an Overseas Trading Corporation (OTC) and as such relieved of UK income taxes on undistributed profits. Nearly 1,000 such OTCs were established. However, this experiment was short-lived and these corporations were abolished in the 1965 Finance Act. There were two other important provisions in that Act. First, it was decreed that in future credit for overseas tax paid by UK companies would be given against corporation tax only. Thus whereas a company paying tax overseas at a rate of, say, 50 per cent could previously credit the whole of this sum against its UK tax liabilities (the combined weight of income tax and profits tax being greater than 50 per cent) it was no longer able to do so with a corporation tax rate of 40–45 per cent and a separate withholding tax on dividends. To ease the transition it was agreed that relief should be given for a limited period to the most hard-hit companies. Second, the system of relief to UK shareholders in receipt of dividends from overseas companies was tightened up in that unilateral relief in respect of foreign 'underlying' taxes (e.g. corporation profits taxes) was abolished except where the shareholder was a British company owning at least 10 per cent of the shares in the foreign company.

Latterly, other issues have come to the fore. The debate in the early 1970s about the rival merits of split-rate and imputation taxes on companies focused attention on the division of a given total of tax revenue between governments when there is inward investment in the UK. And in addition all these matters now have to be looked at from an EEC viewpoint.

It will be noted that these questions all relate to property income rather than earned income. Although the latter is not without its conundra, as the fracas about the 1974 Finance Act and the remittance basis demonstrated, the bigger issues do arise with property income and we shall therefore confine ourselves to them for the rest of the chapter.[1]

2 GENERAL PRINCIPLES

Before we can arrive at any judgement whether the present position in the UK is satisfactory, we must see what guidance can be obtained from general principles. We shall start by assuming that one wants tax systems to be neutral in respect of capital exports and then examine the implications. Subsequently, we shall ask whether the neutrality position is wholly defensible and, if it is not, what general modifications in tax systems are implied. Then we shall be in a better position to assess the specific modifications, if any, needed in the present UK arrangements. It must be stated very explicitly at this point that the subject is immensely complicated and we cannot do more here than touch on some of the most germane points.[2]

2.1 *Tax neutrality*

It is generally argued by economists that there is a fundamental case for the free movement between countries of factors of production as well as goods. World production will be increased if, the marginal product of any given factor being sufficiently higher in B than in A to offset the cost of movement from one country to the other, the factor in question were to move from A to B; and if there are no impediments to factor movements, this is what will tend to happen. This principle is subject to refinement if there is a greater divergence between marginal and average values in goods or factor markets in one country than another due to monopolistic competition, or if there are discrepancies between social and private costs or benefits. Thus, for instance, the effects of such divergences might be to make the reward to any one factor less in country B than in country A, despite a higher marginal productivity in the former. However, this essentially amounts to saying that one should look at the underlying rather than the superficial relationships

[1] For further discussion, see M. A. Pickering and A. R. Prest, 'Some Aspects of the Remittance Basis for the Taxation of Overseas Income', *British Tax Review*, 1974, No. 6; and 'Overseas Earnings', *Accountancy Age*, 3 March 1978.

[2] For fuller discussion, see J. D. R. Adams and J. Whalley, *The International Taxation of Multinational Enterprises* (Institute for Fiscal Studies and Associated Business Programmes, London, 1977); and M. Sato and R. M. Bird, 'International Aspects of the Taxation of Corporations and Shareholders', *IMF Staff Papers*, July 1975.

between factor rewards and factor values and that, if we do this, there may be cases where government intervention will produce a better factor allocation than would obtain in its absence.

Given the general principles on which inter-territorial movements of factors of production should take place, can anything be said about the sorts of ways in which the imposition of taxation by national governments may lead to a less than optimum allocation of resources among countries? It will be convenient to concentrate on the effects on the movement of capital, as this is most relevant to the subject-matter of this chapter, but the arguments can be applied, mutatis mutandis, to other factors as well.

Suppose we imagine first that country A levies taxes only on its residents, whatever the source of their income, whilst country B levies taxes on all income originating within its territory. In any such case, a resident of A who owns capital located in B will have to pay tax to both governments. Therefore even though the marginal productivity of capital be higher in B than A, there will be a clear deterrent to capital movement and it seems likely that the flow of capital from A to B will be less than it would be if the taxing jurisdictions did not overlap. It would also follow (on the assumption that country B does not tax income accruing to its residents from country A) that residents in B with capital in A would escape tax entirely. It does not therefore seem likely that such a combination of tax codes would produce the 'right' flow of capital across national boundaries. And if we had the converse case where A taxed incomes originating in its territory and B taxed incomes received in its territory, inhabitants of A would pay no tax at all on their investments in B and therefore a more than optimum outflow of capital from A to B would take place. It might, of course, be argued that if residents of A were willing to migrate to B with their capital, they would then escape double taxation of dividends, but this is unlikely to be an acceptable solution in many individual cases, as there may be major disadvantages in being tied geographically to one's property. This may, however, be a relevant solution for companies in some circumstances.

A second case is when country A taxes income originating within its territory and country B does the same. If we assume for the moment that tax rates are the same as in the first case, then there will obviously now be greater incentives for the international movement of capital. There will no longer be a deterrent to a capitalist in A to invest in B where the gross return is higher, at any rate if the cost of moving capital can be thought to be negligible and the rate of tax much the same in both territories. If, however, for one reason or another the rate of tax on dividends and profits were much higher in B than A, even the absence of tax in A on income originating from B might be insufficient to direct capital to B.[1]

Parenthetically, it might be noted that the system of taxation of investment income in the country of origin of income but exemption in the country of receipt is the one which is favoured by some Continental countries, e.g. France, Belgium and in effect Holland. This system can be characterized as being one of capital import neutrality in the sense that taxation on investment proceeds is levied at the same rate whatever the source of the investment funds. But for the reasons indicated above it would not result in capital export neutrality.

A third case would be that in which both country A and country B levy tax on a residential and not on an originating basis. This can be seen to have advantages over both the first and second cases. The flow of capital from A to B in search of a higher yield is not impeded by two bites of tax; nor is it repelled by a higher rate of tax in one country than the other (e.g. the citizen of country A will suffer the same percentage tax deduction irrespective of whether his capital invested in A or B). Provided that the cost of moving capital is zero, capital will move from the territory with the lower to that with the higher yield. And even if the cost of movement is not zero, it will still be worthwhile shifting capital, provided that a sufficiently large part of the additional yield is left after tax to compensate for the cost of movement.

Fourthly, let us take the most realistic case, where both A and B tax on a world-wide basis (i.e. covering income originating and income received by residents) but where credit is given for foreign taxation. Provided that foreign tax liability is no greater than home tax liability, we shall in effect be left with a residential tax basis and so we are back to our third case.[2] If foreign tax liabilities exceed home liabilities, it is then possible that capital flows may be in the 'wrong' direction, e.g. if

[1] Strictly speaking, it is not legitimate to assume the same tax rate in A as in the first case, for we should not then have the same revenue yield unless income from investment in B (after B's tax) were exactly the same as investment income (before tax) flowing from A to B. If the former exceeds the latter, the tax rate in A would be higher in the second case and vice versa. However, it may be legitimate to neglect this further possible complication.

[2] It should be explained that the neutrality result only follows when *both* countries impose taxes on income. If the foreign country had an income tax and the home country an expenditure tax, we should have double counting were the foreign tax to be allowed in full against the expenditure tax and the investment outlay itself to be deductible against expenditure tax. Cf. *Meade Report*, *op. cit.*, pp. 412 ff.

the B rate of tax is sufficiently greater than the A rate to make the net return in A greater than that in B to a resident of A.

Finally, it should be noted that even a residential (or a residential plus originating with double tax credit) basis may not lead to the same capital flow as would take place in some hypothetical no-tax situation or with equivalent yield poll taxes, once risks of foreign investment are taken into account. It does not seem rash to assert that in general foreign investment is likely to be more risky than home investment (e.g. less knowledge and slower appreciation of adverse political or economic developments) and so the general argument about adverse effects of income taxation on risk-bearing is likely to be stronger than in the purely domestic context we examined in Part I, Chapter 3.

2.2 *Further complications*

This simple notion of tax neutrality has to be modified a good deal in practice. The first point is that one may have different views about the desirability of foreign investment depending on whether one looks at it from an international, a national or an individual viewpoint. This can be illustrated by comparing the effects of a tax system based on the residence principle with one which combines residence and origin, with credits for double taxation (i.e. our third and fourth cases in the preceding section). We saw that, on the assumption that foreign tax could be credited in full against home taxation, these two systems would amount to much the same thing from the viewpoint of the *individual* and that capital would continue to flow to the countries with the higher pre-tax returns. But from the viewpoint of the capital-exporting *country* it makes a great deal of difference whether it collects all the tax on the income received from abroad (as it would do if there were no tax on income originating in the capital-importing country) or none at all (as would be the case if the capital-importing country's tax on income originating were at least as great as the tax on income received in the capital-exporting country). In other words, it can be argued that from a national viewpoint one has to look at income from abroad, net of foreign tax, and compare this with whatever other benefits would have accrued if the capital export did not take place. This opens up a number of possible bases of comparison. One is to say that more domestic investment would have been possible if foreign investment were less and in this case one should compare the pre-tax returns at home with the returns from abroad net of foreign tax (see note 1 on page 472). Another is to say that curtailment of foreign investment might be a desirable means of reducing the pressure of demand in an over-extended economy in that the cut in total demand necessary to ensure the same saving of foreign exchange on imports of goods and services, without intensifying inflationary pressures, would have to be much greater.

It is clearly impossible to stop the argument at this point. Even if one is looking at purely national considerations, one has to take into account the many ways in which foreign investment may affect the visible and invisible items in the balance of payments in the future. On the one hand, it may be more difficult to sell our exports if foreign substitutes are developed in the future as a result of British capital investment abroad. Our own capacity to export may also be less than if the same amount of investment had taken place at home. On the other hand, there will be additional invisible earnings in dividends, royalties, etc.; British exports might have been shut out of foreign markets by tariffs, import restrictions etc. anyway; and imports might be cheaper, or at any rate more secure, than if no foreign investment had taken place. There are so many variables here that it is clearly very difficult, if not impossible, to assess with accuracy the long term national advantages of foreign investment.[2]

Even if the balance of national advantage could be easily resolved, the larger question remains whether national or international considerations should be paramount. By and large, foreign investment is likely to flow from richer to poorer countries and this alone would seem to call for some suppression of purely national interests on the part of capital-exporting countries. There is also another point: if it is a 'must' in the world today that the combined total of public sector capital exports, public sector aid and private sector capital exports to less developed countries should be substantial, it then follows that tax arrangements which are unfavourable to private foreign investment are likely to increase the role of the public sector in this sphere. This raises major political, as well as economic, considerations which must be taken fully into account in any overall assessment.

[1] This is not such a clear-cut proposition as it sounds at first sight, as pre-tax returns at home may be less than post-tax returns when there is a generous system of allowances or grants on investment. Therefore it does not follow automatically that if, say, post-tax returns are the same at home and abroad, then from a national viewpoint home investment should be preferred.

[2] See W. B. Reddaway *et al.*, *Effects of UK Direct Investment Overseas, An Interim Report* and *Final Report* (Cambridge University Press, 1967 and 1969) for a detailed analysis of these matters.

So the whole question of how far private interests conflict with or are in line with national or international considerations is immensely complicated. It must be accepted that, in times of serious economic difficulty such as the UK has experienced on a number of occasions in recent years, measures have to be taken to cut foreign exchange demands and overseas investment will inevitably suffer in the process. But this is an entirely different proposition from saying that in the long run there are clear national arguments against overseas investment,[1] quite apart from wider international issues.

3 UK POLICY ISSUES

It may be helpful to clear out of the way some matters which are not of immediate dispute. As far as individuals are concerned, it does not look as if the 1965 arrangements need be changed much. It was always difficult to see why British shareholders of American securities should get relief against US corporation tax. This meant that in effect British shareholders were better treated in respect of dividends derived from the US than in the case of those from the UK – and for that matter better than US holders of US or UK securities.

In the case of companies, the first point is the comparison of UK treatment with that meted out by other countries to their foreign-operating enterprises. It is fallacious to argue that on grounds of equity, UK companies should be treated very generously because some other countries (e.g the US[2]) act this way. It is no more relevant from the standpoint of equity that other countries' tax treatment of foreign-operating enterprises differs from ours than it is that any other aspect of other countries' business taxation arrangements (e.g. taxes on property or on business purchases) differs from ours. The important

[1] Cf. Sir Donald MacDougall, 'Social Choice between Home and Overseas Investment', *Economic Record*, March 1960: 'A conflict between private and social investment optima is entirely possible; what appears impossible is to estimate the presumption of general bias for private overseas investment to be either too large or too small.

[2] US treatment is very liberal by British standards. Broadly speaking, foreign subsidiaries of US corporations – a much wider category than under UK law – are only subject to US corporation tax on a remittance basis, i.e. tax is deferred so long as profits are retained abroad. Then a Western Hemisphere Trade Corporation (i.e. conducting all its business in the Western Hemisphere and having at least 95 per cent of its income from outside the US and 90 per cent from trade or business) pays US corporation tax at a reduced rate. The creation of Domestic International Sales Corporations (DISCs) in 1971 has meant that half of export profits from production and sales has been allocated to them and the deferment principle applied to half this total. See G. C. Hufbauer, 'Taxation of Export Profits', *National Tax Journal*, March 1975; and A. R. Prest, 'G.A.T.T. and Company Taxation', *British Tax Review*, 1977, No. 4.

question is whether tax concessions by other countries increase their ability to compete with us rather than some elusive criterion of fairness; this in turn leads us straight back to the earlier point that risks of foreign investment are likely to be greater than for home investment and so some leniency in the treatment of overseas, relatively to home, income may be desirable. Another point is the OTC experiment.[1] On balance, there does not seem to be much case for revising the 1965 legislation. One snag about the OTC system was that in effect it gave a greater weight to the originating rather than the residential basis of taxation, by exempting undistributed profits from UK tax – and in general principle, as we have seen, this is not a desirable arrangement.

Another point on which no action seems necessary is export taxes. From the equity angle, there is clearly no more case for the relief of British firms trading overseas from foreign royalties or export taxes (in the sense of allowing them as a tax credit) than there is for relief for UK trading firms against the expenses of paying rates, licence fees, etc. In both cases, the royalties, fees, etc. are deductible as expenses in computing assessable profits and this seems to be all that is necessary in equity. From the viewpoint of removing hindrances to foreign investment, the answer turns on whether or not the particular foreign tax concerned can be shifted forward to the purchasers of the firms' products (or, for that matter, backwards on to wage-earners). If it can be so shifted, the firm concerned has little to complain about, but in so far as it cannot be shifted, it will remain a charge on the profits of the firm. It is clearly anomalous that if a foreign tax is an undisguised tax on incomes or profits, it should be allowed as a relief against British income and corporation tax, whereas if it is a disguised tax it should not be so allowed. But the injustice of the case should not be exaggerated. As the disguised direct taxes are treated as expenses when assessing UK tax liability, the reduction in net profits to any firm is far less than the amount of the disguised direct tax.

Nor would there seem to be much disagreement about the extension of tax-sparing arrangements. Since the Finance Act of 1961 it has been possible for the UK to make arrangements with other countries so that, if they tax UK enterprises at specially beneficial rates, the UK cuts its tax rate to the same extent. By this means, the company concerned and not the UK government gets the benefit of foreign tax concessions. Agreements on these lines have now been made with various

[1] See p. 467, above.

countries. Although the US has never made such concessions a number of other countries (e.g. West Germany, Canada, Sweden) have done so.

As has been shown in some detail,[1] there would be many other considerations if the UK were to think of switching in whole or in part from personal income to personal expenditure taxation. We have already mentioned a problem with outward investment.[2] If one looks at inward investment, one must then visualize the retention of domestic income and corporation tax in this context unless the UK were to relinquish its rights to tax such incomes. It may well be that some of the most difficult problems of expenditure tax implementation arise in this area. However, we do not regard this as a pressing policy matter and so will not discuss it further.

We now come to international implications of the imputation system of corporation tax introduced in the UK in 1973. We look first at inward investment and then at outward investment. In both cases there are a number of bases of comparison: the imputation system could be compared with the pre-1965 system, the 1965/73 system, or the split-rate alternative. We shall not attempt to make all possible comparisons but confine ourselves to those which have attracted most discussion, with one or two sidelong glances at the others.

With *inward* investment, the main argument[3] centred around the alternative effects of imputation and split-rate systems in the UK, assuming a non-integrated system abroad (as in the US). Taking the case of direct investment first, the essential point is that with a split-rate system there would be a strong tendency for UK subsidiaries of foreign companies to pay out very large dividends, thereby taking maximum advantage of the reduced rate of tax on distributed profits. This can be looked at in several ways: it means a larger share of tax revenue to the foreign government[4] and a smaller share to the UK government; alternatively, there are larger invisible outflows in the balance of payments; or perhaps most fundamentally, there would be a loss of national income to the UK.[5] All these arguments can be documented

[1] Meade Report, *op. cit.*, Chapters 20 and 21.

[2] See p. 470, n2.

[3] See *Report from Select Committee on Corporation Tax*, Session 1970/71, HC. 622 (HMSO, November 1971), *passim*; also A. R. Prest, 'The Select Committee on Corporation Tax', *British Tax Review*, No. 1, 1972.

[4] In so far as the credit against foreign tax liabilities is reduced by virtue of smaller UK tax levies.

[5] If one took the view that a reduction in corporation tax rates on distributions led to comparable price reductions (i.e. that corporation tax can be 'unshifted'), there need not be a loss of national income under the split-rate system. But this is unlikely.

from German experience with their former split-rate system.[1] Only if it were possible to negotiate differential rates of withholding tax (i.e., higher for dividends flowing from countries with integrated to those with non-integrated corporation taxes than in the reverse case) or differential rates of corporation tax (discriminating in a parallel manner), could these problems be avoided. And neither of these expedients looked at all possible.

With an imputation system the position is entirely different. In that case, corporation profits are taxed at the same rate, whether distributed or not; and no relief is given (nor withholding tax levied) if the distribution is to a foreign parent company.[2] As was clearly brought out in the Select Committee deliberations of 1971, this means that when Double Taxation Agreements are being negotiated, a country with an imputation system is in a much stronger position than one with a split-rate system which has, in effect, deprived itself of its most valuable cards in advance.[3]

As for foreign portfolio investment, a country operating an imputation system is again in a strong position. Although credit is given automatically to domestic shareholders, it is a matter for negotiation whether such credits should be extended to foreign shareholders. In fact, the UK started to renegotiate double tax treaties in 1973 in such a way as to make credits available to foreign shareholders, thereby putting them in essentially the same position as domestic shareholders under the imputation system – and for that matter in the same position as with a split-rate system.

So much for a split rate as against an imputation system for inward investment. It is worth adding that the picture is a rather different one when the 1965/73 system is compared with the imputation system. Whereas the treatment of direct investment is roughly the same that of portfolio investment is more lenient. This is simply the result of introducing concessions to shareholders to avoid 'double taxation'

[1] E.g. With US corporation tax at 48 per cent and German tax at 51 per cent (on retentions) and 15 per cent (on distributions) and withholding tax at 15 per cent in both countries, a German subsidiary operating in the US could not remit more than 44 out of 100 profits whereas a US subsidiary operating in Germany could remit as much as 65 out of 100 (even after allowing for the application of the 51 per cent rate to the total of profits, less sums actually paid out as dividends, i.e. not just to retentions).

[2] Assuming that the UK-US Double Taxation Agreement negotiated during the period 1973–78 is eventually ratified in both countries, there would then be a precedent for giving credits to foreign firms, parallel to, if not as valuable as, those given to foreign shareholders.

[3] Allowance must also be made for any difference in exchange rates prevailing in the two cases. (This point is due to John Whalley.)

at company and shareholder level. Its international extension has to be justified in terms of attracting portfolio investment in this country.

With *outward* investment one debate was about the merits of the imputation system (or for that matter, the split-rate system which has the same properties in this context) compared to that ruling in the UK before 1965. The essential feature of that system was that a UK company had to pay two taxes, profits tax and income tax, on its profits but this absolved dividend recipients from standard rate income tax. Credit for foreign taxation on subsidiaries, whether an underlying corporation tax or a withholding tax on dividends to the parent company, was given against the combined total of the two UK taxes. This was of the order of 50–55 per cent in the latter days of the system. Provided that foreign tax did not rise to inordinately high levels, the tax rate of foreign and domestic investment was the same and so there was no discrimination between them in this respect.[1]

A central feature of the imputation system is that ACT must be paid in respect of every dividend payment. If we take the limiting case of a company with no domestic income and no retentions and a foreign tax rate equal to the UK corporation tax rate we find that the totality of tax paid must be greater than for a company deriving all its income domestically but otherwise similarly situated; whereas ACT is offsettable against the total corporation tax bill in the latter case, this is not so in the former. So we now have a situation where the aggregate tax bite is larger if a given sum of profits is of foreign rather than domestic origin.

The comparison between the imputation system and the separate system prevailing in the UK from 1965–73 can be illustrated as follows. If France and Britain each have a corporation tax at 40 per cent, but it is not linked with their personal income tax structures, then the shareholders of a British company investing in France will (assuming the usual double taxation arrangements) be treated in exactly the same way for tax purposes as if the investment were in the UK; and the same will hold for French shareholders, mutatis mutandis. But now assume one has an imputation system in both countries, say, for simplicity, a 50 per cent corporation tax and a gross-up credit factor of 3/7. In this case the shareholders of a British company investing in

[1] The danger that non-taxpayers in this country might reclaim UK tax which had never been paid was avoided by the device of the 'net UK rate', i.e. a non-taxpayer could only reclaim the excess of the UK rate over the foreign rate on any dividend paid to him.

France will not be as well treated as if the investment were in Britain; and the same will hold for French shareholders investing in Britain. In other words, a form of corporation tax which removes bias between distribution and retention introduces bias between home and foreign investment.

Before discussing the implications, we must note various circumstances in which this differentiation would not apply, or not fully apply.

First, even when all profits come from abroad and none are retained, the degree of discrimination depends on the foreign tax rate. If in fact the foreign tax rate is no higher than 28.57 per cent, and assuming UK corporation rate at 50 per cent and ACT at 3/7, there would be no differentiation against foreign profits.[1] It is only when there is no liability to UK corporation tax (other than ACT) that the full weight of the discrimination is found. Second, even though the foreign tax be as high as the UK rate and all profits come from abroad, the degree of differentiation depends on the pay-out ratio. In the limiting case, with nil distribution there would be no differentiation at all. Finally, when profits are partly earned abroad and partly at home, there may or may not be any differentiation depending on the ratio of undistributed to foreign profits. It was expressly provided[2] that distributions may be assumed to come as far as possible from domestic sources and ACT apportioned against the corporation tax on such income rather than foreign income. So provided that the ratio of retentions to foreign profits is large enough, no differentiation will materialize.[3]

But when all this is said and done, it must be accepted that some UK companies trading overseas will be at a disadvantage compared to others trading at home. Although the scale of the problem is not enormous and, as we have seen earlier,[4] the optimal tax treatment of foreign investment is by no means clear-cut, it has to be accepted that there is a price to be paid in terms of less outward investment, a greater tendency to diversify into UK activities so as to increase the base against which ACT can be offset, and so on. In other words, one simply has to face the clash between a tax structure which differentiates to

[1] Assume foreign profits of 200 and a nil retention: a distribution of 100 would be grossed up to 142.86 and this would involve ACT of 42.86. If foreign corporation tax is at 28.57 per cent, foreign tax would be 57.14, i.e. a tax total of 100, exactly the same as if 200 profits were earned at home.

[2] *Reform of Corporation Tax*, Cmnd. 4955 (HMSO, April 1972), para 30.

[3] This does *not* imply that foreign income cannot exceed undistributed profits; the only requirement is that corporation tax on home profits must be sufficiently large to absorb ACT on dividends without reducing mainstream tax to less than 20 per cent (cf. p. 461).

[4] Cf. p. 471.

some extent against outward investment and one which is free of differentiation between retentions and dividends.[1]

It should be understood that the imputation system bias is against direct rather than portfolio investment. In the latter case, one can reasonably assume that other countries will continue to deduct 15 per cent withholding tax from dividends and that this will be credited against UK income tax liabilities. On the other hand, the higher rate of corporation tax under an imputation system provides more scope for the immediate crediting of foreign taxes.

4 EEC CONSIDERATIONS

4.1 *Alternative possibilities*

The appropriate taxation of profits in the EEC has already received a good deal of attention[2] and will no doubt receive a lot more. There are two separate reasons for this degree of interest: the first is the general urge to harmonize taxes on profits so as to remove any tax inhibitions on capital flows inside the Community; the second is that if a corporation tax were to be a major source of finance for the Community's budget, this would necessitate a fairly common structure throughout the member countries. The second proposition has less force than the first, e.g. it can readily be argued that the ratio of profits to GNP, or that of corporate to total profits varies so much from country to country as to make a corporation tax too inequitable a source of Community finance. But even if this is so, the first argument alone is sufficient to justify a good deal of thought on these matters.

One way of harmonizing corporation taxes within the Community would be to abolish member country taxes and replace them by a single Community tax. Although this is a most unlikely development in the foreseeable future, it should be noted that in many federal or similar type political structures, the main powers of taxing corporations do rest with the central government. If this were a possible longer-term line of development, one would then have to ask what system of corporation tax would be most appropriate. This raises questions which we have

[1] Although the pre-1965 UK system did not differentiate against outward investment nor between retentions and distributions, it depended on the extremely clumsy and awkward device of the net UK rate.

[2] Cf. *Report of the Fiscal and Financial Committee* (Neumark Report) EEC, Brussels, 1963; A. J. van den Tempel, *Company Tax and Income Tax in the European Communities* (EEC, Brussels, 1970); *Draft Directive on Harmonisation of Company Taxation* (EEC, Brussels), 1 August 1975.

discussed at length in this chapter and the preceding ones: the definition of corporate profits, the general merits of integrated versus non-integrated systems, the practical difficulties of integrating one corporation tax with a number of differing personal income tax systems and so on. Although it would obviously be simpler administratively not to have credits against personal income tax liabilities in respect of distributions, such an arrangement would be perfectly possible. It would not seem that any new problems arise in considering the relative merits of different corporation tax systems, if there were to be a single Community-level tax.

Much more complex issues open up once we face the more realistic case, at least in the foreseeable future, of national corporation taxes in each member country. This is a subject to which a great deal of time and effort has been devoted[1] and so we must spend some time on it here.

4.2 *The 1975 proposals*

The general principle underlying these discussions has been that tax arrangements should hinder the free flow of capital between member countries as little as possible.[2] This was to be achieved by a system of corporation taxes emphasizing capital-export neutrality rather than capital-import neutrality, i.e. the location of the investor rather than the location of the investment should be the paramount criterion in determining the relevant tax rate.

It has been generally accepted that these Community harmonization objectives could not be achieved if differing member countries used different types of corporation taxes. Thus if one imputation country were to operate a concessional rate of tax for subsidiaries of another imputation tax country, the amount of unrelieved ACT in the second country would be that much smaller. But if an imputation tax country were to do the same for a subsidiary from a separate tax country, there would be no net gain to the parent company in that less tax in the first country would be counter-balanced by more tax in the second.

What has been much more a matter of dispute over the years has been the form which any common type of corporation tax should take. The split-rate type was in vogue at the time of the Neumark report but

[1] Draft Directive, *op. cit.*

[2] It should be noted that a tax system allowing a free flow within the Community may not be optimal from a world standpoint. Cf. Sato and Bird, *op. cit.*

the van den Tempel report later argued in favour of the separate system. However, since the Draft Directive of 1975, the course seems clear for the imputation system. The majority of Community countries have in fact already adopted the system in one form or another, though it would seem that Holland in particular is still very much wedded to the separate system.

The details of the Community system were not fully settled at the time of writing but there are four main features which are the focus of discussion. First, member countries should levy corporation taxes in the range of 45–55 per cent. Second, there would be imputation credits of 45–55 per cent. This concept needs a little explanation as it follows the French rather than the British imputation technique. Whereas the British tax credit is expressed as a fraction of the cash dividend paid out, the French avoir fiscal or imputation credit is expressed as a fraction of the corporation tax underlying the dividend. The two concepts are related in the following way:

$$\frac{\text{Tax credit}}{\text{per cent rate}} = \frac{\text{corporation tax per cent rate}}{100 - \text{corporation tax per cent rate}} \times \frac{\text{imputation credit}}{\text{per cent rate}}$$

So if corporation tax is levied at 50 per cent the tax credit and imputation credit rates will be identical; if the corporation tax rate is less than 50 per cent the imputation credit rate exceeds the tax credit rate and vice versa.

In fact the 1978/79 UK corporation tax rate of 52 per cent and tax credit rate of 33/67 both fit into the EEC proposals, the corresponding imputation credit being 45.5 per cent.

The third of the EEC proposals is designed to eliminate the bias against foreign investment inherent in an imputation system. In effect the additional tax (ACT in the UK context) payable by a company when profits are made abroad rather than at home is to be offset by imputation credits from the member country where the profits originate. The upshot is, more or less, that the country of profit origin collects corporation tax *less* the credit and the country of profit receipt collects personal income tax *plus* the credit. It should be noted that this system only covers intra-EEC investment and so it is only the bias against these capital flows which is eliminated.

Finally, it is proposed that there should be a withholding tax of 25 per cent on dividends plus credits but that this would effectively not apply to shareholders in EEC countries, whether resident in the country of profit origin or not. But unless some crediting arrangements can be made there would be a bias against non-EEC investment in EEC countries.

It remains to be seen how these proposals are modified before final adoption. But whatever the modifications turn out to be it would be unwise to think that the UK could easily adopt a system, such as the cash-flow corporation tax suggested by the Meade Committee, at variance with these ideas. No doubt the Community proposals have plenty of imperfections (e.g. in neglecting capital gains issues and concentrating on corporation tax integration rather than the definition of the profits base), but they do nevertheless remain the pattern with which we shall have to comply sooner or later and to a greater or lesser degree.

5 TRANSFER PRICING AND TAX MINIMIZATION

5.1 *The nature of the problem*

Our last task is to highlight some of the issues when the cry is that too little rather than too much taxation may be paid on overseas income. It is frequently alleged that multinational corporations arrange their affairs so as to minimize worldwide income and corporation tax payments and there has been a great deal of debate about their tax behaviour in recent years.[1] Much of the debate has been specifically concerned with US corporations and relatively little is known about its applicability in the UK context. So for this reason alone we shall be fairly brief in our discussion.

The simple-minded approach is that if corporate activities straddle more than one country attempts will be made to generate the largest possible proportion of total profits in that country with the lowest rate of corporation tax – whether by underpricing imports to or overpricing exports from that country, charging smaller sums for the supply of knowhow, management or leased equipment or simply lending funds at very low rates of interest. The consequence of any such action will be that less tax will be paid in aggregate than if profits were allocated strictly to the country generating them and also that the allocation of profits, and hence of tax payments, will change between countries.

[1] See, e.g., *The Impact of Multinational Corporations on International Relations* (Technical Papers: Taxation), (UN, New York, 1974); and G. Kopits, 'Taxation and Multinational Firm Behavior: A Critical Survey', *IMF Staff Papers*, November 1976.

It can very quickly be seen that the mechanism is likely to be a good deal more complicated in practice. Calculations of income and corporation tax burdens must take account of withholding taxes on dividends as well as the underlying corporation tax. Overpricing of exports (imports) can run into trouble if there are high ad valorem export (import) duties. Then there are a series of non-tax factors to take into account – exchange control restrictions on dividend payments, expected changes in exchange rates, dangers of running foul of local monopoly or price regulation, generation of funds in a country to finance capital expenditure and so on.[1]

So any attempt to pinpoint the nature and magnitude of the problem must take account of a large number of other variables as well as any simple-minded objective of maximizing profits in the country with the lowest corporation tax. Nevertheless, the general point remains that total tax payments and their distribution between countries will be affected.

5.2 *The evidence*

As usual with tax avoidance, it is extremely difficult to get a clear picture of the magnitude of the problem. First, there is the conceptual difficulty that it is far from easy to determine the correct allocation of profits between countries. It is one thing to say that corporations should follow arm's length pricing principles (i.e. act as if they were dealing with unrelated enterprises), but quite another to translate this concept into practical guidance for tax administrators. International agencies have been trying to grapple with the problem for over fifty years[2] without finality. The rule of adopting the price which would be charged for the supply of particular goods or services to an unconnected body may be quite inapplicable if parents supply goods or services to subsidiaries which they would never supply to outsiders. But despite these and many other difficulties it would be seen that one is utterly lost without the arm's length pricing principle and so one simply has to make the best of a bad job.

Evidence of the extent of deviations from arm's length pricing may be pieced together from a number of different sources. One approach is to compare tax rates in different countries to see how much scope there is likely to be for tax minimization practices. But this really is

[1] Cf. C. V. Vaitsos, *Intercountry Income Distribution and Transnational Enterprises* (Oxford University Press, 1974).

[2] The League of Nations was active in these matters in the early 1930s.

pretty hopeless as one rapidly sinks into a morass as soon as one tries to work out differences in *effective* tax rates (after giving due weight to various concessions, exemptions etc.) as distinct from *nominal* tax rate differences.

A second approach is ad hoc investigations. One of the best-known examples is that of Vaitsos,[1] who found startling evidence of overpricing of various imports into Colombia. But how typical these results are of less developed countries generally, and how far they can be explained by rather special Colombian circumstances, is another matter. Other evidence comes from monopoly control authorities. In the UK this has resulted in one suggestion that parents undercharge[2] subsidiaries and another that they overcharge.[3]

As far as tax authorities are concerned by far the most intensive investigations have been carried out in the USA. A Treasury study of 1973[4] showed that out of 800 US multinationals investigated some 400 so arranged their affairs that US profits declared were less than they should have been on the basis of arm's length principles. Transfers of both goods and services were involved. But from the viewpoint of the US corporate sector as a whole, the underestimation of profits and underpayment of tax were small beer.

A little bit of parallel information has seeped out about the UK position, mainly in answer to Parliamentary questions,[5] but even if examined under the most powerful of electron microscopes the net addition to knowledge is miniscule.

As can be seen from this account, information on the subject is very scrappy. Clearly these practices do go on but neither their magnitude nor the consequences for, say, transfers of taxable capacity from LDCs to developed countries can be stated with any degree of confidence.

5.3 *Remedies*

If these practices are in fact such as to warrant action to curtail them, what form should it take?

Existing tax practices differ widely between countries, both in the wording of the relevant statutes and in methods of translating them

[1] *Op. cit.*

[2] *Footwear Machinery*, HC. 215 1972/73 (HMSO).

[3] *Chlordiazepoxide and Diazepain*, HC. 197 1972/73 (HMSO).

[4] *Summary Study of International Cases Involving Section 482 of the Internal Revenue Code* (Washington DC., 1973).

[5] See Hansard Cols. 512–13, 12 Jan. 1977; Col. 237, 19 Jan. 1977; Col. 412, 24 Jan. 1977; and Col. 758, 25 Jan. 1977.

into guidelines for Revenue officials and corporations. Thus the US Treasury has published elaborate guidelines and has sought court action in some cases. On the other hand, the UK prefers to deal behind the scenes and on a more ad hoc business with individual offenders; only rarely does any information leak out.[1] It is in fact most unlikely that there is any stereotyped procedure which tax authorities in every country should adopt.

This does not mean that nothing can be done to improve existing practices. Governments could do a great deal by putting their own houses in order with, for instance, greater exchange of information between customs officials, income tax authorities and monopoly regulating agencies. Double taxation agreements providing for exchanges of information between different countries can also be a powerful weapon. All the same, some of the suggestions one encounters (e.g. the need for a single world corporation tax, or a system of splitting world-wide profits between countries on parallel lines to that existing in the USA for the division of profits between States) are neither likely to nor deserve to make much progress in the foreseeable future. In short, quiet and unobtrusive moves are more likely to yield returns in this area than the big, bold and brassy ones so frequently advocated from the hustings of international gatherings.

[1] See, for example, *Financial Times*, 16 March 1977 for a discussion of the practices of the Hoover company.

19

THE STRUCTURE OF INDIRECT TAXES[1]

1 THE GENERAL POSITION

1.1 *Introduction*

This chapter begins with the detailed statistics of indirect taxes in the UK and in section 2 the possible justifications for this system of indirect taxation are discussed. In section 3 these criteria are used in analysing the total amount of indirect taxation in the UK today, the allocation between consumers' goods, capital goods and the like and the allocation between the different types of consumers' goods. In section 4 comes the mechanism of indirect tax collection, and in section 5 the sorts of ways in which VAT may need modification over the years ahead.

To reduce this task to manageable proportions we shall not pay much attention to those customs duties which are levied purely for protective reasons. They are not an important element in the total of indirect taxes, and questions of raising or lowering them immediately involve us in international trade considerations outside the scope of this book. Local rates will be discussed in the next chapter and so we confine ourselves here to central government matters. Although subsidies raise questions which are very similar to those discussed here, they raise others which demand lengthy consideration. So although we shall have a few remarks to make on this subject *en passant*, we do not pretend to treat it fully.[2]

These simplifications may seem drastic. But they are essential if we are to come to grips with the main problems involved in a field which,

[1] The theoretical distinction between direct and indirect taxes is a very dubious one; see A. R. Prest, 'On the Distinction between Direct and Indirect Taxation', in W. L. David (ed.), *Public Finance, Planning and Economic Development* (Macmillan, 1973). We use the term here as a purely conventional one.

[2] See Joint Economic Committee, *The Economics of Federal Subsidy Programs* (Government Printer, Washington DC, 1972/1973), for extended discussion. Also A. R. Prest, *How Much Subsidy?* (Research Monograph 32, Institute of Economic Affairs, London, 1974) and 'The Economic Rationale of Subsidies to Industry' in A. Whiting (ed.), *The Economics of Industrial Subsidies* (HMSO, 1976).

despite its great importance, was very much neglected in the UK for many years, at least in comparison with that of income tax.

1.2 *The statistical picture*

We have already seen in Chapter 9 that the ratio of taxes collected by the Customs and Excise Department to total central government budget revenue was of the order of 40 per cent in the earlier years of this century but has fallen to about 30 per cent in recent years. Even as late as 1896/97 it was still only a little under 60 per cent.

Table 19.1

Central Government Indirect Taxes by Classes of Expenditure, UK, 1977

Class of expenditure	*Amount £m*	*Percentage of total*
Consumers' expenditure	11,838	78
Public authorities' current expenditure on goods and services	827	6
Gross domestic capital formation	1,286	8
Exports of goods and services	1,295	8
TOTAL	15,246	100

Source: *National Income and Expenditure 1967–77* (HMSO, 1978); and *Economic Trends*, various.

Notes: (1) Only central government revenue included, i.e. local rates excluded. (The division between categories is approximate.)

(2) Subsidies in 1977 as officially defined amounted to £3,333m (£2,881m central and £452m local) and £2,774m were allocated to consumers' expenditure.

For the purposes of this chapter the more useful figures are those given in the annual *National Income Blue Book*. These give us a somewhat different definition of indirect taxes, which includes items such as stamp duties, motor vehicle licence duties, the national insurance surcharge and royalties on North Sea oil as well as the standard Customs and Excise Duties. They also include social security contributions in the total of central government revenue. On this basis, the ratio of indirect taxes to total central government revenue was 30 per cent in 1977, as compared to 46 per cent in 1938. Thus both approaches give roughly the same overall result. Although some of the items included by the *Blue Book* as indirect taxes are challengeable, the amount involved is not great, as all the additions to the Customs and Excise Department receipts amount to less than 20 per cent of the total of all indirect taxes.

The breakdown of indirect taxes between the main classes of expenditure is shown in Table 19.1.

This shows that although the great bulk of central government indirect taxes are levied on consumers' expenditure, the other end-uses nevertheless account for some 22 per cent of the total. We shall return to this point later.

Table 19.2 shows how the taxes on consumers' expenditure are distributed between commodity groups.

Table 19.2

All Taxes on Consumers' Expenditure, UK, 1977

	£m	*per cent of market value*
Food	485	2.5
Beer	1,135	30.0
Wines, spirits, cider etc.	1,229	44.7
Tobacco	2,524	69.5
Housing	2,236	17.4
Fuel and light	39	0.9
Clothing	552	8.1
Durable goods (incl. cars)	705	11.0
Other household goods	222	9.6
Books, newspapers, etc.	12	1.0
Chemists' goods	105	7.4
Miscellaneous recreational goods	175	8.9
Other miscellaneous goods	116	9.9
Vehicle running costs	2,049	41.4
Travel	105	3.6
Communications services	90	7.5
Entertainments and recreation	191	11.6
Other services	965	10.6
Unallocated	2,225	–
TOTAL	15,160	18.2

Source: *National Income and Expenditure, 1976–77 op. cit.* (HMSO, 1978).
Note: The attribution of 'Unallocated' to the individual categories would change the ratio of tax to market value in each case, but it is reasonable to think that the relative patterns would not differ much from those in the Table.

The nature of the figures presented in Table 19.2 must be emphasized. We exclude subsidies on food, housing, etc. but we are not able to exclude local authority rates attributed to consumers' expenditure. However, a large amount of this rates total is attributable to housing and it seems reasonable to assume that the remainder largely falls into the unallocated group. So for the remaining categories the table does show the percentage burden of central government taxes.

It can be seen immediately how large a role is played by tobacco, alcohol and vehicle running taxes. Tobacco taxes alone account for about 1/6th of total revenue; tobacco and alcohol together make up nearly a third of the total; and when we add the taxes on vehicle running costs we have nearly half the total. These ratios would all be correspondingly higher if rates were excluded. Of the other taxes which it is possible to allocate between different items of expenditure, only the taxes on durable goods, motor vehicles etc. and other services stand out as worthy of notice, if we leave the rating burden on housing out of account at this stage. If we look at the taxes as percentages of market values of the commodity concerned, we find the same pattern again. It is not the importance of tobacco etc. as a proportion of total consumption expenditure but the heavy percentage rates of tax which explain the differing contributions to the Exchequer.

Finally, if a comparison is made with 1938 we find that tobacco tax has gained in importance relatively to alcohol taxation and that the percentage contribution of the two together is considerably less than it was. Other major changes are the reduction in the percentage contribution of food taxes and the increases in those of durable goods, vehicle running costs and other services over the years.

Comparisons with the US system of indirect taxation are vitiated by the very differing importance of state and local governments relatively to the federal government, and by the differing relative dependence on direct and indirect taxes. If we look at the federal government alone, we find that indirect taxes amount to some 7 per cent of revenue, a much lower proportion than in the UK. Of this total, the percentage raised by taxes on liquor and tobacco together is somewhat larger than that in the UK, and the relative importance of the former, greater. If we make a more meaningful comparison by looking at all indirect taxes and all government revenues, we find that the ratio of indirect taxes to consolidated government revenue is approximately 36 per cent in the

UK and 27 per cent in the US.[1] Perhaps the most striking difference in the mechanism of indirect taxation is the much greater reliance on collection at the retail stage in the US; forty-five states have retail sales taxes and there are, in addition, a number of local taxes of the same sort.

2 THE ROLE OF INDIRECT TAXES IN THEORY

The analytical chapters of Part I give the necessary basis for summarizing the criteria applicable to indirect taxes. From the standpoint of *resource allocation* in the sense in which we defined it, there is a general presumption that it is better to confine indirect taxes to commodities for which demand or supply has zero price elasticity, or at any rate very low elasticity. The two main exceptions to this rule were found to be when the degree of monopoly differs a good deal from one commodity to another and when external diseconomies exist on the production side (e.g. smoke and smells) or the consumption side (e.g drunkenness). A further argument is the paternalistic one, that people should be discouraged from consuming what it is not in their own best interests to consume.

To encourage the *supply of resources* coming forward, we found that in respect of work-incentives the first principle was to avoid taxes with high marginal-relatively-to-average rates. Therefore indirect taxes on commodities which do not soak up a large fraction of expenditure from marginal earnings (i.e. commodities not highly competitive with leisure, as far as consumers are concerned) earn higher marks than those which do. Ideally, one would like to tax those goods which are in joint demand with leisure (e.g. afternoon theatre performances), i.e. where the elasticity of demand for leisure is negative with respect to their prices, but this is very difficult to achieve in practice. There is one possible saving grace. In so far as people's cognizance of the slice taken in indirect taxation is less than in the case of, say, PAYE, the effects on incentives to work may give less cause for concern. This effect is likely to be stronger when the earner and the spender are different people; but, as we have seen,[2] this theoretical argument is not a strong one. As for the incentives to save, this is clearly a matter of the sorts of goods

[1] UK data from *National Income Blue Book*. US data from *Survey of Current Business*. Definitions are not exactly the same in the two countries but are near enough for our purposes.

[2] See p. 80.

subject to indirect taxes. Taxes imposed on consumption goods only will discourage their production and consumption relatively to capital goods, and vice versa. The advantages of indirect taxes in favour of saving and investment materialize only if capital goods are not subject to tax.

To fulfil a *stabilization* role in the short period, indirect taxes will work best if they apply most heavily to those commodities with a high income elasticity of demand, so that in a recession consumption falls off more than proportionately to income. It will also be advantageous for taxes to be on an ad valorem rather than a specific basis, so that tax revenue will change in response to price as well as consumption movements.[1] If there is any regular cyclical pattern in the differential price movements of commodities, the right policy is not so clear-cut: on the one hand, ad valorem taxes on flexible-price goods will show greater proportionate changes in yield (for an unchanged quantity of output) than in the case of sticky-price goods, but, on the other hand, the greater degree of price-flexibility may push consumption more in the direction of these goods in times of slump.

For long-run stabilization, we need to combine the criteria for resource allocation and creation with those for stabilization. This immediately brings us face to face with an element of incompatibility: to fulfil one role or set of roles, we need to tax commodities in inelastic demand, to fulfil another we need to tax commodities with a high income elasticity of demand. A commodity on which only a small fraction of income is spent could have a high income elasticity of demand, whilst retaining a low price elasticity of demand; but if only a small fraction of income is spent, then the counter-cyclical tax effect is small. If, on the other hand, we tax a whole range of commodities of this type, the proportion of income spent on them is no longer small, and therefore even small substitution effects will not prevent the existence of high price elasticities, taking the group as a whole. If commodities for which the income elasticity of demand is high are also subject to external diseconomies of production or consumption, our difficulty disappears. But it would obviously be entirely fortuitous if this were so.

Another element of incompatibility arises when goods with a low or zero price elasticity of demand are consumed mainly by poorer people. In this case there is an obvious conflict between minimizing the effects

[1]For discussion of changes in yields of such taxes in the context of inflation, see A. R. Prest, 'Inflation and the Public Finances', *Three Banks Review*, March 1973.

on resource allocation and securing an equitable distribution of the tax burden. This point is clearcut and well known, and so need not be elaborated.

It might also be asked whether some of these difficulties cannot be resolved in principle by levying taxes on goods with high income elasticities of demand but zero or low price elasticities of supply. This immediately leads to other problems, however. If one of the aims of fiscal policy is to secure some *income redistribution*, levying of taxes on commodities in inelastic supply is not likely to be a clear-cut way of achieving these aims, as the burden of the taxes will fall on factory owners rather than consumers. It is most unlikely that we shall find readily available statistical techniques for measuring the impact of such taxes on the size-distribution of income via the changes in relative factor shares in income. If we are interested in taxes with fairly clear-cut effects on income distribution, the attraction of taxes on goods in highly elastic supply or highly inelastic demand is much greater. And quite apart from this point, there is always the very real danger of taxing commodities whose short-term supply is inelastic but whose long-term supply is highly elastic.

Finally, there are the requirements of *administration*. One of the traditional reasons for taxing commodities at all was the difficulty of levying income taxes at low income levels. Now that this has been largely resolved through the PAYE mechanism, is that argument still valid? Even if it is not, is there a case on administrative grounds for taxing rich men's consumer goods as widely as possible as an alternative to endless investigations into devices for avoiding high marginal income tax rates? In other words, is the administrative boot now on the other foot? We clearly need to scrutinize our indirect tax arrangements with a careful eye on these points.

All in all, there are some clear-cut conflicts of principle in the tasks which the system of indirect taxes is asked to perform. There will be very few commodities whose conditions of elasticity of supply or demand are likely to meet all the requirements listed. It is much more likely that it will be necessary to balance the imperfections of any one tax on any one commodity by different imperfections of other taxes on other commodities, so that the overall result of all indirect taxes taken together is of the right order.

3 APPRAISAL OF THE UK STRUCTURE

3.1 *The ratio of indirect taxes to all taxes*

Economic principles cannot help much when deciding on the ratio of indirect to all taxes.[1] Advocates of extreme progression could point to the gradual fall in the ratio of indirect taxes in the UK in the nineteenth century, the sharper fall in the ratio in this century and to the much lower Federal ratio in the US today. This argument does not get us very far as it rests in its crudest form on the implicit assumption that direct taxes are progressive and indirect taxes regressive. In principle the reverse could be the case, and in practice our knowledge of the actual situation is so slender that we simply cannot pontificate. From a political standpoint, there is clearly a lot to be said for collecting a substantial amount in indirect taxes. The fact that they are less obvious than income tax is perhaps not the noblest of political motives but it is certainly a compelling one. From an administrative standpoint, the present structure of indirect taxes does not come off badly.

The expenses of administering the Customs and Excise Department are some 1.63 per cent of revenue collected;[2] the corresponding figure for the Inland Revenue duties is 1.94 per cent.[3] Too much weight should not be put on these figures. The division between Customs and Excise and Inland Revenue is not quite the same as the classification used in this chapter. The ratios of expenses to tax yield partially depend on tax rate structures, so one might expect the direct tax ratio to increase and the indirect one to decrease if there were a reduction in income tax rates and yield accompanied by an increase in VAT rates and yield. And, of course, these costs are those of public administration only and exclude those appertaining to the private sector.[4] Nevertheless, as far as they go, there is no overwhelming administrative argument against the present size of indirect taxes in the UK.

3.2 *Indirect taxes by classes of expenditure*

We must first examine the justification for collecting some of these taxes from final uses other than those of personal consumption. It

[1] For discussion in the optimal taxation framework, see A. B. Atkinson, 'Optimal Taxation and the Direct v. Indirect Tax Controversy', *Canadian Journal of Economics*, November 1977.

[2] *69th Report of Commissioners of Customs and Excise*, Cmnd. 7455 (HMSO, February 1979). See also *Review of Value Added Tax*, Cmnd. 7415 (HMSO, December 1978).

[3] *121st Report of Commissioners of Inland Revenue*, Cmnd. 7473 (HMSO, February 1979).

[4] See C. T. Sandford, *Hidden Costs of Taxation* (Institute for Fiscal Studies, London 1973), for further discussion; also N. A. Barr, S. R. James and A. R. Prest, *Self-Assessment for Income Tax, op. cit*.

should be made clear from the outset that it is not a deliberate aim of the UK tax system to extort contributions from capital investment etc., but a by-product of the system of taxing commodities and transactions which, although mainly on consumption account, are not entirely so. Stamp duties on house purchases, for instance, are incurred partly in the process of exchanging second-hand houses (a consumption of services) and partly in the process of building new houses (capital formation). Duty on petrol is partly a tax on direct personal consumption of petrol, partly on indirect personal consumption (e.g. petrol used by firms making consumption goods), partly on that used in domestic capital formation, public consumption and exports.

There seem to be two questions to discuss. First, should we tax non-consumption uses in principle? Second, if so, should taxes be levied in their present form?

The general answer to the first question must be in the affirmative. There is no reason why indirect taxes should be exclusively confined to final consumption, even if this were technically possible. But somewhat separate issues arise in considering each of the three other final uses. With respect to public consumption of current (or, for that matter, capital) goods and services, we have to differentiate between the central and local layers of government. It is pointless for central government departments to pay taxes to the Treasury, and this has been recognized in the past by such devices as the issue of stamps on a non-payment basis to government departments and their exemption from duties on petrol. On the other hand, it may be administratively easier in some cases not to exempt departmental purchases (e.g. value added tax, liquor and tobacco taxes on goods bought for official receptions). With regard to local authorities, it might seem pointless that they should pay, say, VAT on supplies, especially as the end result may simply be a larger grant from the central government. This does raise a fundamental issue of principle, however. How far should local authorities be regarded as subsidiaries of the central government and how far as separate entities, more akin to business concerns? We shall argue in Chapter 20 that there are a number of functions which local authorities should perform on a purely commercial basis and that there are others to which the benefit principle has a good deal of relevance. If these points are accepted, it follows that there is a case for treating as many central-local transactions as possible on business lines, e.g. the central government collecting value added tax from such local authority activities and the latter collecting rates from the former's property.

With respect to exports, there would obviously be a good short-run case for levying taxes on commodities for which foreign demand is highly inelastic. It does not seem an over-bold assessment of the real world to assert that these conditions are in fact unlikely to prevail very frequently or for very long in respect of any one of this country's exports. We then have to decide whether there are any special reasons for mulcting factor incomes derived from exports. There obviously may be cases in which there is need to direct production from the foreign to the home market, but it seems unlikely that these will be common in the UK. And in any case the more general and direct method of doing this would be to revalue the currency.

In the case of capital formation, it is perfectly reasonable to argue that it may be necessary at times to reduce or increase output, and that one way of bringing this about is by the taxation of investment goods. Sweden is often cited as an example of a country which has used this technique in the past. One must be careful here, however. A tax on investment goods may be an anti-inflationary measure, but it may also have the effect of encouraging the use of labour-intensive methods of production.

It should be observed, moreover, that encouragement has been given to capital formation in the UK in recent years by the various species of accelerated depreciation and the like discussed in other countries. It is quite true that this encouragement has been essentially restricted to business capital formation and that some of the indirect taxes on capital formation apply to public and personal capital formation. Nevertheless, there is quite clearly some conflict: a tax policy which boosts business capital formation with one hand and knocks it down with the other can hardly claim high marks for consistency. Furthermore, the indirect taxes on capital formation will affect public capital formation as well as private.

This leads us to our next main question: given the need to tax non-consumption use goods, are we doing it in the right way? Although the position has improved since value added tax was introduced – it is unambiguously a tax on consumption whereas the same could not be said of its predecessors, purchase tax and SET[1] – there are still some unsatisfactory features of other indirect taxes. The degree of discouragement of capital formation, for instance, is not related to general policy aims in any way at all. It is difficult to believe that the authorities really intended to levy nearly £1,300 million in tax on capital formation

[1] See Chapter 9, section 3.2.

in 1977; it is more difficult still to believe that they wanted to direct it at the particular types of capital formation which it did hit, not least because it is so difficult to determine statistically what it did in fact hit. In principle, the way ahead is quite clear. In the main we should aim our indirect taxes at those commodities which are destined entirely for either personal consumption or private capital formation. We must try not to tax commodities whose end-usage is not readily determinable. There is not likely to be any real justification for taxing exports, and although taxation of local authority purchases is by and large justifiable, there is no strong need to set this up as a main objective. Perhaps even the twin objectives of personal consumption and private capital formation are too wide a field, in so far as encouragement or discouragement to capital formation can be readily given by other fiscal or indeed monetary methods. However, other fiscal techniques do not apply so readily to the discouragement of personal housing construction and so there may well be a case for keeping this additional weapon.

We must conclude therefore that there is a strong case against taxes on commodities the ultimate usages of which are not readily ascertainable. Correspondingly, the case for a value added tax or excise duties on, say, liquor and tobacco which are essentially consumed on personal account only, is stronger.[1] The other main conclusion is that there is a case on these grounds against stamp and similar duties which may work themselves out almost anywhere. The case for and against stamp duties is complicated, but one can still agree with J. A. Hobson[2] that 'for the most part they are the cumbersome relics of a past haphazard method of catchpenny improvisation which has no place in any scientific system of finance'. The moves in the 1960s to cut down stamp duties on house transactions might have been a starting point for more substantial and sweeping reductions but unfortunately they were reversed in the mid-1970s.

3.3 *Indirect taxes by classes of consumers' expenditure*

In 1977 the major sources of revenue of this kind were tobacco, liquor, motor vehicles and petrol. We can concentrate on these items and look at the rest of the indirect tax structure in less detail afterwards.

Although the relative importance of *tobacco* as a source of revenue

[1] The *National Income Blue Book* assumes that 2 per cent of beer and 8 per cent of other alcohol consumption is on business account, but a major part of the corresponding tax must in turn be indirectly allocatable to other forms of personal consumption.

[2] J. A. Hobson, *Taxation in the New State* (Methuen, 1919), p. 125.

has fallen in very recent years, it was still accountable in 1977 for something like 5 per cent of central government revenue. And over the period from 1938 to 1977 its yield certainly increased substantially, despite the specific nature of the duty. The explanation is that the tax has been successively raised to a level where it amounts to something near 70 per cent of the retail price; in addition, the volume of consumption rose by some 10 per cent over these years.

If consumption has risen over this period despite the very large increase in rates of duty, this might seem to suggest that the income elasticity of demand for tobacco is very high. Such a conclusion would not be justified, however. First of all, the rise in the price of cigarettes relatively to other commodities has not been as great as one might think from the increase in tobacco duties; whereas retail prices rose about elevenfold between 1938 and 1978, the prices (including tax) of, for instance, cigarettes only rose about ten times. Second, such statistical evidence as there is suggests that both income and price elasticities for all types of tobacco are low and that trends in long-term consumption are explained by other factors. It would seem reasonable to ask that those who cling to the idea of a high income elasticity of demand for tobacco should produce some evidence for their beliefs.

Tobacco would therefore seem to pass the important test of low price elasticity of demand.[1] Furthermore, it can be plausibly argued that there are some clear external diseconomies of consumption, in the form of irritation to others and the intensification of fire risks, quite apart from personal medical consequences for those concerned. As the tobacco plant is not easily grown in the British climate, the administration of the tobacco duty is essentially a matter of dealing with imports and offers no difficulties of any magnitude. An important aspect of the whole question is that of income redistribution. There is no doubt that the major part of consumption of tobacco in the UK is by lower income groups.[2] As we have stressed repeatedly, the determination of tax incidence is fraught with difficulty, but if it is possible to pronounce at all in this field, it does seem reasonable to say that the demand conditions for tobacco imply that, as compared to a distributionally neutral equal-yield tax, the tobacco tax imposes a much greater burden on the lower income groups.

[1] See Chapters 3 and 4, above.

[2] This has been confirmed by successive issues of the *Family Expenditure Survey*, e.g. that for 1976 (HMSO, 1977) shows that peak consumption (4.8 per cent of household expenditure) was reached in the £60–£70 a week income group.

It is possible to produce many arguments against this state of affairs. One is that the degree of regression introduced into the tax system is too great; another is that if this degree of regression is required, it should be effected openly and obviously through the income tax system, and another is that the tobacco tax is highly discriminatory within income groups. None of these seems persuasive, however. Given the amount of government expenditure, and the relative percentage of total personal income accruing to the 'upper' and 'lower' groups, a sizeable contribution to government expenditure simply has to be extracted from lower income groups. And it is very difficult to believe that a mechanism for collecting a comparable amount of tax from the same income groups through the PAYE system could work nearly as smoothly.

Finally, in so far as one allows that governments may in some cases override individual preferences, there is a ready defence for tobacco taxation, i.e. that it is a 'demerit' good to use Musgrave's terminology in that people commonly underestimate the health dangers involved.[1] Although these medical aspects are too modern to explain the origin of high tobacco duties in the UK, they are an extremely strong argument against removing them.

In the case of *alcohol*, the arguments are similar to but not identical with those arising in the tobacco case. The whole group of alcohol taxes produces about £2400m per year, almost as much as the revenue from tobacco. In pre-war days alcohol brought in some 25 per cent more revenue than tobacco, the explanation of the change being found in differential changes in duty rather than in the volume of consumption. In fact, in recent years the volume of alcohol consumed has risen sharply whilst that of tobacco has stayed much the same.

The general conclusion, though with perhaps a little less certainty than in the tobacco case, seems to be that there is good evidence for believing that income and price elasticities of beer, wine and spirits taken as a whole are fairly small and that other factors explain the long-term trends.

As with tobacco, therefore, we may conclude that alcohol passes the test of low price elasticity as a candidate for taxation. External dis-

[1] One has to be careful here of the argument that national health costs rise because of tobacco smoking; if more people lived longer as a consequence of not smoking, the reverse could be the case. Cf A. B. Atkinson and T. W. Meade, 'Methods and Preliminary Findings in Assessing the Economic and Health Services Consequences of Smoking with particular reference to Lung Cancer', *Journal of the Royal Statistical Society*, 1974, Pt 3.

economies – the domestic and public (e.g. road accidents)[1] consequences of drunkenness – are obviously of major importance, as are those of impairment of mental or physical abilities of the consumers themselves. As far as wine is concerned, there are virtually no vines growing in the UK and therefore no policing is necessary. Although the same does not hold for hops or barley, the problems of illicit brewing or distilling do not seem to rank large. From the viewpoint of income distribution, there is perhaps less to be said than with tobacco. If the conclusions about inelastic demand are accepted (and if they are not, there is really nothing to be said), then it is perfectly true that the weight of beer taxation falls on the lower income groups, but it is not nearly so true in the case of wines and spirits taxation.[2] Historically, the revenue from beer exceeded that from other components in the group, but that is not true in the 1970s. As a consequence, it is no longer so clear that the main impact of alcohol taxes is on lower income groups.

The next major category is the taxes on *motor vehicles and running costs*. These consist mainly of motor vehicle licences, driving licences, car tax and value added tax on motor vehicles, motor cycles etc. and petrol tax. Any justification for taxing these items must obviously rest on very different grounds to liquor and tobacco taxes, as it is most unlikely that demand for the major items in this group will have a low income elasticity. Hence price elasticity is less likely to be low. In so far as one attaches any importance to the consideration of increasing or decreasing returns to scale, the conditions of production of vehicles obviously tend to be of exactly the wrong type for excise taxes and the like. The standard reasons for these types of taxes are, of course, the costs of road construction, repair and maintenance, and the losses to society which result from any inadequacy of these facilities. No doubt there are good reasons for exacting contributions from those who make use of road facilities. But whether the present system exacts too much tax or distributes the burden between road users in any equitable way at all, one must take leave to doubt. Many issues arise here which we cannot discuss in detail. One is how far road costs, capital or current, should be financed by taxation, even taxation of road users, as opposed to the toll principle; another is the apportionment of tax between the personal car and the commercial vehicle – which in turn takes us back to the amount of indirect taxation to be levied on capital

[1] Though the same medical point arises here as with tobacco.

[2] The Family Expenditure Survey, *op. cit.*, shows some tendency for the ratio of beer to other alcohol expenditure to fall as one moves up the income scale.

goods; another is the relative amount of tax collected from the ownership of vehicles as such and that from the use of vehicles; another is the relative contribution from stationary vehicles and moving vehicles, parking charges dealing with the former and petrol taxes or possible other devices with the latter.[1] Yet another issue in this field is how far the 'benefit principle' should be pursued in any arrangements. Neither general theoretical principles nor actual experience with the operation of a Road Fund in this country lend much support to the idea of a separately earmarked fund, even if one accepts the general idea that taxes of this sort are justifiable as a means of financing road development or maintenance. However, it should be recalled that earmarking is practised in the USA for this purpose.[2]

Other arguments are also brought forward to justify vehicle taxes. One is that they help to divert British goods into export markets, or alternatively that damping down home demand may cut down the demand for imports. This raises the whole issue of how far balance of payments problems should be dealt with by selective measures, as distinct from broader fiscal or monetary methods including those of flexible exchange rates. It also raises the further issues of how far high taxes on domestic usage will in fact contribute to exports in the long run. Many business organizations have argued that it is impossible to conduct trade on the basis of a tiny home market and a large foreign one. Although there is no doubt a great deal of special pleading here, and there are many examples of industries largely based on exports (e.g. cotton textiles before 1914), the arguments should nevertheless not be dismissed completely. It would require another book to deal with this range of issues. Briefly, and inexcusably dogmatically, we shall simply say that our general preference would be for non-selective methods, unless a clear cut and analytically sound argument can be made in a particular case for discriminatory taxation.

With respect to the *other categories* of consumers' expenditure, there seem to be two things to say. First, the large item of 'Unallocated' makes it difficult to be dogmatic about the relative weight of taxation on the various categories. But if it is reasonable to postulate that it largely consists of items like petrol used by many different industries, we should expect the total to be well dispersed between the various categories. This point aside, there is an obvious question which comes

[1] Cf. *Report of Committee on Road Pricing* (Smeed Committee), Ministry of Transport (HMSO, 1964).

[2] See Part II, Appendix I.

to mind: why should the ratios of tax to total spending differ so considerably between different goods and services? One knows that the levying of taxes on some services may be difficult or impossible to administer; it is a principle of many excise and sales tax systems to keep taxes on foodstuffs to a minimum. There are no doubt other cases where special reasons can be adduced: it is difficult to find ways of taxing gambling winnings, for instance, and therefore an excise tax on betting is some sort of substitute. But beyond this it is difficult to see any motif in the patchwork of Table 19.2. It would seem just as easy to pick an entirely different set of taxes, rates and commodities which would produce an identical revenue, without in any way producing worse – and possibly even producing better – effects on the allocation of resources, the distribution of income, etc.

4 THE MECHANISM OF TAX COLLECTION

Although many of the issues debated for years under this head were settled by the introduction of value added tax in 1973, a short account of them is still in order. The first is the case against multi-stage (turnover) taxes; the second is whether a single-stage tax should be levied at the manufacturing, wholesale or retail level; the third is the comparison between a retail sales tax and a value-added tax.

It is not difficult to justify the exclusion of taxes levied as a proportion of turnover. There are in fact three strong objections to them. First, if levied at the same rate in two different industries, they will have a smaller impact on the industry with the smaller number of separate transaction links. In principle, it might be possible to correct for this by different rates of tax in different industries, but this would be a highly dubious operation. Second, even if this were possible, there would be a definite incentive to integration of the various stages in the productive and distributive process. Third, if the general objective of policy is not to tax all end-uses of a commodity but to exempt, say, exports or capital formation, an extremely complicated system of rebates would be necessary at all the manufacturing and, possibly, at the wholesale stages.

There is a large literature on the respective merits of manufacturing, wholesaling and retail bases for tax.[1] We cannot possibly discuss the subject in detail but the salient points are the following ones.

[1]See in particular the work of J. F. Due, e.g. *Sales Taxation* (Routledge and Kegan Paul, 1957) and *Indirect Taxation in Developing Economies* (John Hopkins, Baltimore, 1970).

From a resource allocation viewpoint, the retail stage has a great deal to commend it. One reason is that, by and large, it is easier to determine retail prices than others. If a tax is based on wholesale values, one has to invent a wholesale value when a commodity is sold direct from a manufacturer to a wholesaler-cum-retailer: e.g. the so-called 'uplift' principle which existed in the former UK purchase tax at one time. On the other hand, if the tax is at the manufacturing level and a manufacturer performs some wholesaling functions, we have the opposite problem, a deduction being needed to arrive at an appropriate price. Another reason is that if the tax is based on retail values, prices inclusive of tax will reflect the relative efficiencies of retailers as well as of prior links in the chain; whereas if it is on wholesale values, for instance, the amount of tax payable is invariant to the size of retail margins. Conventional notions about retail margins to be added to wholesale prices *plus* tax may have further distorting effects.

From an administrative point of view, the boot is on the other foot. Not only is the number of collection points inevitably very much larger with a retail tax but the quality is also lower. It is one thing to ask a manufacturer or wholesaler with a well-trained clerical staff to fill in forms and returns. It is a very different matter to get the one-man business to do the same. And it is not possible to dismiss small shops as being of no importance in the UK today. An administrative argument which can be made in favour of the retail stage is that the policing of exemptions then becomes less burdensome. Very few exports of public authority purchases are made at the retail level; and it should also be easier to exclude capital goods from tax in this case. If the basic intention is to tax final consumption, the retail stage will give a rather closer approximation than the wholesale stage, and a much closer one than the manufacturing one.

The extraction of tax at the wholesale stage means that retailers have to finance the tax element in the value of stocks. This means that there is some discrimination between retailers with different rates of stock-turn and between retailers bearing different rates of tax, compared to what would prevail if tax were only payable at the time of ultimate sale to the consumer. There is also a further point to mention: the capital gains and losses on tax-paid stocks due to changes in tax rates will tend to increase the uncertainty of retail trading – at least in the absence of extensive 'sale or return' schemes.

A VAT of the kind which allows capital expenditure to be fully deductible and operates on a destination basis can be thought of as being a very close relative of a retail sales tax.[1] The first difference is that it is collected at all stages in the production process rather than at the final stage only. This means a larger number of collection points;[2] and there may be an element of permanent loan from the private to the public sector in respect of tax-paid stocks which would not apply in the retail sales tax case.[3] On the other hand, one can now collect a large part of the revenue from large organizations; and the self-policing mechanism of VAT outlined earlier improves the collection process still further.[4]

A retail sales tax will give automatic tax exemption to most exports, whereas VAT involves collecting tax at earlier stages and refunding it at the final stage. On the other hand, a retail sales tax cannot cope nearly as well with such phenomena as retailers making purchases from other retailers or the diversion of goods ostensibly destined for production to consumer usage.[5]

5. THE FUTURE OF VAT

5.1 *The UK context*

If the future of VAT in this country were solely a domestic matter there would still be plenty of scope for controversy[6] about the extension or contraction of coverage, the level of the standard rate, the case for additional rates, the mechanics of tax collection and so on. For instance, there was a proposal late in 1978 for eliminating VAT payments on transactions between registered traders. Another argument might well centre round the possibilities of regional differentiation. These would not in fact be very great so long as the tax remains on a destination basis. In this case an attempt to impose a lower rate in, say, Scotland than in the south-east would be quite ineffective in respect of Scottish goods sold in the south-east or south-eastern goods

[1] Cf. p. 50.

[2] 70,000 with the old purchase tax at wholesale level; 1.25 m with VAT in the UK.

[3] But see C. S. Shoup, *Public Finance, op. cit.*, pp. 238–39 for an opposing view.

[4] It was argued that a decisive argument against a retail sales tax in the UK was the impossibility of effective administration at the rate which would be required. Cf. *Value Added Tax*, Cmnd. 4621 (HMSO, March 1971), paras 1–4.

[5] Cf. C. S. Shoup, 'Experience with a Value Added Tax in Denmark and Prospects in Sweden', *Finanzarchiv*, March 1969.

[6] See, for instance, *Review of Value Added Tax, op. cit.*

sold in Scotland; Scottish goods would have no relative advantage in either case.[1]

5.2 *The EEC context*

However, it is quite impossible to discuss the future of VAT in the UK without reference to the EEC context. There would seem to be two main issues when one looks at it from that viewpoint. First, there is the finance of part of the Community budget from VAT levies in the member countries starting with a 1 per cent levy in 1979, but rising to higher levels before long. Second, there is the long-standing plan[2] to abolish fiscal frontiers between member countries. This in turn implies a move from a destination basis to an origin basis[3] for intra-Community trade (a 'restricted origin' basis for short) on the grounds that it would only be possible to eliminate customs inspection at frontiers if taxes on imports from within the Community were abolished.

The preparations for the 1 per cent VAT levy for the Community Budget stemmed from the Sixth Draft Directive in 1977. Originally, there were hopes that a common VAT structure might be adopted in all member countries, i.e. with uniform coverage of taxable supplies, exemption levels and so on, but without any attempt at uniformity of the number or level of rates of taxation. The idea was that if a common coverage could be achieved contributions to the Community budget would be equitably levied[4] and, moreover, would have the great advantage of being a revenue source of its own for the Community – the 'ressources propres' in Brussels language – even though it would not have its own collection machinery. In the end, it was not possible to achieve a common structure of tax in all countries though moves were made in that direction in various individual countries.[5] So the present situation is simply that there is a common definition of VAT coverage for Community Budget purposes and each country contributes at the agreed rate (1 per cent in 1979) on that basis. The fact that

[1] A more complicated scheme such as a common regional VAT rate used to finance a differential regional wages subsidy would be a different matter.

[2] See e.g. *Report of the Fiscal and Financial Committee* (Neumark Report) (EEC, Brussels, 1963) and 'The Common System of Tax on Value Added', *European Taxation*, July/August 1967.

[3] See p. 211, above.

[4] Subject to reservations about variations in the ratio of the value of goods and services subject to VAT to total consumption or GNP from country to country.

[5] However, the gaps are still very wide with standard rates varying from 8 per cent to 20 per cent and the number of rate bands varying from 1 to 8 in 1978.

such a sum has to be paid over to the Community by member governments does not necessarily mean that the amount of VAT collected in any one country is greater than it otherwise would be; member governments simply pay over these amounts and it is up to them to determine how they make room for them in their budgetary arrangements.

It is convenient at this point to deal with a common fallacy. It is frequently argued that if any given country, or for that matter, the EEC bloc as a whole, collects a larger proportion of its tax revenue from VAT (and a smaller proportion from income and corporation tax) than say, the USA, the former has an unfair advantage in international trade at any given set of exchange rates. VAT applies to imports and is rebated on exports whereas, the argument runs, such manipulations are not possible with corporation tax and the like. The fallacy here is the automatic assumption that the domestic price level is the same when a large fraction of revenue is raised from VAT as when it comes from corporation tax. This could be so; but the more likely result is a higher domestic price level with VAT and if so, the rebating of VAT for exports (and a border tax on imports) is essentially a means of reaching normality rather than giving an undue trading advantage.

The adoption of the restricted origin principle would have much more far-reaching implications than the preparations for the 1 per cent levy. It is a well-known piece of economic theory that there is no need for uniformity of rates if the destination principle applies – country A can tax commodity X at 10 per cent and commodity Y at 5 per cent whilst country B reverses the two tax rates, without upsetting relative prices of home and imported X or of home and imported Y in either country. With a restricted origin principle there would be no ill-effects if member country A were to impose a 10 per cent tax on X and Y and country B impose a 5 per cent tax on X and Y, provided that exchange rates and/or domestic wage levels were sufficiently flexible to maintain balance of payments equilibrium between the two countries.[1] But it would not be possible for A to tax X at 10 per cent and Y at 5 per cent, whilst B continued to tax both products at 5 per cent, without upsetting

[1] We ignore the complications which arise if the additional government spending facilitated by additional revenue has a different pattern to the private spending displaced by the tax.

Even the proposition that uniformity of rates within but not between countries will not have trade distorting effects is only true under certain balanced trade conditions. We owe this point to John Whalley.

relative outputs of X and Y in the two countries. In other words, once one moves to the restricted origin principle, there are very tight restrictions on domestic rate structures if one is to avoid interference with trade flows.[2]

If it is likely to be extremely difficult to operate VAT on an origin principle without trade distortion one is naturally led to ask how much would be lost if the destination principle were to stay. The standard answer is that fiscal frontiers would then remain and this would be a real blow to the forces of European integration. However, this argument is by no means as clear as it is often made out to be.[1]

First, even with a restricted origin principle, some customs posts must stay, whether for overseeing trade with non-EEC countries or the passage of dangerous or prohibited goods – or for that matter goods subject to heavy excise duties – inside the Community. Second, suppose such custom posts as could be dispensed with were to be abolished without moving from the destination to the restricted origin principle. For the vast majority of goods there would be no major problem, e.g. French exports to West Germany would be relieved of French VAT and would not be caught at the German frontier but would be caught at a later stage in the German distribution network. So the only difference from the present position would be that such imports into Germany would be taxed at a later rather than an earlier stage. There would be problems in some special cases. One would be sales from VAT registered suppliers in one country to non-VAT registered purchasers in another, e.g. mail order supplies, used cars, works of art and so on. Another would be personal exports. In cases such as these, special measures would be needed to avoid tax avoidance (e.g. apply the origin and not the destination principle to personal exports). But it is far from clear that the destination basis and the abolition of fiscal frontiers are such incompatible bedfellows as has often been made out.[2]

One final point is that if any element of regional discrimination were allowable under the restricted origin system (e.g. VAT rates in Scot-

[1] Cf. C. S. Shoup (ed.), *Fiscal Harmonization in Common Markets* 2 vols. (Columbia University Press, 1967) for extended discussion.

[2] See A. R. Prest, 'Fiscal Policy' in P. Coffey (ed.), *Economic Problems of the Common Market* (Macmillan, 1979).

[3] Of the four possible types of transactions between registered and unregistered suppliers and purchasers, it is only those between registered suppliers and non-registered purchasers which would be troublesome.

land being half those in England), this really would improve Scottish competitiveness. So although the restricted origin principle might be thought to impose a straitjacket on member country VAT rates, it could at any rate be a more effective weapon of regional policy than the destination principle.

20

THE FINANCES OF LOCAL AUTHORITIES

1 PRINCIPLES OF LOCAL AUTHORITY FINANCE

1.1 *Introduction*

We described in Chapter 11 the principal characteristics of local authority finance in the United Kingdom. In this chapter we first discuss the principles on which local authority finances ought to be arranged. In the light of these principles we then consider the desirability of changes in three major areas: the ratio of grants to local authorities' own revenues (section 2), reforms in the grant system (section 3) and reforms in the rating system (section 4). Throughout, we shall draw heavily on recent analysis of these matters.[1]

The limitations of our treatment should be made explicit at the beginning. Relationships between Westminster and local authorities will not be the only form of inter-governmental financial relationships in the country, if the passing of the Devolution Acts for Scotland and Wales in 1978 eventually leads to Assemblies in those countries. Nor are grants from Westminster to local authorities the only way in which central government influences the relative well-being of people living in, say, Liverpool and Birmingham, given the vast structure of regionally oriented expenditures in the country. So it must be remembered throughout that we are confining ourselves to one out of a multiple set of relationships.

In analysing the principles of local authority finance, there are two distinct questions. First how important are the commercial aspects of local authority operations and how should such activities be conducted? Second, what can be said about administrative functions? The first question can be answered quickly but the second will take much longer.

[1] Layfield Report, Cmnd. 6453, *op. cit.*, A. R. Prest, *Inter-Governmental Finances in the U.K.*, *op. cit.*

1.2 *Commercial functions*

In so far as we can think of local authorities as business firms, we do not need to spend too long on the principles which should govern their finances. In essence, these would be the same as those governing the financial operations of nationalized industries. Although there is plenty of room for controversy in this field, the general idea that some adherence be paid to a marginal cost system of pricing for goods produced or services rendered is not seriously challenged. There are many variants of this – prices proportional to marginal costs, two-part tariffs, etc. – which we need not explore here, though it should be noted that there are severe legal restraints on deficit budgeting by local authorities. Considerations such as equity and the encouragement of risk-taking or personal saving which are usually present in central government revenue and expenditure proposals are simply beside the point if there is to be strict adherence to commercial principles.

But how far can a local authority be likened to a business firm? There are some straightforward commercial activities such as the provision of transport which most people would place in this category. Other activities such as the provision of cemeteries, slaughter-houses, and perhaps refuse collection can also be put in the same box. It would not be grossly wrong to charge on a commercial basis for all these services, but a glance at figures of local authority expenditure show that compared with education and other major expenditures these items are a flea-bite[1]. Even in the education field it would be possible to contend that vocational or technical training had some commercial characteristics about it, but such a proposition could not possibly hold for the general run of education expenditure. Although there are a number of schemes afoot[1] for allowing schools to charge fees to pupils with the local authority issuing vouchers to children's parents to meet such expenditures, the effect (of the less radical schemes, at least) would be more a matter of altering the distribution of pupils between schools than one of making a net addition to local authority financial resources. A major area where commercial principles could play a much greater role is local authority housing. There have been many demonstrations of the harmful effects of the present arrangements.[3] But reconsideration

[1] See Layfield Report, *op cit*., Ch. 9.

[2] See e.g. A. Seldon, *Charge* (Temple Smith, 1977).

[3] See e.g. A. Grey, N. P. Hepworth and J. Odling-Smee, *Housing Rents Costs and Subsidies* (Chartered Institute of Public Finance & Accountancy, 1978).

of such policies takes one into the much wider areas of the general case for housing subsidies and the relative treatment of local authority housing.

So, overall, one is forced to conclude that most people would take the view that the extent to which local authorities can really take on a commercial mantle is fairly limited given the nature of their activities and the constraints imposed by national policies relating to resource allocation and income distribution.

There are some further points. First, the extent to which one local authority can and should levy imposts on people living in other local authority areas is quite clear when we are thinking of commercial-type services: 'foreigners' should not be charged more or less than 'locals' for identical services. In one sense, this principle is itself a limitation on the extent of local authority activity which can be run on commercial lines. It is quite impossible to provide clean streets for 'locals' without also providing them for 'foreigners' (i.e. a public good situation) and, short of an octroi or local frontier system, impossible to charge the latter.

Secondly, how does our distinction between local authority commercial and administrative functions tie in with the distinction between onerous and beneficial taxation, which figures so prominently in the work of Marshall and Edgeworth? Although similar, the two classifications are not identical. The onerous-beneficial distinction attempts to distinguish between those activities which are for the benefit of local people (and therefore ought to be locally financed) and those which are primarily of national interest (and therefore merit national support). A sewerage system must be judged beneficial; public education onerous. Our distinction is somewhat different. Whereas it might be true that a particular service is purely for the benefit of local people and of no consequence to the rest of the country, it nevertheless might well be impossible to charge for it on a commercial basis. Thus a local fire service must be judged 'beneficial', but it cannot be placed in the commercial category.

One can reasonably end this section by noting that the Layfield Committee, whilst realizing that the subject of fees and charges opened up very much wider questions, felt that there might be scope for firmer adherence to commercial principles in some local authority activities and so recommended a major review of the area. The results of the review are not yet available.

1.3 *Administrative functions*

It is convenient to abstract from differences in local authority resources and needs per head initially and assume that we have only one pattern of local authority. This is a *representative* local authority in the same sort of way that we talk about a representative firm. It is therefore to be thought of in every way as having modal characteristics, neither corresponding at one extreme to the very large and highly efficient government machines of great cities nor to the small, backward and remote parish councils at the other. When we have explored the ramifications at this level, we can proceed to those which are due to the fact that in practice local authorities differ vastly from one another.

The underlying questions in this section are, first, how expenditure should be divided between central and local government and, second, how revenue raising should be divided between the two levels of government.

So let us start with the expenditure relationship between the representative local authority and the central government, and inquire into the criteria by which expenditure should be divided between the two. The first criterion must be that of efficiency, and the sort of considerations which arise are very analogous to those determining the competing abilities of large and small firms. When economies of large scale arise as in, say, expenditure on international airports, it is quite obvious that this is a job for the central and not the local government. Although it might be said that complex issues could be handled by an agency specializing in advising local authorities (analogous to specialist firms rendering advice to small firms), this does not in practice seem to be a very effective way out. When great flexibility and manoeuvrability is needed, as with, say, the provision of fire services, it is equally obviously a job for the local authority. There are many cases in between where the division of responsibility is not nearly so clear cut. But we may have said sufficient to illustrate the main point.

A broader principle for deciding the division of expenditure is that of the degree of conformity to popular wishes. It is probably true that members of local authorities have their ears more to the ground and are more susceptible to malaise and uneasiness among voters than is the central government. There is therefore a great deal to be said for decentralizing some public expenditure for this reason. However, one must be a little careful here. Closeness to popular wishes can all too easily turn into suceptibility to pressure groups and therefore this argument in favour of the local authority should not be pushed too far.

Another broad problem is to decide the minimum amount of activity which can be left to local authorities without killing all interest in their activities. Suppose, for instance, that on grounds of economies of scale it is thought that the central government should undertake all types of activity, even down to fire brigades, refuse collection and so on. And let us imagine that the 'ear to the ground' argument carries no weight either. If these two criteria were judged completely decisive, there would be no case for having local government at all. This is clearly a *reductio ad absurdum*. The reason why this conclusion is fallacious is, in the last resort, that there is a case for local authorities because there is a case for local authorities, in the sense that for fairly fundamental democratic reasons the powers of government should be separated and devolved on small local units as well as large centralized ones. This is an *ex cathedra* judgement, but we believe it accords with most people's ideas and in a book devoted to the economic aspects of public finance it seems reasonable to assert it without being called upon to justify it in detail.[1]

Although it can also be argued from a political decentralization angle that the more revenue local authorities raise for themselves the better it will be for them, it is not immediately apparent, however, that one would reach the same conclusions when inquiring into the most efficient administrative system of finance. One of the prime necessities of an efficient system of tax collection, especially when progressive taxes are involved, is ease of accurate assessment. This in turn depends on the amount of information available about a man's income, property or consumption. Almost inevitably, a larger public authority is likely to be in a position to obtain more accurate information than a smaller one, simply because the danger of transactions being half inside and half outside the jurisdiction of the authority is far less in this case. It may be that the officials of an *extremely* small local authority could personally know what goes on inside its borders, but this is not likely to be a common case. Therefore one is bound to conclude that the larger the taxing jurisdiction, the more likely it will be able to uncover all or nearly all economic transactions and thereby make accurate assessments.

[1] See R. A. and P. B. Musgrave, *Public Finance in Theory and Practice*, *op. cit.*, Chapter 29, for a discussion of the principles which should determine the optimum size of local communities, assuming no constraints due to historical patterns.

Much the same conclusion follows about the collection of tax. Any public authority is likely to be more effective in extracting tax payments from the residents within its area than from those outside (e.g. US states are not very successful in levying parking tickets on cars bearing out-of-state number plates). Therefore, whilst a local authority may be just as effective in dealing with its own residents as a central authority, the very fact that its area is smaller will mean that many taxes cannot be so effectively enforced.

So even though one can carve out a determinate role for spending by local authorities, nevertheless their revenue raising characteristics are such that even if there were no other considerations to take into account, it might well be desirable for the central arm of government to play a greater role in revenue raising than on the expenditure side. So on these grounds alone there is likely to be a case for transfers of funds from the central to the local level. This may take a number of forms such as grants from general revenue, shares of the revenue received from particular taxes and so on. We are not at the moment concerned with the precise mechanism of the assistance but simply note that, even abstracting from differences in local authority resources, needs, etc., there is likely to be a case for central government preservation of more of the revenue raising than of the expenditure disbursing functions.

There are in fact a number of other roles which central government grants may be called upon to play. There is first of all the externalities argument. Any one local authority's actions may confer benefits or impose costs on the citizens of other authorities as well as on its own. This may come about directly (e.g. a cost transfer in the form of smoke discharge) or indirectly (e.g. a benefit transfer in the form of the movement of people who have received training or education in one area to another). Grants, and for that matter, charges, may well have an important part to play in this context.

A second reason is merit wants. The central government may wish to encourage consumption of certain goods and services. This may again be a case for grants to local authorities, though two caveats should be noted: first, even if it is agreed that certain wants should be promoted (e.g primary education), the further condition has to be satisfied that such promotion should be by grants from the central government to local government rather than to individuals; second, that demerit wants exist as well as merit wants and they would point to negative rather than positive outpayments from the central authority.

Thirdly, there are second-best arguments. Obstacles to competitive forces, whether in the form of pockets of monopolistic practices or impediments to labour migration and the like, may easily interfere with efficient production. It may be simpler, from a number of viewpoints, to counteract such forces by a grant system rather than tackle them at the root.

It will be noted that we have made no reference to any role of local authorities in the pursuance of income stabilization objectives. This was quite deliberate in that the power of a local authority in this context is very substantially less than that of a national government. This is partly a matter of mechanics: a national government with the power to borrow from the central bank is much more likely to be in a position to run a budget deficit than a local authority. One must also recognize that any one local authority's power to pursue a stabilization objective in its own area is severely limited by the extent to which the effects of increases or decreases in revenue or expenditure would in reality impinge on incomes or outputs in other areas with which it has economic links. The same problem arises with measures to bolster incomes in whole regions though in a less accentuated form than with small local authorities. So even though one need not accept some of the more far-fetched claims which are regularly advanced by the Treasury in favour of strict controls over local authorities to ensure compliance with national demand management objectives,[1] one can argue nevertheless that local authorities have not much of a role to play here.

Similarly, if we leave local authorities as their own masters in redistributing income, it is again unlikely that the pattern of post-tax distribution will conform to that which is generally taken as acceptable. It may be nationally acceptable to redistribute from, say, the top ten per cent of income earners to the bottom ten per cent. Attempts to redistribute between the top and bottom quintiles in, say, Scotland and the top and bottom quartiles in, say, south-west England would not fit in with this policy except by chance. It is perfectly true that if labour and capital can move easily from one local authority area to another there will be effective constraints on the extent to which one local authority can pursue a radically different redistribution policy from others. But, even so, the overall results might well differ substantially from those of a national redistribution policy.

If we envisage a role for grants to local authorities even when

[1] See A. R. Prest, *op. cit.*, pp. 27 ff, for illustrations of this viewpoint. What gives the game away is that the Treasury advanced strong arguments in favour of controlling local authorities long before stabilization became an accepted policy of government.

differences in resources and needs are ignored, it is necessary to spend a little time asking which sorts of grants are likely to be needed to meet the various objectives mentioned above. There are various ways of classifying grants, the most important being:

(a) whether the grants are related to rather general or very specific criteria;
(b) whether the criteria are related to revenue capacity or expenditure needs, or both;
(c) whether the grants are tied to levels of local authority spending; and
(d) whether the grants are limited in total amount or not.

Any one grant may embody more than one of these characteristics. Thus supplementary transport grants in the UK are very specific (i.e. (a)); they are tied to local authority spending levels (i.e. they are a matching grant as under (c)); they are also in effect limited in total amount (i.e. (d)). UK police grants, on the other hand, are of a specific and matching nature but are not limited in total amount.

More generally, we can align instruments with objectives fairly readily. By and large, the 'easy' objectives of externality correction, merit wants promotion and second-best provision are met by grants which have very specific criteria and which are also tied to levels of local authority spending. Unless the latter condition is satisfied, the objectives of the donor government could easily be thwarted, in that the donee government would in effect simply have the equivalent of an increment in income which it could use in any way it wished, whether by way of increasing expenditure or reducing local tax rates. But if the grant is of a matching variety, there is a substitution effect as well as an income effect in that the marginal cost of expanding that service is reduced relatively to that of others. The position is then markedly different.

On the other hand, grants reflecting the division of functions between central and local government or grants designed for equalization purposes need to have more general criteria and to be related to revenue capacity, need and the like.

Mention of revenue capacity and need bring us to the point where one must remove the restrictive assumption about the representative local authority and allow for differences in resources and needs per head. This brings us directly to arguments about the case for inter-authority fiscal equalization, i.e. the proposition that there is a general case for levelling down 'rich' local authorities and levelling up 'poor' ones, even if all the specific objectives of grants identified above have been satisfied.

Although the theoretical case for inter-authority equalization is often taken as self-evident, it has in fact some questionable features. The standard argument[1] is that if one partitions a country into a number of different jurisdictions, there will be a differing spatial distribution of tax burdens (and/or expenditure benefits) from that which would arise if there were a single government only. With a number of jurisdictions one would expect some to be better off, or to have lower 'needs', than others and therefore able to provide a higher level of public services at a given tax rate (or the same level at a lower tax rate) than poorer authorities. A man with a given level of income located in authority A may therefore pay a lower total (i.e. central plus local) tax rate than a man with the same level of income in authority B, thus flouting the standard principle of 'equal treatment of equals'. With one administration covering the whole of the country, there is no reason why such a result should occur, it being perfectly possible to arrange the single set of taxes and public expenditures so as to avoid it.

The conclusion can then be drawn that this establishes a case for some sort of redistribution between richer and poorer areas; and this immediately opens up the possibility of a role for a grants system.

The first query about this argument is whether it establishes a case for redistribution between *governments* over and above whatever redistribution takes place between *individuals.*[2] The answer is likely to depend on how far one thinks that the minimization of disparities of treatment at local government level is a goal in its own right as distinct from that of reducing disparities between individuals.

A second query is whether mobility of people out of fiscally disadvantaged areas will not affect rents and property values so as to compensate for fiscal differentials, thus removing the need for intergovernmental equalization grants.

Nevertheless, even though one may have serious doubts about the innate logic of the argument for such grants, there is a very good case for them in terms of historical precedent. It is politically and economically inconceivable that one could in the foreseeable future abandon a

[1] Derived from the pioneering paper by J. M. Buchanan, 'Federalism and Fiscal Equity', *American Economic Review*, September 1950. For another major contribution, see C. Tiebout, 'A Pure Theory of Local Expenditures', *Journal of Political Economy*, October 1956. Cf. A. R. Prest, *op. cit.*, pp. 76 ff, for fuller discussion.

[2] Cf. R. A. and P. B. Musgrave, *op. cit.*, p. 636.

system which is now so deep-rooted. When both politicians and officials are involved and the interests of different layers of government are at stake, fairness and 'equality' have to be construed in the context of what has become customary in inter-governmental grant payments. This does not mean that there is no scope for changing the details, but simply that one must accept inter-governmental equalization grants as a fact of life.

There is a natural presumption that equalization grants should be related to rather general criteria, and that they should pay attention to both revenue capacity and expenditure needs (i.e. criteria (a) and (b) on p. 575).

On the *revenue* side, one may wish to distinguish between taxable capacity and tax effort, in that any given level of revenue may reflect differing combinations of the capacity to pay taxation and the willingness or ability of governments to tap that capacity. In general, the aim should be to arrange grants as compensation for low capacity or as recognition of high effort. As always, it is easier to set out the general principle than to formulate the detailed ways of giving effect to it. Various decisions have to be taken on such matters as, e.g., whether one measures local taxable capacity by income and, if so, whether by income generated or by income received in that area. And in so far as one levies local taxes which are passed on to inhabitants of other areas, the meaning of tax effort is very different to the case where such passing forward or backward is not possible. So one should not run away with the idea that it is easy to derive satisfactory grant bases from the revenue side.

Nevertheless, the problems may well be worse on the *expenditure* side. Differences in recorded expenditure on any particular service (e.g education) may simply reflect circumstances broadly outside the control of the local authority, e.g. the numbers or age composition of children to be taught, the impossibility of achieving economies of scale because of small numbers, the diseconomies of serving a sparsely populated rural area or the specially high costs of inputs (as with London weighting of salaries). But expenditure differences may also arise for other reasons within local authority control, such as when attempts are made to provide better levels of instruction or simply when there is inefficiency, in the sense of not minimizing costs per unit of output. If the general objective is to make larger grants the more the 'needs' of an authority, then one has to distinguish between these two general reasons for expenditure differences, the first one being a basis for such grants but not the second. In other words, if we cannot say for certain what is a given level of output of a service and what costs of meeting it could potentially be avoided, it is very difficult to specify precise bases for equalization grants.

One can obviously construct a grant system on the basis of numbers of inhabitants, numbers of weak or disadvantaged groups, size of area and so on. And no doubt one gets some approximation to a system of making larger grants to the more deserving authorities by this means. But one should not deceive oneself that it is a scientific or objective process.

One final caveat should be entered about equalization grants. Suppose there is a system of compensating poorer local authorities but that *either* these grants benefit better off people in such areas *or* that the revenue to finance such grants is at the expense of poorer people elsewhere. In that sort of a case one might end up by having more equalization between governments but less between individuals.

We can now summarize the principles on which local authority finance should be arranged. Some local authority activities are essentially commercial in character and should be treated as such. Even if we assume that local authorities are all alike in terms of resources and needs per head, there are still arguments connected with the division of labour, externalities, merit wants and 'second-best', why one should have a system of grants. Once we allow for differences in resources and needs, the whole question of equalization grants arises. Although not necessarily easy to pin down in principle or practice, we must accept such grants as an established fact of life.

2 THE RATIO OF GRANTS TO LOCAL REVENUES

2.1 *The major problem*

As shown in Chapter 11, the percentage of central government grants to grants plus local authority revenue from rates has risen from 25 per cent to about 65 per cent between 1913/14 and 1977. This changing pattern has been the subject of much discussion for many years, culminating in the Layfield Committee Report of 1976.

If the view is taken that more and more responsibility should be transferred from local authorities to the central government (the 'centralist solution', in Layfield terminology), the trend increase in the grant ratio is not a matter for concern. But if the view is that local authority independence does matter (the Layfield 'localist solution'), then these figures do arouse apprehension. One aspect is that as the central government increasingly takes on the role of piper it is increasingly likely to call the tune, with a resulting loss of local authority independence of decision-making and gradual demoralization of officials, council members and the electorate. Another view is that local authorities are likely to be less careful than if they were spending monies for which they were accountable to the local electorate. Yet another argument is that when grants loom large in local authority budgets, one group of authorities is more likely to spend its time squabbling with another group about grant allocation than when the prizes to be shared are much smaller.

These sentiments have been challenged[1] on the grounds that much the greater part of government grants is in general form and not specifically attached to particular items of expenditure. In so far as marginal decisions are taken by an authority to incur additional expenditure this will have to be financed entirely from its own revenues; and the electorate always has the power to turn that group of councillors out of office at the next election. As the Layfield Committee pointed out,[2] such a view is only a partial one in that the growth in the ratio of general to specific grants over the years has been accompanied by a proliferation of administrative controls and regulations which closely circumscribe the power of the recipient authorities to spend the allegedly general grants. So it appears that there is not much solace to local authorities here, and we must acknowledge that local power and independence really have diminished substantially over the years.

2.2 *Possible solutions*

One proposal is to correct the disparity between local authority revenues and expenditures by transferring functions (e.g. education) to the central government. This is clearly one of the 'species of remedy which cures the disease by killing the patient', to quote an aphorism by Keynes. For not only is it the case, as we have seen, that local authorities can administer many such services more efficiently than the central government but, even more important, if local authorities are

[1] See F. Cripps and W. Godley, *Local Government Finance and its Reform* (Dept. of Applied Economics, Cambridge, October 1976), Chapter 2.

[2] *Op. cit.*, p. 265.

left with none but the most trivial functions it is only too likely that they would become moribund institutions.

Another general proposal is that local authorities should reduce the disparity between revenue and expenditure by raising more from existing taxes. Although there are various means such as market charges, licence fees, etc. by which local revenue can be increased a little, this proposition is in the last resort an argument for raising the yield of local rates. However, this comes straight up against some vociferous hostility to the level of revenue currently being raised through the rating system. Proposals have been put forward in this country for abolishing domestic rates altogether. And in other countries too (witness the celebrated 'Proposition 13' vote in California in June 1978) great hostility has been shown to local property taxes. It may be that one could raise more revenue from local rates after effecting the various reforms which we shall consider shortly,[1] but it is utopian to think that much more juice could be squeezed out of the fruit at present.

The next proposal for reducing the dependence of the local authorities on the central government is a system of sharing the proceeds of a national tax. In principle, this could take two forms: either an assignment of a certain proportion of the proceeds of a national tax to local authorities or the joint administration and organization of a tax.

Either method *can* work. In the years after 1888, we had a system of assigned revenue (e.g. liquor licences and probate duty) to local authorities in this country. An example of joint administration is to be found in Switzerland where the communes levy a *centime additional* for every franc of cantonal income and capital taxes. The cantons and communes jointly assess the tax and the communes collect it. There are also many other cases of a supplemental rate of local tax being added to the national tax with varying degrees of local authority responsibility for assessment or collection. The difficulties which arise are partly those of politics and partly those of equity. The political difficulty is quite simply that local authorities do not achieve the same degree of independence as when they raise entirely local taxes and are not always able to insist on getting a fair assignment of the total revenue. This political difficulty may well be intensified in the joint administration case, when quarrels about the operation of the tax as well as the division of the proceeds are only too easy. The difficulties of equity are that once again it is likely to be a case of 'to him that hath shall be

[1] See below, p. 528.

given', with the consequent widening of the margin between richer and poorer authority. This difficulty may well outweigh any advantages from sharing even in a buoyant source of national revenue.

Another way of dealing with the present ratio of grants to local revenue is to find new sources of local revenue. Various proposals have been aired over the years on the subject. Local sales taxes, employment taxes, entertainment taxes, tourist and hotel taxes, vehicle duties, motor fuel taxes, as well as a whole variety of charges for local services, have all had their adherents at different times. But there is very little mileage in these ideas, as is shown by the amount of space the Layfield Committee felt it worth while devoting to them – the main discussion occupies only four pages in a report of nearly 500 pages. Thus local sales taxes face difficulties in a small country where a national value added tax already exists. Motor vehicle duties have only recently been 'delocalized' and registrations centralized on a national basis; and even if that were not so, problems of allocating between authorities would be serious, as it was formerly the custom for many companies to register all their vehicles in the district of the head office, even though they might be located in many different parts of the country. And all these ideas have the general drawback that the richer authorities are likely to benefit more from such innovations.

It may be that two other relatively new sources of revenue are more promising: the income from local lotteries and the profits accruing from the operation of the Community Land Act. But even here the Layfield Committee conclusion was that the amounts involved were not likely to be sufficient to make any difference of substance to the grant-dependence of local authorities.

This still leaves us with one other major possibility; a local income tax. This is also an idea which has been under discussion for very many years but it has had a considerable boost recently and so we must look at this proposal in much more detail.

2.3 *A local income tax*[1]

Proponents of local income taxation usually begin their arguments by reference to practices abroad. The USA, Canada and Sweden are all quoted as examples of countries which operate lower-level income taxes alongside a central system. The Canadian lower tier is at provincial level, but Sweden has a comprehensive local level tax and the USA has examples of both state and local level income taxes.

[1] See A. R. Prest, *op. cit.*, Chapter V for fuller discussion.

The precise arguments in favour of a local income tax depend on whether one regards it as a substitute for or an addition to rates. If the former, it is mainly a matter of whether income taxation is more closely related to ability to pay and is likely to show greater buoyancy over the years than rates. If the latter, the main argument is in terms of giving local authorities a larger local tax base, thereby reducing their dependence on central government. All in all, one would seem to be on stronger ground in the latter case (i.e. an addition to local revenue) and this was essentially the basis of the Layfield Committee's case – that one needs a substantial addition to local revenue if one is going for a 'localist solution' and personal income tax is the only likely source.

Arguments against a local income tax divide into two: the general ones which would apply in any country and the particular ones arising from the particular nature of the UK income tax system.

At the *general* level, one has to recognize that local personal[1] income tax revenues may be liable to fluctuations of yield from year to year and then some sort of smoothing device may be needed to enable local Treasurers to budget without too much difficulty. Then there is a whole set of problems connected with the appropriate basis of tax for any one local authority. With employment income, the choice is between allocation on the basis of the place of employment or the place of residence; on the whole, the objections to the latter seem less. With investment income, one could argue for the place of residence of the recipient, the location of the company paying a dividend, or the location of its factory. National treasuries are usually markedly reluctant to let any of the demand management possibilities of income tax variations out of their clutches; and in this respect the UK is no exception.[2] Finally it can be argued that income tax proceeds will vary substantially between richer and poorer areas, but the precise importance of such variations clearly depends on whether income tax is a substitute for or an addition to rates, what accompanying changes take place in the grant structure and so on.

There are some *particular* features of the UK national income tax system which make it more difficult to add on a local income tax system than in other countries. As we have seen earlier,[3] the UK national

[1] It is generally accepted that it would be extremely difficult to apportion taxes on corporations between local authorities.

[2] Thus a Treasury witness to the Layfield Committee (Appendix 1, *op. cit.*, p. 366): 'We need income tax as a fiscal instrument; we need to have it unimpaired; and we need to maintain its flexibility in the hands of central government.'

[3] Chapter 7 above.

system does not necessitate a return of total income by the great bulk of the population at the end of the tax year. So there is no ready basis on which local income tax supplements could be charged at such times. Furthermore, there is no up-to-date knowledge at the national level of the addresses of individual taxpayers. Nor is there any simple mechanism whereby the proceeds of any local income tax supplement levied by the Inland Revenue on behalf of local authorities could be attributed to the areas from which it is derived.

The Layfield Committee considered all these matters at length and did produce a blueprint for a local income tax, in the context of a 'localist solution'. We do not propose to go into this in detail here, but the following were the central features. The Inland Revenue would be responsible for all aspects of tax collection and disbursement and the definition of income, allowances, etc., would be the same for local as for national purposes. Major local authorities would have the right to levy a supplemental income tax at a rate which might vary from one authority to another but only within fairly narrow limits. The mechanism for taxing employment income was that the Inland Revenue would collect addresses annually and an additional element would be incorporated in coding instructions to employers, reflecting the area in which the employee lived and the relevant local tax rate. Self-employed people would also be charged additional tax on the basis of residence. Investment income was to be taxed at a single rate for local purposes and the proceeds paid into a pool to be shared among local authorities. In fact, the pool principle was also of importance for tax on employment income in that the basis of allocation of such tax would be the local tax rate applied to the estimated income total for the area, i.e. it would not be possible to identify the exact amount of supplemental tax paid, individual by individual, in each local authority area. It was estimated that another 12,000 Inland Revenue staff costing (at 1975 prices) about £50m p.a. would be needed to administer the system together with additional private sector costs of the same order of magnitude.

The government rejected the idea of a local income tax – and any other additional local tax for that matter – in its response to the Layfield Committee.[1] So it would seem to be a dead duck at present. But there is one important point to remember. The financial arrangements for Scottish and Welsh devolution admit of no independent source of revenue for the new Assemblies. But it is highly doubtful

[1] See Cmnd. 6813, *op. cit.*, para. 6.10.

whether they would be prepared to exist on central government handouts for long. And if they have to be provided with local revenues, a local income tax will be a very strong runner indeed. If that happens, and also if various changes are made in national income tax arrangements,[1] the local income tax may well come to the forefront again before long.

3 REFORMS IN THE GRANT SYSTEM

3.1 *Criticisms of the rate support grant*

The rate support grant is by far the most important constituent of the grant system and so we must start by looking at the criticisms commonly levelled against it.

First of all, there are some criticisms of a very general nature. One is that the determination of the annual total is a matter of Byzantine complexity, and that it is essentially an exercise in haggling behind closed doors rather than one of setting out explicit objectives and explaining the extent to which they are or are not fulfilled. Another complaint attaches to the uncertainty of the whole process: the lateness in reaching decisions relating to any one financial year and the variability of the grant total from one year to another. Then there are problems associated with the division of the grant between authorities, with some receiving one element of grant on behalf of others as well as themselves[2] but with roles being reversed for the other element.

To see whether there is any justification in another general criticism – that the rate support grant fails to meet its central objectives of making it possible to levy similar rates of local tax for the provision of similar services – we must look at the components of the grant, one by one.

Taking the *resources* element first, it will be recollected that the general idea is that of the ghost ratepayer: the central government pays a grant, at whatever is the local poundage, in respect of the difference between rateable value per head in any one authority and the centrally determined standard rateable value per head. There are in fact four major criticisms of this arrangement.

The first is that rating valuations are frequently of a somewhat

[1] A move towards self-assessment (see Chapter 7, above) would greatly facilitate the levying and collection of local income tax. See N. A. Barr, S. R. James and A. R. Prest, *op. cit.*, for detailed discussion.

[2] See Chapter 11, section 3.

arbitrary character and therefore the equalization of poundages may not in fact lead to the same payments by two individuals living in different areas, even though the 'true' values of their properties are the same and similar services are being provided. It is also most unlikely that the ratio of local tax payments to income will be the same in different areas even though the standards of services provided be similar. Thus it is often maintained that the disparity between rateable values per head in London and elsewhere is greater than that between incomes per head.

The second criticism is that the resources grant works asymmetrically, in the sense that authorities with rateable values per head above the standard level do not suffer negative grants and so there is no real equalization of taxable capacity. Furthermore, those authorities below the standard level are in a poverty-trap situation, in that attempts to attract more industry and hence more rateable value to the area will result in reductions in grant – unlike the richer authorities.

Thirdly, the ghost rate payment is on the basis of whatever is the local poundage and not some nationally determined average figure. This means that this element of grant is of a matching character, in that it not only adds to the resources of the authority (an income effect), but also increases the advantages at the margin of local authority spending relatively to the disadvantages of levying rates (a substitution effect). So it can be argued that the result will be an unnecessary encouragement to local authorities to increase expenditure and that the aims of equalization of resources are being thwarted. How much weight should be given to this criticism depends on whether one thinks it at all important to reward local authorities for their willingness to levy higher poundages to finance higher levels of expenditure.

A final criticism is that the only way of cutting resources grant outpayments under the present system is by reducing the figure for standard rateable value per head. This would affect all recipient authorities, whether responsible or irresponsible, and so might be thought to be rather a blunt instrument.

Turning to the *needs* element, the criticisms are of a different character. There is first of all the point that it is extremely complicated and liable to mislead even the experts on the subject.[1] Actual expenditures

[1] Thus W. Godley, Layfield Committee, Appendix 7, *op. cit.*, p. 45 argued that equalization on a per capita basis is unfair to areas with a high proportion of children. Equalization on an adult basis (*continued on page 526*)

derived from past data may or may not be an adequate reflection of needs, in the sense of compensating authorities for incurring expenditures outside their control. The same holds for the usual indicators of population, numbers of children and the like. It can also be argued that equalization of needs could be achieved by disbursement of a smaller total sum, i.e. the amount nominally appearing under the needs element heading is partly for the purpose of reducing tax rates below the level at which variations in needs can be compensated for.[1]

In short, there is a great deal of subjective judgement in the assessment of relative needs whatever the veneer of complicated formulae and whatever the lip service paid to ostensibly objective criteria.

The third element of the grant is the *domestic* one. The precise consequences of the relief for individual households depends on relative rateable values and poundages, e.g. if rateable values differ but poundages are the same, the absolute amount of relief will differ, but it will be the same fraction of rateable value in both cases.[2] But it is very doubtful whether this relief should appear in a grant which is ostensibly aimed at equalization. The appropriate context is the relative rating burden on domestic and non-domestic properties rather than one concerned with relative resources and needs of different authorities.

There are also a variety of other grants, but these are so unimportant today that it is unnecessary to devote much space to them. The principal bone of contention is whether they should be assimilated into the rate of support grant system or whether there is a role for such grants in respect of long-established expenditures such as police, as distinct from the need for forceful stimulation of some new type of services. As we saw earlier, there are general economic arguments relating to externalities, merit wants and the like which can be used in support of specific grants. But opinion is unlikely to be unanimous on these matters, e.g. whilst the Layfield Committee had little time for specific grants, the government in its reply[3] was rather more inclined to dwell on their merits.

would enable one to differentiate between areas with the same number of people but differing proportions of adults and children.

The trouble with this argument is that if it were extended to the resources element (i.e. use of adult numbers rather than total population in that calculation), the area with the smaller proportion of adults would receive less than before on this amount, even if it were to obtain more needs element grant.

[1] Cf. Layfield Report, *op. cit.*, p. 461.

[2] Cf. A. R. Prest, *op. cit.*, p. 95 for further analysis.

[3] Cmnd. 6813, *op. cit.*, Chapter 4.

3.2 *Possible reforms*

Much the most important suggestion is that the resources and needs components of the rate support grant should be combined into a single Unitary Grant.[1] The essential principle would be to pay grants at such levels as to enable any one authority to provide comparable services with another if it levied a nationally determined standard rate poundage. The actual amount of grant to any one authority would depend on a comparison of its expenditure needs assessment and the yield of the standard rate poundage in its area. Such grants could be paid direct to each authority, thereby eliminating the present unsatisfactory pass-through arrangements.

The great advantage of such a system would be that it could take advantage of such coincidences as exist between high needs and high resources (or low needs and low resources), rather than by operating the resources (needs) side without regards to needs (resources). As a consequence, it would be possible to achieve a given measure of equalization with a lower total of grant outpayments than is possible at present. A further advantage is that it would be easier to exercise marginal control on local authority spending by a system of progressive penalization if an authority raised spending levels more and more above the norm set by needs assessments.

But such a grant system would not be without disadvantages. One would be local authority aversion to central determination of spending needs; another would be their dislike of a national standard rate poundage, with immediate implications that those above and below it would stand in the dock as over and under-spenders respectively.

Other proposals to meet some of the criticisms mentioned above are:

(i) Payments of grant elements to all qualifying authorities without any need for pass-through arrangements.
(ii) The improvement of the rating system so as to reduce the present degree of arbitrariness and make it a better measure of taxable capacity.[2] We shall come to some of the details shortly.
(iii) A system of progressively reducing grants to individual authorities as expenditure rises above a pre-determined level, whether in the

[1] *Ibid.*, Chapter 3 and Appendix 1. Also Layfield Report, *op. cit.*, pp. 231 ff and Annex 28.
[2] The Layfield Committee's ideas for using personal income as a basis for assessing relative taxable capacity of different areas (*op. cit.*, p. 222) were not accepted by the Government.

context of separate resources and needs elements or in that of a unitary grant.

(iv) The development of methods of calculating national average costs of services so as to improve the measurement of relative needs.

At the time of writing all these proposals are in the form of general aspirations rather than detailed plans, but action in respect of some of them is likely in the not too distant future. However, it would certainly be unwise to assume that all the problems of grant determination discussed by so many people for so many years are on the point of solution. Nor is there any reason whatever for thinking that, however much lip-service is paid to the principle of untied grants, the central government will abandon its vast array of administrative controls over the detailed actions of local authorities.

4 REFORMS IN THE RATING SYSTEM

4.1 *Criticisms of the existing rating system*

The rating system is often criticized on *resource allocation* grounds. Domestic rating (responsible for about 40 per cent of all rates collected) can be thought of as a special tax on the annual value of housing and, as such, likely to discourage investment in housing relatively to other assets. Similarly, commercial and industrial rating, whether assumed to work its way forward on to consumers or to impinge primarily on returns to owners of buildings and plant, can also be held to discourage investment in the relevant assets with differentiation against those lines of activity where rates bear heavily.[1]

There are also *equity* objections to rating even if valuation procedures work smoothly. Objections of this sort can be raised against non-domestic rating on the grounds that the incidence of such taxes is obscure; but the main weight of this argument is on the domestic component. The point which is made time and time again is that the rateable value of housing tends to rise less than proportionately with the annual income of the occupier and this, it is argued, is clear evidence that domestic rates are a regressive form of taxation. As we shall see shortly, this line of argument is *simpliste* in the extreme but it is regularly shouted from the house-tops all the same.

[1] The Layfield Committee showed that non-domestic rates could vary from 1 per cent to 5 per cent of value added in an industry. And, as we saw in Chapter 11, agricultural land and buildings have been completely de-rated for many years.

Rates are often attacked as being *arbitrary*, the main point being that there may be marked variations of rateable values both within and between different regions of the country which in no way correspond to 'true' differences in rental values. This is not a new problem; it was a major reason for the concentration of valuation responsibilities in England and Wales on the Inland Revenue in 1949. But there can be little doubt that it has become worse over the years as evidence of market rental values became more and more difficult to collect, this in turn being the result of the persistence of rent controls.

Another problem is the general *unpopularity* of rates. This is partly that the tax basis, rateable values reflecting market rents, means nothing to most people; partly that revaluations in fact take place much less frequently than they are supposed to do and hence give rise to sharp upward revaluations; and partly that the traditional methods of payment (though now substantially modified) was that of bi-annual large sums of money.

Finally, it is often argued that the rating system suffers from a lack of *buoyancy*, at any rate in comparison with taxes based on income. Although this argument can be overdone, the rating base clearly does expand at only a very slow pace between valuations. It may also be that another effect of long-persisting rent control is to prevent revaluations from increasing over time as much as would be the case under market conditions.

4.2 *Possible solutions*

First of all, we shall look at the more extreme solutions which have been proposed and show why these are likely to be unacceptable. Then we shall pass on to the more feasible ones.

One extreme solution is to abandon the rating system altogether, though there are not many proponents of this view. Another view is that domestic rating should be abandoned, whilst leaving that on commercial and industrial properties in being. This was a view put forward by the Conservative Party at the time of the 1974 autumn election. And Ireland has actually done it since that date. Yet another view is the exact converse of the previous one: retain domestic rates but abolish non-domestic.[1]

It must be doubted whether any of these solutions are really acceptable. The first reason is that the deficiencies of the existing system

[1] See R. A. Jackman, 'On the Rating of Non-Domestic Hereditaments', Layfield Committee, *op. cit.*, Appendix 9, p. 180.

which give rise to these views are not really as great as is often alleged. Thus the resource allocation arguments against rating are tempered by such considerations as the zero-rating of house-building under value added tax, the extensive system of subsidies to housing, accelerated depreciation for industrial building, partial de-rating for industrial properties in Scotland and so on. Similarly, the equity arguments against the rating system are often overdone.[1] For instance, when allowances are made for rates concessions to poorer people, the traditional regressive picture loses much of its force. This argument is likely to hold *a fortiori* if lifetime rather than annual income is taken as the reference point. And in any event it is not a sin against the Holy Ghost if one tax happens to be regressive against income; what matters is the combined impact of all taxes, hard as that may be to determine with accuracy. Nor do some of the other objections to rates hold as strongly as may appear at first sight. Thus the lack of buoyancy is less obvious when one compares changes in rateable values between successive revaluation dates.

The second reason is that the rating system does have some very real advantages. These were set out at length by the Layfield Committee,[2] but can be summarized by saying that rates are a tax which is unambiguous, predictable, not easily avoided or evaded and relatively cheap to collect. These arguments can be amplified in various ways, e.g. by dwelling on the fact that increases in rate poundages are highly perceptible (yield cannot increase on this account whilst people are asleep, as it were) and that yields are highly stable over the course of the business cycle (which is a desirable property of local, as distinct from national, finances). So the very real merits of rating, which no doubt help to explain why this form of tax has lasted so long, should never be underestimated.

A third reason for rejecting extreme solutions is that even if they could be persuasively argued in themselves, one would still have to find a very large alternative source of local authority revenue or be willing to contemplate an increase in central government grants or take functions away from local authorities. As we have already seen, none of these three alternatives is both practicable and acceptable.

So we now come to more feasible reforms of the rating system. Many suggestions have been made on this subject and we shall have to content ourselves here with looking at three of them: the ratio of

[1] Cf. A. R. Prest, *op. cit.*, p. 49, for more detailed discussion.
[2] *Op. cit.*, p. 145.

domestic to non-domestic rates, the arguments for site-value rating and the case for basing rates on capital rather than annual values.

Although we have rejected the idea of complete abolition of either domestic or non-domestic rates, there is still plenty of scope for differentiating between the two components, whether by partial de-rating of one or super-rating of the other or some mixture of the two. Opinion has in fact swung in cycles on this subject. Historically, there have been times when partial de-rating of industry has been strongly advocated. In more recent years, domestic de-rating has taken a firm hold and there has been talk of super-rating non-domestic property.[1]

It is easy enough to see that any one local authority will be likely to favour differentiation in favour of domestic ratepayers. Non-domestic ratepayers do not have votes; and in any event they may well pass on local rating burdens to the residents in other areas who buy their products. But if all authorities behave like this there will be a great deal of such tax-exporting from one area to another and whether the end result will be desirable from either a local or a national viewpoint is problematical. In effect, the Layfield Committee[2] had to conclude that so little was known about the economic effects of rating on industry and commerce that no really sensible verdict could be given on the appropriate division of rating burdens between domestic property owners and others.

There is, however, one major area where something more can be said; the exemption of agricultural land and buildings from rating. The Layfield Committee was strongly in favour of re-rating such property,[3] but the Government decided against it,[4] partly on grounds of cost and partly on principle. The former argument is very thin in that annual costs of public administration, once the initial problems were out of the way, would only be about 1 per cent of revenue yield, i.e. much less than with many other taxes. And the grounds of principle appeared to be nothing more than the fact that local authorities would not be better off as a whole in the end in that grant income would be reduced as rate income rose. This is patently an absurd argument. One can only conclude that politics rather than economics was in the ascendant at this stage of the discussion.

Arguments have frequently been put forward in favour of site value

[1] With the exception of industry in Scotland which is still 50 per cent de-rated.

[2] *Op. cit.*, p. 178.

[3] *Ibid.*, pp. 165–7.

[4] Cmnd. 6813, *op. cit.*, para. 6.23.

rating, either as an alternative or as an addition to the existing system. Site value rating, which takes as its basis the *unimproved* capital value of land, has a number of desirable properties, e.g. it would not discourage land development in the same way as the existing system, in that tax payable is the same whether a site is developed or not. It has been used extensively and successfully in Australia and New Zealand. But it does not appear that the case for it is as strong in a highly developed and highly urbanized country such as the United Kingdom. Valuation difficulties are bound to be considerable in an economy of this sort. If the tax is conceived as a supplement to the existing rate system, it seems unlikely that the yield could be large, especially when the psychological difficulties of pushing up poundages are borne in mind. If, on the other hand, it is to be a substitute, the valuation difficulties would be all the more likely to attract attention. One must conclude, therefore, that such a change of system does not look very likely for the UK. At the same time, the Layfield Committee argument[1] that the case for site value taxation no longer holds since the Community Land Act and the associated Development Land Tax, is somewhat overdone. There is first of all the general distinction between taxes on capital values and taxes on their increments; and, secondly, the permanence of the new arrangements is by no means assured.

Finally, the case for a capital valuation basis for rates – at least for domestic property and in England and Wales – was strongly argued by the Layfield Committee on the grounds that evidence of rental values was insufficient today to permit any other method. Although some of the details of the proposals might be questioned (e.g to secure comparability with non-domestic property -it was proposed to convert domestic capital values to annual values rather than convert non-domestic annual to capital values), the general proposition must clearly be welcomed. Although the government accepted the proposal in 1977,[2] it was announced in 1978 that the next revaluation in 1982 was after all to be on the old basis.[3] So it remains to be seen whether this proposal for rating reform has suffered only a temporary reverse, or whether it will join the many others which have been quietly buried over the years.

[1] *Op. cit.*, p. 438.
[2] Cmnd. 6813, *op. cit.*
[3] It was announced in June 1979 that this revaluation was to be cancelled.

REFERENCES (PART III)[1]

I. BOOKS ETC.

Aaron, H. J., *Who Pays the Property Tax?* (Brookings Institution, Washington DC, 1975).

Aaron, H. J. (ed.), *Inflation and the Income Tax* (Brookings Institution, Washington DC, 1976).

Adams, J. D. R. and Whalley, J. E., *The International Taxation of Multinational Enterprises* (Institute for Fiscal Studies – Associated Business Programmes, London, 1977).

Atkinson, A. B., *Unequal Shares* (Allen Lane, London, 1972).

Atkinson, A. B., *The Economics of Inequality* (Oxford University Press, Oxford, 1975).

Atkinson, A. B. (ed.), *The Personal Distribution of Income* (Allen and Unwin, London, 1976).

Atkinson, A. B. and Harrison, A. J., *The Distribution of Personal Wealth in Britain* (Cambridge University Press, Cambridge, 1978).

Blackaby, F. (ed.), *British Economic Policy 1964–76* (National Institute of Economic Research – Cambridge University Press, Cambridge, 1978).

Break, G. F. and Pechman, J. A., *Federal Tax Reform: The Impossible Dream* (Brookings Institution, Washington DC, 1975).

Brittain, J. A., *The Payroll Tax for Social Security* (Brookings Institution, Washington DC, 1973).

Brookings Institution, *The Role of Direct and Indirect Taxation in the Federal Revenue System* (Princeton University Press, 1964).

Cain, C. G. and Watts, H. W., *Income Maintenance and Labor Supply* (Markham, Chicago, 1973).

Crick, B. and Robson, W. A., *Taxation Policy* (Penguin Books, London, 1972).

Cripps, F. and Godley, W., *Local Government Finance and its Reform* (Department of Applied Economics, Cambridge, 1976).

Culyer, A. J., *Need and the National Health Service* (Martin Robertson, Oxford, 1978).

David, M., *Alternative Approaches to Capital Gains Taxation* (Brookings Institution, Washington DC, 1968).

[1] See introductory note to References (Part I) on p. 170.

Dow, J. C. R., *The Management of the British Economy, 1945–60* (Cambridge University Press, 1964).

Due, J. F., *Sales Taxation* (Routledge and Kegan Paul, London, 1957).

Due, J. F., *Indirect Taxation in Developing Economies* (Johns Hopkins, Baltimore, 1970).

Flemming, J. and Little, I. M. D., *Why We Need a Wealth Tax* (Methuen, London, 1974).

Fromm, G., *Tax Incentives and Capital Spending* (Brookings Institution, Washington DC, 1971).

Gilbert, B. B., *The Evolution of National Insurance in Great Britain* (Michael Joseph, London, 1973).

Ilersic, A. R., *Taxation of Capital Gains* (Staples Press, London, 1962).

Institute for Fiscal Studies, *Conference on Proposals for a Tax-Credit Scheme* (London, 1973).

Institute for Fiscal Studies, *Local Government Finance* (London, 1973).

Krzyzaniak, M. and Musgrave, R. A., *The Shifting of the Corporation Income Tax* (Johns Hopkins Press, Baltimore, 1963).

Krzyzaniak, M. (ed.), *Effects of Corporate Income Tax* (Wayne State University Press, 1966).

Liesner, T. and King, M. A. (eds.), *Indexing for Inflation* (Institute for Fiscal Studies, London, 1975).

National Bureau of Economic Research, *Public Finance Needs, Sources and Utilization* (Princeton University Press, Princeton, 1961).

National Bureau of Economic Research and Brookings Institution, *Foreign Tax Policies and Economic Growth* (Columbia University Press, 1966).

Oates, W., *Fiscal Federalism* (Harcourt Brace, New York, 1972).

Pechman, J. A. (ed.), *Comprehensive Income Taxation* (Brookings Institution, Washington DC, 1977).

Pechman, J. A. and Timpane, P. M., *Work Incentives and Income Guarantees: The New Jersey Experiment* (Brookings Institution, Washington DC, 1975).

Posner, M. (ed.), *Demand Management* (National Institute of Economic Research – Heinemann, London, 1978).

Prest, A. R. (ed.), *Public Sector Economics* (Manchester University Press, Manchester, 1968).

Prest, A. R., *Social Benefits and Tax Rates* (Institute of Economic Affairs, London, 1970).

Sandford, C. T., Willis, J. R. M. and Ironside, D. J., *An Accessions Tax* (Institute for Fiscal Studies, London, 1973).

Sandford, C. T., Willis, J. R. M. and Ironside, D. J., *An Annual Wealth Tax* (Institute for Fiscal Studies, London, 1975).

Shoup, C. S., *Federal Estate and Gift Taxes* (Brookings Institution, Washington DC, 1966).

Shoup, C. S. (ed.), *Fiscal Harmonization in Common Markets*, Vols. I and II (Columbia University Press, New York, 1966).

Sullivan, C. K., *The Tax on Value Added* (Columbia University Press, New York, 1965).
Surrey, S. S., *Pathways to Tax Reform* (Harvard University Press, Harvard, 1973).
Tait, A. A., *The Taxation of Personal Wealth* (University of Illinois Press, Urbana, Illinois, 1967).
Van den Tempel, A. J., *Corporation Tax and Income Tax in the European Communities* (EEC, Brussels, 1970).
Vickrey, W., *Agenda for Progressive Taxation* (Ronald Press, New York, 1947).
Ward, T. R. and Neild, R. R., *The Measurement and Reform of Budgetary Policy* (Institute for Fiscal Studies – Heinemann, 1978).
Wheatcroft, G. S. A., *Estate and Gift Taxation* (Sweet and Maxwell, London, 1965).
Wheatcroft, G. S. A., (ed.), *Value Added Tax in the Enlarged Common Market* (Cassell/Associated Business Programmes, London, 1973).
Willis, J. R. M. and Hardwick, P. J. W., *Erosion of the Income Tax Base* (Institute for Fiscal Studies – Heinemann, 1978).

II. ARTICLES

Arrow, K. J., 'The Welfare Economics of Medical Care', *American Economic Review*, December 1963.
Bhatia, K. B., 'Accrued Capital Gains, Personal Incomes and Savings in the US, 1948–64', *Review of Income and Wealth*, December 1970.
Break, G. F., 'Effects of Taxation on Incentives', *British Tax Review*, June 1957, and 'Income Taxes and Incentives to Work', *American Economic Review*, September 1957.
Buchanan, J. M., 'Federalism and Fiscal Equity', *American Economic Review*, September 1950.
Davis, J. M., 'Aggregate Time Series Analysis of the Short-Run Shifting of the UK Company Tax', *Oxford Economic Papers*, July 1972.
Domar, E. D., 'Depreciation Replacement and Growth', *Economic Journal*, March 1953, and 'The Case for Accelerated Depreciation', *Quarterly Journal of Economics*, November 1953 (both reprinted in *Essays in the Theory of Economic Growth*, Oxford University Press, New York, 1957).
Fields, D. B. and Stanbury, W. T., 'Incentives, Disincentives and the Income Tax. Further Empirical Evidence', *Public Finance*, 3, 1970; and 'Income Taxes and Incentives to Work. Some Additional Empirical Evidence', *American Economic Review*, June 1971.
Goode, R., 'Accelerated Depreciation Allowances as a Stimulus to Investment', *Quarterly Journal of Economics*, May 1955.

Harbury, C. D. and Hitchens, D. M., 'The Inheritances of Top Wealth Leavers', *Economic Journal*, June 1976.

Musgrave, R. A. and P. B., 'Fiscal Policy' in R. E. Caves (ed.), *Britain's Economic Prospects* (Brookings Institution, Washington DC, 1968).

Prest, A. R., 'Negative Income Tax Concepts and Problems', *British Tax Review*, Nov.–Dec. 1970.

Prest, A. R., 'The Select Committee on Corporation Tax', *British Tax Review*, Jan.–Feb. 1972.

Prest, A. R., 'The Political Economy of Tax Reform', *Economic Papers*. Economic Society of Australia and New Zealand, July 1971–April 1972.

Prest, A. R., 'Proposals for a Tax-Credit System', *British Tax Review*, No. 1, 1973.

Prest, A. R., 'Inflation and the Public Finances', *Three Banks Review*, March 1973.

Prest, A. R., 'The Select Committee on Wealth Tax', *British Tax Review*, No. 1, 1976.

Prest, A. R., 'The Meade Committee Report', *British Tax Review*, No. 3, 1978.

Prest, A. R., 'The Structure and Reform of Direct Taxation', *Economic Journal*, June 1979.

Prest, A. R., 'Expenditure Tax Implementation', *Annual Conference Proceedings*, Canadian Tax Foundation, Toronto, 1979.

Prest, A. R., 'Fiscal Policy' in P. Coffey (ed.), *Economic Problems of the Common Market* (Macmillan, London, 1979).

Samuelson, P. A., 'An Exact Consumption – Loan Model of Interest With or Without the Social Contrivance of Money', *Journal of Political Economy*, December 1958.

Tiebout, C. M., 'A Pure Theory of Local Expenditures', *Journal of Political Economy*, October 1956.

Wheatcroft, G. S. A., Prest, A. R. and Stout, D. K., Articles on Value Added Taxation, *British Tax Review*, September–October 1963.

Wheatcroft, G. S. A., Peacock, A. T., and Tress, R. C., Articles on Wealth Taxation, *British Tax Review*, November–December 1963.

III. OFFICIAL PUBLICATIONS

A. *United Kingdom* (All HMSO, London).

Inflation Accounting, Report of the Inflation Accounting Committee, Cmnd. 6225, 1975.

NEDO, *Investment Appraisal*, 1967.

NEDO, *Value Added Tax*, 1969.

The Rate Support Grant Order, 1979–80.

Report from Select Committee on Corporation Tax, Session 1970–71, 1971.

Report of Committee of Inquiry into the Impact of Rates on Households Cmnd. 2582, 1965.

Report of Committee on National Debt and Taxation, Cmd. 2800, 1927.

Report of Committee on Taxation of Trading Profits, Cmd. 8189, 1951.

Report of Committee on Turnover Taxation, Cmd. 2300, 1964.

Royal Commission on Taxation of Profits and Income, *First Report*, Cmd. 8761 (1953), *Second Report*, Cmd. 9105 (1954), *Final Report*, Cmd. 9474 (1955).

Select Committee on Tax-Credit, Session 1972/3, Vols. I, II, III HCP 341-I, II, III, 1973.

Select Committee on a Wealth Tax, HC 696, 1975.

Small Firms: Report of Committee on Small Firms, Cmnd, 4811, 1971.

B. *United States* (All US Government Printing Office, Washington DC).

Committee on Ways and Means, *Tax Revision Compendium*, Vols. 1–3, 1959.

Committee on Ways and Means, *Tax Reform Studies and Proposals*, 1969.

Committee on Ways and Means, *Tax Reform*, 1975.

Joint Economic Committee, *Federal Tax Policy for Economic Growth and Stability*, 1956.

Joint Economic Committee, *Economics of Federal Subsidy Programs*, 1973.

Joint Economic Committee, *Federal Expenditure Policy for Economic Growth and Stability*, 1957.

US Treasury, *Statistics of Income* (Annual).

C. *Other*

Kaldor, N., *Indian Tax Reform* (Dept. of Economic Affairs, Ministry of Finance, India, 1956).

Report of the Fiscal and Financial Committee (EEC, Brussels, 1963).

Sixth Draft Directive on Value Added Tax (EEC, Brussels, 1973).

Draft Directive on Harmonisation of Company Taxation (EEC, Brussels, 1975).

Revenue Statistics of OECD Member Countries 1965–74 (OECD, Paris, 1977).

Report of Royal Commission on Taxation (Carter Commission). Queen's Printer, Ottawa, 1966.

Taxation Review Committee, Preliminary Report 1974 and Full Report 1975 (Australian Government Publishing Service, Canberra).

Shoup Mission, *Report on Japanese Taxation* (GHQ, SCAP, Tokyo, 1949).

United Nations: The Impact of Multinational Corporations on Development and on International Relations: Technical Papers, Taxation (New York, 1974).

INDEX